THE OPERAS OF VERDI

The Operas of Verdi, Volume 1

The Operas of Verdi, Volume 3

JULIAN BUDDEN

The Operas of Verdi

2

From *Il Trovatore* to *La Forza del destino*

Revised edition

CLARENDON PRESS · OXFORD

Oxford University Press, Walton Street, Oxford OX2 6DP
Oxford New York
Athens Auckland Bangkok Bombay
Calcutta Cape Town Dar es Salaam Delhi
Florence Hong Kong Istanbul Karachi
Kuala Lumpur Madras Madrid Melbourne
Mexico City Nairobi Paris Singapore
Taipei Tokyo Toronto
and associated companies in
Berlin Ibadan

Oxford is a trade mark of Oxford University Press

Published in the United States by
Oxford University Press Inc., New York

First published in 1978 in Great Britain by
Cassell & Company Ltd., London. First published in the
United States in 1979 by Praeger Publishers, Inc.

First issued in paperback in 1984

This revised edition published in 1992 by
Oxford University Press, Oxford,
and by Oxford University Press, New York

ISBN 0-19-816262-6

3 5 7 9 10 8 6 4 2

Printed in Great Britain
on acid-free paper by
St Edmundsbury Press Ltd., Bury St Edmunds, Suffolk

CONTENTS

PREFACE

Seven operas in Volume 2 against seventeen in Volume 1 may seem a curious distribution; but it is not an illogical one. First, there is the length of the operas themselves. Of those already discussed more than a third fall short of two hours of music. Of those to come not one contains less than two and a quarter, while two (*Les Vêpres Siciliennes* and *La Forza del destino*) if performed in their entirety are among the longest in the repertory. Both *La Forza del destino* and *Simon Boccanegra* exist in two versions, the latter providing the most radical case of an operatic revision that Verdi ever made.

Then there is the increasing complexity of the musical organization. As Verdi ventures further from the self-sufficient world of the post-Rossinian tradition to link hands with his contemporaries in the mainstream of European music, his structures become more continuous, his ideas more subtly connected and developed, so requiring a greater wealth of quotation to illustrate their working. The more characters and situations are particularized through an ever-widening vocabulary, the less it becomes possible to describe a given dramatic moment merely by reference to a routine procedure of the past, even though traces of that procedure may still be present. As a man of property, now settled in life, Verdi was able to take more time and trouble over his operas, which assume a correspondingly greater musical and dramatic density.

Inevitably, too, as Verdi's fame increases so do the number of surviving documents relating to his works. He seems always to have been a prolific letter-writer; but from the time of *Rigoletto* onwards his correspondents were less disposed to throw his letters away. Consequently we can trace the genesis of individual operas in greater detail than before. The works of the so-called middle period from *La Traviata* to *Aida* have for the most part a tortured and complicated history which the biographers of the inter-war years had been at no great pains to unravel. Since then a new generation of scholars, many of them associated with the Istituto di Studi Verdiani in Parma, have set themselves to find out the facts and so have succeeded in correcting many a picture distorted by misplaced piety and uncorroborated hearsay. Prominent among them was Frank Walker, whose discoveries far exceed those embodied in his famous study *The Man Verdi*. New documents are continually coming to light, new theories constantly being propounded through all of which the conscientious commentator must pick his way with care, giving the appropriate signposts. To take an example: it is only during the last decade that Verdians have turned their attention to the wealth of material that exists in the Bibliothèque de l'Opéra, the Bibliothèque Nationale and the Archives Nationales in Paris. Two items of especial interest are the singers' rehearsal books, which contain a skeletal version of their music at a comparatively early stage of composition, and the booklets of directions for staging.

Indeed the so-called *mises-en-scène* and their Italian equivalents, the *disposizioni sceniche*, deserve a word of explanation. In the nineteenth century there were no producers as such. In Italy the responsibility for directing the stage movements and for specifying the costumes (always within the impresario's budget) devolved upon the librettist. Most theatres kept at least one poet on their payroll whose business it was to supervise the mounting of revivals and repertory pieces, adjusting the text where necessary. At the Paris Opéra the procedure was more systematized. From about the middle of the nineteenth century instructions for décor, costumes and action were set down in a printed production book in the utmost detail, complete with diagrams. Exactly when this practice spread to Italy is difficult to determine. Most probably it followed the vogue for grand opera on the French model which began during the 1850s. The earliest surviving *disposizione scenica* is that for *Giovanna de Guzman*, the first Italian version of *Les Vêpres Siciliennes*. Mostly it is a straightforward translation of the original *mise-en-scène* with some of the more sensational features toned down. For instance, Act IV of *Les Vêpres Siciliennes* includes the figure of a headsman in full regalia; in *Giovanna de Guzman* he is merely the captain of a platoon standing with drawn sword by a 'kind of catafalque which will serve as the scaffold but which must not be such as to cause revulsion'. The next extant production book is that for *Un Ballo in maschera* devised by Giovanni Cencetti, resident poet of the Teatro Apollo, Rome, for the première of 1859 (Somma, the author, had firmly dissociated himself from the production). There is likewise a *disposizione scenica* of *La Forza del destino* (first version), which may or may not be based on Piave's original specification. All were published by the Casa Ricordi. That for *Don Carlos* (1867) is described as 'compiled and set out according to the *mise-en-scène* of the Imperial Theatre of the Paris Opéra'. From then on it became Ricordi's practice to print *disposizioni sceniche* with each new opera, no longer as miniature booklets in the manner of a libretto, but in full octavo format with illustrated covers. The author is always Giulio Ricordi; the ideas, at least in the case of *Aida*, are probably Verdi's. Others exist for *Simon Boccanegra* (1881), *Don Carlos* (1886) adapted from the earlier book, and *Otello* – not, disappointingly, for *Falstaff*. It is interesting to observe the subtly changing tone of the instructions over the years. The earlier books are full of drilled movements which freeze at the end of a scene into 'tableaux'. The later tend to be more wordy and at the same time less precise. Sometimes there is a note to the effect that the singer should rely on his own intelligence and histrionic ability rather than on any written instructions. The chorus are urged to remember that 'they must not depict an indeterminate mass, but that each represents a character and must act as such and move of his own accord as his own feelings require, merely preserving a certain unity of action with the rest so as the better to ensure a good musical performance'. A counsel of perfection if ever there was one. Clearly the age of the producer was already envisaged.

In the analytical chapters I have quoted from the production books in footnotes either where they explain the action more clearly than the libretto or the vocal score, or where they offer a different interpretation from the traditional one. Producers no less than students of Verdi are recommended to consult the originals, copies of which can be found both at the Istituto di Studi Verdiani in Parma and at its sister organization, the American Institute of Verdi Studies in New York. To resurrect a Verdian production of a hundred years ago in the course of a modern opera season would be unthinkable. The costumes alone would be too costly, the scenery too heavy and prosaic. There is no reason to suppose Verdi's visual taste any more than Wagner's would be acceptable today. Indeed the tableau he prescribed for the priestesses in Act I, scene ii of *Aida* would not be out of place in a Bluebell Girls revue. Likewise his, or Boito's, directions for the self-cursing Paolo in *Simon Boccanegra* take us to the world of *Sweeney Todd, the Demon Barber of Fleet Street*. What the production books provide is an invaluable starting point for the realization of the composer's dramatic conception; they show us where the emphasis should be laid and why.

Despite the growing complexity of the subject I have not departed from the method of exegesis used in Volume 1. Even when two versions of an opera differ from each other as widely as those of *Simon Boccanegra* it still seems to me preferable to discuss them side by side if only to demonstrate directly and without cumbersome back-reference how often the original conception has been sharpened or transcended. Only when the original is fitted to a new plot, as in the case of *Stiffelio/Aroldo*, does it warrant a new chapter. In view of the length and number of the music examples I have not provided a stave for the singers when their line doubles the orchestral melody. Where they have a separate line of declamation which is not relevant to the point of the illustration I have indicated the voice-part by unpitched notes (e.g. Ex. 32a).

As in Volume 1 the title pages of each opera do not literally represent those of the original published score – for which the reader is referred to M. Chusid, *A Catalog of Verdi's Operas* (New Jersey, 1974) – but are set out so as to convey as much information as possible within the style of the period.

Finally, in addition to the acknowledgements given in Volume 1, I would like to express my grateful thanks to Ursula Günther, Andrew Porter, David Rosen and Flynn Warmington, all of whom have allowed me access to their material before it has appeared in print; to Marcello Conati and Mario Medici of the *Istituto di Studi Verdiani* for their unfailing assistance in my researches; to the authorities of the Teatro la Fenice, Venice, for permission to print the two facsimile pages of the manuscript full score of *La Traviata* held in their archives; to the Casa Ricordi for permission to quote from Verdi's unpublished correspondence with the firm; to Michael Rose and Michel Noiray for their assistance in lending or procuring important documents; and finally to the Reverend Peter Southwell-Sanders, himself a Verdian author, for help in proof-reading my typescript.

J.B.

1978

I THE COLLAPSE OF A TRADITION
(ITALIAN OPERA 1840–70)

Up to 1850 the background to Verdi's artistic growth and the influences that nourished it are fairly easy to trace. The two main landmarks stand out clearly enough: on the one hand the more or less static tradition of post-Rossinian romantic *melodramma*; on the other the cosmopolitan world of Parisian grand opera. Thereafter the pattern becomes more confused as the landscape itself changes. In France grand opera declined in importance, though the yearly supply was scrupulously maintained till 1870. Meanwhile at the Théâtre Lyrique a more truly native opera came of age with works by Gounod, Bizet and, later, Massenet; and from the Bouffes Parisiens sprang a rejuvenated lyric comedy under Offenbach, which was to epitomize the heady gaiety of the Second Empire. All these composers were to leave their mark on Verdi. Though not a note of Wagner's music was to be heard in Italy before 1871, his theoretical writings were widely read in translation. Even the fiasco of *Tannhäuser* in Paris in 1860 enhanced rather than diminished his fame as a force to be reckoned with. Above all the sturdy tradition of the primo ottocento in which Verdi had been reared was tottering. Verdi apart, Italian opera of the mid century was in a state of decay.

A 'tradition' or 'school' in the sense in which it is applied here is easier to point to than to define. It embraces a host of generally accepted rules and procedures which by narrowing the creative choice allow a rapid rate of composition and put a premium on craftsmanship rather than originality. In the eighteenth century 'tradition' reigned supreme, especially in music, which the aesthetics of the time rated rather low in the canon of the fine arts since it is not representational. A good tradition can sustain the minor craftsman—composer; he will be listened to with pleasure not for his individual voice so much as for the ease and resource with which he exploits the current idiom. Who can doubt that if Arne or Boyce had had the opportunity of writing within the continental tradition his stature would be higher than it is? Likewise the Storace of *The Pirates* or *The Iron Chest* has little more to offer than a handful of pretty tunes; but in *Gli Equivoci*, written for a Viennese public to a libretto by da Ponte, he takes on the strength of the tradition which he serves.

Now it is obvious that most so-called 'schools' of the nineteenth and twentieth centuries are of a very different order. They may, like the Russian 'kutchka', proclaim a number of common aims and even rules; but the merit of each member depends largely on the extent to which he goes his own way in spite of them. The 'school' turns out to be nothing more than a label. Rimsky-Korsakov, the most tradition-minded of the 'mighty handful', by common consent ranks below Mussorgsky, Borodin and even Balakirev. In the nineteenth century the composer however great or small is required to have an individual voice if he is to command our attention. In the eighteenth century genius makes itself felt in less obvious ways. Mozart has no stylistic fingerprints such as are to be found in the works of the leading romantics. His biographer Eric Blom observed this fact and drew the wrong conclusion from it – namely that pronounced individuality of style is the hallmark of the minor composer.* His instances include Bizet, Tchaikovsky and Puccini; but they might just as well have extended to Brahms, Wagner and Mendelssohn, not to mention middle-period Beethoven. The truth is that while Bach, Handel and Mozart worked within a living tradition the romantics were obliged to make their way alone. Greatness has nothing to do with the matter.

Various factors have been made to account for the persistence of 'tradition' in Italian opera just when in other countries it was beginning to break down: the slow penetration of romanticism south of the Alps, the theatrical conditions of the time, the unique strength of the personality of Rossini, who codified if he did not make the rules. But the reasons may well lie deeper, in the realm of Italian society with its strong network of family relationships, where a man can feel sure of his aims only as part of a larger unit. It is surely no coincidence that the leader of the revolt against native traditionalism in music was a half-Pole who grew up unacquainted with any of his Italian relations; while the composer who triumphed over the tradition's collapse had fought all his life to make himself independent of his family.

Italians, it could be said, have always profited more than other nations from the existence of fixed traditions; hence their undisputed hegemony of music in the seventeenth and eighteenth centuries, and their decline into semi-provincialism in the years that followed. Not only that. Three years before Verdi produced his last opera the Rossini phenomenon was repeated and in very different circumstances. In 1890 the young Pietro Mascagni produced his *Cavalleria Rusticana*. A new tradition was created; and in the eyes of both Italy and the world Italian opera was reborn. Leoncavallo and Puccini, both Mascagni's seniors by five years, found their artistic feet through his example, with *Pagliacci* (1892) and *Manon Lescaut* (1893) respectively. The minor composers – Giordano, Cilea, Zandonai – followed, all writing within the same so-called 'veristic' style, often indistinguishably from one another. Yet we enjoy *Adriana Lecouvreur* and *Andrea Chénier* without caring about their lack of true originality. We should never extend such tolerance to the followers of Mendelssohn or Brahms. The verismo tradition produced only one genius – Puccini; when he died and the modernism of the 1920s invaded the scene causing the tradition itself to wither, the minor composers languished with it. Giordano and Cilea both survived the Second World War without producing anything of greater value than they had written before the First. The pattern of the previous century was being repeated. Meanwhile between the fall of post-Rossinian tradition and the rise of verismo there stretched a musical wilderness in which Italian opera was trying to seek a new identity, partly with the aid of foreign models, yet was unable to shake off the encumbering relics of the past.

When Verdi began his long operatic career with *Oberto Conte di San Bonifacio* the primo ottocento romantic tradition was set for its final flowering. Donizetti, its foremost representative, had four more years of active life ahead of him; these were to see the birth of *Maria Padilla*, *Linda di Chamounix*, *Maria di Rohan* and *Don Pasquale*, not to mention the French *La Favorite*, which in translation and without the ballet was to become one of the cornerstones of the Italian repertory. With his *Il Giuramento* of 1837 Mercadante had launched a series of grandiose dramatic operas that were to crown his reputation – *Elena da Feltre*, *Le Due Illustri Rivali*, *Il Bravo*, *Il Reggente* and the neoclassical *La Vestale* and *Orazi e Curiazi*. Pacini emerged from five years'

* E. Blom, *Mozart* (London, 1935), pp. 195–6, 264–5.

operatic retirement to write his single masterpiece, *Saffo*. Luigi Ricci after several failures had turned his energies to church music and his duties as maestro concertatore at the Teatro Grande, Trieste; but for his brother Federico, whose *La Prigione d'Edimburgo* had triumphed in 1837, the year 1841 was to see the double success of *Corrado d'Altamura* in Milan and *Luigi Rolla* in Florence.* Vaccai was about to sign off an honourable career with the carefully wrought, dignified *Virginia* of 1845.

But this fruitful period did not last long. In 1842 came the impact of *Nabucco*, whose effect was soon to kill off the less hardy operatic growths and polarize the theatrical world between Verdi and Mercadante, one, as before, the people's favourite, the other the darling of the academics. The state of contemporary opera was neatly parodied in the youthful opera buffa of Antonio Cagnoni, *Don Bucefalo*, written in 1847 when he was still a student at the Milan Conservatoire. The plot, taken directly from Fioravanti's *Le Cantatrici villane* of 1806, is one of those evergreen theatrical satires that can be adapted to fit any age. In the aria 'Mettiamo un andantino' Don Bucefalo is setting a text of Metastasio in the modern manner ending with a phrase of swaggering triplets designed to bring the house down.

At once he is seized with remorse. 'Forgive me, ye classics,' he cries; 'these triplets are not mine!'

Indeed the triplets are not his – they are Verdi's – so a contemporary audience would have concluded; and doubtless the cap was intended to fit. Viewed from

* *Corrado d'Altamura* even reached Her Majesty's Theatre, London, in 1844 though it was not especially well received; the plot, incidentally, is identical with that of Verdi's *Oberto* with the addition of a 'travesti' part as the heroine's honourable suitor.

today it would seem to fit Mercadante almost as well, since this style of grandiosity was a feature of the 1840s, being directly due to the choral element that invaded opera during the decade. How far this in turn is attributable to the example of *Nabucco*, which earned Verdi the sobriquet 'Papà dei cori',* and how far to the Risorgimento spirit in general is hard to determine. The truth is that in most operas of the time there is scarcely a solo number which is not padded out with choral intervention. Federico Ricci's *Griselda* of 1847 begins with a choral introduction of five episodes; and for the whole of the first act the chorus never leave the stage. Vaccai's *Virginia* is mostly a succession of choral tableaux in the Spontini manner, many of them built round some dispensable comprimario.

It is the failure to assimilate them into a fast-moving drama that was responsible for the decline of Mercadante and his contemporaries. Mercadante's famous letter to Florimo of 1838 certainly reads like a manifesto of reform: 'I have continued the revolution begun with *Il Giuramento* – varied the forms, abolished trivial cabalettas; concision, less repetition, more novelty in the cadences; due regard paid to the dramatic side; the orchestration rich but without swamping the voices; long solos in the concertati avoided, as they oblige the other parts to stand idle to the detriment of the action; not much big drum and very little stage band.'† All this holds good for the operas of the next few years; and in particular for *Il Bravo* of 1839, arguably Mercadante's most dramatic work. But as the choral element begins to predominate so the pace of his operas slackens and he is driven back more and more on slow-moving neo-classical plots. Musically he never ceased to advance; his harmonies become more inventive, his part-writing more ingenious. It is his dramatic movement that stagnates. For him and most of his contemporaries the only way forward was through elaboration. The basic structure of their operas remained as before: a succession of finite scenes each surrounding a solo or an ensemble, and each marked off from the next by pauses for applause. Only the constituent units were expanded. The scene would be tricked out with all manner of 'parlanti' beneath snatches of instrumental solos, the cantabili extended by repetition of words and musical phrases, the cabalettas by long modulatory excursions. Concertati become grandiose as never before with rolling periods and richly detailed accompaniments. Yet the effect whether monumental as in Mercadante, meandering as in Pacini, is that of the mixture as before but in larger doses. By the side of Mercadante's *Oriazi e Curiazi*, Pacini's *La Regina di Cipro* and Federico Ricci's *Estella di Murcia*, all written in 1846, Verdi's *Attila* of the same year, with its swift bludgeoning choruses and terse cabalettas, could well have been judged nasty, brutish and short. But at least it contains no superfluous tissue; it never sinks beneath its own weight.

The scoring of the period shows the same tendency towards complexity, while remaining strictly in the Rossinian manner with opaque tuttis and brilliant contrasting splashes of wind colour. There is nothing here like the organic use of full orchestra to be found in Wagner or Berlioz. The result is both garish and heavy. Verdi's scoring at its crudest is plain, Donizetti's rudimentary by comparison. Pacini in his latest works is tireless in his search for new, exotic orchestral tints. In his last

---

* Gatti, I, p. 207.

† Letter from Mercadante to Florimo, 1.1.1838. G. De Napoli, *La Triade nella drammatica altamurana* (Milan, 1931), p. 155.

opera *Niccolò de' Lapi*, posthumously performed in 1873,* the woodwind used in the prelude includes a basset horn; the opening ballabile combines harp and glockenspiel with a popping bassoon pattern of semiquavers. In his *Don Diego di Mendoza* (1867) there are two stage bands of brass and woodwind respectively, the first accompanying the good spirits, the second the bad in their contest for the soul of Don Enrico. A similar device – here called a double fanfare – is to be found in *Margherita Pusterla* (1856) to depict the supernatural activities on St John's Eve. In both cases the result would have been more impressive if there were the slightest attempt to give each of the two forces an appropriate harmonic colour. Neither shows any advance on Verdi's *Giovanna d'Arco* except in length. Curiously, at the time when Verdi was lightening and refining his orchestration Pacini and Mercadante were thickening theirs. We have already noted how the trombones and tuba in the tenor cavatina of *I Lombardi* are removed in the French revision, *Jérusalem*. In Mercadante's later works the brass choir is rarely absent for long, and his use of trumpet to double a vocal melody in whole or part far exceeds Verdi's. Liszt, it is true, maintained a great admiration for the author of *Le Due Illustri Rivali*, doubtless because his own orchestration has something of the same hard brilliance; but one can understand the slightly amused contempt of Eduard Hanslick for a musical culture in which Mercadante passed for a supreme contrapuntist.†

Apart from the filling out of inessential moments – the expansion of introductions with ever more intricate instrumental concertini, the prolongation of codas and codettas – a tiny symptom of the degeneration of the primo ottocento tradition can be noted in the increasing use of rapid dotted rhythms at moments where Verdi and Donizetti would be content with simple quavers and semiquavers. Both composers when they do employ this device usually restrict it to one part only so as not to impede the rhythmic flow. With Mercadante it continually invades the full orchestra, sometimes creating a spurious sense of excitement, sometimes giving a no less spurious dignity to a passage that might otherwise sound too cursive and trivial. In Federico Ricci's music, the standard form of the 'polonaise' accompaniment is ♪♫♫♫ etc., usually marked 'allegro trattenuto' as though to warn the performers not to treat it lightly.

Obviously so long as theatrical conditions, the demands of leading singers and the taste of the public remained constant no radical reform was possible. Pacini describes how he attempted to strike out in new paths in his setting of Cammarano's *Merope*, based on Alfieri's tragedy:

> I had in mind to depart completely (insofar as the Italian musical art permits it, since, as I say, without melody one can only write chords) to depart, I say, from all the accepted forms, following the action and expressing in music the different passions and natures of the characters. For Merope I devised an impassioned style of singing; for Egisto a vigorous and agitated style; for Polifonte a reserved, dissimulating manner. All this I did, flattering myself with the prospect of winning praise; but the effect failed to match up to my hopes; and the opera was never revived.‡

---

* Recent research has discovered this opera to be more or less identical with *Lidia di Brabante* (1858).
† E. Hanslick, *Die moderne Oper* (Berlin, 1880), I, p. 227.
‡ Pacini, *Le Mie Memorie artistiche* (Florence, 1873), pp. 102–3.

Such were the consequences of attempting to step out of line; though of course had such a revolution been possible it may be doubted whether Pacini was the man to have carried it through. He adds later: 'In my *Regina di Cipro* I entirely abandoned the declamatory style to give myself up if not wholly at any rate in part to my first manner – which won me much praise from the most illustrious and distinguished Avvocato Brofferio. Did I do wrong?'* For such as Pacini there was no escape from the operatic straitjacket or the verdicts of the various Avvocati Brofferii who made up his audience. His *Saffo* might be accounted a classic; but it remained subject to spare-part surgery as any work of the 1830s. Two years after it was written he was informed by Cammarano that the contralto Marietta Brambilla 'demands that you send her at once a new aria for Sappho because the cavatina is not suited to her vocal means and besides it was never successful with audiences'.† At the same time for the part of Phaon Moriani requested 'a broad impassioned cantabile and a lyrical cabaletta'.‡ Twenty years later when its author was approaching the status of a grand old man, Adelaide Borghi Mamo, a famous Azucena of her day, did not hesitate to ask him for 'two cabalettas in place of the duets between Phaon and Sappho and between Sappho and Climene'.§

After the political events of 1848–9 censorship was strict as never before and the variety of subject matter, itself an important source of innovation, severely curtailed. Even for the composer with strong artistic objections there was no remedy. With Italy divided as well as ruled by Austria piracy continued, and with it the practice of interpolating irrelevant arias according to the whims of the singers. In 1856 Verdi could only beg his friend De Sanctis to try to persuade the management of the San Carlo theatre to hire the material of *Giovanna de Guzman* (*Les Vêpres Siciliennes*) from its rightful owner, i.e. Tito Ricordi, rather than have the music re-orchestrated from a pirated vocal score.¶ The following year *Simon Boccanegra* was revived at Reggio Emilia with Amelia's cavatina replaced by that of Donizetti's *Lucia*.‖ It was during this period that Verdi brought a lawsuit against the manager of the Théâtre des Italiens in Paris for using pirated versions of his operas, and lost. Our own House of Lords meanwhile had passed a law which recognized as 'protected' only works which had been composed in England. The result in the case of the first English performance of *Luisa Miller* has already been noted.** Milan was now a police state in which visitors were required to surrender their passports in exchange for *carte di sicurezza*, failure to produce which could lead to arrest and imprisonment. The Austrian rulers had reversed their policy of leniency in matters theatrical. Bass and baritone soloists in *I Puritani* were forced to amend 'gridando libertà' to 'gridando lealtà'. Grandiose choruses even in the most blameless of neo-classical contexts were now suspect. Mercadante's *Virginia* of 1851 had to wait sixteen years for its first production, although Alfieri's plot had been familiar to operatic audiences since the

---

* Pacini, pp. 104–5. Here Pacini's memory seems to be playing him false; in fact *La Regina di Cipro* came before *Merope*.

† Letter from Cammarano to Pacini, 8.1.1842. Fondo Pacini, Pescia, No. 1191.

‡ Letter from Moriani to Pacini, 31.1.1842. Pescia, No. 1128.

§ Letter from Mamo to Pacini, 19.9.1863. Pescia, No. 1186.

¶ Letter to De Sanctis, 17.7.1856. *Carteggi Verdiani*, I, p. 36.

‖ See letter to T. Ricordi, July 1857 (precise date not given). Abbiati, II, p. 430.

** See Vol. I, p. 445

beginning of the century.* Sexual permissiveness as so often was considered to go hand in hand with political subversion. The liberties that Verdi had won by dogged persistence and the authority of his own eminence for *Rigoletto* and *La Traviata* were just not possible to his contemporaries; and even he was to fall foul of the Neapolitan censors in 1858 with a plot that Auber had made famous in 1833 and that Bellini had considered setting the next year with every confidence of its being permitted. While *Rigoletto* was going the rounds of the Italian theatres with comparatively minor mutilations, the librettist Giuseppe Giannini thought fit to caution Pacini not to set *La Mendicante* 'because the censorship does not allow adulterous loves of any kind whether punished or unpunished'.† While Verdi was crying out for 'new subjects, new forms'‡ his lesser colleagues were retreading well worn paths, often choosing plots that had been set a hundred times before, but giving increasing emphasis to their more sensational aspects.

Indeed the fashion in operatic dénouements was to describe a full semicircle in the course of the century. In Rossini's time, with few exceptions, all operas ended happily. By 1830 the pendulum had already begun its swing. In Mercadante's *Vestale* (1840) the heroine suffers the fate from which she is rescued in Spontini's setting. In Federico Ricci's *Griselda* (1847) her well known patience, rewarded in every other setting of the legend from Scarlatti to Massenet, is exhausted at the end of her trials and she decides to go home to her father. By the 1890s no serious plot was allowed to end in anything but tragedy. Hence in Catalani's *La Wally* Wilhelmine von Hillern's story is altered to allow the hero and heroine to die in an avalanche.

Meanwhile during the mid-century librettists devised increasingly complex variants on the themes of passion, poison and paranoia (for mental derangement still offered the best field for a virtuoso prima donna's display of talent). If the end was a cataclysm – the flooding of Holland in Petrella's *Elnava* (1856) or the eruption of Vesuvius in his *Jone* (1858) – so much the better, since it gave the scene-painter a chance to show his paces. But in general the star singers remained the axis round which Italian opera continued to revolve, and in consequence they were a conditioning factor in its structure – and all the more since choral competition had been reduced. Not an aria, not a duet but contained a cadenza – that strange survival from the age of improvisation – and its full stop for applause. The basic separation of lyrical and declamatory elements remained what it had been since Rossini's time. Orchestral interest was still confined to the 'scena' and prelude. Once launched on a lyrical flight no one would permit the distraction of anything more than a strict pattern of pounding or thrumming in the accompaniment. Concertati were still dominated in most cases by one singer. Hence the persistence of generic rather than specific characters: the standard bellicose baritone (Rocco in Pedrotti's *Isabella d'Aragone* (1859)); the faceless, ranting tenor (Gallieno in Petrella's *Morosina* (1859)).

As might be expected the 'convenienze' still obtained, though, in accordance with that linguistic inflation which results in the longest note being called a 'breve' and the slowest train being described until recently as 'accelerato', the terms were subject to a steady devaluation. In the 1850s an operatic bill could list as many as six 'primi'. A comprimario was anyone who had a certain scenic importance (Gastone, for

* It had supplied the Christian names of Verdi's two children by his first wife.
† Letter from Giannini to Pacini, 18.6.1853. Pescia, No. 973.
‡ Letter to De Sanctis, 1.1.1853. *Carteggi Verdiani*, I, pp. 16–17.

instance, and the Baron in *La Traviata*, neither of whom has more than the occasional line to sing). Further sub-categories were invented like consolation prizes. Dr Greville (*La Traviata* again) is called 'basso profondo' although not only is his line not especially deep, but he sings *above* the Marchese in the ensembles. To the category of 'buffo' is added the newly devised 'baritono brillante', of which the most notable specimen is Fra Melitone.

For one unexpected outcome of the escapist mood engendered by the new censorship was a revival of opera buffa and opera semiseria, both forms at a relative discount in the earnest Risorgimentale atmosphere of the 1840s (*Linda* and *Don Pasquale* were written for Vienna and Paris respectively). At the time of Verdi's *Un Giorno di Regno* a critic had remarked that it was not easy to find anything new to say in traditional operatic comedy. Ten years later, with tragic opera nearing the end of its resources, the balance of the two genres was redressed. Doubtless too the fact that the field of comedy had not been cultivated by the formidable Verdi emboldened lesser and younger composers to try their hand at it. Significantly, it was in 1850 that *Un Giorno di Regno* began a successful run at the Teatro San Benedetto in Venice. The same theatre saw the production of *Crispino e la Comare*, the fourth and most successful collaboration by the brothers Ricci, in which Luigi's more forceful personality is nicely balanced by Federico's more refined musicianship. Despite the obloquy heaped upon it by Bernard Shaw when it reached London as a companion piece to *Cavalleria Rusticana*,* *Crispino* was to prove a minor landmark in Italian operatic comedy – an early prototype of those charming, puppet-like operas in which Wolf-Ferrari was so extraordinarily fertile. Piave's libretto about the poor cobbler who with the aid of a fairy godmother becomes a famous doctor unites Molière with that element of the fantastic that Rossini had deliberately excluded from his *Cenerentola*.

It was in comedy, too, that Errico Petrella, Verdi's exact contemporary, achieved his first success, with *Il Carnevale di Venezia, ossia Le Precauzioni* – a vigorous piece notable for its use of extended 'parlanti' (i.e. declamation over orchestral melody). The same year Antonio Cagnoni followed up his student *Don Bucefalo* with *Amori e trappole*, to the plot of Rossini's *L'Occasione fa il ladro* expanded into a full evening's entertainment. Opera semiseria triumphed in Petrella's *Elena di Tolosa* (1852) and Mercadante's *Violetta* (1853), with their stories of innocence calumnied, then vindicated to a brilliant coloratura rondò finale.

Yet the sad truth is that there was scarcely more novelty in these comedies than in their tragic counterparts. Cagnoni's essay in neo-Rossini seems almost consciously archaic, with cantabile and cabaletta immediately juxtaposed and even the occasional 'open' melody, as in Virginia's cavatina. In the last analysis *Il Carnevale di Venezia* does little more than exaggerate the tricks of twenty years earlier, with consequent disproportion of means to ends. True, there are original moments; e.g. the declaimed strophe ('Ho due ragazze') used as a refrain within a highly formal movement in Muzio's aria di sortita; but the hydrophobic cabaletta that follows ('Ah mi sento un fremito') is little more than a variant of the chattering-buffo-with-chorus formula to be found in *Torquato Tasso* and many other works of the 1830s. *Crispino* is undoubtedly the best comedy of the decade for both melodic freshness and unpretentious suppleness of form; yet here too the idiom is ultra-conservative. The

* G. B. Shaw, *Shaw's Music*, ed. Dan H. Laurence (London, 1981), II, pp. 437–8.

popular duet 'Vedi, o cara, tal sacchetto?' follows in the wake of Rossini's 'Dunque io son' from the *Barber* with the man syllabating on the bass line and the woman indulging in flights of coloratura. Incredibly, all operas of the buffo or the semiserio genre preserve the tradition of recitative with keyboard as if *Don Pasquale* had never existed.* Luigi Ricci's *Piedigrotta* (1852) uses the equally outdated convention of speech in Neapolitan dialect between numbers, as in the first version of Bellini's *Adelson e Salvini*. In each case the effect is pretty and decorative, but without any of that humanity that make *L'Elisir d'amore* and *Don Pasquale*, like all genuine comedy, living documents of their time, and which doubtless led Donizetti to insist that the latter should be given in modern dress. True, the young Bizet was sufficiently intrigued by the Italian musical scene to offer to the authorities of the Paris Conservatoire an opera buffa as the main fruit of his year in Italy as winner of the Prix de Rome. But *Don Procopio* is decidedly an opera buffa with a difference. In it Bizet finds room for such characteristic ideas as a march theme from his first symphony and an early more extended version of the serenade that re-appears in *La Jolie Fille de Perth*. You will search in vain for anything as striking in the works of Petrella, Pacini or Mercadante. The most modest of French composers was always ready to enrich his idiom by means of the exotic whether from Spain, Scotland or the Far East. The mid-century Italians apart from the occasional Spanish rhythm preferred to keep to unadulterated Italian currency, no matter how devalued. The melody that dominates the ballroom scene in Mercadante's *Il Reggente* may be marked 'contradanza inglese' (the setting is in fact Scotland); the opening chorus of Pacini's *Malvina di Scozia* ('Cingi, salvata Scozia') may require the dancers to 'perform characteristic dances'. In either case the music is as straightforwardly Italian as can be imagined, apart from a certain pointing of the rhythm, possibly intended to suggest the 'dot' and 'snap' of the Strathspey. Neither approaches the overture to Mayr's *Ginevra di Scozia* (1802) let alone Boieldieu's *La Dame blanche* (1825) in striking a recognizably Scottish note. This harmonic stasis is yet another by-product of the tyranny of star singers whose special talents showed to best advantage over a basis of simple progressions. Composers who lacked the somewhat academic resourcefulness of a Mercadante were only too ready to fall back on alternations of tonic and dominant to accommodate the coloratura of a prima donna or the logorrhea of a buffo.

Yet by the end of the 1850s the means to reform were becoming ready to hand. Orchestras were improving; the old three-string double bass was giving way to an instrument of four strings (the modern bass with four or five strings was not established in Italy until the 1880s) so permitting a fuller, deeper sound to the string section as well as a more rational proportion of basses to cellos than that of which Berlioz had complained. Above all the direction, previously divided between the 'maestro al cembalo' or 'maestro concertatore' who rehearsed the singers and the primo violino who conducted on the night with his bow from a first violin part, passed by degrees into the hands of the professional conductor, with far-reaching consequences.

Here too Italy had been far behind the times. By the 1820s the conductor's authority had been established in the opera houses of Germany and Austria, so helping to shape the course of German romantic opera and ultimately paving the

---

* A remark by Bernard Shaw in the above mentioned passage suggests that 'recitativo secco' was accompanied in this case not by a keyboard instrument but by spread chords on solo cello.

way for Wagnerian music drama. Not till the 1850s did Italy produce a crop of conductors, mostly recruited from the orchestral strings, who could ensure a comparable standard of performance: Luigi Arditi, Michele Costa, Giovanni Bottesini *et al.* Foremost amongst them was Angelo Mariani who became resident conductor in Genoa in 1852. He it was who introduced to Italy works such as Meyerbeer's *Le Prophète* and *L'Africaine* as well as Verdi's *Don Carlos* in performances far worthier than they had received in Paris. In 1871 and 1872 he was to give the first Italian performances of *Lohengrin* and *Tannhäuser* respectively. His first collaboration with Verdi occurred in Rimini in 1857 over the première of *Aroldo*. Its fruit was the 'burrasca' in the fourth act of that opera – an essay in orchestral virtuosity which the composer would never have risked without the presence of an authoritative baton. From then on Verdi never ceased to insist on the importance of a central direction; of a conductor who assumes total responsibility to the composer and whose rule is absolute over singers, orchestra and stage director – as the producer was then called.* Naturally it took time for the new system to be adopted throughout Italy. In many theatres the dual reign of 'primo violino' and 'maestro concertatore' persisted. As usual at that time it was the South that lagged behind. By 1869 Verdi maintained that theatres such as the San Carlo were not suitable for performance of his latest operas but only for the classics of the cabaletta period and their unworthy successors.† For him the presence of a conductor represented the watershed dividing the operas of today from those of yesterday.

Another area to come under the conductor's authority was the stage band, which thus ceased to be a heterogeneous collection of instruments and became a properly balanced ensemble. In many operas including Petrella's *Caterina Howard* (1865) and Pacini's *Niccolò de' Lapi* (1873, posthumous) it consists of brass instruments only, mercifully free from the bleating of clarinets. In this respect such theatres as Genoa and Bologna were already in advance of the Paris Opéra where throughout the 1860s the stage bands remained under the separate direction of Adolphe Saxe, and where the principal conductor, Dietsch, until his dismissal in 1863, directed from a first violin part, precision being achieved only by months of previous rehearsal which left the players bored and resulted in dull performances. Here too Verdi never tired of contrasting the alert playing under conductors such as Costa and Mariani with the listless thrumming of the Parisians.‡

Another event of importance was the rise of the professional, musically informed critic, a phenomenon unknown in Italy before the middle of the century, if we discount the correspondents of the *Allgemeine musikalische Zeitung* of Leipzig who wrote for Germans. In Italy, as we have seen, the critic was no more than a reporter; it was the public's verdict which counted and from it there was no appeal save to the public of another city. A fiasco in Milan might be redeemed in Venice or Bologna; but unless it were merely due to the production's being behind schedule, as with

---

* Incredible as it may seem in an age which refers to 'Visconti's' *Don Carlos,* 'Béjart's' *Traviata,* and 'Bergman's' *Zauberflöte,* the producer had a very minor role in nineteenth-century Italy. In most cases he was the librettist and his business was to supervise the stage machinery and direct the singers' movements (see preface). The faithful Piave ended his career as a notoriously inefficient stage director at La Scala, Milan.

† See letter to De Sanctis, 21.5.1869. *Carteggi Verdiani,* I, pp. 111–12.

‡ See letter to Escudier, 11.6.1867. *R.M.I.* (1928), p. 525.

Bellini's *Beatrice di Tenda* in Venice and Pacini's *Giovanna d'Arco* in Rome, composers generally attributed it to a fault in their own music and either modified the score accordingly or else cut their losses and used the best material in a new work. No journalist would presume to speak in defence of an opera that had met with general disapproval. However when in 1857 *Simon Boccanegra* was badly received one authoritative voice spoke up firmly in its defence: that of Filippo Filippi, future editor of the *Gazzetta Musicale di Milano* and critic of the periodical *Perseveranza*. In this capacity he delivered a most perceptive eulogy of *Un Ballo in maschera*, an opera whose success was continually frustrated by difficulties of casting. Throughout the '60s Filippi's judgement and that of his colleague Francesco D'Arcais carried the same weight as that of Chorley and Davison in England, Reyer and Berlioz in France. For men of Verdi's generation this was clearly a mixed blessing since it was not easy to blame their strictures on mere contingencies. Moreover, independence of judgement carries with it the possibility of disagreement amongst the critics themselves – a fact which, astonishingly, even today arouses mistrust. Verdi wrote irritably to a friend: 'Put a young [composer], for example, between D'Arcais and Filippi who are in fact among the best critics yet are always at odds with each other, and tell me what should the young man do when he hears one approve of what the other condemns? What a fine thing if there were no newspapers! Everything would be all right and the good things would be just as good.'* True, but they might be less appreciated without informed leadership of public opinion. Like many a composer Verdi forgets that a critic's function is to help the listener, not the creative artist. His preposterous disclaimer to Filippi about his 'somma ignoranza musicale' amounts to no more than putting up a 'No Entry' sign outside his musical workshop.†

In 1859 the Austrian army was defeated at the battle of Solferino by a combined force of French and Italians. Within the next two years, Lombardy was ceded to Piedmont by the peace of Villafranca, the north Italian duchies were permitted to vote themselves into King Vittorio Emmanuele's enlarged realm, Garibaldi invaded the Kingdom of the Two Sicilies, and the State of Italy was proclaimed. So from most of the peninsula the long nightmare of censorship was lifted: and works such as *La Battaglia di Legnano* and *Les Vêpres Siciliennes* could at length be performed under their original titles. But theatrical conditions could hardly change overnight, since many of the old economic factors continued to operate as before. The tyranny of the star singer was less easily shaken off than that of the Austrian governorship. But one important result of political freedom was a ferment of new ideas especially among the intellectuals of North Italy, such as was bound in due course to impinge even on the conservative world of Italian opera.

In 1862 two young students from the Milan Conservatoire, Franco Faccio and Arrigo Boito, set out on a travelling scholarship to France and Northern Europe. Both were filled with a sense of mission – to bring the new Italy into the mainstream of European culture. They had already collaborated on two patriotic cantatas, *Il 4 Giugno* and *Sorelle d'Italia*, which were produced at the annual Conservatory concerts. Both had attracted unfavourable attention from the more conservative press, which accused composer and librettist of reckless experiment and of not respecting the limitations of their art. Such a criticism would hardly have dismayed

---

* Letter to Piroli, 22.1.1872. *Carteggi Verdiani*, III, pp. 89–90.
† See letter to Filippi, 4.3.1869. *Copialettere*, pp. 616–17.

Boito; for he belonged to a new generation of musicians and writers who under the guidance of the writer Teodoro Rovani believed that the future would see a merging of the arts – indeed that the value of a modern work existed in proportion to the extent that it broke down the frontiers that tradition had erected between them. They wore Bohemian clothes, congregated at the Caffè Martini, read Baudelaire and Hugo, and drank absinthe; they raged against the established order with a fury worthy of the German *Sturm und Drang* movement of a century earlier; and like the *Sturm und Drang* their movement took its title from a work by one of its members: Cletto Arrighi's novella *La Scapigliatura e il 6 febbraio*. As so often happens the iconoclasm of the 'scapigliati' was all the more violent for having occurred late. 'Christ has died again!' cried the poet Emilio Praga in a blasphemous attack on Italy's literary 'saint', Manzoni.* More balanced and self-disciplined than his fellow rebels – though for a time he lived as flamboyantly as they – Boito seems deliberately to have set himself up as the converse of the average Italian composer. This was the easier in that Boito himself was only half Italian. His mother was a Polish countess who had married – and been deserted by – a brilliant but ne'er-do-well miniature-painter. Although he never regarded himself as other than Italian Boito grew up as essentially an outsider, his mother's relatives being the only part of his family known to him. He was thus free from many of his fellow-countrymen's tabus.

Was the Italian a craftsman first and foremost? Boito was a theorist with the most lofty and extravagant ideas. Was the Italian composer wrapped up in his own art with no pretensions to a wider education? Boito was a polymath, a man of letters who wrote poems, stories and libretti; and just as certain poems of Praga are little more than a succession of brightly coloured images like impressionist word-paintings, so those of Boito often form ingenious assonances worthy of Edith Sitwell, as though deliberately encroaching on the domain of music. Was the Italian composer orientated almost entirely towards the human voice? Boito associated himself with the revival of instrumental music, which had begun with the foundation of the Società del Quartetto at Florence in 1859; but it was none the less in the field of opera that he hoped, like Wagner, that the final union of the arts would be achieved.

Boito pursued his aims on three fronts: as composer, as librettist for his colleague Faccio – musically the more accomplished of the two if less original in his ideas – and as theatre critic first for *Perseveranza*, then for the short-lived *Figaro* (an artistic weekly founded and edited by himself and Praga), and finally the *Giornale della Società del Quartetto*, the Milanese equivalent of the Quartet Society of Florence. As critic Boito was fairly insufferable, whether on the subject of operas or spoken plays. The unfortunate author of *Un Male Esempio in famiglia* was compared to a man who finds that by blowing into a flute he can make a sound of some kind and therefore imagines himself to be a virtuoso flautist.† Lodovico Muratori's *I Figli dell'arrichito* prompted a long essay on a more famous writer of the same name, at the end of which the playwright is thanked 'for having so kindly awakened memories of his namesake and so giving us the opportunity of devoting our entire column to him'.‡ Of the play

---

* 'Cristo è rimorto' instead of 'Cristo è risorto', i.e. 'Christ is risen again'. The pun is untranslatable.

† See review in *Figaro*, 21.1.1864. A. Boito, *Tutti gli scritti* a cura di P. Nardi (Milan, 1942), pp. 1102–5.

‡ *Figaro*, 3.3.1864. *Ibid*, pp. 1132–3.

itself not a word. A review of Rota's opera *Ginevra di Scozia* begins with the ominous word 'Tekel'. Thereafter Boito relentlessly pursues the biblical parallel to the point of declaring that if thrown into the sea the entire score would float, so light are its contents. Then comes the sermon.

> If ever there was an age in which the splendid revelations of the aesthetic theorists have far outstripped the idleness of artists and public it is this age of ours. At this hour, at this very moment the path that music must follow is picked out in brilliant light. Its laws have been laid down; its lofty theories deeply implanted in the visionary spirit of many a noble intellect. He who will not or cannot recognize these laws and theories, he who casts them aside with loathing is a stranger to the True, the Beautiful, the New.

Rota's chief sin was conformity to an outworn tradition. Even a trace of ugliness in his music would be welcome provided it evinced some originality.

> But no; he follows the procession of deacons, subdeacons, clerics, sacristans . . . with candle in hand and censer swinging, saying Amen at every step and bowing at every altar with the material devotion of a monk and the timid humility of a nun.*

In other words the old ideals of modest craftsmanship which had served Italian music for generations were no longer to be tolerated; and Boito set about attacking them with the fury of Siegfried smashing the handiwork of a Mime. Eduard Hanslick had waxed satirical over the wealth of obligatory forms which made post-Rossinian opera resemble Chinese or Negroes, mutually distinguishable only by each other.† Boito, reviewing Cagnoni's *Il Vecchio della montagna*, was moved to similar observations which he conveyed characteristically, through a lesson in linguistics. The Italians, he said, confused 'form' with 'formula', the second being in every way a diminutive of the first and having as much in common with it as Ruscelli's rhyming dictionary has with an ode by Horace. Formula, he maintained, had dominated Italian opera from its inception; it had acquired strength, development and variety with each successive genius but it always remained *formula*; witness the array of terms such as aria, rondò, cabaletta, stretta, ritornello, pezzo concertato and so on. Likewise the very term 'libretto' is in itself a trivializing diminutive of 'libro'. Conclusion: it is impossible to write good music not only to a bad libretto but to a libretto of any kind. The modern musician must therefore think not in terms of 'libretti' but of tragedy as did the ancient Greeks.‡

Having diagnosed the disease Boito was less specific about the cure. Salvation, he believed, lay in the pursuit of the lofty and the sublime, unfettered by petty rules; and the loftier the conception the more simple it will be. 'The sublime is simpler than the beautiful. The beautiful can incarnate itself in all sorts of forms, the most strange, the most multiple, the most disparate; but for the sublime only one great form is fitting — the divine form, universal, eternal — the *spherical* form. The horizon is sublime, the sea

---

* Review from *Figaro*, 21.1.1864. *Ibid*, pp. 1106–8.
† Hanslick, *Die moderne Oper*, I, p. 218.
‡ From *La Perseveranza*, 13.9.1863. Boito, pp. 1079–82.

is sublime, the sun is sublime. Shakespeare is spherical, Dante is spherical, Beethoven is spherical; the sun is simpler than a carnation, the sea simpler than a brook; Mendelssohn's Adagio [Op. 87] is simpler than Mozart's Andante [from K. 387].'* This 'spherical' theory provoked much derision, not least from Verdi and his friends.

Boito's hierarchy in the instrumental world was dominated by Beethoven – 'As Dante in poetry† . . . Bach comes up to his chest, Mendelssohn to his head, Schumann to his elbow, Haydn to his knee.'‡ From Wagner, curiously enough, he held himself strictly aloof, regarding him as a false prophet; one who had diagnosed the ills of the age but had proposed the wrong remedies. 'Richard Wagner was the Bar Jesus of the art of his time.'§ The 'was' tells everything. Not only was Wagner's music unknown in Italy, but no opera of his later than *Lohengrin* had been performed anywhere in Europe; and a young man of Boito's age might be forgiven for assuming that the firebrand of the north had given up composition for aesthetic speculation. Later, when Wagner's music began to penetrate to Italy, Boito became his self-appointed public relations officer, so earning a long, characteristically involved letter from the composer setting out his beliefs about the musical genius of Italy and Germany respectively and the need for a marriage between the two.¶ Boito also made translations of *Rienzi*, *Der fliegende Holländer* and *Der Liebesmahl der Apostolen* and finally *Tristan und Isolde*. But for the music even of the mature works he could muster no enthusiasm. 'A tasteless plot that moves more slowly than a stopping train, with an interminable succession of duets . . .' thus he described *Die Walküre* in a letter to Verdi in 1893.‖ Yet this was at a time when young Italian composers were at last beginning to come to terms with Wagner and to benefit from his example. Doubtless it was partly the nationalist element at the heart of Wagner's writings that repelled the cosmopolitan Boito. The fact remains that the laborious theorizings of *Oper und Drama* did at least offer a new and workable basis for operatic construction. The rhodomontade of Boito too often suggests the bombinations of the painter Lypiatt in Aldous Huxley's *Antic Hay*, masking a certain creative impotence.

In opera, he considered, nobody had advanced beyond Meyerbeer, 'whose works, once appreciated, caused Italian operas to collapse by the hundreds like the bricks of the walls of Jericho: most of Bellini's, the greater part of Donizetti's, almost all Rossini's . . . and some of Verdi's'.** For Verdi himself Boito's admiration at the time was genuine if qualified. There is no evidence that he shared the views of his brother Camillo, who classed Verdi with Petrella as a writer of cabaletta-operas and dismissed *Un Ballo in maschera* as an 'operaccia', the worst he had ever written. He praised *Rigoletto* as eternally youthful in contrast to *I Lombardi* which he felt to have aged beyond repair.†† *Les Vêpres Siciliennes* he found somewhat faded as a whole but full of exquisite detail; and he drew attention to the important role played by the French language. 'French verse, being less measured than our own, and having smoother and less definite accents, has helped the music since it has removed the

* From *Giornale della Società del Quartetto*, 7.5.1865. *Ibid*, pp. 1169–72. In English, Walker, p. 455.
† From *Figaro*, 28.1.1864. Boito, p. 1110.
‡ *Giornale della Società del Quartetto*, 6.4.1865. *Ibid*., p. 1168.
§ 'Mendelssohn in Italia', from the *Giornale della Società del Quartetto*, 1864. *Ibid*., p. 1257.
¶ R. Wagner, 'Lettera ad un amico italiano', 7.11.1871. Quoted in its entirety, Abbiati, III, pp. 491–4.
‖ Letter from Boito, 31.12.1893. M. Medici & M. Conati: Carteggio Verdi–Boito, 2 vols (Parma, 1978), I. p. 221.
** From *Figaro*, 11.2.1864. Boito, p. 1122. †† From *Figaro*, 7.1.1864. *Ibid*., pp. 1092–7.

tedium of cantilena of symmetry, of that mighty dowry and mighty sin of Italian prosody which *generates a meanness and poverty of rhythm within the musical phrase.'*

Here once more from his vantage point half in and half out of the Italian tradition Boito has diagnosed one of the chief causes of the stagnation of Italian opera during the mid century. Indeed the whole subject of Italian metre and its determining effect upon operatic structure has received very little attention until recently.†

The classification of the metres themselves, though logical enough, is not easy to make clear to the non-Italian reader. Like English and German, and unlike French, Italian words carry a tonic accent which makes itself felt in the structure of its verse. But whereas our metres are classified according to the type and number of feet employed (iambic pentameter, trochaic tetrameter, etc.) Italian verses are categorized first by the number of syllables to a line (quinario, senario, etc.); secondly according to the position of the stress in the final word ('tronco' if it is on the last syllable, 'piano' if on the penultimate, 'sdrucciolo' if on the propenultimate). This second method at first sight appears to contradict the first. A seven-syllable line will only contain seven syllables if it is a 'settenario piano'; if it is tronco it will have six, and if sdrucciolo eight. However, for practical purposes

> Mi lagnerò tacendo (piano, Metastasio)
> De' miei bollenti spiriti (sdrucciolo, Piave)
> Parlo d'amor con me (tronco, da Ponte)

are all variants of the same settenario metre and all three may coexist even in the same quatrain.

The metres are six in number – quinario, senario, settenario, ottonario, decasillabo (10) and endecasillabo (11).‡ With all their variations they constitute the most flexible and wide-ranging system of operatic verse ever devised, as is proved by its survival from the age of Metastasio, when it was perfected, into the middle of the following century, through more than one revolution in musical style. (Metastasio's verse, it should be remembered, was still being set as vocal chamber music in the salons of Milan in Verdi's time.) None the less as in the early decades of the nineteenth century the melodic structure of the aria became simpler and more schematic so the special properties of each type of metre began to make themselves more strongly felt than in a previous age, when the greater independence of the orchestral part and a greater degree of verbal repetition often combined to mask the basic shape from view; so that for instance in 'Non so più cosa son cosa faccio' Mozart is able to change from decasillabi to settenarii without the listener being aware of it.§ At no point did any Italian metre exercise the tyranny that the German stressed iambics wield over the rhythmic structure of *Tannhäuser* and *Lohengrin*;

---

* From *Figaro*, 11.2.1864. *Ibid.*, pp. 1117–20. Italics mine.

† 'Der italienische Vers und der musikalische Rhythmus. Zum Verhältnis von Vers und Musik in der italienischen Opera des 19. Jahrhunderts, mit einem Rückblick auf der 2. Hälfte des 18. Jahrhunderts', I. Teil, in *Analecta Musicologica*, XII (Cologne, 1973), pp. 253–369; 2. Teil, *ibid.*, XIV, pp. 324–410; 3. Teil, *ibid.*, XV, pp. 298–333. The author is Friedrich Lippmann.

‡ The novenario (9) was not then an accepted operatic metre in Italy; but it occurs quite frequently in German *Singspiel* of the late eighteenth century when most German librettists were content to adopt Italian metres. Thus it figures amid the settenari and ottonari of *Die Entführung*; in *Die Zauberflöte* it actually predominates over all other metres.

§ See Lippmann, *An. Mus.*, XII, p. 272.

yet for that very reason its dangers were all the more insidious, forcing the mid-century Italian composers into an automatic adoption of formulae of which they were hardly aware themselves.

Moreover, as Lippmann has not failed to notice, certain special laws operate within the system. First, metrical accent makes itself far more strongly felt in the even as distinct from the odd syllable metres. The ottonario is invariably trochaic, the metre of Longfellow's *Hiawatha* with accented and unaccented syllables in strict alternation; and its rapidly recurring accents make it particularly suitable for fast movements such as strette and cabalette. The ♩ ♫ ♫ ♩ ♫ ♫ ♩♩ ᵥᵥ so often encountered in strette from Rossini onward springs from the use of ottonario verse. Likewise the senario with its perpetual canter of broken anapaests lends itself to those short self-extending rhythmic patterns so dear to Donizetti.* The anapaest also dominates the decasillabo, rare in the eighteenth century but very common in the nineteenth and familiar as the metre of Verdi's rolling Risorgimento choruses – 'Va pensiero sull'ali dorate', 'O Signore dal tetto natio', 'Si ridesti il leon di Castiglia'. Despite variations in the tempo and the melodic figuration the rhythmic structure is identical in each case. In planning the exiles' chorus for the first *Macbeth* Verdi did well to ask Piave for a metre other than the decasyllabic for fear of repeating himself.† The decasillabo can also generate the stretta rhythm instanced above, with the quavers carrying a syllable each in the second and third bars. In both ottonario and decasillabo such is the force of the metrical accent that it is rare to find any setting of a line that exceeds four bars of fast tempo or two of slow.

The odd-syllable verse-types are altogether more flexible. The commonest of them, the settenario, was from the start the slow lyrical metre *par excellence*, its iambic basis never obtruding like the trochees of the ottonario or the anapaests of the decasillabo. Not only is the first syllable often accented, as in 'Parmi veder le lagrime'. Even where it is not composers often set it on a strong beat; and the same tradition applies to the quinario – hence such apparent solecisms of scansion as '*Di* tanti palpiti', '*La* donna è mobile'. However, as Lippmann points out, the downbeat usually turns out to be a 'Nebenakzent', or subsidiary downbeat such as occurs in the middle of a bar. In both the melodic line can sprawl in irregular three- or five-bar designs (e.g. 'Si, ritrovarla io giuro' from *La Cenerentola*) without any verbal repetition.

The metrical physiognomy of the endecasillabo is still more various. Mostly an iambic pentameter, it can assume the form of the Catullan line ('Tutti accusan le donne ed io le scuso' – *Così fan tutte*); it can consist of four dactyls ('Gaie comari di Windsor, è l'ora' – *Falstaff*); it can even fall into two irregular parts ('Com' è gentil – la notte a mezzo april' – *Don Pasquale*). As Wagner was to find out, opera thrives on short lines, and for the lyric forms the endecasillabo was in general found too long for comfort and therefore confined to recitatives where it co-existed with the settenario in so-called 'versi sciolti'. Not surprisingly the most memorable settings of hendecasyllabic verse come from those two masters of the long melody – Bellini and the Verdi of *Aida* and *Otello*.

A glance at the libretti of the 1830s and '40s will show the prevalence of certain unwritten rules. Where the cantabile uses settenario metre the cabaletta tends to

---

* See also the present Italian national anthem.

† Letter to Piave, 10.12.1846. Abbiati, I, pp. 667–72.

ottonartio, and vice versa. Where ottonari are used for slow melodies the first two syllables are normally set as part of the upbeat.* In this way one of the four trochaic accents can be eliminated or at least softened so as not to disturb the lyrical flow. Here lies the explanation of an otherwise incomprehensible remark by Verdi to Boito in connection with the revision of *Simon Boccanegra*. Verdi had asked for some lines for a new duettino between Fiesco and Gabriele to replace the original 'Paventa o perfido'. Instead of cursing Boccanegra Fiesco was to bless bride and bridegroom to be and also introduce 'a bit of local patriotic feeling. Fiesco can say, "Love this angel . . . but after God . . . our country."'† Boito then supplied eight ottonario lines beginning 'Vieni a me ti benedico'. Verdi wrote back, 'I don't much like the ottonario rhythm because of those two cursed syllables on the upbeat . . . but I shall avoid that effect.'‡ He did indeed avoid it but with rather strange consequences; for the line as he set it runs 'Vieni a me ti benedico'. The rule was evidently not without its reasons.

Rhyme was another factor in the standardization of lyrical forms. The prevalence of the Metastasian double quatrain with its rhyme scheme of *abbc* for each verse brought with it a standard pattern of melodic construction apparently designed to mask the central assonance by making the first and third lines musically identical. Examples can be found in the late eighteenth century especially in comic opera where melodic simplicity was aimed at (compare for instance Paisiello's 'Nel cor più non mi sento' or even Mozart's 'Mit Zärtlichkeit und Schmeicheln'). The Bellinian scheme mentioned in Volume I of a^1 a^2 ba^2 and the variants of it to be found in Donizetti and early Verdi all spring from this same principle. Only when the tradition itself became stale did this procedure degenerate into an automatic formula. Cammarano, who more than any librettist between Romani and Boito understood the problems of operatic word-setting, often preferred to rhyme his second and fourth lines only, leaving the first and third free and so producing the so-called 'settenario doppio' (examples: 'Regnava nel silenzio' from *Lucia* and 'Condotta ell'era in ceppi' from *Il Trovatore*). The settenario doppio was to survive into the age of Boito and in fact dominates much of *Otello*.

The dilemma of the mid-century Italian opera composer can be glimpsed from the memoirs of Pacini. Speaking of his early cabalettas he denied that they were thrown off purely in the heat of careless inspiration. On the contrary, 'I studied ways of giving accentuation to poetic metres so as not to fall into melodies that recalled some other idea, as can happen all too easily, especially in the first bar.'§ He goes on to quote actual examples of settings by himself and Rossini of the 'quinario sdrucciolo'. If such problems presented themselves as early as the 1820s and '30s, how much more pressing they must have been twenty years later — if indeed Pacini is not merely

---

* At first sight this rule appears to be contradicted by the most famous of all examples of 'ottonario' slow melodies, 'Casta Diva'; but once again the first syllable turns out to be placed on a 'Nebenakzent', so forming a large-scale up-beat to the much stronger accent on the syllable *di*, which in his usual fashion Bellini has fortified with a long appoggiatura.

† Letter to Boito, 8.1.1880. Walker, p. 482.

‡ Letter to Boito, 10.1.1880. Walker, p. 483. Evidently unaware of the technical meaning of the phrase 'in levare' ('on the up-beat') Walker assumed it to be an idiosyncratic variant of 'da levare' ('to be removed') and translated it accordingly.

§ Pacini, pp. 70–1.

projecting his feelings at the time of writing to an earlier period of his career. Elsewhere, he writes,

> I believe too that the invention of new forms depends more on the author of the libretto than on the composer of the music. And in fact I notice that in *Norma* and *La Sonnambula*, sublime works by the genius of Catania, there are pieces woven by Romani in a manner quite different from so many of his other libretti with the result that the musical formulas also differ considerably from those used by Bellini himself in *Il Pirata*, in *Beatrice* and other works by him. Rossini in his great musical poem *Guillaume Tell* proceeds quite differently as regards the construction of his pieces from the Rossini of *Il Barbiere*, of *Mosè*, etcetera and the same will be found true of *Dom Sébastien* by the swan of Bergamo. And why? Because the text which served these compositions . . . was not conditioned by Italian poetry but by the French manner of articulation.'*

In other words Pacini had reached the same conclusion as Boito, but drew a different moral.

> Our sweet-sounding language and in consequence our poetry, ruled as it is by rhythm and uniformity of verse, are the principal factors in our musical phrase construction. The German and English peoples will never be able to overtake us because of the roughness of their tongue; nor will the French, though their language is rich in conceits, due to the irregularity of their verse, the poverty of their vocabulary, their diphthongs and finally because certain of their letters produce nasal sounds. . . .†

Yet observe the strenuous efforts of Pacini's contemporaries to escape from the straitjacket imposed by this 'poetry ruled by rhythm and uniformity of verse'; to avoid the inevitable caesura half-way through the second or fourth bar; or merely to exorcise the demon of mechanical symmetry. A few examples taken at random from between 1840 and 1870 will suffice to illustrate the point. In every case the metre is standard post-Metastasian. In the first and third it is tortured into a three-bar and six-bar phrase respectively; in the second the line is extended by pointless repetition so as to fill out the fourth bar; in the last it is twisted by coloratura and syncopation into a semblance of irregularity; and the result in all four examples is both laboured and trivial.

Mercadante : IL REGGENTE (1843)

---

* Pacini, pp. 54–5.   † Pacini, pp. 31–2.

Mercadante : ORAZI E CURIAZI (1846)

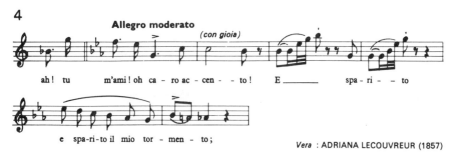

Vera : ADRIANA LECOUVREUR (1857)

Petrella : CATERINA HOWARD (1866)

Boito's answer to the problem is to be found first of all in his libretto for Faccio's *Amleto* (1865). It is not a radical solution, like the Stabreim of the *Ring*, the short cadenced phrases of *Tristan* or the freely scanned, irregular rhymed couplets of *Die Meistersinger*; but it breaks up the set patterns through a much freer intermingling of verse types, and always with a dramatic justification. The ghost, for instance, speaks throughout not only in hendecasyllabics but in the *terza rima* of Dante, as befits a spirit from Hell or Purgatory. While King and courtiers carouse in decasyllables Hamlet's 'O that this too too solid flesh would melt', like most of the soliloquies in the opera, is in Shakespearean blank verse. Hamlet's feigned madness is expressed in a curiously accented jerky design of quinari, to which Ophelia replies with orthodox senari. 'To be or not to be' begins with blank verse and ends with a double octave, each stanza of which begins with settenari doppi and ends with a Metastasian quatrain. Ophelia's mad scene is couched in rhyming couplets. Throughout the libretto we find an intricate play of verbal assonance and a recherché vocabulary that are to be a constant feature of Boito's libretti. The musical effect of this new style can be gauged to some extent from Hamlet's famous monologue. For the first part the standard lyrical forms are out of the question; Faccio responds to the challenge with a thoughtful 'parlante' over a simple yet well nourished orchestral texture rich in pregnant motifs.

Faccio : AMLETO (1865)

When the settenari take over a certain conventionality sets in, and indeed Boito's 'Ah se bastasse un rapido' (Ex. 6b) looks suspiciously like a compromise. It would be asking much of an Italian tenor to expect him to sing what everyone would recognize as his chief solo without the reward of a lyrical plum at the end. Even so the setting is clearly that of a man who wrote quartets and symphonic works as well as operas.

Amleto, though attended by every kind of publicity, achieved no more than a *succès d'estime*, like its more traditional predecessor *I Profughi fiamminghi*. Faccio's teacher, Mazzucato, might write enthusiastically to his colleague Ronchetti-Monteviti (who taught Boito), about the 'truthfulness of the dramatic concepts, the novelty of the forms, the passion of the melodies, the magisterial harmonies' and declare that another opera written in this style would demonstrate to the world that the decline of Italian opera was a fiction.* A more reliable account is that given by Mariani to Verdi during the rehearsals: 'It's a pity that what is good in the opera isn't new, and what is new is a little boring. . . . Faccio is a good musician, his scoring is extremely well calculated, he harmonizes with elegance, but it's all rather heavy, too much licked into shape and even too prolix.'† The reception given to a further performance at La Scala six years later convinced Faccio that the career of opera composer was not for him.

But of course it was from his own example as a composer that the real justification of Boito's theories was awaited. Not until 1868 was his *Mefistofele* ready for public view. It was both more unorthodox in form and considerably longer than the work we know today though it lacked the duet 'Lontano, lontano, lontano', imported from the unfinished *Ero e Leandro*, and Margherita's 'Spunta l'aurora pallida'. It included a scene at the Emperor's court, taken from the second part of Goethe's play, and a symphonic intermezzo representing a battle. As might be imagined, Boito's Faust opera is far more faithful to the original than any written before or since. Where he is obliged to depart from Goethe – as in making Mephistopheles appear first as a grey friar rather than a poodle – he never fails to provide elaborate justifications. Inevitably Helen of Troy speaks in classical hexameters.

The first night was an unqualified disaster. Whistles and jeers persisted until the end. Later it was revived in two parts, corresponding to those of Goethe's *Faust*, each given on a different evening, but with no better result. Rossini, to whom the preface had been sent, remarked to Tito Ricordi that Boito was obviously trying to run before he had learned to walk and quoted the example of his own development from *Demetrio e Polibio* to *Guillaume Tell* as an instance of how a composer should serve his artistic apprenticeship.‡ But the fault lay deeper. Far more even than the Meyerbeer whom he so much admired, Boito lacked the ability to develop his musical thoughts; and the failure was all the more conspicuous in that with far less theatrical experience Boito was aiming so much higher. His musical ideas are often highly individual (where they shock it is with conviction and a certain sureness of touch), but they are juxtaposed, not organically linked. Occasionally their continuity takes the form of a 'loop' of infinitely perpetuating sequences, as in much of the prologue. Mephistopheles' famous 'Son lo spirito che nega' borrows a device from late

* Letter from Mazzucato to Ronchetti-Montevito, undated. Abbiati, III, p. 22.

† Letter from Mariani, 20.5.1865. Abbiati, III, pp. 17–18.

‡ Letter from Rossini to G. Ricordi, 21.4.1868. L. Rognoni, *Rossini* (Milan, 1956), pp. 264–5.

Meyerbeer which may be described as the overblown couplet – two verses in which a succession of heterogeneous ideas are loosely bound together by a recurring refrain (see *L'Étoile du Nord*, passim). In a word Boito had shown himself incapable of bringing forth the Italian opera of the future whose imminent birth he had proclaimed. It was an ignominious failure; and for the next seven years he retreated into hack work for Ricordi and Lucca, translating foreign libretti, providing new but conventional texts for other composers under the pseudonym of Tobia Gorrio, and in his spare time turning out poetry and short stories. With the relative success of the revised *Mefistofele* at Bologna in 1875 and its subsequent diffusion throughout Europe he regained something of his lost dignity and to the end of his life he remained a figure of great respect, a powerful force on committees dealing with musical education, an *éminence grise* for the young writers of North Italy such as Giuseppe Giacosa; while as the librettist of *Otello* and *Falstaff*, the man who 'caused the bronze colossus to resound twice',* he enjoyed a unique position; yet he was never again that powerful voice that had echoed during the 1860s through the land. The dawn that he had heralded had been a false one.

Yet his work had not been entirely in vain. It was partly due to his preaching and the intellectual atmosphere it generated, partly to the impact of foreign novelties such as Gounod's *Faust* and *Roméo et Juliette* and Meyerbeer's *L'Africaine*, all of which soon acquired an Italian circulation, that Italian composers of the 1860s found themselves forced to experiment in a way which would have seemed unthinkable twenty years before. The result was to hasten that loosening-up of the post-Rossinian conventions that can be observed in certain works of the late '50s and for which Verdi had paved the way in *Rigoletto*. At the same time the basic habits of thought which Boito had hoped to sweep away remained to shackle the imagination of all who lacked Verdi's power to re-think old and new into a unique personal synthesis. Italian opera of the 1860s therefore presents a strangely confused picture. Of the older generation Mercadante was by now blind and no longer active in the theatre. Pacini, indefatigable as ever, continued for the most part to elaborate old formulas. Luigi Ricci had died insane in 1859; his brother Federico, like several of his eighteenth-century predecessors, had taken the road to St Petersburg (he was to return by way of Paris to enjoy a late success with his comedy *Una Follia a Roma*).

The field was now dominated by Petrella in the south, Cagnoni, Pedrotti and Lauro Rossi in the north, with Ponchielli about to rise to prominence. In all their works the pendulum swings back and forth between tradition and cautious innovation; but certain basic features and tendencies remain constant. The operas are still 'number' operas, each solo or duet ending with a cadenza and a break for applause. But the two-movement aria or cavatina which was the norm throughout the 1840s and '50s becomes increasingly rare in the new decade. As with the old *da capo* aria of the eighteenth century it was the first section that survived, usually expanded by declamatory episodes, 'parlanti' of various kinds or by mere melodic extension. Yet the function of the cabaletta could not be ignored, since sopranos like Antonietta Fricci and Marcellina Lotti Della Santa had to be accommodated with bravura somewhere. One solution was to extend the coda of the cantabile into a long repetitive pendant festooned with fioritura as in Leonora's cavatina in Petrella's *La Contessa d'Amalfi* (1864) (no relation to Webster's heroine). Another is for the prima

* See Walker, p. 510.

donna to make her entrance with a brilliant genre piece such as the polacca 'O felice avventuriera' from Pedrotti's *Mazeppa* (1861), though after Bellini's *I Puritani* this could hardly be called a novelty. Even the Queen of Naples in Petrella's *Giovanna di Napoli* (1869), who mostly proceeds in plain grandiose phrases like a soprano Amneris, is given a showy bolero in the third act similar to Hélène's Siciliano in *Les Vêpres Siciliennes*. Sometimes the single movement will seem to be pitched half-way between the old-fashioned cantabile and cabaletta as in the baritone's cavatina 'Non sai tu ch'il genio chiede' also from *La Contessa d'Amalfi* – a ternary piece with again a polonaise-like rhythm and some light fioritura to match the volatile nature of the character portrayed. But nowhere in the cases cited above do we find the formal characteristics of the cabaletta with its central ritornello and full melodic repeat. The purpose of such a repeat, as we have noted, was to slow down the dramatic action in preparation for a break. Where there is no repeat the break becomes less of a full stop, more of a semicolon. In other words by modifying the cabaletta form Italian opera was gradually moving in the direction of greater continuity.

The same principle holds good for the duet, which like the aria loses the architectural quality it had possessed in the earlier part of the century. Three-fold repetitions of duet–cabalettas – first voice, second voice, ritornello, both voices – are very rare after 1860. The final movement is usually plain ternary with a vocal distribution that varies. Quite frequently the final statement of the melody will be in the orchestra with the voices *parlanti*. Likewise the preceding movements (or movement) are articulated with greater freedom and variety than before. What we have called the 'similar' scheme in which voices share the same material is obsolete. One voice will often start out in a bold allegro that will recall the beginning of many a Donizetti or Rossini duet; after an emphatic cadence the second voice will follow with a dissimilar reply which soon modulates and leads into a new movement which in turn may take the form of a slow cantabile, a 'parlante' to a rapid orchestral melody, a passage of scena material, or even a strophic song. The duet finale from Act I of Petrella's *Caterina Howard* may serve as an example. Caterina is being courted by the king with lavish presents. Her lover, improbably named Etelvoldo, resolves to avert this threat to his happiness by tricking her into drinking some drugged wine which will produce the appearance of death. The duet begins with an ingenious 'parlante melodico' of about forty bars for Caterina ('Questi superbi doni'), the thematic interest neatly balanced between voice and orchestra almost in the manner of a Welsh penillion. Etelvoldo's entrance prompts an exchange of exclamations together with conventional surprise gestures from the orchestra, modulating from the original G flat to a full close in D sufficiently emphatic to warrant a cadenza. Then comes a 40-bar tenor solo in G ('Ah se tu m'ami') of strictly Rossinian first-movement cut, even down to the reiterations of ♪♪♪♪ ♪♪♪♪ etc., before the cadence. Thirty-six bars of scena follow including a reminiscence of the tenor's solo where Caterina drinks the wine. Seeing her lover's anxious face she tries to rally his spirits in a skittish 8-bar verse ('Brillare, ognor brillare'). Then through a furtive transition she proceeds to her strophic song ('Di Ricciardo il franco arciero') which plays a part in the opera similar to that of 'La donna è mobile' in *Rigoletto*. At the end of the second verse the poison begins to take effect. She breaks off for seventeen bars of agitation and fainting through related keys, eventually reaching the final movement ('No, non morrai'), which begins with a sixteen-bar extended period for the tenor in 3/4 allegro rhythm. There is a short episode, a sketchy recall of the main theme and the curtain falls. From the first tenor solo the music has not so much modulated as 'gravitated' from G, through C and F to a final B flat. There is enough thematic repetition to hold the duet together. But the structural solidity afforded by the Rossinian convention is gone; so too that equilibrium of music and action that informs even the weakest of Donizetti's operas. Moreover despite the new freedom of design the traditional Italian metres still dominate the melodies themselves, which tend to be either hackneyed or inept according to whether the composer bows to the metrical tyranny or makes a frantic attempt to evade it.

Yet whenever the librettist himself strikes out in a new direction the effect is noticeable at once. Thus for the tenor's opening romanza in Cagnoni's *Claudia* (1864) Marco Marcelliano Marcello sets his metrical scheme as follows:

> Un fior pareva dalla bruma colto
> Quel caro volto.

The accompanying melody not only recalls nothing from the Donizetti era but sends a premonitory beam towards the operatic renascence of the end of the century, as the following extract shows:

7

(e) quan - to a -mar mi li - - ce, t'a - - mo in - fe - li - - ce!

ric - co non so - - - no, ma cos-tan - te af - fet - - to, cos - tante af-fet - -

- - to m'ar - de nel pet - to.   A - - ma-mi, o Clau - dia

Cagnoni : CLAUDIA (1864)

Likewise an unorthodox combination of metres in the duet finale of the same composer's *Un Capriccio di donna* (1870) affords an effect that foreshadows the final scene in *Aida*.

The grand central finale is still *de rigueur*; but largo concertato and stretta no longer form a structural unit – and indeed quite often occur separately in different acts. Here as so often one notices a difference between the conservative south and the progressive north. Petrella's Neapolitan works preserve many of the characteristics of the old concertato – the rolling triplets, the Bellinian groundswell, the chorus senselessly syllabating on the off-beats in the manner parodied in Sullivan's *Trial by Jury*; Cagnoni on the other hand favours a plainer and at the same time less rigid movement. Likewise in the matter of recurring themes, Petrella, like Mercadante, rarely recalls a melody after its first appearance. Cagnoni at times approaches the conception of Leitmotiv. The almost Brahmsian arpeggio theme that usually announces the love-sick Silvio in *Claudia*, the chromatic figure that labels the sinister

Enrico in *Michele Perrin*, the tremolo gesture associated with Rodrigo in *Giralda*, are purely instrumental in conception and in the second case even capable of a certain development. Most striking of all is a tiny curving pattern which occurs casually in *Michele Perrin* and as a leading theme for the suffering maiden in *Un Capriccio di donna*, and which Verdi will stamp once and for all with his patent in *Aida*:*

Cagnoni : UN CAPRICCIO DI DONNA (1870)

Parisian grand opera casts a powerful shadow over the scene. Therefore genre pieces abound as never before – a cappella choruses, barcarolles, ballades, and strophic songs of various kinds including the *couplet*. Even Petrella makes use at times of the French ternary form, with a middle section that modulates and develops (see Enrico's cavatina from *Caterina Howard*). Rarely does one find anything as obviously French in inspiration as the galloping, witty first-act finale to Cagnoni's *Michele Perrin*. In general the rule that minor-key movements should end in the major still held good, though the final major section needed to be no more than a brief coda. One of the first composers apart from Verdi to set his face against this practice was Faccio. Indeed the minor-key close is the one genuine novelty of *I Profughi Fiamminghi*, the opera which had prompted Boito to hail its composer as the man 'destined to cleanse the altar of Italian opera now befouled like the walls of a brothel'.† Otherwise Faccio's first stage work shows a disconcerting tendency to relapse into the most commonplace of formulas. A cavatina remains a cavatina even when labelled 'sortita'.

Plots, it is true, show more variety during the late '60s, with no censor to stand at the librettist's elbow. The fashion of romantic dementia was by no means dead so long as there were star sopranos to keep it alive; and Petrella's *Celinda* of 1865, with her coloratura cacchinations of laughing madness (feigned in Act II, genuine by the end of the opera), is not an isolated phenomenon. However, heroines no longer wilt and die as a matter of course. In *Giovanna di Napoli*, *La Contessa d'Amalfi* and *Un Capriccio di donna* it is the tenors who are apparently helpless under their spell. Tragedy and comedy are freely mixed in such works as *Michele Perrin*, about the simple Don Camillo-like priest who saves the life of the First Consul, and *Claudia* which combines elements of opera semiseria with anticipations of verismo. But obviously genuine verismo was precluded so long as the language of libretti remained what it had been since the beginning of the century, with flowery circumlocutions, poetic word-forms ('core' for 'cuore', 'loco' for 'luogo', etcetera) and a fund of clichés for every emotional situation. Even Ghislanzoni, who for a time succeeded Piave as Italy's most fashionable librettist, continually falls back on such time-honoured conversational gambits as 'fa cor' . . . 'ed io vivo ancor?' . . . and so on. Boito extended the scope of traditional language, but not in the direction of

---

* As Verdi was staying in Genoa at the time when *Un Capriccio di donna* was first produced there in the spring of 1870 – at precisely the time when he himself was at work on *Aida*.

† P. Nardi, *Vita di Arrigo Boito* (Verona, 1944), p. 128.

realism. His own libretti are studded with quaint words and expressions that both intrigue and exasperate. Hence the nineteenth-century paradox that while the characters of Manzoni's *I Promessi Sposi* converse in the colloquial idiom of the writer's own time those of *La Traviata* speak a fustian that would be quite out of place in the salons of Louis-Philippe's Paris.

By the same token, as set by Petrella (Lecco 1869) Manzoni's novel is filtered through the jargon of Ghislanzoni – a fact which would matter less if Petrella were at all capable of coming adequately to grips with the humanity of his subject. As it is, his treatment of it is trivial and conventional with (inevitably) many of the main characters removed, Renzo and Lucia a nondescript pair of romantic lovers, and Don Abbondio a chattering buffo bass. A more serious attempt to do justice to the novel was made by Ponchielli as early as 1856 for his native Cremona. He revised it sixteen years later for Milan with the help of Praga; and this is the version that is published. Its basic design is curiously antiquated for the 1870s, with two-movement cavatinas for most of the principals, including the Nun of Monza. The finales on the other hand are more adventurous in both form and harmony. As for the final result one can only echo Verdi's verdict: 'Ponchielli is a good musician but his opera lacks individuality and quite apart from the discrepancy between the new music and that which he wrote sixteen years ago the trouble is that both the old and the new are behind their respective times . . .'* It was a dilemma all too typical of the age. If Ponchielli was constantly rewriting his operas in an attempt to bring them up to date, his contemporary Pedrotti ended by refusing to allow revivals of his own works as being out of date. Had Verdi set *Don Rodrigo*, with which Piave tried to tempt him in 1847, it might not have matched up to the Manzonian original, but it would have had pace and sureness – qualities that Ponchielli would not acquire till the time of *I Lituani* and *La Gioconda*. *A fortiori* had Verdi persisted in his plan to set *Ruy Blas* for St Petersburg his opera would have surpassed Hugo's play as surely as Marchetti's opera of 1869 with its clogged harmonies and overloaded scoring falls below it. Yet such was the dearth of good Italian operas at the time that Marchetti's piece remained in the repertory for the rest of the century. Again Verdi's comment was to the point. 'What I find worst about it is the construction and the scoring. By construction I don't mean the music itself so much as the musical drama.'†

In a word Italian opera had lost its way. Composers liberated alike from the tyranny of the censorship and from what had become the straitjacket of the primo ottocento convention were at a loss as to what to do with their new freedom. Like prisoners released after a long confinement they seemed to yearn for the safety of the cells that they had left. Hence their readiness to relapse into the commonplaces of thirty years before – a tendency shown no less by the apparently progressive Faccio than by the conservative Petrella. Increased harmonic and instrumental resources and a sharpened artistic conscience only led to irrelevant displays of academic technique which are never assimilated into the theatrical style as in Gounod or Bizet and merely obstruct the dramatic movement. Petrella, Pedrotti, Cagnoni, Marchetti and the like are so many composers in search of a tradition; and it is significant that their happiest work is in the field of comedy where such a tradition did to some extent persist. Cagnoni is perfectly at home in the nostalgic Donizettian world of *Don Bucefalo* and

---

* Letter to Arrivabene, 7.3.1874. Alberti, pp. 166–76.

† Letter to G. Ricordi, undated, c. Jan. 1871. Abbiati, III, p. 432.

Amore e trappole; but when he sets out on the stormy experimental seas of *Claudia* or *Francesca da Rimini* his command wavers. Likewise Rossi, while showing a neat touch in *I Falsi Monetari* and *Il Domino nero*, merely bores and exasperates in *Cleopatra* and *La Contessa di Mons*. Over and over again he and his contemporaries in their search for originality are betrayed into pointless ugliness. Bellini's sometimes naive tonic–dominant discords made musical sense within the sharply defined idiom of his time. The same cannot be said of the theme of Glauco's brindisi in Petrella's *Jone* (1858):

Petrella : JONE (1858)

If Cagnoni intended the harmonic piquancy of a Bizet march in the music associated with the heroine's father in *Claudia*, it certainly eluded him.

Cagnoni : CLAUDIA

If the sequences and 'conjugations'* of the Risorgimento operas may weary the sophisticated palate, they are surely preferable to passages such as the following (from Marchetti's *Ruy Blas*):

* I have borrowed the word from M. Mila's *La Giovinezza di Verdi* (Turin, 1974), meaning a simple, predictable extension of an idea in the form of a sequence.

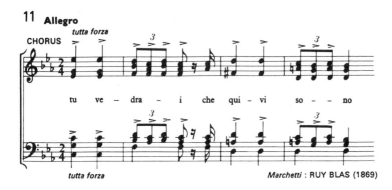

11 Allegro

tutta forza

CHORUS

tu ve – dra – i che qui – vi so – – no

tutta forza

Marchetti : RUY BLAS (1869)

Yet the start of the new decade was to see one striking exception to the rule. In March 1870 *Il Guarany* by Carlos Gomes created a sensation at La Scala. Its composer, Brazilian by birth and educated at the Milan Conservatory, was able to confront Italian opera without preconceived notions. His musical ideas are a little naive, not to say old-fashioned; but he grasped far better than his Italian coevals the problems of pace and dramatic continuity. He understood, as only Verdi understood, the formal implications of that diminishing stress on the final cadence of a number that was a feature of nineteenth-century operatic evolution. The result is that his operas move swiftly and confidently where those of Petrella stumble and stray. Who can doubt that it was Gomes's decision to include a brilliantly scored, exotic ballet in *Il Guarany* in defiance of Italian tradition that induced Verdi to follow his example in *Aida*?

Few contemplated the musical scene of the 1860s with pleasure. 'In this unhappy Italy of ours,' Pacini wrote to his son in 1867, 'things are turning out badly in every sphere and in particular in the fine arts . . . our great theatres like Milan and Naples, etc., etc., are invaded by foreign music and we bear the full burden of neglect.'* The grumbling of a sick lion, no longer able to hunt? But the closure of theatres and the frequent bankruptcy of managements throughout the peninsula tells its own story. 'In Venice the general situation is quite wretched – the Theatre quite deserted.'†

Foreigners had the same dismal story to tell. The English baritone Charles Santley had been engaged for the season of 1865–6 at La Scala. It began with *Norma* followed by *La Juive*. As both bore heavily on the soprano and tenor it was decided to vary the programme with an *opera di ripiego*, which turned out to be *Il Trovatore*. There followed a fortnight of piano rehearsals, three with orchestra and a general rehearsal 'at which what they were pleased to call the Artistic Commission presided'. There was also a production rehearsal directed by the resident stage manager, Piave. 'I was highly amused, for the old gentleman wandered about the dark stage with a coil of wax taper directing us. . . . He told me to come in on the wrong side for my first entrance and was highly indignant when I suggested that he was mistaken, but he soon afterwards begged my pardon when he found his mistake led to a muddle.' All the principals were excellent, Santley thought, 'but the audience had determined otherwise. The tenor they hissed from his first note to his last – very unjustly, I think; the prima donna came off almost as badly; the contralto they would not listen to, and

* Letter from Pacini, 21.11.1867. Pescia, No. 58.
† Letter from Pacini to his son, 28.12.1866. Pescia, No. 181.

even the bell in the tower scene received a volley of hisses for tolling out of tune.' Santley himself was well received, however (autobiographical singers usually are), but the opera had to be taken off and the tenor dismissed. After much discussion it was replaced by Nicolai's *Il Templario* of 1840. 'I do not know how many rehearsals we had, but I was saturated with the music long before we got through those in the green room. We had several on stage with full orchestra and with a multiplicity of directors – Cavallini directing the orchestra with his fiddle stick and taking the time from Mazzucato, who, seated in front of the stage, beat time with his hand, while the chorus master stood in front of his regiment also beating time. Altercations between the conductor and the principal instruments were not uncommon.' At the last moment the Artistic Commission decided to replace the Rebecca, whereupon 'the disapprobation of the public was displayed in a most brutal manner, and again I thought we had laboured in vain; but the prima donna of *Il Trovatore* was induced to undertake the part, and with her we managed six or seven performances, the greater part being on nights assigned to certain charitable benefits.* Soon afterwards Meyerbeer's *L'Africaine* was mounted. Santley, who had been engaged specially to sing the part of Neluska, found the role assigned to another artist and left in a fury, never to return.

A witty comment on the current operatic fare comes from Lauro Rossi, head of the Milan Conservatoire, whose one-act satire of 1867, *Il Maestro ed una cantante*, shows our old friend Don Bucefalo – for it is surely he – at work on a grand *scena ed aria*. But his conscience has deteriorated since 1847. As he searches for themes 'Stride la vampa' floats into his head. A good tune, he thinks, but alas, not his. But what does that matter? Nowadays it is the fashion to plagiarize. So within the space of a few pages he comes out with 'Di quella pira', 'Tu che a Dio spiegasti l'ali' (*Lucia*), the chorus of judges from *L'Africaine*, and 'Ah bello a me ritorna' (*Norma*), which he ingeniously combines with 'Il suon dell'arpe angeliche' (*Poliuto*) before winding up with the finale of the overture to *Guillaume Tell*. Each of these works, be it noted, belong to an earlier decade with the exception of *L'Africaine*; and clearly the last fourteen years had produced nothing to rival *Il Trovatore* in popularity, since it alone rates two quotations.

The carnival season at La Scala in 1868 that included Verdi's *Don Carlos* and Boito's *Mefistofele* prompted the notorious open letter to Rossini by Emilio Broglio, Minister of Education, about the state of music in Italy 'or rather throughout the world'. Rossini's music was certainly 'alive and immortal . . . but we are by now reduced to the condition of never being able to hear it because there's no longer anyone who can sing it. . . . And after Rossini what have we? Four operas by Meyerbeer and. . . . ?? These interminable operas that last five hours have become a wretched habit for the public; these colossi, these musical mastodons can only crush a budding talent, what with their Mephistophelian presumptions. . . .'† His proposed remedy was the formation of a society of wealthy music lovers with Rossini at its head to take the financing of the conservatoires off the hands of the state.

The letter was too grotesquely provincial and ignorant to be taken seriously, least of all by Rossini himself; but it had far-reaching effects. For the first time Verdi and Boito found themselves behind the same barricade. Boito published a witty, satirical reply in the form of a 'letter in four paragraphs' which appeared in the *Pungolo* for 21

---

* C. Santley, *Student and Singer* (London, 1892), pp. 232–7.
† Nardi, p. 314.

May 1868; here he defended the theatre of Verdi as 'glorious, fascinating, fecund . . .'.* Verdi himself, having relieved his feelings by returning his recently awarded decoration as Commendatore of the Crown of Italy, was moved to one of his few cautious expressions of musical optimism:

> As for this perpetual bugbear of decadence which has arisen in every period since the time of Marcello, it is something quite ridiculous. In every case one would have to make a thorough examination before pronouncing sentence. I am the last person to need to defend my own period or accuse others of the past, but it would be easy enough to point, even in certain operatic masterpieces of an earlier age, to the brainless conventionality of the numbers, the pedantry of the pezzi concertati, melody more often than not turning into singing exercises, false expression, a hard, heavy and monotonous scoring without poetry and above all without purpose. We too have our failings, and they are considerable, but there's less conventionality, more dramatic truth in the form; the ensembles speak a language proper to the passions expressed (an ugly language perhaps but it's a great step forward); the expression is more truthful; and above all the scoring has a meaning and a purpose which it didn't have before.†

As a description of Italian opera in the 1860s this is distinctly flattering. But it sums up the progress of the one composer who retained the capacity for self-renewal without the prop of a tradition – Verdi himself.

---

* See Nardi, p. 319.
† Letter to Piroli, 30.5.1868. *Carteggi Verdiani*, III, pp. 53–4.

2 FORMATION OF THE MATURE STYLE

By 1850 Verdi enjoyed one material advantage over his colleagues: he was a man of property. He could, like Rossini, have retired from the theatrical world altogether as he had so often talked of doing – and was so to talk to the end of his career. In fact he merely accommodated his rate of output to the incidence of inspiration. *Luisa Miller* inaugurated a period of astonishing fertility that came to an end with *La Traviata*. Then the pace slackened; yet each successive opera was to encompass an ever widening range and depth of ideas so that poor Basevi, whose discovery of Verdi's 'second manner' in 1849 has provided all subsequent writers with a useful point of reference, was driven to discover two further manners* in a study which stops short of *Un Ballo in maschera*. Indeed the variety of the operas that lie between *Rigoletto* and *Aida* is such as to make it impossible to group any two of them under the same heading. All represent different solutions of different problems. However, broad tendencies can be observed. The operas continue to fall into two main categories: the pioneering and the conservative. In the first Verdi blazes fresh trails; in the second he enriches old, well tried forms with the fruit of his ripening experience. To the first group belong *La Traviata, Simon Boccanegra, La Forza del destino*, and *Don Carlos*; to the second *Il Trovatore, Les Vêpres Siciliennes, Un Ballo in maschera*, and finally *Aida*. *Aroldo* stands apart, being a re-make of *Stiffelio*; while as French operas *Les Vêpres* and *Don Carlos* form a subcategory which cuts across the other two; for in both the French language and the conditions of French grand theatre impose special conditions and formal characteristics. Though it opens up a new scale of thought *Les Vêpres* will be found essentially a work of consolidation, whereas *Don Carlos* is arguably the most ambitious opera Verdi ever wrote. If the pioneering works are more exciting, the others usually strike the better formal balance. But the picture is not a simple one. *Il Trovatore*, the most conservative of all in form and musical language, has an overwhelming force such as one associates with the pioneering *Macbeth*. *La Traviata*, which undoubtedly breaks fresh ground, at the same time shows the structural equilibrium characteristic of all the so-called romantic trilogy. At the other end of the scale *La Forza del destino* and *Don Carlos* both reflect the chaos of the contemporary scene in Italy. Both are in a sense musical mastodons which cost their composer much thinking and re-thinking; and it is doubtful whether he was ever fully satisfied with their final shape. Not that it matters; for the range and quality of the musical thought more than outweigh any defects of overall design. Verdi like Shakespeare can afford such imperfections without loss of stature. Many Verdians of today prefer the complex emotional turmoil of *Don Carlos* to the classical poise of *Aida* where all formal problems have been resolved.

Most writers have confidently dated Verdi's maturity from *Rigoletto*. From then on, they say, his melodic style is entirely and recognizably his own – an assumption made all the easier by the fact that the tunes of the 'romantic trilogy' are all well known, those of other operas of the time hardly at all. Nowadays, however, the fashion for reviving rare Donizetti operas has revealed an embarrassing wealth of

* Basevi, pp. 230, 264.

musical anticipations of *Il Trovatore* and *La Traviata*. The most notorious is Ghino's cry 'O Pia mendace' from Donizetti's *Pia de' Tolomei* whose first repeated phrases are identical with Violetta's despairing outburst 'Amami, Alfredo':

Donizetti : PIA DE'TOLOMEI

Verdi : LA TRAVIATA

But observe the continuation: how Donizetti's theme dissolves into recitative, while Verdi's takes wing in a huge concluding phrase which gives the melody both its significance and its true individuality. Of the moment of coincidence we shall find more than one anticipation sufficiently striking for commentators to have drawn attention to it – in *La Battaglia di Legnano*, in *Rigoletto*, not to mention *Norma*. By itself it is mere ottocento commonplace; yet in the form and the context, musical and dramatic, in which it appears in *La Traviata* it is unique to Verdi. Mozart affords more than one parallel instance. The finite melody that begins the quartet 'Non ti fidar, o misera' (*Don Giovanni*) is a slightly varied form of the heroine's first aria in Martín y Soler's *Una Cosa rara*; but the 'sculpting' of the last two phrases, the purposeful simplicity of the final cadence that generates its own repetition, stamp it as uniquely Mozartian, not with any melodic fingerprint, but merely by virtue of expressing more within a restricted compass than is possible to a minor composer such as Martín. Likewise the pattern of notes that starts Clementi's Sonata in B flat major, Op. 47 No. 2, bears unexpected fruit in the overture to Mozart's *Die Zauberflöte*. As Alfred Einstein puts it: '. . . what with Clementi was nothing more than a striking idea . . . is filled by Mozart with meaning; it becomes by means of polyphonic treatment and polyphonic experience highly symbolic and significant and rises into the realm of eternity.'*

* A. Einstein, *Mozart: his character, his work*, translated A. Mendel and N. Broder (London, 1946), p. 137.

Like Mozart Verdi was born into a tradition; unlike Mozart he survived it. While it was still vigorous he used the common language of his time and place inflecting it to suit his own artistic personality; but as the personality grew so the inflection changed. The idiom of the early operas is that of the primo ottocento made massive and plain yet with elaborate accompanimental trappings. That of *La Traviata* is its distilled essence, the bel canto style pared down to its simplest, most direct and at the same time most profound utterance. Alternatively it could be described as the language of the drawing-room romanze enriched by the dramatic experience.* Then as the tradition decays into uncertainty Verdi, half vulture, half phoenix, can still draw nourishment from the carcass, at the same time taking ultramontane features into a style sufficiently confident and flexible to assimilate them. Right up to *Falstaff* and the *Four Sacred Pieces* that style never ceased to develop and extend. Consequently he avoided the dilemmas and limitations that beset many of the greatest of the nineteenth-century composers in their maturity. He is not restricted like Brahms in the range of emotional states that he can express; he does not, like Dvořák, find a cleavage developing between the demands of an increasingly personal idiom and those of structure. In a word his capacity for self-renewal is infinite; hence the difficulty experienced by so many of his contemporaries – and even by certain music lovers of today – in reconciling in their minds the earlier and later operas; a difficulty which transpires from the respectful, slightly embarrassed tone of the first reviews of *Falstaff*. Apart from Ford's monologue there is so little in it that recalls the composer's earlier manner.

Yet there is no inconsistency in his artistic approach; not even a fundamental change of direction such as occurred with Wagner after *Lohengrin*. Much that is new in middle and late Verdi comes from abroad; but equally much of it will turn out to be an achievement by subtler means and with greater resources of something more modestly attempted earlier on. Verdi was of course fully justified in rebutting the charges of Wagnerianism in the French press after the premiere of *Don Carlos*: 'If the critics had paid a bit more attention they would have seen that the same ideas were already there in the terzetto of *Ernani*, in the Sleepwalking scene in *Macbeth* and in so many other pieces. . . .'† Only the manner changed through ripening experience.

Of the external influences that of France is still the strongest, as it is on all nineteenth-century Italian opera, and especially on Verdi who had already in *Jérusalem* written for the Paris Opéra and spent two years in the French capital. He was well in advance of his fellow-countrymen in his use of 'couplets' as a normal aria movement as distinct from a stage song, of ternary aria form with modulating episode, of 'ethereal' thematic reminiscence, i.e. high up with accompaniment of shimmering strings, of grandiose musical and scenic superimposition, such as we associate with Meyerbeer. In the long melodic limbs of *Les Vêpres Siciliennes*, the result of setting the alexandrines and near-alexandrines of Scribe's vers libre, we find the precursors of those gossamer-light yet infinitely strong settings of eleven-syllable verse without caesura in the final scene of *Aida* and in Fenton's sonetto. Yet, unlike Pelham Humfrey, Verdi did not return from France, in Pepys's words, 'a veritable Monsieur'. The standard Italian verse-forms of *Simon Boccanegra* elicited the usual type of phrase-length which he never tried to disguise artificially as so many of his

---

* 'In *La Traviata* Verdi brought chamber music on to the stage with real success.' Basevi. p. 231.

† Letter to Escudier, 1.4.1867. *R.M.I.* (1928), pp. 524–5.

contemporaries were doing at the time. The French experience operates beneath the surface loosening the grip of ingrained habits. In his early 'Risorgimento' choruses Verdi accepted the metrical authority of the decasyllable verse. Then, as we have observed in the opening chorus of *Il Corsaro*, 'Come libero volano i venti', he ventures to inflect it in a French manner. In *Il Trovatore* he goes still further. The chorus 'Squilli, echeggi la tromba guerriera' presents an entirely new rhythmic pattern with the first syllable squarely on the downbeat and the anapaests totally submerged, yet without any falsification of the verbal accent:

13 **Allegro**

Squil - li, e - cheggi la trom-ba guerriera, chiami all' ar- mi al - la pu-gna all' as - sal - - to

IL TROVATORE

Elsewhere the Parisian style raises its head in semi-martial triplets; while *Un Ballo in maschera* abounds in gallicisms, especially in the scenes depicting Riccardo and his court. Both of Oscar's solos are in the style of French couplets. The Offenbachian high kick can be heard in the finale to the first scene, which incidentally contains, as will be noted, a remarkable instance of alternative verbal accentuation such as the French language encourages due to its lack of a tonic accent. The ghost of Meyerbeer's Consecration of the Daggers stalks the drawing of the lots in the third act. The ceremonial scenes of *La Forza del destino* Act II, of *Aida* and, inevitably, the auto-da-fe scene of *Don Carlos* are all Parisian grand theatre.

'I detest pointless things,' Verdi was fond of saying; and indeed the sentiment broadly sums up his attitude to the Italian tradition. The language of *Il Trovatore* is that of mid-nineteenth-century melodramma purged of all inessentials. The old stock patterns and procedures are, so to speak, burned up in the white heat of a dramatic force that Italian opera had not yet known. This attitude alone would be enough to make Verdi an innovator *malgré lui*. To determine how far the new procedures observable in the early 1860s were due to his example would be far beyond the scope of this study. If there is an instance of an Italian aria movement that stays throughout in a minor key before Amelia's 'Morrò, ma prima in grazia' it has not yet come to light. No one has yet discovered a one-movement cavatina combining the functions of cantabile and cabaletta before those of Riccardo and Renato in *Un Ballo in maschera*: but there are plenty in the next decade. In fact Verdi's transformation of the solo cabaletta could form a study in itself. *Les Vêpres Siciliennes* provides the first instance of what might be called the 'cabaletta surrogate' in the brief allegro that follows Henri's 'O jour de peine'. It is matched in *Don Carlos* by a similar coda to Eboli's 'O don fatal et détesté'. Carlo's 'Egli è salvo' (*La Forza del destino*) balances the cantabile 'Urna fatal' in the manner of a cabaletta; only it is in plain ternary form with no ritornello. However the variety and richness of this middle period would be less than they are were it not for Verdi's readiness to avail himself of the most old-fashioned procedures if they suited his dramatic purpose. So it happens that in this same *Forza del destino* (1st version) Alvaro, having, as he thinks, killed Carlo, leads his men to battle in a Manrico-like cabaletta whose central limb supplies a suitable moment in which to express his resolve to enter a monastery should he survive the war. It is the last appearance of the orthodox solo cabaletta, however, and it vanishes in the revision of 1869.

The duet-cabaletta survives longer. When two people finally decide to run away together the standard Rossinian form, its three statements reduced to two, or two and a half, still seems to Verdi to be the best solution; and for a specific reason which will be considered in the context of each. The same form is used in its full extension for the lovers' farewell to life at the end of *Aida*. At the time Verdi's conservatism in this respect was censured by the leading critics such as Filippi. But he himself remained impenitent. Ten years after *Aida*, when he was looking at the first act of *Simon Boccanegra* with a view to revising it, he wrote to his publisher: 'Musically one could keep the cavatina of the prima donna, her duet with the tenor and the other duet between father and daughter, although they contain cabalettas!! (Save the mark!) But I haven't so great a horror of cabalettas and if tomorrow a young man should rise who could write one of the calibre of for instance "Meco tu vieni o misera" or even "Ah perchè non posso odiarti" I would go and hear it with all my heart and I would give up all the harmonic frills and fancies and all the trimmings of our learned orchestrations. . .';* and there followed the usual diatribe about modern tendencies, false realism, Shakespeare, etcetera. Yet the solo cabaletta he actually took out; that of the duet between tenor and soprano he rewrote so as to remove all the formal characteristic of a cabaletta while preserving the original theme. Only the final movement of the duet between father and daughter bears any resemblance to the species as we know it; and even that is heavily modified, formally, melodically and harmonically. The reason is obvious. By 1881 operas even in Italy were expected to be continuous within each act or scene. A cabaletta is in every sense a 'show stopper', its carefully balanced repetitions being designed to prepare for a halt in the action followed by bursts of applause. If the more seamless continuity of the second as compared to the first *Boccanegra* reflects Verdi's growing mastery of the long reach we should remember that it was also forced upon him by the taste of the time.

The same mixture of conservatism and a tendency to cautious reform marks Verdi's attitude towards that old-established institution, the central finale. Before *Rigoletto* what might be called the 'largo concertato' of dramatic shock was obligatory in at least one act of the opera; and where no suitable occasion for it existed in the original drama (as in *I Due Foscari*) one had to be manufactured. The last instance of the factitious concertato occurs in the first version of *Simon Boccanegra* where Amelia, whose abduction by person or persons unknown has just been announced, reappears in the public square causing the whole population to freeze in its tracks. Thereafter all 'concertati' are characterized by some kind of dramatic motion, even if it is no more than an emotional tug of war, one side pleading, the other resisting. In *Un Ballo in maschera* the shock twice dissolves into an untimely laugh. In *La Forza del destino* there are no concertati that are not ceremonial. With *Aida* and *Otello* there is a return to orthodoxy with, in the latter, a concertato grafted quite gratuitously onto Shakespeare's drama, but Verdi was most concerned that it should not bring the drama to a halt, and that Iago must be seen and heard knitting together the threads of the intrigue while the rest are passively giving vent to their feelings. Likewise he insisted that in the new Act I concertato of the revised *Simon*

---

* Letter to G. Ricordi, 20.11.1880. *Copialettere*, pp. 559–60. Both cabalettas mentioned are by Bellini, from *La Straniera* and *La Sonnambula* respectively.

Boccanegra Amelia should address her pleas for peace to Fiesco, once again in order to give a sense of something happening.

The importance to Verdi of forward momentum has been already noted as early as *Nabucco*; we have seen too how it found expression in a style of melody which throws its weight towards the final phrase and in a propulsive use of the 6/4 chord. During the 1850s this same concern will manifest itself in yet another way. In a paper recently published Joseph Kerman has drawn attention to the incidence of 'three-limbed' melodies in Verdi's operas beginning with Amelia's cavatina in *Simon Boccanegra*.* In fact the germ of this procedure is already present in the Duke's cantabile 'Parmi veder le lagrime' from *Rigoletto*, fostered by the six-line form of the text.

Here the third line is welded to the fourth in a fairly traditional manner: but the impulse continues beyond the cadence, bringing forward the rest of the melody to form a single unit with what has gone before. Later Verdi will apply this method to the quatrain, eliding the last two lines in single sentence which combines the typical third-phrase lift noted by Dallapiccola with the conclusive weight that we associate with Verdi's final phrases. The foreshortening is counterbalanced by an increase in the rate of harmonic change and therefore of the emotional charge. In every case the effect is to throw the emphasis forward and at the same time to concentrate the musical significance in the smallest possible space. But the process does not stop there; it is also reflected, platonically, in larger designs such as the bar-form, increasingly used by Verdi during the '60s, either with refrain (*a x a x b x*) or without (*aab*). Early instances with refrain include Amelia's 'Ma dall'arido stelo divulso' (*Un Ballo in maschera*) and Carlo's 'Son Pereda, son ricco di onore' (*La Forza del destino*). In the Act II duet between Carlos and Elisabeth in *Don Carlos*, bar-form without refrain is the underlying principle of construction for all the movements

* J. Kerman, 'Lyric form and flexibility in *Simon Boccanegra*', in *Studi Verdiani I* (Parma, 1982), pp. 47–62.

being uniquely calculated to convey the psychological overtones of the dialogue. Both singers are constrained; both begin their utterances calmly and formally with repetitions (near or exact) of a thematic idea; the third phrase, more extended than the other two, forms an Abgesang with a built-in climax; and its effect is to suggest a sudden over-spilling of repressed emotion. The entire duet is rounded off with a three-phrase cabaletta followed by a long, crowning phrase in the major for Elisabeth when Carlos has left in despair.

As might be expected the 6/4 continues to figure more and more prominently in Verdi's vocabulary, and with it the similarly propulsive 6/4/3. The pentatonic 'tinta' of *Simon Boccanegra* is precipitated in Fiesco's 'Il serto a lei de' martiri' – a melody whose *incipit* might have occurred to Mercadante; but not the entirely Verdian displacement of the bass notes so as to yield a crop of 6/4 and 6/4/3 chords at unexpected points (*x*).

Though it defies text-book orthodoxy there is nothing arbitrary about this procedure; it is the logical outcome of that compression of melodic thought that is so evident throughout the later Verdi – the harmonic counterpart of the three-phrase rhythmic structure. Everything in Fiesco's first aria is compressed; and once again the melody takes its character from the end. Without that apparently unorthodox E in the bass the transition from the third to the final phrase could not be effected with any cogency; change the E to a well mannered A and the modulation would sound too abrupt. The juxtaposition of the two 6/4s is the only possible solution.

Verdi's harmony develops along more general lines as well: firstly through a frequent contrapuntal loosening of the texture that results in a fleetness of movement rare in his predecessors; while his successors, as the gradual disappearance of coloratura removed that facile rapidity that marks many an old-style cabaletta, tended to fall into rhythmic inertia aggravated by static and impoverished harmony.

It is precisely at the moments when he recalls an earlier style that Verdi's superior energy is most apparent. The duet cabaletta from Act I of *La Forza del destino* is based on a settenario pattern of marching crotchets which turns up twice in Donizetti's *Poliuto* and three times in its French revision, *Les Martyrs*. In fact similarity of the melody to that of 'Il suon dell'arpe angeliche' from Donizetti's opera was remarked on by Russian critics at the time of the première.* Put the openings of both side by side and it will be seen at once that what distinguishes Verdi's melody is the rapidly moving bass, which gives it a momentum at which neither Donizetti nor yet Rossini ever aimed.

Donizetti : POLIUTO

Verdi : LA FORZA DEL DESTINO

* See *Journal de St Petersburg*, 14.11.1862. G. Barblan, in 'Un po' di luce sulla prima rappresentazione della *Forza del Destino* a Pietroburgo', in *I.S.V. Bollettino*, No. 5, p. 849.

In middle and late Verdi a moving bass line often brings with it rapid changes of harmony which again leave the Donizettian tradition far behind. Here Verdi resembles the maturing Beethoven, who harmonizes more and more freely and in defiance of traditional harmonic rhythms, as Hans Gal has pointed out.* In the later operas, the variety of harmonic pace is remarkable. Sometimes a dominant will be prolonged endlessly; sometimes the harmonies will shift as in a kaleidoscope, as in the concertato of Act III of *Aida*:

Non-functional harmony, which colours a vocal line without affecting its tonality, becomes increasingly common in middle and late Verdi; as when the Marquis of Calatrava bids his daughter good night:

* H. Gal, 'Stileigentumlichkeit des jungen Beethovens', in *Studien für Musikwissenschaft*, IV (1916).

It is at least possible that in his own very frequent recourse to non-functional harmony Richard Strauss may be indebted to the example of Verdi whose later works he greatly admired – even to the extent of sending his own first opera to Verdi for his advice and criticism. There is something almost Straussian about that free association of chords in a loosely defined tonal area that opens the Council Chamber scene in the revised *Simon Boccanegra*:

It was inevitable that as each successive opera of Verdi's carried contemporary audiences further beyond the bounds of ordinary musical experience they should have reached for Wagner as providing the clue to the composer's aberrations. Even Basevi solemnly admonishes Verdi for, as he imagines, straying into German territory in the first version of *Simon Boccanegra*.* After hearing *Don Carlos* in 1867 Bizet wrote to a friend: 'Verdi n'est plus italien, il veut faire du Wagner. Il n'a plus ses défauts. Mais aussi plus une seule de ses qualités.'† In his notice on *Aida* the critic Filippi stated that to deny Wagner's influence on the composer would be like denying that the sun gave light.‡ ('A fine result,' Verdi commented bitterly, 'after a career of thirty-five years, to end up as an imitator.')§ Here a distinction must be made between Wagner the theorist and Wagner the musician. Before 1870 only one of his operas, *Tannhäuser*, had been given outside Germany. Of this Verdi appears to have heard only the overture when it was given at a miscellaneous concert

---

* Basevi, p. 279.

† Letter from Bizet to Lacomb, quoted in M. Curtess, *Bizet et son temps* (Paris, 1961), p. 163.

‡ F. Filippi in *La Perseveranza*, 10.2.1872. Alberti, pp. 138–43.

§ Letter to G. Ricordi, April 1875. Walker, pp. 469–70.

in Paris; 'he's mad,' was his only comment.* Wagner's prose works, on the other hand, were generally known in intellectual circles and their concepts – the 'Art Work of the Future', the 'Total Art Work that is a transcendant combination of music, scene-painting and literary drama' – were common coin among the 'scapigliatura'. Yet it was not until 1869 that Verdi wrote to Camille du Locle asking him to send him copies of Wagner's literary works since, 'You must know that I want to get acquainted with that side of him as well.'† For all that, in so far as Wagner's theories crystallize aesthetic concepts that were already in the air, they had certainly impinged on the still relatively enclosed world of Italian opera and on Verdi in particular. Their traces are felt in Verdi's own instructions for the performance of *Macbeth*. He was to show an increasing pre-occupation with the visual side of his operas – not, it must be said, that in visual matters he showed much taste or imagination; but then neither did Wagner; and indeed this is one of the rocks on which the essentially romantic theory of the Gesamtkunstwerk founders. Where is the artist whose genius manifests itself equally in all three of the arts employed; and where is the human faculty that can apprehend *simultaneously* the highest achievements of the visual and aural arts? If the arts are to be combined it must be in a hierarchy with, in the case of opera, music at the head. However the fact that this union of the arts cannot transcend the highest manifestation of any one of them does not invalidate the detailed, profoundly cogitated rules for their combination set out in *Oper und Drama*. But for Verdi these theories could only have held a marginal interest, partly because he himself was the most untheoretical of creators, partly because they were ill adapted to the language in which his own genius first expressed itself and which he never wholly forsook. The exploration of emotional states through variety of harmony was a favourite preoccupation with the early German romantics, beginning with E. T. A. Hoffmann, whose Kapellmeister Kreisler draws up a list of different chords each with its own expressive significance. For Mendelssohn music was a language more precise in its meaning than that of words. Much of Schumann's music seems to be carrying on a dialogue of sensibilities expressed in a variety of appoggiature and suspensions. Wagner's theory of 'tone language' as set out in Part III of *Oper und Drama* grows out of this essentially German attitude towards music. Even at its most extrovert, there is an 'inward' quality about Wagner's mature music which accords with his belief that the orchestra should act as a vehicle of remembrance and premonition. His characters are concerned with thought rather than action. Tristan, Wotan, Sachs, Gurnemanz – even Siegfried and Brünnhilde in their later moments are above all ruminative creatures, each carrying an increasing burden of memories, embodied in evocative leitmotifs from which the symphonic web of the score is spun. It is thus perfectly logical that *Götterdämmerung* should have a far more complicated texture than *Das Rheingold*. Verdi's characters are less introspective. Initially they are concerned merely to vent a primitive, undifferentiated emotion whose force harmonic elaboration would only diminish. When Nabucco cries out that he is a prisoner he expresses himself in plain D flat major; when Alberich proclaims his bondage the music plunges on to an appoggiatura over a diminished seventh. When he curses the ring the orchestra dwells on one of the most extravagant dissonances in the language of the time. Monterone curses Rigoletto to a D flat major 6/4. In both cases Verdi depicts the

---

* Letter to Arrivabene, 31.12.1865. Alberti, p. 61.   † Letter to du Locle, 23.1.1870.

release of emotion: Wagner prefers to dwell and brood on the emotion itself. In later years Verdi's characters become more complex and inward. (Leonora in *La Forza del destino* could be called the Leonora of *Il Trovatore* endowed with a memory and a conscience.) Their musical language becomes correspondingly more subtle and the orchestra plays an increasingly important role in the delineation of their feelings. But the primacy of the human voice remained a fundamental part of his musical thinking: the vocally conceived period remains at the heart of his most complex structures and he was highly critical of those who allowed their music to crumble into a string of 'parlanti'. Thus of Petrella: 'His chef d'œuvre, *Le Precauzioni*, may appeal to the superficial listener because of a few brilliant violin tunes, but when you consider this piece as a work of art it won't stand to be compared not only with real operatic masterpieces but not even with operas like *Crispino, Follia in Roma*, etc., etc. In these operas Ricci proceeds not with *parlanti* but with good tunes.'* Lack of true vocal melody was also, Verdi thought, the besetting weakness of French grand opera. 'For the Opéra I have written *I Vespri* and translated two of my operas. . . . Now, as then, I whisper to you in confidence, I still have a fair facility in thinking up *tunes*, and it seems that there is no market for these at the Opéra. Later perhaps I shan't be able to think of any more and then I too shall write *frum-frums* for orchestra. . . . In the *Vespri* there are two or three tunes, which may be good or bad, but they're real tunes. Perhaps that's why the score is on the shelf.'† No one who thought in that way could have developed his operas through a Wagnerian tissue of leitmotiv. Nor was Verdi concerned to present a dramatic experience on more than one level. Strongly felt emotion must come across the footlights unencumbered by premonition or memory.

Even at intensely pathetic moments the major key of release is apt to supervene, though never in the mechanical fashion of earlier times. Otello and Ford both conclude a monologue of unrelieved bitterness with a sweeping sentence in E flat major such as could hardly be reconciled with the doctrines of *Oper und Drama*. This is one reason too why even in late maturity Verdi's music never reaches a Wagnerian norm of dissonance. The chromaticisms of *Tristan* would not have served his purpose, since none of his characters are introspective to the same degree. Another reason is aesthetic. He could no more abide a long succession of discords that resolve into another than could Berlioz. Hence he scouted the bizarre but to modern ears reasonably euphonious prologue of *Mefistofele* ('hearing how the harmonies of that piece relied almost throughout on dissonances I seemed to be – not in *Heaven* certainly!'‡), Mascagni's *L'Amico Fritz* ('I started to get on with reading the music but soon got tired of all those dissonances, false relations, interrupted cadences . . .'§) and Bruneau's *Le Rêve* ('There's a frightful excess of dissonance that makes me want to cry out like Falstaff for the "tiny vent-hole" of a perfect chord.')¶ He would hardly have endured the chain of suspensions in the overture to *Die Meistersinger* however sunny the mood of the piece as a whole. For all these reasons the kind of cross-fertilization that took place between Haydn and Mozart, two men of opposite temperament yet both working in the same tradition, was impossible between Verdi

* Letter to De Sanctis, 13.1.1871. *Carteggi Verdiani*, pp. 128–9.
† Letter to Escudier, 20.10.1858. Prod' homme, pp. 20–1.
‡ Letter to Arrivabene, 30.1.1879. Alberti, pp. 226–33.
§ Letter to G. Ricordi, 6.11.1891. Abbiati, IV, pp. 426–7.
¶ Letter to Boito, 5.7.1891. *Carteggio Verdi–Boito*, pp. 191–2.

and Wagner. Any similarities between parts of *Don Carlos* and *Tannhäuser* can be accounted for by common roots in the Parisian grand opera that had served Wagner as model for his first success, *Rienzi*. For the rest Verdi was not above taking hints from Wagner in the matter of practical details, whether of scoring, or of dramatic and scenic construction; but not until the time of *Aida*, when he had seen *Lohengrin* performed on stage. The possibility that *Falstaff* owes something, however small, to *Die Meistersinger* will be considered later. Yet neither this nor his approval of Wagnerian ideals such as the lowered pit and the darkened auditorium makes him a follower of the Meister.

In fact Verdi was a Wagnerian only by analogy. He was borne on the same current of romantic idealism which by the later part of the century had caused the act to replace the scena as the structural unit of an opera. Here Wagner was undoubtedly ahead of his Italian rival. In a letter to Mathilde Wesendonck he talked of a belief in 'the art of transition' – in which he himself certainly excelled. No one has ever depicted two people falling gradually in love as convincingly as he in the first act of *Die Walküre*. The Rossinian tradition from which Verdi sprang depended for its effect on balance and contrast, abruptly changing moods and sudden happenings. In the hands of the young Verdi it became a swift dialectic of reaction and counter-reaction. Gradual transition remained foreign to it until in the late 1840s Verdi achieved a more plastic style of melody that breaks down into motifs capable of development. From then on the trend towards a seamless continuity within the act becomes more marked with each successive opera, reaching its apogee in *Falstaff* where, practically speaking, each idea evolves from its immediate predecessor. A comparison of the love duets of *Giovanna d'Arco* and *Un Ballo in Maschera* illustrates this very clearly. Both have the characteristic three-movement form – tempo d'attacco, cantabile and cabaletta. In the first, all three are steeply contrasted. In the second the tempo d'attacco actually prepares Riccardo's cantabile 'Non sai tu che nell'anima mia'; while the cabaletta contains at its climax a quotation from the same cantabile – a solution casually anticipated in the Enrico–Giovanna duet from Donizetti's *Anna Bolena*. An old pattern has been transformed from within so as to express a new ideal.

Like Wagner, Verdi wished to reform the musical theatre, and to work for a closer integration of music and verbal expression, but on a greater level of immediacy. Hence the notion of 'la parola scenica' which begins to surface during the 1860s. This is how Verdi describes it: 'I mean the word that sculpts the situation and makes it clear and vivid. . . . Sometimes in the theatre it is necessary that poets and composers should have the talent not to make poetry or music.'* Its origin for Verdi may well have gone back to *La Battaglia di Legnano* and a letter of Cammarano's stressing the importance of setting the word 'infamia' into suitable relief.† The intention is clearly to harness the energy of individual words and phrases into the musical and dramatic structure; but more significant still is the corollary: 'neither music nor poetry'. For just as the parola scenica is supposed often to make its effect divorced from any scheme of verse or rhyme, so its musical equivalent will, in the interests of theatre, boldly snap the bonds of conventional musical logic in a way that might well have caused Wagner to wonder. The moment at which Leonora staggers in after having

---

* Letter to Ghislanzoni, 17.8.1870. *Copialettere*, pp. 641–2.
† See letters from Cammarano, 9. & 29.10.1848. Abbiati, I, pp. 771–3.

been stabbed by her dying brother in *La Forza del destino* (1869) or where Eboli prepares to confess her adultery in *Don Carlos* (1884) resist harmonic analysis more than the most complex procedures of *Tristan* or *Götterdämmerung*, but their effect is sure and immediate.

The best opportunity of gauging Verdi's progress as an artist is afforded by those operas which were revised many years after they were originally composed – notably *Simon Boccanegra* (1857, rev. 1881) and *Don Carlos* (1867, rev. 1884). The differences are similar to those noted between the two *Macbeth*s. The altered passages are for the most part shorter and sharper than the originals; the harmonic palette is richer and more varied. As in the two versions of *Leonore/Fidelio* the later one discards and compresses. In the first *Don Carlos* the duet between Philip and Posa proceeds by contrasted lyrical sections; in the later single phrases are made to do duty for whole periods. Glancing at the intervening works one is astonished by their growing variety of form and expression, aided by Verdi's ability to reach back as well as forward. Side by side with three-limbed melodies are others basically four-square from which some natural phrase extension or contraction removes all danger of rhythmic monotony. Just as the subjects and the plots become more individual so Verdi finds the means of expression and form unique to each. The duets as always occupy a central position in the scheme, each conceived according to the relationship of the parties concerned; from that of Leonora and the Father Superior in *La Forza del destino*, where though the subject is deep and spiritual neither is in the slightest degree involved with the other, to that of Aida and Radames whose personalities have been merged by true love and self-sacrifice into a spiritual identity; from the intellectual argument of King Philip and Posa in *Don Carlos* to the massive spiritual confrontation of King Philip and the Grand Inquisitor or the unresolved emotional conflict between Henri and Montfort in *Les Vêpres Siciliennes* – the list is endless; not one can be compared with any other except descriptively since each has its own points of reference. Consequently the primitive drama through the clash of vocal archetypes observed in *Ernani* or *Nabucco* is now superseded, for the characters portrayed are too subtly individualized. King Philip and the Inquisitor are poles apart; and the fact that both are basses only emphasizes the spiritual gulf that separates them. In the early operas, with the exception of *Giovanna d'Arco*, it could be said that the love duets were less interesting than those involving paternity. Yet in *Un Ballo in maschera* Verdi has written a duet of almost Tristan-like intensity and surely one of the finest in all opera. Even where the characters are generic rather than particular, as in *Il Trovatore* and *Aida*, they no longer need to clash in order to define themselves. Unlike Ernani, Manrico emerges firm and distinct from his first note; and in fact the characters of *Il Trovatore* rarely do encounter one another head on. Leonora and Azucena remain in two different worlds; on the only occasion on which they meet one of them is asleep.

The definitive *Simon Boccanegra*, like the definitive *Don Carlos*, stands on the threshold of *Otello*; and many passages in it are in the composer's maturest manner – the touches of modal harmony in the duettino of Gabriele and Fiesco, of plainchant in the herald's recitative from Act III, the classical figuration in the rebellion of Act I. The fact that the two styles match in the same work is the surest evidence of the consistency of growth which is such a striking feature of Verdi's genius. In gauging this growth we have so far taken harmony and form as our parameters; but we could as easily have begun with the scoring which would have led us round to the same point. Following what must have been a common practice of the time Verdi was accustomed to draft out his vocal numbers on full score manuscript paper as melody and bass with the occasional 'cue' during long rests to indicate the continuity. In this form they would be handed to the copyist who would transfer the music on to two staves, and hand it to the singer and the coach, the latter presumably improvising the harmonies implied by the material in front of him. Verdi would then complete the scoring and the harmonization together; at no point would he himself make a piano reduction, as do many composers of today before they begin to score a note. For Verdi the piano reduction was the work of a publisher's hack. (His own publisher Ricordi usually employed Muzio who had the advantage of having been Verdi's one pupil.) The result is that as Verdi's harmonies became more various his scoring becomes correspondingly more subtle and refined. There is no division between idea and orchestration as in Meyerbeer who rescored the same idea several times; nor did Verdi ever, like Rimsky-Korsakov, mistake orchestral brilliance for musical thought. The thick daubs of colour that mark the early operas give way to a palette that is richer and more varied; though even at its most sophisticated Verdi's 'mean sonority' is always rather higher than Wagner's. In his most majestic tuttis we still hear the squeal of the piccolo. It is significant too that while Wagner in his most ambitious ventures enriched his orchestra with a family of tubas, Verdi for his Requiem and *Otello* was content merely to add to the traditional orchestra the two extra bassoons and two cornets of the Parisian Opera. Nor should it be forgotten that whereas Wagner's sense of the orchestra is based like Beethoven's on the organic tutti, Verdi's evolved from the prismatic conception of Rossini; and it is to this, refined by the assimilated craft of Bizet and Delibes on the one hand and the conservative Germans such as Mendelssohn and Hiller on the other, that we owe the diaphanous miracle of *Falstaff*. The plentiful use of flute and harp is a French legacy; though it is not until *Otello* that Verdi exploits the full resources of the latter instrument. Decidedly un-French, and even worthy of Brahms, was his prejudice against the valve horn, which led him to begin the second act of *Don Carlos* with a unison passage for four horns each crooked in a different key so as to neutralize each other's stopped notes. In the matter of trumpets he preferred the rotary valve instrument (tromba a macchina) to that with the up-and-down 'piston' in vogue in France and England ('Your trompettes à piston are neither one thing nor the other').* The valve trombone reigned in Italy without interruption throughout Verdi's lifetime; hence the chromatic scale figures which abound in the storms of *Aroldo* and *Otello* and which inevitably sound like glissandi on modern instruments.

In a word, Verdi's steadily developing genius is like a world seen through an ever stronger lens. As the images spring into sharper focus so their variety becomes more marked, and their different colours stand out with an increasing diversity of shade. Perhaps the most instructive of the few sketches of his that have come down to us is that for *La Traviata* reproduced in facsimile in Gatti's *Verdi nelle immagini*.† Here in a nutshell compressed into two pages is the whole of the first act of the opera with the two principal melodies – the brindisi and 'Ah fors' è lui' drafted on a single line, a few instrumental figures and the rest mere stage instructions (clearly as yet Piave had not written a line of the text); yet there are all the main lineaments of the act, seen as

---

* Letter to Escudier, 3.2.1865. *Copialettere*, p. 456.   † Milan, 1941, pp. 64–5.

though from an immense distance. In evolving the final result Verdi's creative eye never wavered; he never allowed himself to be seduced by an attractive idea into prolixity. This certainty of purpose is just one of the factors which make him stand out so sharply from his benighted contemporaries.

In his last published writings Alfred Einstein was moved by his consideration of *Falstaff* to comment: 'Indeed the brightest ones amongst us have already come to the conclusion that Verdi's secret (I am not now speaking of the so-called secrets of form) lies as deep as Wagner's and is much less obvious than is that of the calculating Wagner – rationalizing something to the point of excess.'* Certainly Wagner leaves nothing unexplained in his concept of music drama; while for those to whom no composition can be valid unless it coheres as an autonomous structure there are Alfred Lorenz's somewhat laborious attempts to explain Wagner's works in terms of predetermined form independent of the dramatic idea.† Verdi has left us nothing but a few chance references to be picked up in letters and what our own observation of the music can tell us. The International Congresses of recent years have thrown up a number of highly interesting attempts to discover Verdi's secrets whether of form, or dramatic effect, sometimes in terms of key, sometimes of 'constants' which recur from one opera to another whose meaning we apprehend without necessarily formulating it. It may be traditional and thus hold good for other composers as well; or it may apply to Verdi only, and even to one particular opera. The ground is treacherous even when the strictest principles of inductive logic are applied. The problem of proving in Verdi connections between musical procedures and states of mind is not that it is too difficult but that it is too easy. Limit your symbol to a figure of three or four notes, associate it with an emotion such as 'jealousy', 'power', 'love' or what you will, and you will have no difficulty in extracting that pattern from an aria or scene in which those concepts occur. If they are not present where your theory requires them you can argue that the composer is imparting a special message over and above the text, as Wagner does with the recurrence of the Valhalla motif in *Die Walküre* at the words 'Den Vater fand ich nicht'; and as 'love', 'power' and 'jealousy' are never very far from the surface of any nineteenth-century melodramma you will not easily be proved wrong. But unless the said pattern presents the constant physiognomy of a leitmotif or of one of Verdi's own explicit thematic reminiscences the game cannot be played without allowing for modifications according to context. The question arises, in an orthodox tonal system can the leap of a sixth from tonic to submediant be equated with one from dominant to mediant? Can a rhythmic pattern in 4/4 beginning on an up-beat be equated with the identical pulsation beginning on a downbeat in 3/8? Obviously the listener must make up his own mind.‡ Meanwhile

* A. Einstein, *Essays on Music* (New York, 1962), p. 87.

† See A. Lorenz, *Das Geheimnis der Form bei Richard Wagner* (4 vols, Berlin 1924–33). For a useful summary of Lorenz's theories as they relate to the first act of *Die Walküre*, see G. Abraham, *A Hundred Years of Music* (2nd ed, London, 1948), pp. 124–9.

‡ Among the most valuable contributions from this school of thought should be cited: P. Pal Varnai, 'Unità musicale e drammaturgica nel *Don Carlo*', in *Atti del II° Congresso del I.S.V.* (Parma, 1971), pp. 402–11, and 'Leonora e Don Alvaro', in *I.S.V. Bollettino*, No. 6 (Parma, 1963–6), pp. 1695–710; P. Petrobelli, 'Per un' esegesi della struttura drammatica del *Trovatore*', in *Atti del III° Congresso del I.S.V.*, (Parma, 1974), pp. 387–400; F. Noske, 'Ritual Scenes in Verdi's Operas', in *Music and Letters*, Oct. 1973, pp. 415–39. These and others will be further mentioned in the context of individual operas to which they refer.

the limitations of this analysis are illustrated in Frits Noske's substantial and stimulating essay 'Verdi and the Musical Figure of Death'[*] in which he explores the composer's use of rhythmic figures (♪♪), (♫♪) and (♫♫♪) all of which at various times and in various countries have connoted fatality. This phenomenon Professor Noske traces to French tragédie lyrique, placing its entry into Italian opera at the time of Mayr and Paër, when Italy was producing the native equivalent of the French Revolutionary pièce de sauvetage. Historically the thesis is convincing; one may even suggest a plausible origin for the convention in the funeral drum that conducts the condemned man to the scaffold. Certain it is that at moments when characters are brought face to face with death in La Traviata, Il Trovatore and Les Vêpres Siciliennes — to name the most obvious cases — such figures will be hurled at you with a force that leaves no doubt of their significance. But can we connect every appearance of each of these motifs with the idea of death?

Alas, that is just what we can do, if we have a mind to it. After all, as Verdi himself said, 'Is not all death in life?'[†] When in the recitative preceding her famous 'Ah fors' è lui' (La Traviata) Violetta asks herself whether a 'serious love' would prove her undoing, the orchestra replies with ♫♫♩ twice stated — a clear presage of death, so Professor Noske would have us believe. But does it produce that effect on the listener? Consider for a moment the beginning of the overture to Rossini's Il Barbiere in which this same motif predominates. It is hard to think of an opera in which death has so little place. Granted, this same overture originated with an opera seria; but if the meaning of this figure had been fixed in the mind of the spectator the overture would have been generally judged a nonsense in its new context. Here we may cross-check with a figure which undoubtedly did have a fixed significance in Verdi's time — namely the nucleus of notes with an acciaccatura on the offbeat which regularly signifies navigation. In Un Ballo in maschera it figures very prominently in the song sung by Riccardo — naturally, since it is part of his sailor's fancy dress. The Neapolitan censorship wished to change the hero's disguise into that of a hunter. Verdi scribbled in the margin of the revised text: 'Anyone who has the slightest familiarity with the theatre knows that seafaring music has a special character, and that hunting music has another one which is quite different. . . . All composers, even the most mediocre, have made a distinction between these two types, and those ideas have been so implanted in the mind of the spectator that if I had put my seafaring, undulating music into the mouth of a hunter the public would have been doubled up with laughter and rightly so!'[‡] It is one of those rare observations that break the vicious circle of musicology, whereby we wish to know what people took for granted at a certain period, but precisely because they took it for granted they do not bother to tell us. Whether Verdi's public would have interpreted the orchestra's comment on Violetta's 'Saria per me sventura un serio amore?' as a wordless answer 'Yes!' it is impossible to tell. Varnai is on safer ground in limiting the connotation of death to the single pattern (♪♪).[§] Yet in both cases it is difficult to make the

---

[*] Atti del III° Congresso del I.S.V., pp. 349–86.

[†] Letter to Clarina Maffei, 20.1.1853. A Luzio, Profili biografici e bozzetti storici (Milan, 1927), II, pp. 515–16.

[‡] Carteggi Verdiani, I, p. 252.

[§] P. P. Varnai, Contributi per uno studio della tipizzazione negativa nelle opere verdiane', in Atti del I° Congresso del I.S.V. (Parma, 1969), pp. 268–75.

argument operate in both directions. To anyone who remarked that the repeated hammerings of the Miserere scene of *Il Trovatore* are fraught with a sense of impending doom Verdi might well have retorted, à la Brahms, 'Any fool can see that.' So many other factors combine to make the significance plain: the minor tonality, the pitch (the three-string basses of the time were instructed to lower their A strings), the menacing use of full orchestra pianissimo. But can we be sure that the same figure when it accompanies Leonora on her way to the convent, played by strings only and in a major tonality, is intended to carry the same message, or to imply that life in a convent away from Manrico will be a living death? Or is it merely meant to suggest the heroine's faltering footsteps? The truth is that where the idea of death is unequivocally present, as throughout much of *Les Vêpres Siciliennes* or in the passage in Act I of *Simon Boccanegra* where Amelia warns her lover against political intriguing, it is always reinforced by other means. In other words it is difficult in this field to make an intermediate judgement between the obvious and the purely speculative.

Indeed there are reasons for thinking that as Verdi's language increases in subtlety his musical procedures tend to lose any constant significance that they have hitherto evinced. A case in point is the single note with acciaccatura which until the time of *Don Carlos* had always served as a symbol of grief. Note, however, the following instances of it in Verdi's subsequent works:

20

Of Ex. 20 we can say that Amneris has here a premonition of the grief she will suffer when she knows for certain that Radames is in love with Aida and not herself. We can explain Ex. 22 as Desdemona's attempt to keep back her tears. But there are no tears in Ex. 21; nor could the most extravagant imagination devise any association of

21

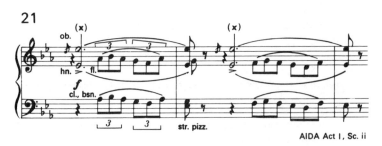

OTELLO Act III

grief. Rather than rationalize from the example of previous operas it is surely more valuable to ask ourselves how we experience the device (x) in the three contexts cited above, whether it has not the effect of an archly raised eyebrow (Ex. 20), an attempt at wheedling slyness (Ex. 22) or a mere decoration (Ex. 21). This need not alter the fact that elsewhere in *Aida* (e.g. Amneris's 'Io pregherò') and *Falstaff* (Nannetta's entry in Act II, Scene 1) the same figure carries its traditional meaning. It is merely that in his later music Verdi found the means of conveying more than one feeling through the same device.

The problem of explaining the unity of a Verdi opera still exercises the minds of scholars. Some, like Roman Vlad, look for a Grundgestalt,* others following the example of Edward T. Cone† see it in an unobtrusive tonal scheme – a difficult argument to sustain without recourse to ingenuity. The truth is that such coincidences of tonality as occur within the same piece too often occur at illogical moments or more often do not occur at all. Choral and dance scenes tend to be more symmetrical in the later operas with the same theme returning always in the same key; but this hardly argues for the existence of an overall tonal pattern. It is much easier to show that Verdi tends to use keys as areas of contrast; that by couching Paolo in C minor and the Doge in F sharp major in the revised *Simon Boccanegra* he was concerned to emphasize as far as possible the distance between them rather than to perfect a tonal scheme whereby the opera itself is sited in A flat major with C major and E major as subsidiary keys. If the alterations of key in the revised version of an opera improve on the original (as for instance in *La Traviata* or *Don Carlos*) it is in relation to their immediate context rather than to the scheme of the whole.

In accounting for the unity of a Verdi opera it is difficult to go beyond Basevi's 'tinta', as described in Vol. 1 of the present study, except to point out that in the later works this can embrace more than one element. It reveals itself in the pentatonic contours of so much in *Simon Boccanegra*; the smooth melodic swell combined with an abundance of death-figures (whose meaning here is quite unequivocal) of *Les Vêpres Siciliennes*; the wealth of delicate waltz-like ideas in *La Traviata* mostly centred round small intervals; the wide arpeggio reach that marks many of the themes of *Il*

* R. Vlad, 'Structural Unity of Verdi's *Simon Boccanegra*', in *Atti del IV° Congresso del I.S.V.*

† See E. T. Cone, 'On the Road to *Otello*: Tonality and Structure in *Simon Boccanegra*', in *Studi Verdiani I* (Parma, 1982), pp. 72–98.

Trovatore. All these features will be discussed more fully in their context. Meantime it will be useful to repeat what was said in the chapter on *Rigoletto*; that however 'motivic' Verdi's later music becomes – as in the revised Act I of *Simon Boccanegra* – it will always at some point need the symmetrical vocal period as a coping-stone to the structure of a scene.

Two problems of Verdi's developing art should be mentioned, the first affecting the performer, the second the musicologist. Precisely because he extends the older lyrical forms instead of abolishing them in order to widen his range of dramatic expression so he makes increasingly heavy demands on his singers. Donizettian opera abounds in obtrusive little conventions designed for the performer's comfort. Thus an opening recitative will parade the singer's extension so as to allow him to 'sing himself in'. As late as *Il Trovatore* Verdi for the most part observes this practice. His Count of Luna apostrophizes Leonora with a widely arching phrase that enables him to check the 'placing' of his voice at the outset. In *Un Ballo in maschera* Renato is required to plunge *in medias res* in his first entrance with a subdued, but highly charged warning about Riccardo's safety; he then proceeds directly to his aria. Generally it is the tenor that suffers most. In *La Forza del destino* he is required to burst on to the stage to a rapid scale passage from the orchestra and at once pick up a brisk allegro of passionate joy. In the first scene of *Aida* he must run the entire gamut of expression from the heroic to the most tenderly lyrical within fifteen minutes. Otello is arguably the most taxing role in the entire operatic repertory, not because it requires sustained volume, but because it calls for infinite degrees of control. Were the opera itself of Wagnerian length it would be unsingable. If by comparison the late soprano roles seem less exacting, this is partly because Verdi made heavy demands on the soprano voice from the start. His Elviras, Abigailles and Odabellas must all display power below and above the stave. Light lyric roles such as that of Gilda, who sings in tenths with the tenor as well as the baritone, are exceptional. In his middle years Verdi came to make a distinction between the 'donna di forza' who in *Aida* and *Un Ballo in maschera* needs the vocal means of an Isolde, and the lighter type of singing actress such as he considered ideal for Violetta. To this period, too, belongs Verdi's discovery of the dramatic mezzo-soprano, which, as we shall see, occurred almost by accident. At the same time the basso profondo emerges from comprimario status with Fiesco in *Simon Boccanegra*. It should be emphasized, however, that after *Il Trovatore* Verdi is concerned not with types but with specific characters; hence his readiness to break with traditional casting practice, as for instance when he sets Oscar in *Un Ballo in maschera* as a light florid soprano instead of the contralto musico as Mercadante had done in *Il Reggente*. Only in the classical *Aida* is there a momentary reversion to vocal archetypes, though richer and infinitely more various than those that had served him before.

The musicologist's problem is more surprising in view of Verdi's own repeated assertions about the integrity of his works, rather less so if we take into account the tradition from which he sprang. However much he might protest his indifference to the way in which his works were received, public opinion continued to play an unackowledged part in the final shaping of an opera. When *La Traviata* triumphed a year after its initial failure, Verdi announced in a letter to De Sanctis that he had not changed a note of it in the meantime. In fact he had changed a good deal. Likewise, when the duet cabaletta of *Aida* Act III was adversely criticized Verdi took care to modify it before making the orchestral score available. In other words there was no question of writing only for the future. Contemporary reaction was for him an essential factor in that dialogue with the public inherent in artistic production; nor did it ever lead to a weak compromise on the composer's part, but always an improvement. Mostly these revisions were intended to be definitive; but not all. Certain alterations that Verdi made for theatres abroad he did not think fit to incorporate in later Italian editions. Instances include the extended finale ultimo of *Le Trouvère* (the French adaptation of *Il Trovatore*); the modifications to *La Traviata* for its performance at the Théâtre-Lyrique in 1864; and, most problematic of all, the French version of *La Forza del destino*, evidently prepared by Verdi in 1881 and intended for consumption in the lesser French-speaking theatres. The same questions will arise again when we consider the final edition of *Don Carlos* as performed in Modena in 1886, and lastly the Parisian revisions to Act III of *Otello* which Ricordi never published in Italy, presumably because the composer told him not to do so, though theatrically speaking there is much to be said in their favour. Evidently he harboured a residual belief that the public had a right to what it wanted of him; he was ready to guide their choice but not to dictate it. Where no autograph exists it is all too easy to mistake for someone else's lash-up what is in fact a version made by the composer for a particular public.

The most bewildering aspect of Verdi's genius remains that unending capacity to take in fresh experience and in each successive work present something new yet deeply rooted in the past. He himself was in no hurry to unveil the mystery. Not only did he deliberately abstain from propounding an artistic theory of his own; his surviving obiter dicta seem designed to confuse a later generation, being both mutually inconsistent and at variance with his own practice. He might publicly set his face against the modernizing tendencies in the 1860s, and then in *La Forza del destino* and *Don Carlos* coolly perpetrate audacities on which the younger generation would never dream of venturing. He might tell the critic Filippo Filippi that since his student days he had never studied a piece of music in his life and that he never kept a score in his house.* But his private library contains scores of all ages from Palestrina and Bach to Wagner and Reyer.† He would oppose the institution for String Quartet Societies with the suggestion – since this was Italy, not Germany – of founding a vocal quartet,‡ conveniently forgetting that five years before he himself had blessed this un-Italian form with an offering of his own. Only once, in a letter to Arrivabene, do we find a statement of artistic belief which, however general and even nebulous, accords in all respects with his practice.

There are those who want to be melodists like Bellini and harmonists like Meyerbeer. I wouldn't want either . . . and I should wish that when a young man sets out to compose he should never think of being either a melodist nor a harmonist nor a realist nor an idealist nor a futurist nor all the devilish ideas that such pedantry brings about. Melody and harmony should merely be tools in the

* Letter to F. Filippi, 4.3.1869. *Copialettere*, pp. 616–17.
† For further details and comment on the musical library at S. Agata see L. Magnani, 'L'ignoranza musicale di Verdi a la Biblioteca de S. Agata', in *Atti del III° Congresso del I.S.V.*, pp. 250–7.
‡ See letter to Arrivabene, 20.3.1879. *Copialettere*, p. 627.

hands of the artist for the sake of making Music; and the day will come when there won't be any more talk of melody or harmony or German schools and Italian schools nor of the present nor of the future, and then perhaps the reign of art will begin.'*

* Letter to Arrivabene, 16.7.1875. Alberti, pp. 182–3.

3 IL TROVATORE

IL TROVATORE

Opera in four parts
by
SALVATORE CAMMARANO
with additions by Leone Emanuele Bardare
(after the play *El Trovador*, by Antonio García Gutiérrez)

*first performed at the
Teatro Apollo, Rome,
19 January 1853*

IL CONTE DI LUNA, a young noble in the service of the Prince of Aragon	PRIMO BARITONO	Giovanni Guicciardi
LEONORA, a lady-in-waiting to the Princess of Aragon	PRIMA DONNA SOPRANO	Rosina Penco
AZUCENA, an old gipsy woman	PRIMA DONNA MEZZO-SOPRANO	Emilia Goggi
MANRICO, an officer in the army of Prince Urgel, and supposed son of Azucena	PRIMO TENORE	Carlo Baucardé
FERRANDO, officer in the Conte di Luna's army	PRIMO BASSO PROFONDO	Arcangelo Balderi
INES, Leonora's attendant and confidante	SECONDA DONNA	Francesca Quadri
RUIZ, Manrico's henchman	SECONDO TENORE	Giuseppe Bazzoli
An old gipsy	SECONDO BASSO	Raffaele Marconi
A messenger	SECONDO TENORE	Luigi Fani

Leonora's female attendants – nuns – servants and armed retainers of the
Count – gipsies – partisans of Manrico, etc.

The action takes place in Biscay and Aragon

Epoch: 1409

The triumph of *Rigoletto* in March 1851 left Verdi understandably jubilant. He had accomplished what had seemed like a revolution in Italian opera and he had carried his public with him. At thirty-eight his creative energy was at its peak; and the man who had found the strain of composing two operas a year well-nigh intolerable was now proposing to the impresario at Bologna to compose a new opera for the coming autumn, 'the libretto to be my responsibility and, I hope, by Cammarano!'* While still in Venice he had already written to the Neapolitan poet proposing *El Trovador* by García Gutiérrez, foremost among the Spanish romantic playwrights who followed in the wake of Victor Hugo. Produced in Madrid in August 1836 with a success that no other Spanish author had equalled and which Gutiérrez himself would never repeat, it is a high-flown, sprawling melodrama flamboyantly defiant of the Aristotelian unities, packed with all manner of fantastic and bizarre incident. It is partly a love story, partly a drama of vengeance with the underlying irony that the two rivals in love – who are also enemies in a civil war – are brothers without knowing it. Otherwise there is little to distinguish Don Manrique and Don Nuño from conventional hero and villain respectively. The main interest centres on the two women. Eleonora, the heroine, is a high-born lady of strict ideals and deep religious faith whose devotion to her lover plunges her more and more deeply into mortal sin. She elopes with Manrique after having taken the veil, makes an infamous bargain with Don Nuño and finally commits suicide. The more she loves the greater her feeling of guilt and remorse. Nowhere is her internal conflict more powerfully expressed than in the scene where Manrique persuades her to escape from the convent with him. The prime mover in the drama, however, is an old gipsy-woman, Azucena, whose obsessive desire to avenge her mother, burned as a witch, leads her to destroy the one being in the world whom she loves. The fantastic plot all hinges on an incident which took place twenty years before the rise of the curtain. After her mother had been burned by order of the Count of Luna for having as he thought cast the evil eye on his eldest son, Azucena had carried off the infant intending to throw him on the still-smouldering fire; but in the excitement of the moment she threw her own son instead. Only in the high noon of the romantic era could such a premise have been tolerated – and only in Spain. No Italian translation has ever been discovered. How Verdi himself got hold of it is still a mystery. Madrid, however, was on the international operatic circuit. It was not uncommon for singers who were friends of the composer to send him plays and libretti from foreign parts. Once acquired the play would seem to have been translated for Verdi by Giuseppina Strepponi.†

The story had obvious attractions for one who tended to follow the trail blazed by *Rigoletto*. Hugo's Triboulet was one of a pair of characters in whom good and evil were strangely compounded; the other was Lucrezia Borgia. If Verdi had been

* Letter to Lanari, 18.3.1851. *Copialettere*, pp. 116–17.
† 'Hurry up and give OUR *Trovatore*'. Letter from Giuseppina Strepponi, 3.1.1853. *Carteggi Verdiani*, IV, pp. 263–4.

forestalled in the latter area by Donizetti, he had a worthy alternative in Azucena. In fact his first intention – if we can believe the notoriously untrustworthy Monaldi – was to make Azucena the title role with Leonora as a comprimaria.* As for the extravagance of the plot, this could only appear a blessing to Verdi in his present frame of mind. More surprising was his decision to entrust the libretto to Cammarano rather than Piave, whose value to Verdi in his most adventurous undertakings had been so abundantly proved. The truth is that during the twenty-five years of their collaboration he never overcame certain reservations about the Venetian poet. Even after *Rigoletto* he regarded him as an able versifier prone to lapse into the prolix and the pedestrian without the composer at his elbow. Cammarano, however, was the born operatic poet with whom Verdi hoped to enter the promised land of *King Lear*.

In his essay 'Donizetti, an Italian romantic' the late Edward Dent had some hard words for Cammarano whose fustian language he contrasted with the lucidity and elegance of Felice Romani.† This is a purely literary judgement. In a different time and place Romani might well have aspired to the status of a Dryden or a Pope. Cammarano could only exist in the world of opera. Deprived of their musical clothing his verses have the mannered absurdity of a poem by Alfred Austin. But they were never intended to stand on their own. The phrases and sentences, always euphonious, cry out for a musical setting. No librettist showed a greater flair for precipitating the atmosphere of a scene through a carefully constructed nucleus of words: 'Viva Italia forte ed una / colla spada e col pensier' (for heroic patriotism); 'Il pallor, funesto, orrendo / che ricopre il volto mio' (for romantic horror); and so on.‡ For a composer who attached increasing importance to the 'parola scenica' the advantages of such a collaborator were obvious. Above all Cammarano was not afraid of unusual subjects – witness *Belisario* and *L'Assedio di Calais* with their lack of a conventional love-interest, and *Luigi Rolla* with its starving artist-hero in the manner of de Vigny's Chatterton. What Verdi seems to have overlooked is that Cammarano's skill lay precisely in bringing all such plots within the pale of the contemporary operatic convention, carving them up into the statutory cavatine, arie, pezzi concertati, eliminating or amalgamating all characters, however interesting, that are not central to the main action (a comparison of his *Lucia di Lammermoor* with the French libretto written for Carafa in 1828 is instructive here) and removing anything which might offend the godly or the Neapolitan censor. How typical, for instance, that in *Il Reggente*, forerunner of Verdi's *Un Ballo in maschera*, the heroine should long ago have been engaged to her would-be lover, but subsequently forced by the wishes of a dying father to marry the hero's friend instead, precisely as in *La Battaglia di Legnano*.

Verdi can hardly have been unaware of Cammarano's basic conservatism, which he had already experienced in his treatment of Schiller's *Kabale und Liebe*. Possibly he hoped by the example of *Rigoletto* to persuade him to bolder courses. If so he was soon

---

* Letter to Cammarano, 2.1.1850. Monaldi, *Verdi (1839–1898)*, 4th ed. (Milan, 1951), p. 151. The authenticity of this letter has since been established. The postmark however, indicates the date as 1851.

† *Fanfare for Ernest Newman* (London, 1956), p. 100.

‡ For a more detailed defence of Cammarano as librettist see F. Carena, 'Salvatore Cammarano e il libretto ideale del *Trovatore*', in *Atti del 3° Congresso del I.S.V.*, pp. 14–19.

to be undeceived – a fact that must be borne in mind when considering the correspondence which followed as well as the result of their labours and its unique position in Italian opera.

When the whole of March went by without any answer from the poet Verdi wrote to their common friend De Sanctis, 'I am furiously annoyed with Cammarano. Apparently he takes no account of time which for me is extremely precious. He has not written a word about this *Trovador*; does he like it or doesn't he?' Then in reply to what must have been *a priori* objection from De Sanctis: 'I don't know what you mean about the problems of good sense or of theatre. For the rest, the more novelty, the freer the forms he presents me with the better I shall do. He can do exactly as he likes; the bolder he is the happier he will make me. Only let him keep in view the demands of the public which always likes brevity. As a friend of his, then, do beg him not to lose a moment more time.'* By now, however, the Bologna contract had fallen through since neither composer nor impresario could agree about the ownership of the score. This was fortunate, since when Cammarano's letter arrived it was full of objections. Verdi dealt with them patiently.

The scene where Leonora takes the veil must certainly be left in; it's far too original for me to give it up; rather, we must make as much of it as possible and get all the effect we can. If you don't want the Nun [Leonora] to escape of her own accord, make the Troubadour [Manrique] and his followers carry her off in a faint [*presumably the censor could not object to that*]. It is true that the Gipsy [Azucena] gives Manrique to understand that he is not her son after all; but she lets it slip out in the course of her story and she takes it back when the Troubadour, to whom such an idea had never occurred, can't believe that it is true. The reason why she refuses to save herself and Manrique from execution is because her own mother had cried out, 'Avenge me!' Elsewhere she says, 'The grim phantom stretched out its arms and cried out, "Avenge me!"' . . . and she sored up into the clouds, crying out, 'Avenge me!'; and the last words of the play are, 'You are avenged!'

Verdi went on, 'You don't say a word about whether or not you like this drama. I suggested it to you because it seemed to me to offer fine theatrical effects and above all something original and out of the ordinary. If you didn't share my opinion, why didn't you propose another plot?' As to the layout of the pieces, the more unusual and bizarre the better.

If in opera there were neither cavatinas, duets, trios, choruses, finales, etcetera, and the whole work consisted, let's say, of a single number I should find that all the more right and proper. For this reason I would say that if you could avoid beginning with an opening chorus (all operas begin with a chorus!) and start straightaway with the troubadour's song and run the first two acts into one it would be a good thing because these separate numbers, with changes of scene in between, seem to be designed for the concert hall rather than the stage.†

* Letter to De Sanctis, 29.3.1851. *Carteggi Verdiani*, I, pp. 4–5.
† Letter to Cammarano, 4.4.1851. Abbiati, II, pp. 122–3.

These are the words of a Wagner or Berlioz. But they meant nothing to Cammarano, whose synopsis, when it arrived, nearly caused Verdi to drop the project altogether. He wrote to Cammarano:

> I may be mistaken, but it seems to me that various situations don't have their former power and originality, and above all that Azucena hasn't retained the novelty and strangeness of her character; I find that this woman's two great passions, filial and maternal love, no longer emerge in all their strength. Then for instance I wouldn't want the Troubadour wounded in the duel. This poor Troubadour has so little for himself that if we take away his prowess, what does he have left? How could he interest a woman as nobly born as Eleonora? I wouldn't like Azucena to tell her story to the gipsies, or that in the third act she should say in the pezzo concertato, 'Your son was burned alive, etc., etc.', 'but I wasn't there, etc.'; and finally I don't want her to go mad in the last act. I would like you to drop her grand aria!! Eleonora has no part in the hymn for the dead and the canzone of the Troubadour, and this seems to me one of the best places for an aria.*

To clarify his views still further Verdi appended his own synopsis of the action in which the main lineaments of *Il Trovatore* as we know it now are firmly established though with one or two divergencies which will be touched upon later. As in the case of *Luisa Miller* he had conceded a great deal to his librettist's conservatism. If these concessions were not enough it was still not too late to change to another plot. 'I have ready another subject which is simple and tender and almost ready made, you might say. If you like I'll send it to you and we won't think any more about the *Troubadour*.' Carlo Gatti's surmise that Verdi was referring to *La Dame aux camélias* is on the whole improbable, for reasons that will become clear in the next chapter.†

But Cammarano was content with Verdi's scheme. By June Verdi was able to write to him, 'Let us have done with politenesses – just continue the *Troubadour* in the way that you have done the introduction and I shall count myself extremely happy. . . . Keep on sending me the verses.'‡ There was no hurry since it had still not been decided at what theatre the opera was to be given. As early as March Verdi had received an offer from the San Carlo, Naples, but had turned it down, partly because of the patronizing way in which it had been made and partly because he had no faith in the management's artistic policy or its purse. Six months later however he was induced to reconsider his decision because of a still more pressing problem – the casting of Azucena. His ideal choice for the part was Rita Gabussi-De Bassini. Had she by any chance been engaged for the coming season at the San Carlo? If so, Verdi told Cammarano, he would be prepared to reopen negotiations. If not, and she happened to be free, perhaps he could arrange for her to be contracted by the Teatro Apollo, Rome, where the company included a natural Manrico in Gaetano Fraschini.§ Cammarano replied that la Gabussi was not on the San Carlo roster; that the season's cartello had already been fixed, with a new opera by Pacini, and the management

---

* Letter to Cammarano, 9.4.1851. *Copialettere*, pp. 118–21.
† Gatti, I, pp. 363–4.
‡ Letter to Cammarano, 25.6.1851. Abbiati, II, p. 135.
§ Letter to Cammarano, 9.9.1851. Abbiati, II, p. 142.

could hardly be asked to change their plans at this stage. He understood that la Gabussi would be willing to accept a contract in Rome to sing Azucena, provided she were allowed to choose another opera during the course of the season. Meanwhile she would like a line from the Maestro so that she could arrange her commitments; she had already been asked for in Madrid. Verdi was in no mood to countenance so many ifs and buts. 'Let la Gabussi do what suits her best,' he replied shortly, but would Cammarano send him more verses, please.*

Work on the opera had been progressing slowly. Cammarano was his usual dilatory self; besides which certain of Verdi's ideas about the finale of Act II had put him 'in grave embarrassment'. Verdi on his side had been beset by domestic troubles – his mother's death, the administration of his newly acquired property at S. Agata, his father's debts and claims on his money (he and Verdi were now corresponding through a lawyer) and the hostility of the Bussetani to Giuseppina Strepponi, the composer's wife in all but name. Offers of fresh contracts were coming in, not all of which could be turned down out of hand. The plan to compose an opera for Madrid to a libretto by his old partner Solera came to nothing; so too the invitation to write a work for the Venetian theatre of Antonio Gallo, violinist turned impresario. But a visit to Paris in the winter of 1851–2 resulted in the contract for *Les Vêpres Siciliennes*. About the same time Verdi resisted Benjamin Lumley's offer of a première at the Théâtre Italien; but he yielded to the blandishments of Marzari of la Fenice, Venice, so setting in motion the chain of events that led to *La Traviata*. During this period a furious quarrel developed between the composer and Ricordi over the translation rights of *Luisa Miller*, resulting in much acrimonious correspondence (the fault was in fact Verdi's for not having read the small print on the agreement). Finally Verdi's father fell seriously ill; not until mid-May was he out of danger.

And still *Il Trovatore* had not been written. Through De Sanctis Verdi made a final attempt to interest the San Carlo in the first performance. The company should include Teresa de Giuli, Raffaele Mirate, Ferri and 'another prima donna of the Gabussi type to sing the part of Azucena'. The opera to be staged between 20 and 30 November 1852.† This time it was the management who refused, having found Verdi's financial conditions too steep. Verdi then opted for the Teatro Apollo, Rome, on three conditions: that he had encouraging reports about the prima donna, Rosina Penco; that another dramatic prima donna be found for Azucena; and that the censorship gave its blessing to Cammarano's libretto. The opera could then be given in the carnival of 1852–3. All this Verdi set forth in a letter to the impresario, Jacovacci, in June.‡ Next month he read in a theatrical journal that Cammarano was dead. It was not only a blow to his plans but a deep personal loss. He wrote again to De Sanctis asking him to procure from Cammarano's effects both his own programma and the librettist's draft of *King Lear*. The first was available; but the second might prove a source of income to Cammarano's widow and six children, who were otherwise ill provided for. So Verdi for the present renounced his claim. There remained the problem of finding a suitable poet to complete the libretto of *Il Trovatore* to the composer's satisfaction. De Sanctis recommended Leone Emanuele Bardare. Verdi accepted the choice, though he seems to have

---

* Letter to Cammarano, undated. Abbiati, II, p. 143.

† Letter to De Sanctis, 3.5.1852. *Carteggi Verdiani*, I, pp. 6–7.

‡ See letter to Jacovacci, undated. Abbiati, II, p. 167.

communicated with the new librettist only through De Sanctis, who told the composer that 'the young poet is beside himself with joy at the idea of working for Verdi'. He also provided reassuring news about the company at the Teatro Apollo.

> La Penco has one or two faults but also many virtues. She is not a perfect soprano. I must tell you that she is very pretty, but beware, Maestro! I warn you she's a devil and will certainly give the other prima donna a drubbing! They tell me that la Goggi is an old stager, but you will certainly make her young again with the magic of your music. We are all expecting a masterpiece from *Il Trovatore*. Verdi with his music will give eternal life to the last work of Cammarano. Remember that the last piece he wrote, eight days before his death, was the tenor aria.*

From this one might conclude that the entire last act is the work of Bardare. A glance, however, at Cammarano's libretto preserved in the Villa S. Agata will show that it was in all essentials complete and could certainly have been set as it stood. It follows Verdi's synopsis of 1851 to the letter except in two details: the hero, whom Verdi called Alfonso, reverts to his proper name italianized into Manrico; and where in Part III the composer had specified the Troubadour's Dream followed by a duet with Leonora, Cammarano gives us the grand aria for tenor with which we are familiar today and no duet. There is no cavatina for Leonora, so that Part I, Scene 2, begins with the entrance of the Count. In the second scene of Part II the count has only a brief recitative before Leonora appears. By way of compensation he has a lengthy romance after the opening chorus of Part III, an apostrophe to Leonora, beginning:

> I miei giorni tu rendesti
> Un sol giorno di martoro.
> Tu mi sprezzi, mi detesti
> Ed io t'amo, ed io t'adoro.

Like many another operatic villain he goes on to lament that he was not born to crime; love alone was the cause of his misdeeds. The finale to Act II is lengthened by a few lines suitable to a stretta. The end of the opera is longer, and perhaps slightly more plausible than what was eventually set: twelve lines of double quinari whose sense is as follows:

COUNT   Let him be taken to the scaffold.
MANRICO Well, let us be gone. Death for me. Mother, farewell!
     (*Exit, dragged off by the Count's retainers*)
AZUCENA (*waking up*) We shall go back to our mountains! My son? Ah, what do I see? . . . Is it my son?
COUNT   Tremble! . . . You will soon look upon him.
AZUCENA What would you tell me? That he . . . ?
COUNT   He is hastening towards his doom.
AZUCENA Quell your insane fury. . . . Hear me. . . . Hold! (Mother, I cannot bear it . . . I must reveal the truth to him.)
     (*Day dawns; the Count drags Azucena to the window.*)

* Letter from De Sanctis, 23.10.1852. *Carteggi Verdiani*, I, 10–14.

COUNT   Behold!
AZUCENA   Ah! The scaffold!
            (*A sound is heard like that of an axe falling*)
COUNT   He is dead!
AZUCENA   He was . . .
COUNT   Who?
AZUCENA   Your brother!
COUNT   Oh horror!
AZUCENA   A late vengeance is yours, mother, but how cruel!
            (*She falls fainting by the window*)
COUNT   (*casting a glance at the scaffold, then at Leonora and drawing his hands
            desperately through his hair*) And I still live!!!!!

The metre and the rhymes all imply a fast movement, though nothing that could
resemble a conventional stretta. An extravagant dénouement, certainly, but it at least
allows time for Manrico's execution to take place. The present whirlwind conclusion
was Verdi's doing without even the aid of Bardare. To De Sanctis, who demurred,
particularly at his condensation of Azucena's final outcry, Verdi replied:

> You tell me that Azucena must say these [Cammarano's] words because they are a
> consequence, etc., etc. Oh, allow me to say that I understand these things
> perfectly well but the greater part of the drama (as you say yourself) is summed
> up not in those words but in the one word 'Vengeance!' . . . To say, 'Mother,
> you are avenged,' and, 'Yours is a late vengeance, mother but how cruel!' means
> exactly the same as far as the drama is concerned, except that the former is shorter
> and more suitable. For the rest, if you don't agree let us print all the lines
> Cammarano wrote with a little note in the libretto: the following lines have been
> changed for the sake of brevity.*

Indeed it may well have been respect for Cammarano's memory which induced
Verdi not to include in the score the numerous alterations made in his own
handwriting on the original text. Had he done so many of the best known aria titles
would be other than they are today.

The various changes and additions required from Bardare show very clearly that
Verdi had changed his mind about the distribution of characters. Il Trovatore was
now to be a two-women opera. Therefore Leonora's part needed to be filled out.
Having first asked for her cavatina to be removed Verdi wanted it restored; hence
'Tacea la notte' and its cabaletta 'Di tale amor'. Likewise her part in the Miserere,
though it included the cabaletta 'Tu vedrai che amor in terra', still was not big
enough for Verdi, since 'it lacks a cantabile. The very beautiful lines "Quel suon,
quelle preci" lend themselves only to a slow "declamato"; therefore it will be
necessary to add eight or ten lines of great beauty and passion after the recitative
"Arreca ai miei sospiri".'† Instead of the romanza in Part III the Count was to have a
double aria at the start of Part II, Scene 2 'as Cammarano and I had already agreed
between us. We should need, however, an adagio cantabile of eight or ten lines . . .

---

* Letter to Cammarano, 1.1.1853. *Carteggi Verdiani*, I, pp. 16–17.

† Letter to De Sanctis, 29.9.1852. *Carteggi Verdiani*, I, pp. 10–11.

then when he says to his followers, "Hide in the shadow of the beeches," I would like
the chorus as they go away to sing a verse in "settenari" to be sung piecemeal
[*spezzata*] and sotto voce, which I would then intersperse with the cabaletta, perhaps
rather effectively.' But of course if their music is to be interwoven with the cabaletta
the followers cannot go away though they repeatedly urge each other to do so. From
which results a typical operatic absurdity beautifully parodied in Sullivan's *The
Pirates of Penzance*. The verses of Azucena's 'Stride la vampa' were to be changed
from four lines to six, to suit the 'canzone caratteristica' which Verdi had in mind and
'with which I would make play musically speaking at various points in the drama'.
Finally he wished to omit Cammarano's stretta at the end of Part II chiefly since he
had set the pezzo concertato not as an adagio 'as is the usual way' but in a lively
tempo. 'A largo,' he wrote to De Sanctis, 'would have been impossible. For this
reason I have decided to suppress the stretta especially since it isn't necessary to the
drama and perhaps Cammarano only wrote it for the sake of tradition.' Then comes
the series of interjections that we know today beginning with Ruiz's 'Urgel viva'
and ending with the Count's 'Ho le furie in cor' (Curtain). 'This I find has more
novelty of form and is perhaps more effective: and above all it's shorter (and that's no
bad thing especially in this libretto which is on the lengthy side).'* In the event he
was to find a still more striking and original way to bring down the curtain.

Rehearsals began immediately after Christmas. Needless to say the libretto did not
go entirely unscathed by the censor. As early as 1851 Cammarano had consulted
Jacovacci of the Teatro Apollo, Rome, on this point in case the opera should be given
there. The reply had been reassuring. There must be no mention of the 'stake' which
might remind people of the Holy Inquisition. Leonora must not be seen to take the
poison as suicide was forbidden (presumably, then, Leonora must appear to die of
love). Liturgical words were not allowed. Yet surely the censor might have spared
himself the ludicrous alteration of the Miserere, whereby:

> Miserere di lei, bontà divina,
> Preda non sia dell'infernal soggiorno!

became:

> Ah pietade di lei che s'avvicina
> Allo splendor dell'immortal soggiorno.†

A soul that is about to enter the glorious realm of everlasting light hardly needs
anyone's pity.

The first performance on 19 January 1853 triumphed mightily despite a cast that
included only two stars, Carlo Boucardé and Rosina Penco. The final scene was
encored *in toto*. There were a few critical cavils about the prevailing gloom, and the
number of deaths; 'but,' Verdi wrote to Clarina Maffei, 'is not life all death
anyway?'‡ Life is not perhaps very like *Il Trovatore*. However the public was not
deterred; and from the Teatro Apollo, Rome, *Il Trovatore* began a victorious march
throughout the operatic world. With none of his operas, not even *Nabucco*, did Verdi
reach so immediately to the hearts of his audience. Within months parodies of it were

---

* Letter to De Sanctis, 14.12.1852. *Carteggi Verdiani*, I, pp. 14–16.
† Letter from Cammarano to Jacovacci, 18.11.1851. *Carteggi Verdiani*, I, p. 8.
‡ See Chapter 2.

springing up in Italy and abroad – a sure sign of overwhelming popularity: baby-swapping figures in two of Sullivan's most popular operettas. Verdi's latest opera became and remained for many years the property of every barrel organ and street band in Europe. It was the music of Antonio and his ice-cream cart; and Fritz in the music-hall song who '. . . plays twiddly bits / On the big trombone' was almost certainly decorating the Miserere from *Il Trovatore*. Of all his output *Il Trovatore* was the most loved in Verdi's own day.

Take a composer at the height of his melodic vitality; fire his imagination through an extravagant and bizarre plot; then channel it through the most conventional of libretto structures – such is the recipe for one of the strangest and most powerful phenomena in the world of Italian opera. Not that Cammarano's libretto deserves all the obloquy which is usually heaped upon it. True it is full of complex narrations, but so is Gutiérrez's play: what is more, Cammarano actually finds room for an encounter to which Gutiérrez merely alludes. Unlike for instance Gaetano Rossi's *Il Giuramento* and *Il Bravo* which are incomprehensible without a knowledge of their literary source, *Il Trovatore* gives us all the relevant facts in legible if not audible form. The elimination of marginal characters, such as Leonora's brother, Don Gullen, guardian of the family's pride, and the two gossiping *criados* whose functions are incorporated in Ferrando, is carried out with the poet's usual skill. The language is always appropriate to the dramatic situation; but the libretto as a whole remains cast in an old-fashioned mould with the static set number as its basis. Verdi, who had wanted a poem with the freshness and flexibility of *Rigoletto*, found himself forced in another direction. The solution that he chose and which required even further traditional elements from Bardare is no less artistically compelling than *Rigoletto*; only it is totally opposite. Where the earlier work is conceived as a steadily evolving action like that of a spoken play, *Il Trovatore* is a drama of the expanded moment. While much of *Rigoletto* develops from a basis of recitative with the orchestra often in the forefront, *Il Trovatore* is an explosion of closed lyrical forms with the orchestra relegated to its traditional role of accompanying the voices. Recitative in the later opera is reduced to a minimum; and indeed the only substantial passage of free declamation in Part II, Scene 1 is marked to be sung as quickly as possible. That *Il Trovatore* conceived in such a form nevertheless can maintain a consistent dramatic impetus is due to the nature of Verdian melody in its latest evolution. Its propulsive quality has already been noted. Here the stresses and contours are so finely graded as to produce even in the most apparently static numbers a sense of continuous forward motion. In several of these he shows himself the equal of Bellini as a melodist. But the essentially dynamic core of 'Tacea la notte' or 'Il balen' was something right outside the earlier composer's experience. Bellini could still surpass him in length of line; for in the new refinement of his style that came with *Luisa Miller* Verdi had, if anything, shortened the rhythmic span of his melodies, though he was to lengthen it, but in quite a different way, in the operas that begin with *Les Vêpres Siciliennes*. In *Il Trovatore* the symmetrical structure of each number helps to concentrate the emotional fire.

Again while Rigoletto, the Duke, Gilda and Sparafucile are all specific characters, Leonora, Manrico and the Count are the merest vocal archetypes; and Ferrando, for whom Verdi had specified a 'rather baritonal bass', is not even that. Only one character is sculpted in depth: Azucena, a figure entirely new in Verdi's female gallery. So far he had made no significant use of the mezzo-soprano or contralto voice in a principal role. Cuniza in *Oberto* is distinguishable from her colleagues merely by her range. Federica (*Luisa Miller*) and Maddalena (*Rigoletto*) certainly exploit the contralto colour; but both are comprimaria roles, and not particularly grateful to the singer (especially Federica). But Azucena is the first of a glorious line which includes Ulrica (*Un Ballo in maschera*), Eboli (*Don Carlos*), Amneris (*Aida*) and in a different vein Preziosilla (*La Forza del destino*). It is usual, following Dannreuther,* to trace her ancestry to Meyerbeer's Fidès (*Le Prophète*), the first of the great mother-figures of romantic opera, and without doubt the model for Ponchielli's La Cieca. Now Verdi was certainly familiar with *Le Prophète* at this time as his letters to Scribe show.† But the two maternal roles have very little in common. Pauline Viardot Garcia was not a 'dramatic prima donna' in Verdi's sense and the part of Fidès is 'noble' throughout. Besides Verdi had originally asked for Rita Gabussi and when she proved unavailable a singer 'of the Gabussi type'. She herself was always described as a soprano, though one with the bad habit of always attempting roles that were too high for her – 'The old story of the right way to ruin your voice,' so Donizetti had written.‡ Relevant here is a letter from Verdi to Piave in the spring of 1853. *Il Trovatore* was to be staged in Venice with Marianna Barbieri-Nini playing Leonora. She was unenthusiastic about 'Tacea la notte'. Verdi wrote:

> You will give la Barbieri my greetings and tell her that I find the cavatina in *Il Trovatore* a good one and that I therefore cannot and must not change it. It would be suicide! But if I'm allowed to express an opinion in the matter, why does la Barbieri undertake that part if it doesn't suit her? If she wants to do *Il Trovatore* there's another part, that of the Gipsy. Don't lets talk about the convenienze or say that its a comprimaria; no indeed; it's a principal, *the* principal role; finer and more dramatic and more original than the other. If I were a prima donna (a fine thing that would be!) I would always rather sing the part of the Gipsy in *Il Trovatore*.§

How, one might ask, could Azucena as eventually realized be regarded as lying within the compass of a soprano? How could a singer feel that she had a choice between the two parts Azucena and Leonora? The real explanation lies in the nineteenth-century attitude to vocal registers, a subject which has not so far received the attention it deserves. Musicologists who are eager at all costs to revive the performing traditions of a past age would do well to remember that some of them might prove unacceptable today, as for instance the alternative method of portamento which Niccolò Vaccai advocates for fast movements in his singing method of 1833 and which now exists only in pop and folk music. The ideal of an even vocal quality from top to bottom of a singer's compass was unknown to Verdi's contemporaries. A sharp break, like a change of gear, between registers, so objectionable today, was tolerated then and indeed this yodelling effect can still be

---

* 'Azucena is Fidès in Romany'—E. Dannreuther, in *Oxford History of Music*, 2nd ed. (London, 1932), VI, p. 63.

† See next chapter.

‡ *Enciclopedia dello Spettacolo* (Rome, 1958), V, p. 810.

§ Letter to Piave, 17.4.1853. Abbiati, II, p. 241.

heard in certain pre-electric recordings. The tenor of Bellini's and Rossini's day was expected to reach d″ or e flat″ but not with full chest support. Anything above a″ was sung falsetto. Likewise a soprano disposed, in theory at least, of two and a half octaves from g to c‴ or d‴; but the lower fifth would inevitably have only a chest resonance. Different singers had their own favourite areas; those who concentrated on the bottom notes, especially if they had a penchant for travesti roles, were known as contraltos. But in Italy categories were loose at least up to the middle of the century, and a singer could describe herself much as she liked. For many the term 'mezzo-soprano' (lit. 'half soprano') suggested a limitation incompatible with prima donna status. Thus Antonietta Rainieri-Marini, star of *Oberto* and *Un Giorno di regno*, though described in cast lists of both operas as a soprano, was really a mezzo-soprano; and a careful examination of the music written for them will show that this was true of several other 'dive' of the time – Maria Malibran, for instance. It is certainly true of Rita Gabussi, whose most famous creations were the *Medea* of Mercadante and above all Giovanna (Madge Wildfire) in Federico Ricci's *La Prigione di Edimburgo*. It is in this half-crazed creature, daughter of a venomous old hag believed to be a witch, the kidnapper of the heroine's illegitimate child, that the true forerunner of Azucena can be discerned. Highly characteristic is the little crooning melody that she sings to the child which serves later as a thematic reminiscence:

F. *Ricci*: LA PRIGIONE D'EDIMBURGO etc.

From here it is a short step to 'Stride la vampa'. What really distinguishes the part of Giovanna is its range of violent dramatic contrasts – the same qualities which appear even more vividly in the role of Azucena. Marianna Barbieri-Nini was a superb dramatic artist, if not a glamorous one ('If she can get a husband,' Giuseppina Strepponi remarked, on first noting the double-barrelled surname, 'none of us need worry!').* Further, she was nearing the end of her career and her area of vocal comfort might well be expected to have dropped somewhat. Verdi's suggestion may not have been so eccentric as it appears.

The word 'dramatic' applies in a very special sense to Azucena since it describes a

* Letter from G. Strepponi to Lanari, 1842. Walker, p. 83.

principle of musical organization whereby Verdi for the first time achieves the kind of polarity between his female singers that in previous operas such as *Ernani* (the nearest in character to *Il Trovatore*) existed only between the males. But whereas the three lovers in the earlier work had defined themselves through their mutual encounters, Leonora and Azucena inhabit different spheres. Leonora's music is purely lyrical. When she describes her first acquaintance with Manrico, the events of her story have not the slightest importance; all that matters is that we should be aware of the flowering of a transcendental love. But when Azucena recounts how her mother was led to execution, the vivid horror of each happening is impressed on us by every possible device including thematic reminiscence. Such distinctions in narrative method were not entirely unknown in Italian opera – compare Donizetti's 'Regnava nel silenzio' (*Lucia di Lammermoor*) with 'Nella fatal di Rimini' (*Lucrezia Borgia*), where again the greater verbal projection of the lower voice is turned to advantage. In Verdi's case not only is the contrast very much greater; both methods exist side by side in the same opera.

The polarity between the two female roles does not end there; rather it is extended into every possible field of comparison. Leonora's music moves in long phrases mostly characterized by a soaring, 'aspiring' quality; her melodies are minted from the purest gold of the Italian lyrical tradition; and if this means sacrificing the element of conflict to be found in the character of Gutiérrez's Eleonora, the loss is a small one. Azucena's melodies evolve in short, often commonplace phrases based on the repetition of short rhythmic patterns. Most striking of all, each woman inhabits her own sphere of tonality – Leonora moves in A flat and its related keys, Azucena hovers ambiguously between E minor and G major, the first associated with her thirst for revenge, the second with her love for Manrico; and her influence reaches to A minor and C major as well. Again it must be emphasized that in Verdi, even when keys are exploited, it is merely as contrasted systems of pitch designed to keep the dramatic elements apart; there is no attempt to use their manifold relationships as a principle of structure. Yet, curiously enough, in *Il Trovatore* their effect is for once architectural as well, since it results in a series of scenes dominated alternately by Leonora and Azucena and their respective tonalities. Only in the last scene of all do they meet but without making contact. When Leonora is conscious Azucena is asleep, and when she wakes Leonora is dead.

The principal men on the other hand are characterized mainly by their respective voice-types. Manrico, the essence of heroic tenor, has no tonal area of his own; but is drawn now into Leonora's orbit, now into Azucena's. The Count, as an aristocrat, remains closer to Leonora, though in moments of isolation he tends to revert to a personal tonality of B flat. *Il Trovatore* obeys its own idiosyncratic system of laws.

PART I

The Duel

Scene 1: A hall in the palace of Aliaferia. On one side a door which leads to the apartments of the Count of Luna.

For the first time Verdi, possibly following the model of *Le Prophète*, has dispensed with a self-contained prelude or overture. The instrumental opening forms an integral part of the recitative which follows, setting the scene with an atmosphere of pomp and medieval chivalry, the spiralling arpeggios giving a foretaste of the wide melodic span of the opera. It is the world of *Lohengrin* and *Euryanthe* transported musically speaking south of the Alps.

The small notes (*x*) indicate the composer's first thoughts, discernible in the autograph. They are logical enough; but the revision is subtler. The corresponding figure in bar 19, no longer a direct contradiction, suggests all the more effectively the mysterious shadow that blights the E major splendour of the Palace of Aliaferia. The G natural is of course a harbinger of Azucena's key of E minor. E major, so often the key of power in Verdi, is re-asserted over a long dominant pedal; but low triplets on the trumpet sustain the underlying sense of menace as the music draws to an ambiguous half-close.

A group of liveried servants are keeping watch by the door, while in the background sentries are pacing up and down. It is late at night, and the retainers are finding it difficult to stay awake. Ferrando, the Count's henchman, rouses them with a brusque 'All'erta, all'erta' and the orchestra responds with bars 1 to 4 of Ex. 24. Their master, he reminds them, insists that they keep a particularly careful watch this evening. He himself is spending night after night under the balcony of the woman he loves, fearing the rivalry of a certain troubadour whose voice is often heard in the gardens. The servants beg Ferrando to tell them the story of the Count's younger brother Garcia. 'Us too!' cry the sentries, coming forward to listen, and Ferrando launches into the first of the opera's many narrations. Long ago, while watching over Garcia's cradle, his nurse saw an old woman fixing him, as she thought, with the evil eye. She called for the servants, who drove the gipsy away; but later the child fell ill with a lingering fever, and the old Count, convinced that he had been bewitched, hunted down the gipsy woman and had her burned at the stake. Next day the infant Garcia disappeared; but on the embers of the funeral pyre was found the charred skeleton of a baby. The witch was known to have had a daughter no less evil than herself. This, it was thought, was her revenge. Yet the old Count refused to believe that his son was dead and commanded that a search be made for the gipsy's daughter – in vain. She had vanished without trace. But were he to see her again after all these years Ferrando would still be able to recognize her. Meanwhile the lost soul of her mother continues to wander the earth. It is said that she had the power to change into a crow or an owl. One of the Count's servants who had once struck her on the forehead died of fright when she appeared to him as a nightjar. 'The clock was striking midnight' . . . and at that moment the midnight bell does indeed ring out from the tower, causing servants, retainers and even Ferrando to scatter in a panic.

Since Verdi had originally wanted to begin with what is now Scene 2, the introduction was presumably Cammarano's idea. It is certainly naif. As if a Spanish grandee of Luna's calibre would have tolerated such a slack and timorous household! Yet Cammarano is following a tradition that Guttiérrez would certainly have understood, whereby the lower orders are cowardly and faintly comic (was there ever a greater coward than Sancho Panza?). Besides, the story has to be told at some stage; and if Gutiérrez put it in the mouth of the servant Jiménez and in rather more plausible circumstances, we should remember that an opera with four principals can with difficulty afford a Jiménez *and* a Ferrando. The only other solution would have been a printed 'antefatto'; but by 1853 such an expedient was becoming outdated, nor does it ever seem to have appealed to Cammarano, who always begins his dramas at the beginning. In the event Verdi turned his scheme to brilliant account, since he uses Ferrando's narration to present us with Azucena musically before she appears on the stage, and in an ingenious and original way. The main part of Ferrando's narrative is divided into two pairs of parallel verse-sections. The first of each pair is rhymed but metrically rather free; the second consists of short lines in strict quinario metre. The musical setting that results suggests the formula of verse and refrain, but with an unusual degree of contrast between the two. The 'verse' sections (Ex. 25a) with their mixture of quavers and triplets have an arioso-like flexibility that permits an element of strophic variation, so that important words like 'bugiarda' and 'ammaliato' in verse 2 emerge in high relief. Each 'verse' begins in a suave B major as though to depict the once comfortable, secure world of the Count – note the ceremonial trill (x), clearly a reflection of that in Ex. 24. With the 'refrain' (Ex. 25b) the rhythm switches abruptly to 3/4, to unfold a melody of the type to be associated with Azucena: primitive, demotic, tricked out with grace-notes, flourishes and, later, displaced accents; and located in Azucena's area of E minor–G major.

The music evolves in short, urgent sequences, each scored for the same block of woodwind and strings with none of the usual 'colorations' where there is a hint of modulation. Only in the last five bars is the piccolo added to the strength in preparation for the choral and orchestral explosion at the cadence. Also characteristic of Azucena is the tendency to insist on the note B in the final period. That the second verse is still referring to the witch not to the old Count, that the witch herself is not Azucena but her mother is true but irrelevant. *Il Trovatore* does not function on this

level of subtlety. Where the music drama is concerned, Azucena is her mother's reincarnation. It is she who takes command of the opening scene – so completely as to engulf the personality of Ferrando. Any doubts of this will be resolved in the transitional recitative – characteristically in strict time – with its patent, if not literal anticipation of themes from the first scene of Part II. The conversational use of the chorus here is a direct legacy from Act II of *Guillaume Tell*.

The final movement ('Sull'orlo dei tetti') has the function of a stretta dell'introduzione, the effect of which is an intensification of everything that has gone before. The sequential pattern is that of 'Abbietta zingara' but the phrases are swifter and shorter; the waltz-like accompaniment is replaced by relentless pizzicato pulsation. The main idea has a bizarrerie, a counterpoint of accent and contour that suggests Meyerbeer, except for that quality of spontaneous combustion that Meyerbeer never achieved but which informs every note of *Il Trovatore*.

The music is at first shared out between the armed retainers, servants and Ferrando. As it moves towards its climax the chorus accompany Ferrando's line with wordless lamenting figures and graphic repetitions of his words. They have so thoroughly frightened themselves that when the bell chimes out (and Verdi specified a really large one) they break out in a cry of terror, made all the more startling by the incursion of a side drum.* The huge vocal and orchestral outburst dwindles away into a coda based on repetitions of Ex. 27. It is the traditional method of emptying the stage, to which a chromatically rising inner part on the cello supplies an attractive Tchaikovskian touch. As in so many Gothick scenes a comparison with Wagner or Weber suggests itself; but this time it is not to Verdi's disadvantage. Wagner arouses terror; Verdi depicts it, and with wonderful immediacy. For the first time he has ventured to remain in the minor key right up to the last bar.

Scene 2: The palace gardens; on the right a marble staircase leading to various apartments. The night is far advanced. Thick clouds cover the moon.

Here the opera seems to take us back to the world of *Ernani* with its soprano cavatina and its quarrelling men. Indeed since the scene has no exact parallel in the play and Cammarano, like most of his kind, was a poor inventor, what more likely than that he based it deliberately on the earlier opera? A neutral preludizing of orchestral strings introduces us to Leonora, strolling in the garden with her attendant Ines. The queen has already sent for her, and Ines is worried. She knows her mistress is in love and dangerously so, but like all good operatic confidantes she is willing to hear again a tale with which she can hardly be unfamiliar. One day a knight clad in black armour appeared at a royal tournament and carried all before him. No one knew who he was or where he came from; but to Leonora fell the honour of placing the victor's wreath upon his brow. Then civil war broke out; the Count of Urgel decided to press his claims to the throne by force. The unknown knight vanished and his memory became a golden dream. At this point Verdi throws a splash of instrumental colour into the austere texture of the 'scena', so reinforcing the magic of the favourite Franco-Italian topos – the rising sixth of romantic love (Ex. 28).

'But then,' continues Leonora . . . 'What happened?' obliges Ines. 'Listen!' says her mistress as she prepares for the cantabile of her cavatina. One night she heard a minstrel singing in the palace gardens. His songs were pious and chaste, as of one who prays to God; but their refrain was always 'Leonora!' She ran to the balcony. There before her stood her knight of the black armour. From that moment the earth became a paradise (the heroine of *Ernani* had likewise talked about an 'Eden' of love). The rest is according to Gutiérrez except for the 'black knight' touch which seems to have been borrowed arbitrarily from *Ivanhoe*.

For concentration of lyrical poetry 'Tacea la notte' is unsurpassed in all Verdi's music, while as a tour de force of melodic craftsmanship it is without parallel anywhere. We have become used to his practice of throwing the main emphasis further and further towards the end of his melodies; but the steady gradient of this andantino is quite new. It is as though throughout 28 slow bars the melodic centre of gravity continually rises, to culminate in that final soaring flight up to B flat enhanced

---

* In early libretti it is implied that the side drum is sounding a call to arms which the Count's soldiers are bound to obey – without any imputation of cowardice!

by chromatically rising inner parts, a roll on the timpani and the introduction of further instruments (Ex. 29).

The melody is repeated with small strophic variants in the 'minore' section, less because the structure requires it (for the major/minor pattern is normally self-sufficient) than because Leonora has not yet finished her story. Note however that in this purely lyrical narrative the words are not allowed to condition the musical events. At the end of the first verse the minstrel of Leonora's tale is still singing melancholy songs ('e versi melanconici un trovator cantò'). Anything less melancholy than the final phrase of Ex. 29 can hardly be imagined. But to the conclusion of the second strophe ('Al core, al guardo estatico la terra un ciel sembrò') it is entirely appropriate: and as if to dispel all ambiguity Verdi makes the final climax even more towering, with its soaring flight first of all diverted into a half close, then repeated over a crescendo of the full orchestra with tremolo strings, the final cadence prolonged by a cadenza of nearly two octaves marked *Adagio ed eguale*, i.e. evenly and in slow tempo. A further subtlety: this is the first time that Leonora has reached a full cadence in the major key, since in the previous verse her final note had been dovetailed into the restatement of the four-bar ritornello.

But there is no moment of repose. The violins that accompany the final A flat move swiftly into the transition or so-called 'tempo di mezzo' with a pattern of semiquavers. Ines is deeply disturbed. The unknown warrior fills her with forebodings (and is it mere coincidence that at the words 'ma tristo presentimento in me risveglia' her line should recall the rhythm of Ex. 26a?). Her mistress should try to forget him. Leonora replies that she would live and die for her troubadour. 'Di

30

Allegro giusto

LEONORA

Di ta - le a-mor, che dir - - - - - si   mal può   dal-la pa-

vln. II , vlas.   vln. I   [fl. added - - -]

pp   *pp*

cellos pizz.
basses

- ro - - - - - la,   d'am-(or)

[fl. added - - - -]   etc.

vln. I

tale amor' with its excited pizzicato cellos and its violin and woodwind 'tintings' seems a reversion to the pre-*Rigoletto* manner. But then Leonora inhabits an older, more ideal world than that of Gilda; her bravura, like Donna Anna's, is part of her aristocratic finery. More to the point, the well-worn Verdian devices are here purged of all vulgarity. If the manner is old-fashioned the matter is fresh, vital and a suitable complement to what has gone before, with Leonora's aspiring lyricism reflected in joyous leaps and trills (Ex. 30).

Between statements of the cabaletta there is the usual noisy ritornello during which Ines must reflect inaudibly on the dangers of loving not wisely but too well. The coda introduces a fresh idea with both women singing and sweeps the aria to a triumphant conclusion. Exeunt Leonora and Ines amid a storm of applause.

Another short murmur of strings brings on the Count. He sings of his passion for Leonora in a short but expressive recitative that moves from C major to a cadence in his home-key of B flat; then 'blind with love' he prepares to climb the staircase to Leonora's apartments. But his last note is covered by the far-off sound of a harp. 'The Troubadour!' exclaims the Count; and, sure enough, the voice of Manrico comes floating over the night air. It is a wonderful stroke of romantic theatre. True, Bellini and Mercadante also used the device of making a singer heard before he or she is seen; but here it carries special overtones. The troubadour was a potent symbol for the romantic age: the lonely outcast, the champion of freedom, whose love-lorn melancholy songs were a constant reproach to the heartless society that would have none of him. 'Deserto sulla terra' plants straightaway the musical language of Manrico the minstrel – simple, regular in its construction (only the final phrase is extended by a bar), somewhat popular in Azucena's manner but with an additional touch of mystery – witness the exotic cadence (*x*).

31

The passionate intensity of the line 'e sola speme un cor' will be echoed in the Miserere scene. The melody is repeated nearer at hand while the Count mutters in fury. Meanwhile Leonora at the first sound of the harp has come down the marble stairway and seeing a man standing in the darkness she flies into his arms, murmuring ecstatically. (The Count's embarrassed 'Che far?' is a nice touch. Villain he may be, but he is too much of a gentleman to take advantage of the situation.) The moon comes out from behind the clouds to reveal another figure on the terrace, his face covered by a visor. So begins the first movement of a terzetto packed with action.

Leonora breaks away from the Count and throws herself at Manrico's feet, babbling excuses and protesting her undying love. Manrico gently raises her to her feet. The Count challenges his rival to reveal himself unless he wishes to be thought a coward. Manrico lifts his visor, to be recognized by the Count as a follower of the now proscribed rebel Urgel. There is nothing for it but a duel. Predictably the scene is launched by a rapid, agitated orchestral theme (Ex. 32a) carrying the voices in dialogue. Observe how Verdi's 'action' melodies no longer repeat or 'conjugate' themselves but actually develop. By the twenty-ninth bar Ex. 32a has flowered into a G major melody with a chromatically rising bass (Ex. 32b); by bar 56 it has become itself a turbulent bass line (Ex. 32c) preparing for the key of the following movement.

32c

This takes the form of a stretta, since a cantabile or pezzo concertato would lower the temperature at once. In the approved fashion Cammarano has given each singer a strophe of his own. The Count in jealous fury cries out for Manrico's blood; Leonora implores him to relent; Manrico reassures Leonora and defies the Count. Verdi, following the example of *Ernani*, combines the verses of Leonora and Manrico in unison so that each render the other's words inaudible. But on the emotional level the point is made: the Count is on one side, Leonora and Manrico on the other. The contrast is vividly stressed through mode, contour and scoring:

No time is wasted in ritornelli. No sooner has 33b run its course than the Count restates 33a in more elliptical form then joins in a repetition of 33b with a staccato counterpoint of his own, like Miller's in the first-act duet of *Luisa Miller*. As passions mount ever higher in the coda, the Count echoes, though more powerfully, his equally jealous compatriot Almaviva in the last act of *Figaro*, both composers having used the classical device of a heavy unison to express negative emotion.

At the end Leonora faints as the two men leave with drawn swords. This whirl of action interspersed with moments of straining at the leash is typical of Italian romantic opera of the previous twenty years. If the effect is particularly exaggerated here, this is due partly to the energy of the music, partly to the fact that Cammarano has deftly combined in reverse order two incidents in the original plot – the duel between Manrique and Nuño and the reconciliation of Manrique with Eleonora after her gaffe.

PART II

The Gipsy

Scene 1: A ruined hovel in a fold of the Biscay mountains. At the back, which is almost entirely open, a huge fire is burning. It is dawn. Azucena is sitting by the fire. Manrico, wrapped in a cloak, is reclining on a mattress by her side. His helmet is at his feet and he is grasping a sword at which he gazes fixedly; a band of gipsies are scattered about the stage.

From Leonora's world to Azucena's. In medieval times gipsies were tinkers by trade, which explains why the anvil plays such a prominent part in the opening chorus ('Vedi le fosche notturne') where the dawn is greeted as a widow who has put off her mourning weeds. The first and third ideas, orchestral and vocal respectively, both have their counterparts in Part I (Ex. 35a, b, c; compare Ex. 26a, b).

The chattering 2/4 rhythm, the acciaccature, the abundance of triangle are all recognizable ingredients of the Turkish style as used by Haydn, Mozart and Gluck. But the abruptness of the motifs themselves, the wandering key scheme (E minor, G major, C major), the frequent shifts of the principal accent from first to third beat of the bar all suggest a deliberate essay in the bizarre, like the witches' music in *Macbeth*. The climax set in relief by a characteristically steep modulation is the unison C major refrain ('Chi del gitano gli giorni abbella') where the men strike their anvils in alternation, tenors on the weak beats, basses on the strong. This, quite new to Italian opera, would be sufficient to ensure the piece's popularity. But the tune itself is a

strong one and helps to give shape to the loose design of the chorus as a whole. The scoring for full orchestra, unashamedly banda-like, enhances its bold simplicity.

The chorus is repeated with a little scenic diversion in which the men ask their womenfolk for a glass of wine and are duly obliged. Then attention is focused on Azucena, who has begun to sing to herself. The gipsies crowd round to listen:

It is not a cavatina but a canzone caratteristica, a popular ditty, to be used as a dramatic counter later on, like 'La donna è mobile' (both songs occur as such in the original plays). 'Stride la vampa' has an extra dramatic dimension, traceable to the note B which recurs with the quality of an idée fixe. Twice it appears as the third of the key of G major; everywhere else it is the dominant of E minor, and as such is prolonged in a trill of four bars in the final phrase while the accompanying harmonies seem to twist and turn in an effort to escape. The B in the melody is a bee in the bonnet.

The resemblance to Ex. 25b is unmistakable. Like Ferrando's it is a narrative song though vaguer and more impressionistic. Azucena is reliving the scene long ago when she saw her mother burned at the stake – the crackling flames, the cries of the victim, the cruel joy of the persecutors. Above all it is the flames which are mirrored in the jagged rhythm of the opening phrase.

The gipsies find the song depressing; but Azucena pays no attention to them. Utterly absorbed she murmurs 'Avenge me' to a diminished seventh on oboes and clarinets. 'Again those mysterious words!' Manrico exclaims. The gipsies meanwhile have work to do. They gather up their tools and wander off down the mountain singing snatches of their anvil chorus. Alone with Azucena Manrico now demands to be told the story of his grandmother. Azucena supplies it in all its horrifying details in the racconto 'Condotta ell'era in ceppi'. This is the largest and most complex of Verdi's narrative arias since Francesco's dream in I Masnadieri, with which it has much in common. Both pieces recount a terrifying experience, the mere memory of which leaves the narrator prostrate; and both start from a schematic basis. Azucena's, however, reaps the benefit of Verdi's so-called second manner, being articulated in shorter, more pliable phrases which permit a wealth of nuance, harmonic and rhythmic, to set the various events in due relief. What is more, the regularity established by the opening strophe soon gives way under the singer's emotional pressure. The accompaniment with its lamenting oboe and violin and its recurring shudder on the pulsating strings (an effect anticipated by the witch in Mercadante's Il Reggente) recalls the somnambulism of Lady Macbeth but in sharper, more concentrated form (Ex. 38).

Her story begins where Ferrando's left off. Azucena saw her mother being dragged to the stake; she followed her, carrying her own infant son. Several times she tried to approach the victim but was driven off by the brutal soldiery. The old woman's last words to her daughter as she was hoisted on to the pyre were, 'Avenge me!' Her terrible cry was for ever engraved on Azucena's heart.

Over and over again the music is drawn back to A minor as though by a magnet.

38

As Azucena recalls the taunts of di Luna's guards the shudders redouble in frequency, reinforced by timpani. Azucena's words tumble and falter; and what should have been an 8-bar transition to the reprise of Ex. 38 is shortened by a bar. With the end of the paragraph the accompaniment breaks into semiquaver motion. 'And did you avenge her?' Manrico asks. 'I stole the Count's son,' she resumes, 'and brought him to the spot where the flames were still burning' (we must take for granted here that, gipsy-fashion, she carried her own infant son with her on all occasions); Manrico's cry of horror brings the sequences to a halt. There is a pause, then a striking harmonic *non sequitur* as Azucena remembers how the sight of the Count's baby weeping desperately moved her to pity. Flute and piccolo depict the whimpering child, the turn into G major Azucena's sudden upsurge of maternal feeling. The progression is as illogical as the emotion that it reflects. Azucena is scarcely less full of contradictions than Kundry (Ex. 39).

A third phrase is cut short by a stabbing high B (the eternal pivot of Azucena's emotions) on the violins, which develops into a tremolando reprise of 'Stride la vampa' (Ex. 37) with elaborated harmonies, as the gipsy tells how at that moment a vision of her mother 'barefoot and dishevelled' rose before her, and again she seemed to hear the cry: 'Mi vendica!'

This orchestral reminiscence is the linch pin of the racconto. It drives home the point of the story by means of an image in sound whose associations have already been established. It accounts for the growing incoherence of the musical narrative and at the same time compensates through its own symmetrical structure. It is the usual periodic kernel to be found in all freely evolving movements in Verdi's operas. The rest of the piece consists mostly of scena-like gestures proceeding in strict time

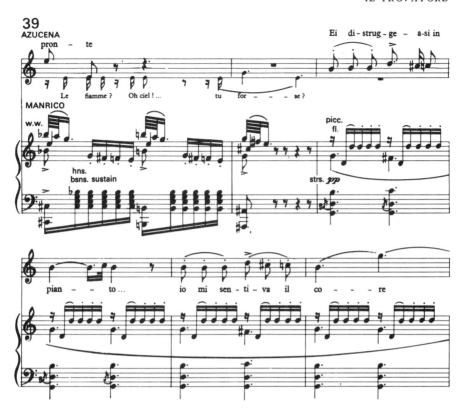

and with a certain measure of formal repetition, while the halter of A minor continually tightens its grip. In a daze Azucena had seized the child and thrust him into the flames. The vision faded; she saw the fire devour its victim; and there beside her was the Count's son. It was her own child that she had murdered. As the music mounts to its climax Manrico joins in with expressions of horror. There is an eight-bar cadence centred on a dominant minor ninth like a shriek of prolonged agony, then a subsidence of twenty-two bars that allows Azucena to descend into the hollow register of her voice ('Sul capo mio le chiome sento drizzar ancor'). In its last pages Azucena's racconto takes on a scale far exceeding that of the traditional Italian solo number, and one that was only possible to a composer who had already written the storm scene in *Rigoletto*. Experienced with this degree of force and dramatic truth the story of the wrong baby consigned to the flames no longer makes us smile.

Manrico is understandably bewildered. If Azucena had burned her own son then who is he? She interrupts him hurriedly (all this recitative is directed to be sung as fast as possible). Of course Manrico is her son. The dreadful memories of her mother's death had confused her. When he had been reported dead at the battle of Pelilla had she not hastened there to give him a Christian burial? When she had found him merely wounded had she not nursed him back to health with truly maternal devotion? The Count of Luna's troops had utterly destroyed the army of Count Urgel; only Manrico, fighting gamely to the last, was thought to have survived. And yet earlier he had had the Count of Luna at his mercy (i.e. after the duel at the end of Part I). He could have dispatched him there and then, but some instinct held him back (this last detail an invention of Verdi and Cammarano as we have seen). Azucena is unimpressed by such scruples and hopes they will not occur again. The incident is recounted in the first movement of the duet ('Mal reggendo') – a dissimilar piece in which Manrico's contribution is remarkable for the beauty of its final, cadential phrase, Azucena's for its suggestion of the grizzling and grumbling of a rather pathetic old woman.

A horn call is heard in the distance; it is the signal agreed upon between Manrico and his squire Ruiz. Manrico takes a horn from his belt and blows an answering blast; at which a messenger enters sent by Ruiz with a letter which (as this is a Cammarano libretto) Manrico reads aloud in recitative, not speech. Urgel's forces have rallied and captured the fort of Castellor. Leonora, believing Manrico to be dead, has gone to a near-by convent intending to take the veil. The news sparks off an anguished C minor parlante as Manrico calls for his horse to be saddled. Despite Azucena's protests he is determined to set out for Castellor immediately. From their conflict Verdi distils the dissimilar cabaletta ('Perigliarti ancor languente'), Azucena pleading in G minor (Ex. 40a), Manrico replying in G major (Ex. 40c). All Azucena's maternal tenderness is in this movement. Her line is reinforced at the third phrase by clarinet and bassoon, then as she becomes more urgent by oboe and violin, and her verse ends with a cadenza which takes her up to high C. In the climbing chromatic line for cello and low clarinet at the words '. . . (poss')io, il tuo sangue è sangue mio' (Ex. 40b) we may recognize a device that will depict the agony of Violetta in *La Traviata* with powerful effect. Manrico's melody ('Un momento può involarmi') carries off-beat accents which heighten the suggestion of agony at

parting, while the persistent pedal G proclaims his unshakable fixity of purpose.*

In his original synopsis Verdi had demanded for this whole duet a freedom and novelty of design. In fact its only novelty lies in the pace and the concision, the dynamic quality of the melody, articulated as in so many of the Azucena scenes from small self-propagating rhythmic motifs, and the deceptive simplicity of the accompaniments. There are no complex patterns of quavers and semi-quavers relentlessly beaten out in bar after bar as in the early operas, but simple dance-like pulsations that leave the vocal lines unencumbered. Some aspects of the duet seem primitive, as for instance the straight repetition of the period 40c; but it is the

* In 40c both voice and orchestra are marked with an accent on the first semiquaver only but there is a verbal instruction to the effect that both should be strongly accented.

deliberate simplicity of a sophisticated artist depicting primitive, elemental feeling. Close attention will disclose a number of unobtrusive touches that give a unique flavour to what may look like the most commonplace of tunes. Such for instance is the cello line beginning at bar 9 of Ex. 40c, which reproduces the voice line at bar 2 in augmentation and at the same time imparts a distinctive harmonic tang. Yet the moment has passed almost before we are aware of what has happened. As in *Ernani* Verdi still has the power to generate such tension by the juxtaposition of contrasted ideas (Ex. 40a and c) that there is no sense of dramatic falsity when the opposing voices join in the same melody.

> *Scene 2: The porch of a place of retreat in the neighbourhood of Castellor.*
> *Trees at the back of the stage: it is night.*

'Place of retreat' is of course a stage euphemism for convent, doubtless imposed by the Roman censor. Stealthy string pizzicati announce the Count of Luna, advancing cautiously with his followers and Ferrando, hoping that he may be just in time to prevent Leonora from taking the veil. Like her he believes Manrico to be dead and therefore all obstacles to his happiness removed. He apostrophizes her in the famous 'Il balen', a counterpart to 'Tacea la notte', which it matches in richness of poetic content. The accompaniment is low-lying and velvety in sound – clarinet arpeggii, cello and bass pizzicato, sustaining violas, shot through with the occasional dark glow of horns and bassoons.

41a

The design is a personal variant of the Bellinian $a^1a^2ba^2$, both simpler and more elaborate than the model. All three statements of *a* are harmonically identical except for the progressive 'gracing' of the melodic line – a rare feature of Verdi's baritone writing at the time; *b* consists of a long phrase modulating to the dominant, again repeated with decorations. The reprise is followed by a pendant (Ex. 41b) too long to be called a coda in which in effect the rhythm is compounded into 12/8 with a corresponding acceleration of the harmonic motion. As in Leonora's cavatina the melodic centre rises towards the end but with a steeper gradient. If in Ex. 41a it is fractionally too low for the comfort of the Verdian dramatic baritone, in Ex. 41b it

41b *con espansione*

CONTE

Ah! l'a - mo - re, l'a - mo - re ond'- ar - do le fa - vel - li in mio fa -

fl., cl., vln. I

strs.
hns.
bsns.

ob.
cellos
added

dim. dolce

- vo - re, sper -da il so - le d'un suo sguar - do la tem-pes - ta del mio cor.

rises to tenorial heights, while a cadenza carries the voice to bass A, for good measure. Nowhere is the singer given a moment's respite. No wonder most baritones view this aria with dread.

A bell rings out — a signal, says Ferrando, that the 'monacazione' of Leonora is about to begin. The Count orders him to conceal his men amongst the trees. Once more we are reminded that this is a drama of the expanded moment, though the music itself is pregnant with action. The men are frozen in the act of departure, the Count in a gesture of defiant glee. The cabaletta 'Per me ora fatal' harks back to that of Nabucco in Act IV in its tonal relationship of soloist and chorus in keys a fifth apart but the contrast is far greater. The 'spezzato' whispered chorus (Ex. 42a) — an unusual effect which Basevi traces to Rossini's *Edoardo e Cristina** — forms a background from which the Count's vigorous assertions (Ex. 42b) emerge with all the greater force. Again, while Nabucco's interventions have a slightly episodic character, the Count is unmistakably in the forefront and finally succeeds in drawing the chorus into his own key. His underlying brutality is reflected not only in the accents and the double-dots of the melody but in the brash scoring (woodwind, brass and at one point cellos doubling the melody, four horns reinforcing the bolero-style accompaniment) and even, one might say, in the insensitive verbal scansion. Verdi's first thoughts for the final cadence, still visible in the autograph, are indicated on a separate stave – a couple of angry flourishes which, though not ineffective, would be unduly tiring to the singer at the end of such a forceful period (Ex. 42b).

Rather unusually the finale begins with a tonal non sequitur. After the Count's emphatic cadence in D flat — doubtless followed by prolonged applause if successful and equally prolonged whistling if not — the offstage chorus of nuns, who sing of the vanity of all earthly things ('Ah se l'error l'ingombra') begins in E flat major; but as if to repair the gap the Count and his followers reply to each strophe with another 'spezzato' chorus ('No no non può') in the new key. Then Leonora arrives with Ines

* Basevi, p. 217.

and a group of attendant women, of whom she takes a sorrowful farewell. Her tears and her faltering steps are indicated by the simplest of orchestral means:*

Touchingly simple too in its sense of heartbreak, with harmonies that recall Nemorino's 'Adina credimi', is the brief ariosos ('Degg'io volgermi a quei') in which she expressed the hope that she may meet her beloved among the souls of the elect in Heaven. 'Never!' cries the Count stepping forward; a tense figure on cellos, basses

* See Chapter 2 about the possible associations of the string motif with the idea of death.

and bassoons against tremolo violins and violas carries the shocked reaction to his behaviour. Then a rocketing violin scale and a pealing tutti in E major (F flat) seem to hurl Manrico on to the stage as though from a catapult. The action freezes once more, much as at Edgardo's entrance in Act II of *Lucia* and in a thousand operas of the 1830s. The pezzo concertato follows, led by Leonora with a phrase beautifully expressive of her tremulous happiness (Ex. 44a). Then as the certainty of joy takes possession of her, her voice soars in one of those endless ascents which are so characteristic of her role (Ex. 44b):

44a

44b

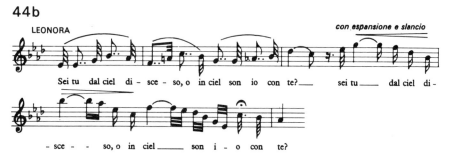

The pezzo concertato is constructed with all Verdi's new-found craftsmanship and can easily be spoiled by oversinging (very little of it is in fact marked above piano). Leonora's part is to be sung 'leggierissimo, brilliantissimo'. The men proceed with a measured gait of almost unbearable tension. 'Has the grave given up its dead?' the Count wonders. Manrico assures him that he is no ghost – he has survived the murderous attack of the Count's men. 'Flee if you wish to remain alive!' cries di Luna. 'God will confound the wicked!' Manrico retorts; and there for the moment the argument ends. There is a breath-catching pause, and then a concluding section based on Ex. 44a with all present joining in supported by an elaborate orchestral filigree. The chorus, syllabating their words with pauses in between in the old Bellini–Donizetti manner, make suitable comment: the nuns that Heaven has taken pity on Leonora, the Count's men with Ferrando that their master is pitting his strength against fate. Nor are they mistaken. For the last cadence brings in Ruiz crying, 'Long live Urgel!' He and a group of Manrico's followers surround the Count who, 'with gestures and accents of maniacal fury', cries out that the light of reason is extinguished in him. Leonora flies into Manrico's arms. In a stage performance very little of this is apparent. It is night, the scene is crowded, and the entrance of a few more soldiers makes little difference. It is left to Leonora to illuminate the situation with a resumption of Ex. 44b backed by the full orchestra. The effect of this after the short action-packed interlude in faster time is to crown the finale far more effectively than any stretta could have done. The emotional function of a stretta is cathartic. It opens the sluice gates of the emotional reservoir that has generated the lyricism of the previous adagio. In this case, as Verdi himself pointed out, the concertato is not an adagio at all; yet beneath its light tripping surface there is a wealth of pent-up feeling due to a certain quality, typical of so much of Il Trovatore, that Basevi happily describes as 'insistenza'.* For the first time (but not the last) Verdi discharges it in a single musical sentence in which the soprano voice is paraded in its full extension. Modern practice is to paint the lily by making Manrico join in the final phrase, to show that it is his victory as well as hers. Possibly this stems from the Paris version (see below) and it may even have had Verdi's sanction. Yet it seems a pity. Leonora, the most brilliant of all Verdi's heroines, is less of a person than a vocal archetype, an embodiment of 'das Ewig-Weibliche'; her most transcendent flights should be left free from the intrusion of another vocal timbre. The conclusion of this finale represents a homage to the soprano voice as devoted as any in the operas of Richard Strauss.

PART III

The Gipsy's Son

Scene 1: An encampment. On the right the Count of Luna's tent over which flutters the Spanish flag as a token of the supreme command. In the distance the towers of Castellor can be seen. Groups of armed men are scattered about the stage. Some are playing at dice, some are polishing their arms, some are walking about.

The scene is set for a typical soldiers' chorus ('Or co' dardi ma fra poco'). As in Act I the men are divided into two groups, the players and the polishers. The first will soon be playing at something more serious than dice; the second hope to renew the bloodstains they have just wiped off. The music is nothing out of the ordinary; but the C major tonality and shrill figuration in the orchestral prelude warn us that this is to be another Azucena scene. Half-way through the number the men turn to look at a detachment of crossbowmen traversing the back of the stage. 'The auxiliaries that were sent for,' remarks one group; 'they look brave enough,' adds the other; and both resume the opening phrase of the chorus extending it into a coda in which they double the bass of the orchestra with massive effect. All are straining at the leash, longing for the assault on Castellor to begin. Ferrando enters from the Count's tent and in a short recitative tells them that the attack will be mounted the following day; the spoils, he adds, should be rich indeed. To this happy news the men react with the famous 'Squilli, echeggi la tromba guerriera', possibly the best-known of all Verdi's unison choruses after 'Va pensiero', both the vigour and the charm of which lie principally in the refreshingly novel rhythm already discussed in Chapter 2 (Ex. 13). All that is most muscular in Il Trovatore is summed up here; nor does Verdi mitigate the sense of exhilaration with any refinement of scoring. After a brief episode of four bars, trumpets and trombone blare out the tune in unison with the voices while the

* Basevi, p. 219.

rest of the orchestra pounds away uninhibitedly in each beat. When the third limb of the melody is repeated ('No, giammai non sorrise la vittoria') violins, flute, oboe and clarinet supply a rudimentary descant (*pp*) in 'broken' dotted rhythm. To the final reprise of Ex. 13 is added a typical pattern of pizzicato semiquavers. Both are used effectively in the final fadeout, the dotted rhythm dying away on a solo trumpet.

The Count comes out of his tent and looks sombrely at the fort of Castellor: 'In my rival's arms' (this to a Verdian commonplace which has attracted undue attention in other contexts). As so often the libretto has jumped ahead of the play, though not implausibly. According to Gutiérrez Manrique had prevented Nuño from carrying off Eleonora *after* she had taken the veil. But some time elapsed before he could persuade her to elope with him. It was her brother Don Gullen who had induced her to enter a convent as the only alternative to marrying the Count if she were to save the family's good name. In the opera she is free to join her lover without moral scruples. If Cammarano's simplification of the issues makes her less interesting as a person, never mind; as the 'beautiful but ineffectual angel' of Verdi's score she does well enough.

Manrico, meanwhile, is commanding the forces of Count Urgel in Castellor — another reason why di Luna is so eager to attack the city. The fact that his final 'Ah Leonora' was originally designed to lead into an aria makes Ferrando's interruption all the more effective. The soldiers, he says, have taken prisoner a gipsy woman found wandering about the camp. A moment later Azucena is brought on in fetters.

The scene which now develops has all the excitement of a Greek 'anagnorisis'. Questioned by the Count, Azucena replies that her home is in the mountains of Biscay. Ferrando starts into attention. She has nothing in the world, she says, but her son who left her to go to the wars, and she is now desperately trying to find him. Her narrative ('Giorni poveri vivea'), in E minor and with characteristic offbeat accents, is all subdued pathos, but where she dwells on the depths of her maternal tenderness she moves into the major with one of those arching phrases which light up the melody in a glow of lyrical poetry:

93

The phrase is so similar to Leonora's 'E versi melanconici un trovator cantò' (see Ex. 29) that it is tempting to read into it a Freudian significance regarding Azucena's relationship with her 'son'.* More probably the likeness is due to the prevailing 'tinta' of the opera of which both phrases are an expression. In each case the singer is referring to the most precious object in her life. But observe how Leonora's phrase is underpinned by a firm dominant suggestive of joyous certainty; with Azucena the harmonic motion reflects her poignant sense of loss.

Di Luna, however, comes back to the subject of the Biscay mountains. Did she ever remember hearing of a Count's son stolen by gipsies some fifteen years ago? Azucena starts. 'Who then are you?' she asks. 'The brother of the stolen child!' Azucena's terror is so palpable that Ferrando is no longer in doubt. She must be the witch's daughter, the gipsy who murdered Garcia. The Count's interrogation, carefully casual, is conducted to an orchestral melody in the same tempo as Azucena's solo.

At the moment of Ferrando's recognition we may note the dramatic use of an empty bar. But the full force of his reaction is delayed. The orchestral theme continues its unhurried progress for seven more bars, to be suddenly cut short by Ferrando with a violent change of key and tempo. As the Count's men secure her still more tightly Azucena calls upon Manrico in a despairing descending phrase, another pre-echo of Violetta in *La Traviata*. But Violetta is a younger woman and her line has more energy even when she is in the throes of consumption. Azucena is old and ravaged; she moves by shorter intervals and her 12-bar phrase has a mortal weariness about it.

* See Petrobelli in *Atti del 3⁰ Congresso dell' I.S.V.*, p. 396.

47

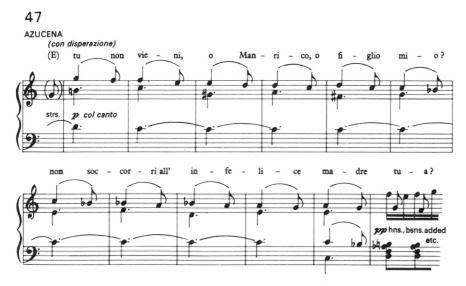

The Count is exultant. He has captured his rival's mother as well as his own brother's murderess. Sheer force of hate causes Azucena to rally. In the final stretta ('Deh, rallentate, o barbari, crudeli mie ritorte') she reviles the Count – 'cruel son of a still more wicked father' – but she is led away to suffer the same fate as her mother. It is a stretta which wastes no time. Of the two thematic ideas, only Azucena's is repeated. The one associated with the Count is a prime example of 'insistenza' applied to vocal melody.

48

The chorus sustain the forward momentum with a strong chromatic inner part. The rest is all chattering quavers with horns and middle strings pounding relentlessly on the offbeat. The entire so-called 'scena e terzetto' is the most dramatic number in the opera with Azucena parading every facet of her character. Nor is it illogical that in her final outburst of impotent rage she should lose something of her identity, and that having begun in her own key of E minor she should end in that of 'Squilli, echeggi la tromba guerriera', close to the Count's area of B flat.*

* A retired mezzo-soprano of international standing once told me that German and English audiences reacted quite differently to the different events in Azucena's tragedy. The English with their well known sympathy for the underdog responded more readily to her capture in Act III; the Germans reserved their enthusiasm for her outburst of 'Sehnsucht' in Act IV.

Scene 2: A room adjoining the chapel of Castellor. A balcony at the rear.

At last Manrico and Leonora are to be married, though in the teeth of danger. For Castellor is under siege and the attack is expected at any moment. Manrico has entrusted the defence of the fort to Ruiz while he turns his attention to pleasanter things. But we are never allowed to forget the persistent menace of the situation, summed up by Leonora in an expressive phrase ('Di qual tetra luce il nostro imen risplende') accompanied by sinister poundings in cellos and basses in which the connotations of death are unmistakable.

49

In the adagio of his aria ('Ah sì, ben mio') Manrico gives her the doubtful comfort that if the garrison is destroyed he will die with her name on his lips. In its rich, expansive lyricism this movement follows in the steps of 'Tacea la notte' and 'Il balen'. It is a large three-quatrain structure similar in rhythmic cut to Edgardo's 'Fra poco a me ricovero' (*Lucia*) and here again a new twist has been given to an old formula, that of the minor/major cantabile. Of its three sections the first two prepare the key of the last (D flat major) from different points in the tonal gamut – F minor on the sharp side, A flat minor on the flat, so that the third quatrain arrives with a special sense of finality, while the melody as a whole preserves that forward progression to be found in the cantabili of Leonora and the Count. Characteristic of the *Trovatore* 'tinta' is the rising arpeggio contour of the crowning period, each stop picked out by 3-note anacrusis (*x*). Notable too are the graceful eighteenth-century style cadence and, at the repeat, the clarinet syncopations illustrative of the 'dying gasp'.

50

To the sound of an organ behind the scenes* Leonora and Manrico prepare to enter the chapel. Their twenty-bar arioso ('L'onda de' suoni mistici') is their nearest approach to a full love duet: a discourse of overlapping phrases which merge into a chain of sixths and thirds. (Ernani and Elvira were likewise restricted to a few bars for the undisturbed exchange of mutual vows.) Here the organ with its religious overtones stresses the purity, the transcendental quality of their love, as befits the tradition of medieval chivalry to which they belong.

But scarcely have they finished protesting their 'casto amor' than Ruiz enters with the news that the Count of Luna's men have captured the old gipsy woman and are even now preparing the stake for her execution. Crying out to the astonishment of Ruiz and Leonora that the gipsy woman is his mother, Manrico orders a sortie to save her. As usual in opera the followers materialize with improbable promptitude; and Manrico makes ready to lead them forth with the celebrated cabaletta 'Di quella pira' (Ex. 51b), an expanded moment of heroic resolution. There are many such in romantic opera, beginning with the famous 'Suivez moi' from *Guillaume Tell*. Meyerbeer added a similar aria for Duprez as Raoul to Act IV of *Les Huguenots*. Verdi himself had done the same for Ivanoff in *Ernani*. Here the aria is more than ever an integral part of the musical and dramatic organism. The contrast with 'Ah sì, ben mio' has genuine dramatic significance. Manrico brings about the Aristotelian 'peripeteia' of the action by moving from the world of Leonora to that of Azucena; from D flat to C major; from the long lyrical flight to the style of melody articulated in repetitions of a short rhythmic pattern. The two movements are linked none the less by the pattern of three notes observed in Ex. 50(*x*).

A tantalizing sentence in Adriano Lualdi's *Viaggio musicale in Italia*† mentions the existence of a sketch for this cabaletta in 'tempo pari' i.e. 2/4 or 4/4. But the final working out in 3/4 shows the operation of what is surely unconscious memory. For

* The impresario, Jacovacci, had specified a large 'fisarmonica'. See letter from Jacovacci to Cammarano, undated (1851). Abbiati, II, pp. 192–3. In default of an organ a note in the autograph score suggests a wind band consisting of clarinet in E♭, clarinets in B♭ (2), flügelhorn in B♭, trumpets in C (2), horns in F(2), bombardino, bassoons, trombones, bombardone.

† Milan, 1927, p. 88.

Donizetti : MARIA STUARDA

the Milan première of *Maria Stuarda* in 1835 Donizetti altered the opening of Leicester's cabaletta 'Se fida tanto' (following the significant words 'Vo' liberarla') to run as in Ex. 51a. Verdi, who was studying in Milan that year, is unlikely to have missed a performance; and the echo is surely unmistakable, though it would not necessarily have struck Verdi's contemporaries, since the definitive version of Leicester's cabaletta begins quite differently. In any case the comparison is all to Verdi's advantage. His own melody has far more grit harmonically and rhythmically, which more than compensates for the lack of Donizetti's easy grace. Never has he used the device of semi-staccato semiquavers reiterated in pairs to more exhilarating effect. The high Cs at the end as well as at the words 'O teco almeno' are both later accretions. According to one account they were introduced by the original tenor Boucardé in Florence in 1855.* But a verbal tradition, related at a public lecture by the late Giovanni Martinelli, traces them to the tenor Tamberlick, creator of Don Alvaro in *La Forza del destino* – he who wished to astonish Rossini with his high C sharp 'de poitrine' and was told politely to hang it up in the hall and retrieve it on his way out. Verdi was more complaisant. Before asking his permission to include the note in question Tamberlick had already experimented with it in various provincial theatres where, he told the composer, it was in great demand with the public. 'Far be it from me,' Verdi had answered, 'to deny the public what it wants.

* Hughes, p. 155.

Put in the high C if you like, provided it is a good one.' From then on, good or bad, it has come to stay. Few tenors, however, are prepared to sing the cabaletta twice, as prescribed in the score; hence we seldom hear the minor key ritornello with Leonora's anguished outcries, but only the coda where Manrico's followers join in massively to bring down the curtain in a blaze of sound.

PART IV

The Execution

Scene 1: A wing in the palace of Aliaferia. At one corner a tower whose windows are secured by iron bars. It is darkest night.

High up in a room in the tower Manrico lies in prison. His attempts to save Azucena have miscarried; the Count of Luna's forces have taken Castellor and Urgel's rebellion has finally been crushed. Low clarinets and bassoons conjure up an atmosphere of sinister gloom. Leonora enters guided by Ruiz who points to the tower where the state prisoners are lodged. She tells him to leave her. He need have no fears for her safety, since her salvation lies *here* – and she caresses a signet ring on her right hand containing a phial of poison. Her cantabile ('D'amor sull' ali rosee') is one of those purely Italian melodies which begin in the minor key and end in the relative major without any sense of incompleteness. It is the complement to 'Tacea la notte' from Act II. Then Leonora's hopes had been high, and the melody had worked towards a soaring climax with the melody opening out like a flower. But now her lyrical wings are drooping and her melody dissolves into a series of dying falls. Both the harmonic and the orchestral palette are unusually delicate, with only one horn in the wind group and all doubling instruments except first violins removed from the summit of a phrase so that the voice can emerge in all its beauty (Ex. 52).

The funeral bell tolls near by and a chorus of monks are heard praying for the souls of those about to die. (As in *Lucrezia Borgia*, there is nothing to account for their presence, since there is no monastery near by.) The declamation which follows ('Quel suon, quelle preci') recalls the passage in Rossini's *Semiramide* where the ghost of the queen's murdered husband appears – the same tonality and the same abrupt orchestral figure with its associations of death. Rossini had confined it to strings only.

Here played by the full orchestra (*ppp*) with the funeral bell tolling in E flat in every second bar it suggests the menace of Ex. 49 suddenly made palpable (Ex. 53).

As Leonora's cantilena descends in broken 'lamenting' triplets Manrico's voice floats down from the tower with harp accompaniment in what used to be the best-known of all *Trovatore* melodies in the days of the barrel organ and the street piano (Ex. 54).

The scene offers another example of that device, Meyerbeerian in origin, whereby different scenic and musical ingredients are presented in succession and then combined. Verdi had experimented with it before: crudely in *Giovanna d'Arco*, more expertly in *Jérusalem* and *La Battaglia di Legnano* but not without a certain self-consciousness. In *Il Trovatore* the solution is perfect. The chanting monks, the sinister rapping of the orchestra, the plaint of Manrico unite with a sense of inevitability, to be crowned by Leonora's passionate cry (Ex. 55).

53

Andante assai sostenuto

LEONORA

Quel suon, quelle pre - ci so-len - ni, fu -

tutti without flutes : bass drum

etc.

- ne - - ste empi - ron que-st'a - e - re di cu - po ter - ror!

54

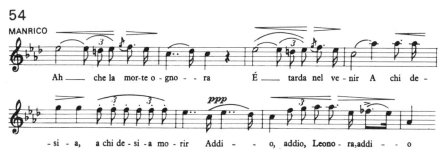

MANRICO

Ah — che la mor-te o-gno - - ra É — tarda nel ve - nir A chi de -

- si - a, a chi de-si-a mo-rir Addi - - o, addio, Leono - ra,addi - - o

55

LEONORA

(Di) te, di te scor-dar-mi! di te, di te scor-dar-mi!

MANRICO

(addi-o! Scon-to col san - gue mi - - o l'amor che po - si in

CHORUS

Mi - se - re-re! mi - se - re-re!

ppp tutti harp tutti harp

After Leonora has repeated her promise of eternal remembrance, rising to a high A flat the music modulates rather artificially from A flat major to F, the key of her final cabaletta ('Tu vedrai che amor in terra'). She has regained her courage, and with it that 'aspiring' quality of mind that distinguished her first two acts. It is a noble piece of music, brilliant and moving with the minor-key ritornello conveying the right suggestion of underlying tragedy. Yet its range is cruelly taxing and its position between two scenes dominated mainly by the soprano causes many Leonoras to omit it. Indeed, if there is one piece in *Il Trovatore* that is expendable this is perhaps it. Though considered in isolation it is one of Verdi's best cabalettas, its effect is that of a concert aria. Nor (though this is a minor consideration) do the words say anything that Leonora has not told us before.*

The Count enters with some of his followers. 'For Manrico the block, for Azucena the stake,' such are his orders. As the men leave he reflects that he is certainly abusing the powers granted to him by the prince whom he serves. 'To this pass you have brought me, fatal woman!' Yet since the fall of Castellor he has had no news of her. Then suddenly she appears before him. She has come to beg for mercy for the Troubadour. But the Count remains adamant; the only God he knows is the God of vengeance. (No such vehemence distinguishes his counterpart in the play. Don Nuño is by now listless and apathetic, and it requires all Eleonora's charm to reawaken his interest in her.) The duet opens in straightforward traditional style with dialogue against a rapid orchestral melody. Soon the voices take charge and the orchestra falls into the background with simple throbbings and doublings, as Leonora throws herself on her knees and begs the Count to kill her, torture her, trample over her dead body but save Manrico. The more she pleads the more strongly he resists. The argument continues in the andante ('Mira, di acerbe lagrime'), a dissimilar movement, naturally, but one in which the tension is increased by the fact that both voices keep strictly to A flat. It is another remarkable instance of Basevian 'insistenza'. There is no pathos in Leonora's appeal, only a desperate will to succeed. Witness the taut intensity of the phrase to which she returns, like a refrain ('Calpesta il mio cadavere, ma salva il Trovator').† Here too there exists an instructive parallel in the tenor cantabile 'Alma soave e cara' in *Maria di Rohan* (Ex. 56a), a comparison which enables us to observe some of the means whereby Verdi keeps up the music's immense driving force: the sustaining bassoons that weld together the first two phrases (Ex. 56b), the pizzicato cellos that underlie the Count's intervention (Ex. 56c).

Finally Leonora plays her trump card. She offers herself to the Count in return for Manrico's life. Incredulously the Count accepts. While he summons his men to give them the appropriate orders Leonora surreptitiously swallows the poison from the

---

* A note in the autograph requires the basses to lower their A string during the Miserere scene. The reason is that at the time of *Il Trovatore* most double basses in Italy had three strings only and played the line written for them at whatever octave they found most comfortable. In this case A″ flat is essential to the harmony and could only be reached in the manner prescribed. Nowadays the problem no longer exists. Conductors who hope by lowering the pitch of the string concerned to produce a hollower sound than normal will be disappointed. Any such effect will be lost in the general sonority.

† A sketch for this movement published by Gatti in *Verdi nelle immagini*, p. 186 and containing the voice-parts only reveals little about the composing process since the music is the same as in the finished version except for the omission of the four bars that prepare for the final unison climb.

signet ring, adding in a hollow voice, 'You will have in me a cold and lifeless prey.'
On being told that Manrico will live she breaks into the final movement ('Vivrà!
Contende il giubilo'). As Leonora lives purely in the present, there is nothing
incongruous in her expressing joy in the same language as that of 'Di tale amor'. She
has saved her lover's life, and that is all that counts. The Count responds with a
simpler variant more suited to his more limited compass and flexibility. As at the end
of Part III, Scene 1, the form though basically conventional (here a duet cabaletta

56a

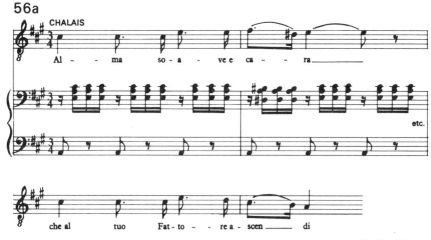

Donizetti : MARIA DI ROHAN

56b

56c

with both voices singing through the ritornello) is highly compressed. The drama which had relaxed its pace in the Miserere scene to create a tableau has now regathered all its former momentum.

> *Scene 2: A gloomy prison. A barred window at one side. A door at the back. A torch half extinguished hangs on a bracket. Azucena lying on a kind of rough mattress.*

Up to this point *Il Trovatore* has been organized chiefly as a succession of formal numbers. The final scene however gathers up the threads in a continuity approaching that of *Rigoletto*.* A succession of sustained pianissimo chords for full orchestra conveys a sense of solemnity and resignation. Already Azucena feels the hand of death upon her. When they come to take her to the pyre they will find only a lifeless corpse. All at once she is seized with hallucinations. The scene of fifteen years ago rises before her: the fierce crowd, the flames, her mother's screams. She gives a despairing cry and falls convulsed into Manrico's arms. It is a magnificent scena to which the recurrence of Ex. 37 high up on the strings gives dramatic depth and perspective. The final outburst exploits almost the full range of the mezzo-soprano voice from a″ to b′. One realizes now why Verdi was so insistent that Azucena should not be mad in the final scene. In the trappings of conventional operatic insanity she would lose all dramatic identity. The truth is that she is slightly crazed throughout the opera.

After this Azucena is ready to sleep. Manrico prepares the way with a soothing recitative as he leads her back to the couch. To the first verse of their duet ('Sì, la stanchezza m'opprime') sung by Azucena in a subdued G minor Manrico replies with one in G major ('Riposa o madre') which with its tremolando 'leggierissimo' accompaniment for strings suggests a lullaby. Then just when we might expect a modified repeat of previous material Verdi springs the surprise of an entirely new melody, the famous 'Ai nostri monti'. The style with its short phrases in triple time is unmistakably Azucena's, but in the arpeggio-born theme to which the mezzo-

* See Vol. 1, Chapter 2.

soprano voice in its middle register gives a horn-like quality Verdi seems to join hands with Brahms at his most romantically 'volkstümlich'. No wonder German audiences often become lachrymose at this point.

57 **Andantino**
AZUCENA

Ai nostri mon - ti... ri-tor-ne - re - mo... l'anti - ca pa - ce... i - vi go - dre- mo!...

Manrico repeats his verse, its expression heightened by its new context. Then the two voices unite in a coda as to a low sustained D on the flute and a hypnotic pattern of muted violins divisi Azucena sinks into slumber. In all this Verdi has idealized the gipsy of Gutiérrez's drama to some extent. The original Azucena is entirely consumed at this point by blind unreasoning terror. With Carmen-like fatalism she accepts her destiny to be burned alive, though she knows that it is the most painful death imaginable. When at last Manrique persuades her to rest she cries out like a whimpering child, 'But don't let them take me away while I am asleep!' This line Cammarano managed to include in the G minor verse of the duet; but Verdi was artistically on sure ground when he failed to reflect its sense in the music. As he had foreseen, Azucena gains from being allowed to retain a measure of dignity until the end.

The door now opens and Leonora enters. The long-breathed phrases with which Manrico greets her have all the verve and sweep of Verdi's most rapturous moments but both voice and orchestra are marked pianissimo since presumably Manrico does not wish to wake Azucena. Soon a note of suspicion creeps into his voice as Leonora, while urging him to flee, seems to have no intention of following him. The music moves into an agitated G minor; and at last Manrico questions her outright: what is the price she has paid for his freedom? When she refuses to meet his gaze he guesses the worst. So begins the first concertato of the finale ('Parlar non vuoi') with declamatory phrases in dialogue with the orchestra, beginning in G major then moving to D as he bursts into a torrent of lyrical fury. The main idea is a variant of one which he had already used in I Lombardi (see Vol. 1, Ex. 49) now enhanced by a more sophisticated technique. Note how the sustained B flat in first violins, horns, bassoons and clarinets flowers into counter-melody when the phrase is repeated. This kind of variation was unknown to Verdi at the time of the earlier opera (Ex. 58).

Leonora replies in agitated D minor patterns of agitated sextuplets. So far it is all strong romantic stuff charged with surface emotion. Then unexpectedly a new vista opens up. The wrangling subsides into a *piano* and Azucena's voice steals through the ensemble singing 'Ai nostri monti' (Ex. 57). A rare touch of enchantment is reserved for the end of the movement – a characteristic harmonic epigram (Ex. 59).

The orchestra introduces a transitional melody in the vein of Ex. 32. As it develops Manrico realizes that Leonora is dying. In the final concertato ('Prima che d'altro vivere') she explains why she had taken poison. It is rare for Verdi to have two slow concertati in a finale; the second one therefore is of a very different type from the first. There is no rolling compound rhythm, merely a succession of simple phrases in

plain 4/4. During this the Count enters and adds his voice to the ensemble bitterly realizing how completely he has been tricked. Leonora's death throes are expressed in a line of semiquaver gasps and displaced accents already anticipated in the finale to Act II of *Alzira*; beneath it Manrico pours out his remorse in a more sustained melody in which syncopation is also prominent. The Count supplies a neutral bass to balance the internal rhythmic structure. Leonora dies; and then everything happens with improbable swiftness. The Count orders Manrico to be led to execution. As he is taken away he bids a last farewell to Azucena. The gipsy wakes up crying, 'Where is my son?' 'He is hastening to his doom,' says the Count. 'Hear me! Hold!' but the Count drags her to the window to see Manrico beheaded. As the axe falls she cries out, 'He was your brother. Mother, you are avenged!' 'And I live on?' exclaims the Count, having barely had time to take in what he has been told. The curtain falls to repeated chords of E flat minor.

Théâtre de l'Opéra, Paris, January 1857

Such was the opera's success that it was not long before the Théâtre des Italiens and the Opéra, Paris, decided to feature it successively as they had done *Luisa Miller*. Verdi, still smarting from the treatment meted out to the earlier work, was determined to prevent *Il Trovatore* from suffering a similar fate. He therefore refused to allow the hire of the score until he could be assured of a suitable cast. For the season of 1855 the Théâtre des Italiens had secured the services of the tenor Ludovico Graziani and an excellent contralto, Adelaide Borghi-Mamo. Fortunately too Verdi himself was in Paris at the time for the production. Calzado, impresario of the Italian Theatre, succeeded after some acrimonious correspondence in enlisting not only Verdi's sanction but also his practical help. But for this the composer received not a sou. Somewhat unreasonably he blamed Ricordi for having sold the printing rights instead of the scores, from the hire of which Verdi would have been entitled to royalties.[*] Peace was soon restored between them; but the following year Verdi decided to institute proceedings against the management of the Italian Theatre for having performed *Rigoletto* and *La Traviata* from pirated material. The case was heard in November 1856 and the judgment went against Verdi. By way of compensation Crosnier, General Administrator of the Opéra, commissioned him to adapt *Il Trovatore* for the Opéra, adding a ballet to the third act. For this he would be paid as for a new work. He agreed to supervise the production which would take place in January 1857, even though the scheduled première of *Simon Boccanegra* at Venice was uncomfortably close at hand. The translation he commissioned personally from Emilien Pacini, whom he persuaded to cede the rights in return for a lump sum.

Here we come to a slight mystery. The Paris score diverges notably in one or two places from the Italian version. Yet neither for the alterations nor even for the ballet music is there any autograph. In a letter to Tito Ricordi sent shortly after his return to Italy Verdi writes, 'A copy will be sent to you of the ballet music I composed for *Trovatore*. . . . If ever some impresario should conceive a fancy for producing it as it was done at the Opéra you can make use of it and pay me. Otherwise keep it under lock and key until I ask for it.'[†] Likewise that the remaining additions and changes are authentic is made clear by a review of the première which appeared in Escudier's periodical *La France musicale*.[‡] Many of the modifications are of the kind that

---

[*] See letters exchanged between Verdi and Tito Ricordi, Oct.–Nov. 1855. *Copialettere*, pp. 166–85. 166–85.　　　　　　　　[†] Letter to T. Ricordi, 30.1.1857. Abbiati, III, p. 377.

[‡] See D. Rosen, 'Le Trouvère', in *Opera News*, 9.4.1977. References to changes made by E. Pacini in letters to Giulio Ricordi (27.1 and 28.2.1891, *Copialettere*, pp. 706–9) are too vague to establish him as author of the variants.

Verdi very often brought to his later revisions, and one or two have even been reflected in modern performances of the Italian version. The first of them occurs in Leonora's cabaletta in Act I, where the cadential phrase is delayed by a pause then expanded from 2 bars to 4 with a skittish little caper of 'picchettate' and syncopations. Possibly the ascending and descending scale seemed too naif for a Parisian audience. The gain here is in technical brilliance rather than musical worth.

Most of the divergencies, however, regard Azucena. In her duet with Manrico in Act II the rising dotted crotchets under the words (poss'io) 'il tuo sangue è sangue mio' – or 'De terreur mon sang se glace' as they have now become – are dissolved into 'sighs' rising chromatically from second to third beat ($.\,\int,\int$). The bass rhythm at the end of her solo ('Ah ... ah ... cède, cède') is broken up, the following tutti changed into a plain sequence of repeated chords with an upward scale on the violins, and her cadenza considerably extended – this last obviously for the benefit of Adelaide Borghi-Mamo, the chief star of the Théâtre des Italiens whom the Opéra had been fortunate enough to engage. Next, in Manrico's entry (Ex. 40c) the woodwind tune that doubles the voice is filled out in thirds at the end of the first two phrases and at the same time embellished with a rising chromatic inner part for cello – a touch of harmonic interest that somehow diminishes the music's fleetness.

There is a cut of eighteen bars in the coda, the end of which is re-written so as to allow the two voices a two-bar cadenza-like flourish in unaccompanied unison before signing off to tumultuous applause. If the cadence is unduly conclusive, as if both parties were satisfied at separating, the cut is standard practice today and not particularly regrettable. The Count's accompaniment in the Part II concertato is now elaborated, and the final Ex. 44b sung by Manrico and Leonora. Changes in Part III are designed partly to prepare for the ballet, partly to suit the more sophisticated Parisian taste. Ferrando's recitative is altered so as to lead from C major into the key of E. This enables him more easily to take a separate melodic part here and there in the famous chorus of Ex. 13 (in the Italian version he had been merged with the chorus basses). A rapping dotted rhythm, varied with the occasional semiquaver triplet, and a vigorous bass line replace the simple tonic and dominant poundings of the original accompaniment, which thus takes on a more obviously martial swing. Gone is the primitive orchestral descant that embellished the reprise; gone too the long diminuendo play-out since the soldiers and Ferrando are to remain on stage for some time yet, to be entertained by a troupe of gipsies.

The ballet which follows is in fact Verdi's third (he had written one in Les Vêpres Siciliennes two years before as well as that for Jérusalem discussed in Vol. 1). In character it is nearer the earlier work though a considerable improvement on it. There are more than a dozen movements all grouped into four set numbers.* The first of these, Pas des Bohémiennes, is of interest in that the first and last of its three movements make use of material from the opening of Act II. In the initial allegro we find Ex. 35b developed in rising sequences towards a long cadential phrase (Ex. 60).

In the final movement we meet Ex. 36, the so-called Anvil Chorus, followed by a more extended version of Ex. 60, cleverly suggesting a compressed reprise of the original Ex. 35b. Here to the traditional gipsy instruments, the cymbals and

---

* The programme of the ballet is set forth in detail in the MS. full score in the Bibliothèque Nationale, Paris (D. 14.199). A less complete score exists in the Bibliothèque de l'Opéra (A. 593a).

60

triangle, are added castanets and tambours de basque. Castanets also figure in the second movement, a rousing Bolero entitled *Gitanella* and danced by eight men.

The next number, *Sevillana*, is a pas de deux danced by a soldier and a vivandière. As the vivandière enters to a whirling violin melody like a rustic perpetuum mobile, the soldiers do not actually whistle but bang their goblets on the table in time to the music. There are various touches of local colour. Most of the opening movement is all'ungherese in the manner of Haydn and Schubert. There is a Tyrolean flavour about the vivandière's solo (*Echo de la vivandière*) but the soldier's solo (*Echo du soldat*), very heavily and brassily scored with double dots and cornet flourishes, shows that he is every inch a Frenchman:

61

The third group, *La Bohémienne*, is the most interesting of all. It is also the only part of the Divertissement to have a programme. The first dance, subtitled 'la bonne aventure', is framed by a short section in what might be called narrative 6/8, during which a fortune-teller enters. Throughout the scene which follows she dances to a little 2/4 refrain, twice in A minor, the third time in A major. In between she deals a pack of cards and tells the fortunes of the soldiers who have meantime gathered round her (an ingenious way, this, of weaving the ballet into the opera plot and so breaking down the barrier between chorus and corps de ballet). To one she predicts that he will be unhappy in love and advises him to challenge his best friend to a duel. ('Astonishment of soldier', read the stage directions.) To another she foretells that he will return home covered in glory. ('Contentment of soldier'.) Finally she sets out the cards and performs a secret ritual; she looks at them again, nods as if to find her apprehensions confirmed, then goes out to the same narrative theme that introduced her. The entire scene seems to have caught Verdi's imagination and may well explain why eight years later he asked for so much of the *Macbeth* ballet music to be mimed. The threads of fate are reflected in a woodwind tapestry of increasing complexity, reaching its highest point of elaboration at the moment where the gipsy makes her final examination.

After an 'Echo de la Bohémienne' the stage fills with eight little Moorish boys and fifes and triangles, who give us a foretaste of *Aida* Act II (Ex. 63).

The coryphées enter and mingle with them to a more graceful melody introduced by cello (Ex. 64).

From these two themes Verdi spins a piquantly tuneful movement. The final number is a pleasant but undistinguished galop with a hint of Offenbach in its phrase-endings. It is followed by a transitional decrescendo (*sortie de la danse*) of no musical interest whatever to allow soldiers and dancers to leave the stage.

The next change is decidedly for the worse, musically and dramatically. In the Italian version the interrogation of Azucena is conducted as a 'parlante' to Ex. 46. Possibly la Borghi-Mamo found this inadequate to her status as chief star. Anyway, following the empty bar Ex. 46 is resumed as a 24-bar cantabile for mezzo-soprano ('Prenez pitié de ma douleur') ending with an emphatic full close. Only after that does Ferrando cut in with a cry of triumph. The action is thus slowed up just where it needs to move forward, while a commonplace narrative tune is made to carry more weight than it can bear. No less surprising is the re-scoring of the stretta ('Ah, barbares, laissez-vous toucher') with a busy bass line of quavers, the viola semi-quavers removed, horns intermittently sustaining instead of playing off the beat and all trace of invigorating 'syncope' abolished. Evidently Verdi regarded the original scoring as being too primitive for so august an institution as the Opéra.

In Part IV the cabaletta 'Tu vedrai che amor in terra' is suppressed altogether. But the most disconcerting change of all is reserved for the end of the opera, which is lengthened by a coda of thirty bars. As Manrico is led away an offstage chorus of monks recall the Miserere chant, during which Azucena calls out brokenly, 'My son, where is he?' As if in answer Manrico is heard in the distance calling down a blessing on his mother to Leonora's intervention in Ex. 55, while Azucena reacts with a descending phrase in the manner of Amneris in *Aida* after the priests have pronounced their sentence. Again the monks sing their chant and Manrico apostrophizes the dead Leonora with his original contribution to the Miserere scene (Ex. 54). There is an orchestral crescendo; then to the roll of a side drum in the wings the Count drags Azucena to the window to see her son executed. Once again he accepts without question the truth of her final words.

All this amounts to no more than musical cobbling. Except for Azucena's descending phrase everything else is a reminiscence — a fact which might suggest a hand other than Verdi's, as if the author were afraid of obtruding his own personality into an established masterpiece. The reason for adding the coda would appear to be twofold: to allow plausible time for Manrico to be beheaded, as in Cammarano's original libretto, and to give more prominence to the Azucena of Mme Borghi-Mamo. Fortunately it never found its way into later reprints of the Italian version. Most of us will prefer the ending we know, however precipitate.

In a letter of 1862 Verdi wrote, 'In the heart of Africa or the Indies you will always hear *Trovatore*.'* At the time this was no exaggeration. Critics and musical writers have had their reservations, beginning with Basevi who described the work as written in Verdi's second manner but with a touch of exaggeration carried over from his first.† Edward Dannreuther, source of many traditional judgements on Italian opera that have become current coin in English academic circles, roundly condemns it as a backsliding into vulgarity after the prodigious advance shown in *Rigoletto*. Another Wagnerian, George Bernard Shaw, writing at about the same time, is more sympathetic but in the last resort equivocal. '*Il Trovatore* is in fact unique,' he wrote, 'even among the works of its own composer and its own country. It has tragic power, poignant melancholy, impetuous vigour and a sweet and intense pathos that never loses its dignity. It is swift in action and perfectly homogeneous in atmosphere and feeling. It is absolutely void of intellectual interest; the appeal is to the senses all through. If it allowed you to think for a moment it would crumble into absurdity like the garden of Klingsor.'‡ This distinction between the 'intellectual' and the 'musical' is one of the great fallacies of Shavian criticism and the cause of many of his more absurd judgements, especially as regards Schubert and Brahms. But his view of the opera is not an uncommon one. Modern writers tend either to confess their admiration with a note of humorous apology,§ or else to exalt the opera in the feverish D'Annunzian manner of Bruno Barilli.¶ Today, while forming part of the charmed circle of operas which no repertory company can afford to do without, it has lost some of its former ground. The nineteenth century was an age of moral confidence and certainty which found its ideals mirrored in an opera in which no one hesitates for one moment as to what action he or she should take. The present age finds it easier to identify with the torments and uncertainties of Violetta or Don Carlos. Moreover *Il Trovatore* continues to be dogged by Caruso's famous obiter dictum to the effect that all it requires is the four greatest singers in the world. True the vertical range of three of the principal parts is unusually wide, a consequence mainly of the extended arpeggio contour that stamps so many of the melodies and is one of the determining elements in the tinta of the opera as a whole. Rarely, however, does this apply to the part of Azucena, the obverse of the coin; and indeed a singer who cannot capture and hold her audience with this most rewarding of mezzo-soprano roles has no business on the operatic stage. For all that *Il Trovatore* is unlikely to depreciate with the years. If it is not the composer's supreme masterpiece it is none the less without parallel in the whole operatic literature − a late flowering of the Italian romantic tradition possible only to one who had seen beyond it. It is a valuable reminder that the laws of musical theatre in its widest sense do not have to conform to those of literary 'drama' in order to produce a coherent masterpiece.

---

* Letter to Arrivabene, 2.5.1862. Alberti, pp. 15–17.

† Basevi, p. 224.

‡ *Shaw's Music*, III, pp. 688–9.

§ How many people will claim that they have heard a performance in English in the course of which Manrico declared, sword in hand, 'Mother is roasting!'? I do not believe that such a translation exists.

¶ Cf. B. Barilli, *Il Paese del melodramma ed altri scritti* (Florence, 1963), pp. 303 ff.

4 LA TRAVIATA

LA TRAVIATA

Opera in four parts
by
FRANCESCO MARIA PIAVE
(after the play *La Dame aux camélias* by Alexandre Dumas *fils*)

*First performed at the
Teatro la Fenice, Venice,
6 March 1853*

VIOLETTA VALERY, a demi-mondaine	PRIMA DONNA SOPRANO	Fanny Salvini-Donatelli
FLORA BERVOIX, her friend and fellow hostess	MEZZO-SOPRANO COMPRIMARIO	Speranza Giuseppini
ANNINA, Violetta's maid	SECONDA DONNA	Carlotta Berini
ALFREDO GERMONT	PRIMO TENORE	Ludovico Graziani
GIORGIO GERMONT, his father	PRIMO BARITONO	Felice Varesi
GASTONE, Vicomte de Letorières, friend of Alfredo	TENORE COMPRIMARIO	Angelo Zuliani
BARON DOUPHOL, Violetta's protector	BARITONO COMPRIMARIO	Francesco Dragone
IL MARCHESE D'OBIGNY, friend of Flora	SECONDO BASSO	Arnaldo Silvestri
DOTTORE GRENVIL	BASSO PROFONDO	Andrea Bellini
GIUSEPPE, Violetta's servant	SECONDO TENORE	G. Borsato
Servant to Flora	CORIFEO BASSO	G. Tona
Commissioner	CORIFEO BASSO	Antonio Mazzini

Ladies and gentlemen, friends of Violetta and Flora – Matadors, picadors
and gipsies – servants of Violetta and Flora – masks, etc.

The action takes place in and around Paris

Epoch: *c.* 1700 [*sic!*]

(N.B. The first act takes place in August, the second in January, the third
in February.)

It will be remembered how, in a letter to Cammarano of 1851, Verdi had spoken of 'another subject which is simple and tender' to which they could change if *Il Trovatore* did not appeal to him. This is taken by Carlo Gatti to refer to *La Dame aux camélias*.* Verdi had by that time no doubt read Dumas's novel even if he had not seen the play. But the hypothesis is unlikely. For the 1850s the story of Marguerite Gauthier was not so much 'simple and tender' as bold and rather shocking, and we may be certain that it would have scared Cammarano out of his wits. But for his next commitment, planned for the carnival season of 1853 at the Teatro la Fenice, it would seem that Verdi had a prima donna opera in mind, since before signing the contract he showed particular interest in the leading soprano proposed for the season. He must be assured of a 'donna di prima forza', he wrote to Marzari. Cruvelli would be excellent but was under contract to London and Paris for the next three years; Medori had been applauded at St Petersburg; Barbieri might be free . . . 'but,' he concluded in April, 'please engage as soon as possible someone who will make up the triad with the tenor and baritone.'† As Verdi had been in Paris in February when Dumas's play first saw the stage it is possible that he was already setting up an ideal operatic cast for it in his mind. But the names suggested as well as the term 'donna di prima forza', i.e. the powerful, bravura soprano such as he emphatically did not want for Violetta, make one doubtful – though of course it is possible that he originally intended to realize the part quite differently. Eventually the terms of the contract were fixed by a special visit to Busseto from the theatre secretary, Guglielmo Brenna, in April. Piave was to be the librettist; the opera was to be staged in March the following year. Brenna's report to the President shows that Verdi was not entirely happy about the choice of prima donna assoluta; also that his ideas about contralti in male attire had not changed since the days of *Ernani*. 'Verdi would have preferred that the prima donna should be Alaymo rather than Salvini-Donatelli. None the less he won't refuse to write for the latter. Under no circumstances will he hear of writing for Alboni. He says that he writes his operas so that they will circulate and a score written for Alboni wouldn't be hired out more than two or three times a year. Still less will he agree to write a trouser role for contralto. He hates transformations of this type.'‡ Few rules in Verdi's book are without exceptions. The next year he was writing to Antonio Somma about casting the fool in *King Lear* as a contralto. Brenna continues:

The opera which he seems disposed to undertake to write will probably require two women. In any case if *Il Corsaro* is chosen as one of the operas in the season we shall need two women, that is a principal and a comprimaria. For the latter Verdi would like us to engage a certain Giani Vives who made her debut during the last

* Gatti, I, pp. 363–4.
† Letter to Marzari, 14.4.1852. Conati, *La bottega della musica*, p. 276.
‡ Letter from Brenna to Marzari, 26.4.1852. *Ibid.*, pp. 285–6.

Carnival season at the Carcano Theatre, Milan, actually as the comprimaria in *Il Corsaro*, and aroused fanatical enthusiasm. Verdi himself has never heard this artist, but since she has been described to him as being very good and having strong vocal resources he would reserve the right to use her as assoluta if need be.

Was this a cunning scheme for making sure of a suitable Margherita? The part of Medora is tender and ultra-feminine. Giani Vives was young and relatively untried. The Violetta who first launched *La Traviata* on the road to success seems to have been a soprano of a similar type.

Anyway Vives was not engaged; and Verdi put off the choice of subject as long as he could. On 26 July he wrote again to Marzari asking for a further postponement until the end of September, since 'apart from the fact that I don't want any of those ordinary subjects which crop up by the hundred, there's the difficulty of the censorship and besides that the mediocrity of the company. If there was at Venice a 'donna di prima forza' [*again that forbidding term*] I would have a subject all ready and one sure of making an effect.'* Some weeks later he wrote to the baritone Varesi thanking him for sending him a copy of the play *La Tour de Nesle* by Dumas père but adding that, 'after having seen the piece performed several times in Paris I'm all the more convinced that you could make magnificent pieces of music out of it but never an opera'.† The search for a libretto continued throughout August and September. He turned down Piave's suggestion of *L'Ebrea di Costantina* and when the poet tried to throw in his hand Verdi rallied him sharply. 'You mustn't refuse to write this book. You must do it, though the heavens fall. . . . Certainly you've set to work on the job a little late but no matter; it must be done, do you understand? . . . If you can't find a subject anywhere else try and find it in your own head. . . . *It must be done.*'‡ But it was not; and by the beginning of October the management were getting worried, since they were being pressed by the police. They decided to allow Piave to visit Verdi in his new home at S. Agata. It was during this visit that the breakthrough occurred. Piave wrote back to Brenna: 'It was the same story as *Ernani* all over again. I had got the libretto almost finished' – which one we may never know – 'when suddenly Verdi got carried away by another idea and I had to throw away what I'd done and start all over again. I think that Verdi will write a fine opera now that I've seen him so worked up.'§ No word as to what caused this last-minute decision.

Anyway the synopsis was dispatched to the Venetian censorship, who, accustomed by now to conceding the spirit if not the letter of Verdi's requirements, merely insisted on changing the proposed title of *Amore e morte*. On New Year's Day 1853 he wrote to De Sanctis: 'For Venice I'm doing *La Dame aux camélias* which will probably be called "*La Traviata*". A subject for our own age! Another composer wouldn't have done it because of the costumes, the period and a thousand other silly scruples. But I'm writing it with the greatest of pleasure. Everyone cried out at the idea of putting a hunchback on the stage; well, there you are. I was very happy to write *Rigoletto*. (I'm sorry to hear they're doing it at Naples; they'll do it very badly and

---

* Letter to Marzari, 26.7.1852. *Ibid.*, p. 297.
† Letter to Varesi, 18.9.1852. *Ibid.*, p. 299.
‡ Letter to Piave, 17.8.1852. *Ibid.*, p. 298.
§ Letter from Piave to Brenna, 20.10.1852. *Ibid.*, p. 301.

without any understanding – and it's my best opera.)'* Verdi might have remembered that ten years ago he himself had baulked at setting Hugo's *Marion de Lorme* because he disliked the idea of prostitutes on the stage. Times had certainly changed.

La Dame aux camélias was a bold choice but a very sound one. Wagner, it may be remembered, held that myths made the best subjects for music drama. The plot of Dumas's novel is essentially a myth, none the less universal for being modern and for having received its definitive form at the hands of a mediocrity, nor is it any less mythical for having had its roots in personal experience. The story of the courtesan, beautiful and doomed to an early death, who falls in love with a young man of limited means, gives up her life of luxury to live with him, and then sacrifices their mutual love for his sake, is one of those simple classical tales which permit as many variations as the legends on which the Greek tragedians built their plays. The difference is that, whereas the myths of Ancient Greece have come down to us ready made, we can trace the growth of this one. It can be seen dimly emerging in a far greater work of art than that of Dumas fils – Abbé Prévost's novel *Manon Lescaut*. This is important to establish since in his own work Dumas is continually using Prévost's as a point of reference. Here too the subject is a beautiful, amoral young girl genuinely in love with a man who is unable to give her the luxury she cannot do without. The problem is insoluble within the framework of society and it ends in prison, deportation and death. The author of *La Dame aux camélias*, like that of *Manon Lescaut*, places himself outside the action, which is narrated at a remove by someone he claims to have met. The occasion of their meeting was the auction of the heroine's effects at which the author bought a copy of *Manon Lescaut*. In it was inscribed 'Marguerite to Manon – humility'. At a key moment in the play the hero picks up a book which Marguerite has left lying open – *Manon Lescaut* again. His eyes fall on the passage:

I swear to you, my dear chevalier, that you are the idol of my heart and that there is no one in the whole world whom I could love as I love you; but can you not see, poor dear soul, that in the condition to which we are reduced fidelity would be a foolish virtue? Do you think it possible to be loving on an empty stomach? Hunger would cause me some fatal mishap and one day I would utter my last breath thinking it was a sigh of love. I adore you, you may count upon that, but leave me to manage our affairs for a little. Woe to him that falls into my clutches! I am working to make my chevalier rich and happy. My brother will bring you news of your Manon; he'll tell you that she wept at having to leave you.

Armand closes the book and adds, 'She was right but she did not love him, for love knows no reason.'† (It is impossible to render the French play on words between 'raison' and 'raisonner'.) During her decline, we are told, Marguerite read Prévost's novel over and over again.

If the literary parent of *La Dame aux camélias* was *Manon Lescaut*, the other point of origin was Dumas's own experience. The heroine Marguerite Gauthier was drawn from life. Alphonsine Duplessis was one of the most celebrated demi-mondaines of

* Letter to De Sanctis, 1.1.1853. *Carteggi Verdiani*, I, pp. 16–17.
† *La Dame aux camélias* (Paris, 1852), III, vii.

her day. Théophile Gautier and Jules Janin (who just met in the company of Liszt) both confirm the description of her that Dumas gave in the preface to the 1867 edition of his play. 'She was tall, very thin, dark-haired and with a pink and white complexion. Her head was small, her eyes long and slanting like those of a Japanese woman but lively and alert. Her lips were the colour of cherries and she had the most beautiful teeth in the world. She was like a Saxe figurine.'* She was born in the country at Nonant the daughter of a mercer, came (or was sent) to Paris at the age of fifteen, where she swelled the ranks of the grisettes, working as a shop assistant by day and cheering the solitude of artists and students by night. Within a short time she had risen to the highest circles of the demimonde, aided, we are told, by a natural grace and distinction which would have become a duchess. She was kept successively by the Duc de Guise and an elderly Count Stackelberg, who installed her in a luxurious apartment in the rue Madeleine with her own carriage and horses. For the purposes of the novel and play Dumas invented the fiction that the old man had met Marguerite at the spa Bagnères where she had gone to recover her health, already endangered by the life she was leading; and he had been so struck by her resemblance to a daughter of his who had died from consumption that he wanted to adopt her, promising her half his fortune if she would forsake her old way of life; and so for a while she did until the partial recovery of her health brought a fresh craving for excitement. In reality, Dumas later admitted, the old Count was just another of her lovers to whom she had no intention of remaining faithful. It was while she was his mistress that Dumas first was introduced to her in 1844. One day while entertaining some friends in her apartment she began to cough blood. Dumas followed her to her bedroom and his genuine concern so touched her that she admitted him as her lover. It was a stormy and unhappy affair. He could not provide her with the luxury she required; and for this reason she could never renounce her other lovers. Dumas himself reproduced many years later the savage letter of farewell that he wrote her: 'MY DEAR MARIE, I am not rich enough to love you as I would wish and not poor enough to be loved as you would desire. So let us both of us forget – you a name which should be almost indifferent to you, I a happiness that has become impossible for me. There is no need for me to tell you that I am sad, since you already know how much I love you. Adieu, then. You have too much heart not to understand why I write this letter and too much intelligence not to be able to forgive me for it . . .'† And Dumas, one might add, was too much of a Frenchman to forget his epigrams even at the height of his grief. This was in 1845. The next year Alphonsine, or Marie as she preferred to call herself, went with a certain Vicomte de Pérrigaux to London and was married to him at the Kensington Registry Office. Apparently they did not remain together for long. A letter has survived in which she tells him that he is entirely free to lead whatever life he chooses as far as she is concerned. She herself went from spa to spa trying to regain her health; but it was too late. In February 1847 she died in her apartment in Paris. She was only twenty-three. Both Pérrigaux and Stackelberg attended her funeral: Alexandre Dumas had gone abroad to forget. The next year he published his novel, which became a best-seller overnight. In 1849 he made of it a play; but its production was delayed for three years because of difficulty with the censorship. (However, he was more fortunate than Victor Hugo who had

---

* A. Dumas fils, *Théâtre Complet* (Paris, 1867), pp. 9–10.
† See E. Newman, *More Opera Nights* (London, 1954), p. 570.

had to wait fifty years for the second performance of *Le Roi s'amuse*.) Due to his father's influence in high circles, which he later freely admitted, *La Dame aux camélias* was at last shown at the Vaudeville early in 1852. Verdi's opera was produced a year later. It could hardly have been more topical.

In its progress from novel to play and then to opera we can watch fact gradually being transformed into a great work of art. As Dumas fils is little more than a minor practitioner his novel is more interesting than the play since it bears the stamp of authenticity, an experience through which he himself has lived. Verdi's opera is greater than either.

The main fictional contributions to the novel are two. First of all Marguerite and Armand do realize their ideal of a house in the country where they can be happy – though not entirely alone since Marguerite has not cut herself off from her female Parisian friends, nor even from the elderly Count. Secondly the lovers' separation is brought about by Armand's father who visits Marguerite during his son's absence and induces her to give him up both for his sake and for that of his sister whose coming marriage will be jeopardized by Armand's association with a notorious courtesan. She then writes Armand a letter telling him that she had decided to become another and richer man's mistress and so leaves him. Here then is a most important mythical element – hostile society and worldly values represented by the father (the Rothbart of the Swan Lake legend more rationally portrayed). Yet throughout most of the novel the flavour of realism is very strong. Not even the grosser details are shirked. Of that first supper party in Marguerite's apartment he writes: 'There was much laughter and eating and drinking.' (There were only five present.) 'The mirth soon descended to the lowest possible level, and every so often Navette, Prudence and Marguerite would greet with delight words which some people think amusing but which soil any lips that utter them. . . . Gradually I became cut off from the din, my glass stood unemptied and I was almost miserable to see this lovely young creature of twenty drinking and talking like a coster and laughing all the louder the more scandalous the joke.'* During Armand's confession of love it is clear that his friend Gaston and Prudence are making good use of their time. As the two friends left the house Gaston was able to assure him that, 'She's still pretty good at it, that fat old Prudence.' Marguerite herself, according to Dumas, always wore white camellias except during the last five days of every month when the flowers were red. When she promised to become Armand's mistress she took a red camellia from her corsage and gave it to him telling him to return when the flower had changed its colour since, 'You cannot always carry out treaties the day you sign them.'† The French have a delicate way of expressing the cruder facts of life.

After she has left Armand, he begins persecuting her in society. He takes as his mistress one of her friends, a certain Olympe, and encourages her to insult Marguerite whenever she meets her. At last Marguerite comes to his lodgings to remonstrate. The lovers are temporarily reconciled and spend the night together. Next day Armand goes to her apartment and sees the carriage of her latest protector outside the door. In a fury he returns home, and sends her 500 francs in an envelope with a note, 'You left in such a hurry this morning that I forgot to pay you. Here is

* *La Dame aux camélias* (tr. Barbara Bray, London, 1975), p. 79.
† *Ibid.*, p. 88.

your fee for last night.'* When next he goes back to the rue Madeleine he is told she has left for England. He is abroad when he hears of her death; but a certain Julie Duprat has kept for him the diary which Marguerite had written during the last two months of her life. Her thoughts were with Armand till the end. It is all harsh bitter stuff; and how far the last part is true can only be a matter for conjecture. Certainly the real Marguerite did leave for England when her association with Dumas ended; and the incident of the last night together, occurring as it does *after* she had made the great sacrifice, may well be a detail which slipped into the myth from the true course of Dumas's affair. Anyway it is not allowed into the play any more than the red camellia, the reference to four-letter words or the misbehaviour of Prudence and Gaston. The pain of Dumas's experience was beginning to subside and he was more ready to idealize the woman who had caused him so much suffering. Not that he had much choice, if he wished to see his play performed. The Marguerite of the novel could not possibly have found her way onto any stage at that time without some modification of her character. The supper party, at which there are now several more guests, is a perfectly decorous affair; Marguerite's promiscuity is toned down, and the myth further enhanced. The country idyll is strictly *à deux*; and Armand's vengeance is presented in a different way entirely. Meeting her at a party some months after their separation he picks a quarrel with her protector. She, afraid that he will be killed, begs to see him in private. Alone with him she implores him to escape while he can; he agrees on condition that she goes with him; but she, true to the promise she made to his father, refuses. Armand furiously summons the other guests, throws at her feet his winnings of the evening and asks them to bear witness that he has finally paid 'this woman' for her favours. The Baron steps forward, strikes him across the face with his glove to a resounding, 'Monsieur, vous êtes un lâche!' Between this act and the next Armand fights a duel with the Baron and wounds him, though not mortally; as a result he has to flee the country; but he arrives back in Paris in time for a final deathbed reunion with Marguerite.

The play was the starting-point for Piave and Verdi, and they kept to it very closely, the only real hiatus occurring between the supper party which takes up most of Act I and the establishment of Marguerite and Armand in the country. The omission of Dumas's Act II where Marguerite lays her cards on the table rather like Manon in the passage quoted is very much regretted by Ernest Newman (*More Opera Nights*) on the ground that it is the psychological core of the play. Neither Verdi, he says, nor Italian opera as it then existed had the means of doing justice to so complex a character as Marguerite in whom there was something of the saint as well as the *grande amoureuse*. 'The borderline between the two temperaments is frequently a very uncertain one and the merest chance my decide in a particular case on which side of that line the subject's life will be lived. . . . Modern music with the instruments for psychological probing forged for it by Strauss in his *Salome*, his *Elektra* and his *Don Quixote* would be much better equipped for the realization of a character so complex as that of† Marie Duplessis than the Italian music of Verdi's day was. . . .'† Here speaks Newman the iconoclast. In fact the interest of such characters as Mlle Duplessis lies entirely in their effect on others. They may be generous, amiable, intelligent even (Marie Duplessis was certainly a great reader) but they live too much in the present to be capable of those finer, nobler feelings with which their lovers are

* *Ibid.*, p. 196. † E. Newman: *More Opera Nights* (London, 1954), p. 565–6.

always trying to endow them. Where Dumas says in one of his prefaces, 'She was one of the last and indeed the few courtesans with a heart; and that is undoubtedly why she dies so young,'* he is the victim of his own sentimentality. She died young because she was consumptive, and because her disease in its turn produced a craving for pleasure which accelerated her decline. Heart had nothing to do with it. Later, however, with typical Gallic realism, Dumas adds, 'But Marie Duplessis never underwent all the poignant experiences which I have given to Marguerite Gauthier. . . . To her great sorrow she could only have played the first two acts of this play. She began them over and over again like Penelope her embroidery except that in her case it was the day that undid the work of the night.'† Marguerite Gauthier is a different, more noble person altogether; and as Violetta Valéry she is nobler still – a kept woman, a demi-mondaine, but not necessarily promiscuous. Nor is it essential to the myth that she should be. Terence Rattigan in his *Variations on a Theme* (in which he supplies the same myth with a different ending as any Greek dramatist might have done) made his Violetta a respectable divorcee, and changed Armand's father into an equivocal 'protector'. Yet the myth remains fundamentally intact. Piave's Violetta, idealized as she is, becomes in Verdi's hands intensely human and yet heroic as well; and no one need feel the loss of the novel's realistic detail. In *La Traviata* the myth achieves its most perfect form. Dumas's play remains a faded period drama needing the talents of a great actress to restore it to life; *La Traviata* is an undying masterpiece.

It was not surprising that *La Dame aux camélias* should have appealed to the composer of *Stiffelio*. Both subjects were bold and contemporary; and both combine unorthodoxy with a strong vein of morality, being essentially products of the new age of humanism with its growing sympathy for the individual in whatever walk of life. The consumptive heroine may not seem much of an innovation today since the *Tales of Hoffmann* and *La Bohème* but it was very daring for those days, particularly since clinical detail is not shirked. The false recovery at the end was taken over by Bernard Shaw in *The Doctor's Dilemma*. The situation in which Marguerite returns to her former life, though for the most altruistic of reasons, produces the same unbearable tensions that we experience in *Götterdämmerung* when Siegfried in Günther's likeness seizes the ring from Brünnhilde. One feels the agony of a betrayal which is at the same time not really a betrayal. There may be something repulsive about it but it is very gripping as theatre. Clearly Venice, so complaisant towards the daring of *Ernani* and *Rigoletto*, was the only venue for such a subject, not least since Dumas's play was about to be performed there during the season – which makes it all the more difficult to understand why the management had insisted on altering the date of the action. Piave had proposed the period of Richelieu, doubtless with Manzoni's *I Promessi Sposi* in mind. Verdi was determined on a contemporary setting, as he explained to the impresario Lasina, who visited him in Rome during the rehearsals of *Il Trovatore*. On his return to Venice, Lasina sent a memorandum to the directorate of la Fenice to the effect that 'The Signor Maestro Verdi desires, demands and begs that the costumes for his opera *La Traviata* should remain those of the present day. . . . [He] has declared to me formally that unless his request is met part of the opera will be sacrificed since he is counting on obtaining a certain effect in the first two acts whereas otherwise he would have to compose two numbers which, however

---

* Dumas, *Théâtre Complet*, p. 10. † *Ibid.*

different, would recall *Rigoletto*. He declares that he is ready to assume responsibility for this as regards the public and that he will get the press to print the reasons already quoted.'* From Lasina's somewhat illiterate, mis-spelt prose we may gather that Verdi was referring to the party music which he intended to sound contemporary. Strange that he should have imagined the first scene of *Rigoletto* to be an example of sixteenth-century period style.

Anyhow he was forced to give way. A little while later Piave wrote from S. Agata: 'As for the costumes Verdi agrees very much against his will that the period should be put back in time, but he won't allow wigs, so it will be necessary to warn Sig. De Antoni to use the costumes of the period immediately preceding that of the wig.'† But to judge from the date finally arrived at — *c.* 1700 — it seems that Sig. De Antoni did nothing of the sort.

The chief difficulty however remained the prima donna. The archives of the Fenice Theatre contain a codicil to Fanny Salvini-Donatelli's contract dated 4 October stating that she is to be released from her part in the new opera if Verdi found her unsuitable, and provided he let the management know this before 15 January. Presumably this had already been stated in Verdi's own contract of 5 May, of which no copy can be found. Unfortunately, by mid-January Verdi was still fully occupied with *Il Trovatore*. It was not until the end of the month, during his journey home, that he wrote to Marzari. 'The news I receive from Venice, especially after *Ernani*, is so appalling that I am compelled to declare that I will certainly not give the part of La Traviata to Salvini-Donatelli. I believe it to be in my interest and the theatre's to engage another prima donna.'‡ He offered various suggestions including Rosina Penco, heroine of *Il Trovatore*; and he ended by asking the management to release Piave for a visit to S. Agata so as to put the finishing touches to the libretto. This last request was granted, and soon Piave was adding his voice to the composer's asking for the removal of Salvini-Donatelli. 'He [Verdi] insists with renewed firmness that to sing Traviata one must be young, have a graceful figure and sing with passion. Every effort of mine to modify that opinion was in vain.'§ When he realized that the management were not disposed to yield, Verdi wrote to Marzari (or rather made Piave write since he himself was suffering from a rheumatic right arm):

> Legally the directorate is in the right, I admit, but artistically it is in the wrong, because not only Salvini but the entire company is unworthy of the Gran Teatro la Fenice. I don't know whether my indisposition will allow me to finish the opera, and with this uncertainty it is pointless for the management to engage other artists. All right; let it be Salvini and the rest of the company. But I tell you that, supposing the opera is performed, I have no hopes of the result — in fact it will be a complete fiasco and so the interests of the management will be sacrificed (for which it could be said that I'm to blame), also my own reputation and a considerable sum of money in the ownership of the opera. Well, that's that. I'm going to write to Lasina straightaway and tell him to cancel everything. . . .¶

---

* Memorandum from Lasina, 11.1.1853. Conati, pp. 306–7.
† Letter from Piave to Brenna, 5.2.1853. *Ibid.*, pp. 316–7.
‡ Letter to Marzari, 30.1.1853. *Ibid.*, pp. 312–3.
§ Letter from Piave to Marzari, 3.2.1853. *Ibid.*, pp. 314–5.
¶ Letter from Piave (in Verdi's name) to Marzari, 4.2.1853. *Ibid.*, p. 315.

That was too much. An indignant memorandum signed by all three directors on 8 February empowered Brenna to go to S. Agata and recall the composer to a sense of his obligations. Apparently the visit was successful. Brenna and Piave returned to Venice leaving Verdi to complete the still unfinished opera for which Piave was to supply further verses by post. The composer's last letter before setting out for Venice ends on an ominous note: 'I've just had from Venice an anonymous letter telling me that unless I get the tenor and bass changed I shall have a complete fiasco. I know, I know, and I'll prove it to you. . . .'*

The events of 6 March on the whole bore out Verdi's predictions, though he may have exaggerated the extent of the failure. After the first night he dispatched a series of curt notes to his friends of which the one addressed to Muzio is typical: 'La Traviata was a fiasco; my fault or the singers'? Time alone will tell.'† To a new acquaintance, the conductor Angelo Mariani, he was a little more expansive: 'La Traviata has been an utter fiasco, and what is worse, they laughed. Well, what about it? I'm not worried. Either I'm wrong or they are. I personally don't think that last night's verdict will have been the last word.'‡ The press, though sympathetic to the composer, left no doubt that the opera had misfired. Cesare Vigna, of Ricordi's Gazzetta musicale di Milano, wrote of the audience's indifference to the many fine things in the score§. Locatelli of the Gazzetta di Venezia condemned the singers with the exception of Fanny Salvini-Donatelli, about whom he waxed enthusiastic. The first act, he said, was applauded throughout with the composer called several times on to the stage. 'In the second, fortune was reversed, alas. Three things are required in the art of music – voice, voice and voice. . . . And in truth a composer's invention is hard put to it if he has no one who is able or knows how to perform his music. . . . All the numbers which were not sung by Salvini-Donatelli . . . went overboard.'¶ Felice Varesi came in for most of the blame. As a result he wrote to the editor Lucca, asking him to print a letter, the gist of which was that his performances in Il Corsaro – the season's 'opera di ripiego' – had shown that he was in perfect vocal form and that if La Traviata had failed, the composer had only himself to thank. 'I don't intend,' he wrote, 'to set myself up as a judge of the musical worth of La Traviata, but I certainly maintain that Verdi has not known how to make proper use of the vocal resources of the artists at his disposal. In the whole of Salvini's part there was only the cavatina of the first act; little or nothing for Graziani. For me only the adagio of an aria and this was highly resented by the Venetian public who expected that I would be very suitably parted since Verdi had already written for me those two colossal roles of Rigoletto and Macbeth.' Audiences, be it understood, are never angry with great singers; only on their behalf. Varesi continues: 'This is what happened yesterday evening; the third performance, given for the benefit of the poor. A wretched house. A little applause for the brindisi and a good deal for Salvini's cabaletta with two curtain calls. In the grand duet between Salvini and myself there was some applause

* Letter to Piave, 16.2.1853. Ibid., pp. 323–4. Like many composers of the time Verdi retained the old-fashioned habit of referring to the principal baritone as a bass.

† Letter to Muzio, 7.3.1853. Copialettere, p. 533.

‡ Letter to Marzari, 7.10.1853. G. Monaldi, Il Maestro della Revoluzione Italiana (Milan, 1913), p. 90.

§ See Gazzetta Musicale di Milano, 9.3.1853. C. Bongiovanni, Dal carteggio inedito Verdi–Vigna (Rome, 1941), p. 24.

¶ Gazzetta privilegiata di Venezia, 6.3.1853. Conati, pp. 324–5.

for the adagio and the cabaletta. Applause for the finale of Act II and two curtain calls for the composer and the artists. Third act – no applause; one curtain call to say good-bye to the composer who was known to be leaving the next day.'* So much for Locatelli's optimistic view that at the second performance, 'the minority of the opera's admirers changed probably into a majority'.

Varesi's ungraciousness is not hard to understand. From the other roles which he had created it can be deduced that he was one of those dramatic baritones who concentrate exclusively on the upper part of their voice. When the tone begins to wear thin and the intonation to slip through lack of proper support from below they have no remedy except bluster, of which there is plenty in the part of Pasha Seid but none in that of Germont. In vain did Verdi in 1853 keep the baritone floating above the stave for bar after bar. Varesi's career was already coming to an end; indeed, it barely survived the year. He was to create no new roles. His last appearance was in 1857 in a revival of *Rigoletto* in which doubtless his experience and dramatic sense pulled him through.

Of the other principals Graziani was to render Verdi signal service in the 1860s as Riccardo in revivals of *Un Ballo in maschera*, though on this occasion in poor health (one of the performances had to be cancelled because of his indisposition). Fanny Salvini-Donatelli seems to have been a good singer in the old-fashioned, cabalettistic style with a penchant for brilliance. She had a comfortable disposition with figure to match; her colleagues and the audience loved her, but she was not the woman to sing Violetta.

La Traviata did not recover in the course of the season; and though Ricordi as usual published the vocal score it was not taken up elsewhere for more than a year. But this was Verdi's doing. Other impresarios and conductors were only too ready to come to the rescue of the fallen woman; but Verdi himself was determined not to risk a revival unless he could be sure of a suitable cast. Angelo Mariani wanted to mount a performance at Genoa with the original singers; it was the composer who prevented him. De Sanctis hoped to interest the San Carlo in the opera. Verdi wrote to him: 'Ah, so you like my *Traviata* – that poor sinner who was so unfortunate in Venice. One day I'm going to make the world do her honour. But not at Naples where your priests would be terrified of seeing on stage the sort of things they do themselves at night on the quiet.'† Vigna urged him to try his luck again at la Fenice, with Luigia Bendazzi (future heroine of *Simon Boccanegra*) as Violetta. Verdi however was not convinced that she had the right appearance or the right capacity for expression. She was too much the 'donna di forza'. He had more hopes of a certain Noema De Rossi who had just sung Leonora in a revival of *Il Trovatore*. He wrote to Luccardi. Which was the better, she or Penco? Had she a good stage presence? Which was the number she sang best? . . . 'Why all these questions you'll say!!! . . . Because it's just possible that I may be coming to Rome to put on *La Traviata*.'‡ But in the end it was not Rome but Venice once again that made an honest woman of Violetta. The same Antonio Gallo who had tried to persuade Verdi to write an opera for him as manager of the San Benedetto theatre two years ago proposed reviving *La Traviata* with a cast

---

* Letter from Varesi to Lucca, 10.3.1853. F. Schlitzer, *Mondo Teatrale dell' Ottocènto* (Naples, 1954), pp. 157–8. Conati, pp. 327–8.

† Letter to De Sanctis, 16.2.1853. *Carteggi Verdiani*, I, pp. 23–4.

‡ Letter to Luccardi, 22.12.1853. Monaldi, *Verdi 1839–1898* (Milan, 1925), pp. 159–60.

that included the baritone Coletti (creator of Gusman in *Alzira* and Francesco in *I Masnadieri*), Francesco Landi and Maria Spezia. Verdi was in France at the time, at work on *Les Vêpres Siciliennes*, but at long last he yielded to the insistence of Ricordi and gave the project his blessing since Piave was at hand to assist with the production. He asked the publisher for a copy of the score in order to adjust the part of Germont to the lower range of Coletti. He wrote back to Vigna: 'After a whole year I've examined this poor *Traviata* of mine in cold blood and I persist in believing that it's not as devilishly bad as people make out. The third act is far superior to the rest of the opera. The first is the weakest; the duet and finale of Act II should have made a better effect than they did.'* Having received the score in March he held back five numbers which he dispatched to Ricordi the following month duly altered.

The success of *La Traviata* on 6 May 1854 was all that could have been wished for. Maria Spezia, young, pretty and as frail as her predecessor had been robust (so much so that her performance in *I Due Foscari* some days before had given Piave serious cause for concern)† carried all before her. Verdi, on receiving the news, wrote triumphantly to De Sanctis:

> You may as well know that *La Traviata* which is being performed at the Teatro San Benedetto is the same, exactly the same as the one performed last year at the Fenice apart from one or two transpositions of key and a few *puntature* which I made to suit it better to the capacity of these particular singers; the transpositions and the *puntature* will remain in the score because I consider the opera as having been written for the present cast. For the rest not a single piece has been altered, not a piece added or taken away, not a musical idea changed. Everything which was in that was there for the Fenice is there for the Teatro Benedetto. Then it was a fiasco; now it has created a furore. Draw your own conclusions!'‡

In fact the alterations that Verdi made for the second performance are a little more extensive than he would have us believe. The autograph tells us little, since as usual Verdi has covered his tracks very thoroughly tearing out double pages and replacing them. But a manuscript score of the 1853 version held in the archives of the Fenice Theatre enables us to examine the changes in detail; and very interesting they are. They will be discussed in the course of the commentary below.

The phenomenon of two such utterly different works as *Il Trovatore* and *La Traviata*, produced within two months of each other and written, it would appear, to some extent concurrently, is one of those astonishing creative feats that sometimes occur in the lives of great artists. Beethoven's seventh and eighth symphonies are a parallel case. It is as though in the stress of creation each idea throws up its complement. Verdi was still in the throes of *Il Trovatore* when *La Traviata* was begun, and the later opera, written in an incredibly short space of time, grew up as the feminine counterpart of the earlier one. Both speak the same language of melody but what is virile and expansive in the one is feminine and intimate in the other. *Il*

---

* Letter to Vigna, 23.3.1854. Bongiovanni, pp. 32–3.
† See letter from Piave, 4.5.1854. Abbiati, II, p. 271.
‡ Letter to De Sanctis, 26.5.1854. *Carteggi Verdiani*, I, pp. 24–5.

Trovatore carries to its ultimate conclusion the tradition of *Ernani* and *Attila*; Violetta is the successor of *Luisa Miller*, but more vividly and consistently realized.

The sketch for Act I of *La Traviata* printed in Gatti's *Verdi nelle immagini** is a unique document in Verdian literature. Nowhere else are we permitted a glimpse of so early a stage in an opera's genesis. It is undated. All we can be sure of is that it was jotted down before Piave had begun the libretto. Marguerite Gauthier is 'Margherita'; Armand is 'the tenor'. But it is proof, if any were needed, that Verdi like Wagner tended to conceive main dramatic events already 'musick'd'. The two pages are an impressionistic jumble of notes, speech and stage-directions, many, alas, illegible in facsimile: but a sample may be quoted:

> Supper in Margherita's house
> Recitative: orchestral tunes . . .
> Brindisi of tenor:
> [*Here follows the melody and bass of 'Libiamo nei lieti calici' set out in C major, not the definitive B flat.*]
> Short ripieno
> Margherita repeats the brindisi
> Then everyone:
> [*The same melody in the subdominant F. The bass clef suggests that Verdi may have had in mind a male rather than a mixed chorus with Margherita more 'hetaira' than Parisian hostess. In consequence the choral line differs from that of the final version in the concluding refrain.*]
>
> Margherita feels ill. Everybody disperses. Only the tenor stays behind and declares his love. She laughs and advises him not to think of it. 'Could I love? Should I [*illegible*].' Everyone returns [*illegible*]. Good night, and they leave: Margherita alone. 'Could it be true? Suppose I did love him? I who have never felt love? Ah, love?' Andantino follows.
>   Duettino in which there will be a phrase which is repeated in the aria.
>
> 'But what am I dreaming of? Am I made for love? [*illegible*] I must enjoy life . . . drown myself in pleasure . . .'
> Brilliant cabaletta
> [*Eight bars of 'Sempre libera', melody only, with penultimate E flat instead of D flat.*]
> At the end of the cabaletta a voice is heard repeating a phrase from the duettino, which speaks of love: 'It is the sun of the soul. Life is all love!'
> 'More of love! Be still, be still, my heart.'
> [*The page ends with a 16-bar melody in settenario metre marked 'grand duet' and doubtless intended to cover part of the action of Dumas's Act II. In the end this was happily dispensed with.*]

The most interesting feature of the sketch is of course the early version of 'Ah fors'è lui' (Ex. 65) with its — in retrospect — clumsy upbeat, its climax in the relative major and its relapse into the original key: an unusual touch, this, in the days when cantabili, having won into the major key relative or tonic, were expected to stay

* Gatti, pp. 64–5.

65

there, and not inappropriate to one who sees a ray of hope gradually extinguished. Though Verdi's jottings are a little ambiguous here, it would seem that even then the phrase (*x*) was intended as an echo from the duettino, not only because its position corresponds to that of the eventual 'Di quell'amor, quell'amore ch'è palpito', but because it alone fits the line 'È il sol dell'anima' quoted further on (never a great literary inventor, Verdi here had recourse to the Duke's verse from the cantabile of his duet with Gilda); in which case Alfredo's declaration of love first took musical shape in the soprano aria and not the preceding duettino. But what emerges most clearly from a comparison of sketch with finished product is that search for simplicity and directness of expression which is the hallmark of the opera as a whole. The number of bars is the same in each case; but the final realization is purged of all superfluity. The lyrical melismata towards the end of Ex. 65, however beautiful in themselves, however expressive in a purely musical way, are discarded in favour of a strictly syllabated line that sets the words 'croce e delizia' in high relief so that their effect is immediate.

The prelude is a musical picture of the heroine. Eight first and eight second violins portray the frail consumptive. (In the final act, as the end draws near, Verdi will revert more and more to this diaphanous scoring for strings reduced and *divisi*.) Note too the diminishing phrase lengths – four, three and two bars, likewise hinting at a decline.

At the twelfth bar the first violins reach upward in a climbing figure strikingly similar to the last phrase of 'Tacea la notte' in *Il Trovatore* but here with an effect of piercing sadness.

The main melody presents Violetta in all her beauty and charm. Simple, song-like, not yet a cry of anguish as in Ex. 12b. It is an inspired use, worthy of Mozart, of the small change of contemporary Italian opera,* to which the full-throated scoring gives warmth and eloquence. The final cadence is interrupted; then, as in the prelude to *Ernani*, the melody is repeated by cellos with at the lower octave a semiquaver countermelody, here entrusted to first violins divisi. What in the earlier opera was merely a routine device, giving added interest to a restatement, here conveys that sense of coquetry which is an essential part of Violetta's character. If the prelude melody has all the radiance of Violetta in love the embellishment gives us the frivolous hostess of Act I. Both elements figure in the coda dying away into a

* For the relationship of this melody to Donizetti's *Pia de Tolomei*, see Chapter 2, Exs. 12(a) and (b).

pianissimo final cadence. Like that of *I Masnadieri* the prelude to *La Traviata* is an independent musical statement, a miniature sufficiently complete in itself to bear being performed out of its context.

ACT I

Scene: A salon in Violetta's house. At the back there is a door leading to another room; there are two other lateral doors. On the left a fireplace surmounted by a mirror. In the middle of the room is a table laden with food.

The brusquerie of the opening orchestral flourishes is more than a device for arresting attention. It anticipates that jarring quality that will mark most of the choral interventions throughout Verdi's most intimate opera, even if the scene before us is a cheerful one, that of the first act of Dumas's play. But as this is opera a larger scale is permitted. Marguerite's guests can only speak as individuals and are therefore limited in number; Violetta's can be swelled by an impersonal chorus who utter in unison. The opening music, confined at first to woodwind and brass, is a brash variant of that theme first encountered in the overture to *Oberto*:

It assumes a more delicate quality when re-stated by an octet of strings (4 violins, 2 violas, 1 cello and 1 bass) as a new group of guests arrive and Violetta goes to meet them. They have come from another party given by her friend Flora Bervoix and have brought their hostess. Violetta sings the praises of wine and good company in a unison phrase, which, insignificant in itself, adds a new element to the rhythmic pattern of the scene.

The entrance of one Gaston with his friend Alfredo Germont is marked by a new melody in graceful conversational style, the last four bars attractively foreshortened to three. Again the scoring is reduced.

Gaston is a young spark, a long-standing friend of Violetta's though not a former lover (Dumas if not Piave is quite clear on that point). He presents Alfredo to Violetta who receives him graciously. Then she announces that supper is ready and bids everyone take their places. She herself sits between Gaston and Alfredo; opposite are Flora, her friend the Marquis and Violetta's protector the Baron. Ex. 70 returns this time in F major with the same octet of strings and an oboe added to the top line. Gaston confides to Violetta that when she was ill two years ago Alfredo came to her house every day to ask after her. 'You were never so attentive,' she says to the Baron. 'But I have only known you for a year.' 'And he,' she indicates Alfredo, 'has known me only a minute.' Amid the cheerful resumption of Ex. 68 the Baron's growing antipathy to Alfredo becomes evident, aggravated by Flora's praises of him. Here is certainly one good reason for describing both characters as comprimarii. It is rarely possible to distinguish their words, with so much interest centred on the ever changing orchestral texture. All the more important, then, that they should be sufficiently good actors to project their feelings by gesture and facial expression. During all this Alfredo is solemn and silent. At Gaston's suggestion Violetta pours him a glass of wine. The dialogue is pure Piave and a long way from Dumas. Violetta compares herself to Hebe; and Alfredo gallantly wishes her the goddess's immortal youth (Giuseppina Strepponi used to wax satirical over Piave's habit of larding his correspondence with classical references). To the rhythm of Ex. 69 Violetta then calls for a toast. The Baron ill-humouredly refuses to lead it; and the task falls to Alfredo, in the famous brindisi ('Libiamo, libiamo nei lieti calici'). He raises his glass to wine, love and the joys of the moment. His guests take up the final line as a refrain; and Violetta replies with the same melody, whose kernel is that leap of a sixth from dominant to mediant which Verdi used so freely in *Ernani*. Here paradoxically by insisting on it in the first four bars he gives sharper focus to the reckless energy and spontaneity of the melody. What the listener will probably not observe unless it is pointed out to him is that the melody is a ten-bar structure, its stresses falling so naturally as to conceal the irregularity of shape.

The chorus abandon themselves to a reprise in the subdominant; after which Violetta pulls the music back into the original key in dialogue with Alfredo – a subtle touch suggesting that amidst all the abandon she remains in control as hostess, and that already the basis of her *rapport* with Alfredo has been laid, that he already exists for her on a different plane from that of her other guests. It is one of those instances where music tells us more than the words which it sets. What could be more absurd than that Alfredo should be the one to lead the party in a hymn to pleasure? It should have been Gaston, as in the play. But the reader will by now have realized why in an opera of this period he could not have undertaken it without a breech of the *convenienze*. He will note too the more sordid aspects of the scene, already less evident in the play than in the novel, have vanished altogether from the opera. Violetta remains a creature of poetry even at the height of her feverish gaiety.

The band strikes up from an adjoining room, much to the surprise of the guests. They had no idea there was to be dancing. Violetta leads the way, then twice has to stop, overcome by a feeling of faintness; she sinks down on to a couch, and tells the anxious guests to go in without her; she will follow in a moment. The preceding scene has shown a new refinement in Verdi's 'festivo' style; a new ability to organize different themes into a well constructed movement. But the banda is always the banda even when its banality is put to good dramatic use; and the next scene unfolds to a string of commonplace waltzes. (In the play they dance a polka, which had just come into fashion in the 1840s.) As usual Verdi does not specify the instrumentation beyond asking for trumpets for the fourth melody (in D flat major).

Violetta looks at herself in the mirror, remarks on her own pallor: then notices that of all her guests Alfredo alone has remained behind. He reproaches her for the life she is leading, which will certainly kill her. She replies banteringly; but Alfredo is not to be put off. The banda music ceases as Alfredo solemnly declares his love ('Un dì felice eterea').

72

In this melody with its intimate expression, its narrow intervals and plain syllabic delivery in which every extension is accompanied by verbal repetition the 'tinta' or 'colorito' of *La Traviata* first becomes fully apparent. It is an idiom redolent of the 'composizioni da camera', as Basevi pointed out, causing several subsequent writers to refer to this misleadingly as a 'chamber opera'. The opening is a variant of that of Verdi's own salon piece 'L'Abandonnée' of 1849. Not only that; every phrase in it is a vivid expression of Alfredo's mood. He is not just any romantic tenor in love. The semi-quaver rests in the first two bars are both an integral part of the melody and an expression of a young man's shyness. The tune seems to gather strength and confidence as it succeeds culminating in that glorious 'slancio' ('Di quell'amor, quell'amor ch'è palpito') which will recur throughout the opera as a symbol of Violetta's and Alfredo's love; a reminiscence motif like 'Stride la vampa' in *Il Trovatore*. (It too has a precedent in the song 'Chi i bei dì', an Italian version of Goethe's 'Erster Verlust'.)

73

We have come a long way from the massively articulated phrases with their elaborately pounding accompaniments of the Risorgimento operas.

Violetta replies that if this is how he feels the sooner he forgets her the better (Ex. 74). (The light coloratura doubled by flute and clarinet is related to the violin motif in the prelude.) Alfredo stubbornly continues his ode to 'love, the soul's delight and its cross' to be rewarded by a tenderly expressive melisma from Violetta in the coda. The cadenza, however, neatly preserves the contrast between the two characters: Armand continuing his steadfast quavers, Violetta her tripping coloratura.

The banda intrudes again the second of its melodies, an episodic theme which serves to remind us that it has been playing all the time and that the cantabile has been, in television terms, a cutaway shot. The intensity of the preceding scene has made it vanish from our consciousness. But now the tension is lowered by Gaston looking in to ask after Violetta's health. Seeing Alfredo he tactfully withdraws. 'No more talk of love then,' says Violetta to Alfredo; but she plucks a flower from her bosom and tells him that he may visit her again when it has faded. 'And when will that be?' 'Tomorrow.' A rising 'rosalia' in the banda music proclaims a typical dance-music coda during which Verdi brings in the orchestra strings on the first beat of each bar to give an extra life to the rhythm and at the same time to mark Alfredo's joy. At last he kisses her hand and leaves. The guests come pouring in to a stretta based on the rhythm of Exs. 69 and 70 rising rather mechanically by semitones in a crescendo to a fortissimo cadence followed by a brief play-out as they too take their leave.

When they have gone Violetta muses on the strange young man who has come into her life, in one of the most famous scenes in Italian opera. It has little to do with the play, still less with the novel, in which Marguerite is portrayed, naturally enough, from the outside. Its nearest equivalent is a short speech in the play's second act which has no part in the operatic scheme. Marguerite is already making plans to escape with Armand to the country.

Who would have told me eight days ago that this man whose existence I never suspected would fill my heart and my thoughts so much and so quickly? Does he love me? Or do I only know that I love him – I who have never loved anyone? But why sacrifice a joy? Why not abandon oneself to the whims of the heart? Who am I? A creature of chance. Then let chance do with me as it pleases? . . . It seems to me that I am happier now than I have ever been. Perhaps this is an ill omen. We women always imagine that we will be loved, never that we shall be in love ourselves, so that at the first assault of this unforeseen trouble we do not know where we are.*

But Dumas's Marguerite takes the initiative, acts with her eyes open. Verdi's Violetta is hooked without knowing it. She refuses to acknowledge her love even to herself, yet she ends by obeying it. This is surely a far subtler stroke of psychology than

* Dumas, *La Dame aux camélias*, II, i.

anything in Dumas. In the recitative she imagines the happiness of loving and being loved in return. Perhaps Alfredo is the man whom she had been waiting for all her life. The andante ('Ah fors'è lui') presents the minor–major design at its simplest; and for the major section it melts into Ex. 73 in the most natural way imaginable. Never one might think has a major section more movingly crowned its minor counterpart. Yet in fact Meyerbeer has an almost identical harmonic scheme in Isabelle's aria 'Robert, toi que j'aime' in *Robert le Diable*, an opera that Verdi knew well. Horizontal brackets placed over Verdi's melody indicate the points of correspondence.

Meyerbeer : ROBERT LE DIABLE

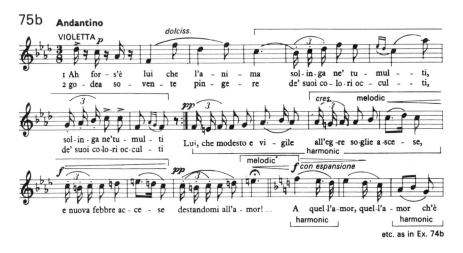

etc. as in Ex. 74b

Indeed the whole movement sounds like an expanded and improved version of Meyerbeer's idea.* Both melodies lead into the major with the same high note from which they subsequently descend. The difference between them lies partly in Verdi's infinitely greater melodic invention but also his artistic courage; he had faith in his own ideas. Meyerbeer who packed each of his scores with enough themes to supply five operas never allowed any of them to take root. Having concluded his maggiore

---

* With the sketch before us (Ex. 66) we can rule out the possibility that the melody was prompted by Meyerbeer in the first place since the resemblance supervenes only in the working out.

section he must needs pass on to another idea for fear that the audience should become bored. Verdi is not afraid to draw for his climax on a theme we have already heard; and here, embroidered with clarinet arpeggios, it sounds still more resplendent than in its previous context, giving the effect of emerging from darkness into light. Though she is not yet aware of it, love, 'the heart's torment and delight', will mean even more to her than to Alfredo. Finally – unthinkable in Meyerbeer – Verdi repeats the whole melody again in a second verse, with Alfredo's words repeated as a refrain for Ex. 75b. The movement is therefore strictly in couplet form (another instance of Verdi's French lessons taking effect) though most of us have yet to hear the second verse performed in the theatre.

A recitative follows in which Violetta jolts herself out of her reverie. Who is she to dream of love? A poor girl lost in the great city of Paris without a friend to help her? Why should she not give herself up to the joys of the moment; and she hails la dolce vita in the cabaletta 'Sempre libera deggi'io folleggiar'. (Many Violettas have a habit of seizing a wine glass at this point.) As she reaches her cadence the voice of Alfredo floats through the window singing his refrain (Ex. 73) to the accompaniment of an offstage harp as in *Il Trovatore*. Violetta listens entranced, then once more shrugs away the thought with a shortened version of her previous recitative. Again the cabaletta is repeated, Alfredo's voice breaking into the coda. But for the present the desire for pleasure has conquered love.

The andante 'Ah fors'è lui' is beautiful music whether heard on its own or in the course of the opera. 'Sempre libera' needs to be heard in its context if it is to seem anything more than a brilliant display piece. The scoring is very much in Verdi's early style with sporadic doubling, rapid pizzicato arpeggios on the cellos to give excitement, and a wealth of trumpet and piccolo. The voice is all scales and roulades reaching higher and higher, and expressing well enough the febrile gaiety that Dumas describes in his heroine. Note the faint suggestion of a Chopin waltz in the harmonies of the third and fourth bar.

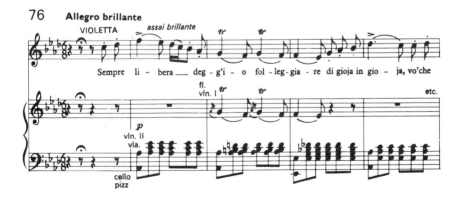

76 **Allegro brillante**

Alfredo's intervention is no less brilliant a theatrical stroke for having been anticipated by Mercadante in an unpublished version of *Il Reggente* given in Trieste in November 1843. Here too the tenor is urging the still dubious heroine to yield to love.

ACT II

Scene 1: A country house near Paris. A room on ground level. At the back facing the spectator a fireplace and above it a clock and a mirror. On either side are French windows leading to the garden. Nearer the front of the stage are two doors facing one another. Chairs, tables, a few books and writing materials.

The plot moves straight to Act III of the play, omitting Dumas's second act altogether; on the whole a sensible arrangement, though its inclusion might have made more sense of the various comings and goings that begin the second act of the opera. Marguerite has taken upon herself the task of making the necessary arrangements for their flight. Armand, who knows his *Manon Lescaut*, has no wish to play the part of des Grieux, spending money which his mistress has extracted from some wealthy lover. Yet in fact this is exactly Marguerite's intention. She sends for her latest protector, the Comte de Giray, and asks him for 15,000 francs to pay off some urgent debts. During their conversation a letter arrives from Armand, who has seen the Baron go into Marguerite's house. 'It does not suit me to play a ridiculous part even before the woman I love. The moment I left your house M. le Comte de Giray entered it. . . . Forgive me my one fault – that I am not a millionaire, and let us both forget that we have ever known each other and that we ever for a moment believed ourselves to be in love. When you receive this letter I shall already have left Paris. . . .' But of course he had not: he was at the house of Marguerite's fat friend Prudence. After a long dialogue the lovers are reconciled, Marguerite has no longer any thoughts of raising funds from the Baron or from anyone else. But the result is that once in the country they have very little to live on.

Verdi's Act II opens with a *vivace* orchestral motif expressive of both his happiness and his restlessness at Violetta's absence. Alfredo enters 'in hunting costume', lays down his rifle and proceeds to give himself up to thought of his beloved and how she has completely changed his life, calming the restless ardour of his youthful spirits. As usual the gradient between recitative and aria is smoothed out by a few bars of arioso. The andante 'I miei bollenti spiriti' is a brief simple movement cast in the same mould as many of the early cantabili but far more compressed. The short phrases and narrower melodic intervals are all typical of the opera's distinctive 'colorito' (Ex. 77, p. 137).

It is one of the few pieces in the score which carries no metronome mark in the autograph: a pity, since this would have helped to dispose of a problem of performance. Most tenors favour a brisk pace since they like to press on to their high notes as soon as possible. But the pizzicato marking of the offbeat violins and violas militates against this. What is more the marking does not extend to cellos and basses. It is a reversal in fact of the usual procedure whereby the lower instruments would be plucked and the higher bowed. Most conductors, Toscanini amongst them, have simply refused to believe it, and have turned the indications upside down. Others, more scrupulous, play the entire accompaniment pizzicato; yet neither the 1914 score nor the autograph leaves any room for doubt. Certainly the bowed quavers can sound ugly unless played with delicacy; but the pizzicati semiquavers are surely vital to the movement's character which lies in the contrast between the serenity of the voice and the restlessness of the orchestra. The 'youthful ardour' of most Alfredos is

still simmering; and rapid pizzicati can illustrate boiling water very effectively.

Annina, Violetta's maid, now comes in much perturbed. She has been to Paris to arrange the sale of Violetta's carriage and horses. Alfredo is thunderstruck. Why had he not been told? Madame had insisted that he should know nothing about it, Annina replies. But life in the country is quite expensive and she still needs a thousand *louis* to cover the housekeeping costs. The orchestra whips up a mood of galloping excitement as Alfredo prepares to set out for Paris to raise a loan, pausing only to protest his chagrin in a cabaletta ('Oh mio rimorso! oh infamia!').

Entirely conventional, apart from its minor key ritornello, it gives Alfredo a touch of the heroic for which most tenors of the day would have been grateful. But its emphasis is not really justified by its context or its verbal content;* as happens more than once in I Due Foscari it is reached by a false coup de théâtre, and above all it causes Alfredo to strike an attitude. If there is one trait foreign to all the characters of La Traviata it is a tendency to posture. Their feelings run far too deep. For this reason the cabaletta is often omitted today. Yet its removal produces the same non sequitur as does that of the Duke's cabaletta in Rigoletto, since one is left with a crescendo and a rhetorical half-close which lead nowhere. Here the problem is still worse since there is no equivalent of the shock of Rigoletto's entrance which might conceivably justify a break in the musical coherence. Toscanini is credited with the solution of two rapid downward scales to bridge the gap to the following string chords. Most Verdians will probably prefer the fault to the remedy, especially as the cabaletta can be quite impressive if well sung.

Violetta comes in, to be told by Annina that Alfredo has left for Paris and will be back about sunset. Meanwhile Giuseppe, her manservant, has brought her a letter from Flora, inviting her to a party that evening. But she has no intention of going. Giuseppe enters again to say that a gentleman is outside and wishes to see her; and from this casual announcement the second act, dramatically speaking, may be said to begin. The long duet between Violetta and Alfredo's father is the core of the opera. Of the various elliptical movements of which it is made up each corresponds to a speech of Dumas's. As usual their meaning has been condensed by Piave sometimes almost to vanishing point; yet the emotional graph is faithfully reproduced. But for a full understanding of the scene two points, omitted by Piave, have to be mentioned. In a conversation with two of her country friends Dumas's Marguerite declares that much as she loves Armand she will never be his wife. 'He has the right to love me but not to marry me; I will gladly possess his heart but I will never take his name. There are certain things that a woman can never efface from her past and with which she should never give her husband the right to reproach her. If I wanted Armand to marry me he would do so tomorrow. But I love him too much to ask such a sacrifice of him.'† The other point is that M. Duval (Germont) does not believe that Marguerite is really ill. 'Let us be calm and not exaggerate. . . . You are young and beautiful and you mistake for illness what is nothing more than the fatigue caused by your restless life. You will certainly not die before the age when one is quite happy to do so.'‡ And he paints a terrifying picture worthy of Somerset Maugham's The Circle of the old age of two people who are outcasts from society, and who have ceased to love each other. Marguerite plausibly enough can see no way out.

In the opera Germont introduces himself without ceremony as the father of Alfredo, the young man whose life she is ruining. To express the cold hostility that underlies Germont's correctness Verdi has recourse to one of music's oldest devices, the diabolus in musica, here a grating tritone between voice and orchestra (Ex. 79).

Violetta interrupts him with a touch of authority. She is a woman, and in her own house, and will not allow him to insult her. Her dignity takes him aback; but all the

---

* That this cabaletta was a later addition by way of a concession to the convenienze is clear from a letter of Verdi to Piave shortly before setting off to Venice for rehearsals: 'I've received the tenor's cabaletta [i.e. the verses]: it means nothing.' Letter to Piave, 16.2.1853. Conati, pp. 323–4.

† La Dame aux camélias, II, iii.

‡ Ibid., III, iv.

same . . . this luxury, these furnishings . . . Violetta shows him a document providing that she has already sold most of her possessions, and gradually his mood relents. There is something fine and noble about her after all; yet he must ask of her a great sacrifice – and not for Alfredo's sake alone. With the mention of Alfredo's sister the formal part of the duet begins. In the previous recitative Verdi's familiar progress of moving from pure recitative through arioso to set piece is geared perfectly to the growing sympathy between Violetta and Germont. The curt exchanges at the beginning are in the most offhand declamatory style; but when Germont has seen the documents of sale pity and sorrow smooth the music into a legato line ('Ah il passato perchè, perchè t'accusa!'). Violetta dispels the gloom of F minor with one of those soaring soprano phrases which encompass a whole world of feeling within two or three bars. Violetta loves Alfredo and her repentance will wipe away the sins of the past.*

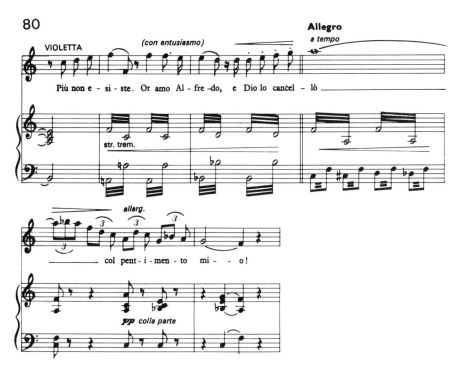

* Martin Chusid in his essay 'Drama and the key of F major in *La Traviata*', in *Atti del III° Congresso del I.S.V.*, pp. 89–121, makes a convincing case for F as the key of Violetta's and Alfredo's idyll. He is less persuasive, however, when he extends its significance to Verdi's operas in general.

Germont is completely won over; and the conversation takes on a new warmth. But at the mention of a necessary sacrifice tremolo strings betray the intensity of Violetta's fear; yet she listens calmly to what he has to say. The duet between them is a chain of short contrasted movements, each marking a fresh stage in the emotional dialectic. It is longer than any of the duets in *Rigoletto* or *Luisa Miller*; its nearest equivalent in the earlier operas is the duet-finale between Lucrezia and the Doge in *I Due Foscari*. But whereas in the earlier work the argument remains static, she, in effect, saying in various different ways, '*Do* something!' and he replying, 'I cannot', in *La Traviata* the argument develops, and as it does so the two characters take on a new dimension of reality. Germont maintains the same position throughout. His is the voice of morality, sympathetic but inexorable, while Violetta moves through the entire spectrum of tragic emotions. For the rest the duet from *La Traviata* is as superior to that of *I Due Foscari* as one would expect from nine years further experience and from the greater poignancy of the situation. The finale to Act I of the earlier opera solves nothing, carries the dramatic situation no further forward. The present piece forms the turning-point of the drama, and reaches a climax in the moment of Violetta's renunciation. When De Sanctis wrote after seeing a performance in Naples that he considered the duet in the second act too long, Verdi assured him that, 'If you saw it produced with two suitable artists this duet . . . would not fail to produce a tremendous effect and you would agree that it is equal to any other duet I have written as regards idea, and superior in form and feeling.'* The outlines are as follows:

A. *Allegro moderato, A flat major 4/4* ('*Pure siccome un angelo*'), *24 bars*
Germont talks of his young daughter, 'pure as an angel', whose marriage to the man she loves is threatened by her brother's notorious liaison.

B. *Transitional movement – animando (A flat – C minor)*
(*'Ah comprendo'*), *16 bars*
Violetta imagines that she need only part from Alfredo until after his sister's marriage. Germont insists that she must give him up ever.

C. *Vivacissimo, C minor/major 6/8* ('*Non sapete quale affetto*'), *44 bars*
Violetta protests that she would die rather than leave Alfredo; she is mortally ill, she has no friends, no family; Alfredo is everything to her and she to him.

D. *Andante piuttosto mosso, F minor/D flat major 2/4*
(*'Bella voi siete e giovine'*), *52 bars*
Germont tells her to think of the future when she will be no longer young and Alfredo, with male fickleness, will have allowed his affections to stray. Their love has not been blessed by the church; they can have no legitimate children, and therefore nothing to hold them together for a lifetime.

E. *Transition, D flat minor – A flat minor – E flat minor*
(*'Così alla misera'*), *22 bars*
Violetta reflects on the hopelessness of her position; Germont begs her to do what he asks.

---

* Letter to De Sanctis, 17.2.1855. *Carteggi Verdiani*, I, pp. 29–30.

F. Andantino, E flat major 6/8 ('Dite alla giovine'), 56 bars
Violetta, resigned, asks Germont to tell Alfredo's young sister how for her sake an unfortunate woman sacrificed her only dream of happiness. Germont praises her generosity and bids her take courage.

G. Transition, sostenuto − Allegro, E flat minor − E minor − G minor
('Imponete'), 30 bars
Violetta and Germont discuss ways of effecting the separation. If she says she no longer loves him he will not believe her: if she goes away he will follow. At last she hits on a plan, which she refuses to reveal to Germont, since he would feel it his duty to forbid it. But she tells him to wait in the garden for Alfredo's return. By the evening he will need his father's comfort.

H. Allegro moderato, G minor − B flat major ('Morrò, la mia memoria'), 81 bars
Violetta's last request is that when she is dead Germont will tell Alfredo that she loved him enough to sacrifice her happiness for his sake. Germont tries to console her.

A is composed of three quatrains, the last of which forms an extended pleading coda. In 1853 the first two verses were set to the same music; in the revision Germont's line was altered by a series of 'puntature' which not only serve to lower it slightly but characteristically hold the melodic climax in reserve for the second verse.* In B Violetta's passage from eager trepidation to the realization of what Germont is about to ask of her is reflected both in the vocal line and the relentless progress to C minor. In C she breaks out in terror with one of those melodies in which the rests are as significant as the notes:

The full expression of her feelings, however, is reserved for its major complement ('Il supplizio è sì spietato'). In 1853 this took the form of a wild soaring and plunging, scored in Verdi's noisiest manner, which took the soprano up to a high C (Ex. 82). As a piece of vocal pyrotechnics it is impressive certainly, despite its inappropriate reminiscence of 'Sempre libera'. The solution found a year later is infinitely better, with the voice remaining on E while cellos, clarinets and bassoons in octaves trace a searing inner chromatic line suggesting a deep-seated agony, and in

---

*For a fuller discussion with appropriate quotations of the original 1853 form of *La Traviata*, see my 'The two Traviatas', in the *Proceedings of the Royal Musical Association*, XCIX (1972–3), pp. 43–66.

82

Ancor più vivo

VIOLETTA

Ah il sup - pli - - - - - - - zio è spie - ta - - to, il sup - pli - zio è si spie -

- ta - - to, che a mo - rir pre-fe - ri - rò, _____ che a mo - rir pre - fe - ri -

- rò, che a mo - rir pre - fe - ri -

- rò, _____ che a mo - rir, _____ che a mo - rir, _____ che a mo - rir, _____ che a mo -

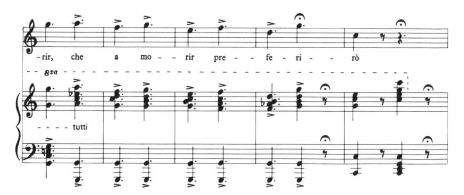

place of the high C a B flat like a scream which by straining at the limits of the C major tonality acts as a fulcrum for the extremely emphatic cadence which ends the movement.

Of all the changes in the score this is perhaps the most important since it sums up within a small compass the essence of Verdi's stylistic development. What in the first version had been done by means of vocal contour alone is now done through

83

harmony and increased orchestral participation. In E Germont expounds his thesis over a repeated rhythmic motif, a method quite common to the Verdi of this period and already noted in much of Azucena's music. Here it is used with great effect to suggest the hammering home of a bitter truth.

84

Again in F Violetta's melody of resignation took a different turning in 1853 nor did it include a part for Germont. Instead of that affecting move at the ninth bar from D flat minor to A flat minor, like the darkening of another horizon, the music remained in the original key for the whole period, ending with an agitated twisting and turning on the dominant like a trapped animal trying to escape; then a portamento took the voice down an octave to begin the central cantabile (G) in E major. Nothing could illustrate better the danger of attributing structural importance to Verdi's key-schemes than the case before us. The alteration of 1854 which brings the new melody into E flat instead of E makes not the slightest difference to the duet considered as a whole. The improvements are purely local — the relief given to the phrase 'L'uom implacabile per lei sarà' with its plunge to a hollow B flat below the stave; the syncopated transition for Germont which allows Violetta a pause before beginning with the utmost simplicity what is the finest moment of the duet and perhaps of the opera. 'Dite alla giovine' is a perfectly orthodox duet-cantabile laid out in 'dissimilar' style; but the melody is one that could only have come from *La Traviata*: plain, 'inward', moving within a narrow compass; a concentration of significance within the smallest possible space. Nowhere in Italian opera is grief more beautifully transfigured than here:

85

After the final melting cadence with its characteristic harmonic twist we reap another advantage from the lower key. The following dialogue had remained orientated in E major from the words 'Imponete' to 'Qual figlia, qual figlia m'abbracciate'. In the present version not only does the initial E flat minor express Violetta's listlessness far better, but the modulation into E major where she begs Germont to embrace her makes the phrase itself stand out like a pearl.* The final cabaletta (H) exploits all the wistfulness inherent in that Italian tradition, beloved of Bellini, which permits a minor key melody to end in the relative major. Both in character and tonal layout it has an ancestor in the soprano and baritone duet 'V'accompagni quella pace' from a favourite work of Verdi's student days, Luigi Ricci's *Chiara di Rosemberg*. The 'dissimilar' scheme however which preserves the dialogue form to an unusual degree is purely Verdian; so too the remarkable stroke whereby a late reprise of the second idea, which belongs only to Violetta, is broken into fragments by the force of her grief, like the reprise of the funeral march in Beethoven's 'Eroica' (Ex. 86).†

When Germont has gone Violetta sits down to write a letter telling Alfredo that the call of her old life is too strong to resist, and that she has decided to leave him. Two orchestral themes convey her true feelings: in the first the 'figure of death' is prominent; the second features a clarinet solo, recalling Luisa Miller in a similar plight (Ex. 87).

* Those familiar with the vocal score of *La Traviata* must often have wondered why in the course of (G) at Violetta's words 'Tra breve ei fia reso' the key signature changes to four sharps just at the point where it has left E major for E minor. The reason is that it was here that Verdi returned to the 1853 version where the key signature had been E major since the end of the andantino (F).

† In 1854 this movement was altered by the omission of – two bars; Germont's phrase 'Premiato il sagrifizio sarà del vostro amore' (Ricordi full score, p. 171) having been originally repeated.

86

While she is still writing Alfredo enters. Quickly she conceals the letter; but she cannot hide her agitation. There follows one of the most remarkable 'false crescendi' ever written – false because for most of the time the dynamics do not increase at all; but the sense of growing tension is maintained for forty bars. The real crescendo takes

87

place only in the last two. Violetta babbles about throwing herself at the feet of Alfredo's father, appealing for his blessing – so that they can be happy. . . . No she is not weeping, she is calm, smiling . . . she only wants to be beside him for ever and ever; then the tension dissolves in a tremendous lyrical outburst, 'Amami, Alfredo' – 'Love me, Alfredo, as I love you' – to the main melody of the prelude but with its last phrase augmented by two bars as in Ex. 12b. It is one of the rare cases in which Verdi has adopted the German practice of indicating a ritardando in note values, a measure of the emphasis needed.

Violetta tears herself from Alfredo's embrace and rushes out into the garden leaving him bemused but happy. He opens a book (we are not told which, but it is of course *Manon Lescaut*). Perhaps after all his father will not be coming today. Then Giuseppe enters to say that Violetta has left in a carriage. Alfredo is not in the least worried; he assumes that she has gone to Paris to sell some of her goods and that Anna will be in time to forestall her. However, just then a police officer arrives with a letter. Alfredo opens it and reads, 'by the time you receive this letter . . .' He gives a cry of despair, turns round, sees his father and falls sobbing into his arms. Here Verdi has made use of a personal device which has been noted more and more frequently in the course of Vol. I: a sudden 6/4 chord in a remote key, here thrown further into relief by preparatory death figures.

88

At this point Dumas rings down the curtain. Verdi and Piave, however, have a principal baritone on their hands who must be accommodated at some stage with a full aria; and where better than here? The andante 'Di Provenza il mar, il suol' in which Germont comforts his son with thoughts of home consists of two musically identical strophes which proceed in small 'conjugations' of the opening phrase like so much of Germont's music. This combined with the woodwind ritornello gives it a curiously Donizettian ring, though the seesawing strings may also suggest Bellini. This is surely intentional: an evocation of nostalgia through echoes of the style of twenty years earlier:

89 Andante piùttosto mosso

It is all in the sensitive baritonic vein of Rolando in *La Battaglia di Legnano* – a further reason no doubt why Varesi found it not to his taste. Verdi may have been exaggerating when he described this to De Sanctis as the finest cantabile for baritone that he had yet written; but detailed markings that accompany every phrase and the predominance of small intervals combine to give it that special flavour of intimacy that informs the score as a whole.*

The same could be said of the cabaletta 'Non non udrai rimproveri' which follows Alfredo's refusal to be comforted. But here it is not a redeeming virtue. In their correspondence over *I Due Foscari* Verdi had insisted to Piave on the necessity of a 'difference of thought' ('distacco di pensiero') between cantabile and cabaletta. In this case no such 'distacco' is possible since Germont has said all there is to say in such a situation. He must therefore say it again differently. The prodigal son will hear no reproaches: a father's and a sister's love will restore his lost happiness. It is a moderato cabaletta evolved on the same rhythmic principle as the andante, though with a different pattern, and it comes uncomfortably close to monotony; hence no doubt the 'tuck' in the reprise, where, as in Rossini's 'Io son docile', only the second half of the melody is repeated after the ritornello. In making the puntature for Coletti Verdi certainly improved it, altering the harmonic scheme for the better and providing a tighter, more effective codetta. The final limb of the original is worth quoting side by side with the revision as an instance of the composer's attempts to keep Varesi in a congenial area (Ex. 90).

The most striking detail in the movement is the caressing two-part introduction for violins, faintly recalling the previous andante. Otherwise it is an undistinguished piece and one cannot entirely blame conductors and producers for skipping to the point where Alfredo catches sight of Flora's letter, surmises quite correctly that Violetta has gone to her party and rushes off in pursuit.

---

* The unusual verse schème, based entirely on ottonari tronchi, was recalled by Verdi in a letter to Ghislanzoni about the versification of *Aida*. The melody, he said, 'would be less bearable if the lines were shorter'. Letter to Ghislanzoni, 16.8.1870. *Copialettere*, pp. 609–10.

90

But what in fact had Violetta said in her note to Alfredo? The play like the opera makes him break off as he is reading it aloud. To find out the full text we must go to the novel. 'By the time you read this letter, Armand, I shall already be the mistress of another man. So all is over between us. Go back to your father, my dear, and to your sister, a pure young girl who knows nothing of all our troubles and who will soon help you forget what you have been made to suffer by the fallen creature they call Marguerite Gauthier. You were good enough to love her for a while and it is to you she owes the only happy moments in a life which, she hopes, will not last long now.'*

> *Scene 2: A gallery in Flora's town house richly furnished and brilliantly lit. A door at the back and two on either side of the stage. On the right slightly forward a large table set out for playing cards; on the left a little table with flowers and refreshment; various chairs and a divan.*

When the curtain rises the ball is in preparation; Flora is chatting to some of her early arrivals, who include the Marquis (her latest lover) and the doctor. The Marquis asks if they have heard the latest news. Violetta and Alfredo are no longer

---

* *La Dame aux camélias*, p. 177.

together. The Doctor is very surprised. He had seen them in the country only the day before and they appeared happy enough. But the Marquis assures him that Violetta's escort at the party will be the Baron Douphol. The music of this scene is in Verdi's brilliant party vein. A little divertissement follows, like a Parisian ballet in miniature, though both numbers are sung as well as danced. The first is provided by a group of gipsies some of whom proceed to tell fortunes during the course of it. They deduce from the Marquis's hand that he is not a model of constancy. The Marquis protests, Flora chides him roguishly with a quotation from Aesop. The second piece in contrasting major and minor sections is sung by Gaston and his friends who enter dressed as bull-fighters. They tell the story of Paquillo the great matador who slew five bulls in succession and was rewarded with the love of a beautiful señorita; Flora, the Doctor and the Marquis join in the matador's praises and the music works up in a grand crescendo, the gipsies beating their tambourines, the picadors stamping their heels. It all amounts to no more than picturesque light music to which the tambourines, triangle, castanets and the exotic sweep of the rhythm all give a certain piquancy: above all they provide a dramatic foil to what follows.

A linking passage of twenty bars marks the entrance of Alfredo, which causes general surprise. Violetta is expected but not he. However, he appears quite nonchalant when her name is mentioned; and everyone, relieved, sits down to a game of cards.

The orchestra now develops an 'action' theme.

91

It is quite suitable to the shuffling and dealing of cards and the punting, but the low clarinets, the acciaccature on every note convey the electric atmosphere that pervades the room as Violetta enters almost immediately on the arm of the Baron. Flora goes to meet them: the Baron whispers to Violetta that she must not say a word to Alfredo. She assents, but three times in the course of the ensuing scene her voice rises and sinks in a desolate phrase, scored slightly differently each time in a typical Verdian gradation, as she begs God to take pity on her. As the one cantabile passage in the movement it not only provides just the right contrast to Ex. 91; it enables the stricken Violetta to dominate the scene with only a few words.*

* The tradition whereby Ex. 93 is extended in a mighty allargando – rightly rejected by Toscanini – is wittily attacked in an article by René Leibowitz, 'Vérisme, Véracité et Vérité de l'interpretation de Verdi', in *Atti del I° Congresso del I.S.V.*, pp. 145–56.

92

Meanwhile Alfredo is consistently winning. 'Lucky at cards – unlucky in love,' he quotes meaningly. Soon, he says, he will have enough money to return to the country. 'Alone?' they ask. 'No; with the woman who recently ran away from me.' Violetta restrains the Baron by threatening to leave; but she cannot prevent him from trying his luck with Alfredo at the table. Again Alfredo wins; but while they are playing supper is announced. He promises the Baron his revenge later, and Ex. 91 dies away on violins, flutes and clarinets.

The company have all gone in to supper when Violetta returns alone, her agitation portrayed in five perilous bars of rapid violin semiquavers. She has sent a message to Alfredo asking him for a word in private. Will he come? He had looked at her with such hate a moment ago. He does come however; and their dialogue is conducted to a brisk, business-like rhythm varied by outbursts of a tense lyricism from Alfredo.* She has sent for him because she wants him to leave at once; the Baron will almost certainly provoke him to a duel. Alfredo sneers; she is afraid of losing her protector? No, she replies, her fears are for Alfredo, and they find musical expression in the incessant 'death figure' (♫♩) in the accompaniment. He agrees to leave but on one condition – that Violetta goes with him. But she replies that she has sworn an oath to leave him for ever. 'To whom have you sworn it?' 'To one who had the right to ask it of me.' 'To Douphol?' And Violetta forces herself to the supreme lie: 'Yes.' 'Then you love him?' 'I love him.' Beside himself with fury Alfredo goes to the door of the supper room and calls in the other guests. 'Do you know this woman?' he cries. 'Do you know what she has done?' (cellos darken the outline of a diminished seventh phrase) and Alfredo denounces her in a speech which is all the crueller for being couched in the form of an ironical compliment. Piave of course condenses it into a symmetrical verse; here it is in Dumas's more extended version: 'She sold everything that she possessed in order to live with me – she loved me so much. That is fine,

* The semiquaver violin figuration beginning at 'Mi chiamaste' is an addition of 1854.

surely? Do you know what I did? I behaved like a wretch. I accepted her sacrifice without giving her anything in return. But it is not too late, I am sorry and I have come to make amends. You are all witnesses that I owe nothing any longer to this woman . . .'* and he flings his winnings in her face. Verdi's setting conveys the irony by means of a straightforward, if tense, melody in the major disturbed only twice by jarring harmonies – a diminished seventh in the second bar and a Neapolitan sixth at the climax, with the line rising to a high A flat. It is an outstanding example of the effect that he can draw from a short-term stanza in the course of a general scene (compare Zamoro's solo in the Act I finale of *Alzira*). It must be admitted that in Dumas's Act IV the situation is more strongly motivated. A month has elapsed since the lovers' separation. Armand has followed his father back to Tours where he has tried in vain to recover his peace of mind. Marguerite meanwhile has plunged deeper and deeper into dissipation. Her present protector is not the Comte de Giray of the second act, but a certain Comte de Varville whom previously she had found unbearably tedious. But now he has taken it on himself to pay her debts, and she in return has offered him her favours. There is therefore additional irony in the fact that Armand fights a duel with a man whom she actually dislikes. But then Armand has returned to Paris deliberately to provoke trouble. When Marguerite tells him to leave the party since she is afraid for his life, his fury crumbles away. He confesses that he still loves her desperately, that if she will only come back to him all his past misery will be forgotten, that he will never reproach her for having left him. Marguerite is thus put to an intolerable strain in her effort to keep her promise to M. Duval and the effect of Armand's curtain speech is all the more annihilating.

The shallower dramatic perspective of Piave's scheme is less damaging than Ernest Newman the iconoclast would have us believe. Words describe an emotion; music conveys it directly. In an opera we do not need to know as much as in a spoken play about the causes of that emotion in order to be persuaded of its strength and depth. Nor is it a disaster if from this point to the end of the act the dramatic element becomes diluted in the interests of musical architecture. To Alfredo's outburst the guests react with horror in a series of irregular unison phrases backed by full orchestra. Suddenly Germont's voice is heard in accusation. He has entered during the previous chorus; and he now launches the *largo concertato*. It is in some respects an old-fashioned piece, appropriate to the figure who dominates it. Germont begins rhetorically in dialogue with the orchestra; then his line gradually assumes a smoother, more periodic flow. To insult a woman, he says, is contemptible; he cannot recognize his son in the man who has done this.† Alfredo murmurs his remorse in an aside of broken triplet semiquavers; a new melody takes over as the guests express their dismay, Germont his pity for Violetta, while the Baron covertly challenges Germont to a duel. There is a brief unaccompanied passage; then once more Violetta's voice emerges from the ensemble like that of the heroine of *Giovanna d'Arco* in a similar situation, as she proclaims her undying love for Alfredo. The line does not lie particularly high; but an illusion of height is given by the dominant tonality (A flat major in relation to D flat). Over the simplest of harmonic schemes

---

* *La Dame aux camélias*, IV, vii.

† At this point the otherwise excellent English translation by E. J. Dent goes seriously wrong. 'You are my son no more, I here disown you' is quite inappropriate. Germont would be incapable of such harshness.

the mood of each principal is beautifully caught in the contour and articulation of their lines — Germont's reproachful nobility, Alfredo's shame and confusion, Violetta's pathos:

93a

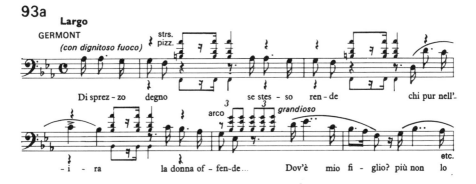

93b

93c

In this number the divergence between the scores of 1853 and 1854 has so far been confined to the lowering of the occasional note for both Violetta and Germont; but now the gap widens considerably. Not only does Violetta's Ex. 93c have a simpler cadential phrase than previously, but the final melodic idea of the concertato, begun by Alfredo and Germont in unison, was developed quite differently. In the definitive score Violetta joins the theme at the third bar in unison with Alfredo just at the point where his baritone pitch forces Germont into a harmonic part. In the original the melody remained chiefly Alfredo's up to the sixth bar at which Violetta emerged in regal splendour to lead the ensembles in a melting descent of four slow bars. The effect is so beautiful, despite its moment of parallel octaves that one might wonder why Verdi wanted to change it:*

* Ironically this very page has always been reproduced in facsimile in the programme book of *La Traviata* published by the Teatro la Fenice. Yet it never struck a single critic that it bore no relation to anything he had heard during the evening.

94

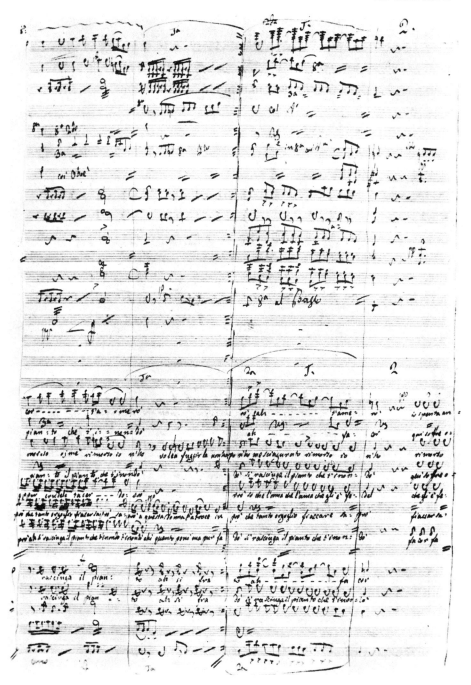

Possibly it gave too much poise and majesty to a heroine who is longing to sink through the floor. Perhaps too it separated the characters in a way that was unnecessary after they had been so clearly and compellingly defined in Ex. 93 – and after all they are continuing to sing the same words. In the revised score Ex. 94 therefore becomes an expression of generic emotion, the kind of lyrical transfiguration such as one expects towards the end of a concertato. Again the new solution has the virtue of greater brevity, always an important consideration where Verdi was concerned.

ACT III

Scene: Violetta's bedroom. At the back a four-poster bed with curtains half-drawn; a closed window with shutters on the inside; by the bed a commode on which is a bottle, a glass and various medicines. In the middle of the stage is a dressing table and near by a couch; another table near by with a nightlight; several chairs and token articles of furniture. On the left a door. Facing the spectator a fire is burning in the grate.

Ex. 67 again assigned to 16 violins introduces the sick-room scene. Violetta is sleeping; Annina is sitting by her bedside, also asleep. At the eighth bar the music, now on full strings, takes on the character of a melody with accompaniment moving from C minor to A flat major; back to C minor and then breaking magically into D flat with an entirely new idea, using the Neapolitan sixth as a pivot:

It is one of the least formal of Verdi's melodies with the freely wandering line of a late Chopin nocturne. The climax is reached with a return to C minor followed by a coda full of descending semitone 'laments' stressed off the beat. In the last four bars the first violins decrease in strength until only two are left on the final trilled C. Throughout the string writing has a rare delicacy, in no way spoiled by Verdi's persistent habit of underpinning important modulations with sustaining wind chords. But then notice how sensitive that palette of wind has become – no longer a routine combination of clarinets and bassoons but a blend of five separate single timbres. Violetta wakes and calls for a glass of water; no sooner has Annina brought it to her than Doctor Grenville arrives and asks how she is feeling. She replies that the priest came to visit her (Ex. 95) since when she has felt calmer in spirit and has passed a peaceful night. In that case says the doctor she will soon be well. But as he takes his leave he tells Annina that her death is only a matter of hours. So far the dialogue has taken place to a light recitative interspersed with phrases from the prelude played by strings sometimes at full, sometimes at reduced strength. But there is a dreadful finality about the cadence which underlines Doctor Grenville's words to Annina, and brings back Ex. 67. Where Chopin is mentioned Bellini is rarely far away; and indeed this opening scene owes much to the beginning of *Norma* Act II, not only in its violin pattern of sighs and gasps but in the use of an instrumental melody to give a lyrical framework to a scene of recitative. The chief difference lies in the more rapid, almost realistic flow of Verdi's conversation as against Norma's sustained soliloquy. The Druid priestess speaks from a remote past; Violetta and Annina are of the world about us.

When he has left Violetta asks Annina to see how much money they have left. Twenty louis, says Annina. Ten Violetta tells her to keep for herself; meanwhile will she please go and see if there are any letters for her. Alone, Violetta takes an old one from her bosom and reads it aloud, evidently not for the first time. 'You kept your promise . . . The duel took place . . . the Baron was wounded but is recovering . . . Alfredo has gone abroad . . . I have let him know of your great sacrifice . . . He will come back and ask for your forgiveness . . . I shall come too . . . Take care of your health . . . You deserve a better future . . . Giorgio Germont.' Here Verdi reverts to the convention of speaking instead of singing a letter, but he has revitalized it in a most original way. While Violetta is reading a septet of strings play a shimmering reminiscence of Ex. 74 – a device which Hollywood has since done to death, but which here has all the freshness of surprise. The last phrase breaks off as Violetta comes to the name Giorgio Germont. Then over a diminished seventh chord (strings, low clarinets, bassoons and horns) she *speaks* 'in a sepulchral voice' the words, 'It is late' ('È tardi'). In recitative she tells us that she has waited and is still waiting – but they have never come. She looks at herself in the mirror. 'How I am changed. Yet the doctor tells me that there is still hope; but I know that for me all hope is dead . . .' Her aria ('Addio del passato') is a farewell to past dreams of happiness with a pathetic oboe to open and close the two strophes and to link their respective major and minor sections, so providing the first instance in Italian opera of an aria that ends in the minor mode. The minor opening (Ex. 96a) is a variant of E in the duet with Germont ('Così alla misera') where she first realizes the hopelessness of her position. The major theme (Ex. 96b) which follows was in 1853 an entirely new melody though evolved rhythmically from the preceding. Due to the revision of the duet in 1854 it now becomes a reminiscence of Ex. 83, transfigured·by the serenity of Violetta's resignation. Whether or not Verdi had this effect in mind when he revised the duet, it would seem to confirm the rule that the most telling revisions in a work of art are those which define more sharply an idea immanent in the original conception. Here too the string writing is remarkable. The first and second violins reduced to eight apiece join with violas in high pulsating chords leaving a gap of two octaves and a third between them and the cellos.

96a

Like the offstage barcarolle in *I Due Foscari* the carnival chorus which breaks in is a deliberate stroke of dramatic irony. Outside a bull is being led in procession, symbol of Mardi gras. The Bacchanal ('Largo al quadrupede') is accompanied by a shrill band of two piccolos, four clarinets, two horns, two trumpets, small drums and tambourine. Thematically its interest is slim to say the least; as a coup de théâtre it is brilliantly effective.

The last note is taken up by the orchestra in a palpitating theme as Annina returns in a state of suppressed excitement and tries to prepare Violetta as calmly as possible for a piece of joyful news. She guesses at once what it is; and at that moment Alfredo appears in the doorway and flies into her arms. It is one of those long passages of dominant preparation which Verdi had used to such good effect in the last act of *Luisa Miller*; but here the sense of over-projection is avoided by a cunning shift from one dominant to another (from G major to E major) in the course of the build-up. United in a glorious tutti cadence the lovers continue their dialogue in the same rhythm and tempo, as they exchange words of love and forgiveness. 'Nothing on earth can ever part us now', and the music again works to a rapturous climax with a typically Verdian vocal *slancio*. Woodwind chords modulate to A flat for the central andante of the duet ('Parigi, o cara'). This again is very much a *Traviata* melody: waltz-like, utterly simple in line and accompaniment and confined mainly within the compass of a few notes.

97

Violetta repeats the melody note for note, since for the present situation nothing less than an old-style 'similar' design will do. Then the symmetry is broken by Alfredo's entry with a new idea over the end of her cadence (that traditional Italian device for giving a touch of urgency to the music without upsetting its structural balance). Violetta replies to him with a phrase of light semiquavers in the accompaniment of

98

which the first violins are again divided into four with only eight on the top two lines.

Violetta's first thought is that they should go straightaway to a church and give thanks to God for Alfredo's return. But as she tries to get up she falls back fainting; she pretends that it is nothing, that seeing Alfredo again so unexpectedly has for a moment deprived her of strength; but it soon becomes clear that she is too weak even to stand. Alfredo orders Annina to send for the doctor. 'Tell him,' Violetta adds, 'that I want to live now that Alfredo has come back.' The agitated motion of the music is arrested by a powerful brass unison; and in a phrase quite chilling in its restraint she tells Alfredo that if his return cannot restore her to health nothing can prevent her from dying.

99

Then despair rises to the surface in the cabaletta ('Ah! Gran Dio! morir si giovine'), a melody whose pathos resides neither in the harmonies nor in the tonality but rather in the accents, phrasing and melodic intervals. Rhythmically it follows a late Donizettian pattern.*

100

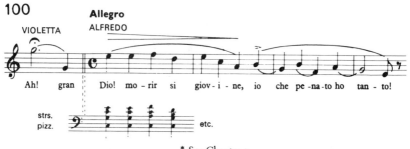

* See Chapter 2.

The archives of the Teatro la Fenice contain an album or Stammbuch belonging to Fanny Salvini-Donatelli to which Verdi contributed the opening phrase of Ex. 100 – but in D flat major; for this is the key in which it was originally sung. Again we have to do with one of those small but masterly alterations whereby Verdi improved the opera of 1853. In the 'tempo di mezzo' or transition, at the point where Alfredo is struck by Violetta's pallor ('Tu impallidisci!') the voice originally rose a semitone bringing the next four bars into E major. In 1854 Verdi exchanged this routine vocal emphasis for a harmonic progression from A flat minor to E flat minor, much as he had done in section E in the soprano/baritone duet in Act II, so intensifying the sense of gloom and anxiety. The contrast with G flat major where Violetta tries desperately to rally with a show of gaiety is all the greater.

There is one more alteration of major importance. 'Gran Dio, morir si giovine' is the most 'similar' of cabalettas. Alfredo repeats Violetta's music; there is an episode in the minor key, like a sung ritornello with voices proceeding in overlapping phrases. Then Ex. 100 returns sung by Violetta with Alfredo sustaining a purely harmonic part. The voices overlap once more in a coda based on a new idea twice repeated. As in all 'similar' cabalettas the result of so much repetition is to prepare the audience for a full stop, torrents of applause for the artists and cries of 'Fuori Maestro!!!' This is clearly what was meant to happen in 1853 and did not. Therefore in his revision Verdi tightened up the coda giving it additional urgency and harmonic strength and cutting off any possibility of applause by a purely rhythmic transition to the key of the Finale ultimo.

101

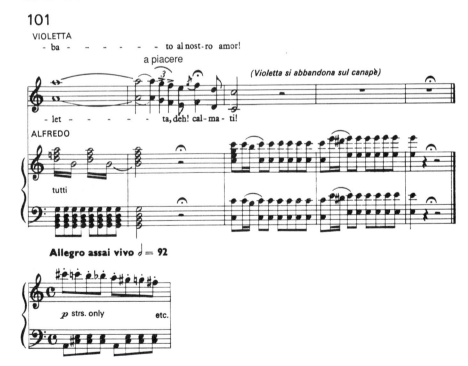

It was an inspired notion but it does not fully solve the problem. To take a banal comparison, it is rather as though a train driver, having slowed up in order to stop at a station, were at the last moment to accelerate past it. The broadening effect of the cabaletta design has now no point. The solution generally adopted is to make a cut from the end of Alfredo's verse to the beginning of the coda (*più mosso*) or, more ruthlessly still, to the diminished seventh at the coda's fifth bar. The dramatic pace is thus maintained but with the sacrifice of some fine music.

The Finale ultimo brings in Germont, now ready to claim Violetta as his daughter. She greets him weakly; and, as he looks at her, for the first time and only time in the opera he betrays strong emotion:

Only now does he realize the wrong he has done her. Violetta meanwhile takes a medallion from a drawer with a portrait of herself and gives it to Alfredo. The final concertato ('Prendi, quest'è l'immagine') starts with the instrumental device found in the Miserere of *Il Trovatore*; a death figure rapped out pianissimo by the full orchestra complete with bass drum beneath a slow vocal declamation (Ex. 103).

Alfredo is to keep the medallion in memory of her; and if he should meet some pure-hearted girl who loves him, he must marry her and give her the portrait, telling her that it is of one who prays for them both. Alfredo is overcome with grief, Germont with remorse; and during the course of the movement the doctor and Annina arrive to swell the ensemble. Basically it is a 'finale concertato' like any other with each principal allotted a characteristic intervention; but in its strict economy and its total lack of melismatic extension it could belong only to *La Traviata*. Then comes the false miracle. Ex. 74 sounds for the last time high up on eight violins and two violas, even more ethereally than in the previous occasion.* (As always, the weaker Violetta

* In a recent paper given at the Fondazione Cini, Venice, Wolfgang Osthoff has pointed out that in the 1853 score this passage was written an octave higher.

103 Andante sostenuto ♩ = 56

VIOLETTA *(cupo)*

Prendi, quest'è l'im-ma - gi - ne de'

tutti *pppp*

miei pas-sa-ti gior - - ni,

becomes the more diaphanous the scoring.) She feels a resurgence of life. The orchestra reflects her growing excitement while her voice remains almost expressionless, low in her register, quasi parlando, then rises with the orchestra to a fortissimo climax at which she falls back senseless. The others exclaim in horror; Alfredo cries out her name; the doctor after feeling her pulse announces that she is dead; and the curtain falls to the usual succession of fortissimo chords.

Théâtre Lyrique, Paris, 1864 (Violetta)

From 1854 onwards *La Traviata* enjoyed a career hardly less triumphant than that of *Il Trovatore*. Nor was it without its humorous aspects. The opera was of course butchered by the censors in Naples and the Papal States as its composer had foreseen. A copy of the libretto censored for a performance in Bologna by a canon of the cathedral exists in the archives of Messrs. Ricordi. There is scarcely a line which escapes unscathed. That 'croce e delizia' should become 'pena e delizia' could be taken for granted. More surprising is the ruthless re-writing of the brindisi whose text was considered far too licentious. Violetta's pagan declaration that 'La vita è un tripudio' is altered by the worthy canon with perhaps a touch of envy to '*Mia* vita è un tripudio'. Even the objective and worldly Basevi found in the descending line of Ex. 74 an image of 'base love', so different from the ideal, pure-hearted sentiments of Arturo's 'A te o cara' from *I Puritani*.* At the first London performance in 1856 Davison, critic of *The Times* and mouthpiece of the English musical establishment, spoke of its 'foul and hideous horrors'. *The Times* further declaimed against it in a leading article. Yet it could be given in concert form at Exeter Hall in the company of *Messiah* and *Elijah* without a voice being raised in protest. In any case the public

---

* Basevi, p. 231.

remained obstinately enthusiastic. If in England *La Traviata* soon exceeded *Il Trovatore* in popularity this was due largely to the soprano Marietta Piccolomini who made it her speciality at both the Haymarket and Covent Garden.

The first performance in France was given in pirated material at the Théâtre des Italiens in 1854. Ten years later Léon Carvalho, manager of the Théâtre Lyrique, obtained permission from composer and publisher to mount a French version in a translation by Edouard Duprez, brother of the singer. What Verdi's part, if any, in the proceedings was we cannot be sure; but the opera's success in this form encouraged him to prepare a revised *Macbeth* for the same theatre. In the French score many of the names are altered for no very obvious reason. Alfredo and his father became Rodolphe and Georges d'Orbel respectively, while the name Germont is transferred to the doctor. Flora becomes Clara, Gaston Le Vicomte Emile de Latorière, Baron Duphol Baron Raynal; Giuseppe and the police officer are fused in a single 'domestique'. The opera is divided explicitly into four acts as is mostly the fashion today (and why not? A journey to Paris from the country could certainly last an interval). The only musical alteration occurs at what is now the end of Act II. Immediately after Violetta's impassioned outburst and exit Ex. 12b is thundered out by full orchestra. Then d'Orbel enters, holds out his hand to the happily absorbed Rodolphe and launches straight into his cantabile 'Lorsque des folles amours' ('Di Provenza il mar il suol'). To the same music as in the Italian score Rodolphe refuses to listen. 'Do you want your mother to die of grief?' d'Orbel asks. It is the first we have heard of her in the opera (indeed the play makes clear that she is already dead) but she it is who forms the subject of Germont's cabaletta 'Ah reviens c'est la vie' ('Non udrai rimproveri'). If this does not amount to a 'distacco di pensiero' it at least advances the argument somewhat. However a note in the vocal score* authorizes the omission of the cabaletta altogether; and indeed the transition is much smoother if this is done. The 'domestique' arrives with Violetta's note which Rodolphe reads and to which he reacts as in the original score with a plunge into D flat major; and in this key the act ends. A page of manuscript in the Bibliothèque Nationale containing the revised ending is catalogued as the composer's autograph, though the handwriting is not easily identifiable as Verdi's. That he authorized it, however, for local consumption is quite likely. It represents one of those scenic 'tidyings' sometimes to be found in the French versions of his Italian operas (*La Force du destin* will provide numerous examples of it). The main weakness of the new scheme, both musically and dramatically, is that it fails to provide a strong position for the baritone aria. Despite the advocacy of Francis Toye† it is unlikely to be revived today.

Two of Verdi's own opinions about *La Traviata* are worth mentioning. When asked in the years immediately following its revival which of his operas written to date he considered his best, he is said to have replied, 'Speaking as a professional *Rigoletto*; speaking as an amateur *La Traviata*.'‡ When many years later Giulio Ricordi recommended Gemma Bellincioni for the part of Desdemona on the strength of her performance as Violetta, Verdi replied, 'I couldn't judge her from *La Traviata*; even a mediocrity could possess the right qualities to shine in that opera and

* *Violetta*, opéra en quatre actes, musique de G. Verdi (Paris, Benois, c. 1864?), p. 142.
† Toye, p. 329.
‡ G. Monaldi, *Verdi 1839–1898*, p. 152.

be dreadful in everything else.'* In other words he did not regard it as a prima donna opera in the conventional sense; it needed sincerity, feeling and a good stage presence as he had written to Vigna at the time. Indeed the heroine of 1854, Maria Spezia, who first carried the opera to glory, never achieved stardom. One of the great assets of *La Traviata* is that while inevitably attracting the great it can make its effect with good artists of the second-rank.

At no time does Verdi seem to have reverted to his original idea of having the opera given in contemporary costume. The first Violetta to have performed in a crinoline was the same Gemma Bellincioni whom he refused to hear in 1886. However, in the days when production was apt to be minimal and when star singers took with them their own *vestiario* from theatre to theatre, the up-dating did not necessarily extend to the rest of the cast. 'As to *La Traviata*,' Bernard Shaw wrote in 1890, 'with Violetta in the latest Parisian confections and Alfredo in full Louis XIV fig, that is familiar to every opera-goer.'† Up to 1914 all printed scores continued to carry the indication 'Paris and its environs about 1700'. However, even if he had had his way in 1853 the modern setting would have seemed purely metaphorical since the language spoken is strictly operatic and 'olde worlde'. The truth is that it does not matter in the least in what epoch *La Traviata* is set. It is Verdi's most intimate music drama; and the feelings it portrays are those of individual humanity down the ages.

Today *La Traviata* is without question the most widely loved opera in the Verdian canon (indeed a poll taken in Italy some years ago showed it to be the most popular in the entire repertoire). Any lingering imperfections in the style can be traced to the problem of the cabaletta, especially the solo variety – a form as fundamentally alien to the world of *La Traviata* as it is basic to that of *Il Trovatore*. Cuts alleviate this problem but can never fully solve it. For all that, few of us would want a note of the score changed. The abiding glory of this opera is that it says fundamental things in a simple, direct way yet with a wealth of poetic suggestion. In this respect it marks the end of a line which began with *I Due Foscari* and passed through *Luisa Miller* and *Stiffelio*. From now on for many years Verdi will point towards grand opera.

No chapter on *La Traviata* can afford to pass over the theory first put forward by the sentimental Luzio,‡ taken up by Lualdi§ and finally embodied in a feature film that in the three principals of his opera Verdi was portraying himself, his first wife's father Antonio Barezzi, and Giuseppina Strepponi. The supposed indications are: (1) Giuseppina's morally not irreproachable past, (2) a letter written by Verdi to his father-in-law from Paris on 21 January 1852¶ – that Barezzi shared the hostility of the Bussetani to Verdi's wife in all but name, (3) letters addressed by Giuseppina to Verdi round about the time of *La Traviata* in which she complains of ill-health and refers to him as her redeemer. In fact there is not the slightest evidence that Antonio Barezzi's attitude to the singer was anything but cordial from the start. In 1848 he visited Verdi and her in Paris and wrote home very appreciatively of his reception.|| His main

* Letter to G. Ricordi, 7.2.1886. *Copialettere*, pp. 343–4.
† *Shaw's Music*, II, p. 229.
‡ *Carteggi Verdiani*, pp. 250–76.
§ A. Lualdi, 'Storia segreta della *Traviata*', in M. Nordio, *Verdi e la Fenice* (Venice, 1951), pp. 76–80.
¶ *Copialettere*, pp. 128–31.
|| Walker, p. 186.

grievance as it transpires from Verdi's famous letter seems to have been that Verdi was no longer taking him into his confidence. Nor can Giuseppina's congenital hypochondria be compared with Violetta's mortal sickness. Leaving aside such minor details the notion that Verdi, while insisting on the respect due to the woman who now shared his life, should then have insulted her himself by portraying her as a demi-mondaine is surely preposterous. One can imagine his blind fury if the idea were put to him.

5 LES VÊPRES SICILIENNES

LES VÊPRES SICILIENNES

Grand opera in five acts
by
AUGUSTIN EUGÈNE SCRIBE and CHARLES DUVEYRIER
(after *Le Duc d'Albe* by the same authors)

First performed at the
Académie Impériale de Musique, Paris,
13 June 1855

GUY DE MONTFORT, Governor of Sicily under Charles d'Anjou, King of Naples	BARYTON	Marc Bonnehée
LE SIRE DE BETHUNE ⎰ French	SECOND BASSE	M. Coulon
LE COMTE DE VAUDEMONT ⎱ officers	SECOND BASSE	M. Guignot
HENRI, a young Sicilian	TÉNOR	Louis Gueymard
JEAN PROCIDA, a Silician doctor	BASSE	Louis-Henri Obin
LA DUCHESSE HELENE, sister of Duke Frederick of Austria	SOPRANO	Sophie Cruvelli
NINETTA, her maid	CONTRALTO	Mme Sannier
DANIÉLI, her servant	SECOND TÉNOR (TÉNOR LÉGER)	M. Boulo
THIBAULT ⎰ French	SECOND TÉNOR	M. Aimes
ROBERT ⎱ soldiers	SECOND BARYTON	M. Marie
MAINFROID, a Sicilian, adherent of Procida	SECOND TÉNOR	M. Koenig

Sicilian men and women – French soldiers – Monks, etc.

Extras and corps de ballet: French soldiers – betrothed couples – pages –
nobles – zephyrs – naiads – fauns – Bacchantes – an executioner

The action takes place in and around Palermo

Epoch: 1282

To conquer the stage of the Paris Opéra at some point in his career was a necessity felt by every Italian composer who aspired to international fame. The advantages it presented have already been mentioned in Vol. I – a greater variety of musical forms than were available at home, a wealth of choral and instrumental resources, more interesting libretti free from the shackles of the Italian *convenienze*, and above all an audience eager for novelty. It represented a challenge, similar to that of the symphony for the German romantic, and on the same analogy not to be undertaken lightly or without due preparation. Verdi had chosen the cautious approach of Rossini and Donizetti. Like the first with his *Le Siège de Corinthe* and *Moïse*, the second with his *Les Martyrs*, he had begun by adapting an earlier work. *I Lombardi alla Prima Crociata* with the aid of a new French text and extra music became *Jérusalem*. This was to have been followed up with an entirely original opera but for the events of 1848 and the subsequent necessity to rescue Cammarano from the threat of imprisonment in Naples. Accordingly he wrote to the directors of the Opéra in November of that year formally breaking off negotiations for the time being.[*]

In 1852, however, he returned to Paris while *Il Trovatore* was in gestation, to arrange a fresh contract. Signed on 26 February, after some characteristic hedging on Verdi's side, its terms show that the composer of *Rigoletto* was well aware of his own worth in the international market. The libretto, in four or five acts, was to be by Scribe himself, with or without a collaborator (not by a team of underlings like Royer and Vaëz, who had concocted the text of *Jérusalem*); it was to be submitted to Verdi in the form of a 'treatment' by 30 June 1852 at the latest and, if acceptable to him, to be delivered complete not later than the end of the same year. Rehearsals were to begin in mid-July 1854. For this purpose the theatre was to be put at Verdi's disposal for three months. The new opera was to be produced at the end of November or the beginning of December 'with all the pomp that the traditions of the Grand Opera render indispensable'. No other new grand opera was to be produced during that season; nothing more substantial than a new ballet to be rehearsed concurrently with M. Verdi's opera – apart from the works that were being revived. All the artists taking part were to be chosen by Verdi himself and the management was to guarantee forty performances within ten months from the première. There was to be a penalty of 30,000 francs for failing to honour the contract.[†]

Verdi in fact was playing for high stakes where the risks were considerable. The monster-opera was essentially a product of the 1830s, its spiritual roots in the age of the Orleanist monarchy which had collapsed ignominiously in 1848. It was an age of good behaviour and wild romantic dreams. People dressed quietly, aping the modes of England; but on stage they demanded every form of extravagance. The more discreet the foreign policy of Louis Philippe and his ministers, the more society indulged in nostalgic memories of vanished imperial grandeur. There was nothing

[*] Letter to Duponchel and Roqueplan, all'Opéra, 25.11.1848. *Copialettere*, p. 65.
[†] See *Copialettere*, pp. 139–40.

here of the radical, genuinely romantic outlook of a Victor Hugo or a Lamartine. Eugène Scribe, the reigning high priest of the Parisian stage, shares with Hugo only his sensationalism. His plays and libretti like the novels of Dumas *père* are designed to please a solid middle-class society bent on stability. The characteristic musical unit of Meyerbeerian opera is not the love duet but the ceremonial march.

The truth was that having launched this new conception of grand opera in 1831 with *Robert le Diable* the directors were hard put to it to attract enough new works of good quality to keep it genuinely alive. Operas in five acts complete with ballet and mounted in the style to which the public was now becoming accustomed absorbed so much time and money that they could only be produced at the rate of one a year. Inevitably the leading Parisian opera house which opened its doors three days in every week – amounting to a season far longer than that of any Italian theatre – was faced with a problem of repertoire. If the new work was successful it could be repeated sufficiently often to pay its way. If not, it must be withdrawn as soon as possible and an old favourite revived in its place. Throughout the 1830s and '40s the graph of success in the field of new grand operas shows a steady descent. *Robert le Diable* (1831), *La Juive* (1835) and *Les Huguenots* (1836) were to prove evergreens, classics of their kind to which the public never failed to respond. *Gustave III* (1833), *La Reine de Chypre* (1841) and even *Charles VI* (1843) were at least capable of being revived; but after *La Favorite* (1840) the only opera to enter the permanent repertoire was *Le Prophète* (1849). This was not surprising. Not only is it arguably Meyerbeer's best opera, but its author had learned by now how to insure against failure.

By 1850 the hazards of grand opera had become even greater, since the social foundation on which it rested was now withdrawn. Paris was entering the epoch of Napoleon III, whose moving spirit was not Meyerbeer but Offenbach. Yet the Académie Impériale de Musique, as it was now called, continued, like some theatrical Minotaur, to demand its yearly diet of new grand operas. Auber's *L'Enfant prodigue* (1850), Gounod's *Sapho* (1851), Halévy's *Le Juif errant* (1852), Niedermeyer's *Le Fronde* (1853), Gounod's *La Nonne sanglante* (1854) were all monumental failures, each withdrawn after a few performances and replaced with the umpteenth revival of *Robert le Diable* or *La Juive*. Two further signs of the times: in 1854 Meyerbeer brought out *L'Etoile du Nord* at the Opéra Comique, so deserting the scene of his former triumphs; the following year a new theatre, Les Bouffes Parisiens, opened under the direction of Offenbach. The first piece presented, *Les Deux Aveugles*, ended with a parody of the gambling scene from *Robert le Diable*.

Even in the 1830s the directors of the Opéra had been forced to eke out the meagre repertoire with works on a smaller scale. As well as *La Juive* and *Les Huguenots*, they had found room for Weber's *Der Freischütz* and Mozart's *Don Juan*, both with recitatives by Berlioz, not to mention Berlioz's own two-act *Benvenuto Cellini*. Nor was an internal ballet obligatory, since if the opera itself was short an independent ballet could be played at the end. The only inescapable rules were that the piece should be given in French and that the dialogue should be 'musicked' throughout.[*] By the 1840s it would seem that the smaller novelties were doing the best business. *La Favorite* even with its ballet and its traditional cuts omitted never attains the scale of Halévy or Meyerbeer. In 1846 *Lucie de Lammermoor*, with a translation originally

---

[*] Berlioz himself had to turn the spoken dialogue of his *Benvenuto Cellini* into recitative when the work was given at the Opéra, and not the Opéra Comique as originally intended.

made for the Théâtre de la Renaissance, settled happily into the repertoire with no important modification apart from a substitute cavatina for the heroine taken from the composer's *Rosmonda d'Inghilterra*. That same year *Giselle* was given together with a revival of Rossini's *Le Comte Ory*; and the two continued to furnish an attractive double bill for many years to come. Both *Jérusalem* and *Guillaume Tell* were revived more often in shortened form than in their entirety. In 1852 *Luisa Miller*, Verdi's most intimate opera to date, was given in French at the Opéra. True, it was withdrawn after eight performances; what is remarkable is that it should have been presented there in the first place, if grandiosity was the order of the day.

In opting for the grandest possible scale, Verdi was running against the current of fashion. His reason for so doing was partly no doubt the desire to measure himself against the unbeatable champion, Meyerbeer – 'to make the Jew die of an attack of publicity', as Giuseppina Strepponi put it on a later occasion.* At a deeper level, however, there was the necessity of self-renewal after the triumphs of *Rigoletto*, *Il Trovatore* and *La Traviata*, which between them had exhausted the possibilities of his operatic language as evolved so far. He was no longer content to capitalize on his assets as he had sometimes done in the mid-1840s. He wanted new horizons such as only vintage grand opera with its infinite variety of forms and scenic devices could offer.

So in the summer of 1852, with *Il Trovatore* still on the drawing-board and *La Traviata* possibly not even thought of, the search for a suitable subject began. First of all Scribe offered *Les Circassiens*, a late *pièce de sauvetage* with an exotic setting in Eastern Europe. Verdi turned it down as Meyerbeer had done before him. Scribe then produced *Wlaska, ou Les Amazones de Bohème*, having in mind Johanna Wagner, niece of the composer Richard, in the title-role. It was a modern version of the Hippolyta legend, in which an officer of Libuse's female army betrays her own side by falling in love with one of the enemy. Having read the scenario, Verdi decided that he preferred *Les Circassiens*. 'The female soldiers strike me as odd. . . . As for Mme Wagner, I agree that we should take advantage of her talent but I wouldn't want to write an opera and entrust it exclusively to her. In *Les Circassiens* there is an equally superb female role and also two others which are very fine. . . .'†

With Giuseppina at his elbow, the 'bear of Busseto' did not scruple to sweeten his objections with uncharacteristic flattery:

> I should like, I need a subject that is grandiose, impassioned and original; a mise-en-scène that is imposing and overwhelming. I have constantly in view so many of those magnificent scenes to be found in your poems, among others the Coronation in *Le Prophète*. In this scene no other composer could have done as well as Meyerbeer; but then too with such a spectacle and above all with a situation so original, grandiose and at the same time so charged with passion, no composer, however devoid of feeling, could have failed to produce a grand

---

* Letter from Giuseppina Strepponi to Escudier, 4.7.1857. *R.M.I.* (1928), pp. 14–16.

† Letter to Scribe, 18.8.1852, unpublished. Bibliothèque Nationale, Départment des Manuscrits, N.A.F. 22552. It is the first of a remarkable cache of letters from Verdi to Scribe recently brought to light by Andrew Porter, who made it the subject of a paper read at the Fourth International Congress of Verdi Studies held at Chicago 1974 and of an article 'Don't blame Scribe!' in *Opera News* (New York, April 1975).

effect! Indeed these scenes are miracles! But you work them so often that I hope you will work one for me.*

It isn't my fault if I am spoilt, difficult and exacting, but yours. Your previous poems have so worked me up, so intoxicated me, that I too must have a poem that will bring on a fever and make me cry out, 'That's it! That's how it should be! To work at once!'†

But there was still plenty of time. Only when Scribe failed to supply a synopsis by the agreed date (July 1853) did Verdi decide to go to Paris that autumn and consult with him in person. The truth was that Scribe was well beyond his prime as librettist and playwright and was beginning to run short of ideas. He suggested adapting an old libretto – Le Duc d'Albe – which he had prepared as early as 1838 for Halévy: its hero is of course the Spanish oppressor of the Netherlands in the sixteenth century, famous from the pages of Goethe's Egmont and Schiller's Don Carlos. The plot runs as follows:

Act I. Spanish officers and their men are drinking in the main square of Brussels watched with suppressed hatred by the Belgian populace. A woman appears dressed in mourning. One of the officers commands her to sing for them; she obliges with a song which develops into a rousing call to the Belgians to free themselves from their oppressors. Sensation at the discovery that she is Amélie, Count Egmont's daughter. An impending riot is forestalled by the appearance of the governor of the Netherlands, the Duke of Alba. The crowds scatter; Henri,‡ Amélie's betrothed, arrives. The Duke cross-examines him about his birth and parentage. Meeting only with scorn and defiance, he has the young man arrested.

Act II. Belgian conspirators, including Henri, mysteriously released, gather in secret at the Bierstube kept by their chief, Daniel. They are surprised by the arrival of Spanish soldiers who discover a cache of arms and barrels of gunpowder. Arrest of Daniel and Amélie, but not Henri.

Act III. Henri pleads with the Duke to spare Amélie's life, only to learn with horror that he is the Duke's illegitimate son by a Belgian woman. He visits Amélie in prison; at first suspicious of his loyalty, she is soon reconciled with him. The execution of Daniel and Amélie is imminent. The Duke promises their freedom if Henri will acknowledge him as his father. After agonized hesitation, Henri agrees. Fury of Daniel and of Amélie, who later in a rendez-vous with Henri declares her intention of murdering the Duke.

Act IV. As he is about to embark for Spain, the Duke is approached by Amélie as a suppliant. She draws a dagger to stab him, but Henri interposes himself and is mortally wounded.

The contract was signed, the text delivered in time; but Halévy withdrew. The libretto was next offered to Donizetti, who seemed enthusiastic at first but took an unconscionable time over the music, continually setting it aside to fulfil more

---

* Letter to Scribe, 27.7.1852, quoted in translation in Opera News.
† Letter to Scribe, 18.8.1852.
‡ In the Italian translation he becomes Marcello.

congenial commissions. The score was still unfinished when Léon Pillet took over the direction of the Opéra. He disliked the subject and refused to consider it. A long wrangle followed between Scribe and the management, both sides safely invoking the name of Donizetti since he himself was mostly in Vienna at the time and his memory no longer reliable. Finally in 1844 Scribe sued the directorate and won his case, with an award of 15,000 francs damages. Even so he was not to let the matter rest. After Donizetti's death in 1848 he induced Pillet's successor Roqueplan to try to recover the score from the composer's effects. After much negotiation with the heirs, they obtained permission for a performance, merely to discover that the music was still incomplete. The first two acts only were orchestrated, the rest existed in short score.* Verdi's visit in 1853 gave Scribe his long-awaited chance for a salvage operation. He described it in a letter to his collaborator Charles Duveyrier, now in retirement from the theatrical world.

I have in no way forgotten our old offspring who has long been asleep in the dust of the shelves: but I don't think he will have lost anything at all by waiting, and I have just found him an establishment worthy of his age and his merit.

Verdi is in Paris – I have been asked for an opera for him. He has a contract with the directorate, according to which the director undertakes to mount this opera next year, in 1854. . . . Verdi, on his part (and modesty should prevent me from bringing this clause to your notice), demands as his first condition that the poem he is to be given should be by your old ally. . . .

As always I had several subjects purely of my own in mind, but then I had the bright idea of resuscitating that poor *Duc d'Albe* whom everyone believed dead on the grounds that he had already had a magnificent funeral amounting to 15,000 francs. But you will recall that in accepting those 15,000 francs I had reserved for you all rights in the dead man as well as the right to bring him back to life at will.

I suggested him to Verdi without concealing from him any of the adventures of the deceased. Several situations suited him: many things about it he disliked.

Firstly that the work had been intended of old for Donizetti, and that it would have been like treating a subject that had been cast off, deflowered, that had been around too long, in a word that had been dug out from the back of the shop. 'The title would have to be changed.' I agreed without difficulty. 'Change the principal character.' That was more difficult, almost impossible. However, I think I got to the root of the matter. We should have to change the scene of the action, to place it in a climate less cold than that of the Low Countries; a climate full of warmth and music such as Naples or Sicily. That was not so difficult and I did it.

Finally we should have to change the whole of the second act since there are no beer halls in that country; likewise the fourth act representing the embarcation and departure of the Duke of Alba, and lastly add a fifth act since he wants a fine, grand work in five acts on the same vast scale as *Les Huguenots* or *Le Prophète*. . . .†

---

* Franco Schlitzer, *Mondo teatrale dell'ottocènto* (Naples, 1954), pp. 98–109. In fact the autograph which exists in Ricordi's archives reveals substantial lacunae even in the first two acts.

† Letter from Scribe to Duveyrier, 3.12.1853. P. Bonnefon, 'Les Metamorphoses d'un opéra', in *Revue des deux mondes* (Paris, Sept. 1917), pp. 887–9; in translation in *Opera News*.

Duveyrier made no difficulty. Scribe then expounded his notions in greater detail.

> Verdi wanted a Neapolitan setting. We have had *La Muette de Portici*, and that would have recalled it; I suggested Sicily and he accepted.
>
> The Duke of Alba becomes Charles de Montfort, hated governor of Sicily under the reign of Charles d'Anjou, brother of St Louis. . . . Charles de Montfort and the French lose no time in paying court to the pretty girls, and carrying them off if need be. Charles de Montfort has carried off or raped one of them, by whom he has had a son: this son, Luigi de Torella, will replace Henri de Bruges.
>
> Daniel, the master brewer, a somewhat insignificant role, will be replaced by Jean de Procida, life and soul of the conspiracy, and as you see we come straight to the *Sicilian Vespers* by way of dénouement.
>
> This title belonging to Delavigne's tragedy doesn't frighten me in the least for the Opéra. It's a fine title and a well known subject at the Opéra always has a good chance of success.
>
> In place of the Flemings, who want to massacre the Spaniards and can't, there will be the Sicilians – furious, outraged and vindictive – who do massacre the French. . . .
>
> The title and the dénouement will be the same as in Casimir Delavigne, but the plot will be different and far more original.*

It was not the first time that a well known title had been borrowed from a different story. Bellini and Pepoli had taken that of a French translation of Scott's *Old Mortality* for their own *Puritani di Scozia*. Later Scribe hastened to assure an unnamed correspondent† that in *Les Vêpres Siciliennes* the Duke of Alba had merely sent his luggage to Palermo.‡ According to Scribe, Verdi had been delighted with the scheme: 'Although it was old he liked the work; he even deigned to tell me that it was like old wine and that it had gained by long bottling'.

On the face of it this flagrantly contradicts Verdi's own version of events recounted many years later. In 1881 Giovannina Lucca acquired Donizetti's autograph, and commissioned Angelo Zanardini to translate the text and one Matteo Salvi to complete the music. The result she submitted to a commission of professors from the Milan Conservatory, who pronounced it basically authentic (standards of editing were evidently free and easy at that period since Salvi's work of reconstruction would certainly not pass muster today). By then *Les Vêpres Siciliennes* had long been a repertory piece; so that when the first performance of the *Duca d'Alba* took place in Rome the resemblance between the two operas did not escape attention – especially since Salvi composed his own prelude very much in the style of Verdi's overture, i.e. in E minor with an abundance of death-figures. Soon afterwards Verdi wrote to a friend, the senator Giuseppe Piroli, 'I never knew that Scribe had made use of the *Duke of Alba* to write the *Sicilian Vespers*. It's true, however, that Vasselli§ did speak to me of it en passant when I was in Rome for *Un Ballo in maschera* in 1859,

---

* Letter from Scribe to Duveyrier, undated. Bonnefon, pp. 889–93.

† Andrew Porter suggests very plausibly that it was Charles Nuitter, himself author of a *Jean de Procida* as yet unperformed.

‡ Undated but evidently subsequent to the opera's first performance. *Ibid.*, pp. 894–5.

§ Donizetti's brother-in-law and one of his executors.

but I took no notice and thought it to be just a suspicion, an idea of Vasselli's. Now I understand and I really do believe that the *Sicilian Vespers* are taken from the *Duke of Alba*.'*

True, Verdi in later life had a way of forgetting what he did not wish to remember. What he may not have realized at the time was that Scribe had made use of actual verses from the original libretto, notably in Acts I and III. After all, Felice Romani was able to write two different texts for Vaccai's *Giulietta e Romeo* and Bellini's *I Capuleti e i Montecchi*. Why should Scribe not have done likewise?

Scribe meanwhile was genuinely enthusiastic about the transformation, of which he gave an act-by-act account to Duveyrier who he hoped would help him over matters of detail. The actual moulding of the verses Scribe would do himself as he had always done for Meyerbeer (Verdi would expect no less). The original scenario was even more grandiose than the final working-out. Act I was to be full of dances and festivities ('I shall not make the French as odious as the Spaniards . . .') during which Procida would try in vain to rouse the Sicilians to revolt. Act II was to be an updated, more ruthless version of 'the rape of the Sabine women' and would take place during a solemn festivity in honour of the Virgin. Acts III and IV as we know them. Act V to begin with a duet between Hélène and Procida in which the latter explains that the vespers bell that will toll for their wedding will be a signal for the massacre. The Archbishop of Palermo to preside over the wedding ceremony that is so calamitously interrupted.

That it was a vast improvement on the original *Duc d'Albe* Scribe had no doubt. It was a plausible subject for an Italian who wished to challenge the composer of *Les Huguenots* on his own ground. It was well known at a time when the unification of Italy was still a burning question and Paris full of exiled patriots. The main difference between Verdi's subject and Meyerbeer's was that while the Massacre of St Bartholomew's Eve was history, that of the Sicilian Vespers is a historical myth though its context is true enough. After the crumbling of the Hohenstaufen dynasty in Southern Italy in the mid-thirteenth century and a brief period of urban republics owing allegiance to the Pope, Manfred, illegitimate son of the former emperor, succeeded in rallying the Ghibelline cause and setting up a feudal kingdom of Sicily. The Pope then appealed to the various sovereigns of Europe for a future ruler of Southern Italy and eventually prevailed on Louis IX of France to send his brother Charles of Anjou. Manfred was defeated at the battle of Benevento in 1266; another Ghibelline force under the emperor's son Conrad and his cousin Frederick of Austria suffered the same fate. In both cases the victors took a brutal revenge. Charles of Anjou moved his capital from Palermo to Naples from which he planned a war with Michael Palaeologue, Emperor of Byzantium. Sicily was ruled in his absence with the utmost ferocity. In 1282 there was a general uprising leading to a war which ended with the expulsion of the French and the establishment of Spanish rule over the island.

So much is fact. The fictional side of the story concerns one Giovanni da or di Procida and his part in the uprising. He himself was real enough; a celebrated doctor of the time, formerly physician to the Manfred who took part in the insurrection of Conrad (or Corradino), suffered the loss of his wife and daughter and went into

---

* Letter to Piroli, 16.1.1882. *Carteggi Verdiani*, III, p. 152.

exile. At the court of Queen Constanza of Aragon he was given a cordial welcome and the governorship of Lusca, Benizzero and Palma.

All this can be learned from Busceni's *Vita di Giovanni da Procida* written not long after his death. According to legend, however, it was Procida who planned the uprising in 1282 in which the vespers bell was used as a signal for a massacre which destroyed the entire French force in Palermo in a single day. No such massacre ever occurred; only an uncoordinated rebellion throughout the island; and Giovanni da Procida was in Spain when it happened. Nevertheless the myth had a wide circulation in the epoch preceding the Risorgimento, when Procida was regarded as a forerunner of men like Giuseppe Mazzini. A play, an opera, even a novel on the subject was excellent material for nationalist propaganda.

A typical instance was Niccolini's *Giovanni di Procida* of 1832 which was developed into the novel *Giovanni da Procida, o I Vespri Siciliani* by one Omero Fiori (Leghorn, 1843), and an opera by Prince Poniatowski given at the Teatro del Giglio, Lucca, in 1840 with Giorgio Ronconi in the title role. Here Giovanni da Procida returns secretly from exile to find his daughter Imelda, who thought him dead, secretly married to the French knight Tancredi. His fury is increased when he finds that Tancredi is the son of the former governor Eribert who had ravished his (Procida's) wife and killed his son. While the massacre is being plotted by Procida and his henchman Gualtiero, it transpires that Imelda and Tancredi have the same mother. Tancredi is killed during the massacre having previously refused to denounce Procida to the French authorities. In the opera, needless to say, Tancredi and Imelda are only betrothed; in the play they have a son.

It was left to another Italian patriot, Michele Amari, to explode the entire basis of this farrago. Though written with passionate commitment which rendered it unacceptable to the Neapolitan censors, his *History of the War of the Sicilian Vespers* of 1846 is fact, not fiction. In his introduction he states roundly:

> I think I have demonstrated that the (so-called) Vespri did not arise from any conspiracy; it was merely a riot which was occasioned by the insolence of those in power and whose origin and strength are to be sought in the social and political conditions of a people who were neither willing nor prone to endure a domination that was both tyrannical and foreign. Such recent documents as can shed light on the origin of this revolt, including letters from Charles d'Anjou himself, and others from the Sicilians not to speak of hitherto unpublished Papal bulls, all confirm this conclusion.*

He mentions, however, an incident which occurred on 31 March during a festival held at the Church of Santo Spirito in Palermo. A French officer, Drouet, and his men joined in the dances and handled the women with great freedom on the pretence of searching them for hidden weapons. At this a riot broke out which proved impossible to control. But of Giovanni da Procida not a word. Traditions die hard, however. In 1855 the year of Verdi's opera, Ricciardi's play *Il Vespro Siciliano* was published with an apology for mixing fact with legend, rather like that of the science fiction writer who exploits the habitual caution of scientific pronouncements to suggest that it is not absolutely out of the question that there should be life on Venus.

* M. Amari, *La Guerra del Vespro Siciliano* (Lucca, 1852), p. 12.

Another more sophisticated working of the theme should be mentioned – namely Casimir Delavigne's *Les Vêpres Siciliennes* first produced at the Théâtre del Odéon in 1819 and revived at the Théâtre Français in 1832 – as it seems to have provided Scribe with a pattern for his treatment of the French as well as with the surname of his baritone lead. Once again Procida returns from exile to set his country free; but this time it is his son Loredan who confuses the issue, having struck up a friendship with the young governor of Palermo, Roger de Montfort, a swashbuckling d'Artagnan-like character, hot-headed but generous. The friendship is shaken by the discovery that Roger aspires to the hand of Loredan's fiancee Amélie, sister of the executed Corradino. High words follow and Loredan joins the conspirators. Amélie, secretly in love with Roger, warns him that his life is in danger. Procida and Loredan are imprisoned, but Loredan, to his chagrin, is set free, since Roger is incapable of bearing a grudge. For the rest of the play Loredan oscillates between allegiance to his father's cause and to Roger. When the massacre occurs (described to Amélie by her confidante in the classical tradition) Roger is stabbed by Loredan in order to save Procida. Loredan then kills himself leaving Procida to close the play with:

> O mon pays
> Je t'ai rendu l'honneur, mais j'ai perdu mon fils,
> Pardonne-moi ces pleurs qu'à peine je dévore.
> Soyez prêts à combattre au retour de l'aurore!

Indeed Delavigne's Procida is not one to spare much thought for the fate of any individual. His programme had been made very clear to Loredan earlier:

> Femmes, enfants, vieillards, tous ceux que l'aillance,
> L'amitié, l'interêt asservit à la France,
> Confondus avec eux, frappés des mêmes coups
> Suivront dans le cercueil leurs ombres en courroux.

In the course of the opera we may have occasion to recall the lines with which Amélie repulses unwillingly the advances of Roger:

> Une invincible obstacle à jamais nous sépare
> L'ombre de Corradin, sanglant, percé de coups
> Terrible vous repousse et se place entre nous.

It will be noted that in all the versions of the Sicilian Vespers legend so far mentioned, Procida, like Massaniello or William Tell, always has a private, family reason for action as well as a patriotic one. This was an essential feature of the nineteenth-century melodramatic tradition, without which the audience's sympathy could not be guaranteed. Scribe was evidently aware of this from the start and wrote to Duveyrier:

> There's a point on which I'm still undecided; you can help me. According to history, Jean Procida, who was a doctor's son and a doctor himself, was dishonoured in the matter of his wife. We could suppose that his wife had been raped by Charles de Montfort, that she had a child by him, whom Procida accepted as his own in order to conceal his shame; but he knows perfectly well it isn't his. It's our old friend Henri de Bruges whom he brings up to hate the French

and above all Charles de Montfort, and he puts a dagger in his hand to kill his own father.

This is very Sicilian. It would be perfect for a play; I'm not sure whether at the Opéra where everything has to be simple it might not complicate the action too much. But it's a good idea. In that case Hélène could be the sister of the young Frédéric who had been beheaded with his friend Conradin by Charles d'Anjou and the French.

Alternatively our old friend Henri de Bruges could be Luigi di Torella, son of a noble Sicilian lady, no matter whom, and Hélène could be . . . Procida's daughter. Think about it and decide.*

Presumably Duveyrier opted for the compromise whereby Hélène is Frédéric's sister, over whom Procida exercises a disinterested guardianship, while Henri remains Henri and independent. Procida is merely a resistance fighter with no personal axe to grind – a fact of which Verdi was to complain bitterly later on.

Once the subject had been agreed, he first directed his attention to Act II. He wrote to De Sanctis in Naples, asking him to send to Paris any treatises that he knew of concerning the customs of Palermo and in particular the annual festival at Monte Solitario or Santa Rosalia. 'Is it a religious festival or also a secular one? Does it have anything peculiar to it, a dance or something of the sort? . . . and during what period was it founded?'†

On the last day of 1853, Scribe's libretto arrived duly completed and Verdi professed himself entirely satisfied with it.‡ By mid-January he was able to write back to De Sanctis with thanks for his information and a further request:

> . . . but for this you'll need to consult Coutreau [*a music publisher*] . . . I would like to know whether the Tarantella is invariably in the minor key and in 6/8 rhythm. . . . If there's an example of one in the major and in a different rhythm please send it to me. . . . I'd also like to know whether there is a local folk dance other than the tarantella; if there is, send me that as well. I know that at Naples they give a ballet called *The Sicilian Vespers* or *Giovanni di Procida* . . . send me the synopsis of it in the same parcel. . . . I still can't tell you the name of the opera because I don't know it [!]. This may surprise you but it's true. All I can tell you is that the scene of the action will be Naples or Sicily, probably the latter; and as the plot is pure fiction I thought of calling it at a later stage *Paolo* or *Pietro* or *Maria* or *Posilipo* or *The Cave of Santa Rosalia* or what have you. *La Muette de Portici* could have had dozens of different titles. . . .§

Presumably De Sanctis read between the lines. One can understand Verdi's reluctance to be explicit since the subject was an explosive one in the Kingdom of the Two Sicilies and he had no wish to prejudice the opera's chances of a later performance in Italian in Naples. It was not until November when rehearsals had long since been under way that Verdi felt able to tell De Sanctis outright, 'The title is:

---

* Letter from Scribe to Duveyrier, undated. Bonnefon, pp. 889–93.
† In letter to De Sanctis, 4.12.1853. *Carteggi Verdiani*, I, pp. 21–2.
‡ See accompanying note from Deligne, 31.12.1853. *Copialettere*, p. 152.
§ Letter to De Sanctis, 18.1.1854. *Carteggi Verdiani*, I, pp. 22–3.

The Sicilian Vespers — a tough subject for our censors!'* By this time, as we shall see, an alternative setting had been found with Scribe's help.

Verdi set to work on it slowly. 'I am writing very slowly,' he told the Countess Giuseppina Appiani, 'in fact you could even say that I'm not writing at all. I don't know how it happens but the libretto is always there in the same place.'† A few days later he had the opportunity of seeing the première of Meyerbeer's *L'Etoile du Nord*, preceded by a barrage of publicity. He wrote in disgust to the Countess Maffei:

> The fact is that I am not a millionaire and what few francs I've managed to earn by the sweat of my brow I don't intend to spend on advertisements, claques and all such muck. Yet that's what you seem to need for a success here. A few days ago Dumas wrote in his paper, '. . . What a misfortune that Rossini didn't bring out his masterpieces in 1854! It is true of course he never had that German flair for knowing how to make a success simmer for six months beforehand on the hot-plate of the newspapers and so prepare an explosion of understanding on the first night.' That's very true. I was at the first performance of *L'Etoile du Nord* and understood little or nothing of it; while this good public understood everything and found it all sublime, beautiful, divine! . . . and this same public even after twenty-five or thirty years hasn't even managed to understand *Guillaume Tell*, and so it's performed in a stunted mutilated version in three acts instead of five and with a mise-en-scène unworthy of it. And this is the first theatre in the world. . . .‡

After hearing the gratifying news of *La Traviata*'s success, Verdi set out for Mandres where, during the next three months, he worked on the new score. By September he could write to De Sanctis, 'I have barely written four acts of my French opera. I still have to do the fifth, the ballet and the instrumentation. When I've finished I shall be very happy. An opera for the Opéra is enough work to kill a bull. Five hours of music? Hauf. . . .'§

Then came an unexpected hitch. Sofia Cruvelli (Sophie Crüwel) who was to create the role of Hélène, was a German soprano with a reputation for eccentricity. During a performance of *Les Huguenots* in October she quietly vanished from the scene and was not heard of for several weeks. Verdi seized the occasion to ask Roqueplan for his contract to be rescinded, on the grounds that Cruvelli was irreplaceable and that it was better to be unknown than to be misunderstood; he refused equally the counterproposals of the minister for the fine arts, Fould, that they should either give one of his Italian works in a French translation or that he should write a new piece for them in three acts. 'There is only one policy for me to adopt; to score a real and decisive success and present myself on your stage with a Grand Opera: either to bring it off or to have done with it ever after.'¶

But his preparations to return home were cut short by the sudden reappearance of la Cruvelli, who proceeded to resume her place as Valentine and to continue

---

* Letter to De Sanctis, 29.11.1854. *Carteggi Verdiani*, I, p. 27.

† Letter to Giuseppina Appiani, 25.2.1854. *Copialettere*, p. 538.

‡ Letter to Clarina Maffei, 2.3.1854. *Copialettere*, pp. 539–40.

§ Letter to De Sanctis, 9.9.1854. *Carteggi Verdiani*, I, pp. 26–7.

¶ Letter to Roqueplan, 28.10.1854. *Copialettere*, pp. 154–5.

rehearsing the new opera. She had been on a premarital honeymoon with her future husband Baron Vigier. But she had cost Roqueplan his job. At the beginning of the year he was replaced by Crosnier from the Opéra Comique. No sooner had the new incumbent taken office than he received a long letter of remonstrance from Verdi.

It is both saddening and humiliating for me that M. Scribe is not taking the trouble to put right this fifth act which everyone agrees in finding dull. I am not unaware that M. Scribe has a thousand other things to do which perhaps he has more to heart than my opera! . . . but if I could have had any suspicion of this sovereign indifference I would have stayed in my own country. . . .

I had hoped that M. Scribe (since the situation seems to me to lend itself to this) would have found to finish the drama one of those moving pieces which bring tears to the eyes and whose effect is always sure. I would point out, Monsieur, that this would have made all the difference to the work in general which is totally lacking in pathos, except for the romance in the fourth act.

I had hoped that M. Scribe would have had the goodness to appear from time to time at the rehearsals to put right certain awkwardnesses in the words or lines which are difficult to sing; to see if the numbers needed revising, or even the acts, etc., etc. For instance, the second, third and fourth all have the same cut: an Air, a Duo, then a Finale.

Finally, I was counting on the fact that M. Scribe, as he had promised me right from the beginning, would have altered everything that attacked the honour of the Italians. The more I think about this subject the more I am convinced that it is dangerous. It wounds the French because they are massacred; it wounds the Italians because M. Scribe, in altering Procida's historical character, has made him – according to his favourite system – a common conspirator with a dagger in his hand. For God's sake, there are virtues and crimes in the history of every people and we are no worse than the rest. In any event I am Italian above all and come what may I will never be an accessory to any injury done to my country.

Certainly, no other version of the Sicilian Vespers story centres so little interest on Procida.

Verdi went on to complain of the superior attitude of various members of the company and ended once again by demanding an annulment of his contract.* When the only reply was a summons to a rehearsal, he retorted with a curt note to the effect that he had no intention of setting foot in the theatre unless either the difficulties he had mentioned were resolved, or his contract was declared null and void.† What steps were taken to appease him, whether the faults of which he complained were remedied and to what extent we shall never be sure; but rehearsals proceeded smoothly once more.

The letter to Crosnier has done great harm to Le Vêpres Siciliennes in the eyes of posterity, since it seems to condemn the opera in advance. It is true that Scribe had not worked the miracle for which Verdi had hoped, and never would; and after the mishaps and delays of the autumn it was natural that Verdi should want to make the most of his grievances. But that Scribe, however tardily, did his best to meet the

---

* Letter to Crosnier, 3.1.1855. *Copialettere*, pp. 157–9.
† Letter to Crosnier, 9.1.1855. *Copialettere*, p. 160.

composer's demands, is made clear both by their correspondence and by the existence of various drafts of the libretto. Not all the changes in the text can be accounted for by Verdi's letters, since he and Scribe had frequent meetings during the period concerned, though not as frequent as the composer would have liked. Then too many of the later letters are undated and their order uncertain. Indeed, Verdi himself often confuses the issue by asking for material with which he later dispensed. To trace the opera's genesis in detail would therefore be difficult and largely a matter of guesswork. We will attempt no more than a brief survey taking the text as our starting-point.

Evidently the plan for Act I as described to Duveyrier was quickly abandoned for a scheme corresponding almost exactly to that of *Le Duc d'Albe*. But apart from Robert when in his cups, the French are altogether more likeable than their Spanish counterparts. They are no less feared, however. Following the insult offered to Hélène there was an interchange between the maidservant Ninette and her fiancé Danieli which obviously had to go:

NINETTE Défends-la! Sois un peu courageux!
DANIELI   Ah j'y tâche
         Car autant que toi je les haïs.
         Mais même qu'en voyant ce français,
         Même qu'en apercevant l'ombre de son panache,
         Un froid mortel se glisse dans mes veines.
NINETTE (*avec mépris*)   Ah, lâche!
         Et tu crois m'épouser.

The quartet was originally a trio for Ninette, Hélène and Montfort, who began by apostrophizing the islanders as 'Race faible et poltronne' – a line that was removed from the score at Verdi's insistence, but which remained in the printed libretto.* At the end of the act, when Henri had disappeared into Hélène's palace in defiance of Montfort, Béthune and Vaudemont entered with a platoon of soldiers. 'Ordonnez-vous qu'il meure?' Béthune asks; to which Montfort replies, 'Pas encore.' As late as mid-September, Verdi was asking for these lines to be retained; but they vanished from the final version of the scene together with Béthune, Vaudemont and the platoon.

The second act began with a different recitative and aria for Procida, which Verdi completed in short score (melody and bass only) with indications for an introduction based on the same material as in the definitive version, though less elaborately developed.† The aria 'O Sicile, ma patrie' is in standard French ternary form with a central episode in which the repeated words 'levez-vous' provide an opportunity of working in the ubiquitous gesture ♫♩. The turn from major to relative minor coincides with the words 'joug de la tyrannie', a clever and sensitive touch, while the vacillation between minor and major in the second limb is a trait that will typify much of the opera, though affecting Henri and Hélène more than Procida as finally realized.

* See letter to Scribe, No. 8, 13.9.1854.
† The autograph is in the Bibliothèque de l'Opéra, Paris (A.Rés. 587 supplt).

104

PROCIDA *cantabile*

O Si - ci - le, o ma pa - tri - e, Du joug de la ty - ran -

- ni - - e Puis - se j'en - fin t'af - fran - chir, te voir li - bre

et puis mou - rir, Te voir li - bre et puis mou - rir

Precisely how Verdi would have harmonized, let alone scored it; whether he would have modified it in the final realization, one cannot be sure. Certainly it is inferior to the aria which eventually replaced it. The substitution must have happened at a late stage since none of the versions of the texts in the Bibliothèque Nationale nor those in the Archives contain the words of 'Et toi Palerme' or the cabaletta that follows it. One of the last of Verdi's letters to Scribe, however, begs him to change the 'tirade' of Procida's henchman Mainfroid, which occurred soon after Procida's arrival:

MAINFROID Des conjurés tremblants à peine un petit nombre
Au rendez-vous donné, dans le caverne sombre
Ont-ils osé venir? 'C'est fête,' disent-ils!
L'on conduit avec pompe à Sainte Rosalie
Les douze fiancés que la ville marie!

'You can talk of the fête,' Verdi wrote, 'but in a different way. Don't worry about the lines [i.e., preserving the metre] because I shall change the music.* There is nothing further on the subject; but in the final version we see the 'petit nombre' assembling at Mainfroid's summons and joining with Procida in the cabaletta 'Dans l'ombre et la silence'. It is now Hélène who mentions the fête as a suitable occasion for causing an affray. In what seems to be a second draft of the scene further contemptuous references to Sicilian cowardice were introduced, which had later to be toned down. For instance the first exchanges between Henri and Procida in the definitive version originally ran thus:

* Letter to Scribe, No. 11, undated.

HENRI   Ce peuple qui s'indigne, impatient d'entrave,
          Ne veut pas être libre et *ne sait* qu'être esclave
PROCIDA Enflammons son courroux! *et contre l'ennemi*
          Marchons!
HENRI   *J'ai tenté*
PROCIDA   *Qu'a-t-il fait?*
HENRI   *Il a fui!*
HÉLÈNE *Le laissant prisonnier.*

In the final version the Sicilians did not flee; they merely hesitated.

Of the grand duet for Henri and Hélène, two spacious parallel verses beginning 'Oh pitié, madame' were replaced by the pithier dialogue of couplets that we know today ('Comment dans ma reconnaissance'). For the barcarole in the finale Verdi first requested a change of metre from seven- to eight-syllable verse;* then he decided for musical reasons to add women to the chorus in order to make a greater contrast with the Sicilians in the foreground; 'Only as they can't say:

> Et toi, ma belle adorée
>
> . . . .
>
> Viens et comme Citherée
> Sois la reine des amours

you will have to adjust the lines so that they can be sung by women too.'† Scribe duly obliged, though for some reason the original lines remained in the printed libretto.

In Act III, whose first scene derives mostly from *Le Duc d'Albe*, there are alternative versions for the start of the Montfort/Henri duet. Nor is it surprising that the original nine-syllable chorus that opens the finale ('Plaisirs joyeux! Transports d'ivresse') had to be changed for one of six syllables ('O fête brillante'). No Italian of that time could be expected to make a period out of a 'novenario'; accordingly that metre is confined to the parlanti throughout the scene. Scribe's first draft of this 'scène à faire' envisaged an ingenious interweaving of chorus and corps de ballet. 'The divertissement ends with a dance from the south, a kind of farandole or galop in which the dancers linked in couples form a column which extends into the adjoining salons. After the dancers have dispersed into the salons on the right the music can still be heard.' Apparently this crocodile would have re-entered the stage more than once during the scene so causing the conspirators to break off their conversation. In the 'farandole' perhaps lies the explanation of Verdi's remarkably late request to De Sanctis: 'I would like you to send me a Sicilian song or air or whatever. But I want a real Siciliana, that's to say a folksong and not a song manufactured by your composers; in fact the finest, the most characteristic that there is . . .'‡ However, when De Sanctis supplied a few specimens, Verdi pronounced them undistinguished and in any case it was now too late. The ballet meanwhile became a self-contained dance of the seasons and the following scene developed against a background of dance music with no specific local associations.

---

* Letter to Scribe, No. 5, 7.6.1854.
† Letter to Scribe, No. 9, 15.9.1854.
‡ Letter to De Sanctis, 10.4.1855. *Carteggi Verdiani*, I, pp. 30–1.

In the shaping of the final two acts Verdi himself played a much larger part than the letter to Crosnier would suggest. An opening scene in Act IV between Robert, Henri and the gaoler was cut. The text of Henri's aria was written three times. First as 'Anges des cieux, éloignez d'elle' it doubtless recalled too strongly the Donizettian 'Ange si pur' which had found its way from *Le Duc d'Albe* into *La Favorite*, to become as 'Spirto gentil' one of the most famous arias in the tenor repertory. The second version is a large ternary design ('D'impatience et d'espérance') with a central episode in a new metre ('Fortune cruelle, tu viens m'accabler') and a brief 'strette' ('Oui mon trouble augmente'). It is presumably to the definitive 'O jour de peine' that Verdi refers in an undated letter 'If you've written the air for Gueymard have the goodness to send it to me, because I've got to give it to the copyist soon so that Gueymard can learn it.'* The original duet for Henri and Hélène was quite short, with Henri revealing his shameful secret straightaway and Hélène at once forgiving him. Verdi however decided to make this the principal love duet of the score and so had it expanded.

From there on the drama was intended to follow the third act of *Le Duc d'Albe*, *mutatis mutandis*. Robert would enter and conduct Hélène and Procida to the scaffold, while distant monks would chant a *De Profundis*. Henri would be joined by Montfort, now willing to pardon the conspirators if the young man will only acknowledge him as his father. Béthune, watching from a window, would describe the proud carriage of the victims and the main formal number would be a trio for him, Montfort and Henri (the equivalents of Albe, Henri and Sandoval in the original libretto). But then we read in a letter of Verdi's: 'Have you thought of the quartet which you said you would be willing to write for the fourth act? If we could find the right situation (apart from the musical advantage) there would be much to gain from making the fine voices of Cruvelli, Gueymard, Morelli and Aubin [sic] heard in a quartet.'† And later: 'I have not yet written the scene of the fourth act. As it is at present I find it very beautiful. It is so well developed, so musical in its contrast between the *De Profundis* offstage and the situation of the characters on stage that we can make something really fine of it; but if you've thought of something still better, so that the quartet will form the most dramatic moment in the opera, I am delighted.'‡

So the Act IV quartet was evidently Verdi's idea, and Scribe accordingly removed the trio and the recitatives associated with it. Verdi himself at first wanted several of these back again so as to prepare more dramatically for Henri's exclamation of 'Mon père!' In a long letter written towards the end of August, he set out in detail his scheme whereby, after the slow concertato of the quartet, Hélène and Procida would be escorted to execution while Béthune as before supplied a running commentary from the window. Henri would then acknowledge his father out of earshot of the intended victims, as in *Le Duc d'Albe*. Later, as we know, he changed his mind, brought forward the cry of 'Mon père!' to the end of the *De Profundis* and made Scribe shorten and even eliminate many of the lines that he had originally asked for. From the start, however, he saw the finale as formed out of the stretta of the quartet

* Letter to Scribe, No. 3, undated.
† Letter to Scribe, No. 5, 7.6.1854. Vincenzo Morelli was of course eventually replaced by Bonnehée.
‡ Letter to Scribe, No. 6, 14.6.1854.

with chorus added. Scribe's scheme had been more grandiose, including a separate 'Choeur des Buveurs' ('Buvons toujours').*

But Verdi's most sweeping changes were reserved for the fifth act. Here Scribe had originally given the prima donna pride of place in a vast, spectacular canvas. There was to be a chorus of bridesmaids offering flowers to the bride ('En ce jour l'amitié fidèle'). Like Agathe, Hélène would shudder at the sight of them. Then came her grand aria ('Tout respire un air de fête') with a central episode where she begs for forgiveness from her brother's ghost, and a coda of prayer to her patron saint, oddly described as a 'cavatine'. Henri would enter to sing a 'couplet' number ('L'ombre descend dans la vallée') with Hélène supplying the final refrain, varied for each strophe with a somewhat irritating neatness ('Je t'aime et j'ai peur. . . . Je t'aime et je n'ai plus peur'). Next a chorus 'Que dans cette heureuse journée' during which Daniéli would slip Hélène a note warning of the massacre to follow her assent to the wedding. Enter Montfort with the Cardinal Legate; all present kneel in prayer ('Dieu puissant, Dieu de justice'). As the Cardinal Legate was about to pronounce the couple man and wife, Hélène would draw back so provoking a concertato of varying reactions. Finally Montfort would overcome her hesitation; the Vespers bell ring out and the massacre begin. Montfort's original rebuke to his murderers was certainly not of the kind to appeal to Verdi:

> MONTFORT Pour eux, honte éternelle!
> Soccomber par la trahison
> Vaut mieux que de vaincre par elle.

Scribe's denouements are rarely satisfactory, though few are quite so preposterous as that of *Le Prophète*. His fifth acts usually move back from the (relatively) intimate plane of Act IV to the spectacular and the impersonal, with the main characters standing out in sensational relief. As first set out, Act V of *Les Vêpres Siciliennes* has all the faults of the weaker grand operas such as *Dom Sébastien* and Bizet's *Ivan IV*, with their pointless comings and goings of choral masses. Verdi on the other hand, once he had reached to the inner feelings of his characters, preferred to stay with them. In defiance of Solera's intentions, he had finished his *Attila* with a confrontation of principals. In the final act of *Les Vêpres*, he was to steer Scribe in the same direction, though somewhat deviously to judge from the correspondence.

He began by asking for the opening chorus to be expanded by a chorus of men in the wings. 'The Sicilian populace, the French soldiers drink, sing and dance for the pardon granted by Montfort. This would be a really happy chorus and we could have it accompanied by nacres, *tambours de basque*, guitars, etc. It would also make a contrast with what comes afterwards.' For the metrical pattern, he took one of the discarded versions of Henri's air in Act IV ('Fortune cruelle, Tu viens m'accabler') as being especially suitable for the 3/8 melody he had in mind. The result was 'Célébrons ensemble, l'hymen glorieux', with the modest castanets and side drums replacing the original specification. The end of Hélène's aria would not do: 'There must be something to suggest an allegro; and Procida, being on stage, could well contribute a line or two.'† Later, 'I've received the chorus and the air of Act V. The

---

* Letter to Scribe, No. 7, 29.8.1854.
† *Ibid.*

chorus is fine. About the air I shall have something to say, but there will be time for us to talk about it.'* With the next reference (undated) a note of irritation creeps in. 'You have written another cavatine for Hélène and all I needed was a simple allegro of eight lines to finish the piece, together with some lines for Procida. Besides, these lines are too short and perhaps have not enough force to finish a grand air for Cruvelli.' He went on to complain that the ensemble of a duo (which?) was not as they had agreed between them; that the design had nothing new about it and 'the lines are insufficiently harmonious for me to write a strongly rhythmical tune for them'. Back then to Hélène's aria. 'For the moment I need a beautiful cantabile in place of "Tout respire un air de fête". I find it impossible to make a melodic sentence from three lines.' (Scribe's original cantabile had indeed a three-line scheme.) 'I must have four, that is to say eight. Try and give them a more pathetic twist, and make the rhythm that of "Ami le cœur d'Hélène"!'† In the end there was a compromise. Scribe supplied lines in the desired rhythm ('Merci, jeunes amies') to be set by Verdi in a single allegro movement. This must have been agreed upon verbally, since there is no hint of it in correspondence about it. However, the letter just quoted contains an important postscript.

> I have thought hard about the finale to the fifth act. It seems to me there is nothing to be done with the prayer 'O Dieu puissant' as we can't have everyone on the stage there and so we would have no musical effect. The ensemble that follows Hélène's 'Non' holds up the action which at this point should move really fast. It's true we could cut the prayer and the ensemble but then we shouldn't have any more music. You will say that that would not be a disaster, but it would be bad business for me. Would you give it a little thought? I will do the same. . . .

Between that and the next letter, it is clear that the problem has been solved by cutting the prayer and replacing the ensemble with a terzetto for Henri, Hélène and Procida.‡ When Henri's air 'L'ombre descend dans la vallée' turned into the present 'mélodie' we have no means of knowing. But meanwhile the act had lost all its meaningless grandiosity. Hélène's solo is as happy and unselfconscious as the Polonaise from I Puritani, Henri's mélodie a poetic declaration of love. If both are decorative rather than dramatic, there is a genuine urgency in the terzetto, which is maintained throughout its considerable length. True the arrival of Montfort brings a moment of scenic absurdity; but thereafter everything proceeds with inexorable swiftness. Like all grand opera Les Vêpres Siciliennes was subjected to cuts when revived; but no one has ever omitted the last act, as used frequently to happen with Les Huguenots.

The Cruvelli incident had inevitably postponed the première; but this in the event was not a disadvantage since the opera could now form one of the attractions of the Great Exhibition of 1855. In the following few months Verdi was able to see the publicity machine of which he had complained swing into action on his behalf.

---

* Letter to Scribe, No. 8, 13.9.1854.

† Letter to Scribe, No. 10, undated.

‡ An extra page (91) of Scribe's libretto contains a dialogue between Hélène and Procida envisaging a solution whereby the former should remain in blissful ignorance of the intended massacre. No final ensemble therefore or even a trio.

During March and April the weekly magazine *La France Musicale,* owned by the Escudier brothers, published regular bulletins and 'puffs preliminary'. More significant is a report in *Le Moniteur* for 27 May: 'It is untrue, as rumour would have it, that M. Verdi has retouched the first two acts of his score. . . . The modifications which anyway are not in the least serious and whose necessity was realized at one of the last rehearsals only concern certain details of the production.' In fact the autograph shows signs of modification at a very late date indeed. As the discarded first thoughts exist fully scored either there or in the material, they will be considered in their context.*

After the première on 13 June Verdi wrote to Clarina Maffei: 'I don't think the *Sicilian Vespers* is going too badly. . . . The press here has been either decent or favourable, except for only three writers who are Italian – Fiorentini, Montazio and Scudo. My friends say, how unjust! what an infamous world! Oh no, the world is too stupid to be infamous.'† Apart from three fulsome articles by Giacomelli, St Victor and Delaforêt in successive numbers of *La France Musicale,* whose eulogies could be taken for granted, the critics found much to admire in the new opera. Ortigues in the *Journal des Débats* found the score 'travaillé . . . fin élégant, spirituel' – words of high praise from a Frenchman; and he gave the composer credit for a dramatic conscience lacking in his Italian predecessors. Adolphe Adam declared that *Les Vêpres* had converted him to Verdi's music. On his return from London, Berlioz added his voice to the general approval:

> Without casting a slur on the merits of *Il Trovatore* and of so many other moving works of his, it must be agreed that in the *Vêpres,* the penetrating intensity of melodic expression, the sumptuous variety, the judicious sobriety of the orchestration, the amplitude, the poetic sonority of his morceaux d'ensemble, the warm colours glowing everywhere and that sense of power, impassioned but slow to deploy itself, that is one of the characteristics of Verdi's genius, stamp the whole work with a grandeur, a sovereign majesty more marked than in the composer's previous creations.‡

The hostile critics mentioned by Verdi were all adherents of the old school of canto fiorito; only Chadeuil of *Le Siècle* touched on a weak spot when he suggested that in this opera superior craftsmanship had sometimes been acquired at the expense of spontaneity.

A libretto cannot make an opera good or bad, but it can determine its terms of reference. Verdi set store by pathos; experience should have taught him that this was not a commodity in which Scribe normally dealt. Yet Verdi could never rid his mind of that scene in *Le Prophète* where before a vast throng in Munster Cathedral the newly crowned John of Leyden forces his mother to deny him. Perhaps only a psychologist could suggest why this should have haunted him so powerfully. But he was to return to it at the time of *Don Carlos*; nor would he be satisfied until his librettists had provided him with an equivalent (a rough one, admittedly, since

---

* All these passages have been reconstructed and edited by Ursula Günther.
† Letter to Clarina Maffei, 28.6.1855. *Copialettere,* p. 542.
‡ Quoted in *La France musicale,* 7.10.1855.

coronation and the betrayal, here more apparent than real, involve different characters). As finally worked out, the libretto of *Les Vêpres Siciliennes* is a competent framework for an opera of effects, of spectacle and theatrical surprise, and Verdi ended by accepting it as such, doing his best to humanize the characters, and at the same time turning it to valuable account in two ways. First he used it as a basis for a new, more ample, more rhythmically complex style of melody. Here the model of Meyerbeer was important though the resulting synthesis was entirely personal. Secondly, he seized the opportunity of solving a problem which had eluded him in a somewhat similar work, *La Battaglia di Legnano*; namely that of reconciling the private and public emotions of the main characters. Arrigo, equally vehement as offended lover and patriot, and in the same way, was a two-dimensional hero; and his dilemma symbolized the unresolved duality of the opera. In *Les Vêpres Siciliennes* the problem is overcome by means of a more varied musical language and above all a new, some might say un-Verdian, restraint in the sector of private emotions. Like Lovelace's hero, Henri and Hélène could not love each other so much, loved they not honour more. This may serve to make them more remote than the blazing, passionate figures of *Rigoletto* and *Il Trovatore*, or the desperately suffering Violetta, but at least they are suited to the historical fresco of which they are part. In other words, Verdi has here solved the problem of grand opera, as surely as Rossini had done in *Guillaume Tell*.

For the first Italian production as *Giovanna de Guzman* Ricordi published a 'disposizione scenica' or production book translated from the so-called *mise-en-scène* printed at the Paris Opéra. Both will be referred to at various points in the analysis.

OVERTURE

This overture is the last and most monumental Verdi was to write in the post-Rossini style, with its roots in sonata form. As usual the themes are taken from the body of the opera and contain a high dramatic charge. The first phrase of the slow introduction is made up of two ideas – a germinal rhythmic motif (a) and what will be the chant of monks intoning a psalm for those about to die (b).

105

Mention has already been made of the traditional association of (a) with the idea of death; the difficulty is always to determine the limits of its application. The basic constituents of tonal music are so few that it is dangerous to endow any of them with the absolute significance of verbal concepts. Everything must depend on context and the degree of emphasis. There are undoubtedly many occasions when Verdi himself leaves no doubt whatever that the pattern of Ex. 105a is meant to convey the idea of death; indeed he gives the 'topos' a vital immediacy to be found in no other composer. In the finale to Act I of *Macbeth* it hammers home all the horror of Duncan's murder. In the Miserere of *Il Trovatore* it illustrates how the chant of the monks has made Manrico's fate rise with frightening clarity before Leonora's vision. In the finale ultimo of *La Traviata* it tells us unequivocally that all is over. But in no opera of Verdi's is it used quite so consistently as in *Les Vêpres Siciliennes*; so much so in fact as to become in certain numbers an almost symphonic principle of construction. At the start of the overture it is a distant but inexorable threat. Important too is the move to the dominant minor for Ex. 105b with its effect of enhanced gloom, already noted in the revised *La Traviata*.

The main melody of the introduction, derived from Hélène's opening aria, seems to offer a promise of relief; but between each phrase the sullen tramp of the death motif persists on strings and brass pianissimi:

106

The traditional function of an adagio in an overture is to prepare for the allegro which follows. Here it is vital to the main theme of the allegro that it should take us unawares. The adagio therefore settles down to a peaceful full close; there is a sudden roll *molto crescendo* on a side drum and the full orchestra explodes into music of the massacre, though, following Verdi's (and Rossini's) usual practice, the time-signature is different (4/4 in the overture, 3/4 in the opera). The juxtaposition of E minor and D minor, modal in origin though curiously modern in effect, adds a further touch of savagery (Ex. 107).

The 'second subject' of the overture is the principal theme of the Act III duet between Henri and Montfort, where the secret of Henri's parentage is revealed. Noble, warm, but in no way incandescent, it furnishes a fine example of the new Verdian melody. The similarity noted by Charles Osborne between it and the 'first subject' from the overture to *Giovanna d'Arco* only serves to throw this novelty into sharper relief. Whereas in the earlier instance all the rhythmic possibilities of the melody are exhausted in the first phrase, here three of the phrases which make up the period have each a different rhythmic cut. As Dyneley Hussey has shrewdly pointed out, the moulding of a melodic line from a free blending of crotchets or quavers with

107

corresponding triplets is a feature of late Meyerbeerian style, as exemplified in Ex. 109 from *L'Etoile du Nord*.* But how much more naturally Verdi manages it!

108

109

Meyerbeer: L'ÉTOILE DU NORD

An orthodox crescendo follows, based on an unimportant theme from the finale to Act IV, and culminating in a powerful development of Ex. 105b upper wood-wind alternating with lower strings, trombones, ophicleide and bassoons, while violins keep up a flurry of semiquaver figures. Treated in this way the theme itself loses its priestly character no less than the Friar Lawrence theme in Tchaikovsky's *Romeo and Juliet* in similar circumstances. To Tchaikovsky the symphonist this scarcely matters. To Verdi the dramatist it may well have supplied the reason for later abandoning this type of overture in favour of the 'pot-pourri', as in *La Forza del destino* where each

* D. Hussey, *Verdi*, 5th ed. rev. C. Osborne, London, 1973, pp. 120–1.

theme preserves intact the emotional aura which surrounds it in the opera itself. The overture has one more theme of importance to offer – Hélène's farewell to her beloved Sicily as the moment of her execution draws near. High strings portray her anguish, while far below Ex. 105a reminds us of the presence of death:

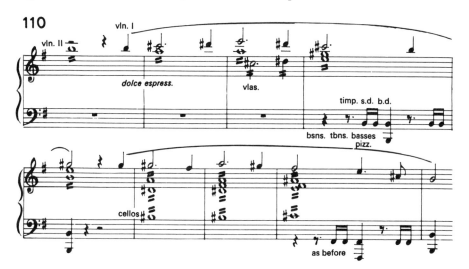

Predictably the reprise begins with Ex. 108, this time with clarinet and bassoon added to the cello line and a new quaver accompaniment of flute, piccolo and oboe replacing the viola triplets of the previous statements. Then the entire melody is repeated after a short transition, scored in a still more full-throated manner; flute, oboe and first violins added to the tune; a new pattern of ascending quavers on second violins, violas and piccolo and a marching accompaniment of ophicleide and four horns. Not only does this extra repetition balance a structure weakened by the lack of a first subject reprise; it also follows the Verdian rule of increasing the emphasis towards the end of the movement, as well as giving due prominence to one of the opera's most memorable themes. The crescendo follows, again with altered scoring, which sets the instrumental groups in sharper relief: full wind and percussion (without trumpets) for the first statement, strings added for the second, trumpets for the third. It is a brilliant effect too often spoiled in performance by an over-exuberant battery which here includes timpani, cymbals, bass and side drum.* There follows the usual coda in faster time based on conventional 'winding-up' material. Like that to *Luisa Miller* the overture to *Les Vêpres Siciliennes* is assured of a place in the concert hall; and its masterly scoring, its neatly calculated proportions are an earnest of the scrupulous craftsmanship which Verdi will bring to the opera as a whole.

---

* The term 'gran cassa', usually translated 'bass drum', in Verdi's time included cymbals unless there is an indication to the contrary.

ACT I

Scene: The main square of Palermo. At the back, streets and the main buildings of the city. On the spectator's right Hélène's palace. On the left the entrance to a barracks with stacks of arms. On the same side the governor's palace to which a flight of stairs gives access. Thibaud, Robert and a number of French soldiers have carried a table in front of the entrance to the barracks and are sitting round it drinking. Sicilian men and women cross the square and form groups here and there looking grimly at the French soldiers. *

The scene is set for a typical double chorus – male for the French, mixed for the Sicilians; a common enough combination in the grander Italian operas, and one which Verdi had used for the opening of *Giovanna d'Arco*. What neither he nor any other Italian had done – not even Donizetti at the corresponding point of *Le Duc d'Albe* – was to make a musical as well as a scenic distinction between the two elements. Here for the first time each has its own distinctive melody, tonality and rhythmic gait:

111

ROBERT, THIBAUD, SOLDIERS

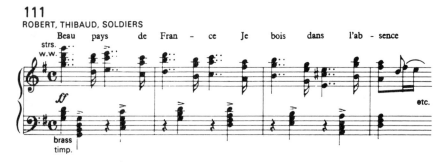

112

POPULACE

In due course the two become rhythmically assimilated as the ensemble builds towards its final cadence. None the less, the contrast has been established and the dramatic situation remains clear. A short episode introduces us to a few of the

* For information on contemporary production there are two important sources: the so called *mise-en-scène* for the première of 1855 published by M. L. Paliantini, a copy of which exists in the Bibliothèque de l'Opéra, Paris; and the so-called *disposizione scenica* published by Ricordi for the first Italian version, *Giovanna de Guzman*. These will be referred to at various points in the analysis, either when they explain the action in closer detail than the vocal score or when either (or both) give different stage directions. In the Italian and French production books only Robert and his men are drinking when the curtain rises. Thibaud enters with a platoon during the first few bars of the introduction; he dismisses them and then joins Robert who pours him out a glass of wine.

secondary characters. Robert and Thibaud drink a toast to Montfort, the scourge of
his enemies and the darling of his troops. The Sieur de Béthune and the Comte de
Vaudemont come out of the barracks. Robert, thoroughly drunk, staggers up to
Béthune, crowing about the delights of foreign occupation. All the women are theirs
for the choosing surely. Béthune chides him tolerantly for being drunk; but agrees
that he can take any woman who happens to like him. The orchestra gives Robert a
little motif of his own, syncopations suggesting his unsteady walk, double dots and a
peremptory cadence his underlying brutality:

113

Warned by Thibaut that the Sicilian is a jealous husband, Robert is undeterred; as a
generous conqueror he is willing to go shares with the conquered.* Violins, violas,
flute and clarinet greet this sally with a guffaw of demisemiquavers and the opening
chorus is resumed in shortened form, the final cadence being reached through
Mercadantian chains of modulating chords recalling similar passages in *La Battaglia di
Legnano*. All in all it is an expertly contrived scene in which every advantage is taken
of the suppleness of the French language and the opportunity it affords for rapid
syllabation. If only its music were a little more memorable and the opera itself not
quite so long, it would doubtless be spared the brutal cut inflicted on it in most
present-day performances.

   Dressed in mourning, Hélène now makes her entrance on the arm of her maid
Ninetta and followed by her servant Daniéli; in her other hand she carries a
prayerbook. The Sicilians greet her with profound respect; as she stops to address a
few gracious words to several of them. All this is in dumb show, without even an
orchestral theme to 'plant' her presence, as happens with Donizetti's Amélie. But this
is appropriate; for Hélène has no wish to draw attention to herself. Vaudemont is
intrigued. Who is this beautiful woman whom the Sicilians treat like a queen? The
Duchess Hélène, Béthune replies, sister of Frédéric of Austria, and held by Montfort
in Palermo as a hostage. Ah, Vaudemont remembers, Frédéric the bosom friend of
Corradino who shared his death on the scaffold. Today is the anniversary of their
execution; naturally she has come to pray for his soul, 'and to call down the wrath of
Heaven on our heads'. 'She is right; our chief was cruel,' Vaudemont murmurs, to
be reproved by his companion: 'It is all too easy to blame one's commander.'† The
conversation is conducted to a suave graceful melody which irresistibly calls to mind
the exchange of the Catholic noblemen in the opening scene of *Les Huguenots*,
though as usual the music is more continuous and periodic:

---

   * *Robert swiftly hands Thibaud the bottle he has been holding, seizes a woman from among the Sicilian populace
[a first soprano] and makes as if to drag her away. A Sicilian [bass] protects her and removes Robert's hand but
without violence. (Mise-en-scène, p. 2.)*

   † It is a pity that Scribe's original epigram was removed. 'It was wrong.' 'Worse still it was pointless.'
The Italian translation is still more austere: 'Such remarks are not for soldiers to make.'

114

At this point the scene was drastically shortened at quite a late stage. As well as the 18 bars which now follow Vaudemont's 'Notre chef fut cruel' there exist in the autograph score 37 bars in which the dramatic situation is still further explained. Here Béthune, who appears to be the senior of the two officers, offers his arm to Hélène. When she draws back in horror he reminds her sharply of her situation. At that moment a side-drum offstage sounds the signal for the parade. Béthune and Vaudemont leave hurriedly; while Hélène abandons herself to thoughts of her brother. 'Touched by your youth Charles d'Anjou would have pardoned you; it was Montfort who had you condemned.'* Not only does this give Hélène an additional reason for wishing to be revenged on Montfort; it adds a new dimension to Béthune's character and plausibly removes him and Vaudemont from a scene in which they have no further part. Musically too there are some effective touches; the tremolo D on cellos depicting the shudder which seizes Hélène at the very mention of Guy de Montfort, and the tiny clarinet solo leading up to the characteristic 6/4 chord at 'O Frédéric, mon frère . . .'

The revision reduces the dialogue to a series of exclamations. First Daniéli† vents his grief at the memory of a day which saw Sicily's hopes destroyed and her land enslaved. Then in a swiftly declaimed prayer to her dead brother Hélène vows vengeance on his murderer. Nothing of importance is lost in the new version, which has the brevity and theatrical intensity by which Verdi set so much store. One curious detail: in the original version the fanfare of woodwind and brass which follows in B flat has a dominant inflexion; in the revision it confirms the tonic of Hélène's previous cadence – a further instance of Verdi's utterly un-Wagnerian approach to tonality.

Freed from the vigilance of his superiors, Robert gives full rein to military licence. He commands Hélène to entertain the troops with a song. After a moment's

---

* For a detailed discussion of this and other changes in *Les Vêpres Siciliennes* see my 'Varianti nei *Vespri Siciliani*', in *Nuova Rivista Musicale Italiana*, Anno VI, No. 2 (April/June 1972).

† In the French score and the autograph; the Italian gives the line to Ninetta.

hesitation she complies.* Her theme is a ship in distress. The sailors pray desperately to God for help; and God replies that their safety lies in their own hands. 'In your hands,' Hélène repeats with quiet emphasis; and from this point on the song develops into a rousing call to action. Robert and Thibaud, having meanwhile returned to their table, become slowly aware that more and more Sicilians have gathered round them. Hélène's song falls into four distinct sections: a recitative with tremolo strings preceded by the ominous re-appearance of Ex. 105a in a pianissimo variant on violins and violas and accompanied by restless darting figures on lower strings and bassoons; a cantabile for the sailors' prayer ('Viens à nous, Dieu tutelaire'), which is formed by Ex. 106 with strings tremolando throughout and arpeggieted triplets on flute and clarinet; a transition (*Allegro moderato*) for God's reply, whose austerity and lack of thematic interest is somehow pregnant with suspense; finally an extended cabaletta with chorus ('Courage, courage'). As the third section dwindles into fragmentary recitative the fatal ♫ sounds pianissimo on strings, is echoed in Hélène's significant 'Dans vos mains' and then serves to launch the melody of the cabaletta:

115

* At Daniéli's solo 'Jour fatal! jour de deuil', etc., *Béthune and Vaudemont slowly and deliberately move back-stage right and leave. [In the Italian they bow to Hélène first.] Robert, increasingly drunk . . . leaves the bottle on the table, runs to Hélène, grasps her by the hand and forces her to front of stage. Movement of fury among the Sicilians, which is as suddenly repressed. This takes place during the four bars preceding 'La belle enfant! Voyons! En savez-vous!' As he says 'Tu chanteras! Sinon!' he makes a brutal threatening gesture and draws his sword. General movement. The soldiers who are still seated rise to their feet. Hélène reasssures the Sicilians with a look, then replies calmly and with dignity, 'Je chanterai.'* (Mise-en-scène, p. 3.)

On the face of it this is in Verdi's earlier style, recalling Lady Macbeth's 'Or tutti sorgete' with energy stored in its minims and released in its semiquavers, and the familiar use of high woodwind to emphasize the melodic contours. But it has more fluency and grace about it, and a new spaciousness of design. The early Verdi would have had a ritornello after the first sixteen bars, then a repeat and finally a coda. Here instead there follows an episode in A minor ('A quoi bon ces prières') leading to a fresh idea in the tonic key ('Debout, debout') consisting of two phrases of five bars each.

As usual in Verdi the effect of the irregularity is mightily propulsive. The rhythm of Ex. 105a which has formed a persistent pattern in the orchestra during the A minor episode now erupts in a slow choral crescendo, to which the insouciant French soldiers latterly provide a background of staccato quavers. Not until Ex. 115 returns in a magnificent climactic unison does it enter their fuddled brains that something is seriously amiss.*

A coda *Un poco più presto* sweeps the movement to a brilliant conclusion as the Sicilians with daggers drawn advance on the unarmed French soldiers. But the final cadence is cut short and the music moves swiftly into E flat as the figure of Montfort appears at the head of the flight of steps. The general fury subsides in a long decrescendo, Hélène however continuing to vent her anger and dismay, till finally

* During what follows several soldiers (extras) remove tables and benches in such a way that the public is as little aware of this as possible. (Mise-en-scène, p. 3.)

nothing is left but the rhythm of Ex. 106a on the strings, a long held note on the horn and a roll on the timpani, all pianissimo.

It is a remarkable tour de force achieved with effortless fluency and able to sustain comparison not only with the loose rondo of the corresponding scene in *Le Duc d'Albe*, whose climax Donizetti left unfinished, but also with a similar scene in Act I of *Le Prophète* where again an angry populace is roused to rebellion and suddenly abashed by the appearance of their overlord. Meyerbeer's scheme is the more original, with its sinister Anabaptist chant, its pounding insistence of question and answer and its culminating march. But Verdi's has the advantage of being floated on a single breath. Berlioz's expression 'a force, impassioned but slow to deploy itself' comes to mind.

The main function of the quartet which follows ('Quelle horreur m'environne!') is to provide a decent interval between the appearance of two of the principals, Montfort and Henri (in *Le Duc d'Albe* it is a trio). It cannot be one of those ensembles whose purpose is to set four different points of view in relief, since two of the characters, Ninette and Daniéli, are too unimportant to have points of view at all; they merely echo the horror of their mistress, mostly in the same words. Montfort meanwhile views with satisfaction the effect of his authority. Verdi has made of it a showpiece of unaccompanied writing and at the same time a discourse on Ex. 105a. Such orchestral interventions as occur are purely by way of rhythmic punctuation except for the doubling by cellos and violas pizzicato of Montfort's chromatic line ('Il tremble sous ma main') which is probably in the nature of a safety precaution. It is a subtle piece, but like all such unaccompanied pieces it poses problems of chording for the developed operatic voice with its wealth of overtones.

The tension is broken by the unexpected entrance of Henri to a typical 'frettoloso' passage on the strings.* His first greeting is to Hélène whose nervousness on his behalf is reflected by variants of Ex. 105a fluttering on violins and violas. For Henri has no idea that he is in Montfort's presence, and freely denounces the cruelty of the governor who had him imprisoned and then for some unknown reason set him free. Yet strangely enough Montfort does not seem to mind. To a bluff string melody which is almost a parody of military pomposity he reminds Henri that he owes his freedom to the governor's clemency. 'Or to his fatigue,' Henri retorts. In vain Hélène and Ninette implore him to keep quiet. If only, Henri says, he could meet the butcher face to face! 'He stands before you,' says Montfort. There is a tutti explosion of surprise. 'Well, have you nothing to reply?' 'I cannot. I am unarmed.' But the death motif given out quietly by the strings leaves us in no doubt as to what form Henri's reply would take if he had a sword.

Montfort dismisses the women and so prepares the duet finale of the first act. It is in two movements only, the first being conceived on a very ample scale. It starts with one of those conversational melodies on the violins which are a familiar feature of *Luisa Miller* and *La Traviata*. Here the prescribed use of the G string gives it a special warmth.

---

* *Hélène proceeds in a semi-circle around the stage and prepares to enter her palace, when the allegro ritornello is heard. Hélène, Ninette and Daniéli all turn to face backstage left from which direction Henri approaches Hélène joyfully and in haste. He does not at first see Montfort who had been about to enter his palace and now stops to observe.* (Mise-en-scène, p. 40.)

117

We might expect it to form a neat period of eight bars, to be repeated as necessary through various keys. On the contrary, it extends itself to thirty following with its modulations the course of the dialogue. Montfort asks Henri about his upbringing. He learns that Henri's mother died a year ago after having placed him in the care of Frédéric of Austria who gave him a father's care.*

As he extols Frédéric's virtues ('Fidèle à ses leçons je prendrai pour modèle') his melody becomes a continuation of the orchestral theme in faster time finally taking shape in a 'cantabile grandioso' in Verdi's new manner:

118

---

* If the French audience knew its Sicilian history it would have been more than a little puzzled by this. The year is 1282 – Frederick of Austria and Corradino were both executed in 1270 at the age of sixteen. But Henri could hardly know that his foster-father was originally Count Egmont before Scribe arbitrarily removed him into another opera.

Montfort, secretly impressed by the young man's boldness, offers him a commission in the French army. The Gounod-esque flavour of this episode reminds us how much that master's style owes to the parade-ground manner of Paris grand opera.

119

Henri refuses emphatically; to a reprise of Ex. 118 he protests that by accepting he would be betraying the honour of his country. Less happy this time is Montfort's counter-melody of private admiration which with its impudent bounce carries associations of Donizetti's Belcore, not to mention Verdi's own Belfiore in a similar situation. In the same tempo there follows a short athematic transition in which the rhythm of Ex. 105a begins to intrude with increasing frequency. Montfort, having accepted Henri's refusal with a good grace, proceeds to offer him a word of advice. Let him keep clear of Hélène if he values his life. Needless to say this is enough to make Henri swear to the contrary. The tug of war finds expression in a 'dissimilar' cabaletta, Montfort threatening with a copious and explicit use of the death rhythm, Henri expressing his defiance in the manner of Rossini's Arnold in the duet 'Où vas-tu?' from *Guillaume Tell*.

With no ritornello and only the most summary of repeats it shows the efficacy of a short sharp movement to wind up an unusually free design. A crowning phrase sweeps Henri to a high B flat and as the orchestra hammers out the final chords he bounds up the flight of steps to Hélène's palace, watched by Montfort 'with emotion but without anger'.

ACT II

Scene: A pleasant valley near Palermo. On the right, hills covered with flowers; here and there cedars and orange trees; on the left, the chapel of Santa Rosalia; in the background the sea. Two men arrive in a sloop and step ashore; the fisherman who has brought them puts out to sea. *

The thirty-one-bar introduction is built on a pair of 'rowing' themes, bristling with offbeat acciaccature, which are a legacy from *Tancredi*. A few bars taken from the final part will give an idea of its refinement both in harmony and scoring.

121

Having disembarked, Procida (for it is he) apostrophizes his beloved country in a conventional recitative. The melody of Ex. 121 repeated on strings tells us the exact moment when the fisherman steers his craft out to sea; then, after a massive tutti to

* The production book carries elaborate instructions for the construction of different planes. The lower slopes of the hills must be 'practicable'. The scene should be 'splendidly illuminated'. (*Mise-en-scène*, p. 5.)

which Procida vows to dedicate his life to his country's cause, a delicate palette of woodwind announces the most famous number of the opera, 'Et toi, Palerme'.* Not implausibly his emotions on seeing once more his native city recall those of Queen Marguerite as she greets the 'Beau pays de la Touraine'.

122a

Meyerbeer : LES HUGUENOTS

Woodwind introductions are common enough in Italian opera from the time of Mayr onwards; rarely do they show the jewelled workmanship of Ex. 122b with each instrumental timbre set sharply in relief. The melody itself has all Verdi's new-found variety of rhythmic articulation; yet the author of *Il Trovatore* has not lost the flair for prolonging a final phrase so as to take the soloist effortlessly up to his highest note (here an E flat). The ternary structure is strictly *à la française* with a central episode that modulates freely. Here Procida recalls how he went from country to country trying to raise help for Sicily. The reply was always the same: 'Rise up, and then I will come.' At the words 'Levez vous . . . et je viens . . . me voilà!' the ubiquitous rhythm of Ex. 105a introduced by cellos and basses at the start of the episode takes command of the vocal line while the full orchestra thunders out a rapid succession of chords in dotted rhythm. Then Procida resumes his tender address with as usual an elaborated accompaniment. Only the coda with its fidgeting woodwind sextuplets and its conventional cadenza recalls the style of the 1840s. Otherwise this cantabile more than redresses the balance which Scribe had tilted against the Sicilian patriot.

A new theme in 3/8 time allegro serves to bring in Procida's followers, some from boats, some from the surrounding hills.† Among them is his henchman Mainfroid.

---

* *Procida steps ashore four bars before the last chord [that is, of the prelude]. As soon as the boat has left R. he exclaims with enthusiasm ['Palerme, O mon pays'], moves forward slightly at the andante and only advances to the footlights to begin his air. (Mise-en-scène, p. 5.)*

† *Mainfroid and ten other conspirators (basses and second tenors) appear at the top of [one of the slopes] from which they descend with an air of melancholy gravity. Some of them come forward and grasp Procida by the hand. (Mise-en-scène, p. 6.) Why second tenors should be required to strengthen a line that is entirely bass in register is not clear.*

All are silent while Procida instructs one of them to gather together his partisans in Palermo, another to summon Hélène and Henri. (As Mainfroid is a tenor while all who take part in the following cabaletta are basses it must be assumed that he is one of the emissaries dispatched.) The cabaletta itself ('Dans l'ombre et la silence') is a variant of the formula used in *Il Trovatore* for the Count di Luna in Act II. Here, however, it is Procida himself who leads the chorus of short, sharp whispered phrases (Ex. 123a) which surround the central melodic solo (b) – a three-limbed period in Verdi's new manner. No need to draw attention to the rhythmic pattern underlying 'La vengeance', rendered even more explicit by the stealthy doubling of violins, cellos and clarinet. (It has already been heard pianissimo on clarinet, bassoon and lower strings in the pause preceding the repeat of the movement.) If 123b has an amplitude befitting the style of the opera as a whole – note the striding crotchets at bar 7 (*x*) – its scoring is only too risorgimentale with the contours picked out by various combinations of wind instruments including – since this is Paris – a solo cornet in place of a trumpet.*

123a

123b

At the repetition of Ex. 123b the chorus supply a tramping bass; then follows the traditional absurdity, admittedly not as prolonged as in *Il Trovatore*, of a chorus protesting its departure while neglecting to depart. Here too, mindful of a more sophisticated audience, Verdi fetches a wide circle of modulation in this coda arriving back in A flat in time for the crowning stroke whereby Procida having continually enjoined silence on his followers advances to the proscenium and cries out in stentorian tones, 'La liberté, et que je meurs après.'† The traditional cut from the end of 'Et toi, Palerme' to the scene that follows is regrettable but venial. The

---

* *At the start of the phrase 'Sainte amour qui m'entraine' Procida advances to the footlights. The conspirators are more or less divided into two groups towards the right. At the repetition of the theme Procida who will meanwhile have joined his friends comes forward again. (Mise-en-scène, p. 6.)*

† *The conspirators retire towards the slope – then disappear gradually always facing the audience. The last words should be sung by all, but only the last two or three conspirators should be visible to the audience. . . . (Ibid., p. 13.)*

care and ingenuity devoted to this scene does not compensate for its lack of that spontaneity to be found in the corresponding scene in the earlier opera.

Henri and Hélène arrive to be given their instructions by Procida. In a long passage of recitative we hear of Procida's travels in Spain and Byzantium. Pierre d'Aragon is standing by with his fleet ready to move in at the first sign of an insurrection. The problem is to induce the Sicilians to revolt. Notable here is a long chromatic ascent of thirteen bars in which Procida declares his intention of acting as agent provocateur to the insolence of the rulers. First he will cause trouble at the imminent Festival at Santa Rosalia. Here the rhythm of Ex. 105a inserts itself into the orchestral fabric, and with good reason, since in the scene of the Festival itself it will play its most important part to date.

Assuring Henri of a special role in his plan of action Procida leaves on other business, so opening the way for a tenor/soprano duet. The first of its two movements ('Comment dans ma reconnaissance payer un pareil dévouement') begins with polite exchanges; then Henri quickly comes to the point. In an extended verse in D flat major ('Vous détournez les yeux') he declares his love with characteristically controlled ardour. Hélène's reaction is reserved for the second movement. Hitherto she has shown nothing but the cold inflexibility of a Donna Anna. Her reluctant yielding to gentler emotions is beautifully realized in this 'dissimilar' cantabile with its progress from E flat minor to major. She is no Giovanna d'Arco, however, to abandon herself completely; on the contrary like Donna Anna once more she makes Henri swear an oath to avenge her brother. But in three successive musical ideas we can see tenderness for her suitor gradually taking possession of her thoughts.

After the hollow harmonies of Ex. 124a, Ex. 124b is like an unexpected shaft of sunlight; while the graceful gesture in the eighth bar foretells the carefree young bride Hélène will become if only for a brief moment in the fifth act. The long descent of Ex. 124c brings her into a chain of melting thirds with the tenor. But immediately afterwards Ex. 124a recalls her to a sense of duty. 'Henri! avenge my brother; and I will be yours for ever.' The duet concludes in a cadenza of unusual difficulty.

Béthune arrives with a detachment of soldiers* and an invitation to Henri to attend the governor's ball that evening. Henri, contrary as ever where Montfort is

124a Andante

HÉLÈNE

con passione

Près du tombeau peut - ê - - tre   où nous allons des - cen - dre,

fl.
ob.

cl.

hns., bsns.

cello

---

* The Italian production book prescribes twelve.

124b

HÉLÈNE *cantabile*

et du haut, du haut des cieux où tu dois ___ nous en-

strs. *ppp*

etc.

-ten – dre, O mon frè – re! o mon frè – re! tu me par-

-don – neras, tu me par-don – ne-(ras)

124c

HÉLÈNE haut, ___ du haut des

(sol)- dat, vous ac – ceptez, vous ac-cep – tez, vous ac-cep – tez ___ ma

HENRI

fl.

cl.

strs.

bsn.

cieux tu me par – don – ne

foi et mon ob – scure mi – sèr – (e)

etc.

strs. only

concerned, refuses with hauteur; whereupon Béthune has him surrounded, disarmed and marched away. All this Hélène tells to the returning Procida. It is a severe blow to the conspiracy, but Procida has no intention of altering his plan of action.

At that moment a festive group of young men and girls invade the scene; from one side twelve prospective brides led by Ninette; from the other their grooms-to-be with Daniéli at their head. Meanwhile Procida is joined by Mainfroid and some friends. Daniéli and Ninette kneel to receive their mistress's blessing. Then the tarantella begins, to which Verdi had given so much thought at an early stage of composition. But the dance which he eventually wrote is an agreeable piece of music in the manner of Auber's *Muette*, written and scored with taste and deploying its themes with great skill. The most important of these is not the opening but the one which is introduced at bar 113 and recurs in different keys as a symbol of the festive spirit.

125

The pattern of the tarantella is essentially abstract; it makes no attempt to follow the complex action which now unfolds on stage, though the texture is calculated so as to help it to emerge clearly.* While the dancing proceeds Robert and Thibaud cross the stage each leading a platoon of soldiers. The dancers hesitate, but Robert gives the signal for them to continue. He and Thibaud halt their men, stand them at ease and dismiss them. All then stop to watch the dance at the centre of which are the twelve couples about to be wed, including Daniéli and Ninette. Procida in his authentic character of doctor approaches Robert and Thibaud, and draws attention to the beauty of the girls; true, they are to be married, but why should that matter to the soldiers of a conquering army? Thibaud recalls a picture of the rape of the Sabine women. Why should they themselves not imitate the example of the Romans? At once the soldiers join in the dance. Robert devotes his attention to the protesting Ninette. But he orders that Hélène be left alone; she is to be the doctor's prize for having suggested to them such an excellent plan. Here the tarantella does at last break up as the soldiers carry away not only the brides but any woman who has taken their fancy. Daniéli and the young Sicilian men hurl themselves at the soldiers, who draw

* The absence of tambourines from the pit does not exclude the possibility that they may have been played by the dancers on stage. (See *Mise-en-scène*, p. 7.)

their swords causing them to retreat in terror. Mainfroid grasps his sword but is restrained by Procida who signs to him to protect Hélène.*

In the movement which follows ('Interdits, accablés') which freezes the action in the manner of a concertato Ex. 105a fully comes into its own. Notable is the extreme economy of the scoring:

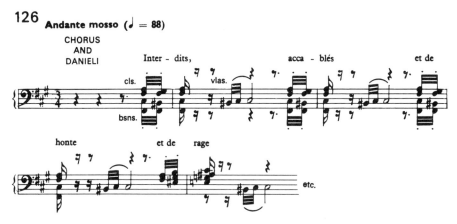

126 Andante mosso (♩ = 88)

Procida and Hélène lose no time in exploiting the situation. Daniéli had not lifted a finger to save Ninette; Hélène herself would have been seized with the rest of the women if only Procida had not been there to defend her. 'C'est juste . . . c'est vrai,' murmur the Sicilians. If the casuistry of Hélène and Procida and their method of working up anger recalls Meyerbeer's Anabaptists, the musical structure shows that careful cohesion noted in the Barbarossa scene in *La Battaglia di Legnano*. As feeling gathers strength two important new elements are introduced by the strings and then spread like a slow fire to the other instruments (Ex. 127).

---

* The production book gives a slightly different programme. Here there are only six affianced couples though they are joined by twelve others with tambourines. The soldiers enter casually, not in formation, and the dance ceases to be general somewhere around bar 128, leaving the first couple dancing alone. Then: *Robert exclaims 'Voilà par St Denis de belles fiancées'. A few soldiers (extras) enter backstage L. and remain there. The couple continue dancing alone up to this sentence: 'Pour les galants exploits ne vendront les fiancés.'* Here the first fiancée dances alone, while Robert, having laid down his helmet, which is picked up by an extra, runs and takes hold of a girl, while a soldier, from the chorus, drags her fiancé away. These and other scenes like them take place front stage left.

At the repetition of the chorus ('Vivent les conquêtes'), the dancing becomes general once more. The men (dancers) beat time with their tambourines. At the end of this chorus and dance, the soldiers mix with fiancées, whirl them round in a pirouette and throw them into the arms of other soldiers, who drag them away. The rest of the dancers on seeing this follow their companions and disappear. The soldiers, now in full possession of the field, continue dancing for a while. Robert dances with the first fiancée. Then, having propelled their partners back stage, the soldiers seize them and run off with them in various directions. . . . The peasants and men of the people try vainly to go in pursuit but are prevented by other soldiers (extras). (Mise-en-scène, p. 7.) An important note tells us that Ninette and Daniéli were not intended to take part in this scene, that their names were indicated in error in the vocal score and that the line assigned to Daniéli should be sung by Mainfroid; the Italian production book adds, however (p. 17), that if the producer so desired they could be included without dramatic incongruity. In fact Ninette's 'Laissez moi! laissez moi!' is omitted in the Escudier edition; but it exists in the autograph as well as in modern Italian vocal scores (see *Les Vêpres Siciliennes a cura di Massimo Mila* (Turin, 1973), p. 33) Verdi was evidently undecided as to the extent to which he could risk making Daniéli look a fool and a coward.

The long crescendo culminates in a presto formed exclusively from Ex. 126 until that
too dissolves into hammered-out quavers as the rage of the Sicilians reaches boiling-
point. There is a pause; and all turn to the shore from which distant singing is heard.
A galley passes across the back of the stage richly decked with pennants. On deck is
Vaudemont with a number of French officers and high-born Sicilian women
reclining on cushions, some playing guitars, some taking refreshments. (Béthune is
doubtless absent because he is on duty.) Their barcarolle transports us again to the
Naples of Auber.

In a short interlude Hélène tells Procida that this splendid equipage is on its way to
the governor's ball. 'Thither,' replies Procida, 'a God of vengeance will guide our
steps.' That evening will see the murder of Montfort and all his suite. 'They have
their swords,' puts in Daniéli, cautious as ever. 'And we our daggers,' retorts
Procida. Then by a stroke familiar to French opera since the Pré aux Clercs scene in
Les Huguenots Ex. 128 is combined with Ex. 126 this time in the major key. This
highly effective piece of theatre, managed by Verdi with all his newly developed
craftsmanship, brings down the curtain on Act II.

ACT III

Scene 1: A cabinet in the palace of Montfort.

Before the rise of the curtain there is a brief entrata of no great dramatic relevance, vaguely prophetic of the party music towards the end of the act. Its happiest touch is a cello counter-melody introduced at the fourteenth bar and giving rise to a characteristic harmonic epigram.

Montfort is discovered seated at a table, thinking of the Sicilian woman whom he had forcibly made his mistress eighteen years ago; who had borne him a son only to vanish soon afterwards taking the infant with her. Then a little over a year ago he had received a letter: 'You who spare nothing, if your bloody axe threatens Henri Nota, the glory of his country, spare at least that innocent head, for he is your son.' Montfort repeats to himself, 'Mon fils! O mon fils!' to a heartfelt cadential phrase so typical of the Verdian father which lights up what has so far been a purely conventional recitative. Béthune enters to ask what is to be Henri's punishment for having tried to resist the Governor's summons. 'Let him be treated in this palace like myself,' Montfort answers, 'but first of all let him be brought before me.'

When Béthune has left Montfort sings his only aria ('Au sein de la puissance') in which he laments the loneliness of power and the sense of emptiness it brings; yet at the thought of his son he feels his spirit reborn. Here the major–minor romance is combined with French ternary form. Montfort is perhaps the most fully realized character in the opera; a King Philip who has not yet become old and bitter. The opening phrase is clearly indebted to Meyerbeer for its rhythmic cut (compare 'Pour cette cause sainte' from *Les Huguenots*) but its mood, despite the martial suggestion of the double dots, is one of gentle melancholy; and as usual the melody is more continuous and formed than in Meyerbeer, whose idea ceases abruptly after two bars.

But it is the second period beginning at the ninth bar which gives the clearest indication of the path that Verdi's style is to take from now on (Ex. 130).

Here is all the flexibility of form, the freedom of rhythm and tonality which make Lady Macbeth's 'La luce langue' stand out like an eagle among the chickens in the second act of *Macbeth*. Note how the wandering chain of sixths in F sharp minor

130

conclude in a characteristic 6/4 in F major which has the effect of jolting the melody back into regularity. After the usual dominant half-close we are prepared for a lyrical effusion of some kind; but it never happens. For three bars the violins trace a tentative line which slowly comes to rest in a new theme given out by the baritone over strangely bare harmonies, somewhat reminiscent of Hélène's Ex. 124a.

131

The triplets which prolong the phrase from four bars to five have the effect of repeated question marks as if to indicate the remoteness of Montfort's hopes. Not even in *Stiffelio* is there such a combination of warmth with austerity. After a central modulating episode in which Montfort declares that he will win his son over by kindness the whole design is repeated with increased figuration in the accompaniment. This time the open sonority of Ex. 131 is enhanced by a pulsating pattern of high violins creating a spread of three octaves and a fifth but still without a third in the chord. This same pulsation breaking into continuous quavers forms the basis of the long-drawn-out coda; then as flute and clarinet in octaves take over the quaver movement in ascending and descending arpeggio figures the upper strings assume the rhythm of Ex. 105a but needless to say without any connotation of death. They merely form part of the delicate filigree of sound which serves as backcloth to Montfort's dreams of happiness.

The dreams are interrupted by the entrance of an indignant Henri. Why, he wants to know, is he being treated with such deference by his country's enemies? A brief argument leads into the grand duet in which Montfort reveals to Henri the secret of his parentage. It is one of Verdi's great pivotal duets whose cut varies according to the particular situation and the relation of the characters. What marks out this one from all those which have preceded it and a good many which follow is the lack of anything approaching a cabaletta. True, this solution was not arrived at immediately. The duet achieved its final form very shortly before the première at the cost of two cuts, one trifling, the other substantial, and the rewriting of an entire movement.

The first movement ('Quand ma bonté toujours nouvelle') is essentially a long solo for Montfort, its design that of a minor–major romanza, its tone one of restrained pathos characteristic of so much of the score.

132

Montfort asks Henri if he was aware of something special in his attitude towards him. Henri's unease is reflected in rapid triplet twitches in the strings between each limb of the melody. The music gathers speed for the central section ('Eh bien donc puisque rien ne t'éclaire!') as Montfort hands him his mother's letter, then resumes the original allegretto for the resolving theme ('Pour moi, pour moi quelle ivresse inconnue!') which is the first statement of Ex. 108, a soliloquy since Henri is now fully occupied in reading the note, and all his interventions merely react to its contents. As Montfort finishes the period his son's astonishment and despair ('La foudre est sur moi!') find expression in a succession of typical orchestral outbursts. Then Ex. 108 is repeated by Montfort to anguished mutterings by Henri ('Je frémis . . . d'épouvanté!'). In a rapid transition Montfort wishes to buy his son's affection by heaping on him all manner of titles and honours of state. But as the rhythm of Ex. 105a reminds us these would be for Henri the trappings of death. His chief sorrow is that he has now lost Hélène for ever. There follows a short, powerful movement of overlapping phrases, with father and son united in private misery. Possibly by design both key and rhythm forestall the music of the final catastrophe.

133

From the noisy diminished seventh in which the previous movement had finished flute and clarinet in a slow unison lead beautifully into the new key as Montfort makes yet one more appeal to his son. This too is very short with the technique of the 'dissimilar' duet condensed within a tiny compass (see Ex. 134).

In the final bars chromatic slithers in the cellos presage the voluptuousness of Saint-Saëns's Delila, after which flute and violins in alternation with cellos and basses bring back a memory of Gilda's last moments. Henri seems about to yield ('Je voudrais courir en vos bras'), but he adds, 'Je ne peux!' The thought of his mother as Montfort's victim makes Henri recoil from Montfort himself, and he ends with an apostrophe to her spirit ('Ombre sainte que je révère'). It is Ex. 108 again but this time in F major, the melody Henri's, the asides Montfort's. Not only is it differently scored with a new pulsing accompaniment but the minor-key preparation has given it a more urgent character. Originally it had grown out of a regular strophe. The F minor section which precedes it here is little more than a series of violent gestures – the same that served to introduce it in the overture. As a result the melody itself seems

134 (♩ = 96)

to move much faster; in fact its metronome marking is scarcely higher than the original: 88 as against 84. Why, it might be asked, should Henri take over Montfort's theme when he does not share his sentiments? The answer is that the theme would only have been Montfort's if Henri had had another to oppose it when it first appeared. In fact it is only a melody of pleading, of unfulfilled longing felt successively by father and son on either side of the barrier that separates them. At the end, Henri rushes desperately out of the room, while Montfort gazes sadly after him.

The discarded material is worth a glance. Originally the central A minor section was much longer. The first statement of Ex. 133 was a solo for Montfort up to Henri's counterpoint at the eighth bar. At bar 17 the music developed as a long solo for Henri starting in A minor and moving a wide tonal orbit through D flat and E major back to the original key. He pleaded to be allowed to spend the rest of his life in obscurity: titles, high honours would only lose him his friends and the woman he loves. A hammering insistence on F, prolonged almost beyond endurance, was broken off by the tenor's sudden plunge into D flat major with a wide-arching phrase that brings to mind Senta's ballade. Here it suggests a frantic effort to escape from confinement rather than a hope of heavenly redemption (see Ex. 135).

Both here and in the E major phrases that follow there is pathos as well as urgency; but whether the tenor was unable to do it justice, or whether it was felt to mar the proportions of the duet as a whole, Verdi made a straight cut so as to begin with the reprise of Ex. 133.

135

Again, the moment where Henri seemed about to yield was longer by four bars; and once more the adjustment was a matter of simple surgery. The final movement, however, was entirely rethought. Originally Henri seems to have had a direct vision of his dead mother ('L'image de ma mère qui se place entre nous') which Verdi embodied in an external musical symbol like that which had served him for the ghost of Carmagnola in *I Due Foscari*.

136

After this brief transitional movement, based entirely on the diminished seventh except for one dominant chord, a kind of cabaletta followed ('Ombre chère et sanglante') whose main section (D minor–major) is dominated by Henri. Neither of its two themes is particularly striking; but the central episode, a solo for Montfort in place of the usual ritornello, ends in a deeply pathetic phrase in which chromatic harmony is used to powerful effect (Ex. 137).

And so to a standard reprise shared out between the two voices and ending with the usual coda with its plethora of reiterated tonic chords. Possibly the experience of Germont's cabaletta had convinced Verdi that there was no point in giving characters new melodies if they had nothing new to say. Possibly he felt that Ex. 108

137

was good enough to benefit from further repetition. More probably he realized that for the dramatic situation anything in the nature of a cabaletta would be quite wrong. The cabaletta 'clinches'; here there is nothing to clinch. The revelation of Henri's parentage brings back the original situation in aggravated form. Hence the new and entirely appropriate solution.

> *Scene 2: A magnificent hall set out for a festive ball. French and Sicilian ladies and gentlemen, the former with and the latter without masks, come and go. Montfort preceded by his pages and officers of the palace guard takes his place on an elevated throne, and signs to all present to be seated. The master of ceremonies comes to receive his orders and gives the signal for the ballet to begin. The ballet of the Four Seasons is played before the Court of Palermo.**

The programme of the ballet is as follows. A preliminary movement in march time introduces the God Janus who presides over the year. He takes out a golden key, inserts it into the ground and up rises a basket covered in ice, out of which steps a young girl wrapped in furs and representing Winter. She is followed by three companions. All are trembling with cold. One of the girls strikes a stone with a piece of flint and so lights a fire. The other two gather round to warm themselves and invite Winter to do the same; but she refuses. The best way to keep warm, she intimates, is to dance, and she proceeds to set the example. Three formal numbers follow, before Winter and her companions take their leave. Next, as zephyrs flit round the basket, the ice begins to melt and discloses bunches of flowers, from the centre of which arises the spirit of Spring. She dances four solos beginning with an adagio. The flowers vanish and are replaced by ears of corn. Summer rises from the basket with her companions, and begins to gather the ears. She and her companions

---

* At this point the French production book specifies a 'changement à vue', i.e., a change of scene in full view of the audience with extras rearranging the furniture and the flats that formed the backcloth withdrawn into the wings to reveal a new depth of stage. *The guests discovered upstage move forward a little exchanging greetings and compliments. Enter Montfort back R, preceded by four pages and a long suite of knights and ladies. All make way for him and bow respectfully. Montfort and the knights each offer an arm to two ladies. Before ascending his dais Montfort greets his guests. As soon as he is seated he makes a sign whereupon all seat themselves. Enter the Master of Ceremonies back R; he makes a deep bow to Montfort. At a sign from the latter the divertissement begins.* (*Mise-en-scène*, p. 9.) This is all very interesting but where is the accompanying music? True, the autograph contains four pages of dominant preparation but these are clearly scored out.

would like to dance, but it is too hot. A group of Naiads appear trailing green transparent sashes to simulate waves. Summer and her attendants decide to bathe; but they are surprised by the sudden appearance of a faun and take flight. The faun tries to pursue them but all at once he hears festive sounds from within the basket which is now covered with vine leaves and fruit. He leaps onto the basket, tears open the cover and out come Autumn and her companions and dance a Bacchic rout. A final galop brings down the curtain.

This is Verdi's second ballet and, at thirty minutes or so, his longest. If it falls short of the classical scores of the century, that is partly because the musical demarcation between pantomime and abstract dance – the former purely illustrative and athematic, the latter thematic but without possibility of development – is too rigid to allow a satisfying continuity and also because in 1855 the 'conquest of the points', which gave to ballet that aerial quality so vividly described in Théophile Gautier's *Mademoiselle de Maupin*, was still a comparatively recent affair. Throughout the 1830s choreographic vocabulary was rapidly expanding; but it took time for musicians to learn how to match it. The great ballet scores of Delibes and Tchaikovsky which mirror the figures of the dance in music of an almost plastic quality do not emerge before 1870, though certain of their traits are to be found in the *Don Carlos* ballet music of 1867; 1855 is too early. Lucien Petipa, brother of the great Marius of Maryinsky fame, had created Albrecht in *Giselle* in 1846. He did not make his début as a choreographer until 1853. His *Ballet des Quatre Saisons* presupposes a score similar to Adam's with a harmless chain of waltzes, mazurkas and polkas. All the more credit to Verdi who without exceeding this brief could so often convey the sense of characteristic steps and even occasionally bend a simple rhythmic scheme to underline a choreographic flourish, as happens in Autumn's Adagio written for the Italian ballerina, Carolina Beretta.*

138

Indeed the ballet, like the opera as a whole, seems to have been written with exceptional care. There is already a tendency to score in blocks of homogeneous tone in Tchaikovsky's manner; † and if moments of noisy 'tinselly' scoring recur this was still the conventional way of lifting the dancers off their feet. Certainly it did not prevent the fastidious Berlioz from singling out the 'airs de danse' for special praise, 'particularly the pieces for Spring and Summer which give the virtuosi of the opera

---

* For an appraisal of the *Ballet des quatre saisons* in relation to the dancers for whom it was written, see Marcello Conati, 'Ballabili nei *Vespri*. Con alcune osservazioni su Verdi e la musica popolare', in *Studi Verdiani I* (Parma, 1982), pp. 21–46.

† *Ibid.*

orchestra a chance to display their talents'.* When the opera was revived in 1863 one critic went so far as to say that if anything could keep *Les Vêpres Siciliennes* alive it would be the ballet. And when all allowances have been made for time and place the music of *Les Quatre Saisons* shows a remarkable vitality, an effortless pouring forth of melodic ideas. Of these the most immediately striking is the B minor Siciliano in which Summer and her attendants try to gather the corn in the blazing noon-day heat. The modal contour, avoiding the leading note, the 'rustic' oboe, the pedal note with the bare fifth above suggesting the drone of the zampogna, all point to a deliberate essay in folk melody:†

139

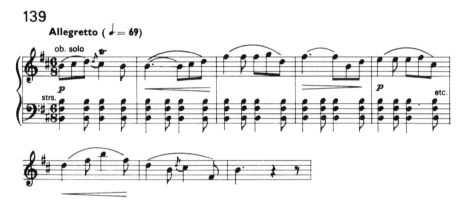

The continuation in F sharp minor, however, with its delicately sophisticated harmonies is invented folk-music, like Pedrillo's serenade from *Die Entführung* or the many 'Spanish' airs from Bizet's as yet unwritten *Carmen*. The major complement is notable for its rich yet pellucid scoring.

140

The other melodies, though more conventional, are skilfully organized and, as in so many of Verdi's scores, there are always more of them than one remembers from the last hearing. The F major allegro with which Spring signs off contains no less than five separate themes. The expected is often by-passed, as in Winter's concluding G major allegro, where the first episode switches abruptly into E flat with witty effect, while the second, in E minor, combines oboe and piccolo in one of those piquant

* See my 'Varianti nei *Vespri*', p. 27.

† Conati, *loc. cit.*, draws attention to the similarity of this melody to 'Il vecchio castello' from Mussorgsky's *Pictures from an Exhibition*.

themes which will characterize Gounod's harmless imps from the Brocken. The adagio for Spring is a clarinet concertino recalling the world of *La Traviata* in its tenderness and unpretentious beauty. Also from Violetta's or Flora's salon is Winter's second dance, whose opening phrase whether by design or accident mirrors that of Autumn's final variation. Of the mime music the sequence for Winter is the most interesting with its ingenious pattern of timbres and intervals. It seems pointless, however, to insist on its modernity when the object is onomatopoeia and little else. In a word few minutes go by without something to arrest the attention: the opening march, more French than the French with its military brusquerie and Meyerbeerian 'tic' reminiscent of the prelude to *L'Etoile du Nord*; the instrumental sparkle of Winter's first variation; the weaving into the Naiads' mazurka of a design of flute triplets taken from the pantomime music for Summer; the unexpected intrusion of a heavy Ecossaise just before Autumn's last variation. The final galop with its aggressively simple up-and-down sweep is worth quoting as an instance of something that Verdi will do much more successfully in the ballet music for *Don Carlos*.

141

The ballet concluded all rise to their feet; the seats are removed except for those on the dais, from which Montfort now descends, a lady on either arm, and proceeds with his suite to one of the adjoining halls.*

The first part of the Finale to Act III proceeds against a background of party music with the double chorus of French and Sicilians this time united in admiring the splendour of the scene in a mass 'parlante armonico'.

142

---

* Mise-en-scène, p. 10.

The scène-à-faire is constructed as a large-scale rondo with Ex. 142 as its main theme whose significance varies according to the situation. For some it is a spontaneous tribute of admiration; for others a smoke-screen of small talk designed to mask the plotting that takes place during the episodes. These are based on two subsidiary themes, the first redolent of the Bouffes Parisiens, the second tense and brooding – compare the card-playing scene in *La Traviata*.

143a fl., picc., ob., cl.

143b

Always kept within the eight-bar structure of formal dance music, although variously extended, 'conjugated' and even intermingled (a new feature, this in Verdian party music), they suggest aptly enough the whirling and eddying of intrigue within confined surroundings. As the guests disperse into adjoining rooms, Henri comes forward, sad and pensive, to be met by Hélène and Procida wearing masks which they now remove. 'Friendship watches over you,' Procida murmurs to Henri (Ex. 143b), and with the sudden turn into the relative minor the festive atmosphere darkens. Henri's first reaction is one of alarm, especially on Hélène's account. In vain he explains that he has no need of protection; he is in perfect liberty (here Ex. 143b in the major is combined with elements of Ex. 142). Their fear of being overheard brings about resumption of Ex. 142 with all three soloists joining in and trying their best to look unconcerned. Then Hélène and Procida explain their plan to murder Montfort and his officers at the height of the festivities. All members of the conspiracy will be recognized by a certain ribbon, which Hélène proceeds to pin to his chest. Henri's terror is now palpable; but just then Montfort himself is seen approaching. Once more soloists and chorus join in Ex. 142. As most of the guests including Hélène and Procida begin to move away, Henri has time to warn Montfort that his life is in danger (Ex. 143b). Montfort mistakes his son's concern for a change of heart (Ex. 143a). 'Never!' Henri cries. 'Then I remain here.' 'But you will die; they will strike you down.' 'They will not dare.' Henri points to his ribbon and explains its meaning. For reply Montfort tears it from him.* From here on the mounting tension is conveyed characteristically by an insistent pattern of semiquavers beneath Ex. 143a, now in the minor key, and finally by a breaking down of the rhythmic unit into two-bar sequences. Father and son are still arguing when Procida and his men surround Montfort; Hélène hurls herself at the governor, dagger in hand, to be intercepted by Henri,† and the music, which has been moving through a wide circle of keys, now switches abruptly and freezes on a prolonged chord of A flat that gradually reveals itself as a Neapolitan approach to G minor. Montfort orders Béthune and Vaudemont to arrest everyone wearing the ribbon of conspiracy, but to let Henri go free since it was he who revealed the plot.

The imposing concertato which follows begins with what can only be called sensation music: a succession of widely separated pianissimo gestures like exclamation marks. From the web of sound which develops the voice of Procida and the Sicilian basses emerge with the rhythm of Ex. 105a ('C'est un lâche!') to be answered by two hammer blows from full chorus and voices. It could be described as the effect writing of *I Lombardi* raised to a higher power by a sophisticated Parisian technique; it has affinities too with the monumental concertati of Mercadante's so-called 'second manner' (Ex. 144).†

From all this emerges a unison cantabile in B flat ('Noble patrie') sung by Hélène, Daniéli and Procida. The model for this kind of two-part texture can be found in Raoul's 'Blanche comme la blanche hermine' from *Les Huguenots*, where it is the subject of some very pungent comments by Schumann ('Behold, Germans, what I can do with so little!').§ The difference is that Meyerbeer was exploiting the two-part combination for its littleness, Verdi for its bigness. There is no sound in music fuller than that of two parts. (See Ex. 145.)

If the sad sweetness of the melody recalls some of the early 'risorgimentali' choruses the combination of smooth contour with flexible rhythm places it firmly in the musical context of *Les Vêpres Siciliennes*. Originally a lament by the Sicilians for the wrongs of their country the melody is now taken up in the dominant by Montfort and Béthune with a more elaborate accompaniment and various anguished asides from Henri. Otherwise there is no attempt to distinguish musically the different attitudes of those present. Whether appealing to Henri's family feelings, cursing him for his treachery, or simply deploring their country's fate all contribute to the monolithic grandeur of the line. An episode follows in rapid 6/8 time with Henri

---

* *After the words 'I tear it from you' the guests return gradually from all directions. . . . From the corner front-stage right about a dozen conspirators emerge gradually, some of them masked, all in party dress. They are preceded by Hélène and Procida and take up their positions on the right of the stage, pointing out Montfort to each other. (Mise-en-scène, p. 11.)*

† Thus the French libretto and the Italian vocal score. The French score has Procida as the would-be assassin; while in both production books Hélène and Procida attempt the stabbing simultaneously.

‡ The influence of this composer on Verdi has so far hardly been touched upon; but in the year of *Les Vêpres Siciliennes* the critic Marco Marcelliano Marcello spoke of Mercadante as the last step in Verdi's ascent. See M. Conati, 'Verdi, il grand' opera e il *Don Carlos*', in *Atti del II° Congresso dell'I.S.V.*, p. 256. If the debt is mostly obscured the reason lies in the greater forward movement of Verdi's early finales. It is only in cases like the present which aim deliberately at a frozen stasis that the hand of Mercadante can be seen.

§ See Robert Schumann, *Gesammelte Schriften über Musik und Musiker*, 5th ed. (Leipzig, 1914), I, pp. 318 ff; trans. *Robert Schumann on Music and Musicians* (New York, 1946).

vainly trying to excuse his behaviour to his friends who of course repulse him with scorn. The new rhythm is now incorporated in the old for the final, glorious resumption of Ex. 145, with all voices in unison and one of the richest orchestral backcloths Verdi ever devised: high woodwind trills; bassoons and horns in pounding triplets; all strings except for basses sweeping upwards in successive patterns of arpeggiated sextuplets. Further elaborations follow until a coda based on material from the central episode brings down the curtain to cries of 'A nous/vous la mort!' The entire finale lasts barely fifteen minutes; the concertato not quite five; yet the sense of scale is enormous and goes to prove how little real grandeur has to do with the clock.*

ACT IV

Scene: The courtyard of a fortress. To the left the hall which leads to the prison cells. To the right a grille giving on to the inner rooms. At the back battlements and the gate of the fortress guarded by soldiers.

In the fourth act of a grand opera interest traditionally shifts from the tableau to the individual. It is the act of the love duet and the great soliloquy. Accordingly Scribe has given his characters greater human interest here than in any other part of the opera. Verdi, while rising nobly to the occasion (this is generally considered the finest act of the five), does not allow his principals to go outside the emotional framework he has laid down for them from the start. Hélène and Henri do not pour out their souls in white-hot passion; even in the grand duet they talk to themselves rather than to each other, sometimes reminding us of Schubert at his most nocturnal.

But it is Beethoven who comes to mind in the prelude with its massive homophony and scoring. It is based on two contrasted themes developed sequentially mostly in regular units of two though without any of the academic quality that the term implies. The first juxtaposes B minor and A minor with a starkness as forbidding as the wall which presents itself to view.

146

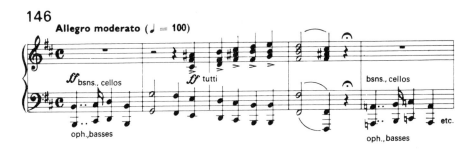

The second theme (Ex. 147) is a ray of light in the darkness. Its first statement, prolonged for six bars, is brutally interrupted by Ex. 146, now evolved in still tighter sequences, rising to a climax, then subsiding into a quiet coda.

The curtain rises to disclose Henri who shows a pass from Montfort and so obtains

* At the change of time signature (allegro 6/8) Procida, Hélène and Mainfroid slowly retire. During this movement Procida is on Hélène's left. After the last syllable has been sung the following movements should be performed as rapidly as possible. A space is cleared in the centre of the stage. The soldiers occupying the terrace on the left advance half-way up the stage and form up on the left of the space, and so face another group of soldiers who occupy the right-hand side and do not move from there. Henri hurls himself after the retreating steps of his friends, who repulse him with contempt. Montfort alone protects him. All the other characters who have likewise retreated a few paces take part in the scene as well. Tableau. The curtain falls. (Mise-en-scène, p. 12.)

147

permission for the prisoners to be brought to him. He waits with mixed feelings; he can explain everything, but will Hélène and Procida listen? Alternations of Ex. 146 and 147 reflect his hopes and fears, often forming a counterpoint to the verbal sense while never relaxing their strictly architectural character. Finally his mood crystallizes in the strophic romance 'O jour de peine!', a remarkable blend of old and new. The rhythmic basis is conventional enough, having already served for 'La donna è mobile'; so too the string writing with violins, cellos and basses pizzicati and violas sustaining in two-part chords – an old Italian commonplace of which Donizetti has made plentiful use. Most unconventional is the tonal scheme which hovers between E minor and E major and their respective related keys, so keeping the singer in a strange twilight of emotion. The woodwind scoring with its use of a 'cool' low flute is entirely French. In the ritornelli a pattern of cello triplets is transferred to flute and clarinet for the second strophe so giving a curious pre-echo of a Tchaikovsky waltz. Tchaikovsky, it must be remembered, was a great admirer of French opera.

148

A pattering allegro agitato suggests both Hélène's footsteps and the beating of Henri's heart. What follows can best be described as a 'cabaletta substitute', based on a single phrase stated alternately in C major by the orchestra and E major by Henri with accompaniment, as though the singer were uncertain which key to choose. Rarely can a Verdian tenor have been less sure of himself than here.

149

It is the first of many Verdian devices for by-passing that most routine of operatic procedures, the solo cabaletta.

Hélène enters and freezes as she recognizes Henri. The duet that follows is very much *sui generis*, proceeding by transition rather than by steep contrasts, so matching the constrained, formal relationship of the two singers. The first movement ('De courroux et de l'effroi') begins athematically with a unison string figure which moves chromatically up and down the tritone – a neat ideogram of negative emotion. To Henri's babbled excuses Hélène returns a series of downward gestures as though slamming a door in his face. Cowardice she might have forgiven; treachery never. This final thrust which takes her down to a low B flat stings Henri into melodic coherence. His reply ('Malheureux et non coupable') with its swift anapaestic gait so typical of mid-century French opera (compare Gounod's 'A moi les plaisirs') turns out to be the main theme of the movement (Ex. 150).

Henri repeats his plea, the cellos reinforcing his eloquence, while Hélène scornfully echoes his words, as though addressing an invisible third party. Still in opposition they drive the music to a climax and a full close. Hélène then rounds on Henri in a recitative. 'Was it not your protecting hand that disarmed me when I was about to strike our enemy, our tyrant?' 'My father!' Here for the first time Verdi has taken care to allow the key word to emerge clearly from the orchestra tissue. In Henri's despairing cry the first syllable of 'père' is completely unsupported, the second underpinned merely by oboes and clarinets and therefore perfectly audible. The inevitable tutti crash that accompanies Hélène's astonished reaction is delayed until

150

the second syllable, by which time nobody can be in doubt as to what the word is. Having now captured Hélène's attention Henri is able to crown his self-defence with a neat antithesis: 'You gave your life to avenge your brother. I have done more: I have given away my honour for my father's sake.' His brief solo is typical of the maturing Verdi in its blend of lyrical with declamatory elements, of melody and neutral syllabation, likewise in its variation of pace from fast to slow and from strict to free as the sense of the words demands. Amorphous to the eye, it reveals itself to the ear as a perfectly organized and satisfying musical paragraph.

151

Once again Hélène echoes Henri ('Malheureux et non coupable') but without scorn in a reprise of Ex. 150 transposed down a tone into D flat, sustaining horns adding a softer glow to the texture. It is an excellent instance of how Verdi uses tonality to reflect an altered emotional situation in the simplest of ways; for the tension between the two parties, like their pitch, has now been lowered. Hélène sings 'avec pitié' and 'très doux'; and even the final climax, though harmonically the same as before, has a more relaxed note about it. In this way the basic property of the 'similar' duet-movement – thematic repetition – is given a new twist. There is a short transition. To a succession of violent orchestral triplets Henri declares that his debt to Monfort is now paid; he will espouse the Sicilian cause once more and claim the right to die with his friends. Here the listener may note the first use of a Gallicism that will figure increasingly in the operas to come. In the chords for full orchestra underlining the phrase 'Je réclame le droit de mourir' horns and bassoons sustain for successively one and two bars while the other instruments cut off after the first crotchet, so allowing the voice to be heard while preserving the illusion of an unbroken tutti. (Again *Faust* is full of this device.)

So to the still centre of the duet which here takes the form of a minor/major romanza of two strophes for the soprano alone ('Ami le coeur d'Hélène'), full of sorrow and tenderness. She can never be his bride, but she can at least die loving him with a clear conscience. This is no outpouring of passion; the music is therefore cool and reflective with exquisite woodwind scoring and distant echoes of Schubert. The oboe adds its familiar lament (*x*).

152

Note how the word 'Ami' has been brought forward for theatrical effect (compare Violetta's 'Morrò . . . morrò la mia memoria'). As the second strophe makes clear the melody itself begins at the third bar. The finest moment is reserved for the coda where Hélène's deepening emotion is expressed in a succession of melting harmonies such as only Verdi was writing at that time – bold, unheard of in the schoolroom but unfailingly sure (Ex. 153). Not surprisingly this movement was published separately as a solo song for soprano. Even out of its context it remains a beautifully fashioned miniature.

153

Henri picks up her words 'En t'aimant' with an appropriate change of pronoun like Raoul in Act IV of *Les Huguenots*. But unlike Raoul and Valentine neither Henri nor Hélène abandon themselves to the ecstasy of the moment. The cabaletta ('Pour moi rayonne douce couronne'), never rising above *piano*, is essentially one of renunciation of a love that will never be consummated on this earth. The piece has all the daring of utter simplicity – a standard 'similar' movement based on an up-and-down arpeggio theme such as will serve Verdi to round off the great love duet in *Un Ballo in maschera*. Although the accompaniment of each statement is different the harp is prominent throughout giving that sense of the ethereal that the text demands. Neither party can look forward to anything but death. But as they toss the triplets lightly back and forth it is as though a great weight has been lifted from their shoulders (Ex. 154).

A coda with the usual strong modulations eventually brings the voices to rest in simple phrases of sixths and thirds.

Procida enters with a letter which has somehow been smuggled into the prison to the effect that Pierre d'Aragon has a ship standing off the island ready to come to the aid of the insurgents. If only he were free for one hour – and here the famous rhythmic motif (Ex. 105a) makes the first of many appearances in this scene. Then he catches sight of Henri and bursts out in a fury. Hélène is trying to defend her lover, when Montfort enters with Béthune whom he orders to summon a priest and the executioner. French soldiers are to occupy the main square in case of trouble from the

populace. Béthune leaves and Procida laments the fate of his country in the telling lapidary manner of the Verdian bass. Henri demands angrily that the captives be freed, otherwise he will share their fate. Despite Hélène's promptings Procida is unimpressed. Henri deserves to die, he says, but not for his country. Montfort, softening his tone, reproaches Henri for being deaf to the call of kith and kin. Procida thus learns for the first time that Henri is Montfort's son. All hope is now lost, he says, his voice tracing a slow C minor arpeggio from E flat to G. The only principal whose faith has not been compromised, he has dominated the scene from his entrance and it falls to him to launch the quartet ('Adieu mon pays, je succombe'), a 'differentiated' concertato in contrast to the generic ensemble of Act III. But since in *Les Vêpres Siciliennes* emotion is more controlled than in the earlier operas the rhythmic separation is less marked. Procida's line with its shifting keys has something of the restless despair of Macbeth's in the second finale ('Sangue a me'); Montfort's intervention is characterized by sharp dotted rhythms; Hélène's ('Adieu, mon doux pays') takes the form of Ex. 110, first heard in the overture. From then on a sad sweetness envelops the quartet whose climax with its rhythmic and harmonic freedom is surely one of the most beautiful that Verdi has written in this vein.

155

Ex. 105b now strikes in from the distance – a De Profundis chanted by a chorus of monks; Hélène and Procida kneel as they await execution and a vast crowd begins to pour into the fortress. Once more Henri pleads for mercy. Montfort puts on a show of severity; then in a long arioso over tremolo strings he declares that if only Henri will acknowledge him as his father before all these people Hélène and Procida shall be set free. Hélène, consumed by a sense of guilt, tells Henri imperiously not to do so. Montfort renews his pleading with a rhythmic variation of the death motif on violins to remind Henri what lies in store for the victims. Once more Hélène gives her veto with a strong downward arpeggio.

At this point the gate on the right is opened to show the place of execution or 'grande salle de justice'.* On a short flight of steps leading to it are seen four penitents in the act of prayer and a few soldiers with torches in their hands. On the first step stands the executioner leaning on his axe. The scene is set for a dramatic and musical tableau of superimposed ideas *à la française* – the finale of *Jérusalem* Act III softened and humanized by the experience of *La Traviata*. Over the inexorable chant of the monks, the pleas of the tender-hearted women bystanders, the 'death' tattoo of the side drum (this time the three-note flam is used), the subdued interchanges of the

---

* *The curtains are raised and the following tableau is presented to the spectators: A hall thronged with monks each of whom carries a lighted taper. Behind them soldiers are drawn up in rank. Alone at the head of a flight of stairs stands the executioner (Mise-en-scène, p. 14). Less sensationally, the platoon captain stands by himself at the head of a flight of steps, his sword drawn. At the back of the hall, which is draped in black, there rises a kind of black catafalque which is to be the scaffold, but must not be such as to cause revulsion. (Disp. scen. p. 30.) The populace lining the back of the stage fall spontaneously on their knees. (Mise-en-scène and Disp. scen.)*

principals, the muted violins take up Ex. 110 and develop it into a long cantabile full of anguished sobs and accents. Two of the monks come down the steps, to lead first Hélène then Procida to the block. Just as the headsman takes hold of Hélène, Henri bursts out, 'Mon père!' twice and throws himself at Montfort's feet. Montfort's happiness is tempered by the knowledge that his son has acted only out of love for Hélène, but he calls a halt to the proceedings. Not only are the prisoners to be set free, France and Sicily shall be united by the marriage of his own son with Hélène. 'Never!' cries the bride automatically; but Procida tells her that her country and her brethren demand that she should obey. Not knowing what he means, Hélène is only too glad to be able to marry Henri without qualms of conscience; and so to the final stretta which begins with a short verse of unclouded happiness for all present almost in the comic opera idiom of *Un Giorno di regno*. Then follows the main melody, which is of the 'conversational' type but here developed on a broad scale and mostly in a joyful unison. Indeed the mood is so unequivocal that the clash of texts in the unregenerate Italian manner is unimportant.

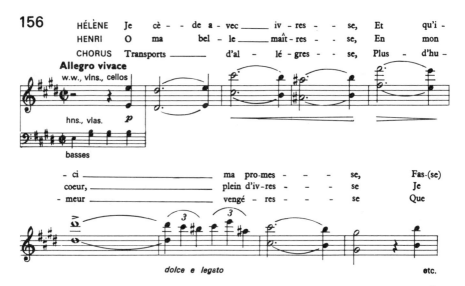

There follows a vital episode in which Henri begs Montfort to allow the wedding to take place the next day. But Montfort will do better; it shall take place at vespers that very day; and here not only the dark modulations but also a stabbing figure on bassoons, violas and cellos give out a danger signal. Henri responds with rapture ('O doux et tendre espoir!'), Procida with savage glee ('Les Vêpres! Dieu vengeur seconde mon espoir'); and when Ex. 156 is resumed it is to a clearly audible moving bass suggestive of vengeful muttering. Ritornello and coda carry the crescendo theme of the overture.*

* *Immediately after the last note a wide space opens up through which Montfort, Hélène and Henri retire. Procida recognizing certain conspirators amongst the populace makes them a sign of complicity. Quick curtain. (Mise-en-scène, p. 14.)*

ACT V

Scene: Richly appointed gardens of Montfort's palace in Palermo. At the back a stairway leading up to the chapel, whose dome is seen rising above the trees. On the right the entrance to the palace. *

By now it is becoming clear that the opera is running short of plot, and the present scheme of three static, purely decorative numbers in succession, though largely dictated by Verdi himself, would seem curiously uncongenial to a composer who liked to speed up and concentrate the action towards the final catastrophe. Nevertheless one of his great achievements in his mid-career following *La Traviata* was the conquest of the episode, nowhere more triumphantly achieved than in *La Forza del Destino*. In *Les Vêpres* the success is more variable. The opening chorus for knights in the wings and young girls on stage ('Célébrons ensemble l'hymen glorieux') with harp and castanets never rises above the level of prettiness, though the scoring of the women's verse ('L'amitié fidèle') is agreeably brilliant and the play of displaced accents and slurs effective. Hélène then comes out of the chapel dressed as a bride to sing the famous Sicilienne ('Merci, jeunes amies').† The title is a mystery since this is quite plainly a Spanish bolero, and indeed in the Italian production book is described as such. Cast in couplet form with a coda of great vocal virtuosity it is one of the gems of the score – a party piece rather than an expression of character, yet so nimble and fresh in its melodies that few would want to be without it. Could Grieg have had the refrain (Ex. 157) in mind when he wrote Solveig's song in the same form and key? In a long play-out Hélène dismisses the young girls and is joined by Henri who has meanwhile come down the flight of stairs from the chapel 'en rêvant' and sings his Mélodie ('Le brise souffle au loin') with Hélène intervening in ritornello and coda.‡ Melody and scoring have a chamber-like delicacy which may account for the unusual title. The piece is both a jewelled miniature in the manner of Meyerbeer and a tone-poem evoking the cool evening breeze with its scent of orange blossom. The 'atmospheric' string tremoli to be found in *Alzira* and *I Masnadieri* are here enhanced by flute and later piccolo trills.

A melisma in the coda takes the singer up to high D – which is usually made an excuse for cutting the piece altogether. A pity certainly, but like Hélène's Sicilienne it is a static, detachable number which bears little relation to the rest of the opera.

Henri bids Hélène farewell while he goes to find his father. Then the drama kindles swiftly into life as Procida enters and explains to Hélène his plan for the uprising, for which the vespers bell will be the signal. In his single-mindedness he has no idea that Hélène could object. When he realizes the truth, that she has given up all

---

* The setting prescribed in the production books is much more elaborate, including columns, some statuary, a terrace with balustrade and a richly decked pavilion.

† *After the chorus Hélène comes out of the pavilion splendidly attired as a bride and preceded by two pages who take up a position at the foot of the pavilion steps, and followed by four maids of honour, who proceed to occupy the extreme right of the stage. The young girls make her a deep curtsey, and offer their flowers which she graciously accepts; she hands them to one of the young girls and comes downstage to sing her Sicilienne. (Mise-en-scène, p. 16.)*

‡ In the production books Hélène retires once more into the pavilion together with pages, maids of honour and the young girl to whom she has given the flowers. She comes out again in time for her intervention at the end of Henri's first strophe.

157   Allegro

thoughts of vengeance for love of Henri, he taunts her bitterly. Very well, as a good Frenchwoman let her denounce himself and all her former friends if she dare. To convey Procida's challenge ('Eh bien, donc! qui t'arrête?') the allegro vivo movement subsides into a chilling austerity. Procida's voice is heard descending to low F just as a flourish of trumpets, cornets and trombones brings back Henri from the palace ('La bannière de France en tous lieux se déploie'). He advances to embrace

158   Allegretto

Hélène, but she remains frozen, repeating Procida's words as in a trance: 'When the bride has answered "I will", when the palace bells ring out the news of their wedding, the massacre will begin.' Strings tremolando, a low clarinet, a roll on the timpani, a slithering figure on violins depict her terror with the utmost economy. Henri implores her to speak. 'If you dare!' adds Procida.

The largo of the terzetto ('Sort fatal', Ex. 159a) has a heavy lowering quality, in strong contrast to the unclouded skies at the beginning of the act. Both key (B minor) and time signature are unusual for Verdi, who preferred to indicate compound time by means of triplets within a 4/4 pulse, and with good reason, since they usually contain 'simple' elements which are intended to form the rhythmic background. But here every quaver carries a special weight of its own. More than half a century later Puccini will use the same means to depict the cloud of menace hanging over Giorgetta and Luigi. In the major section Henri's voice rises in a noble, tender appeal ('De cette voix qui m'est si chère'). Then before the final chord which by tradition must be major Verdi inserts a startlingly poignant coda in B minor for voices and strings. Two features arrest the attention: the clash of A natural and A sharp, and the raising of the cello line above those of violas and second violins – both serve to heighten the sense of anguish, and the second in particular anticipates the kind of string writing to be found in the last movement of Tchaikovsky's 'Pathétique' Symphony, also, be it noted, in B minor.

159a

159b

Hélène now pretends to see the ghost of her brother rising up to forbid the marriage. (Musically he too takes the same form as the ghost of Carmagnola in *I Due Foscari*.) Henri must fly from Palermo. . . . But Henri sees this only as a treacherous volte-face on Hélène's part. The final movement of the trio ('Trahison! Imposture! Le mensonge est ta loi!') is remarkable as being the only piece in which Hélène and Henri give full rein to their feelings. In effect it is a trio-cabaletta with a minor-to-major key scheme and particular weight thrown onto the tenor and soprano. Henri has the first verse entirely to himself as he hurls reproaches at his faithless beloved; Hélène dominates the second, with angry interjections from the men who are both furious with her though for different reasons. There follows a brief episode by way of ritornello in which Hélène on the point of revealing all to Henri, is brought up sharply by Procida who accuses her of selling Sicily to her brother's murderers. Back therefore to the original impasse for the third verse which finds Hélène united with Henri in misery and despair. It is a masterly piece, electric in its sense of drama and its huge melodic sweep. The refrain alone, sung first by Henri, will suffice to indicate the elemental power of the writing, in which the sense of stress is in no way diminished by the major tonality. Montfort now enters to be met by Henri with his tale of woe. Of course he cannot believe that Hélène will refuse to obey the dictates of her heart. 'Soyez unis ô nobles fiancés', he says with all the nobility of a Sarastro or a Don Ferdinando. The same musical phrase takes on an air of parody in the mouth of Procida as he gives the signal for the bells. The music at once drops from F to the dominant of A minor. The tocsin sounds in regular beats; there is a crescendo during which Hélène desperately begs Henri to escape while he can; then to Ex. 107 in 3/4

160

time ('Oui, vengeance!') the Sicilian chorus bursts in armed with daggers and swords, and the curtain falls on the massacre of the French.

Or so it was finally decided. But the printed libretto contains a few lines more which indicate the fate of the principals. Henri runs to Montfort with a cry of 'My father!'; Montfort clasps him in his arms. Hélène places herself in front of both, falls on her knees and implores Procida to spare them or else she will share their fate. The Sicilians fall back for a moment, but Procida rallies them: 'Strike them all down, what does it matter – French or Sicilian? God will choose his own.' And with this he and the Sicilians hurl themselves at Hélène, Henri and Montfort as the curtain falls. Verdi's autograph contains a fully scored setting of this exchange, shortened to his taste, like the ending of *Il Trovatore*, as an episode between two statements of the chorus. Musically it is fairly neutral, but it keeps up the tension while allowing the words to be clearly heard. Why it was abandoned we can only guess. Perhaps it created problems for the producer; perhaps it offended Verdi himself since it presented his fellow-patriot in an even more disagreeable light; perhaps it just 'chilled the action', to use his own phrase. If the public wanted to know what happened to the principals they could always read the libretto.*

* The production books describe the final débâcle as follows, beginning at Montfort's first line ('Erreur! Hélène vainement lutte contre son cœur'). *For some moments past three conspirators clad in brown cloaks have been visible between two columns at the head of a flight of stairs. At a sign from Procida and without being seen by the rest of the characters on stage they swiftly mount the steps leading to the terrace and disappear. Shortly afterwards two other conspirators appear also clad in brown cloaks. At a sign from Procida they too mount the steps and disappear into an upper gallery. Only Hélène has noticed them and her terror redoubles. Then Procida goes to the back of the stage. As he speaks the words, 'Et vous, pour ce grand jour, cloches rétentissez', he climbs five or six stairs and looks towards the right; at the reply, 'N'entends tu pas ces voix', he stretches out his hand as an agreed signal. Soon the chapel bell sounds a mournful chime: Montfort: 'Des chants de rejouissance.' / Hélène: 'Et la cloche*

The performance over, Verdi immediately busied himself with the question of the Italian translation. As early as 29 April he had written to Ricordi: 'If you still have the idea of buying the *Sicilian Vespers*, I will guarantee to send you a copy of the full score with the French text and with the ballet which forms a separate action entitled the Four Seasons; also an Italian translation made under my supervision by a competent poet and changing the subject so as to render it acceptable for the Italian theatres.'*

Scribe himself had a part to play in this, or so he told his unnamed correspondent. . . . 'The other day Verdi learned to his great distress that with its present title the opera couldn't be given in Italy. He asked me what was to be done. I suggested that the Duke of Alba should just pack his bags once more and move to Lisbon.'† Accordingly the Fond Scribe contains three pages entitled *Les Vêpres Siciliennes changés* giving directions for the alteration. The scene is now Portugal in the year 1640 under the Spanish dominion. Vasconcello, the new Montfort, is not a Spaniard but a Portuguese Quisling (this, Scribe noted, should give his son a still better motive for hating him). Hélène would become Helena de Guzman whose sister was married to the patriotic Duke of Braganza; while Procida would be the Duke's secretary, Ribera Pinto, determined to set his master on the throne of Portugal. Henri would retain his Christian name italianized into Enrico. Pedro of Aragon would be Cardinal Richelieu. Alternative endings are suggested. Either Enrico and Vasconcello could be struck down at the altar as in the original, or the Duke of Braganza could arrive just in time to prevent bloodshed. Verdi of course preferred the tragic end. One further change was necessary, since Hélène in Italian (Elena) carries an awkward 'sdrucciolo' accent another name had to be found. Verdi wrote to Ricordi: 'The title we had originally chosen was *Maria di Braganza* but meanwhile I've thought of substituting the name Giovanna; that's why you'll find in the score Maria and in the libretto Giovanna. Not that it matters . . . you can put what you like.' He concluded, 'I now know what it means to translate and I feel sympathy for all the bad translations that are around because it is impossible to make a good one.'‡

---

annonçante' / Henri: *'Mon bonheur.'* At this point the following movements must be performed simultaneously and with all possible speed. A considerable number of young men of the people who have hidden behind the terrace now leap over it in the twinkling of an eye and invade the entire left side of the stage. Others mount the pavilion steps and enter the pavilion itself, from which the women of the castle flee and take up their position on the terrace. Montfort and his men have no arms except the ceremonial poignards that adorn their dress. The Sicilians are armed with swords, lances, axes and daggers. Behind those of the populace already mentioned others pour onto the scene between the two columns. Another crowd of men and women (chorus, corps de ballet and extras) burst in and occupy the remaining flights of stairs. *'Oui, vengeance; oui, vengeance'* / *'Qu'elle guide nos pas.'* Henri, deaf to everything but the call of his blood and the voice of gratitude, places himself beside his father and draws his poignard so causing the rebels to hesitate for an instant. But at a gesture from Procida the bolder spirits amongst the populace to the right hurl themselves against Montfort and his men with swords and daggers drawn; but they fall back wounded mortally by Montfort and Henri. Hélène falls on her knees before her lover intending to shield him with her body. Infuriated by the sight of the first victims, the populace make haste to avenge them. Montfort, Henri and the knights behind whom the women of the castle have taken refuge await the onslaught rooted to the spot. Procida emboldens his followers. On this tableau and during the final held *'vengean–ce'* the curtain falls swiftly. (Mise-en-scène, pp. 17–18.)

* Letter to T. Ricordi, 29.4.1855. *Copialettere*, pp. 160–1.
† Letter from Scribe, undated, in *Revue des deux mondes* (September, 1917), pp. 894–5.
‡ Letter to T. Ricordi, 6.7.1855. Abbiati, II, p. 297.

Eugenio Caimi's *Giovanna de Guzman* is in fact one of the worst ever perpetrated. The wonder is that in all essentials it remains in general use to this day. Not only is it full of slack words and phrases which in the original had been taut and striking; much of the scansion is wildly false. The fact is that when faced with the new metres and more flexible prosody of French verse the Italian translator of that time still tended to reach for the nearest of the standard Italian metres. 'Comble de misère' is a six-syllable line with a strong accent at the beginning; Caimi renders it as 'Parola fatale,' an orthodox Italian senario with the accent firmly on the second syllable. As a result it sits very awkwardly on the musical phrase. Examples of this fault can be found in all translations of French opera up till the time when the Italians themselves extended their system of metres. (Zanardini's translations in *Don Carlos* are on the whole very much better than those of De Lauzières.) When after 1861 the opera reverted to its original title and locale the opportunity was taken to remove some of Caimi's worst *sottises*: thus 'Confortan le guerre il vino e l'amor' becomes 'Viva la guerra! Viva l'amor!' But the text is still far from satisfactory.*

None the less the opera's Italian career made an auspicious start with nine productions at different theatres during the carnival season of 1855–6. Only the ballet was to prove something of an embarrassment. 'The Four Seasons received some applause,' wrote Muzio to Tito Ricordi from Padua, 'but it ended in icy silence.'†

Likewise Mariani from Genoa: 'The opera *Guzman* continues to do excellently, only I find that it's not a show to give in this season with a ballet which lasts an hour and a half. For the sake of brevity we had to leave out the first act and even mutilate the ballet slightly.'‡

Italians of the mid nineteenth century preferred their operas undiluted by the dance. As late as 1867 Corinno Mariotti, a journalist from Turin, wrote about the ballet in *Don Carlos*: 'In my opinion this concession that Verdi has made to the demands of the Grand Opera should be his last since we Italians are being logical when we rebel, as often happens, against this French-bred form of opera ballet.'§ In the end it was Verdi himself who authorized the removal of the dances 'since our choreographers can't think of anything which makes them tolerable or which doesn't damage the Finale Terzo'.¶ His advice was followed for all Italian theatres and with rare exceptions (Florence 1951; Turin 1973) is so to this day.

---

* Both Abbiati (II, p. 297) and Loewenberg, *Annals of Opera*, 2nd ed. (Geneva, 1955), p. 918, credit *Giovanna de Guzman* to Arnaldo Fusinato, a reputable minor poet who in February of that year had expressed through Cesare Vigna an interest in translating *Les Vêpres Siciliennes* or, still better, in writing for Verdi a comic libretto – see letter from T. Ricordi, 8.2.1855 (*Copialettere*, p. 485); but there is no proof that his suggestion was ever followed up. Nor is it likely that if it had been he would have remained anonymous. The first edition of *Giovanna de Guzman* gives the translator's initials as E.C. Loewenberg himself gives Caimi as the translator of *I Vespri Siciliani*, evidently not realizing that the two texts are more or less identical. Another puzzle is provided by the early Neapolitan printed edition *Il Vespro Siciliano* where the Italian text is stated to be by E.C. and S.G. Was S.G. perhaps the man responsible for the trifling changes which distinguish the Portuguese from the Sicilian setting? The reader will find most of these problems discussed in M. Mila, *Verdi: Les Vêpres Siciliennes* (Turin, 1973), together with French and Italian libretti set out with all existing variants.

† Letter from Muzio to T. Ricordi, 6.7.1856. Abbiati, II, pp. 361–2.

‡ Letter from Mariani to T. Ricordi, 30.5.1856. Abbiati, II, pp. 365–6.

§ Conati 'Verdi, il grand opera', p. 254.

¶ Apparently a quotation from an undated letter from Verdi either to Muzio or to Ricordi, written from Venice in early July 1856. Abbiati, II, p. 363.

Paris, Théâtre de l'Opéra, 6 July 1863

Meanwhile in Paris *Les Vêpres Siciliennes* continued to prosper, until the departure of Cruvelli at the end of the year, a blow from which it never quite recovered. Successive revivals with Moreau-Saint, Barlot and Medori failed to restore its fortunes. It was by now clear that *Les Vêpres Siciliennes*, for all the respectful praise lavished upon it, was not destined to enter the charmed circle of repertory classics, such as *Les Huguenots* or *La Juive*. The première of *Le Trouvère* in 1857 did it no good at all; this was obviously the Verdi that everyone preferred.

But in 1863 Verdi himself decided to fan the dying embers. Partly by way of compensation to Escudier for having refused permission for a French performance of his recently composed *La Forza del Destino* he agreed to assist in a revival of the earlier opera with two promising newcomers, Sax and Villaret, in the roles of Hélène and Henri respectively. For Villaret, who had created an excellent impression as Arnold in *Guillaume Tell* two years before, Verdi wrote an entirely new romance ('O toi que j'ai chéri') to replace 'O jour de peine', in which the original tenor Gueymard had failed signally to satisfy the composer.* At one of the orchestral rehearsals Verdi demanded the repetition of a particular passage in faster tempo. The orchestra responded by playing it twice as slowly; it was an incident only too typical of the lack of orchestral discipline under the baton of Dietsch, the permanent conductor, but its effect on Verdi can be imagined. Only with the greatest difficulty could he be persuaded to attend the first performance. He left the next day, and all musical Paris shook with the sound of his departure. Dietsch was belatedly substituted by Hainl; but whether due to the demoralization of the final rehearsals, or because, as the press indicated, the singers with the exception of la Sax were out of voice, the opera had a tepid reception. Villaret, it appears, made nothing of his new romance. Berlioz, one of the few who admired the score as a whole, fails to mention it entirely. The real star of the evening was Mme Vernon who danced the part of Spring in the Four Seasons and for whose sake Auber's *La Muette de Portici* was mounted shortly afterwards. Meanwhile *Les Vêpres Siciliennes* was withdrawn from the affiche after a few performances and replaced by *Le Trouvère*. After one revival in 1865 it vanished from the Parisian stage altogether.

The new romance for Villaret was duly printed as an appendix in the second French edition of *Les Vêpres Siciliennes*, and a copy of the score sent to Ricordi,† but it never found its way into later editions of the Italian score. However, Ricordi's catalogue of 1875 lists it as a separate piece with the title 'O tu che tanto amai'. All copies of this seem to have vanished, so that when in 1969 Nello Santi decided to include the romance in an Italian production in Hamburg he was obliged to commission a new text. Clearly the piece had found few takers – which is in a way surprising since although it lacks the dramatic and musical subtlety of the original it is none the less a fine example of the minor–major tenor romance that Verdi had been writing ever since the time of *Oberto*. In the central idea in A major there is a wide spread of strings recalling the final section of 'Addio del passato', while the F sharp major denouement finishes in one of those sweeping lyrical descents characteristic of the later *Macbeth* and *Don Carlos* (Ex. 161).

---

* See letter to Perrin, ? September 1865. Abbiati, III, p. 46.
† See letter to T. Ricordi, 3.10.1863. Abbiati, II, p. 744.

161

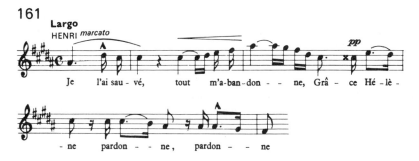

No cabaletta substitute follows, since the full sense of release has already been achieved. Nor is the subsequent key-change a problem. Four bars of neutral modulation had been necessary to introduce F sharp minor at the beginning; but the drop of a minor third from the final chord to the unison E flat that begins the grand duet is a smooth enough procedure – if anything, too much so. The downward shift of a semitone in the original created a greater feeling of suspense.*

Although its best known excerpt is an aria for bass *Les Vêpres Sicilennes* has usually been regarded as a prima donna opera, and rightly. For of all the principals it is Hélène who is required to show the widest range both of character and technique, from embattled virago to joyous, tender-hearted bride to be, from donna di forza to something like soprano leggiero. The problem has been encountered before in *Attila* and *Luisa Miller*. The difference is that here the diverse traits are integrated. In the transitions between one mood and another we are aware of being presented with different facets of the same personality – which was certainly not the case with Odabella. Procida, on the other hand, remains one-dimensional; and his dimension of patriotism becomes rather uninteresting once attention has become focused on the lovers. As compensation Verdi has written for him a bass-baritone part of rare vocal beauty. Montfort's is again a developing personality, harsh and authoritative at first, then rising to heights of nobility and tenderness. Partly because the part is, for a Verdi baritone, unusually low, he achieves an 'inward' quality unusual in his kind. Henri is to some extent a victim of the plot, forced much of the time to cut an undignified figure and nowhere more than at the end when – to quote Massimo Mila – he rushes to his father like a child crying over a broken toy.† But in general he shows a restrained dignity of emotional expression that is rare for a Verdian tenor, though he requires a very considerable weight of voice, due to the long phrases. He is like an adult Arrigo from *La Battaglia di Legnano*. And indeed this is the opera with which *Les Vêpres Sicilennes* so often invites favourable comparison. Both were written with the greatest care and attention to detail. In both the special requirements of an adapted plot impose particular formal solutions, often of a rather classical nature. *La Battaglia di Legnano* is divided into alternating scenes of grandeur and intimacy; *Les Vêpres Sicilennes* is planned in spacious movements using thematic recurrence more widely than in the more 'dialectically' constructed operas. But whereas the first falls into incoherence on more than one level, the second remains an organic whole, in which the same problems are successfully solved. *Les Vêpres* sustains its length perfectly (not

---

* The autograph of the romance is to be found in the Bibliothèque Nationale, MS. 1080.

† M. Mila, *op. cit.*, p. 232.

that it is as long as is often supposed once the ballet has been omitted: an uncut *Carmen* or *Figaro* is considerably longer). If the absorption of new elements into his musical language occasionally disguises the composer's voice, the opera has no less than *Attila, Macbeth* or *La Traviata* its own special 'tinta', to be found not only in the ubiquitous 'death figure' (♫♩) but also in the spacious melodic gait usually epitomized in a smooth descending pattern embedded in the second or third phrase (see Exs. 108, 117, 118, 123b, and 145). Why then is the opera so rarely performed; why is it a 'festival' rather than a repertory piece?

Firstly, like *Jérusalem* and until fairly recently *Don Carlos*, it has suffered from the prejudice attaching to all Verdi's French operas (for his first Italian commentators and biographers could never believe that he could put his heart into the setting of a French text). Then too the story, which Verdi himself misleadingly condemned in his famous letter to Crosnier, suggests a cut-price *Huguenots* using the props of *La Muette de Portici*. Few have bothered to notice that Verdi humanizes it far beyond the capacity of a Meyerbeer or an Auber. True, the formal nature of French-style recitative sometimes obtrudes unnecessarily, as also in *Moïse* and *Guillaume Tell* (the French may have called the lines 'vers libre', but they lack the freedom of Italian 'versi sciolti'). To this may be added a slightly self-conscious quality which contrasts with the 'careless rapture' of a *Trovatore*. However, *Les Vêpres Siciliennes* was not without influence on Italian opera of the mid-century – an influence very marked in Petrella's *Giovanna di Napoli* of 1869. It also had a partisan in the young Arrigo Boito who, somewhat perversely, preferred it in its Portuguese setting.* But it has fared very badly with biographers of this century. Today, when the fashion is all for the primitive force of 'Verdi risorgimentale', *Les Vêpres* is often compared unfavourably with, say, *Il Corsaro* or *I Masnadieri* – a preposterous judgement. Let us hope that a new generation of Verdians will recognize it for the noble, thoughtful and often exciting work that it is.

---

* *Critiche e cronache muscali di Arrigo Boito*, a cura di R. De Rensis (Milan, 1931), pp. 136–7.

6 SIMON BOCCANEGRA

SIMON BOCCANEGRA

Opera in a prologue and three acts
by
FRANCESCO MARIA PIAVE, with additions by Giuseppe Montanelli
(after the play *Simón Bocanegra* by Antonio García Gutiérrez)

First performed at the
Teatro la Fenice, Venice,
12 March 1857

Prologue

SIMON BOCCA-NEGRA, corsair in the service of the Genoese republic	PRIMO BARITONO	Leone Giraldoni
JACOPO FIESCO, a Genoese noble	PRIMO BASSO PROFONDO	Giuseppe Echeverria
PAOLO ALBIANI, a Genoese goldsmith	BARITONO COMPRIMAPIO	Giacomo Vercellini
PIETRO, a popular leader	BARITONO COMPRIMARIO	Andrea Bellini

Opera

SIMON BOCCA-NEGRA, Doge of Genoa	PRIMO BARITONO	Leone Giraldoni
MARIA BOCCA-NEGRA, his daughter, under the name of AMELIA	PRIMA DONNA SOPRANO	Luigia Bendazzi
JACOPO FIESCO, under the name of Andrea	PRIMO BASSO PROFONDO	Giuseppe Echeverria
GABRIELE ADORNO, a Genoese gentleman	PRIMO TENORE	Carlo Negrini
PAOLO, a courtier, the Doge's favourite	BARITONO COMPRIMARIO	Giacomo Vercellini
PIETRO, another courtier	BARITONO COMPRIMARIO	Andrea Bellini
A maidservant of Amelia	SECONDA DONNA*	N.N.

Soldiers – sailors – populace – servants of Fiesco – senators – the Doge's
court – African prisoners of both sexes
The action takes place in and around Genoa
Epoch: towards the middle of the fourteenth century
(N.B. Between the prologue and the opera 25 years pass)

REVISED VERSION

(with additions and alterations by ARRIGO BOITO)
First performed at the
Teatro alla Scala, Milan
24 March 1881

BOCCANEGRA	Victor Maurel	AMELIA	Anna D'Angeri
FIESCO	Edouard de Reszke	Captain of	
PAOLO	Federico Salvati	crossbowmen	Angelo Fiorentini
PIETRO	Giovanni Bianco	Amelia's maidservant	Fernanda Capelli
GABRIELE	Francesco Tamagno		

---

* At the first Venice performance this tiny part was given to a secondo basso.

At the beginning of 1855 while rehearsals for *Les Vêpres Siciliennes* were in progress Verdi twice refused an invitation to compose a new opera for the Teatro la Fenice, Venice, for the following year. 'Various future plans stand in the way; but if I am to be frank the chief obstacle is my unshakable determination not to bind myself any more to a definite period for either the composition or the production.'* A laudable intention; but the time was not ripe for it to be realized. At the time Verdi's future projects were three: to revise *Stiffelio* and *La Battaglia di Legnano* so as to make them acceptable to the Italian censorship; and to fulfil his long cherished ambition to compose a *Re Lear*. Of these only the first was destined to be accomplished. Emanuele Bardare, the poet chosen to remake the text of *La Battaglia di Legnano*, failed to produce anything sufficiently inspiring, and the plan was quietly dropped. Correspondence on the subject of *King Lear* with Verdi's new acquaintance, the playwright Antonio Somma, was to continue for some years, but the libretto was its only fruit.

By the spring of 1856 Verdi felt free to accept yet another offer of a contract from the Teatro la Fenice. This time it is clear that the moving spirit was Piave, who throughout the early months of the year bombarded Brenna and Torniello with letters urging them to approach the composer and agree to his terms, however high. A favourable reply was received from Verdi on 12 May 1856. 'The conditions could be largely the same as for *La Traviata*: but it would be timely to add that if the subject I shall choose requires some new "comprimario" parts the management should guarantee to engage them.'† Two weeks later the contract was duly signed.

But it was not until the eve of his departure for Paris in late summer, to present his law-suit against Calzado, that he wrote to Piave, 'I think I've found the subject for Venice; I'll send you the programme from Paris.'‡ Three weeks later, we hear of the title: 'How is *Simon Boccanegra* going?' §

What led him to another play by García Guttiérrez we can only guess. Possibly the hope of repeating the success of *Il Trovatore*; possibly the Genoese setting, since Genoa was a city for which he had a particular affection (later he was to spend the winter months of each year there). Like *El Trovador*, *Simón Bocanegra* was never published in Italian; so once again we may suppose that Giuseppina Strepponi made the translation. The story of a fourteenth-century Genoese corsair, his elevation to the supreme power, and his death at the hands of a former friend and ally, *Simón Bocanegra* shares a number of features with its better known predecessor. The time-span is huge; much of the action takes place against the background of a civil war – here a Guelph rebellion; and the main pivot of the plot is again the identity of a long-lost child, Bocanegra's illegitimate daughter by his beloved Maria, herself the daughter of his political enemy, the patrician Jacopo Fiesco. Certain of the characters

* Letter to Tornielli, 16.2.1855. Conati, *La bottega della musica*, pp. 336–7.
† Letter to Tornielli, 12.5.1856. *Ibid.*, pp. 363–4.
‡ Letter to Piave, 31.7.1856. Abbiati, II, p. 368.
§ Letter to Piave, 23.8.1856. Abbiati, II, pp. 369–71.

even have their counterparts in *El Trovador*. Just as Eleonora is led by her love for Manrique to betray more and more of the social and religious tenets by which she had lived, so Fiesco, in his thirst for vengeance against his daughter's seducer, increasingly compromises himself to the point where he is blackmailed by Paolo Albiani, Bocanegra's former friend and betrayer, into promising him the hand of his ward, the soi-disante Susana Grimaldi, little realizing that she is in fact his missing grand-daughter. Only when Paolo tells him how he has had Bocanegra poisoned does Fiesco recoil in horror. By now the Guelph revolt has been quelled. Fiesco, its leader, is prepared to face the victorious Bocanegra alone. Paolo, a coward as well as a turncoat, wishes to flee with the remnant of the rebel army. As he leaves hurriedly Fiesco has a brief exchange with one of his followers:

> FIESCO   See that he gets safely away to the mountains.
> LAZARO   And then?
> FIESCO   Show him no mercy.

For reasons of economy this dialogue was omitted from the libretto so that in the first version of the opera we never learn of Paolo's fate. In the second Gutiérrez's plot is radically altered.

Paolo himself shares with the Count of Luna a self-knowledge which is powerless to control his actions. Each might have said with Ovid, 'Video meliora proboque; deteriora sequor.' The Count's love for Leonora has led him to abuse his authority as governor of a province and to pervert the course of justice – he admits as much; but he can do nothing about it. Paolo regards his ambition, his envy of the patricians as a disease for which he asks Bocanegra's compassion. Yet when the Doge denies him the hand of Susana – partly because she hates him, partly because he knows that Paolo is only interested in her money – he becomes a Monostatos to Bocanegra's Sarastro. But love, even as felt by the Count of Luna, is a much more amiable spur than the emotions of greed, envy and family pride, which animate so many of the characters of *Simón Bocanegra*. It is also very much easier to portray in a mid-nineteenth-century Italian opera. In fact, romantic love plays a surprisingly small part in the present plot. Gabriele Adorno, the jeune premier, conventionally in love with the heroine, Susana, does not scruple to lie to her about his part in the Guelph uprising. Susana herself, having discovered that Bocanegra is her father, makes it clear that from now on he comes before Gabriele in her life. All the characters define themselves against an ingeniously shifting pattern of intrigue such as can be highly effective in a play but is well-nigh impossible to follow in an opera. Had Cammarano been alive he might have propounded a drastic solution that Verdi himself would have found acceptable. Piave had neither Cammarano's experience nor his authority. To make matters worse, during the crucial stages of preparation he was in Italy while Verdi found himself increasingly detained in Paris.

As early as September the composer was somewhat irritated to hear that Piave was being badgered by the censor for the completed text. He had already sent a full synopsis.

> What is the point of finishing the story of *Simon Boccanegra* before the end of the month? Haven't the police and the directorate got a sufficiently detailed

programme? Indeed, it isn't a programme – it's the completely finished drama. In the libretto not an idea, not a word will be changed. What does it matter whether for the moment it's in prose or verse? And as you have quite rightly remarked, this *Simone* has something original about it. Therefore the scheme of the libretto, the numbers, etc., need to be as original as possible. This can't be done unless we get together; at present it would be a waste of time.

Just tell our friend Torniello to keep calm and leave matters to us, who know our job extremely well, and if he wants something to do there's plenty that needs doing elsewhere. Let him attend to the decor and the costumes. Oh, the settings could be so beautiful in this *Simone*! In three of them the painter could and should do very well indeed. But the scenes should have double and triple backcloths and the practicable props should be really practicable, not stools like those used in *Guillaume Tell* . . . *

A week later, to make assurance double sure:

Write back yourself to the directorate on my behalf that the *Simon Boccanegra* I sent them in August is not a programme (I don't think programmes are set out in that way) but the libretto as it needs to be approved by the censor. I am obliged to give an opera at the Teatro la Fenice in the carnival season, and this time for the sake of novelty I intend to set a prose libretto. What do you think of that? . . . So I'm perfectly within the rules! . . . For further changes we shall ask for a second approval from the censor, as the President quite rightly says.†

Let no one think, however, that Verdi was serious in this. The structure of his musical thought throughout his career rested on a basis of metrical verse. It was merely a dodge to keep the censor quiet; and indeed the censor acquiesced, if a little stiffly, and insisting on a further examination of the versified result with the hope that Signor Piave might see his way clear to 'moderating certain intemperate phrases encountered in the prose sketch'.‡

Meanwhile Verdi failed to obtain an injunction preventing Calzado from mounting *Rigoletto* and *La Traviata*; but his costs were offset by the commission to assist with the production of *Le Trouvère*, which was to keep him in Paris for the rest of the year. He wrote again to Piave in October asking him to work on the text of *Simon Boccanegra* by himself and send it to him act by act at his leisure.§ Two weeks later he gave Piave news of the lost law-suit with Calzado, adding, ominously, 'About *Boccanegra* I've many things to say to you but we'll talk about it later when you've finished it.'¶ As late as November he hoped to return home within a few days and told Piave to get ready to come to S. Agata for consultations;‖ but it was not to

---

* Letter to Piave, 3.9.1856. Conati, pp. 382–3.

† Letter to Piave, 12.9.1856. *Ibid.*, p. 383.

‡ Memorandum from I.R. Consigliere di Gov. Direttoriale, 27.9.1856. *Ibid.*, p. 386.

§ Letters to Piave, 2 and 7.10.1856. *Ibid.*, pp. 388–9.

¶ Letter to Piave, 21.10.1856. *Ibid.*, p. 391.

‖ Letter to Piave, 27.10.1856. *Ibid.*, p. 393.

be. Unable to work at close quarters with his librettist Verdi felt obliged, not for the first time, to look elsewhere for help. His choice fell on the Tuscan poet and patriot Giuseppe Montanelli, now living in exile in Paris after being sentenced in absentia to hard labour for life for his part in the revolutionary government of 1849. (Later he was to earn Verdi's deepest admiration as a combatant in the war of 1859.)*

The three letters that have survived – two from Montanelli and one from Verdi – clearly represent the aftermath of their collaboration, with the composer now back in Italy. The passages referred to are six – mostly important moments in the original version of the opera: the cabaletta of the heroine's cavatina, the recognition duet between Boccanegra and his daughter, the preparation for the Act I concertato, and three scenes from the end of the opera including that of the Doge's death. All three Montanelli had to write twice before Verdi was satisfied with them. Sometimes, as in the duet, it was a matter of new lines with the *accento tronco* instead of *piano*. Elsewhere it was for reasons of intelligibility and stage effect.

Thus: 'At the Doge's death in the ensemble the pathetic note is lacking or insufficient. These are none of those words which – common as they are – never fail in their effect and draw tears. The stanzas of the Doge ("Gran Dio li benedici"), of Amelia ("Ahime! sull'alma sento") and of Gabriele ("Come passò qual lampo") are too vague; the characters never exchange a word among themselves and that makes the scene dull and not very moving.'† In the end he accepted Montanelli's revised versions of the stanzas for Amelia and Gabriele but used one of his own for the Doge.

Also in Act III: 'Pietro's line "Far cor – tutto disposi alla vendetta" is not sufficiently clear for the public. Perhaps for the stage it would be better thus: PIETRO, "Far cor – tutto disposi"; PAOLO (*with joy*), "È giunta l'ora alfin della vendetta" (change this bad line).'

And it was certainly an economical way of making clear that while Paolo plotted the Doge's murder by poison it was his henchman Pietro who carried it out, though nobody explains how and when. (In the play Pietro puts poison in the chalice from which the Doge traditionally drinks on state occasions.) From the same letter we learn that Verdi himself was responsible for Paolo's grotesquely feeble exit line in the following scene with Fiesco, ('Folle, resta – io coi tuoi riederò'), having in his usual manner set out the dialogue as he wanted it and asked Montanelli to turn it into good verse while preserving the sense.‡ How far these rewritten passages differed from Piave's text it is impossible to say since the autograph of the original libretto has not survived. Nor did Verdi ever give away the name of his new collaborator.

Meanwhile Piave himself, unaware of what was happening, continued to satisfy the composer's requirements as best he could. Thus of the finale to the first act:

> I'm sorry to hear that you're against allegories; but since you are I shall declare myself against them as well and we won't talk about it any further. I don't see however that you say anything about the last chorus I sent you, which has nothing to do with allegories and which I set out in four verses according to an

---

* For this students are indebted to Frank Walker whose essay 'Verdi, Giuseppe Montanelli and the libretto of *Simon Boccanegra*', in *I.S.V. Bollettino*, No. 3 (Parma, 1960), pp. 1373–90, sets forth all the relevant documents and examines in detail evidence for the extent of Montanelli's contribution.

† Letter to Montanelli, 30.1.1857. Walker, *op. cit.*, pp. 1382–4.

‡ See letter from Montanelli, 5.2.1857.

idea you suggested to me yourself; if even this isn't satisfactory tell me what you would like done. . . . I myself, for instance, rather than allow for a formal celebration would have a grand march for the Doge who would proceed to the throne while the chorus were singing, and just as the games were about to begin the interruption would occur caused by the arrival of Adorno, etc., etc. Good heavens! If we were together it could all be arranged so easily! In any case write to me and all will go well.*

But when Verdi did write it was to absolve Piave from all further work on the text. 'Here is the libretto, shortened and altered more or less as it must be. You can put your name to it or not, just as you please. If you're sorry about what has happened I am sorry too, and perhaps more than you, but I can only say, "It was a necessity!"'†

It was not the only bitter pill that Piave had to swallow. On 18 February he was obliged to plead with the management to grant him the agent's fee which he had been promised as an intermediary between them and the composer. Finally, some time after the unsuccessful première, Verdi heard from Cesare Vigna that he himself was rumoured to be the author of the libretto. He concluded that Piave must have started the rumour and wrote him an angry letter, which has not survived. Its contents, however, can be gathered from Piave's dignified reply.

My defence, supposing I wished to make one, lies all in your letter, since it is impossible that I should not have foreseen the consequences of what you say, and you will not think me so foolish as to have wished to expose myself to them. For the rest I have never heard the gossip that you mention and whoever wrote to you about it, if he didn't invent it, must have heard it from someone who deliberately spread it around so as indirectly to put an end to the kindness with which you honour me and for which I am so greatly envied. . . .‡

Good relations were soon restored. Verdi indirectly acknowledged his injustice in a letter to Vigna: 'The story about my being the author of the libretto was just about the last straw! A libretto with Piave's name on it is judged in advance as wretched poetry; and I would honestly be happy if I could have written verses like "Vieni a mirar la cerula . . . Delle faci festanti al barlume" and various others with so many lines scattered here and there. I admit my ignorance; I am not clever enough.'§

But of course 'a libretto with Piave's name on it' is not quite the same as 'a libretto by Piave'; and the lines that Verdi quotes with such admiration may well be Montanelli's, especially since words as 'cerula' and 'barlume' lie outside the normal range of 'librettese'.¶ This would also tally with a letter written on the same day to Tito Ricordi recalling the critical attacks on the libretto of *Macbeth*. Then Piave had

---

* Letter from Piave, 27.2.1857. Abbiati, II, pp. 379–80.
† Letter to Piave, undated. Conati, p. 401.
‡ Letter from Piave, 1.4.1857. Abbiati, II, p. 397.
§ Letter to Vigna, 11.4.1857. *Copialettere*, p. 553.
¶ This view, cautiously advanced by Walker, was developed by G. Vecchi in his paper 'Il . . . libretto del primo Boccanegra', delivered at the Fourth International Congress of Verdi Studies (Chicago, 1974), but as yet unpublished.

been blamed for certain lines which Verdi himself admired and which were in fact by Maffei.* It was all very embarrassing, especially since an attempt on Verdi's part to make practical amends to Piave had been frustrated. 'I'm sorry,' he wrote to Ricordi in February, 'that you have removed the clause I put in for the benefit of the librettist, whose position seems to me neither favourable nor just.'† Librettists' copyright was not recognized in Italy at that time, and Ricordi did not intend to create a precedent.

Certainly none of Verdi's libretti ever came in for more hostile criticism than that of the first *Boccanegra*. Abramo Basevi declared that he had had to read it through SIX TIMES (capitals his) before he was able to make head or tail of it.‡ Like all libretti written under Verdi's direction it is fast-moving and compact – at times exaggeratedly so, as if the librettist had taken as his norm the rapid cross-talk of those thorough-paced villains Paolo and Pietro – and it keeps as closely as possible to the original plot, adapting it to the exigencies of opera by the usual means of elision and omission. Several scenes towards the end are left out, as well as the entire second act of Gutiérrez's drama, and with it the central character at whose palace the action takes place – Lorenzino Buchetto, money-lender and unsuccessful candidate for the position of Doge. The central finale, so important to the architecture of all mid-century Italian opera, had as so often to be grafted artificially onto the story. The point chosen, logically enough, is where the heroine Amelia (Gutiérrez's Susana) reappears after her abduction by Paolo. But in order to assemble the necessary number of people the delicate mechanism of the plot was given a wrench from which it never recovers. The omission of Buchetto was obviously required partly because of the preponderance of male characters and partly because he is essentially a comic figure and the activities in his palace suggest the comings and goings in a Feydeau bedroom or Wodehouse's Totleigh Towers. Nevertheless they are essential to the coherence of the plot; and a brief résumé of the action which Piave and Verdi omitted may help the listener to understand the events that they kept in.

In the play the mutual recognition of father and daughter takes place in two stages. In the first Bocanegra, on his visit to the Grimaldi palace, learns just enough about Susana's identity to be fairly sure that she is his long-lost child; but before he can tell her so he is called away (a contrived touch, this, but necessary to make the plot thicken). He tells Paolo not to think of marrying her. Paolo accordingly resolves to have her abducted by Pietro and lodged in Buchetto's palace. No sooner said than carried out. A page farther on Gabriele has discovered the abduction and is breaking the news to his ally Fiesco, now living under an alias as 'Andrea' and acting as Susana's guardian. The disturbance brings back Bocanegra and Paolo and their men. Bocanegra suspects that Paolo is responsible; Gabriele makes thinly veiled accusations against the Doge. To his surprise the Doge is not in the least offended and refuses to have him arrested. He then goes away, leaving Fiesco and Gabriele with the suspicion that he is himself in love with Susana. Curtain.

At the start of Act II Buchetto receives a visit from one of Fiesco's men bidding him be ready that night to join the Guelph insurgents. No sooner has his visitor left than

* See Vol. I, p. 274.

† Letter to Tito Ricordi, 8.2.1857. Conati, p. 400.

‡ Basevi, p. 259. Six times was evidently not enough, however, since in his own synopsis Basevi gets certain details wrong.

Pietro enters, tells Buchetto that he knows of his treacherous plotting and offers him a choice: either he must receive Susana into his palace and keep her there until nightfall, in which case he will enjoy Paolo's protection: or else he can refuse and be exposed to the Doge as a Guelph rebel. Buchetto naturally chooses the former alternative and Susana is brought in. When the two are left alone Susana has no difficulty in guessing how Buchetto has been compromised. Just then Bocanegra is announced together with Paolo. Despite Buchetto's anxious pleading she refuses to leave the spot. Bocanegra dismisses Paolo, Buchetto and the guard, and in the course of a second conversation with Susana reveals that he is her father. He then recalls the bewildered Buchetto and commends his present loyalty, adding that he knows of his previous plotting; and he orders him to have Susana escorted to the ducal palace that evening. When he has gone Buchetto, totally confounded, blurts out to Susana all he knows of the Guelph conspiracy and Gabriele's role in it. Susana, her worst fears confirmed, retires as Fiesco and Gabriele are announced. To their irritation they find Buchetto now disposed to blow cold on their plans. Then Susana returns. Not for the first time Buchetto wants to sink into the ground. But she tells them coolly that she is in Buchetto's house of her own free will, and adds that she is now to set out for the ducal palace. To Gabriele all is clear. Not only does the Doge, the slayer of his father, love Susana; she loves him in return. 'What else is left me in this world?' To which Fiesco replies, 'The pleasure of vengeance,' and the curtain falls.

Gutiérrez's Act II therefore ends with Susana in complete control of an extremely tangled situation. She must frustrate the conspiracy, save her father and obtain pardon for her lover and, if possible, permission to marry him; and in due course she will accomplish all her aims. Now we can see the point of the eccentric distribution of the play – one principal woman and six principal men. By goodness, courage and, above all, intelligence Susana dominates all the others. As innocent as a dove, she is also as wise as a serpent. From this point the last two acts of the play correspond roughly to those of the opera in its original form, and the proceedings as well as her part in them are logical and clear.

Not so in the libretto. In order to fill the stage for a concertato Amelia's abduction is announced during a public celebration in the main square of Genoa. Then, while Gabriele is hurling insults at the Doge, Amelia reappears. A concertato expresses the reactions of those present: relief in the case of Boccanegra, Gabriele, Fiesco and the crowd, fury in that of Paolo and Pietro. Amelia then tells her story. Finding herself in Buchetto's house she had threatened to denounce him to the Doge unless he released her. He did so, obliging her with the name of her real abductor which Amelia says she will tell the Doge and no one else. The act ends with a stretta in which the people call for justice. Not a word about the Guelph conspiracy. And how has Amelia, from being a recluse in the Grimaldi palace, suddenly become the mascot of Genoa? If threatened by Amelia's 'I have your secret', what was to prevent Buchetto replying, Hollywood-style, 'Yes, my dear, but I have *you*'? These are just two of the questions raised by the operatic abridgement. It could of course be said that the upshot of Gutiérrez's Act II is implied in parts of the dialogue – but only to an audience that knows the original play. In works such as *I Lombardi* Verdi and Solera could afford their manipulations of time and incident since Grossi's poem was familiar to every Italian listener. But it is clear that even Basevi, who could quote readily from Burney's *History of Music*, had never read a line of Gutiérrez's drama.

Despite the risks he was running with such a subject Verdi cherished high hopes for the success of *Boccanegra*. He was as concerned over its staging as he had been over that of *Macbeth*. The prologue needed plenty of depth. There should be a small climbable flight of steps to the church of San Lorenzo and a column behind which Paolo and later Fiesco could hide. The Fiesco palace must be clearly in view so that Simone can be seen when he goes in and when he appears on the balcony and unhooks the lantern:

> I think I have a good musical effect here which I wouldn't want sacrificed because of the scene. . . . The Palazzo Grimaldi in the first act should not have much depth. Instead of one window I would have several right down to ground level; a terrace in fact. I would then have a second backcloth with the moon with its rays reflected on the sea, which should be visible to the public. . . . Take great care, I beg of you, with the scene where the Doge orders Pietro to disclose the balcony: we should see a rich broad illumination occupying a wide space so as to allow a good view of the lights which are extinguished one by one until at the Doge's death all is in the deepest darkness. . . . The first backcloth needn't be far back but the second one with the illuminations must give an effect of distance.*

About the singers he seems to have been less exercised, except in the case of Paolo – one of those heavy comprimario roles which can jeopardize the success of an opera if not carefully cast. While still in Paris he had urged the Directorate through Piave to engage the 'best comprimario available'.† In February he returned to the charge. 'The part of Paolo is very important; it is essential to have a baritone who is a good actor. . . . My stomach is all to pieces.' As usual in the last stages of composition Verdi was troubled with his health.‡

Of the principals Luigia Bendazzi was a fine singer in the somewhat robust tradition of Sofia Loewe. Verdi had spoken approvingly of her in a letter to Vigna, though he doubted whether she would be right for Violetta.§ Indeed one of the greatest Violettas of the time, Marietta Piccolomini, wrote to the baritone Giraldoni: 'I read in the newspapers that Verdi will be writing [an opera] for you and for Negrini. How lucky you are! I really do envy you; I'm only sorry about one thing and that is that since Bendazzi is the prima donna Verdi will write a part entirely "di forza" and I shall never be able to sing it.'¶ In fact la Piccolomini was wrong. Only the cavatina, with its widely arching phrases in the andante, requiring powerful breath-support, and its brilliant cabaletta demand a donna di forza. The tenor, Carlo Negrini, was of the powerful, somewhat baritonic variety (Petrella was to write for him a characteristically barnstorming part in *Morosina*). His line is not a particularly high one; and in adapting it for Tamagno in 1881 Verdi felt obliged to raise it here and there – and always with beautiful poetic effect. Likewise he was to lower for Maurel the part of Boccanegra, originally written for Leone Giraldoni, a sensitive, nervous high baritone, much prone to indisposition (as Renato he nearly

---

* Letter to Piave, undated. Conati, p. 401.
† Letter to Piave, 21.10.1856. *Ibid.*, p. 391.
‡ Letter to Piave, 9.2.1857. *Ibid.*, p. 402.
§ Letter to Vigna, 1.12.1853. Bongiovanni, pp. 26–7.
¶ Letter from Marietta Piccolomini to Leone Giraldoni. *Carteggio I.S.V.* 62/17.

compromised the first performance of *Un Ballo in maschera* in 1859). The remaining principal, Giuseppe Etcheverry, was that rare phenomenon on the Italian stage, a deep bass of principal status, who enjoyed the quaint description of 'primo basso profondo assoluto'. Of Spanish provenance, Etcheverry seems to have had a very short career in Italy, lasting about four years, during which Fiesco was the only important role he created. Had he been more eminent Verdi might not have dared to write for him the part that he did, which could be described as a 'super-comprimario'. Throughout the opera Fiesco is ubiquitous, yet without a single gran scena or double aria to himself. He is Moser or Barbarossa writ large.

Simon Boccanegra was not a success. 'I've had a fiasco in Venice almost as great as that of *La Traviata*,' Verdi wrote to the Countess Maffei; 'I thought I'd done something passable but it seems I was mistaken.'[*] Certainly the singers were not to blame in this case. Luigia Bendazzi acquitted herself magnificently. But: 'The music of *Boccanegra* is of the kind that does not make its effect immediately' (ominous phrase). 'It is very elaborate, written with the most exquisite craftsmanship and needs to be studied in all its details. From this it came about that on the first night it was not fully understood and led to some hasty judgments – judgments so bitter and hostile in the form in which they were expressed . . . as to appear singular and strange, to say the least.' The *Gazzetta Privilegiata di Venezia* continued: 'This first, unfavourable impression can be to some extent explained by the character of the music which is perhaps too heavy and severe, and by that mournful colour that dominated the score, especially the prologue.' The article concludes: 'We cannot . . . conceal the fact that Verdi, or at least his opera, has a few enemies; but to the honour of our kindly country we must declare that certain signs of disfavour, all too eloquent and outspoken, did not proceed from Venetian lips. They were an importation from outside.'[†] . . . This dark saying would appear to be explained by a letter from Vigna: 'The existence of a properly organized hostile clique is now obvious. . . . In particular there were subtle and murky plots on the part of some rich Israelities who were totally committed to the support of a certain Mo. Levi (of the ancient tribe), author of a *Giuditta* which shared the same fate as Holofernes; yet heedless of the lesson he wants to try his luck again in the theatre. . . . Some see in all this the hidden hand of Meyerbeer; a gratuitous supposition if you like but one that does little honour to his character' – and still less to Vigna's, one might add, or to his intelligence.[‡] The truth is that complaints of 'obscurity', 'severity', 'harmonic abstruseness' are heard from even the most respectful of critics.[§]

Indeed the opera's fortunes over the next few years were none of the best. It was rarely successful except when Verdi was there to direct it. It triumphed in Reggio Emilia later that year and again in Naples in 1858 with those two Verdian stalwarts Fraschini and Coletti as Gabriele and Boccanegra respectively. A revival in Rome a

[*] Letter to C. Maffei, 29.3.1857. *Copialettere*, p. 553.
[†] Review in the *Gazzetta Privilegiata di Venezia*, 15.3.1857. Conati, p. 415.
[‡] Letter from Vigna, 23.3.1857. Abbiati, II, p. 395.
[§] 'I have just left the Teatro la Fenice and the harmonies of *Simon Boccanegra* are still ringing in my ears. Can I perhaps give you a detailed account of this work? No, my dear readers, because the music of *Boccanegra* is so severe in general that it is impossible to judge it after a single hearing, and in fact the public left the theatre without having made up their minds.' Marco Marcelliano Marcello in *L'Arte*, 18.3.1855.

few months earlier with the original Boccanegra was again favourably received. On the other hand in 1859 a fiasco at la Scala, Milan, with Sebastiano Ronconi in the title role provoked a well-known outburst from Verdi about the ingratitude and discourtesy of the public since the days of *Un Giorno di regno*.* Meanwhile *Boccanegra* had been laughed off the stage in Florence in a disastrous performance which furnished the basis of Basevi's unsympathetic, not to say obtuse, chapter on the opera itself, which he regarded as a misguided essay in the Teutonic style(!).†

All these criticisms of the first *Boccanegra* make very odd reading today, especially for those who have had the opportunity of hearing it performed. It is gloomy, certainly, but no more so than most Italian melodrammi and certainly no more so than the revised version, which is generally acknowledged as a masterpiece. There is nothing in the second version to compare in vivacity with the scene in the public square from 1857. The abundance of andantino 3/8 recalls *I Due Foscari*; so too does an indefinable 'marine' atmosphere that pervades the score. In general the phrases are shaped more conventionally than in *Les Vêpres Siciliennes* if only because the lines conform to traditional Italian patterns. As to what chiefly troubled contemporary audiences, Verdi himself provides a clue in a letter to Giraldoni: 'If there aren't many melismata in my music, there's no need to clutch at your hair and throw a mad fit.'‡ In fact the word-setting throughout *Simon Boccanegra* is more syllabic than in any previous opera of Verdi's. Declamation, whether forceful or conversational, predominates over lyrical writing. Arias tend to be compact and concentrated, like the racconto of Paolo or Fiesco's 'Il lacerato spirito'. All the devices that we associate with the term 'bel canto' are sparingly used. To the mid-century Italian this amounted to a denial of Italy's national birthright. At the very least Verdi seemed to be treading the dangerous path of Bellini's *La Straniera*. Basevi complains specifically about the use of recitative on a single note or 'vocal pedal', as he puts it, during which the harmonies change;§ and he quotes several instances from the prologue. He later notices with alarm the same principle being extended to lyrical melody in the duet between soprano and tenor 'Vieni a mirar la cerula' – one of the passages which Verdi left unchanged in the revision (Ex. 162).

To a modern listener this is particularly subtle and delicate. We forget how odd it must have sounded to a public brought up on Donizetti and Bellini that a voice should mark time just at the point where it would be expected to announce an arresting melody.

The original *Boccanegra* is a hard, gritty work, austere in its vocal writing and uncompromising in its expression; but it was not a work of which its composer had any reason to be ashamed. Nevertheless once *Un Ballo in maschera* had appeared *Boccanegra* ceased to circulate; and that was a matter of concern for both composer and publisher.

It was Giulio Ricordi, Tito's son, who as early as 1868 suggested that Verdi might revise the score.¶ He returned to the subject in the early months of 1879. But Verdi

* Letter to T. Ricordi, 4.2.1859. *Copialettere*, pp. 556–7.

† 'To judge from the prologue at least I would say that [Verdi] was almost wanting to follow, though at a distance, in the footsteps of Wagner, the well known subverter of the present state of music.' Basevi, p. 264.

‡ Letter to Giraldoni, 9.12.1857. *I.S.V. Carteggio* 48/50.

§ Basevi, p. 268.

¶ See letter to Giulio Ricordi, 2.12.1880. Abbiati, IV, p. 137.

would not commit himself. 'I received yesterday a large parcel which I suppose to be a score of *Simone*. If you come to S. Agata six months, a year, two or three, etc., from now you will find it untouched just as you sent it to me. I hate unnecessary things. . . .'* But Ricordi refused to give up. He had already managed to interest Verdi in the prospect of an *Otello* with Boito as librettist. What arguments he urged in this case, whether he hinted that before collaborating on an enterprise as vast as that of *Otello* Verdi and Boito had better test their compatibility on something less arduous, we cannot tell. But by November 1880 the revised *Boccanegra* was a certainty for the following year.

> The score is not possible as it stands [*Verdi wrote*]. It is too sad, too depressing. There is no need to touch the first act [*he meant the Prologue*] nor the last, or even the third except for a bar here and there. But I shall need to redo all the second act [*i.e., Act I*] and give it more contrast and variety, more life. Musically speaking we could keep in the cavatina of the prima donna, the duet with the tenor, and the other duet between father and daughter although they contain cabalettas. Save the mark! However I haven't such a horror of cabalettas, and if a young man were to be born tomorrow who could write one of the calibre of 'Meco tu vieni o misera' or 'Perchè non posso odiarti' I would go and hear it with all my heart†. . . .

And there follows one of those crotchety diatribes against new-fangled ways that had become habitual with Verdi in recent years. Then he returns to the need for brightening up the first act.

* Letter to G. Ricordi, 2.5.1879. Abbiati, IV, p. 82.
† See Chapter 2.

How? With a hunt, for instance? It wouldn't be theatrical. A celebration? Too commonplace. A pitched battle with the African pirates? Not very entertaining. Preparations for war with Pisa or Venice?

On this point I recall two superb letters of Petrarch's, one written to the Doge Boccanegra, the other to the Doge of Venice, telling them they were about to engage in fratricidal strife, that both were sons of the same mother, Italy, etc. How wonderful, this feeling for an Italian fatherland in those days! All this is politics, not drama; but a man of resource could make drama out of it. For instance, Boccanegra, struck by this thought, would like to follow the poet's advice; he convokes the Senate and the privy council. . . . Horror all round, recriminations, fury even to the point of accusing the Doge of high treason, etc. The quarrel is interrupted by the seizure of Amelia. . . .*

So was born the Council Chamber scene, the crowning glory of the new *Boccanegra*. But as yet it existed only in embryo, as the subsequent draft of a letter to Ricordi makes clear:

As for the libretto, once an *Idea* has been found, vast, grandiose in form and colour, on which to build the *Head* of the finale, the rest will amount to very little.

I say the *Head* because it will be necessary to retain Amelia's racconto of which I should like to change a good deal of the music, and I would keep many things in the stretta, especially the opening.

I don't think there's any point in having one of the usual pezzi concertati. Only when Amelia suddenly appears. I would just have the Doge sing four or eight lines thanking heaven for having saved his daughter from dishonour. Four lines such as Boito can write, to be set to a broad musical sentence in the finest way possible. This sentence I should like to repeat to different words in the middle of the stretta at the point where the harps enter so stupidly.†

Boito then set to work diligently but without enthusiasm. He compared the drama to a rickety table of which only one leg, namely the prologue, was sound. It lacked true sense of theatre; it contained no character that made one exclaim, 'Drawn to the life!' Nevertheless he would do his best to carry out Verdi's wishes while maintaining due regard for historical accuracy. His scheme for the Council Chamber scene ran as follows:

An usher announces a lady who begs to speak to the Doge. The Doge gives orders for her to be admitted, but he will only attend to her when the destinies of the state have been settled. The Doge announces to the Council that Toris, King of Tartary, sends an ambassador requesting a peace-treaty with the Genoese. The whole Council gives its unanimous consent. Then the Doge makes a solemn plea for the war with the Venetian Republic to be brought to an end. Rebuttal from the Council; uproar. The Doge exclaims, 'You agree to grant peace to barbarians

* Letter to Giulio Ricordi, 20.11.1880. *Carteggio Verdi–Ricordi 1880–1881*, ed. P. Petrobelli, M. Di Gregorio Casati and C. M. Mossa (Parma, 1988), pp. 69–71.
† Letter to G. Ricordi, 26.11.1880. *Ibid.*, pp. 77–8.

and infidels, and you wish for war with your brothers. . . . You have carried your victorious standard on the waters of the Tyrrhenian, the Adriatic, the Euxine, the Ionian and the Aegean' — and here we can make use of a few of the finest passages from Letter 5, Book XIV, of Petrarch's letters, especially where he says, 'It is fine to defeat an enemy by the test of steel; yet finest of all to conquer him by greatness of heart and soul' and where he waxes lyrical over the splendours of the Riviera (provided this last digression does not prolong the scene too much); but it is so fine where he says, 'And the boatman, lost in admiration of the new sights before him, let the oars fall from his hands and marvelling stayed the boat in mid-course.' But the Doge's peroration must end in an atmosphere of fury, interrupted here and there by shouts from the assembled company. The popular party are for peace, the nobility for war. . . . Uproar at the door of the hall; the arrest is announced of a nobleman who wanted to enter the council chamber sword in hand. Nobles and plebeians vehemently insist that he come forward. Enter Gabriele Adorno, who accuses the Doge of having had Grimaldi abducted. Surprise and fury of the nobles: the Doge stands thunderstruck and gives orders for the woman who had begged for help and sanctuary in the palace to be brought before him. The woman is brought in. It is Amelia, who throws herself at the Doge's feet and announces that she had been saved. Here we should find room for a few lines in which the Doge thanks heaven for having saved Amelia [*evidently Giulio Ricordi had shown Boito Verdi's letter*] and the act could end as in the existing opera.

But if that scheme had proved unsatisfactory Boito had another, much bolder one to offer, involving a conflation of Acts I and II and the addition of a new act immediately following. The first part of Act I would stand as in 1857, apart from the omission of the duettino between Gabriele and Fiesco. After the recognition duet Boccanegra would refuse his daughter's hand to Paolo, who would then have a short soliloquy threatening to stir up the people against the Doge. Re-enter Boccanegra to take a tender farewell of his Amelia — at which point Gabriele steps out of hiding and tries to assassinate the Doge. Terzetto and finale as in the original Act II. No abduction of Amelia, therefore, and no Council Chamber scene.

The new act proposed is a striking instance of Boito's scenic imagination and (for the time) modernity of outlook. There was to be nothing like it in Italian opera before Zandonai's *Francesca da Rimini*.

Inside the Church of S. Siro, an ancient Benedictine monastery, adjoining the Boccanegra houses. The church is full of soldiers; crossbowmen are standing on the parapets; on the central *rosone* of the façade a catapult is being loaded. Outside, shouting and tumult of the attackers; trumpet blasts: inside a priest is blessing the combatants. Gabriele is on the central parapet by the catapult, keeping watch; Boccanegra is giving orders. Enter scouts: the Fieschi, the Doria and the Grimaldi have joined that section of the rebellious popular party that is attacking the church. The consuls of the sea, together with the entire navy, the crossbowmen and most of the people have remained loyal to Boccanegra. At every step Gabriele asks if he should launch the catapult . . . but the Doge is against this. Meanwhile the doors of the church resound to noisy blows; the great bell sounds the alarm. A message is brought in by a scout who tells how the attackers have been surrounded by a powerful band of crossbowmen who sallied from the Boccanegra palace (the spies come and go from a door which communicates with Simone's house). The church door threatens to fall in ruins. Boccanegra places himself in front of it with a group of crossbowmen; the door collapses; Fiesco enters at the head of a whirling throng of nobles and plebeians and wounds Boccanegra in the hand; but all at once, seeing the church full of soldiers ready to charge, the attackers stop short in dismay. Boccanegra, wounded, shows Fiesco the catapult poised menacingly at the heads of the assailants, and swears solemnly that he will not shoot, and that no outrage will be committed on the rebels if they will solemnly swear to make peace in the sacred refuge where they now stand. Moment of silence. Meanwhile Paolo, who is leading the revolt, quietly asks Pietro, who is among the supporters of Boccanegra (with intent to betray him), if there is any hope for the rebels. Pietro replies that they are surrounded by crossbowmen and that Boccanegra has caught them in a trap. Then Paolo tears the bandage from his sword and after sprinkling it with a few drops of poison from a flask which he takes from his tunic, throws his sword at Boccanegra's feet, kneels before him and begs to be allowed to bind the bloody wound on his hand. Then all the attackers sheathe their weapons. Boccanegra allows his hand to be bandaged, tells Paolo to rise and pardons him. Meanwhile Amelia enters from the door from which the scouts have left. Gabriele has come down from the parapet. Boccanegra solemnly orders an oath of peace to be sworn; he gives out its terms, and expresses his wish that this peace should be consecrated by the wedding of Adorno and Amelia, his daughter – GIURAMENTO, which would have all the proportions desirable for a tranquil and spacious musical number. There the act would end.*

The advantages of this act, Boito maintained, were three. It showed the poisoning of the Doge – a vital factor in the drama which in the first version of the opera was merely subsumed – and at the very moment when he was performing an act of magnanimity. It had a basis in history, and it explicitly connected the marriage of Gabriele and Amelia with the preceding events. But was the opera really worth reclaiming?

Verdi had no doubt that it was. However, much as he admired the San Siro project, from every point of view it could involve him in too much work.

> Having unfortunately to give up this act we must keep to the scene in the Council Chamber, which, I have no doubt, written by you could not possibly be dull. Your criticisms are just, but you, immersed in loftier works and with *Otello* in mind, are aiming at a perfection impossible here. I aim lower and am more optimistic than you and I don't despair. I agree that the table is rickety but if the legs are adjusted a bit I think it will stand up. . . . I agree that there are none of those characters (always very rare) that make one exclaim 'drawn to the life!' Nevertheless it seems to me that there is something to be made of characters like Fiesco and Simone.

* Letter from Boito, 8.12.1880. *Carteggio Verdi–Boito* ed. M. Medici and M. Conati (Parma, 1978), I, pp. 7–12.

(A significant remark this; Fiesco and Boccanegra are in fact the twin poles on which the opera rests.) 'Meanwhile,' Verdi continued, 'I'll try to straighten out here and there the many crooked legs of my notes.'*

The re-fashioning of *Simon Boccanegra* seems to have taken Verdi rather less than six weeks, from early in January to the third week of February 1881; and the collaboration with Boito, despite one or two gaps, remains the most fully documented of any of Verdi's career. As usual the difficulty has always lain in assembling the material from different sources and interleaving the documents correctly (Boito often failed to date his letters). This task, projected by Frank Walker before his death and continued by David Rosen and Flynn Warmington, has now been completed by the Istituto di Studi Verdiani at Parma, whose *Carteggio Verdi–Boito* is already in print. A few gaps remain to be filled, but in general the contents of the missing letters can be deduced.

The first of these gaps concerns the original draft of the Council Chamber scene including Boccanegra's great speech 'Plebe! patrizi! popolo!' which had now been removed to its present position, i.e. after the tumult and the reappearance of Amelia. At the same time Verdi and Boito seem to have decided to abandon the original 'stretta' in favour of the definitive ending in which Paolo is forced to curse himself. Fiesco, in his disguise of Andrea, is added to the assembly, and, as in the next act, Amelia interposes herself between the Doge and the furious Gabriele, so saving her father's life.

On 28 December Verdi professed himself highly satisfied with the new scheme, though he queried three of its details. He did not want any mention of Amelia until she suddenly appeared in the course of the scene as in the original version. Was the affair of Tartary mentioned in the text sufficient to convoke the council, or should there not be some other affair of state such as a raid by the African pirates or even the war with Venice? Finally if Gabriele referred to Amelia as his 'sposa' would that not spoil the moment in the next act where Boccanegra discovers that his daughter is betrothed to one of his bitterest enemies? He added, 'Stupendous from "Plebeians, patricians, people" to the end which we close with "Be accursed".'† The adjustments duly arrived and Verdi turned his attention to the earlier parts of the work since 'I would like to do everything in order as if it were a new opera'.‡

But for the moment let us remain with the Council Chamber scene and follow it through to its definitive form. On 9 January Boito supplied Gabriele's line without the offending word 'sposa' but gave it for the time being to Fiesco. Next, since the average spectator knew nothing about the two letters by Petrarch, Verdi wanted the first of them made clearer. The senators should call outright for war with Venice, to be rebuked by Boccanegra with the reminder that the two cities shared a common fatherland.§ Boito, though reluctant as always to pander to popular ignorance, sent the necessary lines.¶ (It has been left to more recent producers to translate his typically allusive 'Il romite di Sorga' into the explicit 'Francesco Petrarca'.) Then on 24 January came an unexpected development.

* Letter to Boito, 11.12.1880. *Ibid.*, pp. 12–13.
† Letter to Boito, 28.12.1880. *Ibid.*, pp. 14–15.
‡ Letter to Boito, 8.1.1881. *Ibid.*, pp. 15–16.
§ Letter to Boito, 15.1.1881. *Ibid.*, pp. 31–2.
¶ Letter from Boito, 16.1.1881. *Ibid.*, pp. 32–5.

Without intending to I've written a pezzo concertato in the new finale. Of course Simone will first sing all his sixteen lines solo ('Plebe! Patrizi! Popolo!'). After that comes a concertato, not much of one but still a concertato. I am not keen on asides . . . since they force the artist to remain motionless and I would like Amelia at least to turn to Fiesco and urge, 'Peace, let all be forgiven and forgotten; they are our brothers.' The little phrase I've written for Amelia would gain in warmth. Don't forget in this new verse the word 'Peace' which I can make much of.*

Boito sent eight lines with the observation: 'I'd have liked to give a little movement to the part of Gabriele, but it didn't work, and the reason is obvious: if the Doge is speaking to everyone and if Amelia is entreating Fiesco, Gabriele has no one to talk to, since Paolo and Pietro are talking to one another.'† Verdi: 'Eight lines are too many for Amelia. The piece is nothing more than a grand solo for the Doge with other parts added at the end. . . . The first four lines will suit me very well, but perhaps you will want to change the second one for the sake of the rhyme'‡ – i.e. so that it would rhyme with the fourth, in accordance with the usual rule for single quatrains in a concertato. In fact Boito sent four entirely new lines, after further prompting from Verdi. Presumably he had already supplied the verses for the remaining characters with his letter of 31 January. The quatrain for chorus however was certainly present in the original draft since he enclosed the definitive 'variant' with his letter of 9 January.

Then as the music of the preceding revolt developed:

I've managed despite an agitato movement in the orchestra to get all the words across clearly. The orchestra roars, but it roars quietly. However it's essential that at the end it too should make its terrible voice heard, and I would like a fortissimo after the Doge's words, 'Here are the people! . . .' At this point the orchestra would be let loose in all its power, with the populace, patricians, women, etc. added. Therefore I should need two lines for everyone to shout out; and in these lines don't fail to include the word 'Vengeance'.§

Boito went further; he added to the two lines requested by Verdi three more for the Doge, whose scorn is perhaps more typical of the patrician Boito himself than of the plebeian Boccanegra ('So this is the people's voice: from far off the tempest's thunder; near-to, the shouting of women and children . . .').

The outburst of chorus and orchestra [he observed] can thus be put into effect, and if in that outburst you find room for women's voices yelling in their high register the prayers of your poet will be answered and the Doge's sarcastic remark explained. I put in that remark in order to face up courageously to the main difficulty that worried us: namely that of having women appear in the senate. If we draw the public's attention to the fact that women are present and do so

---

* Letter to Boito, 24.1.1881. *Ibid.*, pp. 35–6.
† Letter from Boito, 31.1.1881. *Ibid.*, pp. 36–7.
‡ Letter to Boito, 2.2.1881. *Ibid.*, p. 38.
§ Letter to Boito, 5.2.1881. *Ibid.*, pp. 38–9.

boldly nobody will dream of raising the slightest objection. Besides it's well known that women play an important part in popular uprising; think of the Paris Commune. But where the devil have I got to now? To get back to the libretto. . . .'*

And so apart from a few minor changes, to be noted later, the scaffolding was erected for one of the noblest edifices in all music drama.

Of the earlier part of the opera Verdi wrote: 'The Prologue I'll pass over; I may perhaps alter the first recitative and a few bars here and there in the orchestra.' In fact he was to alter it very considerably, but without any help from Boito. He decided to remove Amelia's cabaletta from Act I 'not because it is a cabaletta but because it is very bad'; to alter the prelude and join it on to the soprano's cantabile 'so as to make them into a single piece. At the end I should take up again an orchestral movement from the prelude over which Amelia would say, "Day has dawned and he comes not." So patch me up a couple of short lines in broken phrases. . . .' Amelia's jealous suspicions were to go, logically enough since they are not in character. Indeed Piave's 'forse altro amor' merely results from one of those elisions typical of libretti. In the play Gabriele does not enter with a serenade on his lips, but is introduced more prosaically by the dueña, Julieta. It is she, with her down-to-earth feminine logic, who hints that Gabriele's frequent absences are making her mistress suspect that there is another woman in his life. But in the libretto there is no Julieta; so Amelia herself must voice the suspicions falsely imputed to her.

A duet for Fiesco and Gabriele was to be replaced since 'it's too fierce and says nothing at all. Instead I should like Fiesco, who is like a father to Amelia, to bless bride and bridegroom to be. This would produce a moment of pathos which would be a ray of light amid so much gloom. To maintain the atmosphere bring in a bit of local patriotism as well. Fiesco can say, 'Love this angel . . . But after God . . . the fatherland,' etc. All good words for making the ears prick up. . . . Eight lines then for Fiesco and as many for Gabriele. Simple, touching, tender, on which to write a bit of melody or something like it. . . .'† He would have liked an unaccompanied terzettino with Amelia; but apart from the difficulty of bringing her back the situation would resemble too closely that of the finale of Act III. The letters now followed each other thick and fast, supplemented by telegrams. It would sometimes happen that by the time Boito had sent the lines required Verdi had changed his mind about them. Thus he decided on second thoughts that Fiesco and Gabriele ought to have four lines apiece, not eight, since otherwise the duettino would become too long and too loud. 'I would like just at this moment something calm, solemn, religious. The tone should be that of a father blessing his adopted children.' Thence to an interesting workshop discussion alluded to in Chapter 2. 'I don't much like the ottonario rhythm because of those confounded two syllables on the upbeat, but I shall avoid this. . . .'‡ To which Boito replied: 'Those confounded ottonari! You are quite right, they are the most boring rum-ti-tum in our metrical system. I merely

---

* Letter from Boito, 7.2.1881. *Ibid.*, pp. 41–4.
† Letter to Boito, 8.1.1881. *Ibid.*, pp. 15–16.
‡ Letter to Boito, 10.1.1881. *Ibid.*, pp. 25–6.

chose them in desperation. I didn't want settenari because almost all of the old libretto is in settenari in the lyrical sections; and I didn't want quinari because the old text had quinari at that point and I imagined you would be reluctant to return to the original rhythm.'*

Note the implication that for a slow, religious piece odd-syllable metres such as the settenario or quinario which do not carry a heavy tonic accent are the most natural ones to choose, and Boito is therefore at pains to point out why he had avoided doing so. Verdi, meanwhile, so as to save time, decided to proceed with the ottonari already supplied; but he deliberately broke with the old tradition whereby the first two syllables are placed on the upbeat; and the result, as we shall see, is some rather odd verbal accentuation. The old rules usually had their purpose.

It was Boito's idea that Amelia should receive the Doge in her garden, where the preceding action had taken place. 'Three scenes in one act seem to me too many; they destroy the sense of unity so essential to the organic life of the act. Remember that in the entire opera this is the only bright scene. All the others are heavy, solemn and gloomy. There are too many interiors. Since at the beginning of this act we're in the open air, let's stay there as long as we can. On one side at the bottom of the garden there could be a pair of curtains representing the entrance to the Grimaldi palace. Amelia could go to meet the Doge on the threshold of the palace and the scene which follows could quite naturally take place in the garden. Besides if the scene were to change there would be no reason for Fiesco and Gabriele to flee from a place where the Doge will never set foot.'†

The Doge's entrance was to be heralded not by a fanfare but by a chorus of huntsmen – until Verdi wired to the contrary, explaining in a subsequent letter that otherwise the act would become overlong. The recognition cabaletta of father and daughter was to be extended by four lines so as to allow it to be more fully developed and to avoid a plain repeat; at the same time one of the Doge's lines was to be altered so as to omit the original word 'aureola' since 'in a cantabile "au . . . e . . . o" give an unpleasant nasal, guttural sound'.‡ In asking for extra lines to clarify the recognition itself he returned to a favourite theme. 'Forgive the heresy: I believe that in the theatre, just as at times it is commendable in musicians not to make music but to show a talent for self-effacement, so it's sometimes better for poets to write instead of a beautiful line the striking theatrical expression ("la parola evidente e scenica").'§

Originally the only modification proposed for Act II was a soliloquy for Paolo during which he would be seen to pour poison into the Doge's goblet (a derivation, this, from the San Siro project). Otherwise the action was to proceed as in the previous libretto, with Paolo trying to persuade first Fiesco and then Gabriele to murder the Doge in his private apartments. The first repulses him with scorn; but Gabriele proves more compliant. The Doge's life is saved by Amelia who interposes herself in the nick of time. On discovering her real relationship to Boccanegra Gabriele changes his political allegiance and, as sounds of an uprising are heard, sallies forth to lead the government forces to victory.

It was not until they came to work on the last act that librettist and composer began

---

* Letter from Boito, 14.1.1881. *Ibid.*, pp. 28–31.
† *Ibid.*
‡ Letter to Boito, 9.1.1881. *Ibid.*, p. 17.
§ Letter to Boito, 15.1.1881. *Ibid.*, pp. 31–2.

to realize that with the altered incidents of the new finale to Act I they had created difficulties for themselves. The plan of the original Act III was a digest of Gutiérrez's Act IV: victory chorus in honour of the Doge; announcement by Boccanegra of rewards to the victors and the marriage of Gabriele and Amelia; exchange of Paolo and Pietro about the poisoning of the Doge; wedding chorus; final dialogue between Fiesco and Paolo, who has admitted the old man by the same secret door into the ducal palace so that he and his men can turn the tables on the victors. But Fiesco's men have deserted him and Paolo also flees. Duet Fiesco/Boccanegra and reconciliation; death of Doge. All this would need to be modified.

Verdi: 'The opening chorus of this act no longer has any raison d'être, and I would like the orchestra to repeat the music of the revolt while the curtain is lowered ending with offstage cries of "Vittoria! Vittoria!" The curtain would rise and the Doge begin: "Brando guerrier," etc., etc. Would the following scene between Pietro and Paolo and Paolo and Fiesco remain in? If only we had finished!'*

Boito:

I go back to my old comparison of the table; now it's the fourth leg that's unsteady. We must prop it up and use a good deal of cunning in the process so that once it has been put to rights the others don't start to rock again.

For the last two days I've been thinking over and over again about this [third] act.†

The idea of an orchestral introduction played with the curtain lowered and accompanied by shouts off stage I like very much; it is very useful, it binds together wonderfully the end of the [second] act with the beginning of the [third] and it gathers up the events of the last two acts in a temporal unity that is rapid, concentrated and highly dramatic. But this idea is not sufficient in itself. The scene between Fiesco and Paolo cannot stand as it is.

We shall have to modify certain circumstances in the scene between the Doge and Fiesco (Fiesco and the Doge have already found themselves face to face in a movement of violence two acts previously, in the ensemble). The Doge's first words in the [third] act must give a forewarning of the catastrophe. In the old libretto when Simone says: 'Brando guerrier,' his state of health is altogether too satisfactory. Anyway tomorrow I will send you an attempt to put this right all set out in verse, and you can judge for yourself.‡

Verdi:

Very well, let's adjust the fourth leg. You alarm me when you say that we must alter the scene between Fiesco and the Doge! If it's a small matter, all right; but if it must be rewritten then there just isn't enough time. Never mind; I await your letter tomorrow. And tell me: couldn't we leave out the whole of the first scene? In that way the Doge would only make one appearance in this act when he comes in feeling the effects of the poison. . . . 'M'ardon le tempia', etc. The act would

---

* Letter to Boito, 2.2.1881. *Ibid.*, p. 38.

† Boito and Verdi frequently refer to Act III as Act IV, looking on the prologue as Act I. Also both refer to Fiesco from time to time as 'Fieschi'. For the sake of clarity I have kept to the correct nomenclature.

‡ Letter from Boito, 5.2.1881. *Ibid.*, p. 40.

begin with the orchestral prelude and the off-stage cries of 'Vittoria'. . . . At the rise of the curtain the off-stage wedding chorus would be heard and the two saints Peter and Paul could say that the Doge has won and that Gabriele will marry Amelia.*

Boito:

This time I'm the one who says that we haven't yet finished. I've got your last three letters on the table in front of me and I study them at every step, but as regards the first scenes of the last act my own ideas are still further crystallized. I've made various unsuccessful attempts at it. However today you've suggested to me an idea which seems highly practical: to open the act with the wedding chorus in the distance (a fine contrast after the warlike vivacity of the prelude) during which a very rapid but indispensable dialogue unfolds on stage between Fiesco and Paolo (we can forget about the other apostle Pietro, no one will notice), and this dialogue must be totally different in character from that of the old libretto.

Paolo must have taken an active part in the revolt of the Guelphs to overthrow the Doge and has been taken and imprisoned and condemned to death by the Doge himself. It is right that the Doge should finally condemn somebody, and since we have on our hands a scoundrel who has betrayed the popular party to ally himself with the Guelphs and has committed all sorts of villainies let's condemn him to the gallows and have done with him. By the same token Fiesco, at the very moment at which Paolo passes by under guard on his way to execution, Fiesco, I say is freed by order of the Doge, and it's right that he should be; he hasn't taken part in the uprising, I'll be bound, since he was in prison; so that the condemned and the liberated meet during the singing of the wedding hymn and in their conversation Paolo reveals the matter of the poison, and their talk can make clear the facts which need to be made clear. . . . About fifteen lines, not lyrical ones, should be enough.

Now we come to the scene between the Doge and Fiesco. Don't be alarmed, Maestro, I realize the importance of that scene which apart from anything else is the finest in the drama. I said we should change some of the circumstances of the dialogue; 'some' is overstating it; one alone is essential by which I mean the one that is summed up in the words 'Have the dead risen from their graves?' But I realize also the great importance of these words and I will not remove them; I will perhaps add a line or two to bring them into the dialogue in a more logical fashion since we have now created certain facts and divergences which did not exist in the first version.†

But in fact Boito's reference to Fiesco's being in prison shows that he had misunderstood Gutiérrez's plot. In the play the act set in Buchetto's palace ends with the bomb of Susana's abduction successfully defused. Even Paolo is apparently vindicated and in the next act continues to beseech Boccanegra for Susana's hand, while at the same time trying to achieve his aim by more dubious means. Neither Gabriele nor Fiesco has been in the Doge's presence since Susana's reappearance.

* Letter to Boito, 6.2.1881. *Ibid.*, pp. 40–1.
† Letter from Boito, ?7.2.1881. *Ibid.*, pp. 41–4.

What is more, at the start of the next act both are still at liberty. Paolo makes use of his still unshaken authority to have them arrested by Pietro and brought into the Doge's palace by a secret door. When Fiesco refuses his infamous proposal Paolo has no choice but to let him go free. He knows that there is no chance that Fiesco will denounce him to the Doge, since his one idea is to keep out of the Doge's way. He cannot afford the risk of being recognized. Gabriele is a different matter. He would have no hesitation in exposing Paolo's infamy, if he should decide not to murder the Doge after all. Therefore, even when he has persuaded Gabriele to carry out the murder, Paolo takes the precaution of locking the secret door with the aside, 'If you default, this room shall be your grave.' All this is taken for granted in Piave's libretto.

Boito, however, assumed that both Fiesco and Gabriele had been arrested at the end of the previous act after the concertato that greeted Amelia's reappearance. Possibly he misinterpreted Fiesco's line in Act III 'Prigioniero in qual loco m'adduci'. At all events he wrote to Verdi:

> As regards Fiesco, before I forget, I should suggest two minute modifications in the scene between him and Paolo in the penultimate act just for the sake of clarity. Instead of Paolo's words, 'Stolido, va,' which are very rough and ready and might raise a laugh with their vulgarity (or rather let us say *realism*) I would rather say:
>
> FIESCO Osi a Fiesco proporre un misfatto?
> PAOLO Tu ricusi? (*After a pause*) Al tuo carcere ten va.
>
> In this way we should make the fact quite clear: *rather than be a party to treachery Fiesco prefers to return to prison*. . . .
> The old text had at this point *Exit Fiesco right*. . . . Where did he go? To prison? Apparently not. So while refusing the cowardly bargain with Paolo he accepted the freedom which was evidently the reward of that bargain. And this is not like Fiesco. It would be to our advantage if Fiesco takes no active part in the Guelph uprising, so as not to saddle him with a further outrage against the Doge, and I repeat, the best way of preventing that is to keep him under lock and key.

But by now Verdi himself was becoming worried by the implications of the revised Act I:

> We still haven't finished!
> The fine, the truly fine finale which you have written for me has slightly prejudiced the scene in the last act between Fiesco and the Doge. In the old libretto they hadn't met again since the prologue. Twenty-five years have passed between Boccanegra's being elected Doge in 1339 and dying in 1364. As it is the Doge knows Fiesco all too well and the latter can no longer appear to him 'like a ghost'. However I don't think it will be difficult to put matters to rights. . . .*

He suggested four changes. In the finale to Act I Boccanegra should no longer say as he observes Gabriele being hounded by the crowd, 'At his side Fiesco is fighting.' Nor should Fiesco himself defend the murder of Lorenzino on the grounds that he had

* Letter to Boito, 15.2.1881. *Ibid.*, p. 45.

abducted Amelia. In the Doge's soliloquy in Act II he should avoid mentioning 'two rebels' but revert to the original, generalized 'traditori'; and finally the captain of the guard in the last act should not say to Fiesco, 'The Doge declares you a free man,' but rather, 'The Doge pardons everyone; you are free.' To which Boito replied:

> *We haven't finished*: The same scruples that have been torturing you have been torturing me as well. I accept and approve all the expedients which you have suggested to me. Let us say, 'Accanto ad esso combatte un Guelfo,' or, 'Accanto ad esso combatte un vegliardo,' or, 'Accanto ad esso combatte un patrizio' – you choose.
>
> The words 'Ei la Grimaldi avea rapita' we will have spoken by Adorno or a section of the chorus. Instead of 'i due rebelli' we shall say 'i traditori' or else 'i rivoltosi', which ever you would like best.
>
> We will not say 'libero il Doge ti proclama' but instead 'libero sei; ecco la spada', or 'libero sei, quest'è il tuo brando', and the officer hands Fiesco his sword.'*

The letter ends with a most involved justification of the new scheme as it stood. Boito pointed out that in Act I Fiesco and the Doge had merely caught fleeting glimpses of each other; they had never met face to face and therefore the expression 'like a ghost' was still in order. Verdi raised no further demur; but it must be admitted that the loose ends remain. Of the alternatives proposed by Boito for the finale of Act I he chose 'At his side a Guelph is fighting'. But how could Boccanegra know that it was a Guelph unless he recognized him as Fiesco? And if he had done so only for a second would he not have made all possible haste to present him with his long-lost grandchild? Then, too, how did Fiesco find himself in prison? Who had him arrested? We learn from Boito's text that Gabriele, though he has his sword returned to him, is put under detention for a night; but there is no word about 'Andrea'.

In reclaiming *Simon Boccanegra* Boito provided Verdi with some splendid theatrical ideas. He piled on the effective incident. Amelia saves her father's life twice instead of once. The Doge offers his naked breast to the slaughter three times, instead of twice. Paolo from being a rather tawdry villain is built up into a satanic figure like Iago or Barnaba. Many bad lines are replaced by good ones. What Boito conspicuously failed to do was to clarify the plot, which is both more obscure and more illogical in the definitive version. It is like one of those mathematical games where at one point the player takes away the number he first thought of. What was in Gutiérrez's play a delicate, highly wrought dramatic mechanism has become a chaos of sensational incident. All this would matter only if we accept the fallacious reasoning which attempts to judge music drama by the same canons as a spoken play. It is true that there are operas – *Die Meistersinger* and *Palestrina* for instance – whose libretti would bear performance even without the music. But no libretto of Boito's ever aims in this direction. What is more, the aspects of Gutiérrez's plot that have been sacrificed are precisely those which could not have been realized in a Verdian opera. One such aspect for instance is the degeneration of Fiesco. Far better musically speaking to keep him noble and haughty till the final scene than to show him beholden to Paolo as in

---

* Letter from Boito, 15.2.1881. *Ibid.*, pp. 46–7. The postal service was certainly prompt in those days.

Act III of the original libretto. Likewise the addition of the Council Chamber scene adds a new dimension of humanity to the musical character of Boccanegra. Lastly the fact that no writer has ever drawn attention to the flaws in the revision, though the first libretto with its more logical plot and clearer motivation was a constant target for abuse, is surely proof of how unimportant such flaws are in the context of the opera as a whole.

For the revival Verdi was even more concerned to pick the right singers than he had been in 1857; and from the beginning he showed little faith in those engaged for the current season at la Scala, Milan.

> Your baritone [Maurel] is presumably a young man. He may have a voice, talent and feeling as much as you like, but he cannot have the calm, the poise, or that quality of authority on stage that is essential for the part of Simone. It is a part as tiring as Rigoletto but a thousand times more difficult. . . . For Fiesco you want a deep voice, audible in the bass register right down to F with something in it that is inexorable, prophetic, sepulchral; things which are lacking in the slightly empty and far too baritonal voice of De Restke [*sic*]: even D'Angeri precisely because of her powerful voice and personality wouldn't be right for the part of a modest young girl, a kind of young nun.*

He would have liked Adelina Patti; but of course she was beyond the management's purse. 'Don't count on this *Boccanegra*,' is the burden of his letter to his publisher, during the weeks that followed. However a secret visit to Milan in February to hear *Ernani* with Faccio and the proposed cast reassured him somewhat. For the part of Paolo he insisted as before on a good actor. A final doubt as to the number of performances and rehearsal dates allowed was laid to rest; and the performance took place on 24 March. Under the baton of Franco Faccio, successor to Angelo Mariani as Italy's leading conductor, the singers acquitted themselves far better than Verdi had ever imagined possible. Two of them, Maurel and Tamagno, were to provide him respectively with his Iago and Otello six years later. Filippo Filippi, critic of the *Perseveranza*, wrote a long, perceptive, generally enthusastic but by no means wholly uncritical review.† After the first few performances Verdi felt justified in writing to his friend Opprandino Arrivabene: 'Now, if you really want to know, I'll tell you that I think *Boccanegra* will be able to go the rounds of the theatres like so many of its sisters even though the subject is a very sad one. It's sad because it has to be sad, but it's gripping. In the second act it seems the effect fell off; but it wouldn't be surprising if in another theatre where the finale primo didn't make such a great effect the second act had the same success as the others.'‡ Here he was over optimistic. *Simon Boccanegra* has had to wait until the Verdi revival of this century to be enjoyed for the masterpiece it is.

The revision of this opera was the most far-reaching that Verdi ever undertook. It is far more radical than that of *Macbeth*, not surprisingly. Not only is the interval between the two versions longer by six years; the musical landscape had changed far more profoundly in the meantime. It was not a matter of adapting an Italian work to

---

* Letter to G. Ricordi, 20.11.1880. *Canteggio Verdi–Ricordi*, I, pp. 69–71.
† Reproduced in Alberti, pp. 69–80.
‡ Letter to Arrivabene, 2.2.1881. Alberti, pp. 285–6.

Parisian taste and reinterpreting it in the light of later experience. The original *Simon Boccanegra* belonged to the age of the cabaletta, when the structural unit was the 'scena', i.e. the period during which the same character or characters are present on stage. By 1881 the cabaletta was extinct, and the structural unit was the entire act. It was like turning a stage-coach into a steam train. That this could be done at all indicates how far ahead of its time was the original opera.

The number of additions, omissions and changes are so extensive as to put considerable strain on the method of analysis so far adopted, whereby the two versions are discussed side by side. Yet this remains the only way in which the development of the composer's thought can be followed, as it suffuses the noble austerity of the original concept with the warmth and humanity of the definitive work.

For the version of 1881 we have the valuable aid of a 'disposizione scenica' published by Ricordi. Like all production books of the 1880s and after it is a much more sophisticated affair than that of *Giovanna de Guzman* with its abundance of drilled movement. On the first page there is a notice directing the chorus 'not to portray an indistinguishable mass of people; on the contrary each member must represent a character and act as such, moving on his own account as his feelings dictate and merely preserving a certain unity of action with the rest so as best to guarantee the musical performance'. From it we learn the ages of the principal characters. In the prologue Boccanegra is 25, Fiesco 40, Paolo 25, Pietro 20; and all are twenty-five years older by the start of Act I. Gabriele is 30 when he first appears, Amelia 27 — somewhat mature for a marriageable young lady of the fourteenth century as the malicious Florentine critic of 1857 was quick to point out; but given the circumstances of the plot there is no way out of this. The 'vestiario' or wardrobe inventory of 1857, made out in Piave's hand, gives a different age-distribution: Boccanegra 36, Fiesco 45, Paolo 30, Pietro 25. The interval between prologue and Act I is shortened to twenty-four years (1339–63); Gabriele becomes 28; Amelia remains inescapably 27. Boito's historical researches are in general more reliable than Piave's; on the other hand it makes more sense for Gabriele to apostrophize Boccanegra as 'vegliardo' if the difference between their ages is thirty-two years rather than twenty. This is not the only puzzle for producers in this score.

PRELUDE
(1857 version only)

This is a thumbnail sketch of the opera's subject based on four of its principal themes. The first is a version of the Hymn to the Doge (Ex. 199) given out by full orchestra in staccato chords with long gaps between each — a rough-and-ready expedient for arresting the attention that has already been used less obtrusively in the overture to *Stiffelio*. Oboe and clarinet forestall the cry of 'È morta' that punctuates Fiesco's 'Il lacerato spirito'. Next the main theme of the recognition duet ('Figlia! a tal nome io palpito', Ex. 194) steals in on high woodwind with a shimmering accompaniment of strings. By leaving the first bar unaccompanied Verdi delays the sense of a key change (E minor to C major), at the same time enhancing the dream-like quality of the proleptic quotation. Trumpets, horns and trombones announce the theme of the Guelph uprising at the end of Act II ('All'armi, all'armi, o Liguri', Ex. 215). Timpani underline the rhythm of the melody while violas and cellos accompany with a rushing pattern of semiquavers which gradually spreads to the other strings as the movement is whipped up to a tutti climax. As it subsides a theme associated with the final reconciliation between Boccanegra and Fiesco (Ex. 221) is heard on flute, clarinet, bassoon and cello. It is Verdi's most elaborate variation to date on a formula already exploited in the preludes to *I Due Foscari* and *Il Corsaro*: arresting gesture; soft lyrical theme; crescendo to brutal climax and descrescendo away from it; ray of consolation piercing the gloom. Not very new perhaps but theatrically sure.

PROLOGUE

*Scene: A square in Genoa. At the back the church of S. Lorenzo. To the right the palace of the Fieschi, with a large balcony; on the wall to the side of the balcony is an image before which a lantern is burning; on the right other houses. Various streets lead to the square. It is night.**

Here for the first time Verdi and Piave opened with a device unheard of outside the prose theatre: two people entering in conversation, as it might be Iago and Roderigo in Shakespeare's *Othello*. Paolo Albiani, the goldsmith, is discussing with Pietro, a leader of the popular party, their choice of candidate for Doge of Genoa. Pietro is for Lorenzino, the usurer. Paolo proposes instead the champion who drove the African pirates from the seas and carried Genoa's fame far and wide. Pietro understands; no need to mention names. The price for his support? Gold, power and money, replies Paolo. Satisfied, Pietro leaves and prepares to gather the plebeian party. Paolo then shakes his fist at the Fiesco palace, symbol of the tyrannical oligarchy of patricians that he intends to overthrow. Simone Boccanegra hurries in, and greets Paolo warmly. Why, he wants to know, has he been summoned from Savona. Mysteriously, Paolo asks him if he would like to be crowned Doge. Not in the least, he replies. 'And Maria?' Paolo insinuates. Boccanegra wavers: Maria, daughter of the patrician Fiesco, whose lover he has been is now kept a prisoner in her father's palace. Could Fiesco refuse her in marriage to the Doge of Genoa? Paolo's arguments carry the day; meanwhile as people are heard approaching he tells Simone to hide.

In 1857 all this had been treated as the barest of *scene*; a lithe, swift-moving alternation of dialogue and orchestral gesture with not an ounce of superfluous musical tissue and nothing that a contemporary Italian audience would have recognized as a theme. The vocal intervals are short and unemphatic – two people conspiring in low voices; the scoring is for strings only except where Paolo's outburst against the patricians provokes a few octave flourishes from the brass. The voices remain unsupported for several bars at a time as in the recitatives in *Don Pasquale*. In 1881 the whole design is transformed by an enveloping orchestral theme – noble, tender, and rich both in emotional nuances and in possibilities of

---

* The production book directs that the superstructure of the church (which is the present-day cathedral) should be incomplete, presumably since the dome was not added until 1567. It also places the Fiesco palace stage right and specifies four columns supporting a balcony with two windows opening on to it, a large iron grille in front of the door and at the rear a staircase that can easily be climbed. The 1857 score requires a 'marble' palace for the Fieschi and adds that the church must later be lit up internally.

development, which are exploited not only by Verdi himself but still further by Liszt in his late piano fantasy *Reminiscences de Boccanegra*. Here too the instrumental palette is more varied and delicate than anywhere in the score of 1857.

From this Verdi spins a prelude of twenty-six bars before the curtain rises. When it does so, Pietro and Paolo are discovered already on stage talking together. There is no gesture to bring them on as in the earlier score; moreover the conversation proceeds at a slightly slower, more relaxed pace, being throughout set in the lyrical framework of Ex. 163. The new score carries the instruction 'all this scene *a mezza voce*'.

Two lengthy quotations will serve to illustrate the entirely different approaches to the same text of 1857 and 1881 respectively (Exs. 164 and 165).

In one sense the second solution was the more orthodox of the two. For by supplying the scene with a thematic basis Verdi was reverting to a practice that goes back to Rossini's time (compare Arsace's 'Eccomi alfine in Babilonia' from *Semiramide*). The difference is that here the orchestral discourse is far more continuous and the theme itself (Ex. 163) more pervasive, so turning the voice parts

PIETRO

-nor di primo a-ba-te Loren-zin, l'u-su-rie-re? Al-tro pro-po-ni di lui più

PAOLO

Più moderato ♩ = 100

de-gno! Il pro-de, che da' no-stri ma — ri cac-cia-va l'a-frican pi-

-ra — ta, e al li-gu-re ves-sil-lo re-se l'an-ti-ca ri-no-man-za al-

PIETRO   PAOLO

-te-ra. In-te-si... E il premio? O-ro, possan-za, o-

into something akin to Wagnerian declamation and eliminating all those commonplaces of recitative in which Ex. 164 abounds (e.g. Paolo's 'rese l'antica rinomanza altera'). At 'Oro, possanza, onore' the original contours are maintained but given greater meaning by the orchestral intervention. Whereas before Paolo's offer was crude, almost bluff, here it takes on a suitably insinuating tone. In the same way Pietro's answer, set to a line of neutral character in the first version, assumes the right affirmative nuance in the second, ending with a cadence well calculated to underline the handclasp that the production book prescribes. The rhythmic flexibility of the four new bars following Pietro's departure, with subtle use of weak-beat stresses and the logical surprise of a simple cadence, reveal the mature composer of the 1880s. The orchestration carries the burden of Paolo's 'Abborriti patrizi'; and the dark scoring with low woodwind, brass and timpani does more to convey his sense of bilious hatred than the simple flourishes of Ex. 164. Finally, despite what the cast-list tells us in both scores, Pietro from being a baritone has now become a bass

165

PAOLO

pre - mio?   O - ro,   possanza,   ono - - re.

PIETRO   (Si dànno la mano; Pietro parte)

Ven - do a tal prez - zo il po - po - lar fa - vo - - re.

obs., cls., bsns.
hns., strs.

tbns.
added

PAOLO (solo) alzando un po'la voce, ma non troppo

Abbor - ri - ti,   pa - tri - zi,   al - le   cime ove al - ber - ga il vos - tro or -

[Hns.

[timp.   ]   [timp.

and is regularly so played today.* The entrance of Simone elicits the first definite theme of the 1857 prologue — not much admittedly but it stands out clear and distinct amid the surrounding austerity.

166

In 1881 it is replaced by something much more graphic. 'Boccanegra enters rapidly from the archway and looks everywhere for his friend who has made the appointment with him. . . . Seeing Paolo he goes up to him, embraces him, then drawing back a little asks him, "What has happened?"'† The hurried footsteps, glances hither and thither, the moment of pleased recognition are all pointed in a brief orchestral vignette (Ex. 167).

However, in making this change Verdi has sacrificed a dramatic point. When he first enters Simone is a simple sea captain with no thoughts of political leadership. At the end of the opera, as he begins to feel the effects of the poison, his thoughts revert to his early life; and we hear Ex. 166 transfigured by nostalgia in a gently rocking 6/8 rhythm (Ex. 218). This passage is common to both versions of the opera; but in the second it is no longer a reminiscence at all since the original statement has been omitted.‡ In general the second version of Simon Boccanegra relies much less on thematic recurrence than the first.

* The most penetrating study of the two Boccanegras so far published is that of W. Osthoff, 'Die beiden Boccanegra', in Analecta Musicologica, I (Cologne, 1963), pp. 70–89. Among the points to which he draws attention are the structural use of rhythm in late Verdi and the tendency in the revision to alter the superstructure of the earlier musical idea while preserving the bass — a tendency which he attributes to the composer's early training in basso continuo.

† Disp. scen., p. 4.

‡ For a similar instance which has puzzled many a commentator see the Act II finale to Mozart's Così fan tutte where to the words 'A voi s'inchina, bella damina' Ferrando sings what ought to have been a quotation but is not. Possibly as in Verdi's case it relates to an earlier idea which was later replaced.

167

From this point the design of 1881 begins to take in elements from the 1857 version – notably the rising violin tremoli which accompany Paolo's tempting offers; but once again cliché is avoided. At the point where Paolo points to the palace of the Fieschi a portentous passage in descending thirds is replaced by a simple design of chords in E minor each with acciaccatura 'lament' to illustrate the word 'geme'. Ex. 163 is heard for the last time as Paolo explains that he has arranged everything. As in 1857 there is a tutti outburst where Simone and he seal their pact with a handclasp.

At this point the two scores converge, though in different keys and with significant differences of detail. What follows is for 1857 a remarkable scene, treated with great delicacy. As Simone leaves* Paolo moves to the 'hiding-place' which the scene-painter decided should be in an angle of the Fiesco Palace, not behind a column of the church as Verdi had suggested. The stage now fills with sailors and workmen led by Pietro.† Will they assemble in force for the election at dawn? They will. Are any of them for the patricians? Not one; they will vote for Lorenzino. Pietro replies that he has been bought by the Fieschi. He prepares them to hear about their new champion; but it is Paolo, not he, who emerges dramatically from hiding to give the name 'Simone Boccanegra' – the first time it has been mentioned. The chorus take it up in a roar, adding as an afterthought, 'The Corsair!' 'The Corsair!' agrees Paolo; and the Fieschi will have to put up with him. The first version of this passage seems to have been inspired by the fortune-telling dance in the ballet of *Le Trouvère* with its chattering high woodwind alternating with strings. The revised score entrusts the

---

* In 1857 he enters the church; in 1881 he merely goes away.

† At the Moderato (♩ = 100) *sailors, artisans, plebeians, etc., should enter gradually from all the streets leading to the piazza. They should form groups of six or eight people; some should greet their friends with hands outstretched, seeming to ask for news or for a password; thence they will gradually gather together in the centre of the square; at about the same time Pietro will have entered. . . . As he goes rapidly from one group to another he will gather them round him, making a sign that he wants to address them; all this must happen without noise or confusion so that the chorus should be in position at the moment when Pietro asks: 'All'alba tutti qui verrete?' (Disp. scen., p. 5.)*

thought almost entirely to strings touched in here and there by sustaining
woodwind.

Ex. 168b is more appropriate to a nocturnal scene; indeed the last act of *Falstaff* is not
far away. Again in 1881 the explosion 'Simone Boccanegra' is more effectively
delineated, partly by a more subtle rhythmic and harmonic preparation* and partly
by postponing the climax from Paolo's announcement to the chorus's surprised echo
of it. The words 'Il corsaro!' are now murmured under the breath, where previously
they had been shouted out. Another detail of Verdian economy can be noticed in the

* See Osthoff, pp. 77–8.

two different transitions as Paolo gathers the plebeians around him to tell them the story of Maria's imprisonment.* In 1857 Verdi had made use of one of those gestures often associated with the idea of death(♫♪); in 1881 he renounces it in favour of a simple brooding passage of four bars for strings. The death figure will then make an infinitely greater impression when it bursts on us for the first time with the entrance of Fiesco, and its meaning will be unequivocal: 'Maria is dead!'

Paolo's solo with chorus ('L'atra magion vedete') has something in common with Ferrando's 'racconto' in *Il Trovatore*. Once again a crowd of simple folk is being frightened by suggestions of the supernatural. Paolo indicates a room high up in the palace where the beautiful young Maria is held prisoner, a prey, it is said, to ghostly visitations – witness the sinister flames that are sometimes seen at her window. At that moment a light inside the palace begins to flicker;† the chorus take fright and slip away making the sign of the cross. The figure (*x*) in the bass line in the second bar of the melody conveys the shuddering uneasiness of the hearers.

169

---

* *The chorus should have taken up a diagonal position, looking at the Palazzo Fieschi: Paolo goes from one group to the other, so as to excite the imagination of the people who should reply with approving gestures and pointing out to each other the Fieschi palace. Gradually the general interest should quicken and likewise the terror which Paolo's words arouse.* (Disp. scen., p. 6.)

† *The stage director should stand ready on the staircase* [i.e., behind the Fieschi palace] *with the lighted torch and at Paolo's words: 'Guardate! la feral vampa appare', pass slowly onto the elevation behind the balcony so that from the two windows of the palace the glow of the lamp should be seen from the stage. The light should be suddenly extinguished and the director should return quickly downstairs onto the stage.'* (Disp. scen., p. 6.)

If the phrases are regular the form itself is unusual: *a–b–c a–b–coda*; *b* is a sequential transition such as one might expect in any romanza leading to the final major section; but the new idea *c* in which Pietro and the chorus comment sympathetically on Maria's fate has the character of an episode, starting in the relative major key then modulating away from it until jerked back into the tonic minor by the reprise of Ex. 169 with a new decoration of semiquavers in violas. At its second appearance *b* is prolonged by four bars continually rising, falls back through a wide orbit of keys onto a cadential phrase which is interrupted as the flame appears at the window – three high woodwind chords in remote keys – and expires in a long coda nailing down the original tonality. It is all swift, lithe and grippingly intense. Here the changes between versions are fewer still. The original is in F sharp minor, the revision in E minor; otherwise the two are identical up to section *c*, where in 1881 more interest was given to the orchestra and a more sensitive, less ordinary idea found for the second 8-bar period. As so often in the revision a double phrase is replaced by a single one with a wider melodic span and no internal repetition. Especially delightful here is the use of offbeat timpani pianissimo accompanying the woodwind – a refinement of percussive scoring that would never have occurred to the Verdi of 1857.

170

There are other changes in the scoring even where the musical thought is the same. At the return of *a* ('Si schiudon quelle porte') the viola semiquavers are doubled by cellos in the original but not in the revision; and the constituents of the ghostly woodwind chords are different in each case – flute, piccolo, two oboes and bassoon in 1857; piccolo, oboe, clarinet and bassoon in 1881. It is significant that the piccolo should be common to both. In *Rigoletto* Verdi had already demonstrated how it can be put to sinister use.

Finally the score in the archives of the Teatro la Fenice contains a variant in the coda which is not to be found in any of the printed editions. Verdi explained it thus in a letter to Tito Ricordi written shortly after the première: '. . . In the introduction at bar 68 of the 6/8 movement I have altered the orchestration for the space of ten bars so as to avoid a difficult passage for the violas and cellos, which in our orchestras are always a *race of hounds*; and I have preferred to change it in the score and so avoid havoc during performance.'* In fact he changed more than the scoring. His original conception developed through modulating cadences like those which followed the reprise of *b* and represented the kind of procedure that earned for the first *Boccanegra* the reputation of harmonic abstruseness.

171

By 1881 the violas and cellos of la Scala, Milan, had certainly improved on their predecessors at Venice; so Verdi doubtless had other reasons for not reverting to his first thoughts at this point. Possibly he felt it was a case of piling Pelion on Ossa; perhaps he just forgot. The standard version is perfectly satisfactory as it stands.

Seven bars of orchestra were sufficient to disperse the chorus in 1857; exactly twice that number are needed in 1881; for it is at this point that Verdi has decided to turn the tiny motif (*x*) of Ex. 169 into the 'death figure' (♫♪), given out first unobtrusively in the cellos and basses then fiercely on all the strings in unison to be answered by baleful brass chords that seem to predict the opening of Tchaikovsky's *Francesca da Rimini*.

This sudden metamorphosis will be surpassed six years later by a similar effect where Iago, all charm and smiles, suddenly lets the mask slip. One consequence of the

* Letter to T. Ricordi, 5.8.1857. Abbiati, II, p. 413.

172

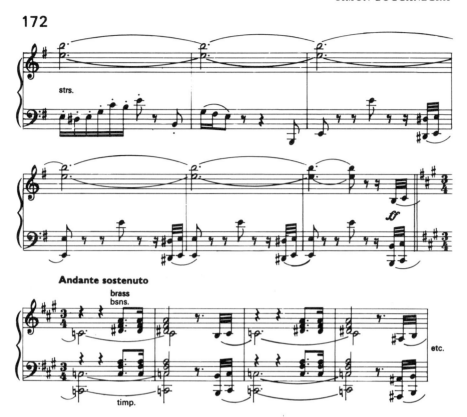

1881 enlargement is that the high open fifth at the beginning of Ex. 171 originally given to solo flute and clarinet must now be taken over by violins since they alone can sustain for the necessary length of time.

By the start of Fiesco's recitativo e romanza 'Il lacerato spirito', the high-water mark of the 1857 prologue, the two versions, which have been steadily converging, are for the moment identical. Fiesco, who now comes out of the palace, could be called the apotheosis of the Verdian basso comprimario. Not for him the baritonal suavities of such as Pagano, Attila or Procida. He must have, said Verdi, 'a voice of steel'.* Each phrase of recitative and aria is compact and granite-like.

The opening 'A te l'estreme addio' carries echoes of Bertrand's invocation from *Robert le Diable*, an opera for which Verdi was known to have had a special admiration.† Like Meyerbeer's villain, Fiesco feels himself to be a lost soul, as he bids farewell to the palace which has been his daughter's grave. He apostrophizes Boccanegra with hate ('O maledetto! O vile seduttore!'), reproaches the image of the Virgin Mary for failing to protect his child, then checks himself in the act of blasphemy and begs forgiveness for a father's heart torn by grief and shame. The romanza itself shows the tripartite minor–major design at its most skeletal, together with the musical consistency of a diamond. The first sentence ('Il lacerato spirito') is a mere eight bars, scored for the same combination of brass as Ex. 172 with timpani

* Letter to G. Ricordi, 2.12.1880. Abbiati, IV, p. 137.
† See I. Pizzi, *Per il I° centenario della nascita di Giuseppe Verdi* (Turin, 1913), p. 187.

thudding after each phrase. Four bars of dominant harmony follow; twice an offstage chorus of women chant 'E morta' and twice a chorus of monks, also behind the scenes, reply with a 'Miserere' on a single note. Thence immediately to the major section ('Il serto a lei de'martiri', see Ex. 15)* with its accompaniment of tremolo strings and intermittent cry of women. The persistence of sorrow in the major key is stressed by the pentatonic contour, faintly suggestive of a highland pibroch. Here the melody is only eight bars long; the rest is repetition and coda with slight choral elaboration. Yet so intense is the banked-up emotion that it seems spontaneously to generate a long instrumental postlude, during which the mourners come out of the palace and disperse.† It is a tender Beethoven-like melody mostly for woodwind and tremolo strings with trumpet minims tolling on the second beat of each bar. The same blend of austerity and compassion will stamp the music for the Monk in *Don Carlos*.

Only in one respect does this scena e romanza show the dilemma of revising after nearly a quarter of a century. Moments in the recitative, such as 'E tu, Vergin celeste', sound curiously old-fashioned in the context of the 1881 score. Elsewhere in the opera all such commonplaces of recitative have been rooted out. Possibly the conventional setting was thought appropriate to such a conventional sentiment, since reproaching heaven and retracting your reproach had been a standard operatic gambit since Monteverdi's *Lamento di Arianna*. However, Verdi did see fit to make one change in the aria itself. In the twelfth bar of the major section Fiesco originally sang an expansive triplet phrase (Ex. 173a) which was later simplified into a plain step-wise descent (Ex. 173b).

173

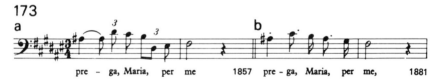

pre - ga, Maria,   per   me   1857   pre - ga, Maria,   per   me,   1881

The change undoubtedly accords better with Fiesco's stern, inflexible character. Then too Verdi seems to have taken a dislike to the shape of the original phrase as such since he also removed it from the recognition duet.

As Fiesco is about to enter the church he finds himself face to face with Boccanegra, who has returned full of hope at hearing his name on everyone's lips. There is a predictable tutti explosion, and Fiesco bursts out in fury and scorn, his line like Barbarossa's doubling the orchestral bass. Simone's placatory reply is conveyed by a pleading melody in the orchestra (Ex. 174).

But even in 1857 this is no ordinary dissimilar duet movement. It moves in a sequence of contrasting periods, sentences and phrases which follow the course of the argument. After Simone has sued in vain for forgiveness he points to his deeds of

---

* See Chapter 2 for the musical example together with a discussion of its characteristic harmonic scheme.

† The 1857 score mentions 'domestic servants and women in mourning'; the production book of 1881 is more specific: *3 women, 1 doctor, 1 monk, 4 valets, 2 boys. Take care that this movement of people across the square should not have the appearance of an organized procession. These are people who are slowly leaving a house where grief now prevails: this is the impression that the public must be given.* (*Disp. scen.*, p. 7.) A diagram indicates the pairing of the mourners and the direction which each pair should take out of the square.

174

valour in a brief military-sounding period in D flat major ('Sublimarmi a lei sperai'). Fiesco is unimpressed; he applauds Simone's courage but cannot forgive him the stain on his own escutcheon. If he aspired to the ducal throne it would be an offence in the sight of God and himself (all this to a slowly upward crawling line in the manner of Silva). Simone offers to let Fiesco kill him on the spot if only he would put an end to their blood-feud; and here the orchestra gives out an anguished derivation from Ex. 174. But Fiesco has no wish to be a murderer. He will forgive Simone on one condition: that he hand over to him his daughter by Maria. The tone of his offer reminds us how much of the priest there is in Fiesco (Ex. 175).

But Simone cannot comply. 'Thieving Fate' has snatched his daughter from him. In all this the alterations of 1881 are small but significant. At the words 'il perdono a me concedi' Simone's line had a few unmanly sobs in it; these were removed and replaced by a more dignified chromatic descent. Then where previously Fiesco and Simone had shouted at one another over chords of F minor ('Tardi omai' — 'Non sii crudel!') Simone's lines and accompanying harmonies were given a great flexibility and warmth, Fiesco remaining immovable as before. At the climax of Fiesco's long climb ('Segno all'odio mio e all'anatema di Dio') the Verdi of 1881 appears to have felt that an anathema to a major-key cadence, however emphatic, could not be a very serious matter. Accordingly he prolonged the passage by two bars underlining the word 'Dio' first with a diminished seventh (Ex. 176 (x)) then with a 6/4 chord (y) both stepping-stones to a still greater climax matching the words 'e di Fiesco

175

l'offensor' and formed from two secondary seventh chords (z) that would have been right outside the Verdian vocabulary of 1857.

Fiesco has thus made it clear that it is a far worse crime to offend one of his name than to offend God; and from this point the music descends smoothly and without repetition to the long dominant preparation for Ex. 175. In the first version this

176

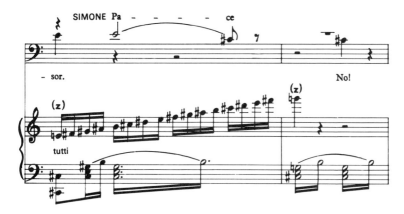

dominant had been arrived at four bars too early, at the word 'offensor', after which it had been necessary to mark time harmonically. Once again short-winded repetition has been dissolved into a seamless continuity. In the next six bars a dominant pedal has been removed; and the final bars of the movement which prepare for Simone's narration are wonderfully enriched and sensitized.* Thus in the phrase 'rubella sorte lei rapì', chromatic inner harmonies replace the stark octaves rapped out in dotted rhythm.

The second movement of the duet ('Del mar sul lido') is a solo for Simone with the occasional prompting from Fiesco. In contrast to the first it is essentially formal and based on the eight-bar unit, though each of its three sections begins and ends in a different key. A final exchange between Simone and Fiesco by way of a coda keeps however to F minor throughout. Simone describes how he had the child brought up in a house on some distant shore with an aged woman to look after her; one day he called at the house to find it locked and the old woman dead. The child had been seen wandering about for three days, then had vanished without trace; Simone had sought her ever since but in vain. Although the ship is not mentioned for some time the motion of the andantino is strictly navigational in the post-*Tancredi* manner. The violas' acciaccatura of the opening motif has a double function: it both 'sails' and 'laments' (Ex. 177).

Despite the underlying regularity of phrase only the first section is purely symmetrical. In the second ('Di là una notte') the voice is cross-phrased with the orchestra in the first eight bars; then as the story mounts to its climax the pace quickens with a semiquaver accompaniment of violins, and the modulations become faster and steeper. The end of the story ('Misera, trista') with its pathetic woodwind accompaniment in thirds is enhanced by those little extensions which are a familiar part of Verdi's technique. In the coda Fiesco returns to doubling the orchestral bass with a phrase of Wagnerian richness and solemnity ('Se il mio desire compier non puoi, pace non puote esser fra noi'). If Simone cannot produce the daughter there can never be peace between them. Simone pleads in vain, and in the second version a little oboe melody adds poignancy to his entreaty. But Fiesco merely turns his back on Simone and goes away with a frigid 'addio' which takes him down to a low F.†

* See Osthoff, pp. 73–5.

† In 1857 he went into the church; in 1881 he merely moved some distance away and then stayed behind to watch.

177

So ends a remarkable duet of 'scontro' between baritone and bass, but not of the purely generic kind to be found in the operas of the 1840s. Simone and Fiesco are sculpted as individuals, each within his own vocal archetype: Fiesco hard and inflexible, Simone infinitely mobile. Even in its original form the duet upset Basevi with what seemed to him its reckless modernity. Not only do the voices never sing together; Boccanegra himself often is content to declaim on one note leaving all the musical argument to the orchestra. 'Not even Wagner,' declares the indignant Florentine, 'would have ventured so far along this road.'*

From here to the end of the prologue both versions of the opera are the same. As soon as Fiesco has gone Simone exclaims bitterly at the pride of the Fieschi. What follows is a mixture of recitative and mime music. Longing for a sight of his Maria, Simone, on an impulse, knocks at the door of the palace. No answer. But the door is unlocked, and he goes in. Fiesco, watching from the shadows,† comments with grim satisfaction at the sight that will greet him. Then Simone appears on the balcony, takes the lantern off the hook and returns inside.‡

If any evidence were needed of Verdi's recent French lessons it is provided by the violin theme which accompanies Simone's movements (Ex. 178).

Suddenly his cry of horror rings out: 'Maria! Maria!' 'The hour of your punishment has struck!' – thus Fiesco from below. As Simone reappears on the balcony distant shouts are heard: 'Boccanegra!' It is the people come to acclaim him as their new Doge, led by. Paolo and Pietro. To Simone they are all horribly unreal. To Paolo's greeting he can only cry brokenly, 'A tomb!'; to which Paolo replies, 'A throne!' while Fiesco fumes helplessly from his place of concealment. The scene is laid out as a

* Basevi, p. 270.

† Appearing at the church door in 1857.

‡ *Meanwhile the chorus should be gathered behind the backcloth. Paolo and Pietro in the wings on the right; 12 extras ready R. with lighted torches: ditto 12 L: 4 large bells to be prepared.* (Disp. scen., p. 10.)

crescendo with more and more people pouring on to the stage with lighted torches. Eventually bells ring out and the curtain falls on shouts of 'Viva!' The banda-like orchestral theme which brings on the populace is without doubt Verdi's most successful essay in deliberate banality. Not that it embarrasses since, unlike many of his melodies actually written for banda, it is not a debasement of something lyrical. It is simple, direct and popular, and in its context brilliantly effective.

It jars on our nerves as it jars on Simone's with a thoughtless cheerfulness which does more to bring home the hollowness of his triumph than any conventional monologue of despair.*

ACT I

Scene 1: The garden of the Grimaldi Palace outside Genoa. On the left the palace; directly in front, the sea. Dawn is breaking.†

Both versions of the opera begin with an evocative prelude played before the rise

---

* At the last bar but ten from the end the curtain should fall quickly. It is vitally important that at the moment that the curtain descends the bell-players should be warned to stop at once since if the bells make too much noise it will be impossible to hear the curtain signal or the point where the orchestra stops. The continuation of the sound of bells after the curtain has fallen makes a thoroughly bad effect. It is also essential that this last crowd scene should be played with the utmost liveliness and the contrast between this scene and the dark, dramatic colouring of those preceding is the aim that the composer has set himself, and it is from this contrast that the desired effect can be obtained. (Disp. scen., p. 11.)

† The 1857 score is more detailed. The sea washes the bottom of the garden. In the far distance there is a view of Genoa behind which the sun rises. This is of course very different from the scene as imagined by Verdi in his letter to Piave in 1856. But like everything else in the first published edition it is based on the second production at Reggio Emilia, by which time it had been decided to divide Act I into three scenes instead of the original two. In Venice scene 1 had been a shallow interior with the sea glimpsed through the windows of the palace. At the start of the finale the backcloth had been removed to reveal the public square in Genoa. In Reggio the first scene was set in the open air. It could afford to be a deep one since it was followed by an interior during which Amelia receives the Doge; meanwhile the still grander scene in the public square could be prepared. The production book of 1881, however, specifies *a very shallow stage. Terrace and gardens overlooking the sea; palace on the right; dawn is about to break . . . Tranquil half-light; then full light.*

of the curtain, and based on the same pentatonic theme – the shell from which Amelia's cavatina emerges – see Ex. 180 (*x*) below.

The first – a mere 22 bars of 6/8 – is simple and direct. Less integrated with the cavatina than its successor it nevertheless prepares for it with a delightful stroke of surprise-logic, moving up into the new key just where it seems about to return to the old. But its air of matutinal freshness is slightly diminished by certain rhetorical gestures recalling the world of *Semiramide*. By contrast the prelude of 1881 is all tone poem, full of glinting colours and rich in melodic and harmonic interest. What does it matter if the imagery is vague? The stage directions speak of the rising dawn; the text of the cavatina of the moon and stars reflected in the sea. The music would suit either; it could even be a portrayal of the dawn chorus. It is enough that the interplay of bright sounds (produced mainly by the piccolo) distils a feeling of magic in the air.

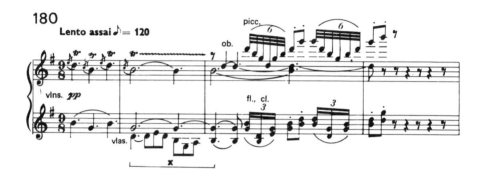

Amelia's cantabile has a grand-opera scale – a three-limbed melody in French ternary form with an eventful central episode and a full reprise, not to mention a distinctly Meyerbeerian modulation at the fourth phrase ('All'onda il tuo chiaror'). She is sitting in the garden admiring the prospect – moon and sea united in soft radiance, 'like the loving embrace of two virginal hearts'.

- l'on - - da il tu - o chia - ror! Ah! ___ a - man - - te am-ples - so

con forza

pa - - re _____ di due _ ver - gi - nei cor!

strs.

Yet the sight also brings back memories of long ago when an old woman on her deathbed recommended her to the care of heaven. The sinister recollection is conveyed by the favourite use of the 6/4 chord in a remote key. In 1857 it is the same progression repeated four times at the same pitch; in 1881 the pitch is varied and the effect like a descent into some mysterious abyss. (See Ex. 182 a and b.)

In the orchestral link that follows the neutral semiquaver pattern of 1857 becomes in 1881 a direct quotation from Simone's racconto in the prologue, where he describes how he found the nurse dead and the child missing. If there was previously any doubt in the listener's mind as to Amelia's real identity, there can be none now.

Resuming Ex. 181, she vows that the pomp of her new home, where love first smiled upon her, will never make her forget the humble seaside hut where she was brought up. We have noticed how from _Luisa Miller_ onwards Verdi's melodies have tended to slough off the self-perpetuating accompanimental pattern. In the 1857 version Amelia's melody was backed first by an unobtrusive design of string quavers and semiquaver triplets, at its reprise by an arpeggiating clarinet. From this point of view the high woodwind filigree and punctuating strings of the definitive Ex. 181

182a

AMELIA

(me) - schina? La not-te a - tra, crudel, quando la pia mo -

strs.

_pp_

- ren - te scla - mò: Ti guardi il ciel.

f solenne

hns.
bsns.
added

_pp_

182b

may seem a regression – were it not that they approach more nearly the evocative patterns of a Schubert *Lied* than those intricate pulsations which merely serve to give rhythmic emphasis to the Risorgimento operas. In fact the solution of 1881 is unique, since, like so much of the revised *Boccanegra*, it explores the realm of what might have been. Had Verdi decided to set the aria anew, it would have been in a different, more harmonically fluid style in which figuration of this kind has no part. As it is he takes the melody of 1857, which implies a static accompaniment, then embellishes this accompaniment with poetic overtures by elaborating precisely those elements which in general his maturing thought was tending to discard. The reprise features a still more striking combination of brass, strings with clarinets and remaining woodwind (Ex. 183) hinting besides at the oppressive grandeur of the Grimaldi palace, which is the subject of Amelia's verse.

183

At the end where she turns towards the sea the orchestra reverts to the first design for a gently diminishing coda which replaces the conventional ending with cadenza of the original. For a 'monachella' or convent girl, as Verdi described her in 1881, Amelia's manner in this cantabile is uncomfortably grand. Even in the revision the shadow of the powerful Luigia Bendazzi hangs over her.

There followed, in 1857, fifteen bars of anxious recitative in the manner of Lida in *La Battaglia di Legnano*, ending with a fine downward-swooping phrase over one and a half octaves. 'Day is breaking. He comes not. Perhaps a disaster . . . perhaps another love.' But Verdi had objected to any suggestion of jealousy on Amelia's part; so the music was removed and Amelia was given a few poetic lines to be draped over the orchestral coda of the cantabile.

Then Gabriele's voice is heard in a distant serenade ('Cielo di stelle orbato'), a snatch of melody which might have come from Manrico were it not unmistakably imbued with the *Boccanegra* 'tinta'.

184

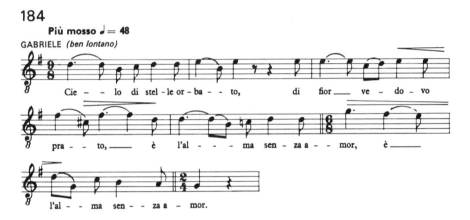

In 1857 the accompanying instrument was a 'fisarmonica' or small harmonium behind the scenes; in 1881 it is a harp. As to the reason, one can only hazard a guess. In the mid-fifties an offstage harp would have suggested that Gabriele was playing it himself – an occupation suitable to a troubadour but unworthy of a Genoese nobleman. By the time of the revised score the device had become sufficiently established as a background to any romantic serenade as to cause no sense of the incongruous. The fisarmonica, whose sound was so small that it could be used for giving singers their notes during a performance, was presumably chosen because of its disembodied quality; but it was an unsatisfactory compromise.

Amelia reacts with breathless excitement; then the song is repeated to a new verse and nearer at hand. Amelia's response in the first version is a brilliant cabaletta ('Il palpito deh frena') in which she asks her beating heart to be still and begs not to die at such a joyous moment. In calling it 'bad' Verdi was exaggerating. Of its type – which is that of Lady Macbeth's 'Trionfai' of 1847 – it is impressive with its wealth of trills and its accompaniment of clarinet arpeggios (rare in a fast cabaletta). But it is too generic or 'poco caratteristica' as Verdi would have put it. Even if the triple rhythm with its triplet subdivisions can be seen as related to the 9/8 of the cantabile, the piece remains one of those disconcerting 'throw-backs' which sometimes occur in the operas between *Les Vêpres Siciliennes* and *Aida*. One can understand Verdi's irritation when for a performance of *Simon Boccanegra* at the Théâtre des Italiens in 1883 the singer of Amelia demanded the original cabaletta. As by this time both score and material had been destroyed Muzio, then the theatre's musical director, sent a copy of the piano reduction and with many apologies begged his old teacher to score it afresh. He recalled how at the first production in Venice 'the arpeggi were performed by Mirko on the clarinet, and on the second crotchet the pizzicato of the basses was followed by that of the violins and violas, and I still remember the tremendous, magical effect at the reprise, when the voice was accompanied by flute and oboe and ended with a chromatic scale amid storms of applause. . . .'* It is typical of the naive Muzio that he should praise precisely those doubling devices that give the cabaletta its faint air of routine and 'déjà vu'. Whether or not Verdi obliged is not known; but a testy letter written to Giulio Ricordi three days before Muzio's was dispatched makes it seem unlikely: 'I declare here and now that I will not make a new orchestration of the cabaletta and that I haven't got the old one. Bit by bit as I revised I cut out the old pages and threw them in the fire and probably this pointless cabaletta along with them.'†

185

In the revision the cabaletta was replaced by a mere eleven bars of eager anticipation ('Ei vien! l'amor m'avvampa') for which Boito supplied the text. It is all in the composer's late manner – a nimble bass of cellos divided into two groups and phrased across the barline, and a delicate web of sustaining instruments. (The older Verdi himself, it seems, the younger his music.) At the last three bars Amelia is joined by Gabriele with an 'Anima mia!', and the versions converge once more. She reproaches him for his delay; he gives as his excuse weighty reasons of state. Amelia recalls with a shudder the times she has seen him in mysterious conversation with her

---

* Letter from Muzio, 30.10.1883. *Carteggi Verdiani*, II, p. 224.
† Letter to G. Ricordi, 27.10.1883. Abbiati, IV, p. 221.

guardian Andrea, Lorenzino the usurer and others. Gabriele is evasive and tries to change the subject. In all this the two death-rhythms |♪♪ and | ♫♪ are unmistakable in their significance, above all at the words 'In cupa notte non ti mirai', where the first is stated alternately on middle strings and woodwind beneath a sinuous pattern of violin and cello triplets.

The cantabile of the duet ('Vieni a mirar la cerula') harks back to the duet between Lucrezia and Jacopo in *I Due Foscari*; it has the same 3/8 rhythm and the same counterpoint of sound and sense. Amelia is pointing across the water to where Genoa 'towers above its foaming bridal chamber' and Gabriele's enemies lie in wait for him. But the melody, the softly fluttering strings and low woodwind trills all speak the language of unclouded affection. It is not till the final limb of the melody that music and words unite in what is to serve as a refrain to an otherwise 'dissimilar' movement.

186

Note once more the pentatonic nucleus indicated by the bracket, and its relation to Ex. 180. Gabriele's ecstatic reply ('Angiolo che dall' empireo') is altered so deftly in the revision by means of puntature, inner harmonic elaboration and rescoring that the original version with its low-lying tenor line seems like a sketch by comparison. While ostensibly making concessions to the higher range of Tamagno, Verdi has contrived to confer on Gabriele a touch of the Fenton yet to come. But despite the different arrangement of sonorities the harmonic scheme of both versions, and with it the bass line in all but two bars, is exactly the same. In the new coda, in accordance with the canons of 1881, the original double cadenza is avoided, and its place taken by a delicious harmonic epigram (E flat⁶, E major⁶, D⁷, G) emphasized by a plunge from *ff* to *ppp*.

Amelia starts; she has noticed another man passing like a shadow in the garden.* A maid comes from the palace and announces a messenger from the Doge. Gabriele wants to get a sight of him first but is restrained by Amelia. Pietro is allowed to enter and tell her that the Doge intends to pay her a visit on his return from the hunt in Savona. When Pietro has left Amelia informs Gabriele that the Doge intends to marry her to his henchman, Paolo: 'Fly in search of Andrea; hasten; prepare the nuptial rite and lead me to the altar.' Operatic architecture, if not common sense, demands a cabaletta at this point. For its time the first 'Sì, sì dell'ara il giubilo' is quite original, with its design of overlapping phrases, but it is still a cabaletta with orchestral ritornello, reprise and vocal climax reached by syncopations as in the cabalettas of *La Traviata*. Thematically the version of 1881 is the same as before but everything 'cabalettistic' has been removed.† It proceeds in a single sweep towards a tutti climax enhanced with a device which is usually associated with Puccini – the doubling of treble and bass with the harmony sandwiched in between.

187

The early cabaletta ended with a coda and a battery of chords followed by applause and curtain calls. No such good fortune for the singers in 1881; for as Amelia enters the palace the music moves to a half-close in a new key. Gabriele, about to go in search of Andrea, is forestalled by the appearance of the man himself – Fiesco under a new identity. He is sympathetic to Gabriele's suit but feels bound to warn him that Amelia is of humble birth. The real Amelia, he explains in a Silva-like arioso ('La figlia dei Grimaldi'), died in a convent in Pisa long ago. His own ward is a nameless orphan who took her place in order to prevent the Grimaldi inheritance falling into the hands of the state, since both her brothers had been exiled. Gabriele declares that he loves the orphan no less than the heiress. Here the two scores diverge once more. In the original, trumpets off-stage announce the approach of Boccanegra. The two men decide to leave. But in the 1857 score they first permit themselves a subdued but savage outburst against the Doge – murderer of Gabriele's father and Fiesco's

* Here once more the sequence of events is confused by the convention of compressing and eliding details from the original play. In Gutiérrez's play the man whom Simone has caught sight of in the garden is never identified then or later. He is just someone whom Amelia has several times noticed at that hour of day and who seems to be spying on her. When Gabriele turns to look the man has disappeared. The opera-goer might be forgiven for imagining that he is Pietro, who is introduced immediately afterwards, and whom both Gabriele and Amelia/Susana know perfectly well.

† For this Verdi had provided his own model in the duettino ('Ora di morte e di vendetta') which ends Act III of the revised *Macbeth*.

daughter. 'Paventa, o perfido' is described by Basevi as the weakest number in the opera.* It is certainly an odd piece of vocal writing. In the play Gabriele is all for violent action at this point, while Fiesco counsels prudence. It is appropriate therefore that Gabriele should lead the duet; but here Fiesco seconds everything he says; and indeed the theme seems to have been calculated with a view to the natural resources of a basso profondo rather than a tenor. Even if he can reach the low B at the fifth bar, Gabriele will sound like a bass manqué, and his personality be entirely engulfed by Fiesco's, since this is Fiesco's musical language. Not only that; from the start the tenor has to compete with continuously rolling timpani and bass drum, and a number of hollow brass chords at moments where projection is difficult.

188

As a piece of musical savagery in the manner of the future 'Dies irae' this Giuramento is impressive. The scoring is murky but economically so, and apart from the steep dynamic contrasts there is a blood-chilling unison climb for the two voices towards the end (from C–A flat–E major–C sharp minor–G sharp minor) followed by a foretaste of 'Mors stupebit' – two pianissimi pizzicato notes in a sudden vacuum.

But few would want to exchange this piece for the duettino religioso which replaced it in 1881. Apart from the wish to lighten the first act, Verdi in late middle age was mellowing in his attitude towards these unforgiving, inexorable old men – witness his treatment of Philippe in the successive versions of *Don Carlos*. In the circle of family and friends there is no reason why Fiesco should not have been a lovable

* Basevi, p. 275.

patriarch. In the second score he is so touched by the sincerity of Gabriele's love, that he makes him kneel and gives him a father's blessing.

189

Heralded by solemn chords for brass and bassoons this duettino is deliberately organ-like in its scoring even down to the use of long pedal notes and surprise modal cadences in the manner of Fauré. Here at least Gabriele preserves his separate identity, with a smooth, mainly cursive line in contrast to Fiesco's wide intervals. Only the prosody leaves something to be desired for reasons that have already been mentioned. 'Vieni a me ti benedicó' is not the best way of setting an ottonario. Immediately after the final cadence trumpets are heard for the first time in the 1881 version and with a far more distinguished fanfare than that of its predecessor. The key, the contour and the orchestral punctuations on offbeats suggest that Beethoven's Choral Fantasia was perhaps not unknown to Verdi. Gabriele and Fiesco have gone by the time that Amelia comes out of the palace with her maidens just as the Doge enters from the other direction with Paolo and a following of hunters.*

So in the revision. In 1857, however, following the performance at Reggio, there was a change of scene here to the interior of the Grimaldi palace, a hall hung with suits of armour and family portraits. The trumpets must therefore sound again to herald the Doge's entry. He dismisses his suite and reminds Paolo of the festivities that are to take place the next day; therefore they must be ready to leave for Genoa when the hour strikes.† In 1881 there were to be no festivities. So 'Il nuovo dì festivo chiede presente la città' is replaced by the vaguer 'Ci spronano gli eventi'. Thereafter the texts converge once more, though the musical setting is changed in the later version so as both to point the verbal meaning more clearly and to avoid those occasional clichés of recitative which still encrust the original.‡ The difference is especially marked where the retiring Paolo gazes wistfully at Amelia murmuring 'Ah, qual beltà!' In the first version the strings mark time on and around the chord of B flat major for four bars; in the second we find in its place seven bars of almost Wagnerian eloquence in voicing Paolo's unspoken thoughts. In much the same way does Siegmund gaze after Sieglinde in the opening page of *Die Walküre*.

190

* The production book specifies four stage trumpets, though two would be sufficient to play the notes; six huntsmen; and four maids in attendance on Amelia.

† Why the hurry? Because in the play the Doge's interview with Susana must be cut short before he can reveal to her the truth about her identity. As usual the sentence is carried over into the opera where it has no real purpose.

‡ For a valuable discussion of this scene see Osthoff, pp. 79–81.

Alone with Amelia, Boccanegra hands her a document recalling the Grimaldi brothers from exile — her own kin, as he imagines. For the moment she is too overwhelmed to speak, so allowing the orchestra four bars in which to prepare the graceful, conversational theme with which violins launch the first movement of the duet ('Dinne, perchè in quest'eremo'). It is the language of Sparafucile purged of everything that is sinister or mocking.

191

Why, the Doge wants to know, does Amelia live such a secluded life? Her blushes tell him that she is in love; she cannot deny it and as mutual understanding grows so the voices tend to double the orchestral theme more and more. But there is a change to the minor as she tells him that there is someone else who is paying court to her to get his hands on the Grimaldi money. 'Paolo?' the Doge hazards. 'You have named the villain,' replies Amelia. Naively — since no doubt the Doge is too taken aback to reply — Amelia changes the subject. As Simone has been so kind to her she will tell him a secret; she is not a Grimaldi. In the second version the music is cunningly prolonged at this juncture to give more emphasis to Amelia's announcement, and above all to avoid the line 'Since you have pardoned my non-brothers', which, as Boito remarked dryly, is certainly not very beautiful.* There is a gain too in lyrical warmth, since Verdi has replaced the scraps of orchestral figuration and short vocal phrases of the original Amelia with a longer string-supported cantilena ('E perchè tanta pietà', etc.). The words 'Non sono una Grimaldi' are preceded by a roll on the timpani and dovetailed into an orchestral tutti of surprise. 'Oh ciel! chi sei?' asks the Doge — so prompting the second movement ('Orfanella, il tetto umile').

Like that of the Fiesco/Boccanegra duet in the prologue it takes the form of a 'racconto' in three parts and a coda and is in a similar andantino, for Amelia's

* Letter from Boito, 16.1.1881. *Carteggio Verdi–Boito*, I, pp. 32–5.

story is Boccanegra's told from a different angle. Boccanegra was the seafarer and his music was permeated by the active 'plying' motif. Amelia is the lonely orphan girl who knows nothing of her family or where she came from; hence the poignant melody anticipated by clarinet in 1857, oboe in 1881, and the pathetic harmonies.*

192

Amelia describes her upbringing by an old woman in Pisa; as she died she gave the child various tokens and a picture of her mother. The tonal scheme is simpler than in Simone's narrative, being more akin to that of a minor/major romanza. Inevitably too the end is different; for while Fiesco could only add a frigid comment Simone has become increasingly gripped by Amelia's words. Hardly daring to hope he adds a new idea to the major section ('Ah! se la speme, o ciel clemente') and the voices join in a lyrical conclusion with, in 1857, a prolonged cadenza. In 1881 Verdi rescored the opening part of this and replaced the last ten bars with a coda instinct with a romantic poetry of the most piercing beauty.

193

* There is a certain mystery here. The autograph in the Ricordi archives shows this passage first of all written for oboe, then scored out and rewritten on the clarinet stave. But over the top is written in a hand which is certainly not Verdi's the word *oboè*, the accent on the last letter indicating a nineteenth-century source. All the non-autograph manuscript scores of 1857 place the melody on the clarinet line. The printed score of 1881 gives it to the oboe. It would seem, therefore, that Verdi first imagined it for oboe, changed his mind, and finally, though there is no direct evidence for this, reverted to his original idea.

The Doge has a few further questions to ask. Did Amelia remember anyone else from her childhood? Yes, a man from the sea used to visit them. Was the old woman called Giovanna? Yes. And did the picture of Amelia's mother resemble one which he now produces? They are the same. The mounting excitement is conveyed with great skill by a derivative of the first movement orchestral theme developed in ever tighter rosalias. The ecstatic cadence and long subsidence over a dominant pedal are not new but they retain all their freshness in this context. The cabaletta ('Figlia! a tal nome io palpito') furnishes one of the key themes of the opera. The first period ends differently in both versions.* (See Ex. 144.)

In the 1857 score this is laid out as an orthodox similar cabaletta, with the theme sung successively by both singers and then, after a ritornello, shared between them, with coda and short cadenza to follow. As in 'Gran Dio, morir si giovine' (*La Traviata*) both continue singing through the ritornello and coda. The piece winds up

---

* The D in small type signifies another of the divergences between the old score and the new, and a rather puzzling one. The C sharp has already appeared where the theme is anticipated in the prelude and will appear again in the quotation that recurs in Act II (both in the earlier score). Yet neither the autograph score, the three available MSS. *partiture* nor the printed vocal sore of 1857 leave the slightest doubt that in the voice part Verdi originally intended three consecutive Ds and only in 1881 changed the second one to a C sharp. There is a possible explanation for this. The whole phrase is written everywhere legato and was obviously so conceived. Unlike a voice, however, the wind-instruments which are required to give the quotations cannot so easily reiterate a note without breaking the legato line. Therefore even in 1857 it was necessary to make an adjustment in the prelude and Act II. Later Verdi may well have decided that he preferred the instrumental form of the melody even in the voice part. *The questions of the one, the replies of the other, the eagerness, the ever-increasing interest of the Doge are too clearly depicted in the music for it to be necessary to indicate in detail the movements to be carried out by the two actors; it is one of those scenes of music-drama which derive their effect from the genius and intuition of the artists. Suffice it to say that the Doge should have a miniature painting hung round his neck beneath his robe; that Amelia will have a similar one in the reticule that hangs from her girdle, and that at a suitable moment she should take it out to put beside the picture which the Doge is holding, that when father and daughter recognize one another there will be a huge outburst of joy, that the Doge will press Amelia tenderly to his bosom; that at the end of the duet he will kiss his daughter on the forehead, as he walks with her towards the palace: Amelia will bid farewell to the Doge but after taking a few steps she will turn again and on an impulse of filial love should run to her father, crying, 'Padre.'*

Take care that this final part of the scene should not be played at the footlights but near the backcloth on the right, near where Amelia will make her exit. . . . (Disp. scen., pp. 16–17.)

194

with the cadential variant of Ex. 194 thundered out fortissimo by full orchestra, somewhat crudely voiced since it is designed to cut through torrents of applause.

In 1881 there is no such thing as an orthodox cabaletta. Amelia is therefore given a new idea (Ex. 195) which will be taken up in shortened form in the coda.

195

More striking still is the remoulding of Simone's second period which has already begun at the fourth phrase of his first (see Ex. 194). The 1857 version with its wealth of triplets and dotted rhythms has a faintly military air (not for nothing was Basevi reminded of Bellini's 'Suoni la tromba').* In the second (Ex. 196b) the rugged outlines are softened; melody and harmony take on a new warmth. It is the music of one who has come to terms with the gentle Gounod without losing any of his native strength. He is still the composer of 'Andrem ramminghi e poveri' (*Luisa Miller*).

There is no longer a central ritornello and the reprise is confined to the second half of Simone's period. The coda is simpler and gentler than before and the final, hushed cadence merges into the instrumental postlude – Ex. 194 on violins accompanied by sustaining horns and harp arpeggi. To further prolonged cries of 'Figlia' and 'Padre' it swells to a huge climax, then melts away to the last phrase of Ex. 196b on harp, clarinet and bassoon with horns and pizzicato strings to underpin the final chords. In a letter to Boito, Verdi had talked of giving 'more development to the so-called cabaletta'.† In fact the later movement is twenty-one bars shorter than the earlier; but there is more music in it.

As Simone stands gazing rapturously after Amelia, he is approached by Paolo. 'What was her answer?' The Doge starts; then tells him abruptly to give up all

---

* Basevi, p. 266.

† Letter to Boito, 9.1.1881. *Carteggio Verdi–Boito*, I, p. 17.

196a

Un pa - ra di - so il te - ne-ro pa - dre ti schiu-de - rà

strs. [hn. sustain

pizz.

di mia co - rona il rag - gio au - reo - la tua sa - rà

[fl. cls., bsns. sustain - - - - - - - -] etc.

(1857)

196b

Un pa - ra - di - so il te - ne-ro pa - dre ti schiude - rà

dolciss.

strs.

pizz. [hns. sustain - - - - - - [bsns. sustain - - - - - etc.

di mia corona il rag - gio la gloria - - tua sa - rà

ppp

[fl., cl., bsn.

ob. cl.]

etc.

[strs.] [strs.]

thoughts of marrying her. 'Doge, I cannot!' 'I wish it.' So saying, Simone leaves. 'You wish it!' Paolo exclaims. 'Have you forgotten that you owe your throne to me?' From this outburst a soft but tense allegro theme is launched as from a catapult. Pietro enters to learn during a rapid parlante that Paolo intends to abduct Amelia. He will blackmail the treacherous Lorenzino to harbour her in his palace. Pietro as before will be richly rewarded for his help.

Today this short scene can prove slightly embarrassing not only because there is something slightly comic about the rapid volley of exchanges (taken, however, direct from the play where Paolo and Pietro normally communicate thus) but because the quiet curtain can produce an anticlimax after what has gone before. Sometimes it is cut altogether. *Stiffelio*, it may be remembered, contained a similar scene which at least one modern producer has seen fit to displace. But this argues an ignorance of nineteenth-century staging in Italy. In both versions of the opera – even in the original unaltered staging in Venice – the scene was a shallow one. To change it required only the retraction of the two flats which formed the backcloth; meanwhile extras would rush in and remove unwanted articles of furniture. Indeed the production book of 1881 calls explicitly for a 'cambiamento a vista' during the space of one empty bar.* If there is an anticlimax here the fault must lie with the producer.

> *Scene 2 (Venice)/3 (Reggio) (1857 version): A large square in Genoa. In front is the harbour with craft variously dressed. In the distance on the right can be seen hills with castles and palaces. Nearer on the right magnificent buildings carried by flights of arches with balconies festively decorated, on which beautiful women are attending the solemn occasion. At the back is a broad street; on the left a wide flight of steps ascending to a stately palace; near the proscenium there is a dais richly decked. The anniversary of Boccanegra's coronation is being celebrated. As the curtain rises the square is crowded with people of all ranks, who are milling round joyfully carrying banners, palms and green boughs, and singing.*

A full-scale finale with concertato and stretta might still be current coin in 1857. But Verdi had apparently finished with it by the time he wrote the 'romantic trilogy'; and if he was to return to it four years later we may be sure that it would be a finale with a difference. And so it proves. The opening movement ('A festa, a festa, o Liguri') consists of two ideas; the first (Ex. 197a) a theme designed for those 'spezzato' choral effects with which Verdi had been toying since *Il Trovatore*; the second (Ex. 197b) a piece of straight party music like that of Act III in *Les Vêpres Siciliennes*. The contrast between them is heightened by their being placed in different keys like the first and second subjects in a sonata movement.

197a

197b

But there is no kind of development. The allegro is soon wound up in a short coda, to be followed by a four-part unaccompanied barcarolle for female voices ('Sull' arpe, sulle cetere') ushering in a barge filled with gaily dressed girls. However, the pentatonic 'tinta' of the opening half-phrase makes it almost a quotation from Fiesco's 'Il lacerato spirito'.

198

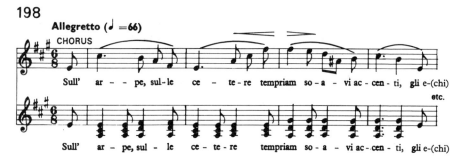

There is obviously no dramatic significance in this. The divertissement is light relief, no more. Thematic links with what has gone before prevent it from falling into musical irrelevance.

Simone now enters, and with him the banda. As he mounts the steps to the throne the banda give out what was one of the principal themes in the early version of the opera; the Hymn to the Doge ('Viva Simon!').

199

Ceremonial music in nineteenth-century opera is rarely very distinguished unless it is either nationalistic or by Berlioz. The above is no exception, though it has the merit of plainness and concision. If it does not uplift the soul neither does it set the teeth on edge. The chorus and orchestra take it up, the latter contributing a separate pattern of crochet triplets to the second stanza – an early essay in that combination of orchestra and banda which Verdi was to manage more successfully in *Don Carlos*. The games begin with the 'ballabile con coro' of the African corsairs. The main theme has a splendidly muscular panache.

200

The women's intervention ('Intreccia, o figlia d'Africa'), first in G major, later in E with banda joining in, is no more than a boisterous re-statement of Ex. 199. No sooner has the final chord died away than the voices of Gabriele and Fiesco are heard in the distance with cries of 'Tradimento!' They have discovered Amelia's abduction. A powerfully turbulent movement builds up, similar to the allegro of the Act I finale of *Macbeth*, though more lightly scored. The dialogue follows closely that of Gutiérrez's Act I, scene xviii: Gabriele hurling insults at the Doge, Fiesco urging caution while keeping as far as possible out of sight, the Doge turning angrily on Paolo, who in turn cringes with fear. The centrepiece is a stanza from Gabriele accusing the Doge of lying and hypocrisy – a counterpart to the curse of Edgardo in *Lucia* or the challenge of Zamoro in *Alzira*, though noticeably lower in range than either. The crowd murmur; Fiesco attempts vainly to hold Gabriele back. 'The Doge is infamous,' cries Gabriele. 'The Doge is innocent,' retorts Amelia, appearing suddenly. It is the moment for a pezzo concertato of surprise; and Verdi, by now more than ever averse to lyrical note-spinning however beautiful, has here aimed at the most direct, naturalistic expression that the form will allow: a series of disjointed exclamations passed from mouth to mouth followed by sighs of relief, barely disturbed by the outraged mutterings of Paolo and Pietro.

201

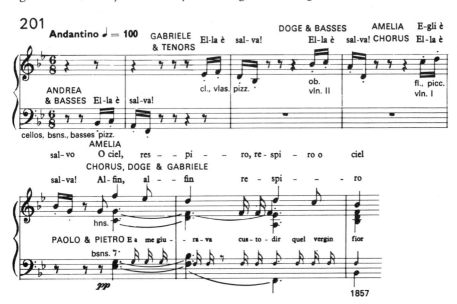

A bold experiment, and a dangerous one. The musical stylization of involuntary reflexes is more for comedy than tragedy; it is after all one of the secrets of the Rossinian 'grande risata'. When motifs such as those of Ex. 201 are worked into a concertato the effect tends towards comic exaggeration, as in 'Freddo ed immobile' from *Il Barbiere*. One can perhaps forgive a sophisticated Florentine audience of 1857 for smiling at such a ploy, if not for overlooking the immense skill with which the disjointed fragments have been knitted into an imposing tapestry of sound over a pattern of pulsating semiquavers. As usual the separate interventions are characteristic, though judged by the standards of the earlier operas the baritone and tenor appear to have exchanged roles. Boccanegra's line is lyrical, Gabriele's powerfully energetic as he appears to hold up the bass line like some caryatid.

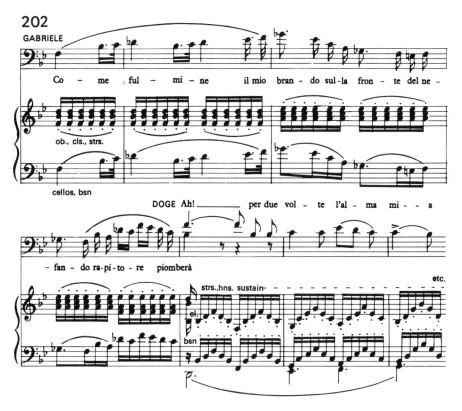

Here, though not in the later version, Pietro's part lies above Paolo's, while Fiesco is soon submerged into the chorus basses, at one point rising to a high G flat – which of course he did not need to take since there would be a full complement of choristers to take it for him. Musically speaking this is as fine a concertato as any Verdi has written to date, with the lyrical and rhythmic element in perfect equilibrium. Theatrically speaking, however, one can understand why he wanted to change it.

The dramatic movement, having ground to a halt, is restarted by the feeblest of feed-lines from Simone ('Amelia, racconta qual fosti rapita') couched in that plain, unthematic style that so infuriated Basevi. Amelia's racconto, however ('Nell'ora soave') is strong enough, musically and dramatically, for parts of it to be incorporated in the revised score. Occurring as it does at a moment of transition it has no need even of the modified formality of Azucena's 'Condott' ell'era in ceppi'. There are no schematic sequences in patterns of three. All sense of the periodic melts away after the first eight bars. But this is no loosely knit scene; it evolves a coherent musical argument from three clearly defined motifs. The first (Ex. 203a) is introduced by a delicate combination of woodwind; the second (Ex. 203b) is notable for that classicizing tendency that becomes increasingly prominent in mature Verdi – it might have come from a sonata by Clementi or the young Beethoven.

203a

203b

203c

Amelia was strolling along the shore (203a on strings) when she was seized and hustled on board a ship. She fainted; when she revived she found herself in Lorenzo's house (*b*). Knowing his cowardice (derivative of *b*) she threatened to reveal his treasonable activities to the Doge. Confused and frightened he let her go free (*c*). The chorus cry out for Lorenzo's blood (combination of *b* and *c* derivatives). But, says Amelia, he is not the real villain, and anyway she promised Lorenzo his life. 'Then let him be banished from Genoa,' says Simone, with improbable promptitude. As for the guilty party, Amelia continues, she will reveal his name only to the Doge; and when Gabriele, Fiesco and the populace all demand that she say it aloud, the Doge forbids her. All this from Amelia's 'Io salva promisi serbargli la vita' forms a coda in faster time with the contour of (*a*) and in the inner parts the syncopated rhythm of (*b*). By a procedure entirely novel for the time the growing excitement causes the music to topple over without a break into the main theme of the stretta 'Giustizia,' based on two contrasted ideas, like the pezzo concertato to which it forms a complement. But here the contrast is far more arresting. The first theme, after a unison start (Ex. 204a) bursts into rugged counterpoint, of which two examples are worth quoting (b and c).

The second idea is no more than a prolonged plagal cadence extended sequentially in a variety of keys (Ex. 205).

In 1857 the major-key conclusion is still obligatory; but as in the final bars of *Stiffelio*, Act I, the tension never slackens. Rather, it is enhanced by a new idea conceived in massive three-part harmony: for Amelia, high woodwind and trumpets, a vigorous, swerving line, heavily syncopated; for the rest, striding crotchets in thirds which circle the related keys before reaching a cadence. Ex. 205 returns now as a sequence of resolving dominants like those in the trio of Mozart's 'Jupiter' symphony. And just as Mozart in the Act I strette of *Don Giovanni* and *La Clemenza di Tito* sustains the feeling of menace in a major key by repeatedly flattening the sixth, so Verdi leans from time to time on the Neapolitan triad to similar effect.

In comparison with his previous strette this one is distinctly learned; but not a whit

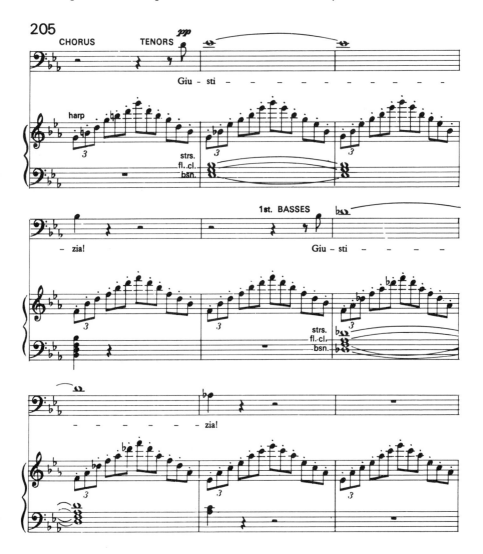

more so than the kind of movement that Mercadante was writing at the time in such works as *Pelagio* and *Virginia*. The difference in that of *Simon Boccanegra* lies in its total lack of musical hedonism. Here everything is bare, dramatic and functional. It is understandable that men of Basevi's generation should have been repelled by its harshness. They could hardly have foreseen that ten years later such composers as Cagnoni and Lauro Rossi would attempt similar but far less successful solutions in their efforts to free themselves from the stranglehold of a dying tradition.

> *Act I, Finale; Scene 2 (1881): The Council Chamber of the Doge's Palace, the Doge seated on the ducal throne. On one side twelve counsellors of the patrician party; on the other twelve counsellors from the plebeian; seated apart, four marine consuls and the constables. Paolo and Pietro on the front benches of the plebeians. A herald.* *

There is a prelude of twenty bars, strong but athematic and based on two gestures to cover the change of scene (see Ex. 19). Then the curtain rises on a passage of recitative. The Doge has two proposals for the agenda: a treaty with the King of Tartary who will grant Genoese shipping in return the freedom of the Black Sea. This is approved without a division. Then in allusive and highly literary terms Simone announces Petrarch's message urging Genoa to make peace with Venice. 'Let the singer of the blonde from Avignon [*i.e., Laura*] attend to his rhymes,' sneers Paolo – a minor-key phrase in unison with strings, clarinets and bassoons ending with a mocking trill. The others agree. Simone is vainly pleading for an end to fratricidal strife, when far-off sounds of tumult are heard. So the finest of all Verdi's 'sommosse' begins – a splendid example of thematic development put to dramatic purpose. Its basic themes are two. The first (Ex. 206a), curiously pianistic on paper, is harmonized during the course of the movement in a variety of ways: sometimes with block chords, sometimes with a bass pedal, sometimes with a bass counterpoint; the second (Ex. 206b) stated first on strings lends itself particularly well to the tight brass writing which Verdi had used to such good effect in the ballet music in *Macbeth*.†

206a

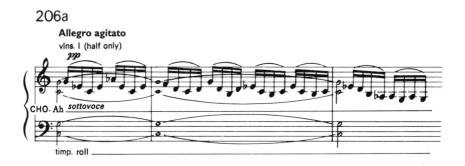

* The detailed stage directions for this scene given in the production book may be summarized as follows: main entrance to the chamber backstage facing the audience; Doge and counsellors seated on a low platform extending in a shallow curve from front to rear stage left, so that the entire council is visible to the audience. The Doge is in the centre of the row seated at a table on which are a water-clock, an inkwell, papers and various parchment scrolls. On the Doge's right, twelve plebeian counsellors (six tenors and six basses); on his right twelve patricians distributed likewise; Pietro and Paolo seated below the platform in front of the Doge. Stage right facing the Doge's table a large window; to the left of it four Marine Consuls, to the right four Constables (all eight to be mimes skilled in sword play). Six Ducal guards and four pages drawn up back stage either side of the main entrance; two pages front stage right. The rest of the chorus are ranged with the chorus master offstage to the right, in due course to be given their note by an electrically operated pitch pipe inaudible to the audience. (*Disp. scen.*, pp. 18–19.)

† The device of trombone and trumpet in contrary motion would have been more effective in Verdi's day when the trombone had valves instead of slides (see Chapter 1). Today the bass of Ex. 206b is inevitably a glissando.

206b

The scene develops as a crescendo. Hearing the distant baying (see Ex. 206a), Paolo runs to the window and announces a large crowd approaching from the direction of the Fieschi palace (Ex. 206b). Gradually the word 'Morte' becomes audible. The Doge looks out and sees Gabriele Adorno with a mob at his heels and 'a Guelph fighting at his side'. He calls for a herald; exeunt two pages to carry out his order.* Pietro urges Paolo to escape while he can; but the Doge forbids anyone to leave the chamber (here Ex. 206a is developed into an authoritative flourish in A major followed by a Berlioz-like chromatic scale of plunging woodwind). Now 'Death to the Doge' is clearly heard; worse still, the plebeian counsellors show signs of supporting the populace. To a development of Ex. 206b he orders the herald to tell the crowd that he is ready to face them unafraid. Again the woodwind swoop, and again to Ex. 206a the crowd call even more violently for death and pillage, to be cut short by the sound of the heraldic trumpet. There is a brief silence, followed by cries of 'Evviva il Doge!', and with this the populace burst into the chamber with Gabriele and Fiesco held fast. If they are no longer out for the Doge's blood they are still in turbulent mood; hence the final statement of Ex. 206a at its noisiest with cries of 'Vendetta' – vengeance on the murderer.† To high staccato woodwind chords with acciaccature (Verdi's usual formula for mockery) the Doge comments ironically on the crowd before him: 'Is this the voice of the people? In the distance a hurricane, near to the voices of women and children?' Here the movement breaks up into scena-like declamation. Gabriele announces that he has killed Lorenzo for having abducted Amelia Grimaldi; but before dying Lorenzo had implicated someone in a high position, without revealing his name. Gabriele has no doubt that he meant the Doge. Breaking away from his captors he hurls himself at Simone and is about to strike him dead when Amelia appears and interposes herself to a pealing tutti ('Ferisci?') from which the tension subsides during a long twenty-one-bar transition based on a rhythmic pattern of two bars (♩. ♪♩♩♩♩) repeated eight times. Gradually the B flat chord of surprise unfreezes; Simone's anger turns to relief at the sight of his

---

* *Disp. scen.*, p. 21.

† *'Many of the plebeian supporters are armed with axes which they brandish above their heads; some of the others carry halberds. Be it noted that the bars of music are few in number; therefore the right of the stage must be kept clear and the space between the main entrance and the backcloth should be sufficient to allow the chorus to enter almost en masse; otherwise it will be difficult to attack the words "Vendetta! vendetta!" The chorus, which must surround the Doge and the Counsellors on all sides* [these having by now left their seats] *must be in position at the point where the women sing their held B. In order to make way for the chorus, the four Marine Consuls should move quickly left of stage and range themselves in front of the counsellors' chairs at the last cry of "Evviva il Doge!" behind the scenes.*

'We would like to give a special warning to producers that the stage movements of this Council Chamber scene are very difficult; the dramatic events follow each other in quick succession with a good deal of variety, and the music points them within rapid tempi.' (Disp. scen., p. 23.)

daughter; he yields to her appeal to spare Gabriele's life; and the change of mood no longer makes his request to hear Amelia's story sound foolish.* In the same way, though still more compellingly, Otello's evaporating fury will be portrayed in Act I of the opera, when he is left alone with Desdemona after his dismissal of Cassio. There follows an improved version of Amelia's racconto of 1857. This time there is no wind introduction to Ex. 203a. Instead, flute, clarinet and bassoon join the strings in accompanying the vocal statement. All the angular flourishes of the 1857 narrative are removed as a matter of course; and so, rather surprisingly, is Ex. 203b in its original form. Its essential features – the syncopation and suspension – are embodied more sparingly in a six-bar climb which avoids some previous parallel octaves between voice and cellos and gives a greater sense of urgency to the narrative.

At the conclusion Ex. 206b makes its appearance as the two groups of counsellors prepare to fight one another – each suspecting the other party of having organized the abduction. Swords are drawn; but the Doge steps between the contending parties with a cry of 'Fratricidi!'

The appeal which follows ('Plebe! Patrizi! Popolo') (Ex. 207a) is Verdi's finest monument to the baritone voice, a hymn to [the ideal of] universal brotherhood as uplifting as Beethoven's 'Ode to Joy' and very nearly as simple – two double periods of sixteen bars, each with a one-bar extension. Here the *Simon Boccanegra* of 1881 reaps the benefit of its hybrid style, as an earlier world is brought back and transfigured. The symmetry within each double period is as unvarying as in, say, *I Mansnadieri*; but small rhythmic variations in the voice part serve both to avoid monotony and to underline the verbal meaning. The second half of the melody ('Piango su voi sul placido') features the old Italian device of a conclusive modulation to the relative rather than the tonic major – and with perfect dramatic logic. The tonic major would have conveyed a suggestion of fulfilment, however slight. By moving from E flat minor to F sharp major Simone is able to sustain to the end a note of earnest pleading. The scoring has all the economy of Verdi's mature style. Gestures such as those at the end of the fourth and eighth bars which once would have been given to strings and woodwind with sustaining brass are here confined to strings alone. The tutti is reserved for the portrayal of chaos at the words 'Voi nei fraterni lari vi lacerate il cor'. In the final phrase piccolo and heavier brass are silent so as to allow the voice to ride clearly over the climatic chord with a high F sharp. The pentatonic tinta of the concluding phrase (Ex. 207b) is very marked.

---

* The exchange between Gabriele and the Doge together with Amelia's sudden appearance are amplified thus in the Italian production book: 'The Doge turns . . . and says to Gabriele, "Adorno, perchè impugni l'acciar?" while at a sign from him the two plebeians who have Gabriele pinned by the arms should release him and withdraw a step. The people, still in a state of excitement, angrily interrupt Gabriele's words. The Doge exclaims indignantly, "Ribaldo!" and withdraws from Gabriele in disgust. . . . During all this Amelia should have entered backstage and taken up a position in the centre amongst the chorus without being visible to the public. (N.B. We beg the artist singing the part of Amelia not to get the chorus to clear a path before her as though to warn the public that a prima donna is about to make an entrance. Amelia herself should have to force her way through the crowd so as to appear unexpectedly.) At the word "Muori!" Gabriele raises his sword and is about to hurl himself at the Doge, but is quickly grasped by two plebeians, while Amelia suddenly rushes out from amongst the crowd and places herself between the Doge and Gabriele, saying to the latter, "Ferisci?" All react with the utmost astonishment crying out, "Amelia!" At the same time the chorus retreats a couple of paces; Amelia approaches and says to him quietly, "Oh, Doge!" He turns to Gabriele and the two plebeians who are holding him fast and says, "Nessun l'offenda." The two plebeians release Gabriele who replaces his sword.' (Disp. scen., pp. 24–5.)

As in 'Il lacerato spirito' the intensity of emotion in the melody generates a postlude, which here takes the form of a concertato. There are two main ideas – that of Amelia, as she urges peace with its one asymmetrical bar of 3/4 (Ex. 208a) and that of Fiesco (Ex. 208b), a stylized groan lamenting the fate of Genoa beneath the yoke of a vile Corsair.*

Ex. 208b is vanquished by a resumption of the Doge's Ex. 207b, after which Amelia's theme is shared by Gabriele and doubled by upper woodwind and violins playing in a serene glow on the G string, enhanced by a continuous tremolo from violas and cellos.

Beneath the lyrical surface, however, dark plots and deeds are being contemplated; Pietro tells Paolo to escape before he is discovered; Paolo replies in effect that he has not finished with the Doge yet. Fiesco continues his lament. Gabriele, on the other hand, is entirely taken up with relief at Amelia's safety. At the end he offers his sword to the Doge; Simone allows him to keep it but insists that he spend the night in the Ducal palace until the plot has been laid bare.

So to the other great novelty of the revised *Boccanegra* – the concluding scene in which Simone orders Paolo as tribune of the people – or so it may be gathered from Boito's rather periphrastic lines – to repeat his own solemn curse on a certain coward who lurks within the city, and whose name he knows only too well. 'Sia maledetto,' cries the Doge in a terrible voice. 'Sia maledetto,' Paolo repeats, pale and trembling; and the whole chorus take up the cry, 'Sia maledetto,' in a violent tutti diminished seventh to which the tam-tam is added. Then they melt away slowly muttering the fatal words as they go; Paolo runs off with a terrified 'Orror!'† This quaint piece of melodrama enabled Verdi to recoup some of the rugged force of the original stretta. The key is again C minor; and of the two ideas on which the scene is based Ex. 209a has

---

* The production book ranges the principals on stage R–L as follows: Gabriele, Amelia, Boccanegra, Paolo, Pietro, Fiesco. (*Disp. scen.*, p. 25.) Evidently Verdi had given up his notion of having Amelia address her appeal to Fiesco.

† The production book gives the following minute analysis of the final scene. *The Doge takes the middle of the proscenium and cries out in a terrible voice, 'Paolo!' . . . The latter, who had tried to hide among the counsellors on the left, hesitates a moment, then comes out of the crowd and in a state of stark terror presents himself to the Doge with a low bow as he replies, 'Mio duce!' He remains there trembling and with head lowered. The Doge,*

a similar character to Ex. 207a, though it carries no contrapuntal implications; Ex. 209b is a non-pentatonic, minor-key version of Ex. 208a: the dark obverse of the coin.

The modal B flat in the first is one of those touches frequent in late Verdi giving a freedom and variety of expression to the melodic line worthy of Berlioz's Prince of Verona. Here it serves to emphasize the effect of the tutti unison trill – the most powerful expression of negative emotion the composer knew. The scene abounds in new and subtle instrumental combinations such as are never found before *Aida*. At the word 'testimon', oboe, horn and trombone sustain a unison B while violas and violins have a tremolando on A flat and F, and the bass clarinet gives out Ex. 209b. The orchestral fortissimo at Simone's and Paolo's 'maledetto,' dispenses with all the brighter instruments, so allowing the baritone E flat with its important consonant to come across without difficulty. In a word, what had begun as an exciting political

---

with terrifying majesty and with an increasingly formidable emphasis, says to him:

DOGE In te risiede l'austero dritto popolar;   *Paolo remains motionless and struck dumb. At these*
     E assolto l'onore cittadina nella tua fede.   *words Paolo's expression becomes less gloomy; it lights up with a ray of hope.*

     Bramo l'ausiglio tuo.   *Paolo is now completely calm: an incubus has lifted from his mind, he raises his eyes, takes a short step towards the Doge saying:* Parla: eccomi a' tuoi ordini.

The Doge moves slightly closer to Paolo and in a low voice, but clearly and distinctly, proceeds thus: V'è in queste mura un vil che m'ode; *then more softly still and stretching out his hand to Paolo he suddenly adds:*

     Ei impallidisce in volto.   *Paolo is troubled: his eyes cannot meet the Doge's, his breathing becomes laboured.*

     Già la mia man l'afferra per le chiome.
The Doge takes a step forward and reaches out as though   *Paolo is terrified. As though he felt himself being clutching at an imaginary being*   *clutched he lowers his head and turns slightly away from the Doge.*

     Io so il suo nome.   *Paolo makes a gesture of terror.*
     E nella sua paura . . .
The Doge ironically points to Paolo's face.   *Paolo is overwhelmed and almost hides his face in his hands.*

     Tu al cospetto del ciel, etc.   *The Doge's words are so frightening that despite himself Paolo is compelled to turn towards him slightly.*

The Doge cries out in a terrible voice: Sia maledetto, *then suddenly grasps with his left arm the right arm of Paolo and with his right hand stretched out towards him, suddenly adds sombrely but in a tone of command:* E tu ripeti il giuro.

Paolo is struck an almost mortal blow by this anathema: his expression is one of the utmost terror: he would like to refuse but then cowed by the Doge's gaze he pulls himself together, takes a step forward, crying fearfully: Sia maledetto; *then he suddenly covers his face with his hands, murmuring:* Orrore, orrore!

Everyone should have followed this scene with wonder and resentment; take care that the movements of the other actors and of the chorus, except in the case of Amelia, should not be those of people who understand the Doge's allusions, since no one suspects Paolo: none the less everyone understands that something terrible is about to happen; this should be the feeling that prevails and that breaks out at the words which everyone repeats: Sia maledetto. *Precisely on the last syllable of* maledetto *all the artists and chorus should take a big step forward stretching out their right arms with a very emphatic gesture, as if they were cursing an invisible character. The Doge is motionless gazing contemptuously at Paolo who is crushed and trembling. Thence everyone as though smitten with some mysterious, inexplicable terror should retreat slowly backwards on the words* Sia maledetto! *which they repeat grimly, in a low voice and with arms continually outstretched. The Doge dominates the centre of the stage: Paolo, flinging up his arms, cries* Orrore! *and flees desperately pushing his way through the midst of the chorus. (Disp. scen., pp. 26–8.)* Further observations follow on the necessity for both the Doge and Paolo to have a natural histrionic talent. But would this type of acting be acceptable today?

intrigue ends as a massive confrontation of good and evil, emphasized not for the first time by polarity of key – F sharp major against C minor. And as though to illustrate the narrowness of evil as against the freedom and variety of goodness Verdi takes care from here on to imprison Paolo in C minor except where he is trying to dissimulate. So another dimension is added to the music drama.

ACT II

Scene: The Doge's room in the Ducal palace of Genoa. Doors on either side. From a balcony can be seen the city. A table and chair with writing materials (1857). A jar and a glass (1881). Night is falling (1857). *

When the curtain rises it is still C minor. Paolo draws Pietro to the window, points to Gabriele and Fiesco below the balcony and orders him to have them conducted to the room by a secret door. In 1857 this was the work of a moment, allowing Paolo a mere eleven bars of solitude in which to exclaim once more against the Doge for having robbed him of Amelia and her money and to add that the three days left to him in Genoa are enough for his revenge. This was replaced by a scene of some forty bars in which Paolo recalls with horror his own self-cursing and disgrace and ends by pouring poison into the Doge's water jug, saying, 'Let Death make its choice between poison and the dagger.' It is a splendid scene, rich in verbal as well as musical significance ('What a pity to put such powerful words into the mouth of a paltry scoundrel!' Verdi had commented admiringly).† Unlike the Paolo of 1857 whose power and, still more, effrontery were as yet unshaken, the Paolo of 1881 is a more consciously Satanic figure, consumed with a guilt like Boito's own Nero yet bent on evil for its own sake. He remembers the curse not with either of the orchestral themes of Ex. 207 but with the actual notes of 'Sia maledetto' thundered out by trumpet and trombone in octaves. But there is also a more subtle link with the preceding act. The Doge's anathema had been punctuated by a chromatic figure of three notes (Ex. 210a) played by bass clarinet. The same instrument repeats it here at

---

* The production book adds a candelabra with three candles alight and substitutes the courtyard of a palace, with a further view of Genoa seen across the balcony.

† Letter to Boito, 5.2.1881. *Carteggio Verdi–Boite*, I, pp. 38–9.

the words 'E suo anatema mi segue ancor' (Ex. 210b). It recurs yet again on clarinet
and bassoon over thudding basses where Paolo pours poison into the jug (Ex. 210c).
From here on it will be a poison motif – the Doge's curse turned back upon himself.

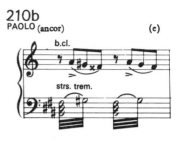

The scene is wound up by a tremendous phrase like a clenched fist ('Scelga morte sua
via fra il tosco ed il pugnale'). Then as Fiesco and Gabriele are brought in Paolo
switches to the smooth, sardonic manner of Sparafucile, whose duettino with
Rigoletto seems to have been the model for his own dialogue with Fiesco – an F
major 'parlante melodico' in rondo form. The contrast in style with the preceding
solo serves only to enhance Paolo's dissimulation (Ex. 211).

Variety of key supplements variety of accompaniment, the second statement of Ex.
211 being in A flat. The only difference between the versions here concerns the text.
In the original duettino Fiesco affects not to know who Paolo is; Paolo retorts that he
recognizes in 'Andrea' the Doge's enemy Fiesco and knows all about his part in the
conspiracy of the Guelphs; Fiesco reacts with a startled 'Io? . . .' Paolo follows up his
advantage with the suggestion that he should murder the Doge in his sleep. This
Fiesco repudiates with scorn; Paolo sends him away, but detains Gabriele. In the
second version there is no mention of Fiesco's alias; and to Paolo's accusation of
conspiracy he replies proudly, 'Sì.' Clearly this all stems from the decision taken in
1881 to keep Fiesco true to his ideals from first to last. In his turn Gabriele is as
contemptuous as Fiesco until Paolo tells him that Amelia is in the palace and the
Doge is enjoying her favours. His words make their effect; but Paolo is taking no
chances. He locks the door by which Gabriele has entered and tells him that unless he
carries out the plan that Fiesco has spurned he will never leave the palace alive. Exit
Paolo by the opposite door, which again he locks after him. Alone Gabriele gives
way to an explosion of jealous fury, conveyed by an orchestral gesture scored in full-

211

blooded *Battaglia di Legnano* style: all strings in unison on the semiquavers, all wind sustaining.

212

From this is forged the accompanimental pattern behind the first movement of his double aria ('Sento avvampar nell' anima'). Both movements show the working of the Parisian experience below the Italian surface. The first phrase of each has the cut of so many 'incipits' from *Rigoletto*, *Il Trovatore* or *La Traviata*. But as it proceeds, each takes on a new scale, throwing out more rhythmic offshoots. The first movement has the kind of tonal scheme that hitherto we have associated with recitatives such as 'Pari siamo', never with aria movements: first period, A minor; second period, B flat–B major–C major–F minor–A major. The major 'sfogo' at the end is arrived at enharmonically by turning the A flat into a G sharp – an unheard-of procedure in Italian opera of the 1850s; but it has the effect of maintaining the murderous tension till the end. Once again Gabriele shows himself a strenuous, baritonal tenor – almost a young Rigoletto, and not surprisingly. There is a certain similarity in their situations, except that with Gabriele it is all in the mind. Rigoletto-like too is the change of mood from fury to pathos, accompanied by a tiny lamenting figure on bassoon and cellos, which is then transferred to oboe.* The emotional graph is that of 'Cortigiani, vil razza' in the ample cantabile ('Ciel pietoso, rendila') – a movement that gains in interest as it proceeds (note the characteristic descent through a remote 6/4 as he talks about the 'cloud of impurity' that hangs over his beloved). The prayer ends with a cadenza which for once Verdi did not consider it worth while removing in the revision.

Enter Amelia for a dialogue of misunderstanding full of agitated flourishes in the orchestra. Simone, she says, loves her with a pure and holy affection which she returns; more she cannot say. This is not calculated to reassure her lover. The scene is virtually unchanged in the revision except for the final bars which are altered to give more urgency and variety to Gabriele's emotion. He continues his pleading in the duet ('Parla, in tuo cor virgineo') whose *Foscari*-like character recalls the duet in Act I though in more sorrowful vein. Amelia pours out the balm of her major-key reply ('Sgombra dall'alma il dubbio') but Gabriele refuses to be comforted. The rather plain coda of 1857 with its ungainly leap between registers (presumably to show off a particular skill of Luigia Bendazzi) is replaced in 1881 by a longer one of graceful flowing lines and appropriately altered words.

Trumpets in the orchestra announce the Doge. Amelia desperately begs Gabriele to hide; Gabriele at first refuses. The argument continues in a final movement ('All'ora stesso teco avrò morte'), as pithy and free from the conventions of the cabaletta as could be wished. Especially effective is Gabriele's entry in an unexpectedly high register ('A te pietade?') which is like a sudden yelp of jealousy. At the end Amelia succeeds in hiding him on the balcony.

The Doge enters reading a sheet of paper, to the following passage.

213

It is not important in the musical organization; but it tells us at once that the Doge is now an old man bowed beneath the cares of state. In the 1867 version of *Don Carlos* King Philip makes an entrance to just such a theme, though without the energy of Simone's triplets. However, to his daughter's solicitous inquiry he denies that he is in low spirits. Yet he is concerned for her. Will she not tell him the name of her lover? 'The noblest, the kindest warrior in Liguria,' she replies. 'Adorno.' 'My enemy!'

---

* For the performance of 1859 at la Scala Verdi sent to Ricordi a variant of this transition designed to lower the following cantabile by a semitone in case the tenor should find the original key too high. (Letter to T. Ricordi, 30.11.1858. *Carteggi. I.S.V.* 61/61.)

Boccanegra exclaims, pointing to the sheet of paper where Gabriele's name heads the list of conspirators. But Amelia insists that she will die with him if her father withholds his pardon. Simone, undecided, rails bitterly against his fate. After his anguished 'Una figlia ritrovo, ed un nemico a me la invola' the string semiquaver patterns that have dominated the 'scena' coalesce into a reminiscence of his desperation in the prologue where he begged Fiesco to kill him ('Si, m'uccidi, e almen sepolta fia con me tant'ira'). For all that, he shows signs of yielding. Meantime he begs Amelia to leave him; she is understandably reluctant to do so and therefore does not go very far. At this point the opera is expanded in the later version to allow the Doge to take the poison that has been prepared for him. In 1857 he merely reflects on the wisdom of pardoning his enemies, before sinking gently into sleep. In Piave's text he concludes that mercy would be taken for weakness, in Boito's that severity would be a sign of fear. In what follows the rhythmic pattern of 1857 is maintained in the definitive version with marching basses beneath a three-note death figure, which persists through the Doge's somnolence (his sleep, we gather, is likely to be a long one). As he pours and drinks the water, the orchestra warns him in unmistakable terms – trombones and bassoons on a chord of D minor, rolls and fatal poundings on the timpani: 'Even the spring water tastes bitter on the lips of the man who reigns,' he remarks once more, his mind still on Amelia and her love for his mortal enemy Gabriele Adorno. As he falls asleep high violins, playing on the point of the bow, trace a pattern of semiquaver chords pianissimo while flute and clarinet give out a reminiscence of Ex. 194. It is a variation of the French 'dream formula' to be found in *Le Prophète*, *L'Etoile du Nord* and later in Massenet's *Manon*. But as the entire passage has been taken over without alteration from the original version of 1857 the quotation ends with the old cadence, complete with the triplets which had been removed in 1881. Design or oversight? The latter seems probable; but to ears unfamiliar with the original *Boccanegra* it can sound like a deliberate variation and, as such, perfectly acceptable.

Gabriele, emerging from the balcony, has to nerve himself to stab the sleeping Doge; and his angry words contrast strangely with the murmuring violins and woodwind melody, now shifted from D major to F sharp. He is about to strike when Amelia interposes herself for the second time with a stage whisper of 'Insensato!', a third lower in 1881, with a consequent gain in realism. The Doge wakes and a furious exchange takes place the rhythm of racing triplets, which cease abruptly for the revelation. Here the decasyllabic metre of the verse is allowed the upper hand in sixteen marching bars of declamation punctuated by soft chords. The deliberate avoidance of expansive melody and the plain prosody give an effect of almost Schumannesque intimacy. It might be an Italian 'Die beiden Grenadiere' (see Ex. 214).

The terzetto ('Perdon, perdon, Amelia') is dominated by the remorseful Gabriele, who has the first section of its bipartite structure entirely to himself with a long asymmetrical melody wandering from key to key. To this the second version brings some notable improvements, condensing the last eight bars into six, topping the vocal line with a high B flat in place of the original repeated A flats, removing certain modulations and in general giving greater sharpness and spontaneity to the expression.* The second section too is modified. Here Simone again debates with

* See Osthoff, pp. 82–5.

214

himself whether or not to pardon Gabriele, while Amelia prays for guidance to the spirit of her mother, events having now got altogether beyond her. In 1881 her phrase 'Solo per troppo amor' becomes identical with the motif of reconciliation (Ex. 221) from Act III, quoted in the 1857 prelude. Even in the revision, however, Verdi does not disdain the old device of bassoon and cello arpeggios in unison. Finally the coda is altered partly to throw into relief Simone's expression of idealism ('Sia d'amistanze italiche il mio sepolcro altar') and partly to make room for six bars of unaccompanied voices – which, however, are usually cut in performance. Inevitably the two men dominate the canvas: Gabriele with his upward leaps, Simone with his mainly step-wise descents in which a mortal weariness is already present.

From the far off come the sounds of martial chorus ('All'armi, all'armi, o Liguri') – men in 1857, men and women in 1881 – arousing the people to rebellion. A glance at the main theme will leave no doubt as to the origin of the sommossa motif in the new finale of Act I (Ex. 206a). Side drum doubles the rhythm throughout and a fanfare of four trumpets and four trombones, both added for the Reggio performance, are brought in during the course of the crescendo.

215

Over this unaccompanied chorus, always offstage but coming continually nearer, the principals conduct an urgent conversation. The upshot is that Gabriele will go out and appeal for peace. If the appeal fails he will fight at the Doge's side against his former friends; and for this he will receive the hand of Amelia in marriage.*

ACT III

Scene: Interior of the Doge's Palace. At the back three apertures through which can be seen Genoa illuminated in festive style. In the background the sea.†

1857 version: This opens with a triumphal double chorus ('Vittoria! vittoria!') to the music of Ex. 199, shared between the populace and banda offstage and the senators and orchestra on. As in the last number of Act II no women are involved. The Guelphs have been put down, Gabriele has distinguished himself in the Doge's service and will receive his just reward. Such is the gist of a powerful intervening recitative from Simone. There is a final burst of sound from choruses, banda and orchestra ('Doge a te gloria, eterno onor'); then as the senators disperse Pietro whispers mysteriously to Paolo that he has made everything ready; Paolo gloats over the prospect of his approaching vengeance (Montanelli's lines). A bridal chorus ('Dal sommo delle sfere') is sung behind the scenes by women only to a stage empty except for Paolo. The sonority of the four-part cappella writing is suitably limpid, but the piece itself arrests our interest only in the twelfth bar ('di pace sien foriere') where a characteristic 6/4 gives a faint anticipation of moments in the 'Ave Maria' from the Quattro Pezzi Sacri. Paolo, having presumably registered those emotions which he will express aloud in the second version, opens a secret door from which emerges

---

* The production book (p. 37) gives very precise instructions for the offstage forces. The chorus is to be drawn up backstage four to six abreast, basses to the fore, women to the rear, and behind them the trumpets and side drums. At the words 'Le guelfe spade cingano' they are to begin marching in the wings right of stage until the front rank is level with proscenium.

† The directions of the 1857 score are as follows: 'Magnificent ducal hall in Genoa. At the back a view of three arcades closed by drapes; these give on to a terrace from which in due course will be seen the Piazza Doria fully illuminated. Doors on either side and a secret door to rear left. A throne and a table on which a silver lamp is burning. The Doge enters from the left followed by Gabriele, Paolo, Pietro, squires, pages etc.' The production book of 1881 confirms most of these details but adds some interesting directions for the illumination: there were to be two extra rows of gas footlights, a small one in front of the backcloth to be controlled by a single tap, and a much larger row stretching across the middle of the stage, each flare controlled by a separate tap. This second row would be concealed by a cut-out in the form of a false parapet. As a result of this arrangement there is no silver lamp on the table, but instead the ducal cloak and cap.

Fiesco. Their dialogue is a somewhat inept conflation of scenes 1 and 6 of Gutiérrez's Act IV – inept because it fails to make clear why Fiesco, having haughtily rejected Paolo's helping hand in Act II, should accept it here, and also because Paolo's exit line was on Verdi's own suggestion taken from the earlier of the two scenes, where it made sense. Here it makes none at all, unless we assume Paolo to be a fool as well as a villain. He begins by telling Fiesco that he has kept his promise (what promise?); but where are Fiesco's followers who were to have come with him? 'I know not; they fled.' 'Let us flee too.' 'Flee?' 'If you do not wish to be marked as an accomplice in the Doge's death.' For the first time in the 1857 version Paolo mentions the poison. Fiesco is horrified but refuses to leave; Paolo hurries off with the excuse of summoning Fiesco's followers. Fiesco retires to the back of the stage as Simone returns, a sick man.

1881 version: Here the act begins with an orchestral prelude played behind a lowered curtain, and based on Ex. 215. The binding effect of this device, so greatly approved by Boito, was not lost on the composer of *Madame Butterfly*; and needless to say the theme itself gains enormously in vigour from the ability of the mature Verdi to make his bass line move. At the end cries of 'Evviva il Doge' are heard and the curtain rises to discover the captain of the crossbowmen restoring to Fiesco his sword and his liberty. But Fiesco can take little comfort from either since the Guelphs have been defeated. About to leave he encounters Paolo surrounded by four guards. So vague and apocalyptic are his words ('Il mio demonio mi cacciò fra l'armi dei rivoltosi') that we need the evidence of Boito's letter to understand that Paolo deliberately took part in the revolt. Once more in C minor he is given a sinuous line doubled by the orchestral basses, which is clearly derived from Ex. 209b. At his words 'Un velen (più nulla io temo) gli divora la vita' the poison motif takes shape on the bassoon beneath tremolo strings. The soft string chords at 'Ei forse già mi precede nell'avel' carry a suggestion of prayers for the dead while at the same time making a seamless transition to the offstage bridal chorus, which in its new context has the character of a C major episode or 'trio' in the C minor movement. Paolo vents his despair at having lost Amelia. Fiesco draws the correct conclusion that it was he who arranged the abduction. He makes as if to strike him dead then thinks better of it; Paolo shall be 'sacred to the block'. The sinuous C minor theme sounds again in the orchestra as Paolo is led away. Fiesco, as in 1857, but to different music, reflects that his enemy deserved a better fate. As he retires into the shadows the captain enters and with him a trumpeter, to a theme on the horns (Ex. 216b) which is like a weary inversion of the confident fanfare in Act I (Ex. 216a). Note the elegiac downward movement of each phrase.*

The trumpet sounds a death-signal; and in a measured recitative with echoes in it of plainchant the captain gives orders for the lights to be extinguished throughout the city out of respect for the dead. Again the melancholy Ex. 216b tolls; and the captain leaves.

With Simone's entrance the two scores coincide again and another of those details, insignificant in the first version, clicks into place in the second (Ex. 217). In 1857 this was little more than a musical portrayal of Simone's sickness; in 1881 it is an inversion of the poison motif. It tells us not only that Boccanegra is sick but why. With burning temples the Doge drags himself to the arcade giving on to the

---

* The production book specifies a straight (i.e. long) trumpet 'without keys'. (*Disp. scen.*, p. 42.)

216a

216b

217

terrace from which he can feel the wind from the sea – the sea that holds so many memories. For the moment he has become Jacopo from *I Due Foscari*.

218

If in the revision this no longer relates to Ex. 166 the loss is a small one, since the Doge has been characterized more powerfully since. Besides that, how many people would recognize Ex. 166 in its new guise after the intervening acts? A connection can be felt with the racconto of the prologue at the words 'Ah perchè, perchè in suo grembo non trovai la tomba?'. These give Fiesco his cue to step forward. Better for the Doge to have found death at sea than that which awaits him. Startled, Simone calls for his guards. Fiesco replies that there is no one to hear. He bids Simone pay attention to what he has to say. This moment, all 1857, is masterly. The harmonic stasis and the fact that Simone even in a state of alarm never leaves the note G already announced by Fiesco suggests a man caught in a nightmarish trance. Note too the bold harmonic ellipses in bars 7–8 and 10–12.

219

Only a pedant would wish to point out that this exchange makes far better sense in the original context where Fiesco had been admitted by a secret door than in the revision where he had been conducted into the hall quite openly by a captain – a hall moreover which seems little less than a public thoroughfare. So begins the opening movement of the final duet ('Dalle faci festanti al barlume') between Simone and Fiesco.

The extraordinary melodramatic text in which Fiesco appears as a prophet of doom, announcing the writing on the wall, makes one think of the opera that Verdi had wanted to write in 1848, based on Guerrazzi's *L'Assedio di Firenze*. If, as Walker and Vecchi conjecture, the words are Montanelli's rather than Piave's, this may furnish a further explanation of why Verdi turned so readily to the Tuscan poet for the retouching of the original libretto. Montanelli had been a colleague of Guerrazzi in the provisional government of Tuscany during the revolution of 1848, and might therefore be expected to understand what Verdi was aiming at in Guerrazzi's novel. In the musical setting Verdi has reverted to the symmetrical phrase structure of his youth varied only by a final break into triplets with full orchestral accompaniment. The result, combined with the old-fashioned doubling of the voice by trumpet, oboe, clarinet and bassoon, gives a monumental simplicity, an antique severity that is wholly convincing in its context. As he finishes the lights begin to go out in the piazza; and the slow climbing transition in which Simone at last recognizes his enemy is heavy with death-figures in the orchestra. The next movement ('Come un fantasima') is an action-piece built, like the sextet in *Figaro*, round a dramatic anagnorisis – in this case Fiesco's discovery of his grandchild's existence. Launched by Fiesco himself, it is characteristically rugged, unyielding, with a powerful rhythmic drive that recalls Beethoven in his *Egmont* vein. Notice how orchestra and voice, beginning out of phase, develop a long, irregular period of eighteen bars which through successive changes of rhythmic emphasis – a kind of thrust and counter-thrust – achieves a sense of perfect equilibrium (Ex. 220).

The polarity between Fiesco and Simone no longer depends on contour or rhythm but rather on harmony. Where Fiesco's progressions are stark and heavily scored, the Doge's are smooth and suave, and his lines less accented. In a long sentence of sixteen

220

bars ('In Amelia Grimaldi a me fu resa e il nome porta della madre estinta') from which Verdi removed woodwind in the revision, Simone reveals Amelia's identity. Fiesco's astonishment is marked by a sudden key change and a pattern of parallel sixths in the orchestra. These coalesce into a series of lamenting figures which persist for no less than twenty-seven bars as Fiesco weeps silently, afraid to look Simone in the face. The Largo ('Piango, perchè mi parla') is a dissimilar duet in which Fiesco has the principal theme, and Boccanegra no more than a comment full of musical sighs; but as the music turns finally into the tonic major it is he who introduces that motif of reconciliation heard in the 1857 prelude. Again the scoring is lightened in the revised version.

221

Fiesco, bitterly remorseful, is won over.* But, as the orchestra tells us in the coda, Simone's death is near. He sinks into a chair and calls for Amelia. At that moment she and Gabriele return from the church followed by senators, knights and their ladies and bridesmaids. In 1857 their entry was marked by an orchestral resumption of the Doge's hymn (Ex. 199), gradually diminishing as the two lovers greet Fiesco with

* By the last bar of the duet Simone and Fiesco should be locked in an embrace. (*Disp. scen.*, p. 44.)

astonishment and are then told by the Doge the happy truth.* In the revision Verdi contented himself with a prolonged extension to the final chord now tending to the subdominant and with Ex. 221 persisting in the bass. Amelia's expression of joy is cut short by the Doge with 'Tutto finisce, o figlia'. He breaks the news of his approaching death to a series of slow dissonant chords alternating with an inexorable C in the basses. But at the words 'Ma l'Eterno in tue braccia, o Maria, mi concede a spirar' the music moves into a kindlier D flat, and then, as Simone prepares to give his blessing, into the key of the final concertato. The Doge's 'Gran Dio, li benedici' faintly hints at the Ave Maria in *Otello*. The replies of Amelia and Gabriele are in a traditional concertato-manner; but a triplet figure in the bass of Amelia's intervention ('No, non morrai, l'amore vinca di morte il gelo') will assume rhythmic importance later on. The later version gives new prominence to Fiesco with a characteristic booming phrase.

222

The Doge begins to fail with the usual lyrical sighs and gasps and it is Amelia who launches one of the longest and most moving final melodies to grace any concertato, its momentum sustained partly by the vocal syncopations, partly by the triplet figure mentioned above, now moved to the weak beats of the bar. This final section, regarded even in 1857 as one of the few undisputed gems of the score, Verdi nevertheless reworked in the revision, enriching the sonority with a female chorus, preserving the same material but rewelding it into longer phrases, smoothing out the contours so as to give a bigger sense of scale, increasing the musical tension with a cross-rhythm between melody and bass and enhancing the final climax with a heart-warming 6/4 chord in a remote key. Observe too the delaying of the subito piano in the later version. (See Exs. 223 and 224.)

The last chord is interrupted harshly but quietly. Simone gives orders for Gabriele to be crowned as his successor.† Part of Simone's blessing is heard once more high in the strings; Simone tries to speak but falls back dead. Fiesco announces to the people in the piazza the name of the new Doge. 'No, Boccanegra,' they reply. 'He is dead. Pray that his soul may have peace.' All present kneel and the curtain falls to the quietest ending that Verdi had ever written up until 1857. Four strokes of the funeral bell – another legacy from *I Due Foscari* – intensify the sense of darkness and mourning.

* *Gabriele should enter from the left leading Amelia: they are followed by Ladies, Nobles and Senators (leaving six basses and five sopranos to make up the final offstage chorus), who should enter from both sides. Behind the bride and groom are six pages with lighted torches and eight guards who proceed to range themselves along the back of the stage. N.B. When the Pages enter with the torches the jets behind the parapet should be turned full on. (Disp. scen., p. 45, slightly paraphrased.)*

† *He cries, 'Senatori!' Three senators come forward from the chorus on the right to receive his orders; Gabriele retires a little. (Disp. scen., p. 47.)*

Like the first *Macbeth*, the first *Simon Boccanegra* was a daring, innovatory work. Without altering the letter of the contemporary Italian forms it certainly altered their spirit. The spare, functional declamation, the abundance of minor key, the wide tonal orbit of several numbers, the frequency of enharmonic modulation – all these are gathered into a synthesis as new and difficult for an Italian audience of the time as anything Verdi had written so far. Quite unheard of was a protagonist without a single extended lyrical solo to himself. (Don Giovanni is the nearest to a precedent.) Simone's role is confined to *scene* and ensembles. His personality is split up into three different facets each limned by a special motif: the lone corsair by Ex. 166 later transformed into Ex. 218 and perhaps deliberately hinted at in the first cadence of his 'racconto' (see Ex. 177); the head of state by Ex. 199; the loving father by Ex. 194. It is an interesting idea; but it has the disadvantage of preventing Simone from rising to his full stature at any one moment. As a result he remains too passively sympathetic and hard done by. Possibly this was in Verdi's mind when he described the original score as 'troppo triste, troppo desolante'. Simone's life had remained shattered into fragments since the death of his beloved Maria.

This fault at least the revision was to put entirely to rights. In the Council Chamber scene Simone rises to spiritual greatness. For the first time his moral authority puts forth all its strength, both positively as in the appeal for peace and negatively as in the cursing of Paolo. The schematic division of character is now otiose. Ex. 166 can be dispensed with in its original form and the commonplace Ex. 199 can be dropped altogether. The richness and subtlety of musical language acquired over twenty-four years suffice to fill out Simone's personality further. Fiesco, likewise, receives a sharper definition in the revised score. Nor was his musical character in any way modified to suit the 'baritonal' timbre of Eduard de Reszke. The priestly tone of the new duettino is already present in the brief passage 'Se concedermi vorrai' (Ex. 175) from 1857. It has merely been amplified in a new context. Elsewhere the hard unyielding quality is further emphasized. Both the concertati contain characteristic interventions, steadily booming round the top line of the bass stave, the main striking area of the basso profondo. 'Give me a low F,' Verdi had written. 'I don't mind about the high notes, which I'll remove if necessary.'*

The raising of Paolo from a trivial villain into an embodiment of evil has already been noted. Amelia benefits from the omission of her tiresomely brilliant cabaletta and of more than one cadenza. Gabriele receives new touches of eloquence and even charm in the revision. Yet of all the principal roles in the opera his remains the least re-thought from one version to the next. Hence Act II in which he dominates has the least alterations in it; and it is here that we find the musical loose ends – the misquotation of 'Figlia a tal nome' and Gabriele's anachronistic cadenza.

It is the central problem of the revised *Macbeth*, if anything writ larger. Here, as there, Verdi has enriched an earlier score from two sources. He has drawn on more advanced structural techniques (for his late additions) while bringing to the pieces conceived in 1857 a new refinement of thought and craftsmanship. He reinforced the 'tinta' of the original work as revealed both in pentatonic turns of phrase and an abundance of parallel sixths, while clearing away much dead wood in the way of marching triplets and trivial ceremonial music. He has re-thought a cabaletta-opera in terms of post-Wagnerian continuity: and again where old and new

* Letter to G. Ricordi, 26.11.1880. *Carteggi Verdi–Ricordi 1830–1881*, pp. 77–8.

223

join the seams are invisible. Yet once more the better is the enemy of the good. The new finale to Act I is Verdi's political testament, perhaps the highest expression of social idealism in opera ever penned. Yet in raising the drama to this transcendental plane Verdi created a problem for himself in the act which follows, which could hardly be solved without rewriting the character of Gabriele. For after the sublimities of Boccanegra's appeal, how can the worries of that young aristocratic hothead seem anything but unimportant? Evidently Verdi relied upon the interval to mask the change in level. But Filippo Filippi, who had been among the few to speak up for the original version, was quick to note the discrepancy. Even today it remains the one obvious flaw in a near-perfect masterpiece. The original version, though it nowhere scales the heights of the revision, remains consistent throughout. But that is not the only or even the chief reason why *Simon Boccanegra* has never been a repertory favourite. The subject, the complex and often illogical plot, the preponderance of lower male voices, the comparative rarity of true bassi profondi such as are needed for Fiesco, and not least the heavy demands made on the acting ability of the singers ('In *Forza* the characters are ready made; in *Boccanegra* you have to make them')* – all these factors inevitably militate against its popularity. But it remains for the Verdian connoisseur a pearl of immeasurable price.

---

* Letter to G. Ricordi, 2.12.1880. *Ibid.*, p. 84.

7 AROLDO

AROLDO

Opera in four parts
by
FRANCESCO MARIA PIAVE
(adapted from *Stiffelio*)

*First performed at the
Teatro Nuovo, Rimini,
16 August 1857*

AROLDO, a Saxon knight	PRIMO TENORE	Emilio Pancani
MINA, his wife	PRIMA DONNA SOPRANO	Marcellina Lotti
EGBERTO, an elderly knight, her father, a vassal [*sic!*] of Kent	PRIMO BARITONO	Gaetano Ferri
BRIANO, a pious hermit	BASSO PROFONDO COMPRIMARIO	G. B. Cornago
GODVINO, an adventurer, guest of Egberto	TENORE COMPRIMARIO	Salvatore Poggiali
ENRICO, Mina's cousin	SECONDO TENORE	Napoleone Senigaglia
ELENA, also her cousin	SECONDA DONNA	Adelaide Panizza
JORG, Aroldo's servant	MIME	N.N.

Knight-crusaders – ladies and gentlemen of Kenth* – Squires – pages –
heralds – huntsmen – Saxons – Scotch peasants

The action takes place in Egberto's castle near [sic! *] Kenth for the first three acts;
by the shores of Loch Loomond* in Scotland for the fourth.*

Epoch: *c.* 1200

* In his autograph Verdi spells both names correctly.

That he would need to alter the final scene of *Stiffelio* if only for reasons of censorship had been made clear to Verdi soon after its first performance at Trieste; and a performance in Bologna in 1852 seemed to offer the right opportunity. Unfortunately the impresario, Lanari, had already decided to use the already bowdlerized version, *Guglielmo Wellingrode*, in which the German pastor is turned into a minister of state. Verdi would have none of it. 'How on earth could you suppose that I would be willing to write a new act . . . for something so ridiculous, so void of sense and character as *Wellingrode?*' he wrote to Lanari;* and with that he returned to *Il Trovatore*. Two years later he came to the conclusion that the entire subject would have to be changed, and wrote to that effect to De Sanctis, mentioning Piave as librettist.† They began work during the spring of 1856 at Busseto. The new Stiffelio was to be an English crusader who returns from Palestine to find his hearth dishonoured. The idea was borrowed from Scott's novel *The Betrothed*, familiar to Italian audiences through Pacini's *Il Connestabile di Chester*. But for most of the new names Piave had recourse to Bulwer Lytton's novel, *Harold, the Last of the Saxon Kings* – Aroldo (Stiffelio), Godvino (Raffaello) and Egberto (Stankar). None of them bear any relation to their counterparts in the novel, in which Godwin, not Egbert, is Harold's father-in-law. Mina (Lina), Enrico (Federico) and Elena (Dorotea) seem to have been chosen at random from operatic stock. Briano, on the other hand, is at a guess Brian the Hermit from Scott's *The Lady of the Lake*; hence the setting of the last act. His original name of Jorg is transferred to a non-singing servant.

As always the revision was a longer business than Verdi had foreseen. In March he had written optimistically to De Sanctis: 'Piave is here to change me the subject of *Stiffelio* . . . and this . . . should be finished about 20 April because I've only got to write various recitatives and two or three new pieces.'‡ In fact it was to last on and off for over a year, with intervals for the law suit against Calzado, the production of *Le Trouvère*, and the composition of *Simon Boccanegra*. Before setting off for Paris Verdi wrote a characteristic letter to his librettist: 'I've received the verses of *Stiffelio* and they would be fine if only it weren't for half-lines and whole lines here and there that are quite unnecessary, paddings, ah's, ih's and oh's that are there merely to fill out the metre. It seems to me essential that in her first recitative Mina should say that there's a banquet to celebrate her husband's arrival, but that she can have no part in the general rejoicing. . . . An inferno is in my heart . . . remorse.'§ Later he sent Piave a draft of the opening chorus to the new act for him to versify. It provides an excellent illustration of how the partnership with Piave worked:

---

* Letter to A. Lanari, undated. Abbiati, II, p. 168.
† Letter to De Sanctis, 6.7.1854. *Carteggi Verdiani*, I, pp. 25–6.
‡ Letter to De Sanctis, 28.3.1856. *Carteggi Verdiani*, I, p. 33.
§ Letter to Piave, 31.7.1856. Abbiati, II, p. 368.

Shepherds, Huntsmen; Reaping or harvesting women

SHEPHERDS

Let day be done; the shepherd	—
Return home with his flock	—

HUNTSMEN

The sun has set . . . the hill is dark	—
Huntsman, let us leave the woods	—

WOMEN

The night is coming . . . let us gather up	—
Our ears of corn and return home	—

Two more lines

SHEPHERDS

Hail!

HUNTSMEN

Friends!! . . .

WOMEN

What a glorious day!   *Two lines here as well*

SHEPHERDS AND HUNTSMEN

For us as well!

HUNTSMEN

On the steepest crags and in the thickest   *First stanza to make a*
Woods no beast can escape   *nice solo – keep to*
The sureness of our aim.*   *eight-syllable verse*

SHEPHERDS

By the streams where the grass grows thickest
We shall lead our flock; then to eat and rest   *Second stanza*
In the hut guarded by a faithful dog.

WOMEN

Laden with grain and ears of corn
Gathered in the mid-day heat, we return home   *Third stanza*
Joyfully to our husbands and children.

ALL

May all our days be as propitious
As today; and to God let us raise
A hymn of thanksgiving and praise.   *Fourth stanza*
     For the
     Night comes on.
     Let us be gone, let us be gone.

A glance at the score will show that Piave as usual followed Verdi's instructions to the letter and displayed considerable ingenuity in the versification.

Evidently the première was originally destined for Bologna the following year.†

* The three lines for each verse are merely the result of tabulating on a narrow sheet of paper. Each strophe would be composed of four lines.

† Letter to Torelli, 2.9.1856. Abbiati, II, pp. 340–1.

Such at any rate was Ricordi's plan. Verdi on the other hand was more disposed to grant it to the brothers Marzi, impresarii at Reggio Emilia and Rimini. Eventually it was decided that it should open the Teatro Nuovo Comunale at Rimini. In the meantime Verdi had good reason to be dissatisfied with the Marzi brothers' management. No sooner had he left Reggio Emilia and the *Boccanegra* which he himself had rehearsed than they allowed several pieces to be omitted and the cavatina from *Lucia* to be introduced.* But the cast for *Aroldo* was a good one: it included the soprano of Verdi's choice, Marcellina Lotti, and the best conductor in Italy, Angelo Mariani, already a warm admirer of Verdi's music. From the start Mariani showed himself enthusiastic. 'The piano rehearsals are going well,' he wrote to Tito Ricordi, 'and Verdi and I take turn and turn about. I shall start the orchestral rehearsals right away to gain time. So far I like the new music to *Aroldo* very much.'† And a little later:

Yesterday evening we had the first orchestral rehearsal with chorus and singers; it went superbly without interruption from beginning to end. Verdi was very pleased with my orchestra. . . . The chorus wasn't as precise as it might have been, but today I've had two piano rehearsals to refresh their minds. . . . As usual teaching the singers their parts has put years on Verdi's life. If Pancani is in good form he should be very effective; Lotti has a magnificent voice but needs more artistic feeling. Ferri excellent, Cornago likewise: As for the music, this *Aroldo* could be one of Verdi's finest operas; it includes pieces which are absolutely certain to make an effect. The fourth act which is all new is a stupendous affair; you'll find in it a storm; a pastoral chorus, and an Angelus Dei treated in canon and beautifully wrought.‡

After the performance: '*Aroldo* created a furore; not a single piece that was not applauded: the composer called on stage an infinite number of times. He is extemely happy about it. . . .'§ From Rimini, *Aroldo* made its way to Bologna and Turin. From Bologna Muzio reported to Tito Ricordi: 'The nail is fixed and *Aroldo* has triumphed.'¶ Verdi was less enthusiastic. 'The reception of *Aroldo* was not what it should have been either at Bologna or Turin. At Bologna it was the fault of the company. . . . At Turin it was the mise-en-scène . . . and the secondary parts about which I actually wrote to you to put certain conditions into the contract. . . . It would be as well to watch out that the settings for the fourth act aren't so ridiculous in other theatres. Rest assured, this fourth act is the least poor in the opera, and if the visual side is neglected it could compromise the whole score and we could have another *Stiffelio* on our hands'|| – which is, in essence, what happened. Performances were few and far between. In Naples in 1859 *Aroldo* was a fiasco. In general it was the public, not the censors, who found it unacceptable; nor is it difficult to see why. Turning the minister into a crusader has removed the heart of the dramatic conflict.

  * Letter to T. Ricordi, 1.7.1857. Abbiati, II, p. 430.
  † Letter from Mariani to T. Ricordi, undated (July–Aug. 1857). Abbiati, II, pp. 425–6.
  ‡ Letter from Mariani to T. Ricordi, undated (August 1857). Abbiati, II, p. 426.
  § Letter from Mariani to T. Ricordi, 16.8.1857. *Ibid.*
  ¶ Letter from Muzio to T. Ricordi, October 1857. Abbiati, II, p. 442.
  || Letter to T. Ricordi, 9.10.1857. *Ibid.*, pp. 444–5.

Stiffelio was by his calling a man of peace. His moment of trial comes when his emotions as a husband prompt him to act against the rules of his cloth. Aroldo as a crusader is a man of war, however righteous. Why should he not smite the ungodly no less than the Philistines? The religious scruples that prevent him from fighting his wife's lover while permitting him to slaughter Mohammedans by the thousand would hardly be understood by an audience of the time, least of all in Italy. In Stiffelio unusual situations had brought forth new musical solutions. In Aroldo the solutions where they differ from those of the original are more conventional. On the other hand the action proceeds far more clearly, and the new music reaps the benefit of seven years' growing maturity. The new last act, lacking as it does the dramatic concentration of the original final scene, belongs to what we have called 'the conquest of the episode'; it contains what is Verdi's most striking essay in orchestral virtuosity to date.*

Overture

This is the same as for Stiffelio except for two details: the reprise of the trumpet cantilena is shortened by eight bars; while the woodwind interjections after each phrase of the De Profundis melody are omitted. The first of these cuts is the kind of neat economy that we associate with Beethoven's revisions of Leonore in Fidelio; the second is a matter of dramatic relevance, since the short woodwind figure is a quotation from the replaced final scene of Stiffelio.

ACT I

Scene: Drawing room in Egbert's dwelling. A large window in the centre from which will be seen the battlements of the castle. Doors on either side and a table with writing materials, chairs, etc. The room is empty. Songs from inside indicate the end of a banquet.

At the rise of curtain the listener's heart may well sink. Instead of that magnificent recitative for Jorg which opened Stiffelio, the most conventional of all opening gambits – a drinking chorus. Nevertheless the unaccompanied 'coro d'introduzione' for four-part male voices ('Tocchiamo! a gaudio insolito') in which Aroldo's comrades welcome home the lord of the manor is far more elaborate and varied than most of its kind. Verdi has here taken advantage of two factors: the superior discipline that could be achieved under Mariani, and the fact that as the singers are off stage there was no need to confine himself to the type of writing which could be memorized without difficulty. (This last he could have taken into account in a similar scene in I Masnadieri but did not: Balfe was no Mariani.) Significantly the second of the two constituent themes recalls the De Profundis, which in turn had given rise to the trumpet melody. One feature of Aroldo as distinct from Stiffelio is a somewhat tighter thematic organization. (See Ex. 225.)

With sixteen bars of orchestral agitation Mina bursts in to deliver the recitative of remorse for which Verdi had asked ('Ciel, ch'io respiri!') followed by a prayer ('Salvami, Tu, gran Dio'). In Stiffelio, it will be remembered, Lina had to expound

* To make sense of the following analysis the reader is advised to consult in addition the chapter on Stiffelio in Vol. 1.

225

her guilt first in the course of a septet, then in a series of asides during a chorus of welcome.* This was, if not ideally clear, dramatically effective, since Lina is essentially a frightened, passive creature who acquires dignity only in the duet of Act III. Her successor, Mina, though no less consumed by guilt, is conceived as a full dramatic soprano with perfect messa di voce down to B below the stave. It is a voice to which the unusually powerful orchestral preamble scored with a post-*Vêpres* expertise can act as a platform, and which can sing the phrase 'Mi lacera il rimorso' twice against developments of it. The prayer is simple and concentrated – a mere 29 bars of which the main melody is scored for woodwind only with cello and bass, each chord so voiced as to give an organ-like sonority (Ex. 226a); particularly striking is the harmonic rhythm of the coda which gives an unusual sense of freedom and asymmetry to the six bars (Ex. 226b).

Many may prefer the more appealing femininity of Lina's equivalent 'preghiera' but Mina's is far more strongly characterized. Here is a woman who is prepared to face the consequences of her action from the start.

Aroldo and Briano now enter to the main allegro theme of the overture (Vol. I, Ex. 303b) here reduced to a mere reminiscence (in *Stiffelio* it had been developed into a full chorus). Aroldo introduces the holy hermit who had saved his life in Palestine; they had visited the holy places together and on the sacred tomb of Christ had sworn a solemn oath never to be parted. Mina welcomes Briano as the 'guardian angel' of the house. Briano replies that he hopes that the hand of the Lord will protect it from

226a

---

* On this and various other aspects of the revision of *Stiffelio* see V. Levi '*Stiffelio* e il suo rifacimento (*Aroldo*)', in *Atti del 1° Congresso Internazionale di Studi Verdiani* (Parma, 1969) pp. 172–5.

guilt and evil. All this is set in a new arioso recitative full of characteristic phrases. Briano's first utterance is accompanied in the traditional hermit style by a combination of brass and bassoons. He then leaves husband and wife together. There follows as in *Stiffelio* a long aria for the tenor with anguished pertichini from his wife. But it is simpler, with fewer twists and turns, and except for certain phrases the music is entirely new. In *Stiffelio* his tale had been of wantonness and debauchery on all sides, and his tone suitably severe. Aroldo on the other hand merely describes how as he fought under the blazing Syrian sun, and as he lay wounded on the point of death, his thoughts were only of her. For the cantabile ('Sotto il sole di Siria') Verdi avails himself of the trumpet melody in the overture for which he had found no place in the body of the earlier opera.* Its combination of the martial with the pious makes it not unsuitable to a Crusader.

In repeating the final limb Verdi extends the melody very gracefully by a whole bar. Mina's asides make copious use of the semitonal lament, as in the earlier opera, and a cadenza at the end reminds us that we are still in the 1850s. Aroldo now observes his wife's discomfort. Both here and later Mina's agitation makes use of material from

* The practice of keeping a neutral melody in hand in your overture to serve as basis for an additonal aria, if one were required, seems to have been fairly common. Instances include Mercadante's *Il Reggente*, where for the Trieste revival a new scene for soprano was quarried from the overture's main theme, and Gounod's *Faust*, where a melody in the prelude was turned into the aria 'Even bravest heart' written for the baritone Charles Santley.

her first scena. As in the overture to *Luisa Miller* there is evidence that Mozart's great G minor symphony was not unknown to the composer.

Such is the turmoil of her thoughts that she is unable to utter a word. Well then, why will she not at least give him a smile? asks Aroldo, taking her hand. Here, for thirteen bars, words and melody are the same as in the corresponding point in *Stiffelio* ('Allor, dunque sorridimi') but with a notable difference: there is no tonic pedal note for the first seven bars of the verse.*

The reason for this lies probably in the different approach in each case. After the long dominant of Ex. 228 a tonic for eight bars would create a sense of stasis; while the continuing dominant of Ex. 229 keeps the expectation alive. Then too the situation is altogether less complicated than in the earlier opera and does not require such nuances as the tension of dominant harmony over a tonic pedal. Like Stiffelio, Aroldo breaks off suddenly as he notices that Mina is not wearing his mother's wedding ring. Horrified asides from Mina; threatening demands from Aroldo; then what can only be called a 'masked' cabaletta ('Non sai che la sua perdita'). 'By the way,' Verdi had written from Paris, 'see if you can write me a cabaletta for the tenor aria. The one that's there is and must be very fine . . . but . . . all the better for you; it

* On this point see also T. Gotti, 'L'opera, appunti per un' analisi', in *I.S.V. Quaderno*, No. 3 (Parma, 1970), pp. 37–73.

can provide a gem for some other libretto.'* He was referring of course to Stiffelio's 'Ah t'appare in fronte scritto' which as far as sense goes would do equally well for the present context. But for the music Verdi clearly wanted something more controlled, whose tone would match that of the 'divorce' duet in Act III – falsely suave, blandly bitter with the hint of an obsession about it. Unlike the fiery outburst in *Stiffelio* it is a slow 'prancing' cabaletta with plentiful use of woodwind in thirds:

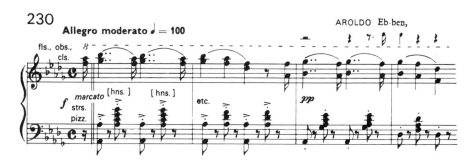

In one sense it is a distinctly old-fashioned design with an instrumental statement of the melody beforehand and a central ritornello in faster time. Two features, however, give it a character entirely of its own. One is the unusual distribution between voice and orchestra, its persistent alternation of 'parlante' and 'cantabile'. The other is the extreme thematic economy whereby Ex. 230 recurs no less than ten times either in the form given above or in a variation. The effect is a masking of the cabaletta design and at the same time that of a cat playing with a mouse. As Aroldo tells his wife over and over again of the 'fatality' of losing the wedding ring we have a foretaste of the frightening sarcasm with which Otello will taunt his wife over the loss of the handkerchief. Over the last chord comes the distant sound of the banda with the *Rienzi*-like theme from the overture slightly modified to allow the orchestra to punctuate the beginning and end of each phrase. Briano hurries in to tell Aroldo that his friends are waiting for him to join them. With Stiffelio's words 'I shall return soon' Aroldo goes out with the hermit, leaving Mina to echo his final word. '"Soon," he said.' The same exclamation led in the earlier opera to Lina's prayer. In *Aroldo* it introduces the scene in which the erring wife writes a letter to her husband making a full confession. As she sinks into a chair, covering her face with her hands, Egberto, her father, enters quietly and observes her. If his opening recitative 'O miei sospetti!' is somewhat subdued for a principal character it is at least an entrance of a sort. In the earlier work Stankar first voiced his suspicions in an ensemble, where they would have been quite inaudible. Egberto employs the same words in a clearly intelligible recitative: 'Godvino, if you have stained the honour of my house, tremble!' Mina rouses herself and begins to write a letter. But after four string bars of 'writing' music the page is snatched from her by her father. He reads, 'Aroldo, I am not worthy of you . . .' and rounds on her savagely. Brokenly Mina admits that she could keep silent no longer. From here on the scene proceeds note for note and word for word as in *Stiffelio*. In the course of a three-movement duet ('Dite, il fallo a tergere') Egberto persuades his daughter to tear up the letter since its contents would

* Letter to Piave, 23.8.1856. Abbiati, II, pp. 369–71.

kill her husband. As the baritone part is the least changed of all the three principals it may be useful to bear in mind that it was created originally for the high, light, flexible baritone voice of Filippo Colini. Hence the floridity of the cadenzas and the sparing use of fortissimi.

> *Scene 2: A suite of rooms illuminated for a grand celebration. In the first there are some pieces of period furniture on one of which rests a book locked by a clasp with a key.*

In *Stiffelio* the soprano and baritone duet had been followed by a tiny scene in which the adulterer had placed a compromising letter in the book (Klopstock's *Messias* in *Stiffelio* – unspecified here, and who, other than a monk, would have been able to read it in the eleventh century?), had then exchanged a word with a minor character (Federico) and left. Briano's counterpart, the old minister Jorg, had seen Federico (Enrico here) but not Raffaello (Godvino) and therefore concluded summarily that he must be the guilty party. In *Aroldo* a similar scene is enacted but within the framework of the Act I finale. Therefore throughout the opening bars of party music the stage directions tell us that the knights and their ladies who are seen greeting one another must 'for the moment' only be visible in the rooms at the back. The melody is the same as in *Stiffelio*, an undistinguished waltz which figures as the second allegro theme of the overture (converted into 4/4 time) and shorn of its upbeat (see Vol. 1, Ex. 304). In *Aroldo* it receives somewhat more sophisticated treatment. It appears first on full orchestral wind and timpani in detached chords, then with a smaller orchestration and a pattern of clarinet quavers in the bass. Strings take over with soft, silken chords as Godvino enters cautiously ('O Mina, tu mi sfuggi ed io cotanto t'amo'): strange words for one who in the play is a cold-blooded seducer.

231

As he opens the book and slips in the letter he is observed by Briano. This time there is no Federico to confuse the issue for the moment: but remember that Briano has only seen Godvino from the back. As he leaves, shaking his head suspiciously, the other guests enter the room at the front of stage with a new melody not to be found in *Stiffelio*.

232

This in turn gives way to the original waltz theme sung by women's voices ('È bello di guerra dai campi cruenti') with upbeats restored and clarinet arpeggios in the accompaniment. Ex. 231 returns as Enrico (counterpart of Federico) enters dressed like Godvino, and holds out his hand to Briano who refuses to take it; for he is certain that it was Enrico whom he saw slipping the letter into the book. When Enrico actually picks up the book, finds it locked and goes off to mingle with the other guests Briano is certain. He approaches Aroldo who at that moment has entered with Mina and Egberto, draws him aside, tells him what he has seen and points to Enrico as the culprit. They converse over a sinuous A minor theme which uses a motif of triplets derived from Ex. 232. Melody and bass carry useful possibilities of development.

233

Aroldo has no time to react for everyone now gathers round him to a resumption of the original waltz melody 'Per te della croce possente guerriero' scored as before but sung this time by the full chorus, and leading to a final triumphant statement of Ex. 232. If in all this Verdi is to some extent at the mercy of his former material he has worked it into a far stronger design which may be set out as follows (action themes being indicated by smaller letters):

A (Vol. I Ex. 304) – b (Ex. 231) – C (Ex. 232) – A – b – c – (Ex. 233) – A – C
E major   E minor   E major – A major A minor – A major E major

It is one of those rare key-schemes that are occasionally to be found in Verdi's party music. In *Rigoletto* and *La Traviata* these were conditioned by the inability of the banda either to develop their themes or to move outside a small circle of related keys; and in any case they were so primitive as hardly to deserve a mention. Two factors make a difference here: the counterpoint of the tonal and thematic pattern and the fact that the action themes develop and modulate while always returning to their original tonality. In other words the above design is essentially that of a symphonic rondo; and it brings a new dimension into the structure of the finale.

In a solemn recitative ('Eterna vivrà in Kenth . . .') Egberto welcomes the guests, who evidently include Aroldo's comrades-in-arms since he asks 'somebody' to recount the exploits of Richard Cœur de Lion in Palestine. All crowd round Aroldo and press him for a story. At first he refuses until goaded by the special plea of Enrico, the suspected adulterer. The rapping figures of the march-like transition tells us that Aroldo has murder in his heart. His story ('Vi fu in Palestina') is a symmetrical double verse, much of it couched in a monotone over an accompaniment which brings memories of the protagonist's death scene in the first *Macbeth*.

234

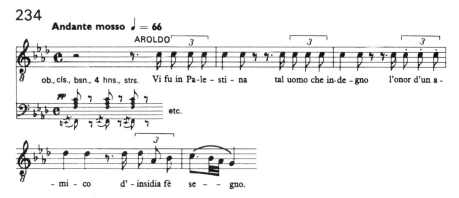

He recounts how in Palestine there was a scoundrel who betrayed the honour of his host and was observed to make a guilty assignation with his hostess by means of a letter slipped into a book. 'A similar tale,' he continues, 'is told by one of the prophets. I will read you his exact words.' With this he picks up the book, only to find it locked. 'Mina has the key,' puts in Elena helpfully. Panic of Mina. 'Open it then,' commands her husband. Throughout this scene largely set in E flat minor Aroldo expresses himself in the apocalyptic tones which he will use in Act II but with more sparing use of high notes. The action then freezes for the concertato 'O qual m'invade ed agita' which is taken over in toto from *Stiffelio*.*

As Mina is petrified with fright, Aroldo himself with all the strength of a seasoned crusader breaks open the clasp; a letter falls out and is swiftly retrieved by Egberto who tears it into fragments. In *Stiffelio* his counterpart Stankar was merely doing what the minister himself had done in a similar situation at the start of the opera; but then he had no idea that the honour of his house was involved. Hence the irony of his behaviour at this point. In *Aroldo* this irony is missing; Aroldo himself is acting as any betrayed husband might be expected to act, angrily demanding the letter and then bursting out in a denunciation of Egberto when the letter is torn up. The stretta ('Chi ti salva, o sciagurato') gives a new line to Aroldo more in keeping with his character. Whereas Stiffelio spanned an octave and a fourth within the first six bars, Aroldo keeps within the octave and shows a tendency to hug the note E; the bass on the other hand leaps and dances with fury.

---

* A detail which went unremarked in the analysis in Vol. I was the derivation of its crowning phrase from the chorus 'A te Stiffelio un canto' which forms the main theme of the overture (Vol. I, Ex. 303b). There can be no dramatic significance in this in either opera, least of all the later one, where the theme in question only appears briefly outside the overture; it is merely a manifestation of the opera's 'tinta' through overlapping fourths (see Vol. 1, p. 457).

235

At its return Ex. 235 has a bass of moving staccato crotchets doubled by Egberto and Briano and the chorus basses; but however full the sound may appear on paper the only people to sing forte are Aroldo and Mina. Everywhere else there is a sense of hush, partly horrified, partly conspiratorial – since as in *Stiffelio* (and to the same theme) the heroine's father is covertly challenging the adulterer to a duel. The full explosion of sound is reserved for a maggiore section, rather like that in the first *Simon Boccanegra* which replaces the few bars of major key that wound up the original finale. The basis is again Ex. 235 with the crotchet pattern, confined to orchestra alone, transformed into a ferocious climbing bass reinforced by trombones. Two further contrasted ideas, both repeated, bring us to the final, noisy cadence. If, dramatically speaking, the protraction of the finale seems unnecessary, it is an inevitable consequence of the earlier architectural strengthening. Despite a similar thematic basis the Act I finale to *Aroldo* has an altogether larger scale than that of its predecessor.

ACT II

Scene: An old graveyard of the castle of Kent. In the centre is a cross with steps; on the right the door of a chapel lit up within, to which a large stairway gives access; on the left further back can be seen the castle; the moon sheds a dim light on the tombs here and there in the shadow of age-old cypresses. One of the tombs is of recent construction.

Little in this act differs from its predecessor of 1850; there is the same atmospheric prelude, the same agitated entrance of Mina followed by a prayer to her dead mother ('Ah dagli scanni eterei') with its luminous combination of string groups. True, a comparison with the vocal score of *Stiffelio* will show that the last phrase of the melody before the cadenza has been shortened by four bars; but quite clearly this cut had already been made in the earlier opera.* Quite different, however, is the following transition ('Mina! Voi qui?') and cabaletta. Mina, unlike her predecessor,

* See Vol. 1, p. 466.

is a tragic heroine in full panoply; so the pattering 6/8, however attractive, which served as background for the nervous exchanges of Lina and Raffaello will not do here. Instead, there is an allegro agitato of no thematic interest against which phrases of bitter scorn can emerge loud and clear. How dare Godvino profane this holy place? Why can he not leave her to her prayers? If there is a drop of honour left in his veins let him return her ring. Godvino refuses; he loves her, he says, and is ready to defend her. In contrast to Lina's conventional 'Perder dunque voi volete' the new cabaletta ('Ah del sen di quella tomba') is a remarkable piece of work, musically and dramatically. Observe first of all the gesture by which it is introduced (Ex. 236a), one of those unisons of negative emotion that will be used to portray Iago. Here it conveys Mina's weary disgust at words of love on the lips of such a worthless creature as Godvino, words which cause her mother's ghost to rise from the tomb. The same sense of horror pervades the first section of the cabaletta, emphasized by the brutal tritone of the opening phrase (Ex. 236b). A novel touch, characteristic of the operas to come, is the delayed bass, founded neatly on the triplet of Ex. 236a, which leaves the first few notes of the melody suspended in mid-air. In the second verse the three-note death figure which permeated the transition with no more than a feeling of vague agitation becomes unequivocal in its meaning. The major key section ('A fuggite! Il mio spavento') is unexpectedly old-fashioned both in its scoring and in its reliance on vocal virtuosity as can be seen from the extended final sentence (Ex. 230c). Never again will Verdi require of his heroines a total flexibility over two octaves. With this cabaletta, we may say, he bids a last, impressive farewell to the age of fioritura.

From then on action and music follow the course of *Stiffelio*. Egberto arrives and fights a duel with Godvino, which is interrupted by the appearance of Aroldo.

236c

Egberto is still determined that Aroldo shall not know the identity of his wife's seducer; but when Aroldo, in his effort to reconcile the combatants, takes the hand of Godvino, he can control himself no longer and blurts out the truth. Aroldo, beside himself with fury, is about to fight Godvino when sounds of prayer are heard from within the chapel (Vol. I, Ex. 303a); Briano appears on the steps and calls on Aroldo to remember the vow they had sworn together (what vow?) and return to his senses. He points to the cross as a symbol of divine mercy; Aroldo still torn by conflicting emotions faints on the steps.

ACT III

Scene: An antechamber in Egberto's house which gives on to various apartments. On the table are writing materials.

Here too differences with *Stiffelio* are few. In a full double aria Egberto prepares to take his own life; then at the news that Godvino has not left the house with Mina, as he had supposed, he exults at the prospect of fighting him once more. It is an aria built strictly round the virtues and limitations of Filippo Colini, the original Stankar; but for his Egberto Verdi was prepared to let it stand. There follows the short scene between Aroldo and Godvino ('What would you do if Mina were free?') and the much longer one between husband and wife. Here the soprano interventions ('Pietade, pietade, non mi scacciate' and 'A me quest'atto') are given greater musical prominence than in in the original, partly because, as has been said, Mina has a stronger personality than her predecessor, partly because the experience of *La Traviata* had suggested new ways of rounding a female character. When Aroldo taunts her bitterly with using tears in an attempt to make him weaken ('Credete che per lacrime si scemi il dolor mio?') she reacts with force and dignity. Here we may notice the subtle use of a rhythmic pattern to bind together two movements, one old, the other new. Mina's snatching of the divorce papers is accompanied by a gesture of two heavy chords (♩♩♪♪) repeated twice in a descrescendo. After an empty bar this is transformed into a rhythmic motif (♩♪♪♩♪♩♩♪♪, etc.) first by flutes in octaves then with strings joining. Harmonically this is all in the *terrain vague* of the diminished seventh. As she signs her name the key of F sharp minor takes shape and the music moves slowly towards the dominant with the rhythmic motif persisting throughout. 'Now we are both free,' she says handing him back the document; he is about to go but she holds him back. At this point the new score joins hands with the old taking up the melody ('Non allo sposo, al giudice' – Vol. I, Ex. 326) but in the higher key of F sharp major and with full woodwind on the top line. Its three marching crotchets now seem to derive from the pattern mentioned above with the beginning transferred from the last to the first beat of the bar. It is a simpler, and more logical approach to the melody which will be crowned by that vital phrase in which the heroine asks her husband Aroldo to listen to her not as a husband but as – what? Here is the great stumbling block of the new text. Aroldo, however religiously inclined, has no spiritual authority. She can only ask him to be her judge: 'Lo voglio, giudicatemi' is as inept a substitute for 'Ministro confessatemi' as that forced upon Verdi and Piave by the original censorship at Trieste. Nor is her following apologia with its altered words to the same cor anglais melody – this time 'ungraced' – any more convincing than Lina's ('If I have sinned my soul is pure!' . . . and 'It was a betrayal').

From here to the end of the act there is nothing to justify fresh music; the action proceeds as before, Egberto reappearing with a bloody sword having dispatched Godvino, Briano calling Aroldo to the church and husband and wife joining in a final, turbulent duet.

ACT IV

Scene: A deep valley in Scotland. The shore of Loch Lomond is seen in the background. Mountains (practicable props) covered with woods to right and left, where there is a small grove of pines and beside it a modest dwelling. Distant sounds of horns and bagpipes approaching. Voices of shepherds, women and huntsmen who come down from the mountains and meet.

A typical evening scene, then, at which many a stag will have drunk his fill. The opening chorus ('Cade il giorno') is made up of three scenic and musical elements – shepherds, huntsmen and reaping women. Of these the first two are allotted a characteristic motif, after which a vaguely rustic theme establishes the G major tonality. (See Ex. 237a, b and c.)

There is no attempt to combine them vertically in the Parisian manner; they are simply arranged with consummate skill into a delicate pastoral landscape more redolent of Abruzzo than Dumbartonshire. Niceties of local colour meant no more to Verdi than to most Italians of his generation. Indeed he is said to have deplored it as a cover for emptiness of musical thought.* Like Donizetti's Lammermoor or Federico Ricci's Edinburgh, Verdi's Loch Lomond is situated south of the Alps. For the bagpipes his model was the Italian piffero; hence his quaint illusion that they were played by shepherds as they tended their flocks. His shepherds therefore are characterized by a primitive combination of oboe and clarinet, aided by bassoon when the compass becomes too low (Ex. 237a). Here and there he suggests the drone with a dominant pedal note (e.g. at 'Dissetollo un rio d'argento') but the italianate quality of the melody not to mention the prevailing dominant harmony prevent any possible northern associations. In the interest of pictorialism Verdi avoids anything too definite in the way of a melody for most of the scene. Instead the music proceeds

---

* See Pizzi, p. 161.

237a

237b

237c

in a kaleidoscope of phrases, half phrases and sentences, often repeated, until the design is drawn together by a broad unison melody begun by the women and repeated by full chorus:

238

There is a conventional coda followed by a long 'play-out' founded mostly on Ex. 237c and with each group signing off in appropriate fashion. Aroldo and Briano appear from the slopes on the right and make for the hut; both are dressed as hermits.

Aroldo contrasts the happiness of the peasants and huntsmen with his own spiritual anguish ('Cantan felice! . . ed io l'inferno ho in core!'). He is of course thinking of Mina whom he ought to hate but cannot. The Angelus bell sounds in the distance. Briano and Aroldo kneel accordingly. The unaccompanied preghiera 'Angiol di Dio' is, as Mariani has said, a beautifully fashioned four-part canon in unison and at the octave, with each of the three choruses entering at intervals of two bars; but it is not a continuous piece of contrapuntal writing, which would have been ridiculous in the present context. It is spelt out in single sentences with the voice-parts fading away in the order in which they entered. Not until the last is silent does the new sentence begin. The effect is of Tennysonian echoes 'dying, dying, dying'. Again Verdi has availed himself of the skill possible to an offstage chorus who can sing from their copies.

Already night has fallen; and the moon which had risen during the Angelus is covered by clouds; a wind gets up and ruffles the surface of the lake. The burrasca which now irrupts is Verdi's most striking piece of orchestral virtuosity to date, forestalling the storm in *Otello*, particularly in its chromatic writing for brass. As the autograph is full of smudges and bars crossed out one may gather that much of it was the fruit of practical experiment in which the skill of Mariani may have played a considerable part.* First violins are divided into three parts, seconds into two. Some of the material recalls Act III of *Rigoletto*: the lightning figure, here shared between all the upper woodwind; the moaning wind, here given to second violins, not voices; the distant thunder of cellos and basses. New, however, is a raindrop motif assigned to the first violins. Within thirty-five bars of the opening all four motifs begin to coalesce in a vestigial counterpoint. As the storm grows the chorus enters from all sides, coming to the rescue of a boat in distress. Sopranos provide the thematic centre of the storm with a wailing prayer which owes something to the fourth movement of Beethoven's Pastoral symphony, and which being worked into a triple pattern ascending by semitones may possibly qualify as a ritual (Ex. 239).†

Aroldo and Briano meanwhile have flung out a rope and are heaving hard. A feature which will recur in the storm in *Otello* is the chromatic runs for brass in unison – inevitably more telling when the trombones had valves instead of slides. As the storm recedes a sailing boat comes into view, its mast broken, its sail torn. In it are Mina and Egberto and two boatmen. The peasants help them ashore, and point to the hermit's hut where they may find shelter ('Bussate a quella porta . . .'). As the chorus leave, the oboe gives out a major-key reminiscence over tremolando strings of Ex. 237a, with a romantic suggestion of clear sky after the storm. Mina is at the end of her strength ('Ah più non reggo'). So too the orchestra tells us still more eloquently with a hesitant motif of syncopations (Ex. 240).

After a pause the motif tries again, now reaching four bars before breaking off in weariness. After five more bars violins make a fresh start with the help of the oboe,

* The spirit of their collaboration is neatly illustrated in an anecdote related by Eugenio Checchi. Mariani was rehearsing part of the burrasca over and over again, striving for a particular effect, when Verdi went up to him and suggested that he pass on to the remainder of the act; Mariani reluctantly consented. Later he asked Verdi for an explanation. Verdi assured him that he intended no criticism of the players or of Mariani himself. 'But,' he added, 'surely you must have noticed that the scoring is at fault. Tomorrow evening I promise to let you have the passage scored afresh.' E. Checchi, *Verdi* (new ed., Florence, 1926), pp. 142–3.

† See F. Noske, 'Ritual scenes in Verdi's operas', in *Music and Letters* LIV (1973), pp. 415–39.

239

Allegro brillante

240

Allegro moderato

this time producing the effect of one of those freely wandering lines to be found in Berlioz and associated with the same wind instrument; with Verdi, as usual, it is orientated more strongly towards its final cadence. Mina is thinking not of herself but of her father's misfortunes('Povero padre mio!') for which she is responsible. At Egberto's comforting words ('Non più! Qui posa, o Mina . . .') a cello countermelody enters the orchestral design with soothing effect; and as he goes to knock at the door the plangent oboe drops out leaving the violins and cellos to continue the discourse. It is a wonderfully delicate piece of mood-painting which owes nothing to the voices, everything to the orchestra. As Mina sinks down on the rock Egberto calls out begging shelter for a benighted traveller. At the sound of Aroldo's words of welcome ('Ben giunto lo stranier al tetto mio') Mina starts up. (Note the use here of a cello 'lamenting' figure *above* sustaining violas, with the same poignancy as in *Les Vêpres Siciliennes*.) Aroldo is no less disturbed. His first reaction is to drive her away. The terzetto which develops is in fact a succession of solos; Aroldo's 'Ah da me fuggi, involati' brings together the old and the new. In the declamatory opening, half in dialogue with the strings, and the smooth continuation there is the faint relic of the Rossinian open melody; and the polonaise-like cadential flourish is equally a relic from a bygone age. On the other hand the growth from short to longer phrases with a more varied rhythmic articulation is a legacy from *Les Vêpres Siciliennes* through *Simon Boccanegra* (first version). The third sentence shares both traits with another – the *Aroldo* 'tinta'.

241 **Allegro**

The relation of mood and contour to that of Egberto's 'Dite che il fallo a tergere' from Act I. Stiffelio, whose character was more clearly defined by his situation, expressed himself in Stankar's language only in Act III of the opera. Aroldo, denied the priestly attributes of his predecessor, resorts far more often to the bitter suavity of his father-in-law. Here, however, Egberto is all dignified reproach. In his reply ('La patria legge vindice') he tells Aroldo how he had to flee from England to escape the death penalty for having killed Godvino. Mina had followed him into exile and suffered all manner of hardships for his sake. If Aroldo cannot call her his wife, will he please remember that she is still Egberto's daughter. This too is a strongly formed periodic melody (C minor–E flat major–C major). Mina is for the moment too crushed to be able to utter more than broken phrases, propped by reminiscences of Ex. 240 ('Taci mio padre calmati'). But even as she prepares to leave with her father her line takes on strength and nobility for one last appeal for which Piave found some rather simple and touching lines. When the years have subdued her heart, her hair is white with grief, her eyes dim with weeping and her last hour is near, may she still have some hope that she will die forgiven? Solo cello and cor anglais are a well-known Italian formula for grief, which Verdi had almost patented in *Rigoletto*. Yet was it ever used more tellingly and economically than at the start of the final quartet

(Ex. 242a)? No less affecting is the major complement (Ex. 242b) with its warm string tone and harmonies conveying the forgiveness that Aroldo will be unable to withhold.*

242a

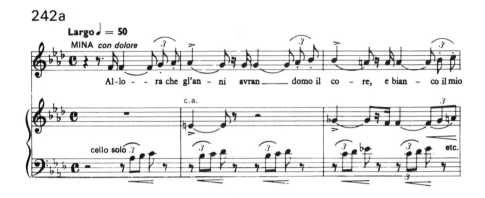

242b

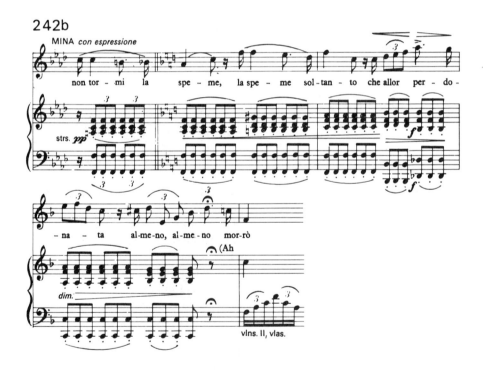

The string triplets now split into sextuplets in familiar fashion as Aroldo and Egberto add their comments. Then Briano appears at the door of the hut and with all the authority of a comprimario bass hermit pronounces the scriptural words, 'Let him who is without sin cast the first stone. . . .' Dramatic in the mouth of Stiffelio, they

* This quartet is used as the finale for Charles Mackerras's Verdian ballet *The Lady and the Fool*, where it winds up the sad sentimental story most movingly.

sound little more than a pious platitude here, though their music adds the right touch of variety to the thematic design. Aroldo's gradual emotional thaw finds expression in a slow orchestral climb opening out into a melting 6/4 from which he descends with a poignant 'Io pur piansi tanto, tanto, tanto'. And now it is he who sings Ex. 242b to 'Sei perdonato'; Mina takes it up with 'Ah grazie, gran Dio' and both voices join in unison on the final phrase. The phrase is repeated with Briano and Egberto beneath, and amid a sense of triumphant happiness the curtain falls. If there is something here that recalls the finale to Act III of *Ernani* a comparison of both scores will show the variety, subtlety and economy of thought which the intervening thirteen years had brought.

To weigh up the merits and defects of *Aroldo* in relation to *Stiffelio* is not easy. At first sight the honours would seem to lie with the earlier work. *Stiffelio* is founded on an unusual play which led Verdi to musical solutions of considerable originality for the time. Everything in it stems from the character and situation of the hero, in whom there is a touch of Manzoni's Padre Cristoforo – a man outwardly controlled, but with strong feelings beneath the surface. He is unique among Verdi's tenors until Otello. By comparison the other two principals are lightly if effectively touched in. On the debit side the action of the opera was often unclear, the stagecraft clumsy and the musical quality slightly uneven. In *Aroldo* the plot is simpler and better paced and the purely theatrical problems are overcome – often, however, at the expense of substituting the conventional for the unconventional and so taking away what was one of the principal merits of the earlier opera. The drinking chorus which replaces Jorg's arioso is one case in point; another is the first part of Act IV with its peasants' chorus, preghiera and tempest, as though composer and librettist had just resorted to the most hackneyed theatrical expedients they could think of. Worse still the hero himself is somewhat compromised. In the first act where his music is nearly all new he is a different character from the Austrian pastor. He is a phlegmatic Englishman, slower to anger but formidable when once aroused. His controlled weightiness is expressed in a line which moves little, which remains mostly in the lower to middle register of the voice and often shows a tendency to remain anchored to one note. How significant that his first solo ('Sotto il sol di Siria') should originate in an instrumental melody. All this nearly brings a new 'tinta' into the opera. In Act II, however, he steps into Stiffelio's shoes. It may be argued that certain substances originally distinct lose their differences when raised to a sufficiently high temperature and that Stiffelio's hysteria, when confronted by irrefutable proof of his wife's infidelity, is no less appropriate to his English successor. But to Stiffelio the revelation comes at the point when he is exercising his authority as a minister of the Gospel. It makes no sense for Aroldo to say to the combatants, 'Di Dio ora parlo nel nome'. Besides if he had preserved the character he is given in Act I he would already be in single-minded pursuit of his wife's seducer. Stiffelio's fluctuations of mood are not for him. In Act III, while it is possible for each to speak with the ironical bitterness of Stankar, Aroldo has no reason to break out in despair when he learns that his father-in-law has killed the seducer. To Stiffelio this means the failure of everything he has preached; to Aroldo it is merely what he had every intention of doing himself. In a word, where Aroldo is himself he is less interesting than Stiffelio; and where he is Stiffelio he has no right to be. Mina on the other hand is limned far more strongly than Lina, as though after *La Traviata* Verdi no longer felt it necessary to apologize for his erring women.* Egberto, who varies hardly at all from his earlier incarnation, makes an important contribution to the 'tinta' of both operas with his bland, often chromatically inflected line. But before closing the balance sheet account must be taken of the richer vein of musical invention in *Aroldo*, the strengthening of the architecture at so many points and the more sustained level of craftsmanship – all the fruits of the intervening seven years' experience. If from the dramatic point of view Verdi in making his revision showed himself a better tactician than a strategist, his musical conscience never slept. There is not a weak point in the fabric of *Stiffelio* that is not immeasurably strengthened in the later work. We may sum the matter up by saying that *Aroldo* is better as music, *Stiffelio* as music drama, and leave it at that.

---

* Another factor here was doubtless the prima donna Marcellina Lotti, 'excellent in strong parts, but I wouldn't know what to make of her as Cordelia'. (Letter to V. Torelli, 16.5.1856. *Copialettere*, pp. 192–3.)

8 UN BALLO IN MASCHERA

UN BALLO IN MASCHERA

Opera in three acts
by
ANTONIO SOMMA
(after the libretto *Gustave III* by Augustin Eugène Scribe)

First performed at the
Teatro Apollo, Rome,
17 February 1859

RICCARDO, Earl of Warwick, governor of Boston	PRIMO TENORE	Gaetano Fraschini
RENATO, a Creole, his secretary, husband to	PRIMO BARITONO	Leone Giraldoni
AMELIA	PRIMA DONNA SOPRANO	Eugenia Julienne-Dejean
ULRICA, a fortune teller, of negroid race	PRIMA DONNA CONTRALTO	Zelina Sbriscia
OSCAR, a Page	PRIMA DONNA SOPRANO (LEGGIERO)	Pamela Scotti
SILVANO, a sailor	SECONDO BASSO	Stefano Santucci
SAMUEL ⎫ enemies of	BASSO COMPRIMARIO	Cesare Rossi
TOM ⎭ the earl	BASSO COMPRIMARIO	Giovanni Bernardoni
A judge	SECONDO TENORE	Giuseppe Bazzoli
Servant to Amelia	SECONDO TENORE	Luigi Fossi

Deputies – officers – sailors – guards – men, women and children of the
populace – gentlemen – partisans of Samuel and Tom – servants – masks
– dancing couples

The action takes place in and around Boston, Massachusetts

Epoch: towards the end of the seventeenth century

Among the new friends and acquaintances that Verdi made in Venice at the time of *La Traviata* was the lawyer and playwright Antonio Somma, his senior by three years. Though completely forgotten today Somma's works enjoyed a considerable vogue in his lifetime, especially a *Parisina* and a *Cassandra* written for the great Italian actress Adelaide Ristori and performed by her in Paris in 1859. Well known for his patriotic sentiments he had been appointed secretary to the Assembly of the short-lived Venetian republic of 1849. Could this be the great national poet to whom Carcano had urged Verdi to unite his genius? Verdi himself apparently thought so; and when in the spring of 1853 Somma offered him amongst other ideas a *Sordello* to set to music, Verdi was in principle delighted. 'Nothing could be better, nothing dearer to my heart than to join your great name to mine.' But *Sordello* would not do; it was too gloomy and severe.

> I find that the opera of our day sins through excessive monotony; in fact I myself would refuse nowadays to set subjects like *Nabucco*, *Foscari*, etc. They present some very exciting theatrical moments, but they lack variety. Everything is on one string – a lofty one if you like but always the same. To make myself still clearer: Tasso's poetry may be the better, but I prefer Ariosto's a thousand times. For the same reason I prefer Shakespeare to all other dramatists, not excepting the ancient Greeks.

His own best opera to date, leaving aside all question of literary merit, was *Rigoletto*, with its libertine Duke. 'Many have set *Ruy Blas* leaving out the part of Don César. Well, if I were going to set that subject to music, it would be chiefly because I like the contrast which that highly original character provides.' The subjects suggested by Somma lacked the variety 'that my crazy brain would like'. Nevertheless he had no doubt that once a suitable subject could be found their collaboration would be a great event for the world of letters. Meanwhile he recommended Somma to have a look at *King Lear*.* So began a correspondence which was to last two years, off and on.

Alas, though he is said to have collaborated with Francesco D'Ongaro on the libretto of Federico Ricci's *Un Duello sotto Richelieu* in 1839† Somma revealed himself even more innocent of the librettist's art than Piave at the time of *Ernani*. Verdi had to teach him from the beginning. 'For a musical setting you need verses for cantabili, verses for pezzi concertati, verses for larghi, allegri, etc; all alternating with one another so that nothing becomes dull or monotonous.'‡ Somma had to learn never to finish a sentence in the middle of a line; to avoid an excess of recitative in the final

---

* Letter to Somma, 22.4.1853. A. Pascolato, *Re Lear e Un Ballo in maschera* (Città di Castello, 1902), pp. 45–8.

† Abbiati, II, 245 and F. Flora, 'Un Ballo in maschera – Il libretto', in *I.S.V. Bollettino*, No. 1, p. 45, adding the name of Gazzoletti as a third partner and giving the composer wrongly as Luigi Ricci. All libretti of the opera in question give D'Ongaro as sole author.

‡ Letter to Somma, 30.8.1853. Pascolato, pp. 52–5.

scenes; not to overload the eye any more than the ear; and in general to observe all those little rules which were the fruit of Verdi's own experience of more than fifteen years. The libretto of *Re Lear* was finished more or less to his satisfaction shortly before the première of *Les Vêpres Siciliennes*. It was already being hinted that the venue of the première should be the San Carlo, Naples – the home of Cammarano, who had drafted the first scenario, and where if the censorship was strict the company was large and the *convenienze* less rigid than in most other theatres. From Paris Verdi had written jokingly to De Sanctis: 'What would your public think if I were to bring them a *Re Lear* fresh from the mint? . . . It would be enough to get me stoned to death!'*

So when in the spring of 1856 Vincenzo Torelli, now secretary to the management of the San Carlo, approached him with the offer of a contract, *King Lear* was the subject he proposed, always provided that he could be sure of a suitable company. Doubtless it was this uncertainty rather than the complicated reasons put forward in his letter of 22 April† that prevented him from signing the contract until the following February for the carnival season of 1857–8.‡ This left him free to undertake *Simon Boccanegra* in the spring of 1857 in Venice. The management of the San Carlo proved amenable; and at intervals during the rest of the year Verdi kept up an intermittent correspondence with Torelli about the singers needed for *Re Lear*. By this time he and Somma had reduced the cast to manageable proportions. He was especially concerned about three of the principals. For the title role he wanted 'a baritone who is an artist in every possible meaning of the word – such as Giorgio Ronconi was. If I had to make choice between Coletti and Colini, all things being equal I would prefer the former. . . . I am very keen to have a contralto§ and I repeat that Giuseppina Brambilla could do the management a lot of good. Quite apart from the new opera she could play important parts in the older repertory, in *Giuramento*, *Trovatore*, etc.'¶ (At last he admits the true vocal register of Azucena.) As for Cordelia, only three sopranos would do: Virginia Boccabadati, Maria Spezia and Marietta Piccolomini. 'All three have small voices but great talent, deep feeling and a sense of the theatre. All three were excellent in *Traviata*.'‖ He himself sounded out la Piccolomini, who, although in the process of negotiating a contract for St Petersburg for that season, showed herself so enthusiastic and disposed to drop everything for the sake of *King Lear* that Verdi drew back in embarrassment, and hastened to put the matter on an official basis between her and the San Carlo, using the English banker Mitrovich as intermediary.** The result was that nothing was concluded.

To all appearance Verdi was in earnest about *Re Lear*; but was he already afflicted by those doubts of being able to do it justice that caused Somma's libretto to remain unset? Even after signing the contract he continued hesitating on the brink. According to the terms agreed he was to send in a synopsis of the chosen plot by June

---

* Letter to De Sanctis, 7.2.1855. *Carteggi Verdiani*, I, pp. 29–30.

† *Copialettere*, pp. 189–90.

‡ For a copy of the contract see Walker, 'Unpublished letters; a contribution to the history of *Un Ballo in maschera*', in *I.S.V. Bollettino*, No. 1, pp. 39–40.

§ For the part of the fool.

¶ Letter to Torelli, 16.5.1856. *Copialettere*, pp. 192–3.

‖ Letter to Torelli, 11.11.1856. *Copialettere*, pp. 196–7.

** See letter to Mitrovich, 13.8.1856. Abbiati, II, pp. 338–9; also *Copialettere*, pp. 194–5, where the addressee is wrongly given as Ercolano Balestra.

1857. But by mid-month he had still not committed himself; and the reason was always the singers. 'Apart from Coletti no one would be right. I know la Fioretti. They tell me that Galvani is a flexible, graceful singer, and I would need a heavy one [*i.e. for Edmund*]. On the other hand Fraschini could well complain that the part isn't important enough for him. La Ganducci is more of a singer than an actress and that's why, for instance, Azucena is not a role for her. To sing the fool in *Lear* you want a contralto who has a real, thorough sense of the stage. . . .'* And so on.

Meanwhile as early as 1855 he had asked Somma to prepare another subject to be held in reserve – 'a kind of *Linda* or *Sonnambula*, though different again because that genre is already too familiar'.† A year later he returned to the idea: 'A quiet simple tender drama; a kind of *Sonnambula* without being an imitation of *La Sonnambula*.'‡ But Somma failed to produce what was required. By September the San Carlo management were becoming as restive as that of la Fenice the year before. 'Give us King Lear,' Torelli wrote, 'for although some other time you may happen upon a better Cordelia you will never have a better baritone, tenor or bass. Set your genius to work; I hear that *La Traviata* – a true musico-social revolution – was composed in a very short time. I hope you will produce a second *Traviata* for us.'§ But: 'I'm working night and day over a subject for the new opera,' Verdi wrote; 'I've chosen a Spanish play which I've had translated; now I'm reducing it to a musical scheme; after that I'll get it put into verse. I would have liked to do a *Ruy Blas*; but you are right, the brilliant part [*Don César*] wouldn't suit Coletti, and on the other hand he wouldn't be able to play the title role.'¶ Ten days later:

I'm in despair! In these last months I've looked through an infinite number of plays, some of them really beautiful, but not one of them will do for me. My attention was arrested by a very fine and exciting play *Il Tesoriere del Re Don Pedro* which I had translated at once; but in drawing up a sketch with a view to scaling it down for music I've found so many difficulties as to make me give up the idea. At present I'm scaling down a French drama, *Gustavo III di Svezia*, libretto by Scribe, performed at the Opéra twenty years ago. It's vast and grandiose; it's beautiful; but it too has conventional things in it like all operas – something I've always disliked and now find intolerable.‖

He suggested as an alternative that he should direct revivals of *Aroldo*, *Boccanegra* and a refurbished *La Battaglia di Legnano*. The management did not regard this as a fulfilment of his contract; so for better or worse *Gustavo III* it had to be. There was no time to prepare anything else.

So what had begun as a search for the new and the transcendental ended with one of the most hackneyed solutions imaginable: a plot fifteen years old, already set by at least three composers of note. True, it must have appeared startling in 1833 since it dealt however unhistorically with events which had happened within living

* Letter to Torelli, 17.6.1857. *Copialettere*, p. 484.
† Letter to Somma, 5.4.1855. Pascolato, pp. 76–7.
‡ Letter to Somma, 7.4.1856. Pascolato, pp. 77–9.
§ Letter from Torelli, 26.9.1857. *Carteggi Verdiani*, I, pp. 300–1.
¶ Letter to Torelli, 9.9.1857. *Copialettere*, p. 561.
‖ Letter to Torelli, 19.9.1857. *Copialettere*, pp. 561–3.

memory. Gustav III of Sweden, a despot of the Enlightenment like Joseph II of Austria, whose reforms had made him many enemies amongst the nobility, was assassinated during a ball in 1792 by a gentleman of the court, one Ankarstrom. He lived long enough to make the necessary arrangements for the regency, his own son being under age. Meanwhile Ankarstrom was sentenced to execution and died without revealing the names of his accomplices or the reason for his action. For Scribe forty years later it was a simple case of 'cherchez la femme'. Gustav must have been having an affair with Ankarstrom's wife. He added a touch of theatrical irony by making the assassin the king's secretary and confidant, and complicated the intrigue still further by inventing a soothsayer, Mademoiselle Arvidson, who prophesies to the disguised king that he will be murdered by the man who next takes his hand. This duly turns out to be Ankarstrom, who has come for the sole purpose of protecting his sovereign. Meanwhile Gustave has overheard his beloved Amélie, also disguised, consult the soothsayer in order to rid herself of a passion for her husband's friend. She is told to pluck at midnight a certain root that grows by the gallows foot. Gustave himself goes to meet her and forces her to declare her love for him. Their idyll is interrupted by Ankarstrom who has come to warn the king that his life is in danger from a party of conspirators headed by Counts Ribbing and de Horn. He exchanges cloaks with Gustave and promises to conduct the heavily veiled Amélie to the city gates and leave her. He then faces the king's enemies. Baulked of their prey, they demand to see the lady's face. General merriment when it turns out to be Ankarstrom's wife. Ankarstrom decides on revenge. He joins the conspirators and murders the king, who, having by this time decided to renounce Amélie, dies with consciousness of rectitude.

It is a cleverly constructed plot in which irony follows irony. It abounds in striking situations and *coups de théâtre*; it offers opportunities for a display of the most intense and varied emotions; and it is full of suspense: in short an ideal work for a theatre that put more value on sensation than on truthful portrayal of character. Moreover, unlike *Les Huguenots* or *Le Prophète*, it was to attract more than one foreign composer of greater eminence than Auber, for whom it was written.

Gustave III, ou Le Bal masqué was produced as a grand opera in five acts in Paris in 1833 with Adolphe Nourrit as Gustave, Nicholas Levasseur as Ankarstrom and Cornélie Falcon as Amélie.* It was no more than a half-success, remaining in the repertoire but rarely revived and then mostly in fragments, like Rossini's *Guillaume Tell*. However, it had a certain circulation abroad. Act I and V are enlarged by ballets, the first supposedly devised by Gustave himself on the subject of his ancestor Gustave Wasa; and it is the music for these that forms the most attractive and characteristic part of the score. Auber's muse is that of the Faubourg, elevated at times by a natural taste that gives the occasional roughness of his melody and harmony a piquant, sometimes haunting quality. Over and over again he returns to march rhythms in which an essentially demotic language can be felt beneath a veneer of Rossini and Cherubini. One of Auber's virtues is that he is incapable of pretentiousness. Where invention runs high, as in *La Muette de Portici* and *Fra Diavolo*, the result is always more compelling than a perusal of the score would lead one to

---

* For an account of its reception and a penetrating analysis of the score, see F. D'Amico, 'Il *Ballo in Maschera* prima di Verdi', in *I.S.V. Bollettino*, no. 3 (Parma, 1960), pp. 1251–94.

expect. Where it flags, as in *Gustave*, the music is mostly trivial, even-paced and dull, with just a progression here or a melodic turn there to remind us that Auber's is a genuine personality. He gives us moments of tenderness as in Gustave's two duets with Amélie, and of mild horror as in the scene with Madamoiselle Arvidson; but high tragedy was beyond him. *Gustave III* remains a rather uninteresting museum piece, though one from which Verdi did not scorn to learn.

The same subject, it seems, tempted Bellini as possible for Naples: 'Magnificent, spectacular, historical,' he wrote to Florimo from Paris. 'We won't have Gustav killed (if that is what they want) but the situations are fine, really fine and new.'* But it was Bellini's own death which put an end to that project. Two other Italian composers however did set Scribe's plot, though in a different historical context. In 1841 Vincenzo Gabussi, brother of the singer Rita, produced *Clemenza di Valois* at the Teatro la Fenice, Venice, to a libretto by Gaetano Rossi; and in 1843 Mercadante and Cammarano produced *Il Reggente* at the Teatro Regio, Turin, with the action transported to Scotland in 1570 during the reign of the infant James VI. Gustave became the Regent Murray, Ankarstrom the Duke of Hamilton, and the conspirators adherents of the imprisoned Mary Stuart. Of the two operas the first would appear to be negligible;† but the second was composed by a Mercadante at the height of his fame, though his creative powers were just past their meridian. Ever since 1838 he had been a reformer eschewing all that was most facile in the Rossinian legacy. *Elena da Feltre*, *Il Giuramento*, and especially *Il Bravo* are noble, distinguished and even exciting. In *Il Reggente* that lack of spontaneity which is Mercadante's besetting weakness is more evident. In the self-conscious avoidance of regular phrase-lengths many of the melodies become laboured. Then too despite moments of great power and a greater sharpness of characterization than Auber could achieve, the drama itself has suffered a sea change at Cammarano's hands. All the irony has gone. An ingenious and highly individual plot has been deftly converted into another tale of star-crossed lovers hounded by misfortune and misunderstanding. Mercadante's Amelia was once betrothed to Murray; but she, believing him to have been killed in battle, married Hamilton in obedience to the wishes of a dying father (where have we heard that before?). In their love duet they are Gualtiero and Imogene, Orombello and Beatrice, the heroine remaining impeccably virtuous, even when forced to admit her love. After the final catastrophe Murray not only pardons the murderer but can assure him with a clear conscience that his wife is as innocent as 'an angel in heaven'. When Amelia is recognized in Act II by her own husband and the conspirators there is no sardonic laughter as in Auber, no changing of tragedy into comedy. As Scots, Howe, Kilcardy and their supporters may lack a sense of humour, but they are quicker on the uptake than Ribbing and de Horn, and together with Hamilton waste no time in launching a martial chorus of revenge. All the comic elements are concentrated into the 'mezzo-carattere' role of Oscar, a travesty part comparable to that of Stefano in Federico Ricci's *Luigi Rolla*. There is no inter-mingling of the two genres. *Il Reggente* remains a melodramma serio in the current romantic style. Though not amongst Mercadante's most clamorous successes it held the stage intermittently until 1870. If Verdi was prepared to attempt the same subject

---

* Letter to Florimo, 21.11.1834. Bellini, *Epistolario*, ed. L. Cambi (Verona, 1943), p. 478.
† See D'Amico, *loc. cit.*

it was because he was confident of being able to treat it in a very different way from Mercadante. None the less, as we shall see, he drew on Cammarano's scheme for two important details.

Anyway the San Carlo management made no difficulties, nor did Somma. He wrote to Verdi in October:

> I will undertake to put *Gustave III of Sweden* into verse in the version that you are sending me with all haste. Apart from the division into scenes . . . it would be useful for the sake of the musical rhythm if you could note down in the margin the form of the verses, the type of line and the number of lines for each verse, . . . I beg you to let me have plenty of instructions. . . . One point I should warn you about: I would like if you don't mind to remain anonymous for this work and put a pseudonym to it instead. In that way I can write with more freedom.*

There are large gaps in their correspondence, particularly on Verdi's side; but it seems clear that in working out the first act Somma was keeping scrupulously to the Auber–Scribe scheme with its parade of painters, sculptors, ministers of this and that, all of whom receive Gustave's exclusive attention, to the fury of the nobles Ribbing and de Horn; but it is drastically curtailed, with the hero's cavatina shifted further forward and devoted only to thoughts of his beloved. (Auber's Gustave had addressed the main part of his aria to his subjects; only in the central episode did he permit himself a brief apostrophe to Amélie.) Ankarstrom was to be called Carlo, the two conspirators Ivan and Mazeppa, the minister of justice Seni and the fortune-teller Locusta. 'The war minister seemed to me quite pointless, so I've taken him out.'†

Verdi's first reply to have survived dates from early November. As in the case of *Re Lear* he was having to teach Somma his business. 'In the quartet‡ "È scherzo od è follia" remember that we have a chorus of conspirators on the stage who will have to be given something to sing; write them a verse as well.' Then referring to the witch's prophecy:

> The whole of this passage isn't sufficiently theatrical; true, you say all that has to be said, but the words don't strike home, they aren't vivid so that neither Gustave's indifference, the witch's surprise nor the terror of the conspirators emerge sufficiently clearly. . . . Perhaps the metre and the rhythm are a hindrance. If so make the passage into a recitative. I prefer a good recitative to mediocre stanzas.
>
> I would beg you to change 'è desso – ad esso'. These rhymes, being so close, sound bad in music. Take out too 'God doesn't pay on the Sabbath'. Believe me, all proverbs, trite sayings, etc., etc., are dangerous in the theatre. . . . At the end of the act you mustn't forget Oscar and Ankarstrom; they are both on stage and they must each sing a verse.§

Throughout their correspondence Verdi's concern is with clarity, vividness and

---

* Letter from Somma, 13.10.1857. *Carteggi Verdiani, I*, pp. 219–20.
† Letter from Somma, 24.10.1857. *Carteggi Verdiani, I*, p. 220.
‡ Later the quintet.   § Letter to Somma, 6.11.1857. Pascolato, pp. 79–81.

verbal and rhythmic euphony. The trio between Gustavo, Amelia and Ankarstrom/Carlo had to be re-written in a different metre since the original lines, 'lacking as they do a regular cadence, are hard and impossible to set to music (that is to say theatrical music)'.* He even has to remind Somma of the classical rule that all recitative passages should end with an eleven-syllable verse. In Act III, 'The first dialogue between Ankarstrom and Amelia has become dull despite the very vivid situation. In the French there's the phrase 'Il faut mourir', which comes over and over again and is very theatrical. I know quite well that 'apparecchiati alla morte . . . ricommendati al Signore' mean the same thing, but on stage they haven't the same force as that simple 'bisogna morir'.† 'In the aria for the bass [as usual he means principal bass, i.e. baritone] the third line has a very ugly sound, "Che m'affidi e con tratto esecrabile." "Con tratto" in music, however much you change it around always becomes "contratto' . . . and makes an ugly effect. If you have no objection, I would leave out the allegro of this aria. . . . The piece becomes too long, the action slow, and besides all those verses are unnecessary.'‡ It would seem, then, that the famous 'Eri tu' was originally to have had a cabaletta.

Amelia's aria in Act II was written three times before it had the warmth and the 'disordine' that Verdi wanted. The finale of the act was too tragic; and so on. Somma who was clearly working from Scribe's original, had various emendations of his own to suggest. One of them, an additional scene for Amelia after the 'stretta dell' introduzione', was obviously designed to deal with the problem of giving the prima donna a cavatina when she first appears.

> I would move the scene to her private room. The public would then make her acquaintance before that scene in the witch's den. For example this room could have a french window at the back, and a terrace with a vast horizon. Amelia, seated on the terrace, plucks the strings of her harp and sings a romance which refers in general to the prayers of a heart in love. Then she puts aside the harp, rises, determines to conquer her passion and her tears; here there could be a brief, exciting recitative; she decides to have recourse to the witch; and here two verses. She rings a bell, a servant enters and is ordered to go to the witch's home, the servant goes away. With two more verses Amelia would close the scene, and with it, if I may say so, the act.§

In fact Mercadante had already included such a scene, though at a later point, for a revival of Il Reggente at Trieste in which Eugenia Tadolini sang Amelia. Whether or not Verdi knew this, he evidently scouted Somma's idea. At her first entry Amelia remains on stage not a moment longer than the drama requires.

Meanwhile a far greater difficulty was looming on the horizon. On 19 October Verdi had sent a synopsis of the action to Torelli for approval by the Censorship. Torelli meanwhile warned him that a change of locale would be necessary at the

---

* Letter to Somma, 20.11.1857. Pascolato, pp. 81–4.
† Letter to Somma, 26.11.1857. Pascolato, pp. 85–8.
‡ Letter to Somma, 30.12.1857. Pascolato, pp. 88–90.
§ Letter from Somma, 10.12.1857. Abbiati, II, pp. 460–1. This letter was unaccountably missed by Luzio, who transcribed Somma's letters to Verdi in Carteggi Verdiani, I, pp. 217–40, together with excerpts from Somma's original libretto.

very least and the poet had better be advised of this. Verdi wrote back: 'I've sent on your letter to the poet and I don't think there should be any difficulty in moving the scene elsewhere and changing the names, but now that the poet is in full swing it's better to finish the drama and then we can think about changing the plot. What a pity to have to give up the pomp of a court like that of Gustav III! Then too it will be difficult to find another monarch on the lines of that Gustavo. Poor poets, poor composers!'*

From the start Verdi had taken care to warn the librettist that changes might be necessary; to which Somma had replied, 'I understand that you're afraid that the Neapolitan Censorship may make difficulties over the subject. I hope that won't happen but in any case we can easily deal with it.'† Not until a month later was Somma fully apprised by a memorandum from the Censorship of what would be necessary. There were seven requirements: (1) The King must become a Duke; (2) The action must be transferred to a pre-Christian age when witchcraft and the summoning up of spirits were believed in; (3) Anywhere in the north would be possible except for Norway and Sweden; (4) The hero's love must be noble and tinged with remorse; (5) The conspirators must hate the duke for hereditary reasons, such as usurpation of property; (6) The feast should conform to the customs of the epoch chosen; (7) No firearms.‡ Somma wrote to Verdi in some perplexity. 'What century are we to choose in which to set the action? . . . To find one that justifies a superstitious belief in witchcraft as the Signor Censore wishes is beyond me; in fact in all ages you come across superstitions that have their basis in human nature.'§ Later:

> I think that if it's a matter of the North, and a Duke and of placing [the action] in a time when pagan barbarism fought with Christian civilization, it would not be a bad idea to go for Pomerania – a part of Prussia – and an independent duchy in the twelfth century when the Teutonic knights fought to banish the idolatry which then survived in many parts of the duchy, whose capital was Stettin. . . . The drama could be called *Il Duca Ermanno*, a name that I've found in the history of those parts, which seems to me better than Steffano, Wantislao, Boleslao, Ottone, Canuto, Stettone and others which you come across. . . . If the King is changed into a Duke, our Ankarstrom would become a Count, and Stockholm Stettin. In remaking the drama I would remove the painter and the sculptor, terrible anachronisms in that time and country, and for the first recitative I'd substitute words dealing with something different. . . .¶

Verdi approved the place but not the period: 'I really think that the twelfth century is too distant for our Gustavo. It's such a rough and brutal time especially in those countries that I find it sheer nonsense to have characters sculpted in the French manner like Gustavo and Oscar. We should need to find a princeling, a duke, some devil or other – all right, in the North – who's seen a bit of the world and had a whiff

---

* Letter to Torelli, 14.11.1857 wrongly dated 14.10 in. *Copialettere*, p. 563, and 23.10 in Abbiati, II, p. 452.
† Letter from Somma, 1.11.1857. *Carteggi Verdiani*, I, pp. 221–2.
‡ See *Carteggi Verdiani*, I, p. 270.
§ Letter from Somma, 17.11.1857. *Carteggi Verdiani*, I, p. 227.
¶ Letter from Somma, 19.11.1857. *Carteggi Verdiani*, I, pp. 227–8.

of Louis XIV's court. Once the drama's finished you can think about this at your leisure.'*

But it was not to be as easy as that. On 14 January Verdi arrived in Naples, attended a performance of *Batilda di Turenne* (his own *Vêpres Siciliennes*), and was recognized and applauded. He then hastened to submit the fully versified libretto to the Censorship. He was more than two months late in doing so; but he had complied with the various clauses in the Censor's memorandum. The opera's title was now *Una Vendetta in Domino*, the setting seventeenth-century Pomerania, the anonymity of the poet modified into an anagram, Tommaso Anoni. The Duke was sufficiently remorseful in his adulterous pursuit; the conspirators made suitable references to ancestral homes and murdered brothers. The Duke was to be killed with a dagger.

Any chance of its acceptance in this new form was ended by the news of Felice Orsini's attempt on the life of Napoleon III on 13 January. The three Censors failed to agree in their verdict and referred the matter to the Chief of Police, who ruled that the opera text would have to be re-written entirely. Verdi wrote to Somma:

> I'm in a sea of troubles! It's almost certain that the Censorship won't allow our libretto. Why? I don't know! How right I was to tell you that you would need to avoid any phrase or word that could be suspect. They began by taking exception to certain expressions, certain words, then from words they've gone on to scenes, and from scenes to the subject itself. They've suggested to me – out of the kindness of their hearts – the following modifications:
>
> (1) Change the protagonist into a lord, taking away any idea of sovereignty.
> (2) Change the wife into a sister.
> (3) Modify the witch's scene, transfering it to a time when this was credible.
> (4) No dancing.
> (5) The murder off stage.
> (6) Cut out the scene where the names are chosen by lot.
>
> And so on and so forth!!! As you can imagine these changes are quite unacceptable; therefore no opera; therefore the subscribers won't pay their advance; therefore the government will withhold its subsidy; therefore the management is suing everyone concerned and theatening me with a fine of 50,000 ducats!! . . . Write to me straight away and give me your opinion.†

There is a touch of asperity in Somma's reply. What kind of opinion did Verdi want? If a legal one the matter was simple: the Censorship had insisted on certain conditions which Verdi and he had fulfilled. If subsequently they decided to forbid the libretto Verdi had no liability whatsoever. But if the opera was not going to be given at all why did Verdi want his opinion? He could only assume that he was asking him in a roundabout way whether he would permit his libretto to be given with all the changes and distortions mentioned above; very well, provided that another author was credited with the words and that the title *Vendetta in domino* was altered. 'I shall be making a sacrifice, because I shall be chopping in pieces a work which harnessed to yours would have swept through Europe, but it can't be helped.'‡

---

* Letter to Somma, 26.11.1857. Pascolato, pp. 85–8.
† Letter to Somma, 7.2.1858. Pascolato, pp. 90–1.
‡ Letter from Somma, 13.4.1858. *Carteggi Verdiani*, I, pp. 234–5.

In fact the management had decided on a different solution, namely to call in an unnamed poet, probably Domenico Bolognese, to remake the libretto entirely into an *Adelia degli Adimari*.* The scene was fourteenth-century Florence. Gustavo became Armando degli Armandi, leader of the Guelph party; Ankarstrom Roberto degli Adimari, his henchman, husband of Adelia. Ulrica (so called since November 1857) remained unchanged. But Oscar was turned into one Arpini, a young soldier in Armando's service. The two conspirators became secret followers of the exiled Ghibelline faction. Even before receiving the revised libretto Verdi had already decided upon his course of action. He wrote to Torelli.

> Transfer the action four or five centuries back? What an anachronism! Remove the scene where the assassin is chosen by lot?! . . . But this is the most powerful and the most novel situation in the drama and you want me to give it up? I've already told you once that I cannot commit the monstrosities that were inflicted here on *Rigoletto*. They were done because I couldn't prevent them. Nor is it any use telling me that it was a success: if here and there one or two or three pieces were applauded that isn't enough to make a music drama. In matters of art I have my own ideas and convictions which are clear and precise and which I neither can nor should give up. †

Needless to say he refused to have anything to do with *Adelia degli Adimari*. The management sued him for breach of contract; he counterclaimed for damages.

As both sides prepared for battle, Verdi drew up a long memorandum for his lawyer, Arpino, enclosing a copy of the new libretto with pertinent and often entertaining comments in the margin. This document has been dealt with in varying degrees of detail by Luzio, Abbiati and Flora.‡ A few sallies are worth quoting. Where in the opening chorus Somma's conspirators opened with the word 'Die!', those of Adelia begin, 'He sleeps.' ('Observe the difference between these two verses and judge whether the notes placed under for example the word 'muori' could stand for the word 'dorme'. Some distinction should be understood between sleep and death.') Oscar's ballad is sung by a young soldier ('This ballad could sound pretty in the mouth of a page but it becomes ridiculous sung by a warrior'). At the end of the first scene Armando announces solemnly that he will pay a personal visit to the sybil in disguise and form a precise view of the rights and wrongs of her case. ('Even a blind man could see how much damage has been done to the action by changing the character of Gustavo in this way; everything becomes false and uninteresting and that quality of brilliance and chivalry, that aura of gaiety that pervaded the whole action and which made a fine contrast and was like a light in the darkness surrounding the tragic moments, has vanished. With the leader of a faction, and a Guelph one, at a time of blood and iron everything becomes gloomy, dark, heavy and dreary.') In several places the number of lines was altered. ('The management adds and removes lines at its pleasure as though to say, 'Signor Maestro, cobble your notes

---

* So Florimo in *Cenni sulla scuola musicale di Napoli*, IV (Naples, 1881), p. 597. As he was there at the time his surmise has been accepted by Luzio, Abbiati and Walker, reasonably enough.

† Letter to Torelli, 14.2.1858. *Copialettere*, p. 566.

‡ F. Flora, 'Il libretto del *Ballo in Maschera* massacrato dalla censura borbonica', in *I.S.V. Bollettino* No. 1, pp. 46–72.

onto this. . . . What, you've already written the piece? What does that matter? Lengthen, shorten, cut around, it will be all right! We want music, we want your name, and you as our accomplice in gulling the public who are paying! Drama, good sense? Bah! Rubbish! Rubbish!' That's how it is and that's the respect they have for the public, for art and for artists.') At the start of Act II the gallows were removed and Amelia referred merely to 'gloomy trees'. ('The scene has been rendered less gloomy and this modification, apart from depriving the scene-painter of the opportunity of creating an important work of art, has made it impossible for me to present a prelude or a kind of overture with dark and terrible colours, suitable to the place'.) When pressed by Armando to declare her love Adelia replies coyly, 'Of whom do you ask this?' (i.e., 'Need you ask?') ('God Almighty! Unless Amelia lets slip the words "T'amo" the whole piece is without life, without passion, without warmth, without the enthusiasm and sense of abandon that's necessary in scenes of this type. . . . The duet loses all raison d'être. . . . In this kind of situation impetus is everything; with the scene so modified this is completely lacking.') Though Adelia is present at her husband's meeting with the conspirators there is no question of drawing lots, though Roberto tells her rather obscurely that her 'innocent hand' is to be armed with a deadly weapon. The dance becomes a banquet where no one wears a mask. ('There are pieces which are imagined, created and designed in such a way that they cannot suffer the slightest alteration without becoming monstrosities. For instance in this duet the poignant, desolate expression of the melody sung by these two characters is so woven into the festive sounds of the dance that it cannot be detached from them. How then can it be possible to accept the radical alteration into a banquet whose musical expression must be a drinking-song?') Verdi wound up his case in a final blast of rhetoric.

> The *Vendetta in Domino* is composed of 884 lines; of these 297 have been changed; in Amelia's part many have been added, many removed. Moreover I would ask whether the management's drama has in common with mine:
> The title? – No
> The poet? – No
> The period? – No
> The place? – No
> The characters? – No
> The situations? – No!
> The drawing of lots? – No!
> The ball? – No!
> A composer who respects his art and himself could not and should not incur dishonour by accepting as material for music written on a completely different plane these bizarreries which violate the most obvious principles of dramatic art and degrade the conscience of an artist.*

The case was eventually settled out of court. All the management's charges were dropped on condition that Verdi returned in the autumn to produce another opera. The draft contract for this suggests that the opera would have been *Re Lear*, since it

---

* See *Carteggi Verdiani*, I, p. 269. The defence, set out in Arpino's more elegant language, can be found in *Copialettere*, pp. 568–70.

mentions Medori, Fioretti (sopranos), Coletti (baritone), Fraschini and Negrini (tenors), a contralto and a 'basso profondo worthy of the San Carlo';* but in the end this idea was shelved once more and replaced by a revival of *Simon Boccanegra* with Coletti, Fraschini and Fioretti. All three would have taken part in *Vendetta in Domino*, together with Penco as Amelia and Ganducci as the witch. The whole affair had cost Vincenzo Torelli his job as secretary to the management of the San Carlo, but the man whose surname was now bandied around as an acronym for 'Vittorio Emmanuele, Re D'Italia' lost neither money nor popularity. The performance of *Simon Boccanegra* was an outstanding success; and Verdi's visit for the occasion is recorded in the set of delightful caricatures by Melchiorre Delfico reprinted at the end of the first volume of Luzio's *Carteggi Verdiani*.

During his struggle with the Neapolitan censorship Verdi had already begun casting about elsewhere for a venue for *Vendetta in domino*. As early as February he had written to his friend the sculptor Vincenzo Luccardi in Rome, asking him for a copy of the brochure of *Gustavo III* performed by the Dondini company. This was a play by one Dal Testa that was running in Rome at the time.† When it arrived he wrote back explaining the reason.

> It's been decided not to give *Vendetta in domino*. Ricordi has written on behalf of the management and the Government to have it given in Milan; but to tell you the truth I would prefer to give it in Rome first so as to spend a pleasant time with you and our dear friend Vasselli; secondly so as to give this opera almost on Naples's doorstep and show them that the Roman Censorship has allowed this libretto. . . . In any case mention it to Jacovacci as though it were your own idea and see what he replies. Fraschini, who is in as good form as he was ten years ago and actually sings better than he did then, would come to sing the main part.‡

Jacovacci, impresario of the Teatro Apollo, with memories of *Trovatore*, rose at once to the bait. However, he warned Verdi that the libretto would not go entirely unscathed. Verdi replied: 'In Rome they allow *Gustavo III* as a spoken play but won't allow a libretto on the same subject. Very strange! I respect the wishes of your superiors and so have nothing to say. But if I was unwilling to give this opera in Naples because they changed the libretto I can't give it in Rome if they want to change it there as well,'§ and with this he asked for the return of the libretto. But Jacovacci did not give up. He met Verdi at Civitavecchia on his return home; and though the composer was far from reassured¶ he was willing to leave the door open. Meanwhile Somma had already got wind of the new plan and hastened to offer his services for the necessary corrections. Verdi sent him a copy of the text with the Roman censor's emendations (the hero was now a Count of Gothenberg) and asked him if he could write new, inoffensive lines to replace those that had been altered. This time it was Somma who dug in his heels.

---

* *I.S.V. Bollettino*, No. 1, pp. 40–3.
† Not, as many authorities assert, Scribe's libretto performed without the music!
‡ Letter to Luccardi, 27.2.1858. *Copialettere*, pp. 570–2.
§ Letter to Jacovacci, April 1858, quoted without date. Abbiati, II, p. 498.
¶ See letter to De Sanctis, 29.4.1858. *Carteggi Verdiani*, I, pp. 41–2.

How could I manage to do that? So long as every variant has a reason . . . and it's a matter of satisfying the Censorship we can come to some sort of terms; but when in place of a variation there is merely caprice, stupidity, ignorance, and an earnest wish to spoil everything, to tell the truth, I despair of succeeding. . . . But after all you're the master and you can do what you like with the poetry, and if you find that this *Count of Gothenberg* can stand, very well; let it be so as long as my name is left out of it.*

Less concerned than Verdi to make the Neapolitans look foolish, Somma could not understand the composer's refusal to give the opera in Milan where the text might have emerged unscathed. However, largely through the good offices of the lawyer Vasselli, Donizetti's brother-in-law, the Roman Censors proved more pliant than at first seemed likely. 'They will permit the subject and the situations, etc., etc., but would like the scene removed from Europe. What would you say to North America at the time of the English domination? If not America, somewhere else; the Caucasus perhaps?'† Somma, it would appear, opted for the first, making his hero Riccardo Duke of Surrey, governor of Boston, but refusing to rewrite more than was necessary to alter the names. Later Verdi wrote back:

Arm yourself with courage and patience – above all patience! As you will see from the enclosed letter from Vasselli, the Censorship has sent a list of all the lines and the expressions it does not want. If on reading this letter you feel your blood-pressure rising put it down and take it up again after having dined and slept well. Consider that in the present circumstances our best course of action is to give this opera in Rome. The lines and expressions struck out by the censorship are many but they could have been still more. . . . As for the gallows in the second act, don't give them a thought; I'll manage to get them allowed somehow. . . .‡

This time Somma's resistance was vanquished; he would even accept the Censorship's refusal to allow the title of Duke. But in that case, he wrote, Riccardo must be at least a Count; 'so let us call him if you have no objections, Riccardo Conte di Varvich (Warwick)'; and so he remained.§ Verdi himself decided that in its new guise the libretto had lost little and even gained something from the change of scene.¶ It remained merely to keep Somma up to the mark in urgency of dramatic expression. 'In the third act you have changed "Sangue vuolsi" into "Rea ti festi" which is all right; but later on the other changes enervate the scene; "Tu m'oltraggi. . . . Menti. . . . Più non t'odo. . . . Spunta l'alba" – these words admit a certain element of logic and reflection in the characters which in this situation is out of place. . . .' Eventually it was finished to his satisfaction if not to that of Somma, who again refused to allow his name to appear on the libretto.

Not so the casting. As an independent impresario, Jacovacci did not dispose of the resources of the Royal theatre of Naples, and in any case it was short notice for the

* Letter from Somma, 26.5.1858. *Carteggi Verdiani*, I, pp. 236–8.
† Letter to Somma, 8.7.1858. Pascolato, p. 92.
‡ Letter to Somma, 6.8.1858. Pascolato, pp. 93–4.
§ Letter from Somma, 11.8.1858. *Carteggi Verdiani*, I, pp. 238–9.
¶ Letter to Somma, 11.9.1858. Pascolato, pp. 94–7.

assembly of a company which would do justice to an opera containing three important female roles. Verdi had taken as his fixed point Gaetano Fraschini, who had guaranteed to make himself available. His hopes of enlisting Coletti as well were to be frustrated; but in his place Leone Giraldoni, the original Simon Boccanegra, acquitted himself well enough as Renato (Ankarstrom). The women were the real problem. For Amelia Verdi was committed to Mme Julienne-Dejean, the prima donna assoluta of the season. She was a distinguished singer who in her time had graced the leading opera stages of Europe but was now in decline.* Vigna meantime sent disquieting reports of a recent performance at Trieste, in which it would seem that she had lost her voice, 'which was the one quality she possessed'.† Though this turned out to be an exaggeration, she made no more than an efficient Amelia, after having caused the composer endless trouble in rehearsal.‡ For the part of the witch Verdi wanted Ganducci, who would have sung it in Naples; but Jacovacci had already engaged Zelinda Sbriscia, much to the composer's annoyance. Oscar presented the greatest difficulty of all. Verdi had set his heart on Fioretti, the petite smiling doll of Delfico's cartoons; but she was unavailable and it was not easy to find a replacement. Pamela Scotti, Jacovacci's choice, justified all the composer's worst forebodings ('a stuffed dummy, made of wax . . . incapable of performing a brilliant role').§

Despite these deficiencies, the performance was as great a success with the public as Verdi could count upon since the days of *Il Trovatore*. The press was variable. Verdi was again accused of succumbing to ultramontane influences. Some critics deplored the disappearance of the solo cabaletta. Others attacked the libretto as a 'profanation in verse'.¶ Yet of the operas written between *La Traviata* and *Aida*, *Un Ballo in maschera* has most consistently held the stage even when the reaction against Verdi was at its height. The reason is simple: in form and musical scope and the balance of its ideas it comes nearer to perfection than any of them, *Don Carlos* not excluded – and this in the teeth of a preposterous story transferred to an inappropriate setting and a libretto which is often held up as a prime example of literary incompetence. True, Somma has not lacked defenders. F. Flora talks about his impressionistic technique‖ – a kind way of describing a jumble of incompatible metaphors. Amelia 'glows with pallor'. 'How everything shines with gloom!' say the women and children in Ulrica's cave. 'What a sweet shudder bedews my kindled breast,' says Riccardo to Amelia. Fire and water, it seems, have abrogated their usual properties. Renato hears not footsteps, but the *print* of cruel footsteps. Later he is accused of wandering through the fields 'as beneath a lunar ray of honey'. Yet, as we have seen, this libretto

---

* For an account of the first and subsequent casts of *Un Ballo in maschera*, see Eugenio Gara, 'Il Cammino dell'opera in un secolo d'interpretazioni', in *I.S.V. Bollettino*, No. 1, pp. 112–33; No. 2, pp. 704–31; No. 3, pp. 1155–64.

† Letter from Vigna, 7.10.1858. *Copialettere*, p. 202.

‡ See the story told by G. Monaldi in *Verdi aneddotico* (L'Aquila, 1926), pp. 75–6, and quoted in *I.S.V. Bollettino*, No. 1, p. 119. Mme Julienne-Dejean: 'Very well, if you think I don't know my part, why don't you go over it with me?' Verdi: 'I am not a coach. When an artist sets out to present herself in a theatre like the Apollo she should be note-perfect and not need coaching.' It needed all Giuseppina Strepponi's tact to restore peace.

§ Letter to Jacovacci, 29.12.1858. *I.S.V. Bollettino*, No. 1, p. 37.

¶ Gara, in *I.S.V. Bollettino*, No. 1, p. 123.

‖ *I.S.V. Bollettino*, No. 1, p. 60.

grew up under Verdi's direction. Is it therefore evidence of that poor literary judgement of which he has often been accused? Not at all. Verdi is writing music drama on terms which are strictly his own. What mattered to him above all was the power of the individual word to shape a situation, to act as a rocket firing the music across the footlights. He knew well enough that in any cantabile, as distinct from a declamato, a line of verse as such tends to become submerged, with only the important words standing out as landmarks. It was a matter of secondary importance that the sentences should make literal sense. Unfortunately for Somma, libretti in the 1850s were still printed in full as an aid to the spectator and their ineptitude as literature could become fair game for a malicious journalist. The growing fashion for the pseudonym is thus understandable. Italian opera had travelled a long way since the days when a melodramma could be read as a poem in its own right.

The unhistorical setting is another common target. Yet Verdi's satisfaction with it (he never wanted to change it back) can be understood. Seventeenth-century Boston was *terre inconnue*. It was never touched upon by James Fennimore Cooper. But contemporary Restoration England was well known from Walter Scott's *Peveril of the Peak* and the Memoirs of the Count de Grammont which he edited; and in fact the court of Charles II possessed all those attributes of gaiety and sophistication by which the composer set such store. What more natural than to imagine a colonial governor who brought this atmosphere with him across the Atlantic? Verdi could hardly be blamed for not knowing the ways of a community that burned the Salem witches.

Even so Scribe's plot may seem a strange choice for the composer of *Rigoletto* and *La Traviata*; but it offered him two advantages: to re-interpret an old plot by means of new musical techniques and to blend the tragic and the comic 'in Shakespeare's manner'* and far more subtly than he had been able to do in *Rigoletto*, where laughter and tears form a variegated background against which the protagonist stands out in high relief. Here the comic and the tragic are elements in an interplay of light and darkness which forms the governing principle of the drama. Not that the comic can always be identified with the light and the tragic with the dark. The unmasking of Amelia in Act II is black comedy, the final assassination tragedy at high noon. The human personalities are themselves incarnations of the two conflicting forces. If Riccardo is not a mere symbol of elemental heroic love like Manrico, neither is he a particularized, fully rounded individual like Stiffelio or Simon Boccanegra; rather he is a paradigm of generous, heedless humanity dancing on the brink of a volcano. That Gaetano Fraschini after twenty years as a 'tenore di forza' could manage the light-hearted elegance of this role to perfection is a great tribute to his technique.

Together with Riccardo on the side of brilliance is the page, Oscar, almost an extension of the hero's personality into the soprano register. The elements of darkness are Ulrica, the contralto, the conspirators Samuel and Tom, whom Verdi unlike Auber or Mercadante made into two basses, and, surprisingly, Amelia. Verdi's choice for this role had been Rosina Penco, the *lirico spinto* who had created Leonora of *Il Trovatore*; but the abundance of middle and lower notes, the prevalence of the minor mode combined with the complete absence of fioritura, have made it the property of the heavy dramatic soprano. Brünnhildes are rarely seen in the fort of Castellor; but they will often be found gathering herbs outside Boston, Massachusetts.

---

* Letter to Cammarano, 24.3.1849. Abbiati, II, pp. 4–7.

There remains Renato, Riccardo's Creole secretary.* Like many a Verdian baritone he is ambivalent. He begins on the side of light, but his constant awareness of the lurking menace casts a shadow over his music from the start. The famous aria 'Eri tu', where he crosses over into darkness and looks back nostalgically towards the light, is the pivot of the music-drama. Not only that. Once he has joined them the forces of darkness for the first time become really formidable. Ulrica, like all her type, is a clever fraud; Samuel and Tom are comically inefficient. Amelia has up to that point merely been haunted by guilt-ridden fantasies. Now her plight is only too real. In sum Verdi has contrived through a variety of nuances unimaginable to Auber or Mercadante to turn an ingenious but mechanical plot into a gripping parable of the human condition.

The French influence in *Un Ballo in maschera* was indirectly acknowledged, as we have seen, by Verdi himself. It appears overtly in the court scenes and in the saucy music of Oscar the page. Here it seems that Verdi has for the first time absorbed the world of Offenbach and Delibes without ever allowing a note of bathos to creep in. This fact alone gives the opera a far wider expressive scope than that of Mercadante. In Auber the contrast of styles is immanent, as in most French grand operas, which draw their ingredients from far and wide, but never fully developed. His Oscar, a light soprano, buoyant enough in the last act, lapses into solemnity in his first aria. Mercadante's Oscar is a typically Italian mezzo-soprano musico. In giving a travesti role to a soprano leggiero Verdi was following the French tradition. But his model seems to have been not Auber's Oscar but rather Meyerbeer's Urbain in *Les Huguenots* (a role which, inevitably, was transposed down in Italian performances.†)

Lastly *Un Ballo in maschera* marks a further stage in the evolution of the composer's orchestral style. Doubtless the experience of working with Mariani in Rimini had helped in this. For the first time in the prelude we notice the use of violin harmonics. Remarkable too is the way in which thematic reminiscences are developed and combined as a way of uniting the various scenic elements. It is a long way from Wagner; but one can see why the conservative critics were alarmed. Beneath its polished surface *Un Ballo in maschera* harbours many a surprise.

Once again for the analysis we have the aid of an Italian production book, which by good fortune happens to be the one compiled by the stage-director, Giuseppe Cencetti, for the première in Rome.

PRELUDE

Although apparently self-contained, this follows the example of *Il Trovatore* in that it is based on material from the opening scene, so that when the curtain rises those

---

* What Verdi understood by Creole must remain a mystery. He can hardly have meant it in the original sense of 'born in America of European settlers' since in the last act we hear that Renato will see England *again*. For the same reason Creole in the sense of half-caste is unlikely, though not impossible, since cases have been known in seventeenth- and eighteenth-century England in which illegitimate, half-caste children have been adopted and brought up in 'good' society. The contemporary production book which ought to explain the matter only makes it more complicated. Here the chorus extras include 'blacks, whites and mulattos' as well as 'Creoles'. A Creole then should be recognizable at sight without being black, white or mulatto. To complete the confusion we are told that at the start of Act III Renato must be dressed in the garb of a Scottish knight (*Disp. scen.*, p. 4)! Was the writer thinking of *Il Reggente*?

† Meyerbeer himself added an aria for Marietta Alboni with which to replace the original soprano cavatina.

on stage are continuing a discourse of which we already have the gist. After six tantalizing bars of inchoate figuration (but woe betide the conductor who fails to establish definition behind the apparent vagueness!) strings and clarinets give out the theme of the opening chorus 'Posa in pace, a' bei sogni ristori'; a soothing melody which, as in Auber, will take in the occasional chromatic caress. The four-note figure (*x*) already heard in the preceding bars is an important element in the design.

Immediately afterwards follows the motif associated with the malevolence of Sam and Tom – an evil which propagates itself in a fugato. It had been anticipated in the septet from *Stiffelio*, where neither its dramatic nor contrapuntal possibilities were exploited:

After reaching the complexity of four real parts it gives way to the melody of Riccardo's cavatina 'La rivedrà nell'estasi', which will recur throughout the opera as a symbol of his love for Amelia. Pizzicato strings mark the weak beats, alternate chords serving to launch the rhythmic figure (*x*), now etherealized as violin harmonics. Clearly Verdi has come a long way from the routine procedures of his youth (Ex. 245).

In the second period violins on the G string take over the melody, while flute, clarinet and oboe follow in pseudo-canon and the piccolo gives out the figure (*x*) whose origin in the cadential phrase of Ex. 243 should now be clear. Ex. 244 returns

245

moving swiftly to a brutal climax. There is a pause; and then three bars of strings (first violins again on the G string) reassure us with a gentle cadence and the prelude dies away on reminiscences of Ex. 245, having prepared us through the detailed refinement of its scoring no less than through its themes for the remarkable chiaroscuro that distinguishes this opera from its fellows.

ACT I

Scene 1: A hall in the Governor's house. At the back the doors leading to his rooms. It is morning. Deputies; gentlemen, populace, officers; in the foreground Samuel, Tom and their adherents, all waiting on Riccardo.

A chorus of officers and gentlemen sing Ex. 243 to the same instrumentation as in the prelude, and sotto voce; for they have no wish to wake their beloved governor before he has slept his fill. Samuel, Tom and their supporters follow with Ex. 244, 'E sta l'odio che prepara il fio', this time in unison. They are quiet for a different reason – they wish to keep their subversive thoughts to themselves.*

The situation has something in common with the first scene of *Les Vêpres Siciliennes* and it poses the same problem: how do the two contrasted elements preserve their identity at the point where the choral groups join forces? In the earlier work Verdi had followed the conventions of the time and allowed the voice of protest to become submerged. Here he devises a brilliant solution of his own. While the group of 'aderenti', all basses, join the bass line of the 'officers and gentlemen' and proceed by smooth crotchets to the reprise of Ex. 245, Samuel and Tom, doubled by violas and bassoons, keep up an intermittent mutter of semiquavers with violin harmonics filling in the gaps and so maintaining the continuity of rhythm. Suavity prevails but with an undercurrent of unrest which is wonderfully effective.

* *Huge doors to left and right. Backstage right a table covered with a rich cloth, with writing materials and a chair with ornaments near by. Guards stationed by the door backstage: officers ranged diagonally behind the table. (Disp. scen., p. 7.)*

Announced by Oscar Riccardo makes a suitably ceremonious entrance and greets the assembled company (one cannot speak of courtiers, though the feeling of a royal levée inevitably survives from the original scenario). Strings give out the first of two conversational themes of the kind which develop as a background for the dialogue.

246

The light-hearted insouciance, the tripping acciaccature all suggest the page rather than the governor; but then Oscar, as we have noted, is to some extent a projection of Riccardo himself, an embodiment of all that is most irresponsible in his character. Everything about Riccardo's first recitative suggests that he is playing at government rather than governing. 'Power', he declares, as he gathers the various petitions 'is nothing if it cannot dry the tears of its subjects,' and as so often in Verdi the conception of power leads into E major. But at once Ex. 246 resumes with added touches of flute and piccolo as Oscar hands Riccardo the list of guests for the masked ball. As he sees the name of Amelia, Renato's wife, his mood becomes one of tender longing;* and – if the producer understands his business – he comes to the footlights to deliver a short cavatina-in-parenthesis 'La rivedrà nell'estasi' to the melody Ex. 245, which combines the lyricism of a cantabile with the motion and character of a cabaletta (note the pulsating accompaniment and restless bass). Its form is the Bellinian *a1*, *a2*, *b*, *a2*, but it has a conciseness totally foreign to the age of Bellini and Donizetti, and for a good reason. Any theme which must function as a motif or reminiscence must make its point in as few bars as possible. In Ex. 245 everything is in the initial phrase: the wide interval, like outstretched arms; the caressing semitones, the faint cloud of the minor key in the third bar. It is a thumbnail sketch of a man in love, as vivid as a Wagnerian leitmotif. A substantial coda uses the traditional device whereby the bystanders comment on the singer's attitude, expression, or character. Here it serves to keep alive the equivocal situation; for once again the two choral groups emerge with contrasted sentiments – officers and gentlemen with a legato top line, Samuel, Tom and their followers with a staccato bass. Towards the end reminiscences of Ex. 244 become palpable; but the final cadence is undisturbed. Elaborate when described, it is all managed with a Mozartian limpidity and grace.

Riccardo dismisses his visitors, who leave not to the usual dispersal music set out in a long decrescendo but to an ingenious combination of Ex. 244 and 245, the first vestigially contrapuntal on lower strings, the second given out in successive woodwind phrases. Oscar, the last to leave, meets Renato who is entering. By now

---

* *Seeing Amelia's name the Count starts with joy – a movement maliciously observed by Oscar. While Riccardo sings his cavatina at the footlights, Oscar should be seen exchanging compliments with the bystanders. (Disp. scen., p. 8.)*

Ex. 244 is sounding still more warmly on first violins while scraps of Ex. 245 persist on violas and bassoons. Renato interrupts the governor's thoughts with a 'Conte!' At once Ex. 245 shuts off abruptly, as though Riccardo fears that his thoughts can be read.

The dialogue which follows diverges from Scribe's text in an important respect. The original Ankarstrom suspects the truth about Riccardo's preoccupation. Renato is totally innocent of it; and the slight absurdity of their conversation illustrates Riccardo's compulsion to play with fire. He admits a secret sorrow; reacts with terror when Renato claims to know its cause; and reassured by Renato's reference to a conspiracy he then says, 'You know of nothing else?' As to the danger from his enemies, Riccardo is not prepared to give it a thought. His protection, he says, lies in the love of his subjects. Two details call for notice; first the sinuous theme in which Renato paints the forces which lie in wait for the governor:

247

This will recur again in a more sinister context. Riccardo announces his defiance in a proud arpeggio, finishing with a declamation punctuated by brass chords ('Del popolo mio − l'amor mi guardi − e mi protegga Iddio') establishing a D flat major which admits of no contradiction. Yet Renato proceeds respectfully to contradict it. The low F on bassoons and lower strings which replaces the expected tonic chord has the quality of a 'by your leave!' Without more ado Renato begins his cavatina ('Alla vita che t'arride') in which he exhorts Riccardo not to underrate his enemies.

248

Significant is the use of the horn in the second part of the phrase. A brass instrument constantly used as a constituent of the woodwind group, it has the ambivalence of Renato himself. Here its velvet tone underlines his benevolent concern for his master's safety. In Act III it will be associated with the same singer to convey a terrifying menace. The form of the movement combines elements of both French ternary and the traditional Italian binary, in that it has both a contrasted central episode in a different key and mood but a shortened reprise. More extended than Riccardo's 'La rivedrà nell'estasi' (it even includes a cadenza rising to high G) it too combines the character of cantabile and cabaletta within the polonaise-like accompaniment in the outer sections. In both movements Verdi has used the distilled essence of the traditional forms rather than the forms themselves and always with specific reference to the dramatic context. Thus the central section in G minor unmistakably warns of the conspiracy as does the descending bass line in the coda; and by transplanting the last line of the first verse 'Te perduto, ove'è la patria col suo splendido avvenir' as a refrain to end the second Verdi reinforces the noble, pleading character of the main idea.

A new action theme, with officiously martial triplets, introduced a judge who has brought Riccardo various dispatches to sign; among them is one calling for the banishment of one Ulrica 'of unclean negroid race', a fortune-teller who is said to be in league with the devil; Riccardo is intrigued and wishes to know more. The judge is all for severity ('Dovuto è a lei l'esilio; né muta il voto mio') and here the orchestral theme, having evolved with great flexibility, yields an impressive tutti in D flat, contradicted now by Oscar as Renato had contradicted Riccardo, though more pertly, by an assertion of B flat ('Difenderla vogl' io').*

His ballata 'Volta la terrea' is in *couplet* form like its equivalent in Auber (Mercadante employs a more elaborate strophic design in three contrasted sections). Yet there is more Gallic wit and grace in a bar of this than in the whole of Auber's pedestrian 'Aux cieux elle sait lire', to which Verdi may have been indebted only for the implied tonic pedal of the first eight bars – a device used by Auber with a persistence worthy of Sullivan. Note the teasing protraction of 'mesto, felice del loro amor', the pause and the explosion of the refrain 'Ah è con Lucifero d'accordo ognor' like a peal of merry laughter (Ex. 249).

In a lesser composer that three-bar extension before the pause might well have upset the formal balance of the piece. But, like so much in *Un Ballo in maschera*, the ballata has an almost classical finish to it, the pause occurring exactly at the mid-point. As in Mozart the wedding of form and dramatic expression is indissoluble.

Riccardo summons the officers and gentlemen, who return presumably with their womenfolk, since the chorus now includes a female component. He announces that they will all pay a visit to Ulrica's cave, but in disguise – a ploy, one need hardly say, far more suited to an eighteenth-century European monarch than to a colonial governor. Renato protests, and a death-figure stirs in the strings. Riccardo's reply 'Sì, vo'gustar la scena' shows musically how much he has learnt from Oscar. Renato again dissuades, while Samuel, Tom and their supporters chuckle at his nervousness. But Riccardo is determined to have some fun at the expense of the credulous. Pleasure is to be the order of the day; and with this sentiment he begins the stretta dell'introduzione 'Ogni cura si doni al diletto' (Ex. 250a), with Renato and Oscar reacting according to character (b and c). If the displaced accent is typically Verdian the anapaestic rhythm is a commonplace of French opera to which Italian composers often had recourse when setting a French text; compare 'Venez, amis, retirons-nous' from Rossini's *Le Comte Ory* and 'Tous les trois réunis' from Donizetti's *La Fille du*

---

* At the words 'Difenderla vogl' io' Oscar who has come forward moves centre and his place is taken by the judge. Naturally all advance to the footlights. (Disp. scen., p. 9.)

249

régiment, not to mention the choral coda to Oscar's couplets in Auber's *Gustave*. Its employment in an Italian opera is unexpected.

250a

Still more French is the second and in fact principal theme of the stretta with its Offenbachian high-kick. Second and third phrases are bridged by an extra bar – in fact a written-out pause – which allows the strings a brief guffaw. Note how the Gallic rhythm results in a typical instance of Gallic alternative scansion ('Nell'antro dèll' òràcolo, nell' àntro dell' oràcolo') more suitable to a language with a weak tonic accent than to Italian. No matter: the Italian metrical shackles have been triumphantly shattered. No one would guess from the music that the text was set out in orthodox settenari.

251

At three o'clock then they will all meet outside the witch's cave. At first there is more disapproval from Renato, while Samuel and Tom confer in whispers; but eventually the joyous vigour of Ex. 251 sweeps all before it in a great vocal unison backed by full orchestra.

Like *Il Trovatore*, *Un Ballo in maschera* has its conservative aspects, not least the use – for the last time, as it happens – of the old fashioned 'introduzione' with associated cavatinas. There is even an approximate model for this one in Mercadante's *Il Giuramento* of 1838. Once again we are reminded that *Un Ballo in maschera* is essentially a classical opera. The components of the foregoing scene – chorus, solo movement, developing orchestral theme – though short, are laid out with a subtly varied symmetry which recalls the first scene of *La Battaglia di Legnano*. The centrepiece, and also the nearest to a point of repose, is Renato's 'Se la vita che t'arride' – and logically so; since Renato is the pivot on whom the drama turns.

> *Scene 2: The witch's dwelling. On the left a hearth; the fire is lit, and the magic cauldron is steaming over a tripod. On the same side is the opening of a dark recess. On the right is a twisting stairway which loses itself under the vault; at the extremity of the stairway to the fore there is a small secret door. At the back is the main doorway with a large window at the side. In the centre is a rough table; the roof and the walls are hung with instruments and furnishings appropriate to the place.*

As in Auber, Ulrica's invocation 'Re dell' abisso affrettati' is in C minor; but, as so often in middle and late Verdi, the key is not established in any obvious way. Three loud diminished sevenths on full orchestra suggesting Beethoven's Coriolan at his fiercest set the scene; then with the same harmony implied (C′ in the cellos, F sharp in the clarinets) violins and violas crawl between C′ and E′ flat.* A chord of G major fortissimo at once gives us the C minor orientation; but twenty more bars will pass before we actually hear the common chord of C minor. The intervening passage wanders towards related keys, notably F minor, with many a sinister tremolando, a rapping-out of brass and the death figure in two of its guises. Nowhere however does Verdi make use of those chromatic scales which occur throughout this scene in both Auber and Mercadante, with somewhat mechanical effect. Women and children murmur in awe ('Zitti, l'incanto non dessi turbar') as Ulrica performs some mysterious ceremony.† The melody of her invocation (Ex. 252) is cast in a distinctive rhythm encountered only once before, in Arrigo's 'La pia materna mano' from *La Battaglia di Legnano*:

252

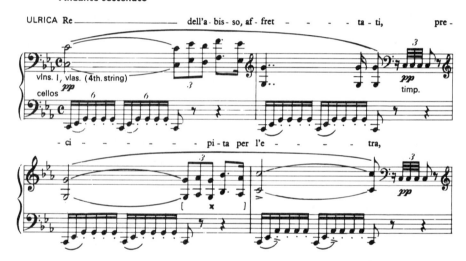

The anticipation of A flat major harmony in the third bar is perfectly grammatical; but it gives the melody a startlingly modal feeling. For the rest it evolves in regular phrases (as befits an incantation), but in a manner observed from the recent operas seems to develop a longer reach as it proceeds. The cadential phrase 'tre volte a me parlò' interposes a spine-chilling D flat before sinking to rest in C minor.

* Winton Dean draws attention to the similarity of this passage to the 'prison' prelude in Act II of Donizetti's *Roberto Devereux* (see W. Dean, 'Some Echoes of Donizetti in Verdi's Operas', in *Atti del III° Congresso dell' I.S.V.*, pp. 122–42). Both composers are obviously drawing on the standard horror vocabulary of their time.

† The Italian production book provides Ulrica with two assistants – a small boy of about twelve and a woman of the people. During the prelude it enjoins the following pantomime: *With her magic wand Ulrica traces a line from the head of the child to the cauldron, then moves in a circle round it, takes a jar and empties its contents into the said cauldron. The chorus, standing around in fearful trepidation and intent on the magical proceedings, sing their first lines while Ulrica advances to the front of stage and after describing a circle on the ground pronounces the invocation: 'Re dell'abisso', etc. When it is finished she returns to the cauldron and dips her wand in it.* (*Disp. scen.*, p. 11.) Once again the book makes clear that we are dealing with a 'deep' stage and that the scene-change has been a 'cambiamento a vista'.

The gloom is suddenly dissipated by a jaunty triplet theme on oboe, piccolo and clarinets. This is Riccardo, arrived before his time in his fisherman's disguise; but when he asks for a consultation the women and children thrust him back ('Villano, indietro!'). The scene grows darker still and Ulrica begins the second part of her aria 'E lui; e lui, che palpiti'), which is essentially a major-key variation of her first with a longer and more powerful conclusion, the increased movement giving it the effect of a cabaletta to the previous cantabile. This time the melody is shared between her and a group of woodwind and trumpets spanning a range of three octaves. On each beat, trombones, cimbasso and timpani thud while strings and horns shudder, as the sorceress feels herself possessed by the spirit of Lucifer. It is all very far from the traditional complement to a movement in the minor key, since the tonality is continually clouded by harmonic inflections derived from the instrumental prelude – notably the malignant F sharp. At the words 'è nulla; più nulla ascondersi al guardo mio potrà', flutes, clarinets, bassoons and cellos unite with the voice over three octaves while trumpets rap an inexorable ♩♪ that persists until the final cadence. From here it is a short step to that doubling of bass and melody with intervening harmonies that we associate with Puccini. Note too the harmonic 'diabolus in musica' and the coiling menace of the line suggestive of some tremendous power rising from the depths (Ex. 253).

The chorus applaud. Ulrica strikes the ground and vanishes. A moment later her voice can be heard, calling for silence, the second time on a low G.*

Light breaks in once more with the appearance of the sailor Silvano. He has endured three years' hardship in the service of Riccardo and is not complaining; but he would like to know if the future holds any reward. Key, rhythm, phrase-length of 'Su, fatemi largo' suggest a familiarity with Auber's 'Vieille sybille qu'on dit habile' in which Gustave in his fisherman's disguise asks to have his fortune told.

If this is plagiary it is the Mozartian kind that puts other people's ideas to better use. Ex. 254a is one of those march-like tunes to which Auber continually reverts, no matter the context. It adds nothing to the musical picture of Gustave. Ex. 254b

253

* The production book explains this somewhat differently: *Behind the row of extras the stage mechanic should be preparing a trapdoor which will make Ulrica vanish; and as she retreats saying the words* 'silenzio, silenzio' *the crowd should assist her movement until she stands upon the trapdoor, and disappears from view. Terror makes everyone draw back leaving the way clear to the door backstage. (Disp. scen., pp. 11–12.)*

254a

Vieil – le sy – bil – le qu'on dit ha – bi – le, par Bel – zé –
– buth apprends moi mon dest – in

Auber : GUSTAVE III

254b

Allegro brillante

Su, fa – te-mi lar-go, saper vo'il mio fa-to. Son ser-vo del Con-te, son suo ma – ri – na – ro:

instantly brings alive the breezy, likable character of Silvano. Nor does it remain like Auber's theme as a mere paragraph to be repeated with choral intervention. Once more the elegant, classicizing tendency of *Un Ballo in maschera* is manifested in a *scène à faire* conducted on much the same formal lines as the quartet 'Non ti fidar, o misera' from *Don Giovanni* with Ex. 254b as its starting point. As in Mozart's work the structural motif is formed from the cadential phrase of the opening melody. But instead of being repeated identically at each recurrence like Mozart's 'Ti vuol tradir ancor' Verdi's phrase is varied each time while remaining recognizably the same idea:

255a

255b

255c

Silvano leads off with a solo of fourteen bars ('Su, fatemi largo', A major), ending in Ex. 255a. The orchestra follows up with what may be called a prophecy figure (*x*). Ulrica reappears, reads his hand and foretells wealth and promotion. Riccardo, who has watched the scene with admiration, slips into Silvano's pocket an officer's commission. By now the music has moved to E major; and the expository section close with Silvano's Ex. 255b. He searches in his pocket for a coin to pay Ulrica, and finds the commission, which he reads aloud 'ecstatically' (triplet movement leading through E major, to C major); the chorus burst out in praise ('Evviva la nostra Sibilla immortale!'). Strings lead into B minor with a new sombre idea in measured minims and crotchets as a servant of Amelia enters through the secret door and announces a visit by his mistress. Ulrica orders the bystanders out; only Riccardo who has recognized the servant remains concealed by the darkness of the recess. Here the music returns through A minor to A major; and Ulrica's final orders are given to Ex. 255c, which is in turn echoed by the chorus. Throughout the scene Riccardo's presence is indicated from time to time with an impudent ($\sqrt{}$) on violins, now on violas and once most effectively on a combination of oboe and piccolo.

Amelia's entrance is marked by an orchestral theme which at once establishes her on the dark side of the drama:

256

The non-sequitur (A major–E minor), since it occurs twice in the scene, clearly has a dramatic intention. Amelia is so taken up with her own inner turmoil that she is unable to take in what is happening around her. Between developments of Ex. 256, her agitation is vented in anguished vocal phrases which span a range of two octaves from b' to b'''. All the more effective is the moment of calm in which Ulrica first hints at the remedy for Amelia's unfortunate passion ('L'oblio v'è dato. Arcane stille conosco d'una magica erba'). Horn and bassoons move from a minor triad to a hollow fifth which has all the dark mystery of Wagner's Tarnhelm. Amelia's shudder can be sensed in the fragmentary resumption of Ex. 256. Ulrica's instructions take the form of a short solo ('Dalla città all'occaso') couched in the insinuating language of Iago when he relates Cassio's dream:

257

Ex. 256 returns, to generate another movement of agitation. Then Amelia pours out her soul in a fervent prayer, 'Consentimi, o Signore', with Ulrica and the concealed Riccardo eventually joining. In both of its melodic ideas the rate of harmonic movement is very slow:

258a

258b

At the end impatient voices can be heard outside. Ulrica dismisses her visitor through the secret door to a whirling coda based on Ex. 256 – whose rhythm even in the calmer passage we have never been entirely allowed to forget. Although this terzetto has proceeded in several stages of dialectic, the 3/8 rhythm has been constant. Variety has come partly from the rhythmic use of harmony, partly from the contrast of Ulrica's steady A major with Amelia's unstable E minor, from which the E major of Ex. 258 gives only a short respite. Just how original this movement is can be judged by a comparison with Mercadante's work, which presents the entire scene as a two-movement cavatina for the heroine. A prima donna of the 1840s would expect nothing else at her first entrance.

Ulrica opens the main door. Enter the officers and gentlemen with Oscar, Samuel and Tom and their supporters. all 'bizarrely' dressed. If they have not brought their womenfolk with them, although the latter were clearly invited, it is because the female chorus is required for the populace. (As may have been gathered male choristers generally outnumbered female on the Italian stage; hence the tradition of the double chorus of which one half consists of tenors and basses only.) The brisk C major theme ('Su, profetessa') brings light and sanity once more. Riccardo whispers to Oscar not to give away his identity to Ulrica; then steps forward and offers his fisherman's credentials in the canzone 'Dì tu se fedele il flutto m'aspetta':

259

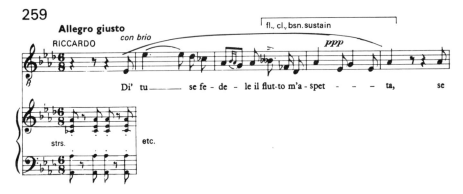

The 6/8 rhythm with its leaping introduction on an E flat dominant recall the Duke of Mantua's 'Quest'o quella'; but the melody itself has a more 'folkloric' as distinct from popular character. Indeed, a critic writing of the first performance noted a similarity between it and the songs of the fishermen of Bari.* The whole piece is permeated by a sense of undulation – sometimes spanning a half-bar, sometimes a bar or more and sometimes a whole phrase. At the words 'con lacere vele e l'alma in tempesta' the 'rowing' acciaccature put in an appearance. In other words, Riccardo is a parody of a fisherman; and the flourish of grace-notes that prepares the final phrase gives once again the effect of a mocking laugh. The chorus repeat the phrase punctually in the manner of a brindisi, and a second strophe follows with small differences in the scoring. The sparkling use of the piccolo is common to both verses and helps to underline the sense of ribaldry. In all this what seems like a routine device of operetta is put to good dramatic use. Ulrica is left in no doubt that she is being made a fool of. In Scribe's text she says so roundly ('O qui que vous soyez tous, dont l'arrogance vient jusqu'en ce lieu pour insulter ma puissance'). In Somma's her words are like a paraphrase of Mozart's Commendatore ('Che voi siate, l'audace parola può nel pianto prorompere un giorno'); and the accompanying music is hardly less horrifying. The relevance of the solo horn will not be missed (Ex. 260).

Riccardo offers his palm, and the 'prophecy' figure is resumed as Ulrica displays her art. It is the hand, she says, of one who has lived under the sign of Mars. 'She has hit the mark!' Oscar exclaims. ('Be silent,' from Riccardo.) But then she draws back, though the prophecy motif does not falter; and in due course Riccardo drags from her the prediction that he will die (a prolonged fortissimo chord of brass). If it is on the field of battle Riccardo has no misgivings. 'No,' replies Ulrica, 'by the hand of a friend.' Here, possibly because the plot was already well known, Verdi has relapsed into the habit of covering the important word – 'amico' – with a deafening tutti, including bass drum and cymbals. The sense of terror is left to reverberate for thirteen bars of low pianissimo scoring. Then the impudent triplets peep out like rabbits from their holes and Riccardo proclaims his amusement and disbelief, as he starts the famous quintet with chorus ('È scherzo od è follia') (Ex. 261b). Once again Verdi would seem to have been indebted to Auber for the 'spunto iniziale', though

* Nicola Cecchi in the *Filodrammatico*, XXXVI, 10.3.1859; quoted in *I.S.V. Bollettino*, No. 1, p. 125. No one seems to have followed up this statement with research into the folk music of Apulia. Sea-shanties, however, are well known for their tendency to travel; and the curious melisma at bars 4–5 can be found in the Scottish folk-song 'The lum hat wantin' the croun'.

260

the phrase in question (Ex. 261a) not only occurs at a later point in the scene but is so transitional in its nature that the similarity may be no more than coincidence.

261a

261b

This quintet, which is among the best known pieces in the opera, is also one of its boldest innovations. Reaction to the witch's prophecy provides the most obvious moment for the obligatory concertato, where the musician takes over from the music-dramatist as he spins an imposing web of sweet lyrical sound. Needless to say, such is the way of Mercadante in *Il Reggente*. In *Gustave III* the moment is shorter and more dramatic – a mere ten bars of G minor–major ensemble. In Verdi's hands the time-honoured convention is transfigured by that interplay of light and darkness that informs the opera. Neither Auber nor Mercadante had found any means of setting their hero's mocking incredulity in relief. In *Un Ballo in maschera* it is this that gives the concertato its prevailing colour, its entrancing un-concertato-like elegance.*

Nor is Riccardo the only one present to be amused. Ulrica has noticed that the alarm of Samuel and Tom is different from and more palpable than that of the others, and she tells them so in a clearly defined solo (Ex. 262a). They in turn babble their embarrassment in a third idea (Ex. 262b), in which they make a half-hearted attempt to resume their conspiratorial manner. It is left to Oscar to contribute the lyrical element (Ex. 262c) as he reflects with a naif, Gilda-like sorrow on the prophecy of doom.

262a

Like the quartet in *Rigoletto* this piece falls into two parts marked by the statement and reprise of Ex. 261a. By way of an added refinement, each idea has its own tonality – B flat major (Ex. 261a), B flat minor (Ex. 262a), F major (Ex. 262b), D flat major (Ex. 262c) – and is for the most part backed by a characteristic instrument: the sparkling piccolo for Riccardo, the lamenting oboe for Oscar, the bassoon, half comic, half menacing, for Samuel and Tom. In the reprise all identities merge in Riccardo's good-humour, with Oscar's Ex. 262c resumed in B flat major like any sonata second subject. Only Ulrica continues to stand out, with a chain of

---

* The credit (or discredit) for introducing the semiquaver chuckles during the rests in the third line belongs to the Emilian tenor Alessandro Bonci (1870–1940). Verdi, however, was quite specific on the subject: '. . . no laughs in the *scherzo od è follia* . . .', letter to L. Escudier, 11.3.1865. M. Conati, *Interviste e incontri con Verdi* (Milan, 1980), p. 27.

syncopations on F and G. The polarity of D flat and B flat is summed up in one of those epigrams which figure more and more frequently in Verdi's codas.

A short passage *a cappella* intervenes before the final cadence. The translucent texture of the quintet, in marked contrast to the heavy if brightly coloured scoring of Mercadante's concertati, shows Verdi far ahead of his Italian contemporaries and already on the road to that miracle of his last years, *Falstaff*.

Riccardo now demands to know who will be his murderer. 'He who first shakes you by the hand,' replies Ulrica, and again we hear the hollow fifth that accompanied her words in the earlier terzetto. Riccardo challenges anyone present to give Ulrica's prophecy the lie; but no one comes forward. Total victory of Ulrica. Just then Renato enters, anxious as usual for Riccardo's safety. He at once clasps Riccardo by the hand. Riccardo's joyous 'Sì perchè la man che stringe è del più fido amico mio' has something of the exultation of the future Otello in his first entrance. Everyone breathes a sigh of relief, Samuel and Tom not least. Riccardo, now that the joke is over, gives Ulrica a purse of gold and revokes her decree of banishment. Touched, Ulrica warns him none the less to be on his guard, since among his followers there is a traitor – 'more than one, perhaps'. Riccardo cuts her short with a brief 'Non più'. There are distant cries of 'Viva Riccardo!'. To galloping figures on the orchestra, the populace burst in with Silvano at their head. In short but characteristic phrases he orders them to bend the knee before their father and friend; and his words suggest that the melody which forms the main theme of the concluding stretta ('O figlia d'Inghilterra', Ex. 264a) is the colonial equivalent of a national anthem.* A second theme (Ex. 264b) is announced by Riccardo and Oscar.

* Even in 1859 censorship had not quite finished with Verdi; in the first complete recording of the opera, made in 1943 with Gigli in the leading role, the words 'dell'Inghilterra' were replaced by 'della patria' – an emendation adopted today in all those productions in Italian which restore the original Swedish setting.

After the delicacy of the concertato the colour is here laid on in bold splashes. This, combined with the fact that both movements are in totally unrelated keys, has doubtless prevented commentators from noticing that, as with the cantabile and cabaletta of Ulrica's invocation, the second is a variation of the first. Ex. 264a and Ex. 261b are basically the same melody. Ex. 264b is likewise related to Ex. 262c, not so much as a variation as by way of a reassuring answer to it, Oscar's fears being swept away in the general acclamation. An episode in F sharp minor scored for woodwind and horns unites Ulrica, Samuel and Tom, and also Renato, for the moment relegated to the dark side of the drama, as he voices fresh misgivings about Riccardo's safety. The conspirators meanwhile express their contempt for the crowd, and Ulrica the conviction that the Count will come to a bad end. Hers is the most important line at this point; and Verdi takes care to make its jagged syncopations stand out in sharp relief from the mutterings of the three men. There is a reprise in which the two main themes (Ex. 264a and b) are combined vertically; and after several of those kaleidoscopic modulations à la Mercadante with which since *La Battaglia di Legnano* Verdi had liked to rivet the final assertions of his tonic chord the act finishes in a blaze of light.

As Ulrica will never appear again, it may be useful at this point to discuss an important problem of production: is Ulrica genuinely possessed or is she merely a clever psychologist? Scribe's original text on which Somma's libretto is mostly based hints strongly at the latter. When Amelia comes to her in disguise, Mme Arvidson makes a few quick deductions from her visitor's appearance before the consultation begins:

MME ARVIDSON (*aside*)   C'est sans doute une grande dame
                    Oui, quelque dame de la cour,
                    Et le trouble agite son âme.
       (*aloud*)   Il s'agit de chagrin d'amour.
AMÉLIE   O ciel, vous savez mon secret!
MME ARVIDSON (*aside*)   J'en étais sûre.

This is the technique of the fortune-teller at the country fair, blessed with the ideally suggestible client. Now admittedly Verdi and Somma omit this passage, possibly because, as D'Amico maintains,* they wished to avoid all suggestion of the rational, but no less possibly for the sake of brevity. Verdi's opera texts are full of omissions, the contents of which have to be subsumed if the passage in question is to make sense. A similar case can be found in the exchange between the king and the witch:

MME ARVIDSON   Gustave, ô mon généreux maître,
                    Pour reconnaître ici tes bienfaits
                    Je ne puis que repétér encore
                    Mes sinistres avis: (*sotto voce*) l'un d'eux te trahira.
                    Plus d'un peut-être . . .
GUSTAVE   (*furious*) Quoi? Toujours des soupçons? Tais-toi, Tais-toi!

In *Un Ballo in maschera* Riccardo's irritable outburst is compressed into 'Non più!' But the original snub to what had been intended as good advice is enough to make Ulrica resume her gloomy predictions with a certain malign satisfaction. We can therefore interpret her behaviour as follows. The opening invocation is hokum, clever conjuring with the aid of a child assistant. The feeling of genuine horror that emanates from the music derives purely from the credulity of the onlookers. Silvano arrives. Ulrica likes him (who would not?) and so gives him a good prophecy – which, however, could hardly have been fulfilled without the adventitious help of Riccardo. (This too, is a clever touch: playing at gods is a common form of 'hubris'.) She has no idea who Riccardo and his friends are; but they insult her and she decides to give them a thoroughly unpleasant shock. Seeing the more serious alarm of Samuel and Tom she realizes that she has hit the mark more nearly than she had any right to expect; and she shrewdly presses home her advantage with the prophecy of the handshake. But once she has received proof of his generosity she proceeds to give Riccardo *genuine* advice based on what she has observed during the course of the quintet. If Ulrica were a real sorceress with absolute faith in her own prophecies, why should she warn Riccardo of treachery amongst his suite? It would serve no

* D'Amico, *op. cit.*, p. 1261.

purpose since he was doomed anyway. As for the advice given to Amelia, this hardly calls for any special explanation. If Ulrica is a good psychologist she knows that Amelia's cure can only come from within herself. The essential question is, how genuine is her wish to be rid of her passion for Riccardo? By directing her to the last place in which a well-born lady and wife of an important government official would dare to set foot, she is making a test of her will-power.

True, this interpretation receives no support at all from the production book. Here Ulrica is a mere vehicle for prophecy who believes implicitly in the truth of her own prognostications. Thus: 'Saying, "Infelice," Ulrica lets fall Riccardo's hand with a look of pity. Then, at the words "Ebben presto morrai", movement of grief among those present, of repressed joy in Tom and Samuel; and at the next words: "per man d'un amico" movement of terror in Tom and Samuel and their supporters, of horror in everyone else except Riccardo. . . .'* And later: 'At the words "Ma v'ha fra loro il traditor" Ulrica directs an inquiring look at Renato and then at the conspirators, who again lower their eyes in consternation.'† This is perhaps another indication that Cencetti was basing some of his production ideas on *Il Reggente*, where at the start of the concertato Hamilton is as fearful of the implications of the handshake as the Regent is careless of them. In *Gustave III*, on the other hand, all present are so convinced that the prophecy has been proved absurd that Ribbing and de Horn attempt the king's assassination there and then, only to be frustrated by the entry of the populace.

In the last analysis, whether Ulrica is genuine or fraudulent does not affect the central issue. Riccardo, like Don Giovanni, is acting under a compulsion which leads him to ultimate disaster. Whether that disaster comes by natural or supernatural means is unimportant (after all, no one has ever tried to rationalize the status of the Commendatore). Yet there are two advantages to be derived from a rational interpretation of Ulrica's role. Firstly, horror stories in general are always more convincing if, like E. T. A. Hoffmann's *The Sandman*, they exist on two levels – the real and the unreal. Secondly, it allows the singer to play the role much more interestingly. After all Ulrica is the dominant figure in a canvas that includes the entire cast. How much more effectively will she dominate if she is a shrewd, calculating fraud rather than a mere vehicle of hellish clairvoyance.

ACT II

A lonely field on the outskirts of Boston, at the foot of a steep hill. On the left towards the back two pillars stand out white. The moon, lightly veiled, illuminates various points of the scene.‡

Like Mina's in *Aroldo* Act I, Amelia's entrance is preceded by several bars of orchestral turbulence. At length she appears on the hillside to a reminiscence of her prayer in the terzetto (Ex. 258a) played by flute over tremolando strings, while between the two phrases a grim descent of bassoons, cellos and basses calls attention

---

* *Disp. scen.*, p. 14.   † *Disp. scen.*, p. 15.

‡ The production book adds a cluster of 'practicable' hills (ramps with concealed steps) stage right, up and down which Amelia can falter and stumble during the prelude. It also indicates the nature of the 'white pillars' by a coy quotation from Amelia's first words, 'where crime is coupled with death'. (*Disp. scen.*, p. 18.)

to the sombre setting. As she prays once more Ex. 258a takes on a new warmth, sung by violins and cellos over sustaining horns and bassoons and arpeggios on flute and clarinet. When she rises, the full orchestra again bursts out in renewed fury; but Amelia has gained the strength to go on with her mission. While she descends the slope the storm of sound gradually sinks to an ominous D minor moan.

Amelia's first recitative ('Ecco l'orrido campo') shows that she is terrified but determined. Fierce gestures from the prelude punctuate her phrases. But it is another thought altogether that forms the subject of her aria ('Ma dall' arido stelo divulsa') with its cor anglais introduction and obbligato (Ex. 265a). Once she has plucked the herb and been cured of her passion, what does life hold for her? Never up till now had Verdi written an aria quite so concentrated in its pathos. Three of its six lines return disconsolately to a minor cadence; only the fifth line (Ex. 265b) brings a faint ray of light, which is at once extinguished in the line that follows. The second verse ('Che piange? qual forza m'arresta?') is a variation of the first, with the melody mostly on the cor anglais and an elaborated accompaniment. The final cadence is interrupted by the sound of the midnight bell. (As in *Rigoletto* it strikes six chimes only, in the mid-nineteenth century manner.) Then a hallucination of terrifying force takes possession of Amelia. Death figures abound in a steady crescendo as she sees a head rise up from the earth and stare at her with balefully flashing eyes. Once again it is prayer that saves her. She falls on her knees with the words 'Deh mi reggi, m'aita, o Signor' to a variant of Ex. 265b which takes her up in a Leonora-like sweep to a high C and down two octaves to a final F major cadence and cadenza.

But behind the regained sense of calm can be heard the thud of the death figure on bassoons, trombones, cimbasso, timpani and bass drum – the most subterranean sound that can be imagined.*

Formally this aria offers a remarkable instance of the way Verdi will compress a traditional form to its limits in order to make it part of a larger structural organism. The opening verse is itself a romanza contracted into three double-phrases. It is repeated by way of strophic variation. What follows appears at first to be an entirely new 'scena'; but the recurrence of Ex. 265b reveals it as a concluding episode – or, if the description seems self-contradictory, an *Abgesang*. In other words we are dealing with a species of bar-form with refrain. Yet there is no deliberate innovation here; merely the bending of traditional Italian designs to meet a particular situation in a particular opera.

The same is true of the duet which follows. Riccardo appears without warning and hastens to comfort Amelia with protestations of love. Amelia puts up what resistance she can muster; but all to no purpose. She ends by confessing her love and falling into his arms. The only other love-duet of this kind to be found in Verdi is that of *Giovanna d'Arco*. Again it is the man who presses and the woman who reluctantly succumbs. Laid out in three expansive movements the grand duet of Carlo and Giovanna is one of the high points of the early score. Given the lapse of time between the two operas, something far more elaborate might be expected for Riccardo and Amelia. However not only does this duet retain the three-movement form of the earlier one ending with a 'similar' cabaletta; it is also shorter. One reason for this is that it is propelled by an underlying sense of imminent danger. The demons who threaten Giovanna are in no hurry; but Amelia is always aware of lurking menace. Then too by 1859 Verdi had learned to say far more with far fewer notes than in 1845. The love-duet in *Un Ballo in maschera* is richer in nuances and variety of musical thought than its predecessor, or indeed than any Verdi had written up till then. Not that the choice is a difficult one. Even in operas such as *Il Trovatore* and *La Traviata* where love is the principal spur its expression is surprisingly limited – sometimes no more than a handful of ardent phrases. Here, however, Verdi faces the romantic challenge with a duet which forms the central climax of the opera.

The start is fairly orthodox: rushing agitation in the strings, a volley of exclamations from both singers punctuated by instrumental barks, leading to what Basevi calls a 'parlante melodico'† – i.e. a continuous orchestral melody (Ex. 266a) doubled by the voices where convenient. In the major-key complement (Ex. 266b) the familiar pattern of excited cello quavers, so often pizzicati in the past, is here played with the bow so as to allow a greater variety of phrasing and a caressing embellishment of the typical mid-Verdian cadences (x).

Riccardo has an answer for everything. He takes up Amelia's Ex. 263b extending it into a long lyrical descent ('Il tuo nome intemerato, l'onor tuo sempre sarà'). Vainly Amelia tries to remind him that she is another's. Riccardo proceeds to silence her with a long outpouring of seductive eloquence.

---

* There is a slight instrumental problem here. Verdi needed an anticipation at pitch of Amelia's noble phrase, for which the obvious instrument was the cor anglais. But since this would take it to the extreme limits of its upper range Verdi cued in the phrase for the first oboe with the instruction 'for greater safety in performance these three bars can be played on the oboe; all the rest on the cor anglais'. In the willow scene in *Otello* he solves the identical problem quite differently.   † Basevi, pp. 30–2.

Note here a striking modification of the traditional Italian design. The essence of the Rossinian tripartite duet is contrast between the movements; if the first is a dialogue, the second will be a joint soliloquy. If the singers alternate in the first they will combine in the second; if the first is a complex of mutually buttressing vocal and instrumental ideas, the second will be an uninterrupted cantilena; and so on. Here, however, the second movement is actually evolved from the first. Instead of contrast we have transition. Amelia's resistance finally spends itself in the long period beginning 'Ma Riccardo, io son d'altrui', which at its climax causes the tempo to broaden with a succession of crotchet triplets ('Io son di lui che daria la vita'). Riccardo's reply ('Ah, crudele!') slackens the harmonic rhythm still further. Cellos then take up the crotchet triplets which, transformed into 6/8, form the basic rhythm of the central cantabile ('Non sai tu che se l'anima mia'). The whole passage is so interesting as to deserve a lengthy quotation:

267

mi - a _____ il ri - morso di - la - cera e ro - de,

etc.

Here it may be useful to recall Basevi's observations about Verdi's so-called 'second manner' – the more flexible rhythms, the lighter style of vocal writing, the more immediately memorable tunes and a certain veering in the direction of Donizetti – the principal difference between them being that 'the former [Verdi], being more passionate by nature, strives the more often to excite and harrow the listener, whereas the latter [Donizetti] almost always wishes to please him'.* The cantabile which follows is full of Donizettian parallels ranging from the archetypal 'D'un pescator ignobile' from *Lucrezia Borgia* for general character to the concertati of *Maria di Rohan* and *Poliuto* and the Roberto/Sara duet from *Roberto Devereux*.† The real difference between the composers lies in Verdi's ability to generate new ideas from a single rhythmic cell where Donizetti is content for the most part to use it to present different aspects of the same melody. Riccardo's opening phrase ('Non sai tu che se l'anima mia'), so touching in its simplicity despite an unobtrusive harmonic richness, is made to yield phrase upon phrase of increasing passion and tenderness. After twenty-four bars Amelia can bear it no longer and seeks escape in a new but related theme in D flat major ('Ah, deh soccorri tu, cielo, all'ambascia', Ex. 268a) with liquid clarinet arpeggios. The phrase with which Riccardo restores F major ('La mia vita, l'universo'), bestriding a prolonged dominant (Ex. 268b), turns out to be a 6/8 variant, differently harmonized, of the one which begins Ex. 267 in the previous movement (Ex. 268).

Amelia's resistance crumbles; the intensity of the music redoubles carrying the melody away from its F major base to a hushed climax in A major of almost *Tristan*-like incandescence, in which the cellos who have been prominent throughout the movement here express the feelings that Amelia herself can only babble disjointedly ('Ebben . . . sì . . . t'amo') (Ex. 269).

More than a quarter of a century later they will make a similar declaration of love in *Otello*. At Amelia's confession Riccardo is 'beside himself' with joy. Farewell to all scruples of conscience, all thoughts of friendship, everything but his passion for Amelia! So twelve bars of exultant recitative lead through F major to a dominant in preparation for the final cabaletta ('O qual soave brivido'). A curious 'sawing' passage for strings in unison and at the octave paints the sweet 'shudder' that thrills the lovers. The melody is not only announced first by Riccardo; with its grace and buoyancy it clearly belongs to him rather than Amelia as a quotation from the later bars will show (Ex. 270a and b).

* Basevi, pp. 158–9.   † See Dean, *op. cit.*, pp. 138 & 142–3.

268a

269

It can be no coincidence that the string figuration that punctuates each beat is the same and in the same key as in the second part of Ulrica's aria. The boldest touch, however, is reserved for the ritornello which deviates into E major for a reprise of Ex. 269 given out 'tutta forza' by all the melody instruments including trumpet.

270a

270b

What is normally a transition is thus elevated to the pinnacle of the movement, and the cabaletta form given a new orientation.

The lovers break away from each other as footsteps are heard.* Amelia swiftly veils herself, and Renato enters, with a warning that the conspirators are on Riccardo's track. He must disguise himself with Renato's cloak and escape at once. Riccardo, with his usual impulsiveness, refuses to leave Amelia alone; but Amelia insists – otherwise she will reveal her identity to Renato. This is of course action music, based on a light-fingered theme sung first by Renato ('Per salvarti da lor che celati lassù') (Ex. 271) then taken up by the orchestra, where its rhythm forms a tight framework to the half-smothered lyrical outcries of Amelia and Riccardo.†

Riccardo gives way eventually to Amelia's wishes and entrusts her to Renato after making him promise to conduct her veiled to the city walls and then leave her. Now, one would have thought, was the time for all three to make themselves scarce. This is what happens in both Auber and Mercadante, though it is already too late. In Verdi all three remain to sing a trio ('Odi tu come fremono cupi') in which Renato and Amelia beg Riccardo to fly while he himself remains rooted to the spot, partly by a sense of guilt, partly because it is in his nature to court danger. Therefore comparison

---

* Towards the end of the duet the moon, which had again been covered by clouds, becomes once again visible. (Disp. scen., p. 19.)

† Producers would do well to consult the Italian production book for the movements – so obvious, yet so apparently elusive – that render this scene plausible.

271

with the policemen in *The Pirates of Penzance* ('Yes, but you *don't* go') is out of place. Besides, if the comic anticlimax of the finale is to succeed, there must first be a precipitation of the forces of terror in a closed formal design. So far these have made themselves felt in the free, often isolated gestures of the prelude and Amelia's scena. Now they must crystallize. The D minor trio has the quality of an infernal hunt with Riccardo and Amelia as the quarry. The death figure in the vocal line, the low clarinet and the softly thudding kettledrum, the subsequent 'lament' of cellos and horns in the third line all contribute to the sense of impending fatality (Ex. 272).*

The movement finished, Riccardo hurries away; Renato offers Amelia his arm and is about to do likewise when the conspirators can be heard in the distance with contrapuntal snatches of Ex. 244 ('Avventiamoci su lui'). They see Amelia's white veil gleaming in the moonlight and make for her escort. Here Ex. 244 generates an orchestral motif, suggestive of soft footfalls – too primitive to be called a theme but destined to play an important transitional role (Ex. 273).

'Who goes there?' Renato cries. Foiled gain! Verdi did not waste a dark, terrifying number on Samuel, Tom and their followers. In his scheme of things they are paper tigers. Their malevolence may be bottomless but they are far too inefficient to carry out their purpose unaided. They have even allowed Renato to penetrate their ranks muffled in his own cloak, as he himself has told us:

---

* For a masterly analysis of this number, with the kind of insight which only a great composer can bring to the work of another, see L. Dallapiccola, 'Parole e musica nel melodramma', in *Quaderni della Rassegna Musicale*: 2 (Turin, 1965). His thesis is based on the tendency of Italian librettists and musicians to lift the third line of a quatrain. Here he shows how this principle was extended by Verdi from an individual verse within an aria to a complex movement of 110 bars to produce a design of faultless classical symmetry.

272

Trasvolai nel manto serrato
Così che m'han preso per un dell'agguato.

However, they despise Renato – another sign of their obtuseness – and now decide to
have some fun at his expense. To a mocking theme in D flat they demand to see the
lady's face. This is the musical language of Alice as she devises her first pranks at the
expense of Falstaff (Ex. 274).

273 Allegro assai moderato

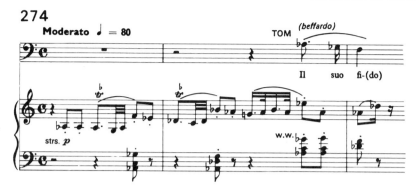

Renato refuses them and an ugly situation is developing when Amelia, in fear for her husband's life, interposes herself, so swiftly that the veil falls from her face, and she stand recognized by all in the moonlight.* Amazement – then laughter. That a man should have a moonlit tryst – with his own wife! What a wonderful story that will make! Thus Samuel, the more prominent of the two leaders; to be joined by Tom in a series of chuckles, which return over and over again and even persist in the distance when the stage is at last empty. If the harmonic scheme of the hilarity owes something to Auber, the rhythmic cut of the main theme ('Ve', se di notte qui colla sposa') is derived in the most logical way from Ex. 274 by way of Ex. 273 with its pattern of two quavers leading to a crotchet on the down-beat:

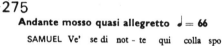

The movement is a rondo with Ex. 275 as its subject. There are two episodes, one dominated by Renato's anger ('Così mi paga') conveyed in brusque gestures on violins and violas, the other by Amelia's tears ('A chi nel mondo ti volgera?') in which her long lyrical line moves by narrow intervals, like a stylized wail. Before he leaves with her Renato demands to see Samuel and Tom the following morning. After a brief demur they consent. Ominous triplet figures in the orchestra point out to us, if not to the conspirators, that death is in the wind. As the conspirators leave,

* As usual Cencetti takes a more solemn view of the action, making Samuel and Tom more dangerous than the music warrants. *The moon once again comes out and lights up the stage. After having said,* 'Vo' quest'Iside mirar,' *Tom take a few steps towards Amelia to remove the veil from her features, passing in front of Samuel, who descends stage right. At the words* 'Non un passo' *Tom halts; and at* 'Non vi temo' *Renato unsheaths his sword and places himself on guard. The chorus saying* 'Giù l'acciaro' *takes a threatening step towards Renato. Saying* 'Vo' finirla' *Tom again draws his sword [not, however, according to the score]. All his companions do likewise; and at the words* 'questo insulto pagherà' *they hurl themselves on Renato who stands his ground unflinching.* (Disp. scen., p. 22.)

still chuckling, the orchestra takes charge of Ex. 275. With frightening calm Renato tells his wife that he has promised to escort her to the gates of the city and offers her his arm. They leave with the sound of mocking laughter in their ears; only when it has quite died away does the curtain fall to four bars of tutti. 'See, the tragedy has changed into comedy,' sing the chorus. It will soon change back again.

ACT III

*Scene 1: A private study in Renato's house. Above a fireplace are two bronze vases; opposite them a large bookshelf. At the back is a full-length portrait of Riccardo, standing; in the middle of the room a table.**

In the instrumental introduction we have Renato in all his formidable strength and fury: brass and bassoons rapping out double dotted rhythms in bar octaves, strings scurrying together in semiquavers, tutti chords like the blows of a monstrous hammer. Renato at length bursts in with Amelia,† puts down his sword and closes the door. Tears, prayers are useless, he says; and adds in that memorable phrase on which Verdi had insisted, 'Blood is needed and you shall die' ('Sangue vuolsi e tu morrai'). Amelia pleads for mercy in a phrase repeated three times in ascending semitones. This movement between unrelated keys is a measure of her desperation, since in Verdi quarrelling couples generally pursue each other in keys a third apart. Renato turns a deaf ear. She admits that she loved Riccardo for a moment but never dishonoured Renato's name. Renato can only return obsessively to his demand for her death. As he draws his sword, she falls on her knees and makes one last request; that she should be allowed to see her son once more before she dies.

The aria 'Morrò, ma prima in grazia' has much the same design as Renato's in the first act with the addition of a cello obbligato to plead her cause. This is Amelia's darkest hour with both her melodic ideas rooted in contrasted minor keys (Ex. 276a, b).

Especially poignant is the Neapolitan F flat in the coda, reinforced by cello solo, violins and horns ('che mai più').

Renato gives way, but without a trace of warmth ('Alzati! là tuo figlio a te concedo riveder'). He points to the door without even glancing at her, and she goes out. So far Verdi has followed Auber as his principal source. Now comes his chief debt to Mercadante and Cammarano: a baritone aria at the dramatic turning-point. In the noble and spacious cantabile 'Nuove ferite' Hamilton voices the monstrous suspicion that the child whom Amelia is so anxious to see before she dies may not be his own. Whether or not a similar thought is implied in Renato's words 'Eri tu che macchiavi quell'anima', as D'Amico suggests,‡ his aria, like Hamilton's, at once sets him in relief as the chief agent of the tragedy, with a singlemindedness that is far from apparent in Auber's Ankarstrom. Indeed the behaviour of the three baritones at this point is quite different: Ankarstrom, having resolved to kill his wife, allows himself to be softened during the course of their duet; Hamilton, in his duet with Amelia, veers from vengefulness to forgiveness then back again; Renato and Amelia have no

---

* The production book adds a bronze candle bracket above the fireplace, writing materials on the table and two chairs: *It is dawn.* (*Disp. scen.,* p. 24.)

† *Dragging her by the hand.* (*Disp. scen.,* p. 24.)

‡ D'Amico, p. 1361.

276a

duet. He hears her out in gloomy silence, then dismisses her with a pitying contempt. She can live out the rest of her life in darkness and ignominy; but for him she is already dead and he can only mourn her memory.

Renato is one of those Verdian characters who, however passionate they appear, are never at the mercy of passing emotions. This in itself would suffice to set him leagues apart from Hamilton whose cantabile is followed by a convulsive cabaletta ('Già scaglio il ferro vindice') festooned with syncopation and fioritura.* The scena and aria 'Alzati. . . . Eri tu' not only has a character peculiar to Renato; it is a far less self-contained piece of music than its performance out of context would lead one to believe. Not that it is ever performed without its preceding recitative, which is as rich in nuances and musical significance as any of Rigoletto's or Macbeth's. The phrase 'Nell'ombra e nel silenzio' recalls Ex. 247 from Act I in which Renato originally warned Riccardo of the conspiracy. Amelia's exit is accompanied by a quotation on oboe and clarinet of Ex. 276b over five bars. Renato does not deign to glance at her. Instead he turns to the portrait of Riccardo; it is *his* blood that is needed to wipe away Renato's shame. At the phrase 'E lo trarrà il pugnale' second violins and violas resume the turbulent string pattern from the prelude. The introduction to the aria proper bursts unexpectedly over Renato's cadence to the word 'vendicator'. Once again a traditional form – the minor–major romance – is given a new perspective. The two ideas of which it is composed are each announced by the orchestra with an instrumental colouring which determines their character.

277a

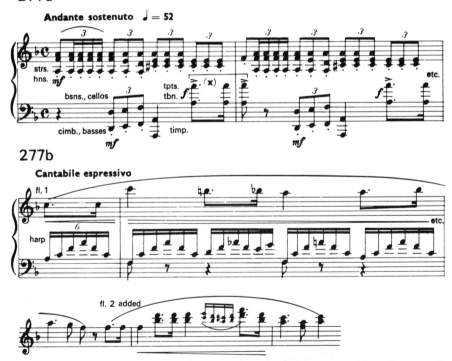

277b

* Charles Santley remarks that Mercadante was about the only composer of the mid nineteenth century who continued to write florid music for baritone (*Student and Singer*, p. 259). Verdi, when confronted with a flexible baritone such as Filippo Colini, confines his fioriture to the cadenzas.

Throughout, the decasyllabic verse is treated with that freedom and flexibility which Verdi's lesser contemporaries were always vainly striving to achieve. The first theme ('Eri tu che macchiavi quell'anima') spreads its opening line over four long bars instead of the usual two, while the repeated insistence on the dominant A with trumpet and trombone pointing a menacing finger (x) and the avoidance of any cadence in the home key invests the entire opening section with a sense of preparation. It becomes a step in the ascent from the declamation of the scena to the pure lyricism of the second idea ('O dolcezze perdute, o memoria'). Throughout the aria there is no direct repetition, only the occasional motivic link; note, for instance, the rapid horn sextuplets at the word 'odio', echoing the pattern of Ex. 277a. The melody (Ex. 277b) is as seamless as in any cantabile of the 'risorgimentale' period but the simple and compound elements in the rhythm are far better balanced. Never was the culminating relative major more aptly used than here, where Renato bids farewell to his lost Eden.

Ex. 244 on cellos and basses announces the arrival of Samuel and Tom. Renato tells them that he has written proof of their conspiracy, and refers them to certain papers. But to their surprise he has no intention of denouncing them. 'I am yours,' he says; and with this the strings launch an action-theme of military stamp with a most important nucleus (x) to which the three converse in 'parlante' melodies:

278

The long scene which now unfolds is organized in a very original and characteristic way. Its basis is the polarity of two ideas. The first (Ex. 278) is a developing theme, beginning in C major and constantly returning to it; the second is a 'resolving' theme (Ex. 279), periodic, non-developing and firmly rooted in A flat. It is an unthinkable scheme for a German romantic but strictly in accordance with Verdian practice. Thematic development came late to Verdi; and he never made it the sole constructive principle for a scene. Sooner or later it is always complemented by a finite melody. Then too, for an Italian of the period, there is no incongruity in resolving a C major idea in the key of A flat. Allowing for the equation of the major and minor modes the system is the same as that of 'Ah sì, ben mio' or 'Dell'amor sull'ali rosee'. Once again, as in the terzetto of Act II the structural principle of a small unit is extended to serve a much larger one.

The first idea (Ex. 278) is evolved in two large periods with a central dominant cadence, each taking E major and E flat major respectively in their orbit. When Renato insists yet again, 'Son vostro,' the full orchestra underlines his declaration with a Mercadantean gesture in rapid dotted rhythm which, precisely because it is so rare in Verdi, stands out with a peculiar emphasis. The conspirators are naturally incredulous, until Renato offers his own infant son as hostage. So to the 'resolving' melody ('Dunque l'onta di tutti sol una') launched by Renato to the same combination of 'bardic' military harp and divided double basses as that to which Otello will bid farewell to pomp and circumstance of war.*

279

If a false note is struck anywhere in *Un Ballo in maschera*, surely it is here. True, in Act IV of *Les Huguenots* the conspiring Catholics express themselves to a melody of similar cut in one of the most famous scenes in all grand opera. But it will not do to compare Meyerbeer's impersonal frescoes with Verdi's canvas of living, palpitating humanity. Besides, Verdi's melody is altogether fresher and more striking; it breathes an air of 'risorgimentale' idealism which the dark sonority cannot conceal. Each of the three singers has his own far from idealistic reason for wanting to dispatch Riccardo, as they tell us to a resumption of Ex. 278 with flute added to the melody and intermittent abrupt or restless gestures in the lower strings. Samuel has been cast

---

* In the autograph the basses are required to lower their A strings as in the Miserere from *Il Trovatore* and for the same reason – namely that on the three-stringed basses of the mid-century A was the lowest note. A further instruction runs: 'When there are not enough basses to double all four notes only the fundamental ones should be doubled.'

out of his ancestral home;* Tom's brother has been killed by the Count. Renato refuses to declare his motive; and unlike Mercadante's Howe and Kilcardy his fellow conspirators are too stupid to work it out for themselves. They decide to draw lots for the carrying out of the deed. Renato takes down the vase from the mantelpiece; Samuel writes their names on three pieces of paper which he throws into the vase. During this time the orchestra traces a particularly subtle pattern of three-fold rising progressions. Schemes of this sort are often to be met with in Verdi's operas from earliest times and are the subject of an important essay by Professor Fritz Noske.† His thesis that all instances of this procedure denote a ritual, either patent or implied, is of course open to the objection that in an age which saw the breakdown of the formal aria the triple repetition of a motif or a complex of motifs is too frequently used as a formal device to bear such rigid connotation. (It will be found in late Wagner, and more often still in Humperdinck.) But that it does often denote a ritual (see *Macbeth*, passim) cannot be denied. Here its significance as such is unmistakable. Bu the three statements instead of being repeated identically, each rising by a semitone, are progressively curtailed, the last one being broken off by the entrance of Amelia announcing Oscar's arrival. It is a hugely impressive passage based on the thematic cell (x) from Ex. 278. As one writer observes‡ much of the effect derives from the precarious sound of the exposed trumpet *pp* above the sweeping string scales and minatory death figures ($\sharp$ ♪) in bassoons, trombones and cimbasso. Amelia's appearance immediately suggests to Renato the cruel notion of making her choose the name of her lover's murderer. So the angry, diminished seventh gestures that the Count's name provokes resolve in an E flat major cadential phrase like a devilish grin ('E tu resti, lo dei; perchè parmi che il cielo t'ha scorta'). Amelia reacts with a series of anguished phrases in E flat minor ('Qual tristezza m'assale'), the thematic basis remaining always Ex. 278 in various permutations. 'She knows nothing,' Riccardo mutters to the conspirators. Ex. 278 dies away on a horn pedal of E flat and a rhythm of reiterated acciaccatura figures on viola coupled with marching double basses, as Renato draws his wife towards the table. He tells her 'in a terrible voice' that there are three names in the urn one of which must be drawn out by her 'innocent hand'. When she asks why he only tells her to obey. Here the stage instructions become very detailed. 'Slowly and with trembling Amelia approaches the table on which the vase stands; Renato continually blasts her with the lightning of his gaze. Finally on the orchestral pianissimo (marked with an asterisk) Amelia with shaking hand draws out a piece of paper which her husband passes to Samuel.' The usual stock-in-trade of romantic horror – death-figures, low chords on the brass, tremolando strings, and the like – are used here with a master hand. A bald shift upward from E flat to E gives Renato's words ('V'ha tre nomi in quell'urna') a razor-sharp definition. Further chromatic shifts take the music to a dominant of C minor and a cadential phrase for Amelia ('Non v'è dubbio, il feroce decreto mi vuol parte d'un' opra di sangue') placed squarely in the mezzo-soprano register, such as only the heavier dramatic voices can manage with ease. It is answered by the entire first phrase of Ex. 278, augmented in a double dotted rhythm and with a scoring of the most inspissated gloom. This is the dark centre of the labyrinth:

* In England, presumably; otherwise he would be either a Creole or a Red Indian. . . .

† F. Noske, 'Ritual scenes in Verdi's operas', in *The Signifier and the Signified* (The Hague, 1977), pp. 241–70.

‡ Hughes, p. 266.

As Amelia thrusts in her hand the music moves to a characteristic 6/4 in D flat major for a pattern of chromatically rising sequences based on the five-note cell (*x*). The tonal centre loses itself in successive diminished sevenths; two solitary drum-rolls aggravate the suspense, as Samuel reads the name on the paper and announces sadly, 'Renato.' Brass and bassoons fortissimo pronounce their sentence of death in the familiar triplet flourish. Renato exclaims to a C major cadence of savage joy: 'O giustizia del fato; la vendetta mi deleghi tu.' This in turn leads to a reprise fortissimo of Ex. 279 ('Sconterà dell'America il pianto'), the conspirators in unison, Amelia supplying a helpless counter-melody in triplets. The scoring is modelled on that of the martial scenes in *La Battaglia di Legnano* with the instruments grouped in 'families' rather than intermingled in an indiscriminate tutti as in the earlier operas. But it retains that curiously banda-like device of broken triplets off the beat on horns and trombones. In other words Verdi has decided to play this grand old conjuration tune for what it is worth, using all his technical skill to emphasize its crude heroics. However inappropriate it may be to the characters who sing it, no one can deny that it winds up the scene very powerfully or that it provides an effective 'sfogo' for the unbearable tension of the drawing of lots.

From darkness to light. A tripping theme in C major brings in Oscar with the Count's invitation to a masked ball. Amelia wants to refuse; but Renato insists that she accompany him; Samuel and Tom will attend as well. So follows a stretta in which each of the three principals has a characteristic contribution. Oscar prattles about the splendour of the occasion (Ex. 281); Amelia, to a minor version of the same melody, reflects on the tragic irony of her situation, while beneath her Renato imagines the possibilities of vengeance offered by a masquerade.*

A subtle detail is the quotation of Ex. 247 at Renato's words 'spira dator d'infamie', to remind us that Renato's special knowledge of a conspiracy, which could once have saved Riccardo, will now destroy him. Samuel and Tom provide that key-phrase which was to have been the original title – 'Una vendetta in domino'. Ex. 281 is repeated softly as a background for a few final exchanges. Amelia wonders whether she can save Riccardo, with Ulrica's help; Renato, Samuel and Tom decide to wear a light blue costume with a vermilion sash on the left side; the watchword will be

---

* In *Adelia degli Adimari* 'la mente mia si pinge' had been altered to 'la mente mia si finge' – pretends, not paints. 'A whole book could be written round that word *pretends*,' was Verdi's comment. *Carteggi Verdiani*, I, p. 263.

281

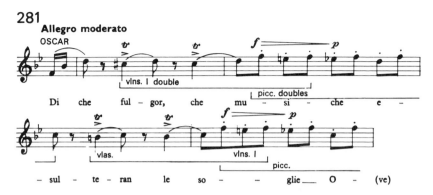

Allegro moderato

OSCAR

Di che ful - gor, che mu - si - che e -

- sul - te - ran le so - - glie___ O - (ve)

'death'. Oscar tells Amelia that she will be the queen of the ball. To a final fortissimo the curtain falls.*

Scene 2: The Count's richly appointed cabinet. A table with writing materials. At the back a large curtain which will discover the ballroom scene.†

A brief oasis of calm in a drama which has been continuously in motion. Riccardo is seated at his desk; before him is the decree recalling Renato and his wife to England.‡ Ex. 241 on the warm G string of the first violins, shimmeringly accompanied, tells us that he can hardly bring himself to renounce his beloved. Even after his decision is irrevocably taken (a pattern of brusque string chords) fragments of the melody keep returning. As he signs, it gives a final poignant turn of the screw; and Riccardo sums up his regret and his resolution in the romanza 'Ma se m'è forza perderti', which at its outset shows every sign of being cast in a conventional if beautiful minor–major mould – so much so that the breath-taking elliptical modulation in the second verse steals on us unawares (Ex. 282).§

Had Verdi moved up his bass to F on the last beat he would have satisfied the grammarians and ruined an exquisite moment. The final bars, though in the major key, are clouded by foreboding, expressed partly in the drooping vocal line, partly in the cello counter-part which joins it at the sixth below, and partly by the violas

---

* Once again the production book emphasies the importance of Oscar in vitalizing the scenes in which he is present. *Before repeating the cabaletta* [i.e. Ex. 280a] *Oscar, who is a youth full of liveliness and courtesy, approaches Renato, Samuel and Tom, so as to share with them his happiness at the prospect of the party; then he returns to Amelia's side; and while she, absorbed in sad thoughts, says to herself,* 'Forsè potrallo Ulrica,' *the three conspirators draw close to one another and talk amongst themselves, apart from the others:* 'E quel costume,' *etc. At the word* 'Morte' *Renato grasps his accomplices by the hand, then politely dismissing Oscar (who leaves with Samuel and Tom from one door) retires with Amelia by the door opposite. (Disp. scen., p. 29.)*

† The production book adds a door covered by a richly appointed curtain, and a candlestick on the table (*Disp. scen.*, p. 30).

‡ In Scribe, Ankarstrom is nominated governor of Finland, so there is no question of repatriation. Likewise in Cammarano Hamilton is to be sent to England, not back to his family estates. Somma's variant is hard to account for.

§ The production book elaborates as follows. *Enter Riccardo left, deep in thought, torn between love and duty: as the latter at last triumphs he seats himself at the table and draws up a decree nominating Renato as Colonial Ambassador to England; but as his heart cannot bear the thought of Amelia's departure the pen falls from his hand; soon however reason gains the upper hand and he signs the fatal document and puts it in his bosom. His sorrow at the sacrifice makes him break out in the words:* 'Ma se m'è forza perderti, *'etc., which the singer will deliver from the footlights.' (Disp. scen.*, p. 30.)

282

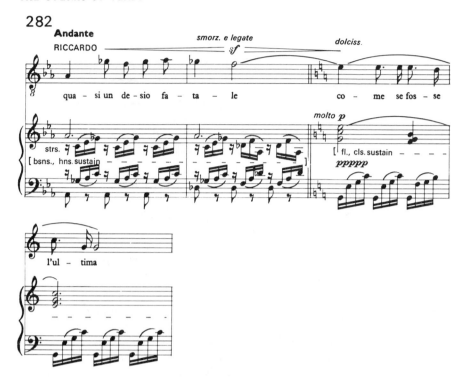

tremolando. A sober cadenza brings the movement to a close. Then the banda is heard behind the scenes with the first of three melodies (Ex. 283) which form the basis of the next scène à faire. During its course Oscar brings in a note from an unknown woman, warning Riccardo that if he attends the ball his life will be in danger. Two thoughts prevent him from heeding it: the fear of being thought a coward, and the longing to see Amelia once more. As he receives the note and reads it, Verdi again uses the technique of the cutaway shot, making the banda cease while Riccardo and Oscar are speaking, but always in such a way as to give an illusion of continuity. When Oscar has left Riccardo indulges in a last, transcendental variant of Ex. 245 ('Sì, rivederti, Amelia'); after which the curtain at the back rises to reveal:

> Scene 3: A vast and richly appointed ballroom splendidly illuminated and set out for a celebration. Joyful music preludes the dances. Already at the rise of the curtain a multitude of guests fill the scene. The greater number are masked, some in dominos, some in gala costume with faces revealed; among the dancing couples are some young Creole girls. Some [of the guests] are on the hunt, some are escaping, some are paying their respects, some are pursuing. The waiting is done by negroes, and everything breathes magnificence and hilarity.*

Three dance melodies alternate:

* The production book adds a series of lateral columns with an entrance between each pair. Strolling choristers are supplemented by a small corps of dancers, the women wearing long skirts. The dance (Ex. 280a) is a Styrienne. (Disp. scen., pp. 32–3.)

283a

Allegro vivacissimo ♩ = 152

banda *f* (*Musica interna di danza*)

etc.

283b

mf (band)

etc.

283c

mf con eleganza

etc.

The opening chorus ('Fervono amori e danze') is to Ex. 283a accompanied by banda with orchestral punctuations. To Ex. 283b Samuel and Tom enter with their followers, all wearing the badge of the conspiracy. They notice Renato approaching slowly 'One of ours,' says Samuel to Tom, helpfully, and for the following dialogue Verdi as usual directs just a few instruments so as not to drown the conversation.*
'Morte,' says Samuel to Renato, as one might say, 'Good evening.' 'Yes, "Morte," '
returns Renato bitterly, 'but he will not be here.' Presumably he guesses that Amelia will have found some way of warning Riccardo, but he has no intention of explaining this to Samuel and Tom. He silences them with a warning that they are being overheard; and indeed at that moment Ex. 283c brings in Oscar, ready like Cherubino to get in everybody's way. The banda is allowed eight bars of reinforced scoring, but must reduce again as soon as the conversation begins. Oscar is determined to make Renato admit his identity. For answer Renato pulls off the page's mask, much to his mortification. He then traps him into an admission that the Count is after all present and demands to know where he can be found. But Oscar wants his revenge. Hence the delightful canzone 'Saper vorreste', a pithy French *couplet* design about half the length of Auber's corresponding rondo 'Non, vous ne le saurez pas', from which it borrows one feature only: the modulation at bar nine to B minor.

---

* The production book adds a number of fellow conspirators who exchange the password among themselves. *They disperse at Oscar's entrance. (Disp. scen.*, p. 33.)

284

Scurrying gestures on violins, flute and piccolo that make up the ritornello are an orchestral laugh. For the moment Renato is thwarted; the chorus (Ex. 283a) returns with another joyous verse; after which Ex. 283b and c permit Renato to renew his insistence. Will Oscar just tell him what costume Riccardo is wearing – it is an urgent matter, for which Oscar himself is likely to take the blame if he fails to do as he is asked. Uncertain, now, Oscar at last lets out the secret; Riccardo is wearing a black hood with a red ribbon on his chest.* Renato wants to know more, but Oscar slips away. In fact, all is not yet quite lost for Riccardo. Ex. 283a returns for the third time worked up to a coda of the utmost brilliance, so concluding a simple, but well balanced design with Oscar's canzone as its central point.

By a final irony the scene of Riccardo's murder is set by the most graceful of mazurkas (so graceful indeed that it is often described as a minuet, which is of course right for the period but wrong as a description of the music), played like the minuet in *Rigoletto* by a small stage orchestra of six first violins, six second violins, two violas, two cellos and two basses.

285

Riccardo, lost in thought, is approached by a woman in a white domino. In a whisper she tells him to leave at once as his life is in danger. As usual Riccardo regards flight as a sign of weakness. He asks to know her name; for repiy she merely becomes more urgent. He no longer doubts that he is speaking to Amelia. Up to this point

* The stage directions give Riccardo a pink not a red ribbon.

their conversation has proceeded in whispers; but at this moment of recognition the music changes from F to D flat major, the stage strings receive help from the pit to the extent of one instrument from each group, and the singers begin to weave lyrical lines in counterpoint to the mazurka. Amelia, desperate for Riccardo's safety, repeats that she loves him and for that reason alone wants him to escape certain death. If Ulrica was a good psychologist, Amelia is a very bad one; and the admission of her love is enough to cause Riccardo to pause and savour it. The main orchestra takes over for a coda-like section in which the voices join. However a distinctive feature of *Un Ballo in maschera*, noticeable in the finale to Act II and in the stretta of Act III scene 1, is a tendency for the main theme of the movement to return pianissimo just when it might be expected to have run its course. So Ex. 285 is resumed with the stage orchestra now reduced to a quintet, while the violins in the pit supply a persistent death-figure. Riccardo tells Amelia, in more conversational style, that he has decided to send her and Renato back to England. The string orchestra pauses twice to allow two long-drawn-out 'addio's'* and Renato steps forward with a thunderous 'E tu ricevi il mio' – i.e., a dagger thrust. Officers and guards hurry in from all sides. Oscar indicates the assassin. His mask is stripped off and the long orchestral crescendo culminates in a chorus of fury: 'Ah! morte, infamia!' When it ceases the mazurka – incredibly – is still playing. Riccardo, gasping, orders his guards to release Renato, manages to draw the dispatch from his costume and beckons to him. By now even the musicians have realized that something is amiss. The mazurka trails into silence.

The final concertato is shorter than usual but highly charged. The opening idea is scored with the utmost economy – a murmured declamato to a mournful theme (Ex. 286a) scored with that transparency that so often betokens the approach of death; the second part (Ex. 286b) is a touching lyrical phrase for the voice, 'Io che amai la tua consorte' – the opera's second debt to *Il Reggente*. Almost to the same words as Murray, Riccardo explains that though he loved Amelia he did her no wrong – a disclaimer that sounds more convincing in Mercadante's opera than in Verdi's. He then shows Renato the decree that recalls him to England.

Ex. 286b is repeated with the full orchestra weighing in for one short sharp chord like a spasm. A characteristic troubled concertato follows back in B flat minor as everyone expresses their dismay and regret, not least Renato. The music then moves into G flat major; harps remind us that Riccardo's thoughts are already turned towards heaven. Chorus and soloists join in what has become a swelling hymn that returns to B flat major through successive modulations which give the effect of increasing light. Riccardo bids a last farewell to Amelia and his people, and falls

286a

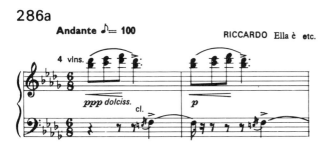

* At the first 'Addio' Riccardo presses Amelia's hand to his breast. (*Disp. scen.*, p. 36.)

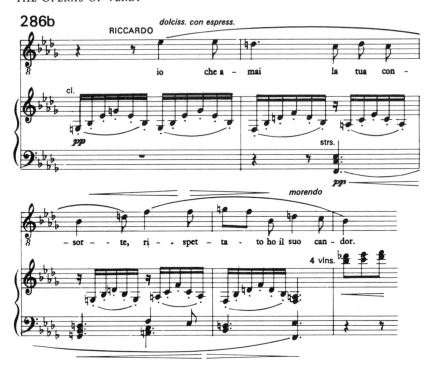

dying. Ten bars of choral and orchestral vehemence ('Notte d'orror!') bring down the curtain.

The immediate fortunes of *Un Ballo in maschera* were more variable than the première might lead us to believe. Verdi was paying the penalty for having followed the French rather than the Italian *convenienze* with five principals whose music is deployed throughout the opera with a regard for the drama rather than the singer. Mercadante and Cammarano had been more astute in this respect. The Oscar in *Il Reggente* has, if anything, less to sing than her counterpart in *Un Ballo in maschera*; but it is organized in two scenes dominated by him alone. The ballade in Act I is in no less than four contrasted sections; that in Act III is an incidental scena and aria in which Oscar pretends to be a fortune-teller, and which could easily be removed altogether if the singer were of comprimario rank only. For Ulrica Mercadante provided a simpler version of her only aria so that the role could likewise be assigned to a comprimaria if no principal were available. In other words *Il Reggente* could easily be adapted to the facilities of a second-rank theatre. Not so *Un Ballo in maschera*. Hence for the first two years every performance foundered on the lack of three adequately contrasted female singers.* Oscar was usually the chief problem since in Italy light sopranos were not accustomed to play travesti roles.

Success came in 1861 with a number of prestigious performances in Italy and abroad. At the Théâtre des Italiens the opera triumphed despite an inadequate performance by the ageing Mario as Riccardo, and the manager's insistence on

* See E. Gara, in *I.S.V. Bollettino*, No. 1, pp. 112–33.

changing the setting yet again to seventeenth-century Naples, with Oscar renamed Edgardo. The same year the rival impresarios Gye and Mapleson mounted two performances within a fortnight of each other, at the Lyceum and Covent Garden respectively; the first with Thérèse Tietjens as Amelia and Antonio Guglini as the Count; the second with Rosina Penco (Amelia), Mario (Riccardo) and Graziani (Renato) under the baton of Sir Michele Costa. ('I was never fully aware of the value of Auber's music,' wrote Chorley, 'until I heard the assault made by Signor Verdi on the same subject.')* Muzio conducted the American première in New York and then took the same company to the opera's adopted city of Boston, having composed for the occasion a galop to be inserted in the last act and danced on the stage by the regular patrons of the opera.† Throughout the 1860s *Un Ballo in maschera* was among the front rank of Verdian favourites, holding its own more successfully than most during the partial eclipse of the repertoire that occurred in the later part of the century. In 1903 it was the battleground for Toscanini's campaign against the encore. The public of la Scala were determined that their favourite tenor Zenatello should repeat 'È scherzo od è follia'. Toscanini took no notice and went on with the opera. Eventually the whistles and catcalls became such that he threw down his baton and walked out of the theatre.‡ The year 1914 saw the debut of the prince of Riccardos, Alessandro Bonci, who, as we have seen, left a well-nigh indelible mark on the quintet.

Yet strangely enough, *Un Ballo in maschera* fared less well than might have been expected in the Verdi-renaissance of the 1920s and after. Though it remained in the repertoire in most countries, critical approval has been for the most part moderate. Toye, though sympathetic, is somewhat defensive in his assessment;§ Walker complains that the drama lacks drive and intensity and that we really do not *know* the characters.¶ The truth is that in the last fifty years attention has centred far more on the 'questing' operas (to borrow a useful term from Schiller) which explore new problems and blaze new trails. The classical poise and balance of *Un Ballo in maschera* have told against it just as, in a different way, they have told against *Aida*, and even led to a misunderstanding of its nature.

Indeed right from the start it was never a favourite with intellectual reformers. Camillo Boito scandalized the Countess Maffei's salon by describing it as Verdi's worst opera.‖ When it was revived in London in 1888 by Signor Lago's company Bernard Shaw derided it as the kind of melodrama from which Wagner had delivered the musical theatre – though, as so often, he retracted much of what he said in a later article.** It would seem that the origin in grand opera, combined with the troubled history that marks Verdi's final struggle with the censorship, prepare us for a particularly sensational kind of melodrama. In fact *Un Ballo in maschera* is Verdi's *Don Giovanni* – a comedy with dark edges. If the tragic border is wider and blacker than in Mozart, this is his tribute to the romantic age. Many grand operas of the 1830s

---

* H. F. Chorley, *Thirty Years Musical Reminiscences* (London, 1862), quoted Toye, p. 124.

† See G. Martin, 'La prima rappresentazione di *Un Ballo in maschera* a Boston, 15 marzo 1861', in *Atti del I° Congresso dell' I.S.V.* (Parma, 1969), pp. 378–82.

‡ A. Della Corte, *Toscanini visto da un critico* (Turin, 1958), p. 95.

§ Toye, pp. 358–65.

¶ 'Verdi' in *Grove* (5th ed.), VIII, p. 738.

‖ P. Nardi, *Vita di Arrigo Boito*, p. 88.

** *Shaw's Music*, I, pp. 516–7 and III, pp. 576–7.

and '40s had an element of comic relief: the buffo duet between Bertrand and Raimbaud in *Robert le Diable*; the 'quartet of Oberthal and the Anabaptists in *Le Prophète*; it was part of the legacy from heterogeneous opéra-comique of the French Revolution. It is present in *Gustave*, and indeed it is precisely Auber's failure to depart from it sufficiently often that weakens the impact of his opera and even devalues the comic scenes themselves. When the chorus weigh in with an operetta-like refrain after Gustave's 'Vieille sybile qu'on dit habile' we seem to be hearing a composer using a convention which comes naturally to him with no suggestion of wit or irony. When the same thing happens in 'Dì tu se fedele' we are left in no doubt that Riccardo is deliberately putting on a charade, that the convention itself is being drawn upon for specifically comic purposes. Don Giovanni is inviting the statue to supper.

By contrast Mercadante is at the mercy of the 'serio' genre which required all characters except that of Oscar to wear the buskin. All possibilities of ambivalence, of subtle interplay of light and darkness, of the rational and the irrational have been removed by Cammarano's tailoring. Even the supernatural element, represented by Meg's prophecy, becomes just another misfortune with which all three principals have to contend. It was left to Verdi in one of the most exquisitely fashioned of all his scores to make a tissue of improbabilities into a great human drama.

Yet misunderstandings persist. Most modern producers make no attempt to come to grips with the central issue, the chiaroscuro of the score; but they will waste time wrestling with the subsidiary problem of the setting, to which there is no obvious solution. Verdi himself clearly felt that there was nothing wrong in keeping it to Boston. He did not seize the opportunity provided by the unification of Italy and the progressive raising of the censorship to restore the original setting, as he had done with *Giovanna de Guzman* (*I Vespri Siciliani*). Not until 1952 was *Un Ballo in maschera* given by a major opera house in a Swedish setting, when Edward J. Dent prepared for Covent Garden a very serviceable English translation which restored the names of Scribe's libretto. Subsequent revivals in Britain have kept to this, though needless to say Renato and Ulrica must remain as such whenever the Italian text is used, since Arvidson and Ankarstrom will not fit the music. In 1960 the Royal Swedish Opera brought to London a supposedly authentic version with a Gustav who was far more interested in Oscar than in Amelia, and so demolished once and for all the case for a historical approach. To make Riccardo's pursuit of Amelia no more than a diversion, a mere test of his own virility, is to destroy the entire premise on which the opera is built. History is mocked no matter what setting is chosen. A producer can do no more than keep to the basic requirements as stated by Verdi in his letters – a sophisticated, frivolous high society and an age and a climate in which people believed in witchcraft. Seventeenth-century Naples will not really do. Mediterranean sunlight is harmful to the plot. One of the most successful solutions of recent times was the one adopted by the semi-professional Gemini Opera company of Richmond, Surrey, in which the action was moved to the French colony of Louisiana, *c.* 1750. At least this was suitably removed from the ambience of the Pilgrim Fathers.

Few Verdians would go as far as the late Gabriele Baldini in regarding *Un Ballo in maschera* as the composer's masterpiece. Rather, as an instance of that discerning appreciation which a master hopes for and so rarely gets in his lifetime, let us end with a review written by the critic Filippo Filippi of *La Perseveranza* during the 1860s.

> In *Un Ballo in maschera*, having rejected convention and formula, having assigned to each character his own particular language and having rendered the dramatic situation with evident effectiveness, in fact having moulded the drama, Verdi can take his seat between the past and the future and turning round to each of the two sides can say to one party: 'Do you want tunes, ideas, proportions, a beginning, a middle, a continuation and an end? Do you want rhythm, phrasing, pure music? You have it and to spare. And you others, gentlemen of the future, do you want general colouring of the drama, faithful interpretation of the words, freedom from hackneyed and conventional forms? Do you want ideals, gracefulness, distinction of character? Do you want banality banished and in its place the new and the elegant? Do you want the orchestra and the stage to be like a single statue? and a kind of aesthetic pantheism to prevail everywhere? Help yourselves; there is plenty for all your needs.*

---

* A. Della Corte, 'Saggio di bibliografia della critiche al *Ballo in Maschera*', in *I.S.V. Bollettino*, No. 3, p. 1179.

9 LA FORZA DEL DESTINO

LA FORZA DEL DESTINO

Opera in four acts
by
FRANCESCO MARIA PIAVE
(after the play, *Don Alvaro, o La Fuerza del sino*, by Angel de Saavedra, Duke of Rivas,
with a scene added from Schiller's *Wallensteins Lager* translated by Andrea Maffei)

First performed at the Bolshoi Theatre, St Petersburg.
10 November 1862

IL MARCHESE DI CALATRAVA	SECONDO BASSO	Meo
DONNA LEONORA, his daughter	PRIMA DONNA SOPRANO	Caroline Barbot
DON CARLO DI VARGAS, his son	PRIMO BARITONO	Francesco Graziani
DON ALVARO	PRIMO TENORE	Enrico Tamberlick
PREZIOSILLA, a young gipsy girl	PRIMA DONNA MEZZO-SOPRANO	Constance Nantier-Didier
IL PADRE GUARDIANO } Franciscans	PRIMO BASSO	Gian-Francesco Angelini
FRA MELITONE }	PRIMO BARITONO BRILLANTE	Achille De Bassini
CURRA, Leonora's maid	SECONDA DONNA	Lagramanti
An Alcade	SECONDO BASSO	Ignazio Marini
MAESTRO TRABUCO, Muleteer, then pedlar	TENORE COMPRIMARIO	Geremia Bettini
A Spanish military surgeon	SECONDO TENORE	Alessandro Polonini

Muleteers – Spanish and Italian peasants – Spanish and Italian soldiers of various ranks –
orderlies – Italian recruits – monks – peasant girls and vivandières
Ballet: Peasants – soldiers – vivandières
Mimes: Host – hostess – inn-servants – muleteers – soldiers – drummers – buglers – peasants –
children – a tumbler – various sutlers

The action takes place in Spain and Italy
Epoch: towards the middle of the eighteenth century

REVISED VERSION
(with additions by Antonio Ghislanzoni)
First performed at the Teatro alla Scala, Milan,
27 February 1869

MARCHESE	Giuseppe Vecchi	PADRE GUARDIANO	Marcello Junca
LEONORA	Teresa Stolz		
CARLO	Luigi Colonnese	FRA MELITONE	Giacomo Rota
ALVARO	Mario Tiberini	CURRA	Ester Neri
PREZIOSILLA	Ida Benzi	Alcade	Luigi Alessandrini
TRABUCO	Antonio Tasso	Surgeon	Vincenzo Paraboschi

(N.B. Curra, Trabuco and the surgeon are promoted to *donna comprimaria, tenore brillante* and
tenore comprimario respectively!)

For two years after the première of *Un Ballo in maschera* music seems to have faded from Verdi's mind, to judge from his correspondence. Friends who asked for signed musical quotations were put off with the excuse that he could not remember a note of his last opera. 'I fear that Verdi has forgotten everything he knew about music,' Giuseppina, now at last Signora Verdi, wrote to De Sanctis; 'in which case it will be up to you to give him some lessons and get him back into practice.'* He was eager to keep in touch with his professional colleagues such as Piave and Mariani, so long as there was no question of a new opera. 'As you know,' he told Piave, 'I am now the complete countryman. I hope I have bidden farewell to the muses and that I shall never again feel the temptation to take up my pen.'† For the present, domestic affairs and political events were all that mattered. These were the years of the battle of Solferino, Garibaldi's liberation of the south, the unification of Italy, not to mention Verdi's own marriage in Savoy, then part of Italy but soon to be ceded to France by the peace of Villafranca. His devotion to the patriotic cause was well known (he and Mariani had already helped to supply rifles to a national guard), and he was soon to find himself, much against his will, nominated as deputy for Borgo San Donnino (renamed Fidenza in 1926) in the new Italian parliament of 1861.

It was during his visit to Turin in a vain attempt to persuade Cavour to allow him to stand down that two letters arrived at S. Agata. The first was addressed to Giuseppina from her old friend, Mauro Corticelli, secretary to the actress Adelaide Ristori, then touring in Russia; enclosed with it was another addressed to Verdi personally by the singer Enrico Tamberlick. The gist of both was, would Verdi consider accepting a commission from the Imperial Theatre of St Petersburg to write a new opera for the winter season of 1861–2? On the face of it, an unlikely prospect – but Giuseppina was not unhopeful. What is more, the idea of a winter spent away from S. Agata in a fashionable European capital was one that appealed to her. 'If I were not afraid of committing forgery,' she replied to Corticelli, 'I would willingly alter that imposing figure of 22 below zero which will make him open his eyes wide in fright. As for myself, I took refuge under the stove. . . . In any case, however poor an advocate I may be I shall gather together on this occasion the shreds of my eloquence to try and persuade him to expose his nose to the danger of freezing in Russia. If I don't succeed by eloquence I shall employ a method which I have been assured succeeds even at the gates of Paradise with St Peter, and that is to insist and make a nuisance of oneself until one gets what one wants. . . .'‡

Her instinct proved correct. Whether because he wished to serve his country's name in a field more suitable to his talents than Parliament; whether because the creative itch would not be denied; whether because he needed money to pay for the extensive alterations recently made to S. Agata, Verdi declared his willingness to

* Letter from Giuseppina Verdi to De Sanctis, 15.10.1859. *Carteggi Verdiani*, I, pp. 64–6.

† Letter to Piave, 2.9.1859. *Carteggi Verdiani*, II, p. 353.

‡ Letter from Giuseppina Verdi to M. Corticelli, 17.1.1861. Original from the Strepponi–Corticelli correspondence in the Museo alla Scala. Gatti, II, pp. 38–9.

accept.* 'You are quite free to choose the subject and the poet,' Tamberlick had written. 'You can make your own conditions and the score will remain your property.'† Verdi chose Victor Hugo's *Ruy Blas*. But even at the relatively liberal court of Tsar Alexander II Hugo was still dynamite, and a telegram from Tamberlick conveyed the censor's veto. Naturally this put the whole venture in the balance. 'If *Ruy Blas* is impossible this puts me in a very awkward position. I've leafed through play after play without finding one which satisfies me completely. I cannot and will not sign a contract before having found a subject suitable to the artists whom I would have at St Petersburg and approved by the authorities. Therefore as nothing can be settled at the moment perhaps the time will be too limited for me to write for the coming winter.' However, 'Rest assured that I shall continue to search for a subject and if I find one I shall write to you at once. . . .'‡

He proposed a meeting as soon as Tamberlick should return from Russia; but in the end it was Achille, the tenor's brother, who visited the reluctant deputy in Turin and, in Giuseppina's words:

> . . . seeing the terrain not too favourable he swore to gain the victory despite the fact that Verdi, taking advantage of the veto imposed on his subject by means of that famous telgraphic dispatch, was much more concerned with the Chamber than the Theatre. He then embarked gently on his mission, correcting the mistake in the dispatch and declaring with the greatest calmness that Verdi could set to music *Ruy Blas* or anything he liked, since he himself had instructions to grant him all the conditions he could possibly require, apart from compelling Tsar Alexander to declare a republic in Russia. Verdi scratched his head, pointing out that for *Ruy Blas* there was such and such a difficulty; that in the other dramas he had skimmed through there was some other; that a certain play he had once read and liked could not be found. That was enough and there we were hunting round the bookshops and second-hand dealers of Turin, leaving no corner unexplored. Nothing! Nowhere to be found! In the end it was granted to Verdi (who, to be fair, was as active as the rest of us, since he saw no way of escape which would be right and proper), it was, as I say, Verdi who seized by the scruff of the neck a certain person who was going to Milan, the only place it would be possible to find the play and from which he did in fact get it after twenty-four hours to Tamberlick's great relief. . . . So now it is ninety per cent certain that Verdi will write for St Petersburg. §

She does not tell us the title of the play; but there is no reason to doubt that it is the one named in the contract which Verdi made out the following June in Paris: *Don Alvaro*, or *La Fuerza del sino*, by Angel Pérez de Saavedra, Duke of Rivas.¶

Don Alvaro belongs to that great flowering of Spanish romantic drama that took

---

* See F. Walker, 'Introduction to a biographical study (Parliamentary deputy at Turin, Opera composer at St Petersburg)', in *I.S.V. Bollettino*, No. 5 (Parma, 1961), pp. 1–16.

† Letter from E. Tamberlick, 11–23.12.1860. Abbiati, II, pp. 625–6.

‡ Letter to E. Tamberlick, 5.3.1861. Gatti, II, pp. 46–7.

§ Letter from Giuseppina Verdi to Corticelli, 17.4.1861. Walker, *op. cit.*, pp. 11–12.

¶ For the terms of the contract see Walker, p. 13. It is unfortunate that the standard English title should be a transliteration rather than a translation of the original. Why not 'The Power of Fate'?

place in the 1830s, together with García Guttiérrez's *El Trovador*, Martínez de la Rosa's *La Conjuración de Venecia* and others mostly by authors who had returned from the exile to which they had been condemned for their liberal views by the previous monarch, Ferdinand VII. Many had undergone the influence of Hugo's *Hernani* and followed in the same path. This was especially true of Rivas, who shares Hugo's strongly intellectual bent. Not only does his first play *El Moro exposito* contain a polemical preface in praise of the new romanticism; his *Don Alvaro* like *Hernani* and *Le Roi s'amuse* is based on an idea, a logical premise; and its chief characters interest only in so far as they illustrate the working out of that premise. At the centre is Don Alvaro, son of a Viceroy of Peru who has married the last descendant of the Inca monarchs. Having attempted unsuccessfully to make himself the ruler of an independent kingdom, the Viceroy has been thrown into prison. Alvaro has come to Spain to plead for his release. None of this is made clear until the end of the drama. At the beginning Don Alvaro is a sad Byronic man of mystery, who has had the misfortune to fall in love with Eleonora, the daughter of the proud but impoverished Marquis of Calatrava.

He is admired for his valour in the bullring, and loved everywhere for his courtesy and generosity, but since he refuses to reveal his origin the Marquis will not consider him as a son-in-law. He and Eleonora decide to elope; but by a fatal hesitation at the last moment she allows time for the plot to be discovered. In the act of surrendering to the Marquis Alvaro throws down his pistol which accidentally fires, wounding the Marquis mortally. The old man dies cursing his daughter. In the scuffle which follows the lovers are separated. Consumed with feelings of guilt and remorse, they make no attempt to find one another. Eleonora believes Alvaro to have sailed for South America; Alvaro imagines Eleonora to be dead. In fact she has taken refuge first with an aunt in Cordova then in a lonely hermitage in the mountains near the Monastery of the Angels. Meanwhile the Marquis's two sons, Carlos and Alfonso, the first an officer, the second a student of law, have set out to hunt down the guilty pair. Alvaro and Carlos meet in Italy, having both enlisted in the war of the Austrian succession. They save each other's lives and swear eternal friendship; but when Carlos discovers his brother-officer's identity he provokes him to a duel, only to be killed himself. Since he has thus violated the King of Naples's new decree against duelling, Alvaro is arrested and despite the appeal of his commander and fellow officers is sentenced to death — a fate for which he is only too thankful. At the last moment an Austrian attack on the encampment saves him; so once more, like some Latin Vanderdecken, he finds himself condemned to live. Finally he retires to the Monastery of the Angels, where he takes orders as Father Raphael. Here he is found by Eleonora's younger brother, Alfonso, who also succeeds in provoking him to a duel and is likewise fatally wounded. He calls for absolution; but Alvaro feels unworthy to grant it. He summons the unknown hermit from near by, to be confronted by — Eleonora! She rushes into her brother's arms; he, concluding that Eleonora and Alvaro have been hypocritically living in sin all these years, stabs her to the heart and dies himself. Alvaro, whom events have driven out of his mind, hurls himself from a near-by precipice, shrieking curses on the human race.

So much is Hugo exaggerated. But Rivas adds a new dimension to the drama by means of realistic scenes set among the common people of Spain, who impinge on the central figures and define them by contrast.

For this he draws on the traditional stock of Spanish drama – the student who peppers his speech with Latin tags, the young spark (*majo*), the gipsy fortune-teller, the hostess who misuses words, and, like Mistress Quickly, takes offence at those she cannot understand, and so on. As individuals these people hardly exist, but they return us from time to time to a world of kindly common sense by the side of which the Calatravas with their obsessive pride and vengefulness take on the quality of a dream. When Eleonora is overcome by remorse at the thought of her imminent elopement, her practical maid Curra paints a comforting picture of what will happen. Her father will go crying to the mayor about the stain on his escutcheon; he will have search-parties for the fugitives throughout the length and breadth of Spain. But after a while he will calm down; and when at the end of the year Eleonora has presented him with a fine grandson or granddaughter he will be only too happy to welcome home the runaways. As for Carlos and Alfonso, they will soon be boasting everywhere of their rich, generous brother-in-law, who gives them costly presents and pays off their debts. Curra might be talking of any aristocratic family of the last century. Surely she must be right, since this is what happens in real life. But events prove her horribly wrong. She has left out of her account Fate, which aided by Spanish fatalism turns the long arm of coincidence into the 'fuerza del sino'. In the opening scene Preciosilla, the gipsy girl, tells the company how to this very day tears come into her mother's eyes when she reads the horoscope of the infant Eleonora. No one doubts for a moment the truth of the prognosis. Eleonora is doomed to misfortune from the start – as Verdi makes very clear, since the menacing 'fateful' theme that dominates the overture is always associated with her.* Carlos is only too eager to fight his brother-in-arms because he believes that 'fate' has brought him from Spain to Italy for that purpose. Towards the end of the drama fatalism and superstition, ignorance and envy are epitomized in the ridiculous lay priest Melitone, who has always felt a grudge against the Father Superior for keeping the secrets of the monastery to himself. Alarmed by the strange appearance and behaviour of Father Raphael he asks the Father Superior if it is true that once the devil dwelt in that very monastery disguised as a monk. 'Yes,' replies the other, 'but the Lord granted a revelation to the then Father Superior and no harm was done.' When finally nightmare takes over, Alvaro in a frenzy of madness calls upon the abyss to swallow him up and the monks cross themselves with fear, only Melitone is meanly pleased. This time it was *he*, a humble lay priest, who was given the divine warning; so much for the high and mighty Father! Written by a liberal aristocrat of the nineteenth century, who had distinguished himself in the Peninsular War, and set in the Age of Enlightenment, *Don Alvaro* could serve as a Marxist tract for the present day.

The première in Madrid in 1835 was a *succès de scandale* after the manner of *Hernani* in Paris five years earlier. In 1850 an Italian translation appeared by F. Sanseverino, which in due course reached Verdi, and evidently found its way on to the composer's list of possible operatic subjects. In 1852 Cesare De Sanctis expressed the hope that he had not chosen it for Venice since the Neapolitan censors would undoubtedly keep it from the San Carlo Theatre.† Four years later with another subject for Venice still unchosen Verdi scouted the idea of *La Forza del destino*, since, said Muzio, 'he is

---

* See P. P. Varnai, 'Leonora e Don Alvaro: Osservazioni sull'impiego della melodia in funzione drammatica', in *I.S.V. Bollettino*, No. 6 (Parma, 1963–5) p. 1698.

† See letter from De Sanctis, 23.10.1852. *Carteggi Verdiani*, I, pp. 11–14.

prudent and after *Trovatore* he doesn't want to treat a plot that might be dangerous'.*
By 1861 however, the dangers of political censorship were over for most of Italy;
while if the court of St Petersburg had given permission for *Ruy Blas* it was unlikely
to baulk at Rivas's play.

In a letter to Léon Escudier Verdi described *La Forza del destino* as 'powerful,
singular and truly vast; I like it very much and I don't know if the public will find it
as I do, but it is certainly something quite out of the ordinary'.† Like so much
romantic theatre it makes curious reading today. Much of its interest is pictorial – for
to his other talents Rivas added that of a painter – and the stage directions abound in
visual detail, much of it being carried over into Verdi's score. As in *El Trovador*,
while the common people express themselves in prose vernacular the aristocrats
speak a stilted rhymed verse in free metre – a distinction however which vanishes in
Sanseverino's translation. Among these only Don Alvaro has a definite
physiognomy; he is second-hand Manfred or Childe Harold with the same penchant
for melancholy self-communings. Eleonora, her father and brothers, and the Father
Superior are no more than vehicles for the bizarre logic of the plot. There is
something absurd about the way Carlos and Alfonso continually taunt Don Alvaro
with cowardice, infamy and dishonourable intentions, having had ample proof that
he is the soul of honour. True, men will swear that black is white in the grip of an
obsession; and a Shakespeare can make their sentiments plausible through a full
rounding of their characters. Rivas was no Shakespeare; his Calatravas swing from
one vehement extreme to another without any transition of mood. They are twice as
large as life and half as life-like. For Verdi this was no great disadvantage, since it was
in his power as a musician to give them inner coherence. The three playwrights who
dominated his dramatic thinking at that time were Hugo, Schiller and Shakespeare,
all of whom he valued above all for the strength and scale of emotion they portray.
All three find an echo in the opera. Hugo is present in the dramatic conception;
Schiller is drawn upon directly for one of the encampment scenes; while in the
portrayal of humanity on a vast canvas ranging from the highest to the lowest in the
land there is the unmistakable sense of a Shakespearean chronicle play.

For his librettist Verdi returned for the last time (if we except the revisions of
Macbeth in 1865) to his old collaborator Piave, now a family man and, thanks to
Verdi's own support, resident stage director at la Scala, Milan. He had already drawn
him into the search for a suitable play before hitting on *Don Alvaro* (among Verdi's
suggestions had been George Sand's daring *Cosima, ou La haine de l'amour* with its
advocacy of free love and feminism). The contract once signed, the poet had strict
orders to present himself at S. Agata in the middle of July. Offers of help came from
other quarters as well. Count Opprandino Arrivabene sent a contribution to one of
the encampment scenes in which soldiers sing the praises of a beautiful vivandière
while she replies in similar style that she is not to be won in that way, as a one-day
bride, 'a somewhat veiled reply to make it clear that she does not intend to become
the camp whore'.‡ However, this was not to Verdi's purpose and he made no use of
it. But he did write to Andrea Maffei asking permission to borrow certain passages
from his translation of *Wallensteins Lager*. In this he was reverting to an idea cherished

---

* Letter from Muzio to T. Ricordi, 18.6.1856. Abbiati, II, p. 360.
† Letter to L. Escudier, 20.8.1861. *R.M.I.* (1928), p. 22.
‡ Letter from Arrivabene, 15.7.1861. Alberti, pp. 11–12.

as early as 1849, which was to compose a panorama of life in a military encampment after the model of Schiller's play 'where there is a tremendous scene of this kind; soldiers, vivandières, gipsies, astrologers and finally a monk who preaches in the funniest and most delightful manner in the world'.* Maffei gave his willing consent after first drawing Verdi's attention to Schiller's unfinished play *The False Demetrius* which he thought might be of special interest to the Russians since it dealt with the history of the Imperial family. 'I will just finish,' he added, 'by telling Piave that if he should think me good enough to botch him a line or two he mustn't spare me. Sometimes two heads are better than one. In a word do you and Piave make use of an old friend, if you think fit, and you will be doing him a real service.'† After the trouble over *Macbeth* this was indeed tactfully put. However, Verdi did not propose a direct collaboration between the two poets. Instead he helped himself, word for word, to Maffei's translation of Schiller's comic sermon; and indeed all the scenic elements of that part of the opera are taken from Schiller, not Rivas.

The correspondence with Piave about the libretto begins at the time of the poet's return to Milan in August after a fortnight spent in Busseto, by which time the basic structure had already been determined. Verdi worked far more closely with Piave than with other librettists, due to a limited faith in his ability; hence we have no idea how they came to a scheme which both simplifies and adulterates Rivas's original play. Operatic economy demanded the elimination of many of the characters and the amalgamation of others. The merging of the two brothers into one was an obvious necessity, which brought nothing but musical gain, even if the mechanics of the plot suffer in consequence. Don Alvaro must *think* that he has killed Carlo in the duel and find out four years later that he is mistaken. If as a result the young Calatrava appears twice as vindictive as before, there is a line of Don Alvaro's in the play to remind us that even if Don Carlos had lived the earth would not have been wide enough to hold them both and sooner or later they would have had to fight again. More questionable, on the face of it, is the combination of Carlo with the student Pereda, since it takes away Leonora's chief motive for demanding complete seclusion – namely that her affairs have become the property of total strangers. When in the play the Father Superior reasonably asks her if she would not be better off in a convent she replies that in the presence of other people she would never be allowed to forget her circumstances; there would always be a word, a look or a gesture to remind her; the other sisters could never treat her as one of themselves. Had she not already heard her brother's companion Pereda holding forth on the subject in the inn at Hornachuelos? All this is suppressed in the opera. To the Father Superior's suggestion of a convent she merely replies that she will behave like a madwoman unless he grants her the asylum of the hermit's cave. But, it must be stressed yet again that motive in Verdian opera is always a secondary consideration; and there is no doubt that the character of Carlo gains in variety from this extra disguise.

Again, the building up of minor, faceless characters in the drama brings consequences which stretch the arm of coincidence almost to the point of dislocation. In Rivas Preciosilla, Melitone and Trabuco confine themselves to Seville, the Monastery of the Angels and Hornachuelos respectively. In Piave's libretto they all find their separate ways to Velletri in Italy – and in Melitone's case back again.

* Letter to Cammarano, 24.3.1849. Abbiati, II, pp. 4–7.
† Letter from Maffei, 31.8.1861. Abbiati, II, p. 656.

Preciosilla, more drum-majorette than gipsy, becomes a symbol of the happy, carefree life from which Leonora, Carlo and Alvaro are shut out; hence she is needed as mistress of ceremonies at the camp where Carlo and Alvaro first meet. Melitone is required for Schiller's sermon to the troops; Trabuco's change of occupation from muleteer to vendor of second-hand goods seems to have been a late afterthought. 'Keep in the Jewish pedlar (one, that is),' Verdi had written to Piave in September.* And the autograph of Act III specifies 'Ebreo'. Only in the first edition of the printed score does he become Trabuco. Work on the opera proceeded throughout the late summer and early autumn with Piave coming to Busseto and S. Agata as often as his duties would permit. His offer to bring some Spanish folk songs with him, however, was curtly refused ('I am not in the habit of studying music . . .'). Verdi meanwhile seems to have followed the method adopted in *Simon Boccanegra*, which was to prepare a prose synopsis act by act dividing the dialogue roughly into lyrical and declamatory sections, specifying where possible the number of verses and the appropriate metre. Frequently Piave would find his verses returned to him with instructions to make them shorter and more vivid. Sometimes Verdi himself would give an example of what he wanted adding, 'These lines are ugly, I know, but you're a poet and should be able to make them better.' Act III had too many changes of scene ('. . . like a magic lantern show'), so Piave hit on the idea of having the battle of Velletri described by an onlooker and Don Alvaro brought back on a stretcher to the place from which he and Carlo had set forth. In the event the first of these suggestions was adopted but not the second. As always Verdi was concerned in the action scenes never to let the tension flag for a moment. In the fourth act, 'Leonora's cantabile when she is wounded is long and dull. . . . Don Carlo has too many words.' The result of shortening the dialogue to the composer's satisfaction was to obscure the lines which made clear just why Carlo stabs his sister after calling for Christian absolution, i.e. his belief that she and Alvaro had been living together in the hermitage. Then too, having left out that part of Don Alfonso's speech which explains to the audience who Alvaro really is, Verdi found it necessary to work in somewhere a reference to what he called 'Don Alvaro's life and miracles'. This was finally managed in the beautiful scena which precedes Alvaro's 'Oh tu che in seno agli angeli'. Most of the encampment scene was worked at by poet and composer behind closed doors since Piave, 'old soldier' as he was, would never dream of moving a step in this area without reference to headquarters. But it seems that the Rataplan chorus was his idea.

The opera was in all essentials complete by the last week in November 'except for the instrumentation', so Verdi told his publisher.† But well before that time he had begun to take thought about the casting. He wrote to Achille Tamberlick:

Please advise the management of the theatre at St Petersburg that . . . besides the soprano, tenor and baritone they will need:

(1) A soprano to do the gipsy girl, a very brilliant and important role, like the Page in *Un Ballo in maschera*.

---

* The letters to Piave about *La Forza del destino* are among the collection of Natale Gallini and are quoted in part in Abbiati, II, pp. 646–67, together with some of Piave's replies which are to be found at S. Agata.

† Letter to T. Ricordi, 22.11.1861. Abbiati, II, p. 667.

(2) A basso profondo to do the role of the Father Superior.

(3) A comic baritone for the role of Fra Melitone, also a very important role. It could be De Bassini, to whom I have even written, but I don't know if he could or should or wants to do such a part.'*

At first sight this seems extraordinary. The forty-two year old Neapolitan baritone had created three Verdian roles in the past: the fierce Seid (*Il Corsaro*), the noble and sorrowing Doge (*I Due Foscari*) and the no less pathetic Miller (*Luisa Miller*). He had no reputation as a buffo; but Verdi, like all experienced theatre composers, had an eye for unlikely talent. 'I have a part for you,' he wrote to De Bassini, 'if you would be willing to accept it – comic, very charming – it's that of Fra Melitone. It will fit you to a T and I've almost identified it with you personally. Not that you are a buffoon, but you have a certain humorous vein which squares perfectly with the character that I've intended for you, assuming that you approve,'† After that De Bassini could hardly refuse; nor did he. In due course the gipsy girl, Preziosilla, became a contralto, but her personality remains as described to young Tamberlick.

At the beginning of December the Verdis set out for St Petersburg by way of Turin and Paris, having equipped themselves against the Russian climate and Russian food. Further letters to Piave make it clear that the score was still not complete in all its details, notably in the tenor and baritone duets. With his last specimen enclosure (an extra verse for Don Carlo in Act III where he felt that the tenor had too many solos) Verdi announced that rehearsals were to begin any day but were being held up by the illness of the prima donna.‡ Then at the end of the month Giuseppina wrote to Count Arrivabene:

> Certainly the news I'm about to give you will make your eyes, mouth and ears all open at once. But though you may exclaim in all the keys in your basso profondo voice 'Ha!' 'He!' and 'Ha!' the news is true none the less. Verdi will not give his new opera in Petersburg – this year.
>
> Alas! Singers' voices are as fragile as . . . (I'll leave you to complete the phrase) and Mme la Grua's voice, to her and Verdi's misfortune, is an appalling example. . . . Such being the case, lacking the prima donna for whom the part was written, and there being no other singer suitable for the role, Verdi asked to be released from his contract. To this request he was given for answer a big 'no', though preceded, followed and seasoned with the fairest words in the world. So they have agreed to give the opera next winter subject to the conditions [*etc.*, *etc.*]§

Verdi suspended work on the instrumentation and among other things undertook a journey to London where he saw his *Inno delle Nazioni*, commissioned to represent Italian music at the Great Exhibition, rejected by the committee on a technicality –

* Letter to A. Tamberlick, 30.10.1861. Quoted in translation in G. Martin, 'Unpublished Letters: a contribution to the history of *La Forza del destino*', in *I.S.V. Bollettino*, No. 5 (Parma, 1962), p. 746.
  † Letter to De Bassini, 26.10.1861. *Carteggi Verdiani*, II, p. 62.
  ‡ Letter to Piave, 7.1.1862. Abbiati, II, pp. 678–9.
  § Letter from Giuseppina Verdi to Arrivabene, 1.2–20.1 (*sic!* – probably referring to the differences in the Russian calendar). 1862. Alberti, pp. 13–15.

much to the indignation of the British public – and subsequently performed at Her Majesty's Theatre in a concert organized by Mapleson with a choir of 200 singers and Theresa Tetjens as soloist instead of Tamberlick for whom it was written. It was not the kind of composition to which Verdi himself attached much value; and he expressed relief at the committee's decision and exasperation at the public reaction to it. But the *Inno delle Nazione* has two points of interest for the student of Verdi's operas: the bold, not to say reckless, combination of different melodies which will be achieved with greater skill in *Aida*; and the fact that it is his first collaboration with Arrigo Boito, who wrote the words. The young poet was compensated by Verdi with the gift of a watch; an auspicious beginning to a friendship that was to weather many a frost before ripening into the summer of *Otello, Falstaff* and the revised *Boccanegra*.

The Verdis returned to Russia in September, two months before the scheduled first night. The opera was by now fully scored and a copy already prepared by Ricordi at Verdi's behest for a performance which was to take place in Madrid early the following year. It seems that he was not immune to second thoughts, for a letter to Tito Ricordi speaks of another cabaletta for the baritone aria.* The soprano was now to be Caroline Douvry-Barbot, wife of the creator of Gounod's Faust. Evidently she was Verdi's choice; and the news that her engagement was being opposed by the contralto Constance Nantier-Didier provoked him to a furious remonstrance with the management. 'I can understand that Mme Didier (though she has no right to do so) should try to get out of singing in my work so as not to find herself singing with Mme Barbot; but that she should want to prevent her engagement and so to hinder my opera and the progress of the repertoire, that is altogether too much. . . . I will not submit to Mme Didier's tyranny.'† Fortunately he did not have to do so. Matters were settled amicably without any unpleasantness arising between Leonora and Preziosilla. The cast proved an exceptionally strong one with a notable Don Carlo in Francesco Graziani, brother of the creator of Alfredo in *La Traviata*. Nor was De Bassini the only old stager to take part: the tiny role of the Alcade was taken by Ignazio Marini, the first Oberto and the first Attila.

The première was not an unqualified success, though it earned Verdi much applause, many curtain calls and the Order of St Stanislas. The extravagant eulogies of the *Journal de St Petersburg* were offset by three very lukewarm notices in the Russian-language papers, *Son of the Fatherland, Petersburg News* and *Russian World*. Disagreeing in detail, they were unanimous in finding the work too long. Despite full houses night after night the *Gazzetta Musicale di Milano* felt bound to record a hostile demonstration at the third performance, whether as the writer surmises from the nationalist Russian school or as Giuseppina declared from the 'Teutonic' faction. If the former, the conclusive reply is surely Mussorgsky's *Boris Godunov*, which could hardly have come into being in its present form without the example of *La Forza del destino*.‡

From Russia the Verdis went to Madrid for the Spanish première. Once again the performances were well attended and the press cool, if not hostile. Verdi was accused

---

*See letter to T. Ricordi, undated. Abbiati, II, pp. 708–9; also *Studi Verdiani*, VI (Parma, 1990), pp. 55ff.

† Letter to the Director of the Imperial Theatre, St Petersburg, 12.3.1862. Abbiati, II, p. 693.

‡ For a detailed account of press comment on the first night see G. Barblan, 'Un po' di luce sulla prima rappresentazione della *Forza del Destino* a Pietroburgo', in *I.S.V. Bollettino*, No. 5, pp. 831–79.

of having forsaken the paths congenial to him, having fallen into imitation and above all having desecrated a Spanish masterpiece – an opinion evidently shared by the Duke of Rivas himself. Verdi was inclined to blame the performers, though he had nothing but praise for the soprano Anne Caroline de Legrange and the indestructible Fraschini. 'The rest nil or bad.'* That the creator of Corrado, Zamoro and Arrigo, not to mention Riccardo, should at forty-six distinguish himself in the exacting role of Alvaro is astonishing – especially since the part contained a double aria with chorus ('Qual sangue sparsi') which was removed in the revision of 1869. However, it was doubtless for Fraschini that Verdi had transposed the cabaletta 'S'incontri la morte' down a tone from C major to B flat and lightened the scoring 'since no one will be able to perform what was written for Tamberlick. Please put it in all the scores which you hire out.'† Early printed scores all contain the untransposed version; both, however, can still be seen in the part-autograph manuscript score in the Bibliothèque Nationale, Paris.‡

Yet Verdi was still unhappy about the score as it stood. What chiefly worried him was the dénouement with its three deaths by violence. The search for an adequate solution was to take him six years, often to his editor's inconvenience. 'It's true,' he wrote in the autumn of 1863, 'that I haven't yet sent you the score of *La Forza del destino* because I counted on modifying the dénouement and making some changes at the end of the third act, but so far I've thought of nothing.'§ He decided for the time being to hire out the opera unaltered to the Italian theatres; but the Parisian performance for which Léon Escudier had been pressing him would have to be delayed until the opera could be adjusted to his satisfaction. He wrote to Piave for ideas, and also to Achille De Lauzières, the future translator of *Don Carlos*. Neither was able to provide what he wanted. 'Let me just say,' he wrote to Escudier, 'that in my view the "power of fate", the "fatality", cannot lead to a reconciliation of the two families; the brother after having made all that bother must avenge his father's death (remember too that he's a Spaniard); he cannot possibly agree to a wedding. De Lauzières wanted to do a trio like the one in *Ernani*, but in *Ernani* the action continues during the entire trio, whereas here it finishes just as the trio begins; therefore it's pointless to write one. . . . I'm now in more of a muddle than ever.¶ The length of the opera was also a problem; but the idea of shortening it, raised by Ricordi as early as May 1863, was opposed by Verdi from the start: 'Up to now,' he wrote to Ricordi in December, 'it is no part of my intention to take out the part of Melitone.' Yet that is in effect what was done at the first performance in Vienna in 1865, where it was reduced to a few recitatives.

That same year, however, while negotiating with Perrin, director of the Opéra, a contract for a new work to be given there in 1867 (it would, of course, be *Don Carlos*)

---

* Letter to Arrivabene, 22.2.1863. Alberti, p. 23.

† Letter to T. Ricordi, April 1863. Abbiati, II, p. 732. This was written just before the London première under Luigi Arditi – in the event postponed until 1867 – in which Charles Santley sang Don Carlos. For Verdi's cavalier treatment of him in Paris see Santley, *Student and Singer*, p. 248.

‡ Bibliothèque National, Rés. 1659.

§ Letter to T. Ricordi, 3.10.1863. Abbiati, II, p. 744.

¶ Letter to Escudier, 29.7.1864. R.M.I. (1928), p. 180.

the question arose once more of a French *Forza del destino*, complete with ballet. Given the dimensions of French grand opera, this would mean adding to the score rather than shortening it. Verdi began by suggesting an extra recitative for Don Carlos as he waits for Alvaro in the last act, explaining how he came to be still alive. Or if that was not enough 'perhaps I should add a tiny act after the third. . . . What do you think?'* By way of compensation he proposed ending the third act with the Rataplan chorus 'cutting out the two numbers which follow'.† In 1865 the first of these was the quarrel duet, the excision of which is standard practice in Italy to this day. In view of the opera's later history it is just possible that this regrettable cut had Verdi's sanction.

Perrin evidently was in favour of including the first scene of the play which Verdi had omitted (the only one in which Rivas's Preciosilla actually appears). It was not an unreasonable thought. Rivas builds up the mysterious character of Don Alvaro by having the customers of an inn near Seville talk about him. At a certain point Alvaro himself appears at the door, glances broodingly at the assembled company and then goes away without a word. It is as effective a dramatic 'cavatina' as could be wished. In the opera, he is obliged to make his first appearance bounding in through an open window, and then with an arm round the prima donna and a frantic eye on the conductor to plunge straightaway into a fast duet movement. Even for the most personable of tenors this is difficult to manage with dignity. Verdi agreed in principle to Perrin's suggestion; but insisted that there should be no ballad for Preziosilla, who would otherwise have too much to sing. Also great care would be needed to avoid duplicating the scene in Act II at Hornachuelos. Perhaps there could be a small chorus of women from Calatrava's household who have seen Alvaro passing by night after night with two horses and a negro servant (an important detail, this, in Rivas's drama since it alerts a passing priest to Alvaro's plans and he proceeds to inform the Marquis). Preziosilla would then have a few lines about Alvaro being 'digne d'une reine'; the scene would close with the silent appearance of Alvaro followed by a muttered chorus 'à demi-voix, mystérieux, fantastique'.‡ He was resistant to the idea of raising the part of Preziosilla, as Perrin suggested, or lowering that of Don Carlo to suit Faure, though in the end he was to do both. In November he and Giuseppina went to Paris to arrange the dual contract with Perrin; but although the translation had already been begun by du Locle and Nuitter§ he was to inform Arrivabene the following month, 'There was too much to do to *Forza* and it was impossible for me to undertake so much work in the space of a year.'¶ 'Friend and enemies' alike had been asked for suggestions for a new ending. At one time Verdi had even considered approaching Rivas himself on the subject. After three years he was back to where he had started.

Not until after *Don Carlos* had been composed and performed did the breakthrough occur. The initiative came from Tito Ricordi, who planned for the carnival season of 1869 at la Scala, Milan, a revival of *La Forza del destino* with a first-rate cast. His aim was two-fold: to bring about Verdi's rapprochement with Milan's

---

* Letter to Perrin, 3.9.1865. *I.S.V. Carteggi* 36/32.

† Letter to Escudier, 12.9.1865. R.M.I. (1928), p. 194.

‡ Letter to Perrin, 27.9.1865. *I.S.V. Carteggi* 36/33.

§ See Escudier's notice in *L'Art mondiale*, 28.12.1865. U. Günther, *R. de M.* LVIII, p. 35.

¶ Letter to Arrivabene, 31.12.1865. Alberti, p. 61.

first opera house and to provide a definite occasion for Verdi to work towards in making any adjustments that would be necessary. He first wrote to the composer in August 1868. Verdi, then taking the waters at Tabbiano, was favourably disposed and agreed to return to the problem that autumn, but without any guarantee of a solution. 'By all means let *La Forza del destino* be announced,' he wrote back, 'but with no mention of any changes, since there might very well not be any.'

A more serious difficulty was the librettist. In December 1867 Piave had suffered a stroke which left him totally paralysed for the last eight years of his life. Verdi rallied to his and his family's assistance with gifts of money. He also organized the publication for their benefit of an album of romanze by different composers, to which he had the quaint idea of asking Wagner to contribute. ('If Wagner can't we shall have to resort to Petrella. . . .')* Piave's mantle as the librettist-in-ordinary to the house of Ricordi and to the North Italian theatres in general fell on the shoulders of Antonio Ghislanzoni, a poet, journalist and jack-of-all-trades, sometimes known as the Lombard Paul de Kock. Born in Lucca in 1824 he had started his career as a baritone in the smaller theatres. In the early 1860s he became for a while associated with the 'scapigliatura',† that false dawn of Italian culture that bears so strong a resemblance to our own 'naughty nineties'. For Ghislanzoni the moment of truth arrived with the première of Faccio's *Amleto* in Genoa in 1865. All the 'scapigliati' had turned out in force to praise. He himself found it full of promise; what disgusted him was the publicity, the friends and colleagues who leaped on the stage to join the curtain calls. He poured out his scorn in a sarcastic article written for the *Rivista minima*, ending with the remark that Faccio will 'succeed in getting out of the rut of mediocrity and create excellent musical works when he cordially thanks his friends for the good services they have rendered him, and tells them never again to meddle in his affairs'.‡ When Clarina Maffei wrote to Verdi about *Amleto* hoping for a word of encouragement for the latest of her young lions, he replied in terms that suggested that he had read Ghislanzoni's article and approved of its content.

A cordial friendship was to develop between the composer and his new librettist. Ghislanzoni recollected his first visit to S. Agata in a charming essay§ contrasting the jovial, middle-aged composer, the picture of rude health, with the pale, hollow-eyed young man with whom he had dined in Venice at the time of *Attila*. Both he and Giulio Ricordi had given much thought to the ending of *La Forza del destino*. A letter of Verdi's to the publisher shows which way their ideas were tending:

> The seams would be too evident if we were to bring back the gipsies at the end; then it would jar with the colour of the final scenes. A gipsy scene would be a distraction; it would prolong the action and, what is worst of all, cool it down. It's pointless; once this cursed subject is admitted, the brother and sister, Leonora and Carlo, have to die. To find a way of killing off Carlo even off stage is quite easy; but it's very difficult to have Leonora die. It hardly matters whether there's a

---

* Letter to Giulio Ricordi, 29.3.1869. Abbiati, III, p. 314. In fact Wagner's place was taken by Antonio Cagnoni. The other contributors were Auber, Mercadante, Federico Ricci, Ambroise Thomas and Verdi himself.

† See Chapter 1.

‡ Quoted Abbiati, III, pp. 25–6.

§ 'La casa di Verdi a S. Agata', in *Libro Serio* (Milan, 1879), pp. 151–68.

duet, a trio or a chorus; the only consideration must be the dramatic spectacle. I wouldn't want to hear the finale to the second act recalled at this point. It is a ceremony, a rite which cannot be repeated. In a word the poet should consider only the spectacle; the music can be left to look after itself. As far as I'm concerned a recitative would do perfectly well. . . . . If the poet can find an ending which is good both logically and theatrically the musical ending will automatically be good.*

Ghislanzoni, apprised of Verdi's objections, hastened to approve them. 'Verdi is perfectly right,' he told Giulio Ricordi, 'when he says that a gipsy scene would slacken the action. My idea was that the gipsies would merely appear for a brief moment so that when the curtain falls the stage should not be entirely crowded with monks. . . . I don't think that the composer realized that I wanted Leonora wounded off stage, so that the death-throes of Carlo should be avoided as well.†. . . In my opinion it would be a great gain to remove the final agony of both.'‡ But it was Verdi himself who hit upon the solution, as may be gathered from the fragment of a letter to Giulio Ricordi, from which the first page is tantalizingly missing: '. . . to see Alvaro finish in so resigned a fahion? I have very great doubts over this which may grow or diminish when I've slept on them. Meanwhile let Ghislanzoni be the judge and if he doesn't like it we'll look for something else.' The rest of the letter refers to changes to be made to the challenge duet in Act III and the finale to the same act which Verdi found somewhat disjointed, 'too many tunes without one which dominates'.§ One would give a good deal to know just what the missing first page contained, and whether the notion of a terzetto with Alvaro, Leonora and the Father Superior (not Carlo as in De Lauzière's plan) had already been arrived at. But to end on a note of Christian resignation is of course the only possible alternative to the original dénouement. The three principals have been carried too far from each other on the trajectory of the drama for ordinary relations to be restored between them. A reconciliation would have had the artificial effect of the eighteenth-century happy ending – no great sin in an age where artifice was the rule, but quite out of place in a romantic melodrama. Moreover, the religious ceremony which forms the finale to Act II (a Verdian addition to the original plot) needs a dramatic counterbalance in the final act. This had been provided in a macabre fashion by the ending of 1862. The later dénouement merely reverses the coin. Alvaro instead of blaspheming accepts his sufferings as the will of God. The religious element, no longer generalized in a chorus

---

* Letter to Giulio Ricordi, 16.11.1868. Abbiati, III, p. 232.

† One of the hazards of this ending is described by Charles Santley who played Carlo to Mongini's Alvaro in the first English performance of 1867. 'He had been a dragoon and used to the broadsword, and when excited laid about him most vigorously. I am no swordsman; I never studied anything except the small sword for a short time, more to acquire greater freedom in my joints than for actual sword practice. I was consequently no match for such an adversary, and I confess he made me feel somewhat nervous in the duel at the end of *La Forza*. He did pink me one night. I thought he had cut off the end of my first finger, the blow so benumbed it. When I dropped dead, my right hand being out of sight of the audience, I felt with my thumb and found the blood trickling freely. I had to lie on the stage about ten minutes before the curtain fell, and a very long ten minutes they appeared. I was very much relieved when I found my finger, except for a tolerably large cut, all safe.' Santley, *Student and Singer*, pp. 249–50.

‡ Letter from Ghislanzoni, undated. Abbiati, III, p. 233.

§ Letter to Giulio Ricordi, 27.11.1868. Abbiati, III, p. 234.

of monks, is personalized in the Father Superior, and the conflict is resolved, as so often in a Verdian opera, through a final confrontation of principals. It is such a characteristic solution that one can only wonder why Verdi took six years to reach it. Was it due to an anti-religious bias? If so how and why was the bias overcome?

The answer may well lie in an event which took place in 1867. Giuseppina, while on a shopping expedition to Milan, had, unknown to Verdi, introduced herself to one of his oldest friends, Clarina Maffei. She in turn presented Giuseppina to Alessandro Manzoni, the eighty-two-year-old novelist and poet, and promised to do the same for Verdi himself. Manzoni's I Promessi Sposi has been called Walter Scott italianized. Certainly the two novelists shared a sympathy for humanity in all walks of life, and an interest in historical detail. But there is a radical difference. Scott's outlook was purely secular, with religion kept for canting Puritans and dogged Covenanters. He could never have written Manzoni's chapter on the Nun of Monza or the conversion of the unnamed robber baron in I Promessi Sposi. For Manzoni religion was as real and all-pervasive an experience as for John Bunyan. Verdi in middle age was to say the least an agnostic; but Manzoni's novel had always touched a responsive chord in him. To Clarina Maffei he described it as 'not only the greatest book of our age but one of the greatest books ever to have come out of the human mind. It isn't only a book, it's a consolation for humanity. I was sixteen when I first read it. Since then I've read many others; on reading them again advancing age has either modified or reversed my youthful opinions . . . but for that book my enthusiasm remains as strong as it ever was; indeed it has become stronger the more I get to know humanity. . . .'*

However, it was not until the following year that the two men met. 'How can I describe to you,' Verdi wrote, 'the new, the sweet, the indefinable sensation I experienced in the presence of that Saint, as you call him? If mortal men could be adored I would have knelt before him.'† These are strong words for Verdi. What is more likely than that the experience of having met Manzoni should have overflowed into La Forza del destino and so prompted a dénouement in the tenor of I Promessi Sposi? Indeed as realized by Verdi the opera has the looseness of design more appropriate to a novel than a stage play; while at least two of the characters have Manzonian counterparts. The Father Superior is kin to Cardinal Federigo Borromeo, Alvaro in his monkish guise has elements of Padre Cristoforo, while Melitone is a variant of the tetchy little priest, Don Abbondio – with the difference that Melitone is not a coward.

The solution found, Verdi began to concern himself with the singers. As in Un Ballo in maschera it was the casting of the peripheral characters which preoccupied him most. 'Don't forget that in Forza you need three artists who are completely at their ease on stage to do Preziosilla, Melitone and Trabuco. Their scenes are comedy, pure comedy. Therefore good diction and an easy stage manner. See to that. . . .'‡ In general he was far from happy about the singers proposed and constantly threatened if rehearsals went badly to return to his winter quarters in Genoa taking the new pieces with him, so that the opera would have to be given in the 1862 version. There

---

* Letter to C. Maffei, 24.5.1867. A. Luzio, Profili biografici e bozzetti storici, II (Milan, 1927), pp. 522–4.
† Letter to Clarina Maffei, 7.7.1868. Luzio, op. cit., p. 525.
‡ Letter to G. Ricordi, 15.12.1868. Abbiati, III, p. 235.

were to be no concessions in the way of transposition or puntatura. In any case only the ending was to be announced as new.

In the event he proved less intransigent. Carlo's double aria in Act III was transposed down from F to E for Colonna; Preziosilla's 'È bella la guerra' was taken up from B flat major to B, so producing a far stronger modulation at the transition into the following number. Meanwhile Verdi drafted out for Ghislanzoni the additional text; then, characteristically, sent his own draft leaving the poet to discard the new lines he had devised and adjust Verdi's so that they flowed more elegantly, while keeping the original metre and inflection. Nor did he neglect the visual side. In Act II, 'The landing must be small and not very high – five or six stairs which lead to the room where Leonora is lodging: it should be at the side and not too far back. The scene to be as spacious as possible, always bearing in mind that the monastery must be prepared behind it.' An interesting reminder, this, of how rapidly scenes within an act were changed by moving 'flats' across the stage from the wings. In Act III, 'Preziosilla must sing her song standing on an eminence, or at least she should get up on one immediately afterward to practise her witchcraft. However that shouldn't worry the stage designer since in an encampment you can always find something to rig up at a moment's notice – a bench, an empty barrel, etc. . . .'*

Finally some interesting instructions about the chorus: 'Urge the chorus master to make his singers learn the part so as to achieve real precision, and above all not to let them get away with a sloppy attack. For massed voices attack is the most important thing. . . . We must at all costs arrange the voices and the effect of the female choruses in the camp scene. Contraltos on their own are intolerable and so are sopranos. So be sure and improve matters by adding some boys to the contraltos and finding some good solo voices among the sopranos. . . .'† His various admonitions were not in vain. 'By this time,' he wrote to Count Arrivabene early in March, 'you will know that the *Forza del destino* had a good performance and was a success. La Stolz and Tiberini were superb; the others good. Chorus and orchestra performed with a fire and precision which I cannot describe. . . .'‡

The event had a double significance. It marked Verdi's rapprochement with the theatre which had seen his earliest triumphs and which, after a sad decline, was about to be restored to its position as Italy's leading opera house; and more sadly it was the final fruit of an artistic collaboration with the great conductor Angelo Mariani. Within months a friendship that had endured for more than twelve years began to go sour for reasons that are not entirely clear even to this day. Verdi's growing admiration for Teresa Stolz, the new Leonora and Mariani's fiancée, may have been a factor; so too Mariani's growing vanity and self-importance, aggravated, no doubt, by extravagant praise which the press habitually lavished on him.§ 'I do not admit the right either of singers or conductors to create,' Verdi was to write two years later. 'Would you like an example? Once you mentioned with great approval an effect which Mariani drew from the overture to *La Forza del destino* when he made the brass

---

* Letter to G. Ricordi, 15.1.1869. Abbiati, III, pp. 243–4.

† Letter to G. Ricordi, 11.2.1869. Abbiati, III, pp. 249–50.

‡ Letter to Arrivabene, 1.3.1869. Alberti, pp. 99–100.

§ Ghislanzoni: 'Angelo Mariani deserves, first and foremost in Italy, the title of creator'; Filippi: 'One might say that . . . he composed another *Don Carlos* within Verdi's' – this of the opera's Italian première in 1867. See *I.S.V. Bollettino*, No. 5, p. 1785.

entry in it fortissimo; I disapprove of that effect. The brass playing *a mezza voce* should according to my notions . . . express the religious chanting of the monks. Mariani's fortissimo alters the character completely and the passage becomes a warlike fanfare – something which has nothing to do with the subject of the drama in which the military part is entirely episodic.'* But at the time he was only too grateful for the conductor's fire, enthusiasm and attention to detail.

From the anthology of criticisms of *La Forza del destino* through the ages assembled by Andrea della Corte and published in the fifth bulletin of the Institute of Verdi Studies it would seem that few of Verdi's operas have provoked such contradictory reactions. Two charges, however, recur with notable persistence: a lack of organic unity and a discrepancy between the comic and serious elements. Some writers regard the work as a backward step after the elegance and finish of *Un Ballo in maschera*; others see it as frankly popular work aimed at the galleries, an old-fashioned but enjoyable mixture of the sublime and the trivial. Such is the gist of Francis Toye's verdict, expressed with typical Edwardian panache: 'If *La Forza del destino* inspires love at all, it is perhaps the instinctive tenderness and worship given by a lover to his mistress rather than the reasoned affection of friend for friend or husband for wife.'†

All this is very far from Verdi's own view. To him *La Forza del destino* belonged together with *Don Carlos* to the rare category of serious music drama. It was for this reason that he refused it the following year to the San Carlo Theatre, Naples. He wrote to De Sanctis:

> You should know that there are operas of *ideas* (bad ideas if you like) and operas of cavatinas, duets, etc., etc. for which some of your celebrities might be good, since your public likes them, but as for me, God preserve me from having them, above all in *La Forza del destino*. . . . Your choruses are small and little use for these operas. Your orchestra has excellent elements but individuals are not sufficient to realize those ideas of which I spoke earlier. For these you need a Head. Have you found one? And the rest? And the mise-en-scène!!! . . . At the San Carlo you have much that's good, that's excellent. Perhaps what you have is the best in the world but for these operas you want something else. You want ensemble. . . .'‡

In fact he consented to come to produce *Don Carlos* for the Neapolitans in 1872; but they were not to see *La Forza del destino* till 1876. For the time being the San Carlo was unsuitable for 'modern opera' (Verdi's words). Like all Verdi's mature operas *La Forza del destino* has its own special terms of reference. Its drama is that of the epic poem, the serial novel, or the chronicle play. A certain looseness of structure is essential to its purpose. The more varied the episodes the more powerful seems the hand of fate which pursues its victims over such vast distances. A shorter, more concentrated dramatic scheme could not have achieved this object.

Inevitably the immense range and variety of the music has lent itself to the sport of reminiscence hunting. An early review by Filippo Filippi detected traces of Schubert's 'Ave Maria' in Leonora's 'melodia' from Act IV.

---

* Letter to G. Ricordi, 11.4.1871. *Copialettere*, pp. 255–7.
† Toye, p. 377.
‡ Letter to De Sanctis, 21.5.1869. *Carteggi Verdiani*, I, p. 111.

In my consummate ignorance [*Verdi wrote*] I really could not say how many years have passed since I heard Schubert's 'Ave'; so to imitate it would have been difficult for me. Do not imagine when I talk of 'consummate musical ignorance' that I am joking; it is absolutely true. In my house there is hardly any music; I have never been to a music library or to a publisher's to study a piece of music. I am familiar with some of the best contemporary operas not from having read them but from having heard them in the theatre. In all this there is a definite policy as you will doubtless realize. I repeat that of all composers past and present I am the least erudite . . . I refer to erudition, not musical knowledge. In that respect I should lie if I said that I had not studied hard and thoroughly in my youth. Indeed it is for this reason that I have a hand strong enough to bend the notes to my will. . . .*

The most important part of this letter is the emphasis on the thoroughness of his early training. Like all his compatriots he was educated on the German as well as the Italian classics; but it was many years before both his own musical ability and the taste of the public permitted the fruits of this training to appear in his own compositions. Verdi, Donizetti and Mercadante were all in their different ways attempting the reconquest for Italy of the German heritage. Donizetti's *L'Elisir d'amore* keeps strictly within the style and language of the Italy of the 1830s. *Don Pasquale* (1843) has echoes of Mozart and Schubert. In *La Forza del destino* the Schubertian influence is not confined to 'Pace, pace, mio Dio'. It will be found just as patently in Leonora's second act aria 'Madre pietosa vergine'; while in the chief motif of the overture (Ex. 287b) can be heard the powerful surge of Beethoven's *Egmont* Overture. Throughout the score new and traditional, plain and exotic exist side by side; but amid the wealth of contrasted elements certain melodic patterns persist which unobtrusively confer a sense of unity on the opera.

A production book survives of the 1862 version in the library of the Accademia Santa Cecilia in Rome. No author is given, but from a letter of Verdi's in 1862 it can be assumed to be Piave himself. Here the various characters are described as follows:

Marchese di Vargas (Calatrava): A very noble, haughty Spanish lord who feels the spirit of his rank very keenly, and still more so, if that were possible, his point of honour. He is about 65: grey hair, moustache and whiskers.

Donna Leonora: daughter of the preceding, about 20 years old, a very gentle and passionate creature who loves her father very dearly but not to the extent of putting him before Alvaro, who is her whole existence and her universe. She suffers deeply at having resigned a hero's love and a better fate.

Don Carlo: her brother – a passionate young man of about 22. Throughout animated by a thirst to avenge the offended honour of his house; he faces every difficulty with resolution and tenacity and spurns every danger in order to arrive at his goal.

Don Alvaro: Indian of royal stock, of the most passionate spirit, indomitable and always nobly generous; about 25.

Padre Guardiano: a true model of evangelical meekness, one whose faith is unshakeable. About 70 with white hair and beard.

* Letter to Filippi, 4.3.1869. *Copialettere*, pp. 616–17.

Fra Melitone: Lay-brother, cheerful, rather quick to anger, but easily pacified. About 40, he is a great snuff-taker and has all the marks of shrewdness.

Preziosilla: young gipsy girl, witty, flirtatious; she will be about 20 with all that sense of propriety to be found in her kind.

Curra: young woman in her early twenties, carefree and desirous of travelling – which is one reason why she favours the love of Don Alvaro and her mistress.

Alcade: a man typical of the innumerable tribe of self-important dignitaries, etc., about 50.

Trabuco: A 'character', an open-hearted, lively wit.

NB: about 18 months pass between the first and second acts; several years between the second and the third; more than five years between the third and the fourth. The artists should take care not to forget this when they make themselves up.*

PRELUDE
(1862)

This shows an extension of the ground-plan that had served Verdi for so many of his preludes in the past. Various ideas from the opera itself are deployed in a pattern whose main features are: a brusque motif to arrest the attention; an ethereal theme, usually a prayer, with high shimmering violins; and a fierce crescendo and descrescendo like a tidal wave, leaving a sense of tragic desolation as it recedes. In the first *La Forza del destino* the scheme is elaborated in accordance with the epic character of the opera. Characteristically the prelude opens with a double motif (Ex. 287a and b).

Of Ex. 287a Verdi might well have remarked like Beethoven, 'Thus does Fate knock on the door.' But it is not a particularly fruitful motif; so it is not surprising to find that after the start of Act II Fate gives up this form of importunity. Ex. 287b, however, an action theme taken from the finale of Act I, assumes huge importance throughout the opera, recurring with a sense of sinister fatality, but always in association with Leonora, never Don Alvaro. For this reason some scholars consider it a Leonora-motif rather than a destiny-motif.† The dilemma is a false one. Leonora is Fate's chief victim. She, not Alvaro, is the one whom Preziosilla in the play describes as being doomed from her cradle. Besides, the theme in question dominates the scene in which she receives her father's curse, from whose consequences she can see no way of escape except that of shutting herself away from all human contact. Alvaro, once he knows Leonora to be alive, continues to hope for a while that with a measure of good will their troubles will be over.

When Italian composers wished to develop in an overture or prelude a theme taken from the opera itself they were careful to change its physiognomy; thus Rossini in *Semiramide*, Verdi himself in *Luisa Miller*. Not so in *La Forza del destino*. At its first appearance in the opera Ex. 287b is the first half of a double idea (see Ex. 298), In the prelude, as in the later overture, it is quoted literally except for the scoring; but instead of proceeding to the second idea it takes on a life its own, forming itself into a double period of 32 bars extended to 34, but not by the usual method of lyrical protraction. Only the first period is static and balanced; the second breaks up into

---

* *Disp. scen.*, pp. 12–13.
† See Varnai, *op. cit.*, pp. 1695–1710.

287a

287b

smaller and smaller patterns until it plays itself out in a flurry of semiquavers which return to the inexorable brass unisons of Ex. 287 a. For once, then, an important motif of the opera receives its fullest statement before the curtain rises; and it seems appropriate to talk about its later appearances as quotations. Usually it is the prelude or overture that quotes from the opera.

Finally note the dramatic use of tonal ambiguity. The start of Ex. 287b seems to convert the E's of Ex. 287a into dominants; but well before the end of the first period we are left in no doubt that E minor is the home key, and A minor merely a false route of escape. Such procedures suggest more than a passing acquaintance with the Beethoven of the first symphony, the Prometheus Overture and the second Razumovsky string quartet. The key of A minor returns again with a quotation from the tenor-and-baritone duet in the last act ('I minacci, i fieri accenti'), where Alvaro as Padre Raffaello counters Carlo's insults in a spirit of Christian forbearance.

288

While flute, oboe and clarinet trace the sad, resigned melody, violins interpose a quotation from the seguidilla from Act II (Ex. 299) between phrases. So normal everyday life persists ,while tragedy runs its course. After 16 bars the melody breaks off just as it is about to reach a cadence. There is a pause; and another important theme steals in, the melodic climax of Leonora's aria in Act II 'Madre, pietosa vergine' where she calls on God not to abandon her to her sorrow and guilt.

289

The interleaving arches, each forming a rising sixth falling back a tone from its apex, are a vital ingredient in the 'tinta' of the opera. What is more, they are associated almost exclusively with hero and heroine.* The 'aspiring' sixth is of course a commonplace of Italian opera which Verdi used almost to excess in *Ernani*, though never without point. Here, equipped with a far wider musical vocabulary, Verdi is able to isolate the procedure to depict that nobility and idealism that mark out Leonora and Alvaro from those around them. But it will avail them nothing, as Verdi reminds us; for beneath the soaring violins and shimmering violas, cellos and bassoons recall Ex. 287b with increasing persistence. The music mounts in a steady crescendo to its final cadence, then abruptly dissolves into a turbulent sequence derived from the original dénouement where Alvaro hurls himself shrieking over a precipice. After a climax *fff* four bars of descending string triplets over wind chords take the prelude down to its final hushed cadence in E minor.

OVERTURE
(1869)

By the 1860s the classical overture, even in its adulterated post-Rossinian form, had had its day. Italian composers preferred to preface their operas with loosely constructed 'trailers' featuring the most prominent themes of the opera. This was the kind of overture that Verdi set himself to write, taking the prelude as his starting-point. For the first 77 bars or so the two pieces coincide except for one or two improved details. Ex. 287a is repeated twice instead of once after the full statement of Ex. 287b; Ex. 288 has as its countermelody not the seguidilla but another reminiscence of Ex. 287b. The interventions of the same idée fixe during Ex. 289 are redistributed more effectively. As so often one cannot speak of two-part counterpoint. Harmonically speaking the two themes fit where they touch, and awkwardly even then. The combination is only possible because they exist on

---

* See Varnai, *loc. cit.*

different planes of sonority. Here Verdi's model can only have been Berlioz, the first composer to deliver orchestral harmony from the tyranny of the keyboard.

With the final cadence of Ex. 289 the overture takes a new turning, plunging into noisy rhythmic developments of Ex. 287b. Hectic semiquavers on the strings prepare for a still more emphatic E minor cadence. There is a pause. Desolate phrases from Ex. 288 seem to close the door on hope; then, unexpectedly a new theme is announced:

290   Allegro brillante

This too is associated with Leonora and will appear in slightly altered form in the course of her duet with the Father Superior, portraying her regained peace of mind. Its harp accompaniment, distinctive rhythmic cut and E major tonality had the unfortunate effect of recalling to more than one commentator the final duet from Donizetti's *Poliuto* ('Al suon dell'arpe angeliche'),* as did the duet-cabaletta of Act I (see Chapter 2) where the similarity extended to the phrase-structure. Like so many of his apparently conventional melodies this one contains a hidden charge of energy. Its smooth texture and lack of dynamic stress all disguise the swiftness of its rhythmic current which only becomes evident where the music breaks into semiquaver motion, with further developments of Ex. 287b, like the limpid surface of a river being churned up by rapids. The same apparent contrast is immanent in the overture's next idea, introduced by a bold harmonic ellipsis.

291

The brass theme is the Father Superior's 'A te sia lode, Dio clemente' from the duet with Leonora in Act II, moulded to a different rhythm. The figure for unison strings has no source in the body of the opera, but its significance is unmistakable; the lightning flash of a drawn sword. If in *Don Carlos* earthly power is subservient to the

* See W. Dean, *loc. cit.*

church, in *La Forza del destino* religion is set at nothing by earthly passion. Once again Ex. 287b is treated in a variety of developing sequences, which culminate in an apotheosis of Ex. 289 in the home key of E major, a simple stroke whereby Verdi gives shape to what would otherwise have been a pot-pourri. From there to the end all is coda. Ex. 290 returns varied by Rossinian violin triplets which wipe out all its religious overtones; but in the bass recurrences of Ex. 287b remind us that the hound of fate is still in pursuit. The final pages consist entirely of festive winding-up material mixed with a few adroit back-references to previous themes. All sense of impending tragedy has gone; the audience is merely being galvanized into attention for an important event, and at the same time asked to admire some unusually brilliant orchestral writing. Such is the way of all self-contained overtures in the opera house.

Although entirely bound up with the opera and constructed on a far from classical design this is Verdi's most popular overture in the concert hall – which alone is enough to indicate that its appearance of inconsequence is an illusion. In fact it is built on a principle that becomes increasingly common in middle and late Verdi – the alternation of a developing theme (Ex. 287b) and one which is static and regular (Ex. 289). This was last observed in the drawing-of-lots scene in *Un Ballo in maschera*, woven throughout from the two motifs in question. Here the scheme is expanded by episodes certain of which (notably Ex. 290) seem at first to belie their subsidiary character until the surprise restatement of Ex. 289 *fff* sets the record straight. Indeed the overture furnishes a paradigm of the opera – chaotic on the surface, logical and coherent beneath, combining the concentration of *Ernani* with the diversity of *I Lombardi* and containing far better music than either.

ACT I

Scene: Seville. A hall carpeted in damask with family portraits and suits of armour and furnished in the style of the eighteenth century, but in a state of dilapidation. Facing, two windows; that on the left closed, that on the right open and 'practicable', through which can be seen a very clear sky lit by the moon, and the tops of trees. Between the windows a large cupboard closed and containing clothes, linen, etc., etc. Each of the lateral walls has two doors. The first on the right of the spectator is the main one; the second leads to Curra's room. On the left backstage is the Marchese's apartment; nearer to the proscenium is that of Leonora. In the centre of the stage is a little table covered by a damask cloth, and on it a guitar, vases of flowers, two silver candlesticks shielded by lampshades which give the room its only illumination. A large chair near the table; a piece of furniture with a clock between the two doors on the right; another piece of furniture on which is a full-length portrait of the Marquis; it is hanging from the left-hand wall. The room contains a raised parapet. The Marquis, with lamp in hand, is taking his leave of a worried Donna Leonora. Curra comes out from the left.

Here is, quite plainly, the model for the opening of the revised *Boccanegra* – a soft, flexible string melody with harmonies in the composer's maturest manner. Although Leonora only utters a brief aside at the end of the period, the melody is hers, not her father's. Her unease and guilt find expression in the restless syncopations, the

chromatic shifts, and the unexpected turns of harmony (see the non-functional 6/4 at *y*). Not only does the minatory Ex. 287a cast its lingering shadow from the overture; the bass of the main melody (*x*) is a variant of Ex. 289. From it we can understand how Leonora's religious feelings are bound up with filial guilt. The three-note climb from E to C natural is a mute plea to her father to forgive and understand; in Act II this same figure will flower into that intense prayer to God already heard in the overture.

The Marquis is tender but uncomprehending. He is convinced that Leonora is cured of her love for the unworthy stranger; there is nothing further for her to worry about, so why is she looking so sad?* For answer Leonora can only throw herself into her father's arms, and the mounting tension is dissolved in a cadential phrase of the utmost poignancy, using yet again that uniquely Verdian device – the 6/4 in a remote key (see Ex. 19).

* There is an unaccountable divergence here between play and libretto. In the first the present scene takes place at the country seat of the Calatravas, whence, presumably, it would be much easier to arrange an abduction. In the opera the Marchese and his daughter have already returned from the country to their mansion in Seville.

Curra sees the master to the door, then returns to find Leonora reclining on the chair in floods of tears. Practical, as in the play, she opens the cupboard and starts packing. ('I was afraid he was going to stay here till the morning.') But now Leonora declares that she cannot decide whether or not to elope. Curra reminds her sharply that if she does not it will mean at the least imprisonment for Alvaro, and probably execution. Evidently she does not love him; but this Leonora vehemently denies. Is she not willing to leave her father and family for his sake? So after a passage of orthodox but gripping recitative to her first aria 'Me pellegrina ed orfana', which is a heartbroken farewell to hearth and home. As is well known the text is lifted straight from Somma's libretto for *King Lear*. Is the music likewise a fragment of that famous opera which Verdi never wrote? Surely not. In Somma's drama it was to have been an aria for Cordelia after she has been disinherited and driven out by her father, and it would conclude the first scene of the opera. Therefore the musical setting would have had a 'conclusive' structure at least as marked as that of, say, 'Ritorna vincitor'. Indeed, since that scheme was drawn up mostly between 1853 and 1855 it is more likely that the final two stanzas would have been set as a cabaletta – a supposition confirmed by 'pertichini' of consolation written for Cordelia's betrothed, such as he would naturally interpolate during a central ritornello and coda. What is more, Cordelia has no choice in the matter of her exile. Leonora's aria is not only transitional in character; it is the music of agonized indecision. It oscillates between major and minor; the phrases beginning regularly break out into new, unexpected shapes with a constantly changing articulation. Appoggiature and semitonal clashes abound. The three ideas of which the piece is made up follow each other with the impulsiveness of a rhapsody rather than a formal cantabile or romanza.

293a

293b

293c

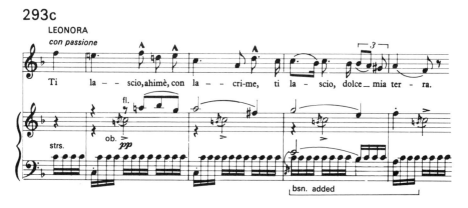

The last of these moves to a climax ('Per me non avrà termin sì grand dolor') of almost 'veristic' intensity – which may explain how Mascagni came within an ace of quoting it in the course of Santuzza's confession to Mamma Lucia. The design is neatly rounded off with a restatement of the opening idea. Yet another feature of interest is the use of solo cello at various points, to add eloquence to Leonora's grief. Twenty years earlier it would have played throughout as part of a handful of instruments designed to give the aria an unusual but also unvarying texture; here it is woven into the normal orchestral sonority with a new ease and suppleness.

Curra's only reaction to this moving outburst is to ask her mistress to give her a hand with the packing. But Leonora notices that it is late. Perhaps Alvaro will not come after all. But a pattern of galloping strings, pianissimo but growing in volume, tells her otherwise. Before she can collect her thoughts Don Alvaro 'without his cloak, clad in a tunic with wide sleeves, and over it a majo's jacket, his hair in a net, booted and spurred enters through the window and throws himself into Leonora's arms'.* The orchestra with its dash and sweep depicts an entrance in the manner of young Lochinvar. Wasting no time on even the most perfunctory of recitatives Alvaro embarks straight away on the first movement of the duet 'Ah per sempre, o mio bell'angiol'. As in the play these are the first words he has to speak, but there the audience has already seen him as a dark brooding presence. In the opera we make his acquaintance more slowly. Leonora's reply keeps up his headlong motion, but the

* *Majo* is an impossible word to translate; 'young spark' is the nearest English equivalent, if the term can be stripped of its upper-class overtones.

minor harmonies betray her reluctance to act. Alvaro counters with the first statement of what is almost his personal leitmotiv, here introduced as an episode within the allegro movement:

294

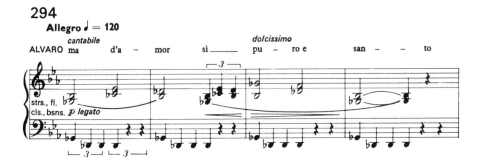

Appropriately it is a declaration of faith. All Alvaro's idealism is summed up in that noble melody with its distinctive interval of a falling fifth, its passionate upward sweep. His love for Leonora is pure and holy; God is with them. After the cadence the primo tempo is resumed and the dialogue continues urgently, Alvaro all for action, Leonora still holding back. He appeals once more in a graceful solo ('Pronti destrieri') with a winning charm such as the Duke of Mantua brought to his wooing of Gilda:

295

Music, however, takes no account of sincerity of motive, as *Così fan tutte* abundantly proves. In opera a libertine and a *preux chevalier* may express themselves identically. Swift horses are waiting below to carry the lovers away. A priest is ready to bless their union; and when the sun, God of Alvaro's ancestors, has flooded the world in splendour they will be man and wife. If Alvaro's theology is a little confused, there is no mistaking the power and grandeur of the 'madrigalism' with which he depicts the rising sun — a sustained climb over thirteen bars from b' flat to the octave above. Surprising but logical is the reminiscence in the tremolo string accompaniment of the introduction to Alzira's dream in the earlier opera (see Vol. 1, Ex. 140). If not related, Alvaro and Alzira are certainly compatriots. As always in such cases the superiority of the later score leaps to the eye and ear. The Verdi of *Alzira* would never have thought of enhancing the last bars of the sunrise by a grandly downward-moving bass-line, nor would the sweetness of that trill on the flute have occurred to him.

296

In the transition which follows, and in which Leonora's inner conflict reaches its greatest point of tension, the scores of 1862 and 1869 diverge again. Her mental state is like Violetta's where she makes her great avowal of love to Alfredo. She protests to Alvaro that she loves him, that her heart is filled with joy, and yet – can they not put off their flight till tomorrow? Not surprisingly, considering the short distance of time that separates them, both Verdi's solutions are powerful, but as usual the second one is better. The Leonora of 1862 expressed herself in broken flights of lyricism, each phrase dovetailed into an orchestral response often with a resolving discord where the phrases overlap (Ex. 297a). The climax is reached with Leonora's 'Oh anch'io tu'l sai, t'amo io tanto' marked *con gaudio* (297b). Strong harmonies convey the ambiguity that underlies her words, but a bass pedal note on C brings a certain unwanted stasis which inevitably persists when the music breaks into quaver motion before the words 'Gonfio . . . di gioia'.

The version of 1869 is the work of one who had already written the final act of *Don Carlos*. Strings with oboes and bassoons set up a pattern of plangent quavers in A flat minor (Ex. 297c). Leonora's line is at first more continuous, more persuasive, until she loses the thread of what she is saying and breaks into incoherence ('Sì, perchè m'ami . . . ne opporti dei . . . Anch'io'). Here both the pattern and tonality also dissolve, to take shape a few bars later with the same ominous C minor theme (Ex. 297d) which had followed the outburst in 1862. In the revision however it acquires a dominant bass with a correspondingly greater sense of propulsion. The climax has been by-passed and with it that momentary stagnation of harmonic movement. The passage has gained in vividness and dramatic truth. As always Verdi excels in the portrayal of present feeling.

297a

297b

297c

297d

LEONORA *(piange)*

Gonfio

The music ends in mid-air, rhythmically and harmonically, as Leonora is overcome by helpless sobs. Alvaro, with sombre irony, takes up her words ('Gonfio hai di gioia il core e lagrime'). In a sustained recitative which grows more chilling with every modulation he offers to release her from her promise; their marriage, he says, would be death for both of them if Leonora were unable to return his love. But she cuts him short with an impulsive avowal of her feelings ('Son tua . . . col core . . . e colla vita'). She will follow him to the ends of the earth.

So to the cabaletta of their duet ('Seguirti fine agli ultimi').* If this solution seems a little old-fashioned for the 1860s it is not the last time that Verdi will use the cabaletta form for two lovers who decide too late to run away, so that the obligatory repetitions play their part in producing the fatal delay and at the same time increase the audience's suspense. Attention has already been drawn in an earlier chapter to the moving bass line which gives the whole movement a fleetness and energy without parallel in Donizetti or Mercadante and which is Verdi's recipe for recovering the brilliance which went out of Italian opera with Rossinian canto fiorito.

There is no central ritornello; instead a characteristic coda of overlapping phrases follows directly upon the tenor's verse ('Sospiro, luce ed anima'). The element of reprise is not lost, however, but worked into the final bars in a most dramatic way. Alvaro and Leonora develop the opening phrase in dialogue; there is a sudden interruption and the sound of someone climbing the stairs; then both make for the balcony singing the last phrase in a climactic unison over an orchestral tutti.

Too late. The courtyard is guarded. Alvaro refuses to hide; he produces a pistol with which, he says, he is ready to take his own life. The dialogue is carried on swiftly over a sustained cello E (*recitativo a dirsi presto* is the description in the autograph). After various blows the door (back left) is flung open and the Marchese enters in a fury brandishing a sword and followed by two servants.

The basis of the following scène-à-faire is Ex. 287b differently scored from the opening (violins and high woodwind on the melody, the rest of the orchestra on the chords) and woven with a complementary 'parlante melodico' (Ex. 298) which is developed with a bold, elementary vigour that, like much else in this score, recalls the Beethoven of the middle years. A shorter sequential idea, introducing the words 'No, la condotta vostra', completes the tally of themes.

In vain Leonora begs for mercy. In vain Alvaro protests her innocence and tries to take all the blame upon himself. He begs the Marquis to strike him dead; but the Marquis refuses to soil his hands with the blood of anyone so vile and baseborn. Alvaro in an act of surrender throws down his pistol with the fatal result of which we know. So far the modulations have been frequent and strong; here they culminate in a violent wrench which takes the tonality by three semitonal stages from C sharp

---

* See Chapter 2, Ex. 16b.

298

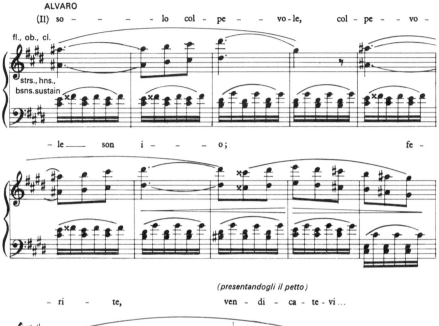

minor to A minor, as Leonora cries out for help. The dying Marquis casts Leonora from him ('Lungi da me. . . . Contamina tua vista la mia morte. . . . Te maledico'). Leonora cries to Heaven for mercy, Alvaro exclaims at fortune as the music returns with tremendous and final emphasis to C sharp minor. The servants remove the Marquis to his rooms while Alvaro drags Leonora to the balcony* and the curtain falls.

'Everyone finds fault with this first act,' Verdi complained to Ricordi, 'but given the dramatic situation I couldn't have developed a full love duet. . . .'† No indeed; nor would a modern critic be disposed to condemn one of the finest single acts in all Verdi, whose only fault here is that he gives the audience too much to take in too soon. Neither Puccini nor even Wagner, at his most demanding, ever made that mistake. They are careful to ease the listener into the drama gently. So too was Rivas with his casual, conversational opening scene. Verdi's first act however is dense with meaning from the first note. The fact that his opening theme is subdued (Ex. 292) is a

* *The Marquis falls back into the arms of his servants, who carry him to his rooms, while Curra and Alvaro try to unclasp Leonora's hands from her father's knees which she has run to embrace. They try to drag her towards the window. (Disp. scen., p. 17.)*

† Letter to G. Ricordi, 10.3.1869. Abbiati, III, p. 257.

further sop to an audience's power of concentration. Alvaro's all-important Ex. 294 is apt to pass unnoticed; indeed no scholar before David Lawton (see below) has given evidence of having noticed that it is the source of the extended clarinet solo in Act III.

ACT II

Scene 1: The village of Hornáchuelos and its neighbourhood. Large kitchen on the ground floor of an inn. On the left is the main door; in front a window and a big cupboard with plates etc., etc. Backstage right a large fireplace, lit, with various saucepans; nearer the front of the stage a little staircase leading to a room; with a door that can be entered. On one side a large table laid for a meal with a lighted oil lamp upon it. The host and hostess (who do not speak) are busy getting supper ready. The Alcade is sitting by the fire; a student is sitting by the table. Several muleteers, among them Mastro Trabuco who is to the fore, seated on one of his pack-saddles. Two peasant boys and girls, a servant and a muleteer are dancing the seguidilla. On another table, wine, glasses, flasks and a bottle of acquavite. Servants, peasants, etc.*

Twice the brass calls us to attention with the three peremptory raps of Ex. 287a. There is a snatch of chorus in the popular, faintly exotic style of *Il Trovatore* Act II ('Holà! Ben giungi o mulattier'); and from its final note a springy dance melody leaps forth (Ex. 299). The opening gesture with its characteristic rising sixth has already been quoted in the original prelude. Note, however, that it is not the 'aspiring' sixth of Leonora and Alvaro since the melody does not fall back within the interval but continues upwards. Perhaps if Verdi had not so curtly refused Piave's offer to bring some Spanish folk-songs he would have realized that the seguidilla is not danced in 2/4 time. But that is a problem for the choreographer only.

299

Peasants and muleteers dance for a full forty-eight bars with no choral intervention except for an occasional 'holà'. Here as in most of the numbers in this most episodic of scenes the form used is the rondo. The scoring, delicate and economical, gradually takes on weight as it proceeds, ending in an emphatic tutti. To the same movement the Alcade announces that supper is ready. (It should of course be the hostess herself, but for reasons of stage economy she and her husband are dumb; in consequence much of the conversation which Piave had lifted directly from the play is awkwardly

* A diagram in the production book has the dancing couples by the footlights.

redistributed.) Most of the company sit down at table with glad cries. The student confides to the audience that he is still searching for his sister and her seducer. This, of course, is not in the play, where the student is exactly what he claims to be. In the opera he is Leonora's brother, Carlo; but apart from that one aside, his disguise throughout the scene remains perfect. The Alcade requires him to say Grace, and he obliges with a suitable display of piety and learning. 'Amen,' reply the others, and the dance music resumes for the benefit of a solitary couple backstage with one of those pizzicato embellishments in the bass to which Verdians have been accustomed since the days of *Giovanna d'Arco*. Here it has an extra touch of thematic relevance beginning as Ex. 299 in diminution.

As everyone falls to with appreciative comments Leonora dressed as a boy appears at the door of her room and withdraws hurriedly with a cry of, 'Whom do I see? . . . My brother!' The student compliments the hostess with a Latin quotation, then turns his attention to Trabuco, who is still leaning on his packsaddle and eating nothing in pursuance of his Friday fast. Who, the student wants to know, was Trabuco's travelling companion? But the question is cut short by the arrival of Preziosilla, clearly a well known and popular figure since each of the male guests asks her to sit beside him ('Brava . . . Qui presso a me') and tell his fortune.

Preziosilla, as she appears in the opera, is a creation of Verdi and Piave, owing nothing to Rivas except her name. Fortune-telling is the least important of her accomplishments. She is a first cousin to Donizetti's Marie in *La Fille du régiment*; a cheerful hoyden who will come into her own in Act III rallying tearful recruits and leading everyone in a Rataplan chorus. Here she appears to have taken upon herself the role of recruiting officer for the war against the Germans in Italy.* Her task is almost too easy. With a cry of 'Death to the Germans!' which a tactful publisher changed to 'Death to the enemy!' in the years of the Triple Alliance the men agree to enlist ('Tutti v'andrem'). 'And I shall be with you,' cried Preziosilla, which, of course, settles the matter, and, incidentally, explains how not only Preziosilla but the entire male chorus will be found an act later on the battlefield of Velletri in Italy. In all this, be it noted, the basic tempo has not altered since the beginning of the act. Indeed Preziosilla's 'Correte allor soldati in Italia' is sung to the same music as Carlo's initial aside to the audience. There can be no possible dramatic meaning in this. It is merely further evidence of the strong thematic coherence of the score.

The upward transposition in 1869 for the sake of Ida Nagy-Benzi begins at the chorus 'Morte ai tedeschi!' which now proceeds from D to E instead of E flat. A choral tutti over Preziosilla's last word dwindles to three bars of solo side-drum which introduce her opening 'canzone' ('Al suon del tamburo'). It is a conventional song in praise of the soldier's life such as might have come from any eighteenth-century opera buffa; nor has it any Risorgimento overtones – obviously, since the unity of Italy was no longer an issue. Its burden is: war is fine; only the cowardly get killed; the brave survive to receive all manner of rewards – and, true to her calling, Preziosilla goes round the company foretelling a colonel's rank for one, a generalship for another and for someone else success in love. It is all in the manner of Donizetti's Marie and her 'Chacun le sait' but the form is Verdi's own. It appears to be a strophic song with refrain; all the verses are musically different but since the refrain (Ex. 300)

* For a description of her character and operatic ancestry, see John W. Freeman, 'The Gipsy Girl', in *I.S.V. Bollettino*, No. 5, pp. 825–30.

is the only 'constant', the effect is that of a rondo with episodes. As in the introduction the side-drum plays a prominent role.

300

The key-scheme with an opening strophe in the subdominant is one of those not unpleasing anomalies to be found in Italian popular music. As later, in Iago's drinking song, the rondo design is extended to take in a scène-à-faire before the final refrain. Carlo asks for his hand to be read; Preziosilla replies that terrible misfortune lies in store for him; then, peering at him more closely, she adds that he is obviously no student, but that she will not give him away. Preziosilla, like Oscar, laughs in her music.

301

The last reprise of Ex. 300 develops into a coda, whose conclusion is by-passed by a modulation to the dominant of G (slightly steeper in 1869 than in 1862 for obvious reasons). A distant chorus of pilgrims is heard singing one of those phrases which without having the slightest melodic interest evoke a world of religious feeling:

302

For this chorus, which never actually crosses the stage, Verdi's autograph advises us '. . . a few voices will suffice; for example 4 tenors, 4 basses and 12 women'. To everyone's question the Alcade replies that these are a band of pilgrims on their way to the 'giubileo' and he suggests that everyone kneel in prayer as they pass. Meanwhile Leonora again appears at the door of her room wondering if this distraction will give her an opportunity of escape. A large-scale choral movement develops in which four separate strands are interwoven; the five-part chorus behind the scenes, the normal mixed chorus of muleteers and village girls, the solo quartet of Preziosilla, Trabuco, Carlo and the Alcade, closely related to the on-stage chorus but showing a greater fluidity of line, and finally Leonora, seeming to stand apart in helpless anguish. Despite its elaboration the movement has the fundamental two-part structure of many an operatic pezzo concertato, though with the two parts more sharply distinguished than usual. The first in four-pulse time uncomplicated except by the occasional triplet from Preziosilla; the second in an equally unequivocal 12/8 – a phenomenon so rare in Verdi as to be remarkable. The muleteers and peasant girls it will be noted express themselves with a more conventional piety then the pilgrims; their opening theme has the character of a congregational hymn:

The second section begins as a dialogue for Leonora and the other soloists over an accompaniment of clarinet arpeggios, then works through a typical Italian groundswell of chorus and orchestra to a climax in which the figure of Leonora springs out in high relief melodically, rhythmically and harmonically.

The cadential figure (*x*) is identical with that in which she took a desperate farewell of her father in Act I (see Ex. 292). Finally the pilgrims whose part in the ensemble has been minimal are heard retreating into the distance and the movement comes to a close.

There is nothing of all this in Rivas's play. But its purpose in the opera is clear enough. On the surface it provides the element of concertato desirable in so vast an opera but unprovided for in the original plot. But it makes sense on a deeper level as well. A basic theme of the opera, as indeed of the play, is the progressive separation of the principals from the kindly, everyday world of ordinary people. This concertato represents Leonora's last contact with that world. While she joins her voice to theirs she becomes from time to time part of the humanity from which she will soon banish herself. At the same time her own feelings of guilt continually detach her from the general mood of tranquillity; note in this connection the occasional use of jagged dotted rhythms in the manner of Abigaille. The pilgrims' chant, as it dies away, has a very special meaning for Leonora.

It is Carlo who breaks the mood with a toast to 'good company'; health in this world, eternal glory in the next – to which the others fervently assent. He then resumes his questioning of Trabuco. What was the sex of his travelling companion? Receiving no satisfactory answer he turns to the Alcade. What was the young person like? Why does he not come down to supper? As the Alcade is no more communicative Carlo turns again to the muleteer. Did his fare sit astride the horse or side-saddle? But Trabuco has had enough of this catechizing; he would rather sleep amongst his mules 'who know no Latin and hold no degrees'; and away he goes amid general laughter. Verdi, it will be remembered, described the character of Trabuco as 'pure comedy'; not surprisingly therefore his exchanges with Carlo anticipate the style of *Falstaff* more directly than anything Verdi had written to date – lively conversational pace, small apparently insignificant phrases tossed from voice to orchestra, rhythms which buttress another in a continual forward motion, light-fingered scoring (much of it for strings alone), and with plentiful use of the piccolo in the busier passages where Trabuco begins to lose his temper (Ex. 305).

It is Trabuco who gives the entire scene its character even though he has less to say than Carlo; but Carlo, like many a Verdian baritone, is Protean, and just now his disguise as a silly pranking undergraduate is impenetrable to all except Preziosilla. He suggests that they all break into the stranger's room and paint a couple of moustaches on the sleeping face. But this the Alcade forbids. Strangers, he says, have a right to his protection. Instead he asks the 'student' to give some account of himself. Carlo obliges with the ballata ('Son Pereda, son ricco di onore'). His name is Pereda and he is a student from Salamanca. He has achieved a baccalaureate and was about to qualify as a doctor 'in utroque' when a fellow student of the name of Vargas enlisted his help in tracking down his sister and her seducer who together had caused his father's death. With Vargas he went to Seville and then to Cadiz where he heard that Leonora had been killed during her escape, while her lover had taken ship to South America. Thither Vargas followed him leaving Pereda to return to his studies.

All this tallies with the play, where the brother concerned is Alfonso, who never appears till the end of the drama, and the student himself no relation; whereas the operatic Pereda is a clever impostor who none the less allows us a glimpse of the

305

cloven hoof. His ballata, again in rondo form, and marked *con eleganza*,* has the gait of Ruiz's from Donizetti's *Maria Padilla* which may unconsciously have inspired it. Here however the dotted rhythm is made to convey a graceful swagger, aided by the grace-notes which launch the final phrase of the melody (Ex. 306).

The suavity is maintained until the second episode ('Là e dovunque narrar che del pari') when the rhythm of Ex. 287b rears its head in the accompaniment, launched each time by a softly menacing brass chord. It is no more than a faint recollection as Carlo imagines the night of the tragedy and at the same time forces himself to lie about Leonora's supposed death. The mounting tension is expressed in restless chromatic patterns in the accompaniment which contrast strangely with the composure of the vocal line. A climax is reached on the word 'Sfuggia' with a tutti of sustained brass and chromatic scales in contrary motion on wind and strings; after which Carlo hastily adjusts the mask and returns to the easy manner of the opening. The chorus take up Ex. 306 and work it to a triumphant close.

All including the Alcade are impressed with the tale. Only the tiresome Preziosilla makes it quite clear that she does not believe a word of it; and she repeats her previous mockery (Ex. 301). The Alcade looks at the clock and suggests that they all retire for the night. General assent and repeated good nights, which do not prevent the dancing from continuing to Ex. 299. Carlo sings a few more snatches of his ballata; Preziosilla mocks as before. So the scene is rounded off by the resumption of three of

* Verdi directed in a letter that it should be sung mostly mezza-voce; see letter to G. Ricordi, 31.12.1868. Abbiati, III, pp. 240–1.

its most important themes. The 'good nights' are of interest not so much because they prefigure a similar device in Britten's *Rape of Lucretia* but because their stylized declamation is such an important part of Verdi's conception of comedy. In a well known letter to Arrivabene he stressed the need for avoiding narrow musical classifications: 'Take the phrase in the *Barber* "Signor, giudizio per carità"; this is neither melody nor harmony; it is precise and truthful verbal declamation; and it is *music. . . .* Amen.'* The same could be said of Mistress Quickly's 'reverenza' in *Falstaff*; and it applies in equal measure to the general leave-taking in *La Forza del destino* Act II, Scene 1.

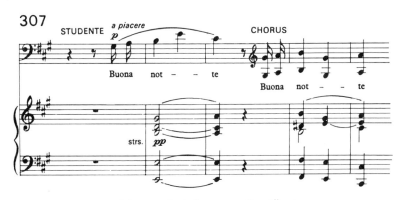

* Letter to Arrivabene, 17.3.1882. Alberti, p. 297.

Note the wealth of innuendo that Preziosilla infuses into her own 'good night'. Her laughing motif (see Ex. 301) is allowed to have the last word in the orchestral postlude.

> *Scene 2: A small plateau on the slopes of a steep mountain. To the right cliffs and rocks; facing, the façade of the church of the Madonna of the Angels; to the left the door to the monastery, with a small window in the middle; on one side the rope which rings the bell. Above there is a small projecting gable. Beyond the church can be seen high mountains and the village of Hornachuelos. The door of the church is closed, but above it a wide semicircular window will show that the interior is illuminated. In the middle of the stage a little to the left is a short flight of steps leading up to a crude stone cross eroded by the weather. The scene is lit by brilliant moonlight.*
>
> *Donna Leonora arrives, ascending from the right; tired; dressed in an overcoat with broad sleeves, a wide-brimmed hat and riding boots.**

The 'destiny theme' (Ex. 287b) reappears in C sharp minor as in Act I but with less urgent, perhaps more sinister orchestration: violins and cellos on the melody; violas, lower brass and timpani on the bass. The last note is interrupted by a tutti outburst. In the succeeding quiet, over a slow descending line of cellos and bassoons, Leonora announces that, thanks be to God, she has reached her last place of refuge. When next the destiny theme sounds in E minor it is scored more smoothly and lightly, as though the pursuit has slackened. In a turbulent scene full of diminished sevenths and silences Leonora relives the moment in the inn when she heard her brother recounting her story. What had grieved her most was the news that Alvaro had abandoned her and set sail for South America – an important detail this, and one which Verdi pointed up by one of those intensely desolate phrases with which he had endowed many a tragic heroine in the past. But how much more vivid it is when, as here, a new harmonic sophistication is brought into play (Ex. 308).

By making much of Alvaro's supposed desertion Verdi and Piave avoided one of those subtleties of motive which make more sense in a spoken drama than in an opera. In his catechism of Eleonora, Rivas's Father Superior asks how she would feel if she were to meet her lover again. She replies that, though she might still love him, she could never be his; an ocean of blood has separated them for ever. In the opera no such possibility is ever raised since Leonora firmly believes that he has sailed home never to return. Possibly, too, this theme of desertion is responsible for another Schubertian reminiscence: as Leonora falls on her knees in prayer strings set up a gently agitated accompaniment together with a lamenting line of flute and clarinet (Ex. 309a). The basis of the famous aria 'Madre pietosa vergine', it carries a clear echo of Schubert's 'Gretchen am Spinnrade', whose poem Verdi had already set years before in an Italian translation. In the sequence that starts the seven bars which lead up to the major-key section (Ex. 309b) the echo becomes clearer still.

---

* The production book adds a ramp reaching below stage up which Leonora should proceed *so as to make more evident the weary path up which she has trodden in her ascent. . . . The scene, which will have been changed in view of the audience, should remain empty for a moment; the spectators' mood must be attuned to the grave and solemn nature of what is about to take place.* (Disp. scen., p. 22.)

308

Otherwise the ancestry of this aria is easy to trace in Verdi's own 'Tacea la notte' from *Il Trovatore*. Both are strophic descendants of the minor-to-major romanza; but the later is infinitely more complex. In the opening bars symmetry of the accompanimental pattern is masked by cross-phrasing with the soprano line, as in many a seventeenth-century ground bass. The major-key section ('Non m'abbandonar, pietà') (see Ex. 289) arrives with the same sense of a transcendental flowering as the final phrase of 'Tacea la notte'; but it makes a far more radical contrast with what has gone before. The agitated semiquavers of Ex. 309b give way to a sustained tremolo above which rise the interlocking arches of Ex. 289, now heard for the first time in all its vocal glory. From the fifth bar wind then timpani intervene gradually to provide a groundswell for the concluding phrase.

As in 'Il lacerato spirito' a musical period of intense concentration generates a long postlude. Here it takes the form of a four-part 'Venite adoremus' sung by a chorus of

309a

309b

LEONORA

(In) que — — ste so — — li - tu - din - i e - spi - e -
rò, e - spi - e - rò l'er - ro — - re... Pie - tà di

monks behind the scene accompanied by organ while Leonora murmurs of hope and comfort. The second verse is not a repetition of the first but a development of it, beginning with fragments of Ex. 309a interspersed with rapid declamation. Leonora is assailed by doubts. Dare she knock at the monastery door at this time of night? Suppose someone should find her there and recognize her? But she summons up her strength of will; and once more Ex. 289 peals out *con più forza*, while the monks take up the end of each phrase with a fragment of their chant. As in 'Tacea la notte' there is yet another statement of the final phrase, here backed by the whole orchestra with timpani reinforced by bass drum. After this supreme outpouring of a full heart seven bars of hushed coda suffice to bring the piece to an end. It is in music such as this that the meaning of Verdi's term 'opera d'intenzioni' (opera of ideas) becomes clear. It needs more than a beautiful tone and an instinctive feeling for the Verdian phrases. Nothing will do here but a soprano who can be a great actress with her voice.

Leonora rings the monastery bell. The little window in the door is opened; from it shines a lantern which throws its beams in Leonora's face. She starts back, terrified. Fra Melitone speaks, always remaining inside. In a brief exchange of recitative she tells him that she has been sent by Father Cleto. The name of that 'holy man' has the desired effect. Fra Melitone invites her to enter; but of course as a woman she cannot do so. Fra Melitone however does not know this and imagines she must be excommunicated.* He goes off with a bad grace to fetch the Father Superior . . . 'And if I don't come back, good night.' Leonora's confidence starts to ebb once

---

* A curious slip in the published vocal score makes Melitone aware of Leonora's sex ('Scomunicata siete').

more; to the point where her 'destiny theme' (Ex. 287b) returns on the strings; but her faith in the Virgin Mary and in the Father Superior's reputation for kindness overcome her fears. By the same token the destiny motif is vanquished by Ex. 289 played over tremolo strings by a solo clarinet. There is a last reference to the coda of her aria. Then Fra Melitone returns bringing with him the Father Superior. On being asked her business Leonora declares that it is secret; whereupon he sends Melitone away. The lay-brother leaves grumbling. Why is it that these holy men are the only ones allowed to know secrets? 'the rest of us are so many cabbages':

310

This is the first time that Melitone has been musically characterized. He is the habitual grumbler to whom everything is a source of irritation; hence the downward line and fussy quaver movement of every phrase, the exasperated lingering on minims and dotted minims. Not that he expects anyone to take any notice of what he says. When the Father Superior asks what is wrong he replies hastily that he was just complaining that the door creaked. The Father Superior's stern 'Obbedite!' is a further cause for annoyance. ('Che tuon da Superiore!') But this time he is careful not to be heard.

The duet which follows between the Father Superior and Leonora presents a situation quite unlike anything that Verdi has confronted in the past. The two characters remain on entirely different planes. There is no personal relationship between them even of the kind which brought together Violetta and Germont. One cannot even speak of a polarity. From first to last Leonora remains a suppliant and the Father Superior her confessor. This calls for a stronger degree of musical separation than Verdi has yet given us in a duet. At no point does either trespass on the other's thematic territory. Otherwise the 'dialectic' of contrasted movements proceeds as usual, except that some of the movements have now shrunk to single phrases. As well as that there is a new sense of repose, a relative lack of urgency in the dialogue which permits the infiltration of recitative to an extent that the early Verdi would have avoided for fear of slackening the dramatic pace. There are places too where the musical argument advances while the verbal remains static. The resulting scene has a subtlety and complexity which may well elude the listener who expects to be swept off his feet in the familiar manner. The scheme is roughly as follows:

A. Allegro assai moderato 4/4 F major ('Or siam soli')
Leonora reveals to the Father Superior that she is a woman. Astonishment of Father
Superior.
[7 bars of declamation in strict time, based on a fragmentary orchestral idea]

B. Allegro agitato 4/4 F minor ('Infelice, delusa, rejetta')
Leonora vents her despair. The Father Superior wonders how he can help her. She
mentions a letter sent by Father Cleto. 'Then you are Leonora di Vargas!' 'Are you
angry?' 'No.'
[Overlapping with next movement. 19 bars beginning with an eight-bar strophe
from Leonora in a style recalling the central part of her aria in Act I and with a telling
use of Neapolitan G flats. The Father Superior's comment dissolves from strict time
into free recitative when he realizes Leonora's identity, and the tonality modulates
steeply through key on the subdominant side to a diminished seventh on E flat.]

C. Sostenuto 4/4 G major–E minor ('Venite fidente alla croce')
The Father Superior bids Leonora put her faith in heaven and the cross.
[10 bars; a double phrase with an appropriately modal inflection; the affinity to
Fiesco in the Prologue and the first act of *Simon Boccanegra* (1881 version) is palpable]:

311

D. Andante mosso 2/4 E minor–major ('Più tranquilla l'alma sento')
This has three subdivisions:
(1) E minor–G major
Leonora kneels before the cross, kisses it and declares that she already feels calmer and
less haunted by her father's ghost.
[25 bars. In fact it is a sixteen-bar period variously expanded to give point to the sense

of the words and the situation. The phrases no longer press hard on each other's heels; even the tonality wanders casually into F minor through a familiar variant of the rising sixth pattern before reaching the heartfelt climax in G major ('nè terribile l'ascolto la sua figlia maledir'). For most of this section the orchestral colouring is constant: high tremolo strings beneath which flute, oboe and clarinet double the voice part, suggesting the cool tranquillity experienced in a high vaulted Gothic cathedral]:

312

(2) *G major–E major ('Sempre indarno qui rivolto')**
The Father Superior confirms the holiness of the place. For that reason, says Leonora, she wishes to end her days among these rocks; 'So you know?' 'Yes. Father Cleto told me.' Leonora will devote her life to God.†
[16 bars, modulating declamation which alternates between strict tempo and free recitative]
(3) *E minor–E major ('Quai per chi si lascia illudere')*
The Father Superior solemnly warns Leonora about the folly of deciding too hastily: Leonora repeats her lines of G (1).
[42 bars beginning as a dialogue in which Father Guardiano leads with a fresh idea while Leonora responds with a derivative from Ex. 312. With the change of key to E major it develops into a richly scored ensemble of overlapping phrases. The sustaining horn and the demisemiquavers for violins belong to the revised version, which allots a more grateful line to Leonora. Symmetrical repetition gives the effect of a coda whose final cadence with its powerful scale for cellos, basses and lower brass is likewise an afterthought of 1869.]

E. *L'istesso tempo. E major–A minor ('E l'amante')*
Questioned, Leonora tells of her father's accidental murder and her brother's vengeance. Father Superior suggests a convent; Leonora cries vehemently, 'No!'

* Hughes, p. 294, points out that the initial B lies outside the compass of a modern flute. An experienced player could 'lip' it easily enough, however.

† How Verdi and Piave expected their audience to know what Leonora and the Father Superior were talking about it is hard to say. Rivas however tells us that a female hermit had once received permission to inhabit a cave not far from the monastery and remain there in total seclusion unknown to anyone except the Father Superior. He it was who arranged for food to be brought to her every day. Leonora is determined to follow her example.

[19 bars of free recitative punctuated in the definitive version only by Ex. 312 treated in a 'ritual' manner—i.e. three statements each rising by a semitone – but with no ritual significance.* Here it is a structural device, no more.]

F. Andante mosso 3/4 A minor–F major ('Se voi scacciate questa pentita')
[61 bars (1862); 69 bars (1869). Leonora threatens to run amok in the hills if the Father Superior will not grant her request. To give emphasis to her words she runs to embrace the cross. At once a sense of peace descends on her. The Father Superior gives thanks to God; Leonora repeats her declaration of faith in the cross's power to heal.]

This movement, the watershed of the duet, falls into two overlapping sections corresponding roughly to the minor and major sections of a romanza. For the first of these Verdi found two entirely different solutions in 1862 and 1869. The original version is lyrical and periodic throughout with an agitated accompaniment that recalls 'Condotta ell'era in ceppi':

313

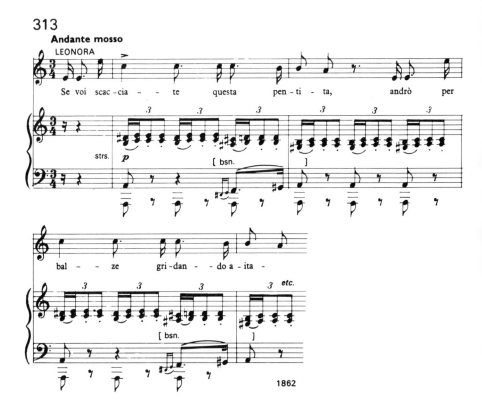

The revision is more eventful and vivid. Its opening is in the declamatory style of 'Tu sei Ernani' but with one of those 'dislocated' accompaniments that figure in many a Beethoven duo sonata:

* Noske, *loc. cit.*

314

Andante mosso

1869

As the rhythm broadens Leonora's distress is mirrored in daring harmonic progressions. What other composer of the time would have resolved a dominant ninth as Verdi does at the start of the second period, or left a 6/4 suspended in mid-air?

315

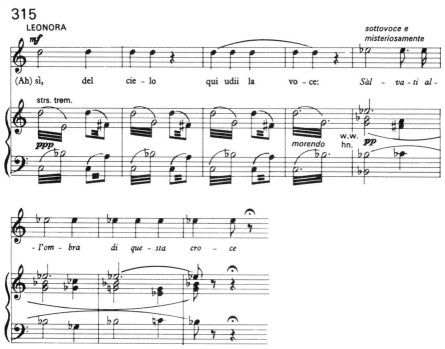

Leonora repeats 'Voi me scacciate' in a hollow monotone, and a death-figure (♩♪) foretells the fate of the outcast. Strings sweep upward as she flies to the cross; at which point the two scores coalesce in a final resolving phrase which is both the culmination of the first part and the beginning of the second. The long flute trill indicates Leonora's new-found serenity.

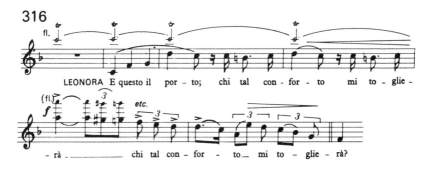

The Father Superior replies with Ex. 291 (see Overture) extended into a full period and converted into 3/4 time. The scoring is for pizzicato strings, timpani and the full brass choir, which from here on play an increasingly important part in the Father Superior's pronouncements, as he summons up all the authority of a man of God.

There is a reprise of Ex. 316 sung by Leonora, with a part for the Father Superior derived more loosely from his previous solo. Note again the evocative flute trill.

G. Allegro moderato 4/4 F major–E major ('E fermo il voto)'

The Father Superior will conduct her to the lonely cave in the hillside; he himself will bring her food every day. He summons Melitone and bids him assemble the rest of the fraternity in the chapel.

[32 bars of transition, much of it pure recitative and freely modulating. A constant – confined to the later version – is the slow march of the brass in D minor before and during the Father Superior's 'V'accolga dunque Iddio' and again in E major at the end. Melitone's entrance is also in strict time; he says not a word but the orchestra neatly conveys his presence through a quotation from Ex. 310, scored in Haydnesque fashion with flute and first violins on the melody, and a pulsating accompaniment for the remaining strings. Fra Melitone may still be burning with resentment at his exclusion from the secrets of the mighty, but he retains his comedian's charm.]

H. Moderato 4/4 E major ('Sull' alba il piede all'eremo')

The Father Superior proposes to have Leonora dressed in a monk's habit and then to set out with her at dawn to the cave. Leonora in her turn gives thanks to God for the Divine grace whereby she feels herself to be reborn.

[73 bars. A cabaletta of comparatively orthodox Donizettian cut, except that the two characters have separate themes, Leonora's being essentially Ex. 290 with the same harp triplets with different modifications in 1862 and 1869.] (See Ex. 317a and b.)

Even now there is something slightly feverish in Leonora's exaltation as the timpani roll at the end of the third phrase tells us, so too the staccato high woodwind chords at the following 'Plaudite, o cori angelici'. It remains to add that in 1869 Verdi

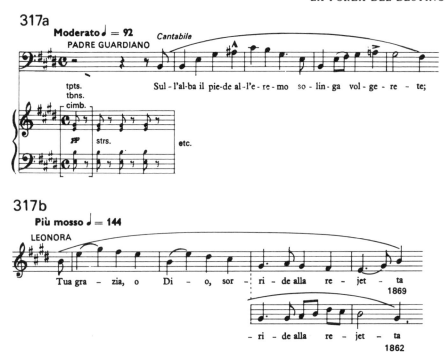

achieved in the coda a better balance between fervour and repose, replacing the hackneyed 'bolero' rhythm in which the final steep modulations were couched by continuous semiquavers, and eliminating many of the syncopations and displaced accents that preceded them. As usual there is not a change in the revision which is not an improvement. Yet what emerges with the greatest clarity in both editions is the masterly use of thematic contour to portray the gradual transformation of Leonora from humble to grateful suppliant. The basic pattern is formed by the twin arches of Ex. 289, which send the melody in an upward spiral. The next stage is Ex. 312 where the width has narrowed from a sixth to a third and the melodic direction is neither up nor down; the line merely revolves upon itself. The final stage is reached in Ex. 317b. Here the second arch covers a fourth and the music aims downward. All this plays an important part in the sense of fulfilment we experience at the conclusion of the duet.

> *Scene 3: The great door of the church opens. Facing, backstage, the great altar is seen, lit up. The organ is playing. From the sides of the choir there proceed two columns of monks carrying lighted wax torches. A little later the Father Superior enters followed by Leonora dressed in a monk's habit. He leads her out of the church; the monks range themselves within. Leonora prostrates herself before the Father Superior, who declaims, with arms outstretched above her head.*

This scene has no counterpart in Rivas's play; indeed it is strictly 'grand opera' both in its design, which is an elaboration of the giuramento formula, and in its somewhat external quality, which is all the more striking after the intimate heart-searchings that have come ·before. It begins with an organ prelude based on the

'Venite adoremus' of Scene 1. In 1869 Verdi expanded his original rather austere scheme, adding moving middle parts to the second sentence and a short episode in a related key before the violins enter with their throbbing semiquavers. Ex. 289 returns played by two muted solo violins high above the treble stave.* The rest of the strings rustle with the same tremolando chords as before. Between two statements the organ is heard again with 'Venite adoremus' and the prelude ends with the coda of 'Madre pietosa vergine' without the voice part.

All this has given the monks time to enter the chapel and take up their positions, and for Leonora to retire from the scene, don a monkish cloak and cowl, reappear with the Father Superior backstage and proceed with him to the point which both had occupied in the previous scene. The Father Superior turns to the monks and tells them briefly that an erring soul has come to seek repentance among the rocks. He then begins a kind of commination ceremony which falls at first into a characteristic ritual pattern, with three identical statements each higher than the other, in this case by a tone. (1) The holy cave is to be opened. Do they know where it is? They do. (2) No one is to approach that sacred place of refuge. They will obey. (3) No one is to cross the threshold. No one will do so. Bassoons, violas and horns lend a dark colour to the accompanying triplets; the vocal line is plain to the point of austerity; so too the unison string figure which bridges one key with the next (Ex. 318).

A curse on anyone who should violate the hermit's seclusion; and here all present break into what appears to be a Risorgimento-style chorus in the major key ('Il cielo, il cielo fulmini, incenerisca'). But the effect is very different, partly due to the 3-bar structure, partly to the far from obvious harmonic direction; and partly because of the special acoustic of a chorus ranged in a partly enclosed building toward the back of the stage (Ex. 319).

In his most religious music Verdi does not disdain theatricality, as the Requiem proves. Here too to convey the mightiness of the oath he plunges from a noisy diminished seventh into what seems a never ending pause. Then oboe and a repeated horn pedal recall very softly the three blows of Ex. 287a, though with no connotations of fatality; the chorus murmur *pppp* 'in a hollow voice' that the wind shall scatter the unclean ashes of the guilty man. They then resume the mood of Ex. 319 and carry the melody to an emphatic cadence with repeated cries of 'maledizion'. In a quiet transition with the rising sixth prominent the Father Superior tells Leonora about the bell outside the cave which she may ring in an emergency; and as if in anticipation of the event second violins and violas begin to toll softly backed by sustaining bassoons. Then the music modulates to G major for the final ensemble ('La Vergine degli angeli') a tranquil hymn in which the internal and the external elements of the two scenes are reconciled. True there is a certain resemblance to the prayer in Act I; but here the mood is transfigured, Leonora repeats the melody of the monks as she too prays for the 'Virgin of the Angels' to protect her days. The men are accompanied by cellos, Leonora by the harp. Note the almost modal half-close (*x*) which adds solemnity to the prevailing sweetness (Ex. 320).

A final touch of mastery is the descending figure – E flat–D–G – played by lower strings, bassoon, third trombone and brass bass under the concluding bars as if to

* So at least according to the score; most conductors choose the safer course of making this a solo for the leader.

remind us that, despite appearances, all is far from well, and that Leonora has not escaped her fate. Leonora now kisses the Father Superior's hand and departs alone for the hermitage. The Father Superior stretches his hand towards her and blesses her, and the curtain falls. Dull would he be of soul who would ask how Leonora would find her own way to the cave of which she only knows from hearsay. It is far more important that the scene should end with a symbolic tableau – the Father Superior speeding Leonora upon her solitary journey.

319

Più mosso ♩ = 100

PADRE GUARDIANO, MELITONE, CHORUS

Il cie — — lo, il cie ___ lo ful - mi - ni, in - ce - ne -

- ri — — — sca sca

320

PADRE GUARDIANO
MELITONE, CHORUS

Adagio ♩ = 69

La Ver - - gine de-gli an - - geli vi

co — - pra del suo man - - to, e

ACT III

Scene 1: In Italy near Velletri. Wooded countryside. Darkest night. Don
Alvaro wearing the uniform of a Spanish Captain of the Royal Grenadiers
comes forward slowly from backstage. Voices within are heard on the right.*

From the peace of a monastery to the din of an army encampment. This is the
pattern of *La Forza del destino*, which proceeds by violent contrasts like a Fellini film.

* The production book specifies a plain 'night' backcloth and the shallowest of stages.

Historically we are plunged into the War of the Austrian Succession, in the course of which Spain with the help of the King of Naples drove the Austrians out of much of Southern Italy. Twenty-nine bars of martial tutti, mostly in unison, set the scene. An equally brusque offstage chorus ('Attenti al gioco') with individual voices occasionally emerging, indicates a card game in progress. Beginning in the plainest of C majors the music moves casually to an A minor triad of which the lowest two notes are taken up by violas and second violins in hushed tremolando. At once we are transported far from the battlefield to a world of dreams and nostalgia. The clarinet solo which Verdi is thought to have written for Ernesto Cavallini, first clarinet at the St Petersburg Opera and a friend of his student days, is the first of its kind since the prelude of *I Masnadieri*, also composed to oblige an old acquaintance. A concertino by way of prelude to the third act was an established convention of which Verdi had availed himself in *I Lombardi*. The movement before us however is a piece of the purest lyrical poetry, like a Chopin nocturne; not a roulade but serves an expressive purpose. It is everything meant by Wordsworth's phrase 'emotion recollected in tranquillity'. The structure is simple binary with coda with a typical F–A flat–F scheme of keys* based on Ex. 294 or, to be more precise, an impressionistic contraction of it (Ex. 321a).

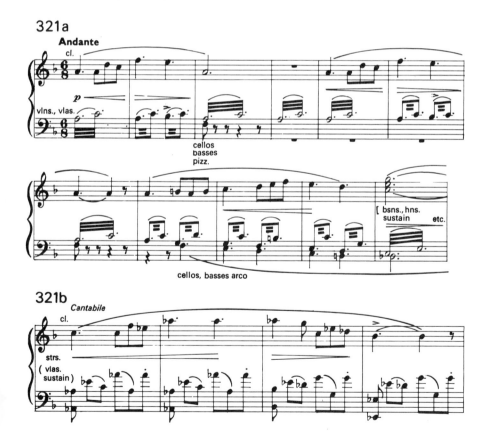

* For a detailed formal analysis of the piece, see D. Lawton, 'Verdi, Cavallini and the clarinet solo in *La Forza del destino*', in *I.S.V. Bollettino*, II, No. 5, pp. 1726–45.

Ex. 294 was unequivocally in G flat major from its first note. Ex. 321a does not establish F major until the penultimate note of the first phrase, by means of a B flat on the violas. Up to that point it could equally well be the A minor that has just been quitted. Stranger still is the melody itself. The first A makes no sense except in relation to Ex. 294, of which it sounds (and is surely intended to sound) like an imperfect reminiscence. The first time, an empty bar restores the four-bar regularity; but at the repetition the phrase is allowed to retain its three-bar form. From then on the recollection of Ex. 294 becomes more definite and the music assumes a more regular gait. Then, at the start of the second section, with a Beethovenian cunning, Verdi proceeds to make sense of that awkward first note (now a C in the key of A flat major) and in so doing reorientates the phrase completely, transferring the dominant harmony to the first beat of the third bar (Ex. 321b). The coda is based on a new idea which has no dramatic relevance but rounds off the movement to perfection.

There is more impressionism immediately after Alvaro's first words 'La vita è inferno all'infelice . . . Invano morte desio', as with the clarinet he tries to summon up remembrance of things past, Ex. 321a returns shorn of its opening note but with an unambiguous F in the bass. There is no empty bar, but between the three-bar clarinet phrases Alvaro murmurs 'Siviglia . . . Leonora'. Then voice and orchestra build up an image of the last eight bars of Ex. 294 which again differ slightly from the original. 'I shall be unhappy to all eternity,' Don Alvaro declares, 'thus it is written.' Here one might have expected an aria to follow; but there were the hero's 'life and miracles' to be recounted. Twenty-six bars of allegro moderato ('Della natal sua terra') inform the audience of circumstances which Rivas had revealed only in the final act – the attempt of Alvaro's father, Viceroy of Peru, to make himself king by marrying the last of the Inca royal house, his failure and imprisonment. Compare this recitation (Ex. 322) with its dark and spare Alberti-bass for bassoon to his compatriot Zamoro's brief narration 'Risorto fra le tenebre' from *Alzira* (see Vol. 1, Ex. 139).

Alvaro has become a defeatist Zamoro with the dark bassoon instead of the bright clarinet, a minor instead of a major tonality. The 'scena' ends with two movements of Ex. 321 played by solo clarinet, the first rendered magical by its augmented fifth, the second beautifully preparing the melody of the aria 'O tu che in seno agli angeli'. If in his youth Verdi had been innocent of the art of transition, he had certainly learned it now (Ex. 325).

Alvaro's prayer to the soul of Leonora to be his guardian angel takes the form of a spacious three-tiered romanza with coda, each successive idea as important and rich in nuance as the last, so allowing us to trace the singer's variations of mood despite some inert verbal repetition. All make use of the rising sixth in different ways. In Ex. 323 it is extended to form two interlocking arches as in Ex. 287.* In Ex. 324a it forms part of a desolate minor arpeggio with both voice and clarinet hinting at the rhythm of Ex. 287b – and very appositely as Alvaro is about to describe himself as 'hated by Destiny'. It is the nearest he comes to a musical idea that belongs exclusively to Leonora. The new theme is developed in two long phrases of which the first breaks

---

* No one should be misled by a cursory glance at the first half-phrase into thinking that the piece is in F minor, ending like so many Italian romanze in the relative major. The opening is merely *inflected* in F minor, but the first cadence leaves no doubt that A flat is the home key.

322

323

off short as if in weariness and accidie. But comfort seems to return with its transformation into Ex. 324b over a softly glowing palette of woodwind (again the double-arch has been traced, the second with its span narrowed to a fifth). A gradual return to A flat follows to be clinched by a transcendent phrase (Ex. 324c) in which the rising sixth again plays a vital part – as it does in the coda (Ex. 324d) which seems to have been generated by the emotional force of the preceding phrase. Throughout the aria the clarinet has played an obbligato role, but so discreetly that we were aware of it only as a constant in the shifting colours of the backcloth.

The tranquillity of the scene is broken by sounds of commotion. While the strings let loose nineteen bars of fairly conventional 'hurry' music, full of syncopations and rushing semiquavers, Don Carlo can be heard in the wings calling for help. Alvaro goes to investigate. There are cries of 'Kill him!' Then several officers enter fleeing in

324a

ALVARO con dolore

non i-scordar di vol-ger lo sguar-do a me ta-pi-no,

b

ALVARO cantabile dolce

Leono-ra mia, soc-cor-ri-mi

c

ALVARO ten.

pie-tà, pie-tà, —— pie-tà del mi-o pe-nar,

d

ALVARO f p

Leono-ra, soccor-ri-mi, pie-tà del mi-o pe-nar,—

disorder with Alvaro and Carlo at their heels. The two principals return and in a bout of swift recitative make each other's acquaintance as far as each permits. Carlo declares that Alvaro has saved his life. The trouble, he admits, was caused by a quarrel at cards. Alvaro wants to know how a brother officer could have fallen in with such low company, to which Carlo replies that he is new to the place, having recently arrived with dispatches from the general. Rivas fills out the story a little more. As the general's adjutant Carlos had made himself cordially disliked by his arrogance. Billeted with a noble family he had further disgraced himself by making a pass at his hostess. It was the military chaplain who, in all good faith, brought him to the gaming house to keep him from doing further mischief. His fellow players made the mistake of thinking that they could cheat him with impunity. Through the suppression of these details Verdi's Carlo emerges as a more likeable character. To Alvaro he gives his name as Don Felice de Bornos; in return Alvaro presents himself as Don Federico Herreros, captain of the grenadiers. Carlo is deeply impressed, since Don Federico's prowess and valour are renowned throughout the army. The two men swear an oath of friendship ('Amici in vita e morte'), a duettino of nineteen bars in which the voices remain yoked mostly in sixths or thirds. The lineaments of Alvaro's Ex. 294, faintly perceptible in the opening, are very plain in the close:

325

Andante maestoso

ALVARO

CARLO

in vita e in mor-te, in vita e in mor - - te entram - bi ne ve-drà

Stage trumpets cut across the last note – first two, then four, then six – together with cries of 'To arms!' In broad noble phrases launched across tremolando strings Carlo and Alvaro vow to outdo each other in heroism. As they leave the music continues but the scene changes.

> *Scene 2: It is morning. A room in the house of a senior officer in the Spanish army not far from Velletri. At the back there are two doors: the one on the left leads to a bedroom; the other is the main entrance. On the left near the proscenium there is a window. Sounds are heard of the battle near by.*

There is a crossfire of trumpet fanfares from stage and pit, and strings set up a battle theme in the tradition of *Giovanna d'Arco* and the first *Macbeth*, to which stage trumpets with their single minims at the end of each phrase add a special note of excitement.

326

As in *Giovanna d'Arco* the fighting is watched from the window by a group of orderlies and a surgeon who carries a pair of field-glasses. They see the grenadiers attack led by Herreros (Alvaro). The Austrians repulse them and the captain is lost to view. Then the Spaniards return to the charge. The enemy are soon in full retreat: 'Victory!'

Unlike Verdi's earlier battle music, this develops with harmonies that are far from predictable and with many an orchestral subtlety of which the vocal score gives no idea. Note the pattern of semiquavers which accompanies Ex. 326 in its appearance in the major key. Here too the combination of strings, clarinets, two trombones and cimbasso is one which lies well outside the conventions of scoring of the 1840s. As the fighting mounts to a climax so the sequence of progressions becomes unnervingly elliptical, impressionistic almost, until a chain of fanfares on the dominant brings in the exultant F major cadence. At once the mood of triumph collapses. To an elegiac passage of slow crotchet chords within the previous tempo the body of Alvaro is carried in on a stretcher by four grenadiers. He is wounded and unconscious. On one side is the surgeon; on the other Don Carlos covered in dust and in deep distress.* A soldier lays a case on the little table. The stretcher is put down almost in the centre of the stage. In the recitative that follows we learn that Alvaro has been wounded in the chest. A snatch of unaccompanied clarinet marks his return to consciousness. Carlo promises him the order of Calatrava for bravery and is amazed at the wounded man's horrified reaction. Alvaro tells the surgeon to retire and motions Don Carlo to approach. Five bars of woodwind and a pause introduce the famous duet 'Solenne in quest'ora', in which Alvaro begs Carlo to search his own pocket for the key of his case. In it, he says, there is a sealed packet; Carlo must make a solemn oath not to open it while its owner is alive and to burn it after his death. Much moved Carlo duly swears, whereupon Alvaro declares that he will die happy.

---

* *At the words 'Approntisi il letto' the five orderlies exeunt backstage right. (Disp. scen., p. 30.)*

So well known is this duettino on gramophone recordings that one is apt to forget that it is an action piece, though designed as a minor–major romanza for two voices. Alvaro's physical weakness and his stoicism are depicted by much the same means that Verdi had used in the final scene of *Stiffelio*; a marching accompaniment of cello and bass on the first three beats of each bar; and a declaimed, fragmentary vocal line of little thematic interest (Ex. 327a).* It breaks off, naturally, at the point where Carlo searches for the key; and the bassoons take over with a deeply pathetic echo of the previous phrase (Ex. 327b). The action performed, Alvaro's line takes on a new strength of purpose. A single flight carries it to its peak in the related key of D flat major before subsiding onto a half-close in the original key. As Carlo makes his vow the weight of care falls away from Alvaro and the duet burgeons into a lyrical C major at a slightly slower tempo ('Or muoio tranquillo') (Ex. 327c). The melody, stated twice, is enhanced at the repeat with a delicate woodwind design of arpeggios in contrary motion woven either side of the sustaining violas. In the final bars the men bid each other a sorrowful farewell. Melodically the duet may not draw special attention to itself; it amounts to no more than a tasteful and sensitive use of mid-century Italian commonplace (note the beautiful arch of the rising sixths in Ex. 327c), but for a similar blend of lyrical and dramatic freedom within a structure of classical poise one can only look to Mozart.

327a

327b

* The fact that Verdi's autograph does not carry the instructions to the basses to lower their A strings suggest that at St Petersburg he counted on having modern four-stringed instruments at his disposal.

327c

The surgeon returns with the orderlies who carry Alvaro's stretcher into the near-by bedroom, leaving Carlo to a long declamatory scena with plentiful orchestral activity. For the first time he reveals in all its force the obsession which has poisoned his life. Alvaro's reaction to the name of Calatrava has aroused his suspicions. Suppose the brave Don Federico Herreras were the murderer of his father! Now is his chance to find out. He unlocks the case and is about to break open the packet when he remembers his sworn oath. Twice during the recitative a menacing combination of brass and bassoons, like a divine warning, deters him from immediate action. He finally throws down the packet, determined not to tempt fate, and addresses himself to the cantabile 'Urna fatal' – in F major in 1862, in E major seven years later through a twist in the preceding recitative (Ex. 328a).*

As in *Un Ballo in maschera* an important turning-point of the opera is embodied in an aria for baritone, and for the same reason. More than its dramatic force the quality that Verdi exploits in the baritone voice is its ambivalence; and nowhere more powerfully than in the course of this double-aria. In the cantabile Carlo is very much the *baritono nobile*. The form is binary but without reprise, since, like that of Alvaro's 'O tu che in sen', its mood progresses. Don Carlo's chief trait is his fixity of purpose, reflected in a tendency at first for each phrase to cling to one note. But as he persists in his resolution not to tempt his fate and break his word, so the line becomes increasingly flexible and the accompanimental texture begins to loosen. The final

* In certain modern vocal scores under the Ricordi plate-number 41381 it is written in the original F.

couplet (Ex. 328b) which is repeated with the most shapely of decorations has been justly compared to the Count di Luna's 'Il balen'.* By the time he has reached his final cadenza he would seem to have put all thoughts of revenge behind him.

All this belongs to the sphere of music drama; but purely as music this piece is remarkable for its fine craftsmanship. Note the characteristic progression of the bass which gives unobtrusive strength to a rather plain theme; the majestic ascent underlined by sustaining brass at 'Un giuro è sacro per l'uom d'onore', in which C major is implied in the entire phrase but only established at the beginning of the next and immediately abandoned; above all the skill with which the subdominant tonality is obliterated before the final cadence in the course of the musical sentence that marks the beginning of Ex. 328b. So an apparently regular melody, extended from 16 to 27 bars by standard devices, follows a key-scheme entirely of its own, yet with such a sense of naturalness that the listener is aware only of a heightened expression and that combination of the inevitable and the unpredictable that is the mark of all good music.

If only Carlo could have suppressed his curiosity with his anger! But in the course of the recitative he continues to search in the case. Eventually he finds a small container and in it a portrait which he recognizes is Leonora's. Just then the surgeon returns to say that Alvaro's life can be saved; whereupon Carlo breaks out with savage exultation (Ex. 329).

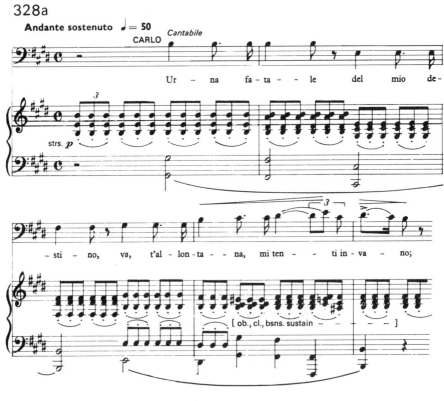

328a

* Hughes, p. 301.

This is a cabaletta, 1860s style, with no ritornello and no second statement. For 1869 if not for 1862 it may seem a rather old-fashioned solution, but it is suitable that a man who has given way to his most primitive instincts should express himself in a more primitive musical form, and that the coarsening of his mental fibre should be reflected by a return to those routine instrumental doublings of the melody that recall the 1840s. But the movement certainly does not lack character. Chromatic inflections obtrude on the vocal line giving the effect of sneering anger. In the central phrase ('Leonora, ove t'ascondi?' etc.) Carlo returns to the declamation on repeated notes, like a bloodhound with his nose to the trail. A rapidly moving bass however averts any suggestion of monotony. In the elaborate coda with its surprise modulation to G sharp major Carlo seems literally to be panting for vengeance. From now on he is a lost soul.*

> *Scene 3: A military encampment near Velletri. To the fore on the left is an old-clothes booth; on the right another stall where foodstuffs, drinks and fruit are sold. All around are soldiers' tents, stalls for second-hand goods, etc., etc. It is night. The scene is deserted. A patrol enters cautiously, spying out the land.*

At this point the differences between the earlier and later versions affect not only the musical substance but the actual order of events. Verdi's original intention was to show the fateful quarrel between tenor and baritone emerging from the cheerful bustle of life in a military camp. It was an amplification of Rivas's play even if many of its details had to be sought outside the original drama. The scheme was therefore: Encampment scene – duet – duel off stage – cantabile for Alvaro bemoaning the destiny which has forced him to kill Carlo – German attack – Alvaro's cabaletta with chorus. It is all logical enough; but there is nothing to prevent the audience from believing, like Alvaro himself that Carlo has been killed. His reappearance in Act IV therefore required a cumbersome recitative explaining how he had survived. But rather than hear from Carlo himself how he recovered from his wounds, set sail for South America, returned and so forth, how much more sensible for the audience to see the duel being prevented. But who was to prevent it? Certainly not the motley crowd of recruits, peasants and vivandières, nor Preziosilla or Melitone. The problem was solved by transporting the fatal quarrel to a point earlier in the day *before* the encampment scene and having the two parties separated by a dawn patrol. But even a patrol needs 'planting'; besides, Don Alvaro needs time to recover from his wounds. The passing of several days is therefore spanned by one of the most haunting *trouvailles* of the 1869 score, the Ronda 'Compagni sostiamo' (see Ex. 330). The revised scheme is therefore: Ronda – quarrel duet – duel – encampment scene; and no double aria for Alvaro. This has the advantage of lightening one of the most exacting tenor roles ever written, but it entails drawbacks as well. The Ronda is hardly long enough to give the required temporal illusion; while in the revised order the encampment scene leads nowhere. The traditional solution is a ruthless one: to cut out the quarrel duet and duel entirely. More thoughtful is the remedy propounded by Franz Werfel in the 1920s and endorsed by Toye and Hughes. This is to follow the Ronda with the encampment scene and restore the quarrel-duet to its original position, but in its 1869 form (see below). The curtain will be rung down on Alvaro's final recitative declaring his intention of entering a monastery. As this is also

---

* *During the singing of the second cabaletta servants will have cleared the room of chairs, the suitcase and the two tables. (Disp. scen., p. 31.) Why 'second cabaletta'? Presumably Piave was referring loosely to the melodic reprise as though it were an old-fashioned restatement in toto.*

peculiar to the 1869 version a few E major chords can be added to give a proper conclusion.*

On grounds of common sense this plan has much to commend it. Apart from concluding the act in E major instead of C, it entails no alteration in the key-sequences. Yet in general conductors and producers are wise not to tamper with a composer's final thoughts. A certain looseness of design is part of the basic concept of *La Forza del destino*. Besides, the revised opening of the quarrel-duet was designed to grow from the end of the Ronda. It would certainly make a very different effect if it were to follow the Rataplan chorus. With all its untidiness the score of 1869 is better left to stand as it is.

The Ronda is for men's chorus in four parts.† On entering they move round the tents, occasionally stopping to listen for a sound; then, satisfied, they move away. The choral theme itself (Ex. 330b) has distant roots in that of the robbers of *I Masnadieri* ('Le rube, gli stupri'); but this time there is meaning in the static bass line, which yields some delightfully piquant harmonies. The phrases peter out after three and a half bars and remain frozen on the last note. The scoring is surefooted and delicate with characteristic embellishments at the reprise. More striking yet is the motif which sets the scene and accompanies the patrol's movements (Ex. 330a): above, the most evocative use of the open fifth since the storm scene in *Rigoletto* (though precisely what it evokes is as mysterious here as there); below, a winding 'circumambulatory' figure for violas and cellos. As an instance of 'bending notes to one's will', in Verdi's phrase, with no regard for the book of rules it is astonishing. Only the fact that chord and melody exist on different planes of perspective make it possible at all. As in the overture, Berlioz is the teacher here. The seventh and ninth bars contain glaring – and deliberate – linear false relations. Only four times in the whole of the fourteen bars preceding Ex. 329a is the harmony completed. Italian models for this kind of writing are hard to find. But a student of Russian music may well be reminded of Borodin – *The Steppes of Central Asia*, and certain passages in *Prince Igor*, notably the dialogue between Igor and Ovlour. True, both works were written later than *La Forza del destino*, which indeed Borodin may have never heard in its second version. But both composers may have drawn from a common source. Although the Russian Nationalists professed little regard for Verdi, Glinka's connections with Italy are well attested. Sparse accompaniments and a movement in even quavers are certainly characteristic of the Russian national style. The ending welds fragments of both the principal ideas in the impressionistic manner noted in the clarinet solo of the first scene (Ex. 330c).

Russian too, at least in its profound melancholy, is the music to which Alvaro comes out of his tent as dawn is breaking, his mind still on the tragedy of his lost love ('Ne gustare mi è dato un'ora di quiete'). The style alone points to 1869, since it indicates beyond any doubt the intervening experience of *Don Carlos*. Following a reappearance of Ex. 294 on clarinet in its minor version the tenor line strikes in with that note of morbid sensibility that stamps Schiller's hero in the opera house.

---

* A modification of this scheme places the Ronda at the start of the act instead of the off-stage gaming chorus. This is obviously a mistake since it no longer offers a contrast with the end of the previous act.

† 'Twelve men will be enough,' Verdi wrote on the autograph, 'three to a line.'

330a

330b

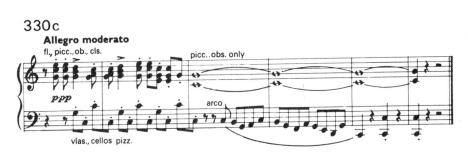

330c

As the last triplet dies away in the bass Carlo's voice is heard calling gently 'Capitano'. So begins the second and most dramatic of the three grand duets for tenor and baritone.

At first the mood is one of unclouded serenity. Alvaro feels nothing but the purest gratitude and affection for the man who has nursed him back to health – witness the Schubertian tenderness of the melody with which he greets his benefactor (Ex. 332).

It is at this point that the corresponding scene begins in the 1862 version. After Preziosilla has drawn off the soldiery, like some female Pied Piper, with her 'Rataplan' chorus, Alvaro and Carlo enter already in conversation; hence a different text to that supplied by Ghislanzoni and a slightly shorter working out of the music. Basically however the situation is the same. Carlo replies with affected solicitude. Is

331

Alvaro completely cured, Carlo wants to know? Could he fight a duel? Alvaro is puzzled; after further prevarication – still to the same bland music centred in G major – Carlo asks in a long crescendo over throbbing violas whether he has any news of 'Don Alvaro the Indian'. So the first surprise is detonated, resulting in a change of key to E major, a powerful tutti beneath Alvaro's cry of 'Treachery!', and an acceleration of tempo to allegro mosso. The cut and thrust of dialogue becomes rapid as Carlo describes how the 'picture spoke', reveals his own identity, and challenges Alvaro to fight him. Alvaro refuses to fight one with whom he has sworn eternal friendship and Carlo in a phrase of the most frightening emphasis repudiates such a description of their relationship. As in *Un Ballo in maschera* effective use is made here of the Gounodesque device whereby tutti chords are cut off at the first beat while violas, horns and bassoons continue to sustain.

333

Alvaro, far from taking offence, realizes that he owes Carlo an explanation of events. He gives it in what appears to be the first movement of a Rossinian duet in 'similar' design ('Non io; fu il destino'); though in the same tempo as the preceding section and incorporating some of its material. And this in the first version of the opera is precisely what it was, with the singers inevitably operating at different pitches. Note how both of the principal ideas are based on the interval of the sixth between soh and mi (x).

334a

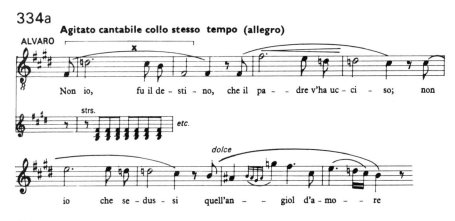

334b

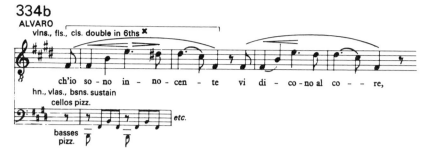

In 1869 Verdi decided to reserve the 'similar design for the final duet, in which Carlo will express his hostility to Alvaro by parodying what he sings. By removing Carlo's double quatrain in 1869 Verdi improved the duet in a number of ways. The original text with its harping on 'vengeance' told us nothing new about Carlo; it merely separated Alvaro's declaration that Leonora was dead from Carlo's contradiction of it. But above all its removal allows Carlo to maintain a 'low profile' throughout the greater part of the duet, so explaining why Alvaro takes so long to realize the full depth of his hatred. In 1869 even the cry of 'Menzogna, menzogna!' is less vehement, as Carlo goes on to recount in four bars of transition how he arrived just too late to surprise Leonora hiding in the house of a relation. The news that his beloved is alive plunges Alvaro into a new world of unreality marked by two prolonged fortissimo chords ('She lives!') and a strong tonal shift to C minor. In the rapid 'tempo di mezzo' which follows ('Carlo! amico, il fremito') Alvaro speaks the language of Leonora in their duet in Act I; but if the line, rhythm and tonality are alike Leonora's harmonic tensions are absent here, for Alvaro's agitation is wholly joyful – so much so that Carlo's baleful fury escapes him completely, even when embodied in a dominant seventh phrase accompanied by full orchestra and so encrusted with chromaticisms that two writers describe it as Verdi's most daring harmonic flight to date.*

335

Traditional methods prevail (though with a difference) in Alvaro's cantabile ('No d'un imene il vincolo') which, at a superficial glance, might seem to have strayed in

* Toye, p. 374; Hughes, p. 303.

from *Attila* or *Ernani*, with its slow parade of string triplets in the accompaniment, its arched phrases broadly articulated (Ex. 336a):

There is a point in this. Beneath his civilized veneer, Alvaro is at heart half a noble savage, a man of uncomplicated heroism, the very stuff in fact of the early Verdian tenor. But he does not regress to musical adolescence; witness the harmonic refinement brought by the flute countermelody at the third bar, the similar chromatic descent coupled with a change of vocal rhythm where just before the reprise he refers once more to his illustrious lineage. Against this simple background Carlo's malignity stands out with a controlled force (Ex. 336b). Fool! he sneers. How could their families ever unite after what has happened? A sea of blood has risen between them; Alvaro must die and after him Leonora. The tempo has become more measured; the accompanying triplets are complicated by a 'fidget' on the second note; chromaticisms have invaded the vocal line doubled by violins and carefully shaded woodwind in thirds with that effect of false blandness so characteristic of Verdian baritones. Not until Carlo has reached the climactic 'E dopo voi l'indegna che il sangue suo tradì' does Alvaro fully grasp what is being said to him. In a telling piece of dramatic realism he can only mutter, 'What are you saying? . . . Be silent . . .' while Carlo insists, 'She shall die,' his line rising in a great crescendo which finally wrenches the tonality to A major. Whereupon Alvaro erupts in total fury ('Voi pria cadrete') and the music returns to the initial E minor for the vigorous cabaletta ('Morte! Ove io non cada') led by Carlo and answered by Alvaro a minor third higher (Ex. 337).

Where the voices combine it will be noticed that Alvaro is the more excited of the two, crying out, 'Morte! Morte!' while Carlo achieves a coherent sentence ('Tinto ancor del vostro sangue quest' acciar le immergerà'). The bold sequence of modulations where the voices combine can be found in identical form, though transposed, in the final trio from Act II of *Guillaume Tell* – logically enough for there too the theme is vengeance. The two men continue to shout at each other over a series of tutti chords whose bass descends over two octaves. Here in 1862 followed a compressed reprise, more tutti chords, cries of 'A morte andiam'; then exeunt both parties 'to the right' to fight their duel. In the later version the reprise is cut, the cadential figures retained and the two men proceed to fight their duel there and then to the music that had originally accompanied their departure. But whereas the original duet had come to a halt in E minor with consequent applause, and presumably the reappearance of Alvaro and Carlo to acknowledge it, here a fierce interrupted cadence brings in the patrol who separate the combatants ('Fermi, arrestate'). Characteristically it is the volatile Alvaro who is the first to cool ('Forse del ciel l'aita a me soccorre'); while Carlo has to be dragged away howling, 'Carnefice del padre!' Left alone Alvaro throws away his sword and determines to seek peace of mind in the seclusion of a monastery. If the passage has no great melodic interest it is finely paced with a rate of harmonic change that produces the effect of a huge rallentando. Alvaro's decision has not been lightly taken.

There is another interrupted cadence and to the sound of trumpets and side drums the camp awakes to life. In the 1862 version, however, the scene that is about to unfold has already taken place, and the duel is fought to its bitter conclusion. Its progress is roughly charted in the rowdy orchestral interlude, all diminished sevenths and syncopations. We can hear the parties advancing and retreating until Carlo fighting desperately is forced back, falls, twitches violently and lies still. Alvaro then appears with dripping sword like Verdi's first tenor in *Oberto*; and he too sings what is basically a romanza ('Qual sangue sparsi') in minor–major form expressing horror at what he has done. But it is quite unlike any romanza that Verdi had written before. What appears to be an elaborate accompanimental pattern is a musical design in its own right, like a Chopin study, with the voice part grafted onto it as a

337

countermelody (Ex. 338a), sometimes producing bold harmonic clashes (Ex. 338b). As the movement proceeds the tenor part becomes more sustained, less fragmented; not until the major-key section ('Miserere di me') (Ex. 338c) does it achieve primacy as it rides over tremolando strings with threatening interventions from low brass and high woodwind.

The final note is covered by an off-stage chorus ('All' armi') crying out that the Germans have attacked and that the royal tent is ablaze. (Twelve choristers enter from the left, say the stage directions; then leave on the right; it is not clear whether they are supposed to be singing.) If the modulation through A minor to a dominant of B flat for Alvaro's cabaletta with chorus ('S'incontri la morte') is unexpectedly feeble, let it be remembered that as originally written the cabaletta was in C major

338a

338b

338c

ending in one of those powerful high C's on the chest which Tamberlick prided himself on having introduced into 'Di quella pira'. But if Verdi therefore transposed the piece down a tone he made few concessions in the rescoring, which remains extremely heavy, with a *fanfare théâtrale* of six trumpets supporting the offstage chorus. The 'bolero-style' rhythm gives way in the middle to soft string pulsations as Alvaro declares that if he cannot find death on the battlefield he will dedicate his remaining days to God. Further cries of 'To arms!' recall him to his immediate duty, and after a heroic martial coda he leads his grenadiers into battle. It is a somewhat obvious expedient, which Verdi was unfortunately to recall in some of his thoughts about *Otello*, but it rings down the curtain effectively enough. So ended the original third act of the opera.

In 1869 the departure of Don Alvaro is followed by a new set of directions:

> *The sun breaks forth. The roll of side drums and the sounding of trumpets give the signal for reveille. The scene becomes gradually animated. Spanish and Italian soldiers of all descriptions come out of their tents, cleaning their rifles, uniforms, etc. Young soldiers play at dice on the drums. Sutlers are selling drinks, fruit, bread etc. Preziosilla standing on a bench foretells good fortune – a scene of the utmost animation.* *

The introductory bars are crowded with side-drum rolls and stereophonic trumpets. The chorus 'Lorchè pifferi e tamburi' makes use of the rapid dotted

---

* The production book adds a guard hut with two grenadiers stationed before it, and Preziosilla surrounded by vivandières.

rhythm that marked the so-called seguidilla theme in Act II. Also there is an episode for unaccompanied off-stage chorus ('Vita gaia, avventurosa') of soldiers in their tents. The first of the principals to utter is Preziosilla. As good as her word she has come to Velletri to do her bit for the war effort by telling fortunes. As always her idiom is highly popular and attractive. Her song with chorus 'Venite all' indovina' is different in both versions apart from its choral refrain. The second (Ex. 339b) not only has a more satisfying melodic shape than the first (Ex. 339a), but for the only time in Verdi's operas (though not in Rossini's) makes use of two piccolos in thirds; with piquant effect:

339a

It is a simple design of two verses with refrain above which Preziosilla must display a long trill, while in the major-key coda a brilliant roulade carries her from e' to c natural above the stave.*

There is a brief transition in which soldiers call for the vivandières to serve them with wine. ('Qua, vivandiere, un sorso'). Healths are proposed by one soldier after another. Preziosilla proposes a toast to 'Don Federico Herreros'; a second tenor counters with one to the captain's 'worthy friend Don Felice de Bornos'. Just then their attention is caught by Trabuco, who has come out of one of the booths dressed as a pedlar and carrying round his neck a tray full of objects of paltry value.

The scene that follows has been traced, plausibly enough, to one in *Wallensteins Lager* in which a German rifleman gulls a Croat into parting with a valuable necklace.† But Trabuco's solo which frames it ('A buon mercato', Ex. 340b) has a more immediate ancestor in the entrance of Isacco in *La Gazza Ladra* ('Stringhe e ferri', Ex. 340a); from which it would seem that in the interests of operatic economy Trabuco is required to change not only his occupation but also his religion. We hardly need Verdi's marking of *Ebreo* to tell us that he conceived this as a Jewish character-part. Like Isacco, Trabuco is given a monotonous, bleating line; the minor tonality and the occasional trill etch the character more strongly than in Rossini's opera.

Like Isacco, too, Trabuco drives hard bargains. The soldiers crowd round him, argue his prices, and are duly cheated. They insult him and finally chase him away but without malice, as the accompanying orchestral theme tells us, frisking along beneath the dialogue like a circus horse (Ex. 341):

* If she can manage it. For those who cannot Verdi has provided an alternative version reaching no higher than A.

† L. K. Gerhartz, 'Verdi und Schiller', in *I.S.V. Bollettino*, II, No. 6, pp. 1589–1610.

340a

Rossini : LA GAZZA LADRA

340b

341

After Trabuco has left, chanting Ex. 340b and highly pleased with his sales, a group of peasants enter holding their small sons by the hand, in the first of two tiny vignettes that weave a darker thread into the general tapestry. These are men whose lands have been devastated by the soldiers and they have come to beg bread from their oppressors. (In Schiller's play, from which the scene derives, there is only one peasant with his son, and his intention is to recover his losses by cheating the soldiers at dice.) The short solo for choral basses ('Pane, pan per carità'), to which the 'voci bianche' of boys are supposed to be added is marked by those Neapolitan depressions which in Verdi no less than in Mozart symbolize extremes of grief. Yet a still more pathetic note is struck by a group of contralti representing tearful recruits who are brought in under escort. Unlike Schiller's solitary recruit, whose song furnished the model for the opening chorus ('Lorchè, pifferi e tamburi') these young men have been empressed; and their song ('Povere madri deserte nel pianto'), which Verdi also intended to be reinforced by boys' voices, has the desolate poignancy that only the oboe above hollow harmonies can bring. The strangely modal inflection, the avoidance of the supertonic suggest that here too a Russian influence is possible:

342

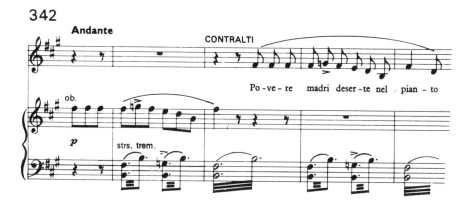

To this lament the vivandières reply cheerfully as they crowd round the recruits and promise to be sisters to them ('Non piangete giovanotti').

In 1862 their music was a variant of Ex. 341; but whether because it featured so prominently the rising sixth from soh to mi which made more dramatic sense if confined to Leonora and Don Alvaro, or whether because he felt that the variety of the scene as a whole was becoming overdone, Verdi replaced it in 1869 with Ex. 341 itself, now in B major, differently orchestrated and embellished by an internal viola figure which does not appear in the vocal score. Preziosilla needless to say has a part to play more bracing, less sympathetic than that of the vivandières ('Che vergogna, che vergogna!'). This too is retouched slightly in 1869. Again her teasing laugh can be sensed in the phrase 'Un'occhiata a voi d'interno e scommetto che indovino'. In fact, she says, there should be quite a few pretty faces around to console the young men for the absence of their dear ones. A particularly happy revision is the new codetta to Ex. 341 in which the melody is shared out between Preziosilla ('Corbellar . . . corbellar . . .') and the vivandières ('No, non piangete, . . . ah no, no, no.').

The ending of the movement seems to have given Verdi some trouble. The original version ends on a half-close in the key of the next number. For 1869 the autograph indicates that he first considered an extensive 'winding-up'. His final solution amounts to a deliberate non sequitur. Preziosilla continues her verbal backslapping ('Su coraggio . . . coraggio . . .'), implying a turn into E major. Then quite unexpectedly a dance movement starts up in C sharp minor, as though to indicate that she and her friends have decided to rely on deeds rather than words and literally sweep the recruits off their feet. The vivandières freely take the young men by the arm and so begins a very lively dance. Soon 'the noise and confusion reach their height'. This too is inspired by *Wallensteins Lager*. But there the site was Pilsen in Bohemia, and the dance was a slow waltz. In Central Italy with troops from the Kingdom of the Two Sicilies it is necessarily a fiery tarantella, carved in the same polythematic mould as that of *Les Vêpres Siciliennes*. As in Summer's variation in *Les*

Quatres Saisons there is a lively interplay of 'exotic' and traditional styles of harmonization: primitive hollow harmonies and a zampogna dominant drone for the opening idea (Ex. 343a); for the second (Ex. 343b) conventional tonic and dominant configurations; the third theme (Ex. 343c) is in unison; the fourth (Ex. 343d and e) has the nature of a choral refrain ('Nella guerra è la follia') similar to 'Vive les conquêtes' from the earlier opera, but with an extra refinement: for while the first limb (Ex. 343d) is harmonized with a tonic pedal and a moving inner part picked out mainly by the horns, the second (Ex. 343e) is recast over a lively bass, which brings a more emphatic cadence.

There is a further episode, a reprise which finds Ex. 343d in the tonic major, and a brief, whirlwind coda,* during which Fra Melitone enters and is caught up in the dance. He has been transformed into Schiller's Capuchin friar, who preaches in the punning manner of the seventeenth-century monk, Abraham a Sancta Clara.† Apart from a few sentences the text is lifted word for word from Maffei's translation of *Wallensteins Lager*, and early libretti acknowledge the debt. Coincidences of language allow one of the puns to work in both Italian and German – and, for the matter of that, English. ('Kümmert sich mehr um den Krug als den Krieg' turns neatly into 'Ben più faccenda le bottiglie vi dan che le battaglie'.) The others are inevitably more laboured, and none more so than Piave's own contribution, intended to explain Fra Melitone's presence in Velletri ('Venni di Spagna a *medicar* ferite, ed alme a *mendicar*'). But the Predica itself ('Toh, Toh, poffare il mondo') is an interesting and remarkably complex piece of writing.‡ In its freedom of rhythm, tonality and form it is part of a direct line which leads from the soliloquies of Macbeth and Rigoletto to those of Iago and Ford. But for once the language is that of parody of the heroic manner ('Venni di Spagna' and 'Ben più faccende') and of priestly chant ('. . . Berteggiar la santa domenica così' and 'Invece di vestire cenere e sacco'). In a central section ('Il mondo è fatto una casa di pianto') in F minor the discourse takes on an apocalyptic note with a pattern of heavily scored semitonal laments reaching from piccolo to double-bass over tremolando violins and violas. Melitone has something of the hellfire preacher in him; and at the words 'Tutto va a soqquadro' a chaotic tutti breaks loose. 'And the reason for this? . . . the reason,' he sneers softly, '. . . your own sinful hearts.'

By this time he has divided his audience, like his Capuchin model, but for a different reason. Schiller's friar had begun to attack the commander Wallenstein. Melitone has merely irritated the Italian contingent by his manner; the Spaniards are readier to defend their fellow countryman. Amid cries of 'Give it him!' from one side and 'Run for it!' from the other Melitone continues declaiming undeterred. As usual the music becomes more periodic towards the end, finishing in an orthodox coda.

As with Macbeth's great 'Mi s'affaccia un pugnal' it is not easy to account for the sense of unity. Partly it lies in the persistence of certain figurations and certain rhythms. Its four sections are so far from being self-contained that not one finishes in the key in which it began. What is remarkable, however, is the Russian flavour of the phrase

* Shortened by Verdi before the first performance, or so it would appear from the autograph.

† Gerhartz, *op. cit.*, p. 1595.

‡ For a close analysis of its structure see G. Ugolini, 'Fra Melitone', in *I.S.V. Bollettino*, II, No. 6, pp. 1716–17.

'Tutti, tutti, cloaca di peccati' which begins the final period with its chromatically sinking 'la' over an implied 'doh' – a mannerism of the nationalists from Glinka to Rimsky-Korsakov.

344

Preziosilla is shocked at the spectacle of soldiers chasing a friar. Her remedy is to take up a side drum whose sound acts on them with the magic of a referee's whistle. The recruits, the Spanish and Italian soldiers come rushing, and so according to the autograph do the peasants who by this time will have donned military uniform. There follows a Rataplan chorus in rondo form unaccompanied for the most part except for two side drums. Here and there an orchestral intervention adds sparkle and vigour to what is essentially a tour de force of pattern-making combined with a clever imitation of fife (Preziosilla) and drums (the rest). At the end everyone mimics the action of firing a rifle. There is a flourish of trumpets; a general exodus at the double; and the curtain falls.

ACT IV

> *Scene 1: Inside the monastery of the Madonna of the Angels. A mean colonnade surrounds a little courtyard with orange trees, oleanders, jasmine. On the spectator's left is the door which leads onto the street. On the right is another door above which is written the word* clausura. *The Father Superior is pacing up and down reading his breviary. From the left enter many beggars of all ages and sexes with rude bowls, pots or plates in their hands.* *

If the 1869 version breaks here the strict alternation of tragedy and comedy which had been a feature of the original, it preserves the contrast of venue and also of pace. We may regret that Don Alvaro has been turned by the revision into a deserter.

---

* *The cloister should present a picture which should approximate as far as possible to reality. A few old men should be seated on benches. Others should be·standing in groups; some old women should be sitting on the ground. Of these paupers some should be elderly and support themselves on crutches. Most should lean on sticks. The women should be leading a few children by the hand. All should be provided with bowls, plates and spoons of wood. (Disp. scen., p. 38.)*

(What will the grenadiers say when they find that their valiant leader has thrown away his sword?) None the less the comedy that now unfolds is so different in kind from that of Act III the listener is made all the more aware of the vast distance of time and place that separates them. Here all touches of the exotic are banished, in favour of a classical, almost Beethovenian idiom, with melodies that move by step and simple harmonies that mostly change with every note of the melody.

345

The poor of the neighbourhood are begging for charity, humbly but with growing impatience at being kept waiting. From the right Melitone appears dressed in a white apron. Assisted by another lay brother he is carrying a huge soup-cauldron with two handles which they place in the middle of the stage. The other lay brother leaves. Melitone with a snarl of reproof ('Che? siete all'osteria?') proceeds to ladle out the soup. The music quickens as they all push forward ('Qui, presto a me!'). So to a melody with 'parlanti' in that post-eighteenth-century *opera buffa* style which was still current coin amongst Italian composers of the 1860s. For the first time Verdi does not enter much into the feelings of his leading character, but stands back and surveys him with a Rossinian chuckle. A horn pedal-note adds piquancy to the rather Haydnesque scoring:

346

The beggars squabble for precedence. One woman demands four portions on the grounds that she has six children. That, retorts Melitone, is because she does not spend her nights telling her rosary and saying the Miserere – at which point the buffo melody makes room for an ecclesiastical cadence. The Father Superior puts in a word of reproof; Melitone grumbles forcibly about the fecundity of the poor; and Ex. 346 is resumed half a tone higher. Another suppliant irritates Melitone by asking for 'a bit more of those dregs' ('Un po' di quel fondaccio') and the cry is taken up eagerly by the other tenors and basses in a vortex of downward modulations ('a me . . . a me . . .'). Melitone's reply is to send them to the Devil – they make him lose his

temper. 'Charity!' murmurs the Father Superior, while the women slyly refer to the
kindness of Father Raffaele. Melitone takes no offence at the implied comparison.
He merely points out that after a week of ministering to the poor the good father
returned to his cell worn out by their importunities. Now it is Melitone's turn to
suffer. His new A major theme ('Sì, sì, ma in otto giorni') is in the comfortable jog-
trot style of Luigi Ricci, one of the last mid-century masters of traditional opera
buffa; but the sense of growing tension is maintained by a busy accompaniment in
quavers. Once more the Father Superior reproves; but Melitone has no patience with
professional beggars who refer to God's benison as dregs.

At this point discrepancies open up between the earlier and later versions. Here at
least the 1862 score has nothing of special interest to offer. Originally at the height of
his annoyance Melitone had ventured into dark, minor-key harmonies; later Verdi
preferred to let his anger vent itself more superficially through rhythm alone, by
bursting into crotchet triplets ('Bricconi, bricconi, bricconi . . .'). Not in the least
abashed the beggars continue singing the praises of the saintly, angelic Father
Raffaele. A derivative of Ex. 346 brings the music round in sequential developments
to a half-close on the original key of E flat. Then after several bars of mutual
provocation Melitone sends the cauldron rolling away with his foot and tells them to
take the rest themselves and get out. The melody of this final movement ('Il resto a
voi prendetevi') is so natural, so spontaneous sounding in its final form that one is
amazed to find it reached through a version as angular and clumsy as that of 1862:

347

As in the previous revision it would seem that the Verdi of 1869 was determined not
to upset the balance of comedy by making Melitone's anger too serious; hence the
dancing intervals of his line were replaced by a smoothness of contour which is
implicit in the theme itself.* During a brief coda in still faster tempo (this also an

---

* There is also a variation in the stage action which could be argued against. In 1862 Ex. 347 had
been approached by a development of Ex. 346 above which the directions both in score and in
production book run: *hurriedly distributing the remainder and saying.* . . . Not until after eight bars of the
allegro brillante is Melitone supposed to kick away the cauldron. This accords strictly with the original
play. In the 1869 version the four preparatory bars to Ex. 347 are altered into a non-thematic figure
which actually suggests the upsetting and rolling away. This coupled with the appropriate stage
direction and Melitone's words 'Take the rest yourselves' indicates that in his fury the monk has
deliberately spilt what was left of the soup. Surely this would bring forth a much greater howl of rage
from the mob and a much severer reprimand from the Father Superior.

addition of 1869) Melitone drives the crowd before him slapping at them with his apron ('Via di quà'). He then returns mopping his brow with a handkerchief, takes a pinch of snuff and joins the Father Superior who chides him gently for his lack of patience. With a return to his punning manner of Act III Melitone retorts that most people after three days of this would end up by doling out not slops but slaps – in Italian the pun is between 'minestra' (soup) and 'ministrare' (administer). He should be humble, the Father Superior rejoins, and not resent it if the people prefer Padre Raffaele. 'Of course not; he is a friend of mine,' says Melitone; but, he continues, the father has some odd ways. 'Yesterday I found him working in the garden, his eyes staring so wide that I said to him joking, "You look like a mulatto," whereupon he looked at me fiercely and clenched his fist. . . . And when the church tower was struck by lightning and he went out into the storm I shouted after him, "You look like an Indian savage"; and he let out a yell which froze my blood. . . . Is it true,' Melitone continues, 'that the Devil once dwelt in the monastery in the habit of a monk? Could Father Raffaele be a relation? . . .' He is reassured. The Father Superior was granted a revelation at the time. Raffaele's behaviour is merely the effect of life's disappointments together with assiduous prayer and fasting. All but the last observation is set as free recitative of no great musical significance. But the argument is summed up in a duettino ('Del mondo i disinganni') which furnishes a neat vignette of the two participants.

348a

The Father Superior's theme with its modally inflected harmonies is an essay in that personal ecclesiastical idiom to which Verdi will return for the new duettino for

Fiesco and Gabriele in the revised *Boccanegra*. Melitone repeats his lines word for word but in a decidedly 'lay' manner, nodding his head sagely the while (what else could the melodic figuration of Ex. 348b signify?). All his ill-humour has passed. He obviously feels flattered that the Father Superior has spoken so frankly to him. He is no longer excluded from the councils of the mighty. Like a typical buffo he chatters on in the coda while the Father Superior supplies a slow marching bass ending on a long sustained F below the stave.

There is a violent ringing of the bell. The Father Superior leaves; and to a pattern of stabbing crotchets with acciaccature Don Carlo enters wrapped in a large cloak, asking arrogantly for a certain Father Raffaele. 'There are two,' Melitone replies, 'One from Porcuna, fat, deaf as a post; the other lean, dark with eyes that . . .' 'I want the one from Hell,' cries Carlo, so confirming Melitone's worst suspicions. . . . 'Whom shall I announce?' 'A knight . . .' and Melitone makes his final exit muttering at Carlo's rudeness. As he waits, Carlo muses on the success of his quest and his renewed determination to wipe clean the family escutcheon with Alvaro's blood. The string-accompanied recitative begins quietly but the progressions are sufficiently unusual to charge the atmosphere with electricity. At the words 'Sete di vendetta' there is an astonishingly bold clash of passing notes:

At the end of the soliloquy a reference to the duel in 1862 was replaced by a fresh couplet ending in a baleful sequence of brass chords.* Alvaro enters to a motif which recalls the sleepwalking scene of *Macbeth* in both shape and scoring (clarinet and bassoon in unison over pizzicato strings). Surely this is not fortuitous. Alvaro for all his piety and Christian resignation is still a haunted man. 'You . . . Don Carlo . . . alive!' he exclaims, forgetting that in 1869 he had no reason for supposing him dead. Carlo loses no time in getting down to the first movement of their final grand duet ('Col sangue sol cancellasi').

The orchestral theme (Ex. 350) is martial, regular and periodic, and already hints at the language of *Aida*, not least in the use of a tutti chord to punch home the end of a

---

* The autograph shows bassoons instead of trumpets; however, a hand which was not Verdi's but which might very well have had his authority has written very clearly 'trombe'. Curiously enough the notes themselves make sense either way; nor is this the only occasion on which the mature Verdi falls victim to his own outdated method of setting out a score.

350

sentence. As in 'Madre pietosa vergine' the symmetry is masked by keeping the vocal and orchestral phrases out of alignment. Alvaro replies to the insults and the offer of a sword in the manner of his entrance theme a few bars back. He will atone for his sins in a cloister, he says, and begs Carlo to leave. When Carlo calls him a coward he starts, then pulls himself together. Threats and cruel words, he says, leave him unmoved. The melody of 'I minacci, i fieri accenti' is that of Ex. 288 in the overture but harmonized simply, without the destiny theme grumbling in the background, and more expansively developed. It forms the central cantabile of the duet and indeed its most important movement; those on either side of it represent merely the 'rump' of a Rossinian tempo d'attacco and cabaletta respectively. Yet here at least the old terms are still applicable; for once again Verdi has succeeded in making a well worn convention yield new fruit. 'I minacci, i fieri accenti' is, for all its elaboration, a 'similar' duet but one in which imitation is designed to give the effect of sneering parody. To the same music as Alvaro's Carlo piles on the indictment ('Una suora mi lasciasti che tradita abbandonasti') but here the cello contributes an angry tic to the accompaniment. When Alvaro wins through to the purer air of 'Sulla terra l'ho adorata' with its ethereal scoring of upper strings and woodwind, Carlo remains earthbound with a major key variant of Ex. 288 ('Non si placa il mio furor') in which the accompaniment is still angrier, full of seething viola demisemiquavers. It is tempting to see in that semitonal inner rise (E flat–E natural–F) another Russianism imbibed at St Petersburg; but it is clearly part of a chromatic design leading the music away from the tonic and bringing it back again with an emphatic modulation. Yet again the sense of vocal 'scontro' emerges strongly, from the contours of each singer's line. In a short postlude once more in the minor key Alvaro offers to kneel at Carlo's feet, as did Manzoni's Padre Cristoforo to the Spanish aristocrat whose brother he had killed in a duel. Here the result is rather different. To Carlo such an act reveals his tainted blood. For the first time Alvaro loses control of himself, grabs the sword and is about to meet the challenge, when the voice of conscience speaks once more in the form of Ex. 288 on flute, oboe and clarinet.* He throws away the weapon and tells Carlo to be gone. This is altogether too much for his enemy. Carlo gives him a slap

---

* The high B flat that certain tenors interpolate at the word 'Uscite' is quite unwarranted; the note in question should be F.

on the face and calls him a coward, so at last producing the desired effect. In a short stretta ('Ah segnasti la tua sorte') the two men cry for each other's blood before hurrying off to fight their duel. Again it is Alvaro who once aroused seems the angrier of the two, with an initial phrase recalling Stiffelio at the zenith of his frustration.

> *Scene 2: A valley amongst inaccessible rocks at the foot of which runs a stream. At the back on the left of the spectator is a cave with a door that can be entered and on it is a bell which can be rung from inside. By one of the rocks is a canister with provisions left by the Father Superior. It is sunset. The scene darkens gradually; the moon appears in all its glory. Donna Leonora, pale and dishevelled, comes from the cave in a state of great agitation.* *

For the first time since Act II the destiny theme (Ex. 287b) is heard again, in a new key and with yet another variation in the scoring (first violins and cellos on the tune, seconds, violas and bassoons on the accompaniment, flute and clarinet joining the melody in the fourth bar). Leonora is heard from within crying, 'Pace.' She appears from the cave and without preamble begins that famous 'Melodia' which reminded the critic Filippo of Schubert's 'Ave Maria'.

351

It was not an unintelligent comparison, since as has been said much of *La Forza del destino* and of Leonora's part in particular does indeed seem to stray towards the

---

* The production book of 1862 adds a precipice, a small path leading up behind the cave, and a concealed dummy which in due course will be hurled into the ravine. There is no moon. See *Disp. scen.*, p. 41.

world of the German romantics. But the listener today would probably find that the design had more in common with Brahms, many of whose slow movements share a similar, freely ranging ternary design, the same nostalgia, the same sense of reflective discourse. Elisabeth de Valois will express herself in a similar aria in the last act of *Don Carlos*. But in 'Toi qui sus le néant' the central section is thronged with a host of recollections. 'Pace, pace, mio Dio' is strung on the single thread of harp arpeggio, denoting that peace for which Leonora constantly strives and which constantly eludes her. Even the incursions of Ex. 287b are not allowed to upset the steady flow. Again the polarity of keys a third apart is in evidence with most of the ideas centred on G minor or B flat minor. The delicacy of the harmonies is matched by the subtly varied use of sustaining instruments to colour the accompaniment. A curious relic here of that 'selective' scoring to be found in the earlier operas is the absence of horns throughout. Nor is the principle of variation-on-repeat ignored. Although the orchestra echoes Leonora's opening phrase melodically the harmonies of both statements are different until the cadence. Even the final reprise carries a new countermelody for the voice ('Invan la pace quest'alma . . .'). Nothing could be less predictable than the ending. Strings take over from harp in what appears to be a pathetic postlude; Leonora meanwhile goes to pick up from a near-by rock the scanty provisions left her by the Father Superior, murmuring that they merely serve to prolong a useless existence ('Misero pane . . . a prolongarmi vieni la sconsolata vita'). Sudden tremolandi warn of some intrusion. Leonora's mood changes from melancholy to stark terror, and with rising screams of 'maledizione!' she hurries back inside the cave.*

To understand Leonora's feelings as she leaves the stage we must return to her dialogue with the Father Superior in the original play. From the Father she learned that her predecessor in the cave had been attacked by three robbers; but God had come to her rescue. A storm arose and they were struck by lightning.

1862. Appropriately a storm does begin in the orchestra with the familiar rumblings of cellos and basses and flashes of flute and piccolo. Alvaro enters with Carlo. 'Those who violate this spot,' he declares, 'are accursed; but this is a day of crimes.' Ten bars of duel-music follow on full orchestra, full of syncopations and rapping death figures. To a diminished seventh crash Carlo falls, mortally wounded. He calls on Alvaro to hear his confession; but Alvaro stands rooted to the spot in horror at what he has done. Here violin and oboe give out a lamenting motif which will assume great importance in the 1869 version (Ex. 352).

Feeling himself unworthy to shrive a Vargas he knocks on the door of the cave and calls on the 'hermit' to perform the office. Leonora at first refuses; but at his third

---

* Although this remarkable piece of music is the same in both versions it is clear that the ultimate form of the melody was not arrived at until the rehearsals in St Petersburg since Signora Barbot's part-book contains ineffective variants of two of the most powerful phrases: 'come il dì primo, da tant' anni dura profondo il mio soffrir' and 'Fatalità, fatalità' with its magnificent octave drop. The harmonies are the same however. See G. Barblan, 'Un po' di luce sulla prima rappresentazione della *Forza del Destino* a Pietroburgo', in *I.S.V. Bollettino*, II, No. 5, pp. 877–8. The manuscript full score, part autograph, in the Bibliothèque Nationale, Paris, shows unmistakable signs of alteration at these points, as well as the illuminating comment on the double bass line: 'For this piece a low G is absolutely necessary' – in other words, those double basses with only three strings must lower their A strings by a full tone. One suspects therefore that this is the score which served for the second performance at Madrid.

352

Allegro moderato assai

vlns., ob.

appeal she rings the bell and comes out, threatening both men with the wrath of heaven, only to recognize and be recognized by the lover whom she believed she had lost for ever. So the fierce B flat minor of her 'Temerarii, del ciel l'ira fuggite!' passes down through F minor to an ecstatic six-four of revelation on C major. Incredibly, to those who know the opera in its final form, a short duettino follows with both voices in unison in Verdi's characteristic 'lovers' meeting' style – melodic sighs and caresses over a throbbing dominant pedal ('Si dunque a me presso tu stavi'). If this is hardly the time or place for such diversions the closed period with its joyous final cadence serves the usual purpose of giving a formal nucleus to what is otherwise a freely developing scene. Formality of a different kind appears in the next passage, where the dying Carlo calls upon his sister to embrace the last of her family. The music builds in units by quadruple repetitions of a neutral bar-long pattern which ends in the false glow of D flat major as Leonora embraces her brother only to be stabbed. She dies protesting her love for Alvaro and forgiveness of her brother. In her final death agony ('Vedi destin, io muoio') the rising sixth plays an important part as it sends the music upward in a spiral to a climax which just stops short of sublimity, possibly because of a slight dominant bias in the bars which lead up to it (Ex. 353).

Her dying gasps ('Alvaro . . . Alvaro . . . t'amo') eked out by the oboe end in a typical 'Leonora' cadence – a minor-key version of x from Ex. 351. Leonora keeps her rising sixth to the end. A despairing snatch of recitative from Don Alvaro tears the music away from F minor to C sharp minor for the final movement – a cataclysm of Wagnerian force. Behind sounds of the rising storm the monks can be heard chanting the 'Miserere' together with Guardiano and Melitone in a curious sequence of harmonies: C sharp minor–G sharp minor–B minor–D major–A minor–E major. At this point descending triads above combine with a rising bass in triplets to suggest Valhalla falling. The monks enter, followed by peasants with lighted torches, and exclaim at the sight of two bodies and the revelation that the penitent was a woman. The Father Superior calls to Father Raffaele; but Alvaro has already climbed a rock, defying the earth to open and swallow up humanity. Declaring himself an envoy of Hell ('I always said so,' comments Melitone) he hurls himself into the ravine beyond.* Amid the thunder-and-lightning music his voice rises higher and higher into hysteria; the progressions culminate in an apocalyptic six-four in E minor then, as the monks fall on their knees with an 'Orrore . . . pietà, Signor . . . misericordia', subsides into a long pianissimo cadence. Whether by coincidence or because he wanted to emphasize the grim logic of 'fatalità', Verdi here reverted to the eighteenth-century practice of beginning and ending an opera in the same key.

1869. Here Leonora's 'melodia' is followed by ten bars of diminished-seventh 'duel' music during which is heard the sound of clashing swords, then the voice of

---

* In fact the tenor climbs up, disappears behind a rock and a dummy in his likeness is propelled into the abyss. See *Disp. scen.*, p. 46.

353

Carlo calling out for a confession. With the appearance of Ex. 352 the scores converge for a while as far as the recognition. This time Alvaro's 'una donna . . . qual voce . . . Ah no . . . uno spettro' are no longer carried forward on a string tremolando. Instead the strings accompany his exclamations with anapaestic figures. There is no exultant 6/4 in C major nor any subsequent duet of reunion. Leonora's phrase 'Io ti riveggo ancora' is firmly orientated in C minor. Her cadence is interrupted and Alvaro's reply is full of guilt and dismay as he seems to step back from her, crying that his hands are steeped in blood. Ex. 352, shortened and transferred to cello and bassoon, furnishes the basis of a transition in which Alvaro briefly tells her what has happened. No sooner has she realized that the dying man is her brother then Leonora hurries to him with a cry of 'Gran Dio', leaving Alvaro to reflect over sepulchral wind chords and brusque gestures on the strings how destiny has mocked him. He has found Leonora only after he has killed her brother. There is a cry off stage. Supported by the Father Superior Leonora staggers in mortally wounded. The motif that signals their entrance − stylized scream in the upper woodwind, with a thudding in the rest of the orchestra − outdoes anything in the first version for stark brutality:

354

Symmetrical repetitions of rhythmical patterns play a larger role in Verdi's music than in that of the German romantics; but the fourfold statements of Ex. 354, unaltered except for a C flat in the last bar, have a dramatic force all their own. The music is frozen in a kind of numb horror as Leonora relates in a monotone her brother's final act of vengeance. The progression from second to third bar is so steep as to amount almost to a non sequitur, since the only element which the two chords have in common is the longing G. But it makes a special Verdian sense. Both to Boito and Ghislanzoni he wrote half jokingly that there were certain situations for which poets and musicians had to learn how not to write either poety or music; that there are times when both must unlearn their training. The present passage is a case of sound-effects raised to a higher power by a musician of genius. Only with the final descent to C flat does a sense of movement return.

Alvaro breaks into curses; but is gently checked by the Father Superior much as Pagano had restrained the blaspheming Giselda in *I Lombardi*. The new terzetto finale ('Non imprecare, umiliati') infuses a note of Manzonian humanity to the drama, softening the music yet at the same time making it more spacious. The original ending, powerful though it was, is articulated through small rhythmic patterns insistently hammered out, since the nature of the action allowed of no other solution. True, the variety and disposition of these motifs kept away any trace of monotony; yet, as so often in Tchaikovsky, they limit the formal perspective. In the final version the absence of violent action allows a musical development in the composer's mature personal style.

Formally the terzetto has two aspects. Its basis is the finite sixteen-bar paragraph formed by the Father Superior's double quatrain of spiritual comfort. This, in turn, yields, in its second bar, a pattern (x) which extends the piece by thematic development making room for other contrasted ideas. For the first time since *Ernani* a bass clarinet colours a death scene.

355

As the Father Superior proceeds, Leonora and Alvaro add appropriate *pertichini*, he muttering in despair, she urging him to pray. Then Ex. 355 is split into a design of syncopations with second trombone, cimbasso and timpani playing a small but important part. As Leonora and the Father Superior admonish Alvaro in turns the motif is further split, and warmth breaks in slowly. Alvaro's bitterness is purged away in a new theme (Ex. 356), which is announced not by the singer but by the orchestra.

And so after a soaring vocal climax to the final period, which reveals itself as the major-key complement to a minor 'romanza'. To a limpid arpeggio melody (Ex. 357) Leonora declares that she is not lost but gone before.

After such simplicity Alvaro's reply ('Tu me condanni a vivere') strikes in with an almost Brahmsian luxuriance of harmony; but there is never any question of departing too far from previous material. The repetition of Ex. 357 is combined vertically with a major-key version of the opening Ex. 355 sung by the Father Superior ('Santa del suo martirio'). After the cadence there is another transition based on Ex. 355, but no longer syncopated. The melodic line whirls with the sense of vertigo to be found in the death agony of Violetta, then descends rapidly for her

356

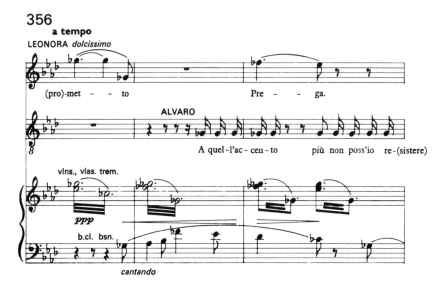

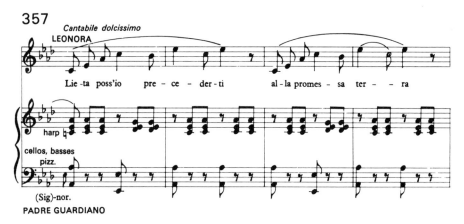

final gasp, rolling bass drum and trilling upper woodwind all contributing to that 'sense of ruin that is worse than pain'. 'Dead!' cries Alvaro. 'Ascended to God,' corrects the Father Superior. The final cadence of Leonora's melody (Ex. 357), etherealized on harp and tremolando strings, brings down the curtain.

Even after its triumphal reception at La Scala in its revised form, *La Forza del destino* was slow in making its way into the repertoire, except in Rome where as *Don Alvaro* – since the days of censorship were not over for the Eternal City until King Victor Emmanuel marched in with his troops in 1872 – it had been a favourite since 1863. The reason was partly Verdi's reluctance to make it available where he could not be sure of a worthy performance. Many of the greatest theatres were not equipped to do justice to this type of work. *La Forza del destino* was a conductor's opera, written at a time when in many Italian theatres the conductor's function was still divided between the *maestro concertatore* and the leader of the first violins. The average buffo who could deal adequately with the generic buffooneries of Bartolo or Pasquale could not approach the individual humour of Melitone. Preziosillas were almost impossible to find. Even the unequivocally tragic part of Leonora was beyond the grasp of most 'prime donne assolute' of the day. Referring to the Neapolitan candidate for 1869, the singer who had served him so well in *Aroldo* twelve years before, Verdi wrote to Giulio Ricordi:

> I can't imagine without laughing the idea of la Lotti with her crinoline and her fichus dressed as a man and as a monk. Anyway you need different blood in your veins to play that part. . . . Besides, the choruses [of the San Carlo] aren't used to that type of opera and don't know how to move. The orchestra would work miracles if I went down there to rehearse them; but unless you want me to get myself killed you mustn't ask this of me. . . . It always comes down to this: who is to be the conductor? . . . To all the questions that you ask me I have only one reply — find a man who knows how to mount and conduct an opera.*

Unfortunately Verdi himself was just about to quarrel with the man who most nearly satisfied these requirements. However before the rupture Mariani was able to turn in two widely acclaimed performances of *La Forza del destino*, at Vicenza and Bologna.

After a mediocre revival at La Scala it was left to the young Franco Faccio to mount a performance at the Teatro Grande, Brescia, in August 1872, which at once led to the opera's being taken up with enthusiasm throughout Europe.

La Force du destin, ANTWERP, 1882. Verdi consented but without enthusiasm to a performance at the Théâtre des Italiens in Paris. 'For the Italian theatre,' he wrote to Escudier, 'you need operas with a simple mise-en-scène which depend much on voices and very little on the orchestra. . . . It is possible that the chorus and orchestra are excellent and that they will do well under Vianesi; and it's possible, as you say, that there is no better conductor than he today, but for my operas I would prefer one of those young conductors that we have here in Italy.'† Presumably he had Faccio in mind. In the event it was his old pupil, Emanuele Muzio, who conducted the Parisian première on 31 October 1876. According to an eyewitness, 'The reason for its failure can only be attributed to the absurdity of the libretto which provoked, not unjustly, laughter among the spectators, although they were predisposed in Verdi's favour, especially in the prologue. Muzio conducted the opera marvellously and the overture, wonderfully performed, was encored amid universal applause. But that pistol that fortuitously kills Leonora's father ruined everything.'‡

In 1881 Léon Escudier died, having previously lost all his money and with it Verdi's friendship. A lawsuit followed between his heirs and the house of Ricordi; it was in connection with this that Verdi paid a visit to Paris in the late spring of 1882. The business concluded, Muzio reported Verdi's departure to Giulio Ricordi, adding, 'He has been working on the French translation of *La Forza del destino*, which has been well and truly put right scenically as well as musically; there are a few cuts,

---

* Letter to G. Ricordi, 7.6.1869. Abbiati, III, pp. 286–7.
† Letter to Escudier, 7.3.1874. *Copialettere*, pp. 289–90.
‡ Gatti, II, pp. 290–1.

tiny new recitatives added; the pistol shot has been removed, etc., etc.'* The French
libretto was by Charles Nuitter and Camille du Locle, who according to a notice in
Escudier's *Revue Musicale* had already completed their translation of the first version
in 1865. As by this time Verdi was not on speaking terms with du Locle all
negotiations were with Nuitter, with whom there was later to be an important
correspondence over the revision of *Don Carlos*. On the subject of the French *Forza
del destino* no letters survive; presumably it was managed within the three weeks of
Verdi's visit to Paris. The first performance of it took place in Antwerp the following
year.† The vocal score published by Choudens‡ is very rare, and the problems
connected with it by no means resolved. Not only is there no autograph of the
altered passages. There is not even a full score in existence which corresponds with the
Choudens reduction. Yet it is clear that the opera was performed in that version as
late as October 1931 at the Théâtre de la Monnaie with Ferdinand Ansseau in the
part of Alvaro. Alas, no one connected with that revival can shed any light on the
matter; the archives of the theatre contain no material relating to it; while the
contemporary reviews are too general to be illuminating. None of the critics
appeared to realize that they were listening to the opera in a form other than that of
1869 – which is understandable, since all were evidently making its acquaintance for
the first time. After six performances it was dropped from the repertory.

Certainly there is no question here of a third definitive edition of the opera;
otherwise it would have been brought out subsequently by Ricordi. Nor was it
intended for the Opéra of Paris for it contains no ballet. It is clearly a rationalized,
'utility' version designed to reduce the opera to a more moderate length, to remove
some of the extravagances which caused laughter in 1876, and above all to ensure a
circulation among French provincial theatres. Despite Muzio's brave words it
remains essentially a *pis-aller*. However, one can learn much about a composer's ideas
by discovering what sacrifices he is disposed to make when faced with the need to
adapt a score to special circumstances.

The first surprise occurs in the course of the duet between Leonora and Alvaro. For
although almost everywhere else the point of departure is the score of 1869, here
Verdi returns to the original version of Leonora's agony, with its lyrical outpourings
in dialogue with the orchestra (see Ex. 297a) – possibly because it is so much easier
for the orchestra and more grateful to the singer; more probably it was a survival
from the score bearing the translation of 1865 and Verdi had forgotten about the
change made here in the definitive version.

Next, the finale to the act is drastically reduced to fit the new story-line. The
recitative after the duet-cabaletta is shortened by three bars and four snatches of
dialogue. One of Alvaro's negro slaves enters from the balcony to say that armed
men are climbing the stairs. Over Ex. 287b now pianissimo on strings alone Alvaro
draws his sword and declares that he will cleave a way through their assailants. At
this point Laura (Curra) puts out the lights; and the stage instructions read: 'By the
door at the back the Marquis's servants are seen to enter with several armed men
wrapped in cloaks.' Alvaro at once goes into the attack to the same orchestral
sequence that had accompanied the Marchese's contemptuous refusal to strike him

* Letter from Muzio to Giulio Ricordi, 19.5.1882. Abbiati, IV, p. 200.
† See A. Loewenberg, *Annals of Opera*, 3rd ed. (London, 1970), p. 959.
‡ *La Force du destin/Opéra en quatre actes* (Plate no. A.C. 5534).

dead; but here (to judge from the reduction) it is more heavily scored as befits a fight. In the mêlée the Marchese is mortally wounded (Ex. 287b in B minor). Leonora recognizing his voice runs to his side. With his dying breath her father curses both her *and* Alvaro, who accordingly joins in her cry of 'Fatalité!'; but, be it noted, this does not entitle him to Ex. 287b thereafter, though one would have thought both theme and concept indissolubly linked. Leonora remains weeping by her father's corpse. Alvaro meanwhile retreats still fighting towards the balcony and the curtain falls. In this way 60 bars of 3/8 allegro have been eliminated together with two subsidiary themes including Ex. 298, its development, and most surprising of all, that violent tonal swing from C sharp minor to A minor and back again. Surely a heavy price to pay for a more rational plot.

The first scene of Act II presents few variants of note, except in the text, where many of the lines which Piave lifted from Sanseverino's translation of the play and which sound so awkward in the context of an opera are rewritten. The food no longer seems to say, as in Alice in Wonderland, 'Eat me.' Carlo no longer addresses the hostess in incomprehensible Latin, preferring to say, 'Horace himself would have celebrated your feast.' Preziosilla's 'Au loin quand résonne' is in the lower, 1862 key of B flat major, and the two-bar link to the chorus of pilgrims is cut. In his teasing of Trabuco Carlo never questions the sex of his travelling companion, nor does he suggest painting a couple of moustaches on the sleeping youth; he merely suggests bringing him (her) out for all to see. In the final 'good nights' (rendered as 'Dieu vous garde') there is no upper alternative for Preziosilla.

The second scene begins normally, but there is a curious puntatura at the start of 'Madre pietosa vergine' where the heroine's first two notes are B and F sharp, not B and D. Was it because the word 'vierge' with its narrower vowel is easier to project at the lower pitch than 'madre'? The 'scène' which follows will cause the reader to rub his eyes unbelievingly. Where is Melitone? He has been written out of the score. In his place is a monk who says not a word, but at Leonora's 'Je cherche le Supérieur' bows and retires. This leads to a resumption of Ex. 287b in E minor corresponding in the Italian versions with its recurrence in C sharp minor after Melitone has closed the little window. What follows is the original, duly transposed and rescored; but Leonora's musings are cut short after no more than two bars of Ex. 289 by the appearance of the Father Superior. As there is no Melitone to grumble behind his back he can appropriate the notes of 'Che tuon da Superiore!' for his dismissal of the silent monk ('Retirez-vous, mon frère') and so proceed quickly to the main body of the duet. No one mentions Father Cleto; Leonora presents a letter which explains her circumstances. From there to the end the duet proceeds as in the 1869 version, though Leonora, in rejecting the idea of a convent, expresses herself more moderately than in either Rivas's play or Piave's libretto. Ex. 310 in its Haydnesque, instrumental version is there as before but of course it no longer has the quality of a back reference. In the organ solo which begins the finale the distinction made by Verdi between 'Organo pieno' for the first 18 bars and 'Organo chiuso' for the last 8 is made more explicit by the terms 'jeux de fonds' et 'jeux d'anches' ('reeds and diapason' and 'diapason only').

The third act starts straight away with the clarinet solo leading to Alvaro's scena and aria. After the fracas, Carlo and Alvaro duly introduce themselves to each other with false names and there is the expected duettino of friendship ('O frère, l'amitié sainte'). But the fanfares immediately afterward summon only Alvaro, who, before sallying forth to what may prove his death, hands over to his new friend the precious packet containing Leonora's portrait. This leads to one of the most ruthless pieces of surgery ever practised on a famous piece of music – the duet 'Solenne in quest' ora'. Yet it is inevitable since the situation is quite different. Alvaro is not at death's door; therefore the funereal opening is inappropriate; so too the bassoon's plangent echo, since there is no need for him to stop singing while Carlo searches him for the key. Instead the central section is spliced into the preceding recitative.

The duet is followed by a much reduced version of Carlo's great recitative 'Morir ... tremenda cosa!' Carlo does not open the packet but the seal awakens a small suspicion which he at once dismisses. So to 'Par toi d'un traître' ('Urna fatal!'), in the 1862 key of F major. Then for the first time we hear a few bars of the 'battaglia' during which a soldier enters and describes to Carlo a masterly feint by 'Alvar' [*sic!*] which has carried the day. So there is no need for the portrait to tell Carlo the identity of his comrade-in-arms. With a cry of 'Sauvé! sauvé! vengeance . . .' he plunges into 'Il respire' ('Egli è salvo') in the 1869 key of E major.

After the Ronde and Alvaro's scena the start of the grand duet is slightly abbreviated with Carlo showing his hand somewhat earlier; for he has no need to waste time on concern for Alvaro's state of health. Thereafter events follow their expected course to the end of Preziosilla's 'Venez, belle jeunesse' ('Venite all' indovina') and the toasts. Then a massive cut eliminates the scene with Trabuco, taking us straight to the entrance of the peasants ('Donnez-nous un peu de pain'). Preziosilla's final words of cheer to the recruits are cut short so that the Tarantella breaks out with still greater suddenness after a chord of B major. Melitone and his sermon are omitted. Instead Preziosilla has a few words of reproof for the soldiers who are more intent on flirting than fighting. Her remedy is the Rataplan chorus that concludes the act.

Act IV opens with an intermezzo based on themes from the opera not all of which have yet been heard. What they all have in common is an association with the heroine, being all taken from scenes in which she has been or will be present. The first is a premonition of Carlo's fatal dagger thrust (Ex. 354) but, incredibly, without the woodwind scream which is so unforgettable in the Italian score. The motif is stated twice in full then developed for six bars to a half-close that brings back the organ voluntary from Act II. This in turn transforms itself into the second part of the great ensemble with double chorus where the pilgrims pass by the inn at Hornachuelos (Ex. 304). The final cadence is interrupted by a quotation from the duet between Leonora and the Father Superior (Ex. 312) which gives way to Leonora's 'Non m'abbandonar' (Ex. 289) played 'avec élan'; but instead of the 'Venite adoremus' a crescendo of two bars brings in the monks' solemn commination 'Il cielo fulmini, incenerisca' (Ex. 319). At the end, Ex. 312 is heard once more in its form of a rising sequence below tremolo strings, this time in preparation for a second premonition – the resolution of the finale terzetto ('Lieta poss'io precederti') with an ending whose tranquillity is disturbed by two waves of violence.

On the face of it this intermezzo looks like a pot-pourri such as any competent arranger could have worked out. It is only when we hear immediately afterwards the destiny motif (Ex. 287b) in B flat minor followed by Leonora's 'Grâce!' ('Pace!')

that its purpose becomes clear. A problem that besets both the Italian versions is Leonora's disappearance from the end of Act II till the middle of Act IV, when she has become little more than a memory for both Alvaro and the audience. The new intermezzo has the merit of gathering up all the threads of her story and so re-presenting her as a living person, before we actually see her again. Not only that; it serves as a dream sequence, a montage of past and future events passing through the obsessed mind of Leonora herself; so that when she rushes out of the cave immediately afterwards her cry of 'Grâce!' takes on a dramatic significance. She seems, like Nabucco – also, be it noted, at the start of the fourth act of the opera – to have awakened from a dream in which she finds herself pursued by dreadful memories and forebodings. The long pendant of the original 'Mélodie' is reduced to four pianissimo final bars. Not till the rough crotchets with acciaccature signalize Carlo's approach does she retreat hurriedly into the cave.

During the next few bars Carlo silently instructs a servant to fetch Alvaro from the near-by monastery. While the servant is gone he delivers his sinister recitative, 'En vain, Alvar, en vain tu pris la fuite' ('Invano, Alvaro, tu ti celasti al mondo'). From there to the end all is the same as the score of 1869 apart from at two points. A tiny transition is needed to bridge the duet and the finale where the repositioning of Leonora's 'Mélodie' had left a gap (and, incidentally, saved a change of scene), and as in the intermezzo Ex. 354 is shorn of its high woodwind, or so it would appear from the piano reduction. But in both places this could have been an arbitrary omission of the arranger, since it is impossible to play all the notes as set out in the Ricordi. Clearly we miss a great deal through the lack of an orchestral score.

Yet we cannot dismiss this third version as unauthentic. Apart from Muzio's testimony, so many of the alterations accord with Verdi's own views on stagecraft – the need for brevity, for avoiding too many changes of scene which reduce the opera to a magic lantern show. *La Force du destin* acknowledges the more serious theatrical liability of the original opera in both its 1862 and 1869 versions; its canvas is too crowded for comfort.

Musically too much happens, most of it too quickly and too soon. It was the first time in his career that Verdi was faced with a problem of proportion – a problem that affects his next opera, *Don Carlos*, in equal measure. In neither can it be said that he ever found the ideal solution. His amputations of healthy tissue in the French *Forza del destino*, though they diminish that variety which is the essence of the opera, also lessen the strain for the listener. The incomprehension evident in so many of the judgements quoted by Andrea della Corte is surely due to the surfeit of good things that the score provides, leaving the critics with a whirl of vague impressions which they have found it impossible to rationalize. Such people might have been guided to a better understanding of the piece if they had approached it first through the French score.

Although during the early years of this century *La Forza del destino* lapsed into an even deeper obscurity than most Verdi operas of this period, it was to play a cardinal role in the German·Verdi-renaissance of the 1920s. As early as 1913 it had enjoyed a short revival at Hamburg in a respectable translation by Johann Christoph Grünbaum; but it was the production at Dresden in 1926 under Fritz Busch that really turned the tide in the opera's favour. The new translator was Franz Werfel, whose scheme for Act III we have already discussed.* Busch was to perform the same service for the English at Glyndebourne and Edinburgh in 1951 with a memorable Italian performance in which Verdi's own sequence was maintained. Present-day performances in Italy still regrettably omit the quarrel-duet in Act III. They would do better to use the French version if they cannot spare the time for Verdi's vision in all its sprawling grandeur.

Whatever the final verdict upon *La Forza del destino*, there can be no doubt that one foreign masterpiece owes it an incalculable debt. Without its example *Boris Godunov* could never have taken shape as we know it today. The procession of holy pilgrims that causes all present to kneel in prayer; the monk who is a figure of comedy; the whining character-tenor who is maltreated by the bystanders – in a word Varlaam and the Idiot have no precedents save in Melitone and Trabuco respectively. There is no one like them in the works of Glinka or Dargomizhky. *Russlan and Ludmilla* ranges more widely in time and place than most traditional opera, but it remains a drama of individuals only; for the panoramic vision of *Boris Godunov* embracing the highest and lowest in society in an alternation of contrasted scenes, only *La Forza del destino* could supply the model. Significantly both operas caused problems of organization for their composers, who had second thoughts about the order in which the scenes should be presented. If this affinity went unremarked by supporters of the Kutchka, this was surely because to the Russian nationalist Italian opera, more even than German, represented the cosmopolitan bogey. It was the product of a race which had held Russian music in thrall since the mid-eighteenth century. In fact *Boris Godunov* has nothing to lose by a comparison with Verdi's opera, especially since it possesses one quality which more than makes up for Mussorgsky's rougher craftsmanship and more limited musical range – namely the fusion of religious and national feeling. In the Father Superior Verdi depicted a man of strong religious faith, but not a Pimen who draws together the threads of national history and the church. The conception of Holy Russia permeates Mussorgsky's masterpiece giving it a rare strength and unity of artistic purpose, which falters only in the Polish scenes.

Verdi's score, on the other hand, lacks such a simple unifying element; and this is a further reason why many find this an exhausting opera to listen to. But it is certainly not incoherent. Variety and profusion of episode are basic to its nature; but over and above the obvious thematic reminiscences there is a musical consistency in the limning of Alvaro and Leonora which as Per Pal Varnai has shown† serves as a point of reference for the whole opera. It depends on the use of the rising sixth in their melodic intervals. One can be even more specific, making a distinction between the sixth from doh to la (as in Ex. 287b) and from soh to mi (Ex. 288) and stressing the importance of the two when combined in a spiral ascent (Ex. 289) or when two of the second form a similar *descent* (Ex. 323a). But as always it is dangerous to analyse too closely the Verdian tinta.

Akin to the overlapping sixths are the overlapping fourths of Alvaro's theme (Ex. 294) in its several manifestations, or even the circling fourths of Leonora's Ex. 312;

---

* If this scheme continued to be advocated in Germany without any mention of its originator, the reason is simple. Franz Werfel was a Jew and unmentionable in Germany after 1933. In his notorious *Lexicon der Juden in der Musik* (Berlin, 1941), p. 402, Herbert Gerigk dismisses him as the author of several debased translations of Verdi opera texts.

† Varnai, *loc. cit.*

but not in a way that can be demonstrated by technical analysis. As in the characteristic patterns of *Macbeth* (see Vol. 1) it can only be sensed when examples are juxtaposed. What matters is that this consistency is sufficient to carry the widest variety elsewhere and so preserve a basic unity in an opera whose only fault is that it is too rich in ideas. It is a fault on the right side.

INDEX